RETAILING

New Perspectives

RETAILING
New Perspectives

Dorothy S. Rogers
New Hampshire College

Mercia M. T. Grassi
Drexel University

THE DRYDEN PRESS

Chicago   New York   San Francisco
Philadelphia   Montreal   Toronto
London   Sydney   Tokyo

Acquisitions Editor: Rob Zwettler
Developmental Editor: Judy Sarwark
Project Editor: Paula Ransdell
Design Director: Alan Wendt
Production Manager: Barb Bahnsen
Permissions Editors: Doris Milligan, Cindy
  Lombardo
Director of Editing, Design, and Produc-
  tion: Jane Perkins

Text and Cover Designer: Stuart Paterson
Copy Editor: Jean Berry
Indexer: Leoni McVey
Compositor: York Graphic Services
Text Type: 10/12 New Baskerville

Library of Congress Cataloging-in-Publication Data

Rogers, Dorothy S.
  Retailing: new perspectives.

  Includes bibliographical references and index.
  1. Retail trade. I. Grassi, Mercia. II. Title.
HF5429.R5793 1988   658.8'7   87-5337
ISBN 0-03-001997-4

Printed in the United States of America
789-039-98765432
Copyright © 1988 by The Dryden Press, a division
of Holt, Rinehart and Winston, Inc.

Address orders:
111 Fifth Avenue
New York, NY 10003

Address editorial correspondence:
One Salt Creek Lane
Hinsdale, IL 60521

The Dryden Press
Holt, Rinehart and Winston
Saunders College Publishing

Cover photo: Courtesy of Triple Five Corporation Ltd.
Visual merchandising photos, following page 298: Jack Gifford, Professor of Marketing,
Miami University of Ohio.

To

Dr. Gertrude C. Shapiro
President Emeritus
New Hampshire College

and

Dean Kenneth G. Matheson
Dean Emeritus, College of
    Business Administration
Drexel University

whose keen insight brought us to the teaching profession.

The Dryden Press Series in Marketing

Preface

Our goal in this preface is much the same as that of the retailer who creates an interesting window display: to offer a sample of the products/ services within.

Retailing is dynamic, exciting, and challenging to its practitioners. The world of retailing is both traditional and trendy. It encompasses the large and the small, national and international, maxi and mini. The only constants are consumers, competition, and change.

SCOPE OF THE BOOK

Retailing: New Perspectives is a practical, readable, user-friendly book intended for use in an introductory course. It is neither too difficult for students in two-year retailing, marketing, or merchandising programs, nor too simplistic for the first retailing course in a four-year institution. Training directors in department or chain stores may also find it a useful guide for management trainees.

The text material can be covered in a one-semester course. With some supplemental reading, however, it could be expanded to two terms.

It is organized into nineteen chapters divided into seven parts. The three chapters in Part I, "A Retailing Overview," were planned to help students understand retailing in a marketing context. Chapter 1 provides historical perspective and also positions retailing in the marketing channel. Chapter 2 describes the retail environment. Chapter 3 focuses on factors that affect consumer decisions and on the decision-making process.

Part II, "Human Resources," describes the opportunities that retailing provides. Chapter 4 on "Retail Career Ladders" is unique to this retailing text. It discusses career options, career paths, personal qualifications for retail executives, the career search, and where the jobs will be. Chapter 5, which addresses the problems of the human resource manager, advocates a human resource plan and budget. Other topics include recruiting, hiring, training, job enrichment, compensation, and unions.

Two of the three chapters in Part III, "Retail Institutions," are not found in other retailing texts. The traditional approaches to the customer are covered in Chapter 6, which describes retail store functions, general merchandise chains, specialty stores, and other major retail categories. Chapter 7, "Direct Retail Marketing: A Nontraditional Approach," explains the growth of nonstore retailing. A variety of nonstore channels are discussed: vending machines, direct-to-home merchandising, telephone retailing, catalog retailing, and electronic retailing. Chapter 8, "International Retailing," explores America's growing taste for foreign goods, foreign retailers in the United States and in their own markets, U.S. retailers abroad, and careers in international marketing.

A "Marketing Approach to Location" is described in Part IV. The three chapters cover researching the trading area, selecting the site location, and layout and design of the store. Key topics include demographic analysis, shopping center types and trends, buying versus leasing, elements of store design, basic store layouts, and reimaging.

The "Merchandise Mix" is the subject of Part V. Chapter 12 concentrates on the planning phase and the merchandise budget. Chapter 13, on the merchandise selection process, is primarily concerned with sources of buying information and the mechanics of buying. Chapter 14, which explains pricing for profit, concludes with an appendix on retail math. Chapter 15 describes ongoing changes in distribution systems and inventory control.

In Part VI, "Retail Promotion," the first chapter differentiates retail advertising from national advertising and discusses the media mix, advertising budgets, and measuring results. A chapter on the visual presentation of merchandise relates the store to a theater. A third chapter describes the sales promotion mix, the promotional activities of the salesforce, and the service mix.

Finally, Part VI looks ahead to "The Future of Retailing." The retailer will need to manage the changes that occur as we move into the information age and as the types and nature of retail institutions change.

The major focus of the text is on career choices and professional training for employment in an established retail business. For the entrepreneur, an appendix written by James F. Wolter, Ph.D., offers a short course on "Starting a Retail Business." Key sections provide a self-assessment questionnaire and outline the rewards and drawbacks of owning a small business. Concise discussions of a five-part business plan, sources of affordable guidance, and an analysis of franchises round out the information provided for those who may consider opening a retail store.

We believe that *Retailing: New Perspectives* will have value to the student long beyond its immediate usefulness in the classroom.

SPECIAL FEATURES

Each chapter begins with an Industry Statement written especially for this book by a prominent practitioner in the retail industry. By sharing insights and strategies, these retailers set the stage for the chapter text.

An outline of Learning Objectives, which also precedes the text, highlights the key topics to be discussed.

Real-world examples of retail activities are given in 35 "From the Field" reports integrated with the text. Many of them explore an idea in the text by describing retail strategy at a particular store. Others expand a marketing theme: the college market, the yuppies market, measuring trends, maximizing department store sales, the revival of small stores, fashion videos, and incentive programs.

The end-of-chapter material includes a chapter Summary and Questions for Review. Both are directly related to the Learning Objectives outlined at the opening of the chapters.

Continuing the emphasis on a practical approach, a Case Study with each chapter gives students the opportunity to apply what they have learned. Each case, several pages in length, concludes with a series of questions. These encourage analysis and often require the student to formulate a strategy or plan.

A short retail math appendix at the end of Chapter 14 explains how to read a profit and loss statement for a retail business. The explanation includes some useful accounting terms.

Retailing terms are defined, when necessary, as they occur in the book. Short glossaries of basic marketing and retailing terms are incorporated in the Chapter 1 text. Chapter 12 contains a list of budget terms. Other key terms are set in boldface type in the text and defined in the marginal area.

An eight-page color insert on West Edmonton Mall, the largest shopping center in the world, enables students to experience the future in retailing. The Canadian mall includes a Fantasyland amusement park and a Fantasyland Hotel.

Available to the student, a **Study Guide** written by Louis Canale is keyed to the 19 chapters of the text. Each unit of the study guide begins with a real-world introduction, followed by a detailed chapter outline and notes. The next section provides objective questions (including multiple choice and true–false), definitional questions, and open-ended discussion questions. Where appropriate, a small-business section is included.

For instructors, a complete **Instructor's Manual** is available. Paralleling the text, it includes lecture outlines, answers to end-of-chapter questions, classroom projects, and suggested answers to case questions, as well as 700 test items and transparency masters.

ACKNOWLEDGMENTS

We are grateful to the many people who participated in the preparation of this book. We especially thank the students who served as proverbial guinea pigs during the writing stage so that we might better meet the needs of future students. We are indebted to the many industry leaders who wrote meaningful introductions to the chapters.

Others whose help and contributions have made a significant impact on the quality of the book include our typists, Patricia L. Rial and Helen H. Snyder; our research assistant, Lori Viet; and the reviewers:

William Black, Louisiana State University
Louis Canale, Genessee Community College
J. Joseph Cronin, University of Kentucky
Raymond Dannenberg, Western Michigan University
Kenneth Evans, Arizona State University
Robert Fishco, Middlesex County College
Ethel Fishman, Fashion Institute of Technology
Thomas Greer, University of Maryland
Stephen Griffin, Tarrant County Junior College, South Campus
Mary Grace Hardin, Santa Barbara Business College
Janice Kelly, Tarrant County Junior College
James Kuhn, St. Louis Community College
Milledge Mosby, Prince George Community College
Katherine Olson, Northern Virginia Community College
Howard Seigelman, Brookdale Community College
Robert Witherspoon, Triton College
James Wolter, Grand Valley State College

Special thanks also go to Louis Canale, who developed the end-of-chapter questions, and James Wolter, who wrote the small business appendix. To the staff at Dryden Press we extend our appreciation for the guidance and patience given throughout this project: Mary Fischer, Paula Ransdell, Judy Sarwark, Bill Schoof, Alan Wendt, and Rob Zwettler.

Dorothy S. Rogers
Mercia M. T. Grassi

About the Authors

Dorothy S. Rogers is Director of the Career Development Center at New Hampshire College, Manchester, New Hampshire. She was Director of Cooperative Education from 1976 to 1982 and a member of the Management/Marketing faculty from 1960 to 1976, during which time she developed the Fashion Merchandising and Retailing curricula and the International Internship Program. Prior to her association with New Hampshire College, she was a retail buyer.

Professor Rogers acts as a consultant to industry and other educational institutions, combining her knowledge of career development, recruitment, and marketing methodologies. She lectures and writes on a variety of marketing and retailing subjects and is a reviewer of marketing and retailing textbooks for a number of major publishers.

In 1981 and 1982, Professor Rogers developed the nationwide New England Life field force internship program and during the same period acted as a marketing consultant to the National Commission for Cooperative Education. She has considerable expertise in international student exchange programs and has conducted a number of student tours of European industry. She is also the co-author of two previous books in addition to *Retailing: New Perspectives*. In 1985, Professor Rogers was selected for listing in *Who's Who of American Women*.

Mercia M. T. Grassi is Professor of Marketing and Director of the Retail Management program at Drexel University, Philadelphia. She served as Fashion Director for John Wanamaker Department Store, Public Relations Director for Bellevue Stratford Hotel, and Public Relations Director for Wermen and Shorr Advertising Agency. She advises several governments and private manufacturing and retailing organizations in the U.S. and abroad. She has developed and coordinated international marketing seminars and conferences for Drexel University students and professionals; has been a guest lecturer and writer on foreign trade, merchandising, and marketing; and has received numerous honors from governments, academic institutions, and professional organizations. She is founder and director of Drexel University's International Forum on Marketing and Merchandising and co-director of Drexel's Specialization in International Business. She was a Fulbright Scholar to Italy and has been active in the field of retail marketing for more than 35 years.

Brief Contents

Contents

Part I

A Retailing Overview

Chapter   1

Retailing, A Dynamic Industry

Source: Courtesy of Macy's New York.

Industry Statement

C. George Scala
Chairman, CEO, and President
Lechmere, Inc.

The essence of American retailing is the management of change. It is a fast, volatile, dynamic, and exciting profession that has grown into a trillion-dollar industry employing more than 15 million people. It is the true and basic industry in our country.

Retailing deals with many societal changes. If our president makes a trip to an exotic foreign country, we will see the art and crafts of that country influence our home decor within a few months of his trip. If a popular singer adopts a unique clothing or hair style, we'll see that influence almost immediately in the fashion forward sections of our stores. The rate of change is accelerating in our society, profoundly affecting the way we live, dress, socialize, communicate, and yes, think about ourselves. Political trends have worldwide influence; competition from foreign markets and makers challenges our ability to stay on the cutting edge of these changes. Retailers face the inevitable fact that quick and appropriate response is the only way to stay current, to differentiate from our competition, and to avoid becoming a me-too retailer.

Retailers are really the nation's purchasing agents for consumer goods. We get a scorecard every day, in the form of sales, on our success in providing wanted, timely, fashionable, basic, and trendy merchandise for our customers. We're in business to please our customers. This is a simple proposition to state, a difficult challenge to execute. Following trends in society helps us to understand the changing demands of our customers. In the latter half of the 20th century, as we progress from an industrial society to an information society, the demand for communication devices (from multifeatured telephones to home computers) has quadrupled.

Retailing is one of the most sophisticated businesses in our country—featuring state-of-the-art computerized merchandise control and distribution systems, magical merchandise presentation, in-depth consumer and market research, and representation of merchandise from worldwide markets. The ever-present constant in this equation is change. Change is inevitable, and we are challenged by it every day. Growth, on the other hand, is optional; we won't grow and expand as a profession unless we commit to trend (change) management. We continually strive to understand our customers—to renew our marketing strategies or to replace them when they no longer serve our customers. Too many retailers exercise their egos by telling customers what is good for them. Marketers ask customers what they want and give it to them. Therein lies the major difference!

This industry (profession) is a series of evolved formats. It began with barter or trading for value. It has moved through specialty, department store, discount store, catalog showroom, direct mail, supermarket, and warehouse club in a relentless search for the low-cost vehicle that will serve most of the people most of the time.

In the end, like any other successful element in our workplace, retailing's strength comes from achieving appropriate balance between continuity and change, between consistency and innovation, between traditional and breakthrough ideas.

Learning Objectives

Upon completing this chapter you should be able to:

1. Understand the qualitative dimensions of retailing.
2. Use retail terminology.
3. Give examples of the "wheel of retailing" theory.
4. Describe the evolution of retail stores in the United States.
5. Understand why today's retailers must think of themselves as marketers.
6. Discuss where retailers belong in the marketing channel.
7. Discuss sources of retail competition.
8. Understand retail classifications.
9. Understand the need for retailers to project a clear-cut image.
10. Understand the importance of controllable and uncontrollable variables in developing specific retail strategies.

In the multidimensional world of retailing, practitioners sell satisfaction to consumers and consumers create profit for practitioners. Because retailing institutions must be as dynamic as the environment in which they exist, retail strategies are subject to constant change. Before we look at specific strategy development or change, however, the retail stage must be set. This chapter focuses on the qualitative dimensions of the industry, a historical perspective of retail stores, definitions of retail terminology, the place of the retailer in the channel of distribution, types of retail institutions and their images, and finally an overview of retail strategy development.

QUALITATIVE DIMENSIONS

Retailing is educational, exciting, dynamic, and demanding. It is as old as biblical markets and as new as the personal computer. It is small town and big city, local and regional, national and international. It is the most important link in the distribution chain from producer to consumer, for

Gross National Product (GNP) Total retail value of all goods and services produced by a country during a specific time period.

almost all of our **gross national product (GNP)** reaches us through some form of retailing.

Retailing is basically defined as the selling of goods or services individually or in small quantities directly to the consumer. Though accurate, this definition does not really address the many qualitative dimensions that make the study of retail principles and practices so fascinating.

Educational Dimension

You have probably never thought of your local retail store as an educational institution. Mention retailing to a group of friends and you will likely hear "profit hungry," "fashion conscious," "a tough business," "over-stored," "long hours," "low pay," "easy credit," but rarely, if ever, "educational."

Yet, observe young children riding in supermarket baskets, their inquisitive eyes darting from shelf to shelf, and you will begin to understand the educational dimension in retailing. Through such questions as "What is that?" and "Can I eat this?" they obtain early lessons. Product knowledge is often followed by a lesson in simple economics. "No, it's too much money" may be said in reference to brightly packaged but more expensive cereals. "It's not good for your teeth" instills an early awareness of the need for good health habits.

A retail store is often the place where a child learns social patterns. When both parents work every day, evening or weekend shopping trips become family events. Thus, in today's world it is in the shopping cart rather than the rocking chair where many values and ideas are formulated.

As an example, a ten-year-old accompanying both working parents to the supermarket in 1980 soon learned that when it came to selecting fresh vegetables, Mom was the decision maker. Eight years later, a five-year-old watched as Dad made the choices. More men than ever before are making the types of basic household decisions that formerly were the responsibility of the woman in the household.

Point-of-Purchase (P.O.P.) Displays In-store displays such as special racks and printed materials, usually furnished by manufacturers.

Many of us are introduced to new products or new uses for existing ones through **point-of-purchase (P.O.P.) displays.** These in-store creations, often located at the end of self-service store aisles, may communicate to us that an old product has been improved or that instant soups have more than one use.

Remote control has cut into the effectiveness of product advertising on television. A commercial can now be zapped away by the viewer looking for something of greater interest on another channel. P.O.P. displays are taking the place of missed messages as they educate even sophisticated consumers about new products.

Basic economics, psychology, and sociology can be added to the list of business courses "taught" in almost all retail stores. Retailers may not try to sell education as they do products or services, but they do not need to. Education is a part of the retail environment as it exists today. Retailers can be proud that they help educate the buying public in many ways.

Dynamic Dimension

Wheel of Retailing
Theory that retail businesses evolve through three stages: entry, trading up, and vulnerability.

The **wheel of retailing** theory[1] hypothesizes a cyclical pattern of retail evolution consisting of three phases: (1) entry, (2) trading up, and (3) vulnerability. According to this theory, retailers usually enter the marketplace as low-price, low-margin, and low-status operators and over time mature into more elaborate and thus higher-cost establishments. As they do so, they become increasingly vulnerable to new, lower-priced, lower-margin, lower-status competitors, who in turn will go through the same process. With its connotation of constant motion, this theory points out the dynamic nature of the retailing industry.

The wheel of retailing theory is illustrated by the Zayre Corporation, a multibillion-dollar retail operation with more than 300 discount department stores throughout the United States plus a number of subsidiary retail companies.[2]

Phase One—Entry

Zayre opened two experimental discount stores in 1956 in Hyannis and Roslindale, Massachusetts. These were immediately successful because they were highway accessible, had plentiful parking, and were modern, well-lighted, and air-conditioned—in contrast to the mill-outlet type of discount stores that were predominant at the time.

Phase Two—Trading Up

Having moved forward one spoke on the wheel because of a new image, Zayre began to move the entire industry up from its humble beginnings, and discounting entered phase two, trading up.

Phase Three—Vulnerability

Today Zayre commands a substantial share of the mass market and, along with other mass merchants, stands side by side with such retail giants as Sears and J. C. Penney, who themselves had started out small

---

[1] This theory was first advanced by Malcolm P. McNair, "Significant Trends and Developments in the Postwar Period," in *Competitive Distribution in a Free, High-Level Economy and Its Implications for the University,* ed. A. B. Smith (Pittsburgh: University of Pittsburgh Press, 1958), 1–25.
[2] Subsidiaries include Hit or Miss, Beaconway, Bell/Nugent Stores, On Stage, Shoppers City, and T. J. Maxx.

Mass Merchants
Group of retailers
engaged in
discount
merchandising.

**Trickle-Down
Process**
Theory that
fashion moves
vertically through
the strata of
society.

with low operating costs. Thus Zayre and other **mass merchants** are vulnerable to continuing new competition in the form of off-price stores and discount catalog operations.

The wheel theory is only one explanation of the dynamic nature of retailing. Many current entrants, particularly fashion retailers, begin by catering to the high-income market but eventually face competition from merchants who copy their strategies to appeal to lower-income groups. Because of this **trickle-down process,** these retailers often trade down instead of up in order to appeal to a lower-income market not originally in their target segment.

The proliferation of branch stores, suburban shopping centers, inner-city malls, and high-priced catalog retailers are only a few examples of change. These new retailing forms do show, however, that nothing remains the same in retailing.

As a matter of fact, some business institutions, never thought of as retail operations, have begun to adopt a retail image. Banks have become retailers as they have made more and more financial products and services, not even in existence ten years ago, available to their customers. Although many bankers might prefer not to be classified as retailers, the list of their offerings shown in Table 1.1 would justify the designation.

Table   1.1   List of Financial Services Offered by Banks

24-hour automatic teller machines	Money orders
Checking accounts	Cashier's checks
Savings accounts	Domestic transfers (rapid funds transfers through other banks)
Savings clubs	
Certificates of deposit	Domestic drafts (negotiable instruments for immediate payment to any payee)
Money market accounts	
Sales of government and municipal securities	Sales of gold and silver, in certificate or metallic form
Personal check guarantees, for cashing	Foreign currency exchange
Overdraft checking	Credit cards
Personal credit lines	Travel and entertainment cards
Personal loans	Trust and estate services
Home-improvement loans	Retirement accounts (IRAs and Keogh Plans)
Residential mortgages and co-op and condominium loans—fixed and variable rates	Investment management services, including fine arts management
Second mortgages, including revolving-type equity loans	Safe-keeping and custodial accounts
	Financial counseling
Mobile home financing	Discount brokerage services
Recreational vehicle financing	Home banking, including bill paying (via computer and telephone)
Automobile and boat loans	
Student loans	Automatic teller machine networks

Source: "Money, Managing It Wisely," special section, *The New York Times.*

Shopping via television also illustrates retail change. (See "From the Field: Home Shopping Network.")

FROM THE FIELD

Home Shopping Network

What started out as a strategy to keep a troubled radio station afloat has added more than $500 million to the net worth of the two entrepreneurs who launched the rescue mission. Their company, Home Shopping Network (HSN) Inc. of Clearwater, Florida, sells merchandise to television viewers via round-the-clock programming on two networks carried by cable systems. HSN offers a discount department store in the living rooms of television viewers, who make credit-card purchases by calling a toll-free number.

HSN-1, the company's original home shopping program, which went on the air in July [1985], reaches an estimated 6 million homes, mostly through cable television systems, according to the company. A clone, HSN-2, offering higher-priced merchandise, went on the air in March and reaches about 2 million homes.

HSN was founded by Roy M. Speer and Lowell W. Paxson, now chairman and president, respectively. The partners ran an AM radio station in Clearwater in the late 1970s. When their advertisers began switching to FM stations, Speer and Paxson decided to stop selling advertising and instead began selling merchandise over the air to listeners.

They later moved the concept to a local cable television channel and developed it enough to offer it nationally via satellite.

A staff of 25 television hosts offers viewers everything from jewelry to furs to household appliances, all purchased in lots from stores that were going out of business or manufacturers who were selling off inventories of slow-moving merchandise. The HSN host might, for example, offer an electric shaver for $12 as he demonstrates it and lists its features. An interested buyer then calls a toll-free telephone number and places an order using a major credit card or payment by personal check. The merchandise is then shipped to the buyer. On average, it is received within four days.

"It's like walking through a department store," said Judy D. Ludin, HSN's public relations director. And yes, she added, people do sit in front of their television sets and watch as dozens of items go up for sale, hour after hour.

Cable television companies get a cut, ranging from 1 to 5 percent, of the sales of merchandise to HSN customers in their system areas. HSN's concept, of course, can easily be copied.

Source: Extracted from Neill Borowski, "Shopping for the Latest 'Hot' Stock," *The Philadelphia Inquirer,* May 21, 1986. Copyright © 1986, *The Philadelphia Inquirer.* Reprinted by permission.

Another indication of the dynamic nature of retailing is geographic movement; retailers have always followed consumers so as to meet their changing demands. In 1983, of 2,006 retail apparel business openings, 435 were in the Central Southwest states of Texas, Arkansas, Oklahoma, and Louisiana, making this the leading area nationwide in clothing store starts.[3] These apparel retailers had tuned in to change and understood the need to move with the market, which was then beginning to shift to these states as traditional Sunbelt states like California and Florida became overcrowded.

A Demanding Industry

In addition to being educational and dynamic, retailing is becoming increasingly demanding. No longer can retailers, whether large or small, small-town or big-city, operate by the seat of the pants. They must search for excellence in every phase of their operation. They must be able to communicate with and understand the needs of their customers if they are to prosper in a highly competitive, technological world. This necessitates a number of basic skills: interpersonal, communications, technological, and research. Only those retailers who meet these requirements will be able to achieve excellence and the long-term success that goes with it.

Because retailing is a "people" business, both short- and long-term success depend on an understanding of consumers' needs, motivations, and lifestyles. For example, automobile salespeople who do not understand why one person wants a red sports car while another prefers a black sedan or why a seemingly reserved customer may choose a flamboyant sports model, cannot sell effectively.

Retailing demands the ability to deal with people at all levels, whether colleagues, superiors, subordinates, or customers. Retail salespeople must get along with other salespeople, department managers, and customers. Retail buyers must deal effectively with sales staff, merchandise and promotion managers, and vendors. Credit clerks must talk to customers as well as computers.

Good interpersonal and communication skills are a must, whether written or oral. A misunderstood directive, memo, or sales presentation can result in substantial loss. In the extremely competitive business of retailing, every loss, no matter how small, affects profit.

Today's retailers cannot exist without technological aids. Computers are as important now as cash registers were in the 1950s. Retailing demands state-of-the-art equipment and the expertise to use it to full capacity.

---

[3] "Dun and Bradstreet Tracks New Apparel Business in 1983," *Fashion Retailer* (June/July 1984).

Figure   1.1   Point-of-Sale Terminal: A Marriage between Cash Register and Computer

Source: Courtesy of International Business Machines Corporation.

**Point-of-Sale
(P.O.S.) Terminals**
Terminals that
supply information
on sales, inventory,
and commission
earnings.

For example, retailers must understand how to utilize **point-of-sale (P.O.S.) terminals** that supply information on sales, inventory, and commission earnings. They must know how to develop programs for payroll or credit and how to use modern technology in site selection, customer profiling, and in pricing, control, and distribution of merchandise. (See Figure 1.1.)

Retailing has unquestionably become more complex since the 1950s and 1960s, when growth seemed limitless, the economy was fairly stable, inflation was low, and competitive battles centered around the question of who could get to the next fast-growing suburb first. Retailing in the 1980s and 1990s demands as much science as art if the dual goals of productivity and profit are to be met.

**HISTORICAL
PERSPECTIVE**

Early Days of Retailing (1600–1850)

Retailers are not necessary in a self-sufficient agrarian economy in which people not only produce all the components of the finished products required to satisfy their total needs, but also complete the process. As life becomes more complex, and there is not time to do it all, they must buy from someone else who produces and/or finishes the goods.

Trading Posts

The first American retailers were the American Indians. They sold skins from animals they had trapped and killed to the early settlers. Although the settlers were mostly self-sufficient, the ability to buy fur skins gave them more time for other chores. As the years went on and farming became more demanding, the settlers began to look for a source of other items that could be purchased along with animal skins. Trading posts made their appearance on the American scene. Here was a central place where Indians could bring their furs to trade for products imported from Europe. White settlers used trading posts to buy and sell. They even competed with Indians in trapping and selling furs.

Trading posts were located along navigable waterways or at intersections of Indian trails, areas that were also natural locations for villages. When settlers did arrive, the trappers who had preceded them into the territory were already waiting to serve them in what could be classified as the first retail stores.

Colonial Markets and Yankee Peddlers

Most of the settlers who came to America during the colonial period settled on the East Coast, where the first cities appeared. Boston, Philadelphia, Baltimore, and Charleston became bustling centers of trade by the middle 1700s, and markets appeared to serve the growing population. Some merchants imported finished furniture, cloth, and clothing from Europe. Carpenters made and sold products for the home, and tailors offered custom-made garments to the well-to-do. Farmers brought their wares to open-air markets so that nonfarming city dwellers could have fresh fruit and vegetables. These markets were the colonial version of today's supermarkets.

In Eastern cities was still another group of retailers. Called Yankee peddlers because their original homes were in New England, these men purchased a variety of goods from importers, auctioneers, and at fairs and then traveled the countryside, first with packs on their backs, and later, as they prospered, with horses and wagons. They sold everything from needles and pins to groceries and patent medicines to their country customers.

As the colonists moved inland, so did the Yankee peddler, who brought the *right goods* to the *right place. Quantity, time,* and *price* were often determined by (1) the peddler's physical strength or the size of his wagon, (2) the ease of travel on terrible roads, and (3) the demand for his items or the ability of the settler to pay either in money or other goods. For many years the appearance of the traveling merchant was a highlight in the settlers' lives. He brought not only needed goods but also news of events in the cities.

The General Store

Life was hard on the road, and eventually one peddler after another settled down in his favorite village or town, sometimes joining forces with the settler who ran the local trading post. At other times the peddler opened his own small store. The result was the birth of the general store, which was to be the most important retail institution of the latter part of the 17th century and most of the 18th century.

General storekeepers in inland towns and villages carried groceries, dry goods, medicines, and other household needs imported from the Eastern cities. They also traded for or bought products produced in the geographic areas where they were located. Their assortments came from three sources: (1) trips to wholesale centers, (2) wholesale peddlers, and (3) local producers.

General storekeepers did not operate on a one-price policy. Instead, they bargained with their customers for the optimum price. They also started the first charge system, often giving credit to farmers for as long as a year or until the crop came in and money or goods was available for payment.

Hollywood has immortalized this early retail institution with many scenes of men in rural outdoor garb, sitting around a potbellied stove, smoking corncob pipes while deep in discussion of local politics or predictions about next year's crops. Such men were permanent fixtures in the general stores of the era and could be found anywhere from Massachusetts to Missouri. They came to buy boots or lanterns, sell milk or meat, and use the post office that was always located in the store.

Specialty Shops

Specialty Stores
Retail outlets that maintain a large selection of a limited line of merchandise.

By the late 1800s, another type of retail store was needed in the Northeast. As cities grew, so did the number of more affluent consumers. Their demand for a broader assortment of goods in all categories resulted in the emergence of one-line specialty stores such as bakeries, shoe stores, and millinery (hat) shops. Home production was not sufficient to supply these new stores and, by 1840, factories that specialized in certain merchandise lines were established on the East Coast. The early **specialty stores** were small shops owned and operated by one merchant in much the same manner as many of today's boutiques. They were clustered together in easily accessible city locations and heralded the start of the city years.

The City Years (1850–1950)

As life in the United States changed, so did the nature of its retail institutions. When our economy was dominated by agriculture, the general store was able to address the few needs that could not be met by farmers themselves, but as we became industrialized, men began to work away from their homes. This resulted in the need to purchase, instead of produce, more and more of the necessities of life.

Industrialization also resulted in expanding urban areas. Large cities dotted the East Coast. They were commercial as well as industrial and were where railroads and ships picked up goods for distribution throughout the rest of the country. Central business districts in these cities attracted residents from every part of town, and public transportation deposited them on the merchants' doorsteps.

Department Stores
Retail outlets organized into separate departments for purposes of promoting and controlling a wide variety of goods, such as apparel for men, women, and children; home furnishings; linens; and dry goods.

The first true city **department stores** were started during this period. After the Civil War they became the focal point for shoppers who also patronized the specialty stores that surrounded them. During the early city years most of the famous American department stores were founded: Boston's Jordan Marsh, Chicago's Marshall Field's, New York's B. Altman and R. H. Macy, and Philadelphia's John Wanamaker, to mention a few. These and many others like them flourished as the commercial cities east of the Mississippi grew. Women took care of their families' needs and became the family purchasing agents. Sales in city stores of all types increased tremendously under their patronage.

Department store growth continued throughout the 20th century. In fact, city department stores were the primary source of family household and clothing needs until the early 1930s. During the Depression years of the 1930s, a slowdown in sales occurred, and many single-owner specialty stores went out of business. Most department stores survived. The reason was that department stores served the family's total needs, so even if Dad or Mom could not buy for themselves, they still purchased clothing, shoes, and other items for their children. Children's needs, like their growth, did not slow down with the economy and somehow had to be met.

Although the 1940s saw the end of the Depression, department (and specialty) store growth remained at a standstill during much of the decade. War and rationing are not conducive to retail growth. Not until World War II ended in 1945 was the American retailer once again able to move forward.

The Suburban Years (1950–1970)

The second and largest spurt in U.S. retail growth took place immediately after World War II. With the war finally over, the American people could get back to the business at hand—a growing economy and increased consumption. Retailers were eager and willing to help in both instances. Because most of the GNP was (and still is) distributed through the retail sector, more stores were needed to serve a growing U.S. population.

In this historic period, the right place was the new suburb. People poured out of the cities to areas where new homes, station wagons, and backyard barbecue equipment were fast becoming a way of life. The American dream was now reality. Real estate developers and highway systems linked city jobs to suburban living.

Instead of redoing their old downtown stores, department store owners from coast to coast decided to follow the newly moneyed consumer to the burgeoning suburban communities, where household needs were proliferating as quickly as home foundations were being dug. The 1950s, 1960s, and early 1970s saw suburban shopping centers become community landmarks. No suburb was without one, two, three, four, or more malls. Some were large, with a department store branch and a supermarket as anchors; others were small with only a few specialty stores. Many had a smattering of department stores, national or regional chains—such as Sears, J. C. Penney, or K mart—specialty shops, supermarkets, and service merchants. **One-stop shopping** was the key phrase of the period.

During the early suburban period, department store owners made one major mistake. In their rush to follow the affluent consumer to the suburbs, they forgot an important market segment, which at that time was still labeled blue collar. Here were families with just as much money to spend as their white-collar neighbors, but who carried the pre–World War II shopping patterns of their nonaffluent parents to the suburbs along with their other baggage. Because new habits do not come as easily as new money, this group did not feel at home in the early suburban **branch stores,** which too closely resembled the upper floors of city stores. Upper floors had always meant expensive merchandise. Because the gap existed in the retail store mix of the new suburbs, **discount stores** were born. These stores succeeded by filling the household needs of the blue-collar family, who had money to spend and no basement level to spend it in.

One-Stop Shopping
Concept of convenience promoted by shopping centers and malls.

Branch Store
An outlet owned and operated by the flagship store, often carrying a modified line of merchandise.

Discount Stores
Stores that buy and sell "low" and depend on fast turnover to make a profit.

Return to Downtown (1975–1985)

While the suburbs flourished, urban blight continued. Twenty years of neglect, Depression, and war followed by another 20 years of suburban growth left most central city districts looking like bombed-out craters.

In the 1970s, urban renewal became a national goal. With funding from both government and private sources, city centers once again began to look clean, fresh, and exciting. Many middle-class and upper-class suburbanites started to trickle back from the suburbs, and by the early 1980s cities from New York to Minneapolis and from Portland, Maine, to Portland, Oregon, were again places where one lived as well as worked. Downtown areas regained some retail focus. In the new center city areas, old flagship stores were renovated and new enclosed malls built. Downtown Minneapolis is a superb example of a modern urban center.

1990 and Beyond

Although the face of retailing is sure to change in the future, one thing is certain: retail stores will remain. Where growth takes place will depend on where the consumer chooses to live, for in the future as in the past, stores will follow their consumers. Chapter 19 will look at the future of retailing.

RETAILING TERMINOLOGY

Every industry has its own terminology, and retailing is no exception. Because retailing is the final stage in the marketing of goods and services, and this text presents retailing in the marketing context, it is im-

FROM THE FIELD

The Four Ps of Marketing

Historically, marketing professionals and educators have used the "Four Ps" of product, price, promotion, and place to describe the functions of marketing; these pigeonholes have long provided a convenient means of telling others what the profession is all about. But to those in the trade, it has always been apparent that not all of the elements fit comfortably into these four over-simplified categories.

Time after time, new words beginning with the letter P are offered as phenomenal discoveries which should be added. Words like "packaging," "persuasion," "purchasing," "production," ad infinitum, are added without any consideration of using the already existing classifications. The time has come to fill in the missing elements, but it must be done with due consideration.

These eight elements have been missing:

Purpose means that the goals, objectives, or mission should be defined or clarified. The most common ones are profit and growth.

Probe means the pursuit of knowledge. This means general education and the collection of data through research, surveys, and testing.

Perceive means analyzing data through the use of intellectual powers of reasoning, logic, and synthesis. It includes market analysis and defining market segments through interpretation of facts and evaluation of (relevant) information.

Perform means proficiency of skills. It runs the gamut of every decision-making area, including, but not limited to: procurement, packaging, persuasion, presentation, positive atti-

portant to define some basic marketing terms before defining specific retail terms.

- *Marketing.* A set of total business functions that includes the planning, pricing, promotion, and distribution (place) of consumer-demanded products and/or services for the dual purposes of customer satisfaction and corporate profit. (See "From the Field: The Four Ps of Marketing.")
- *Market.* A group of people who have the desire and the ability to buy goods and/or services.
- *Target market.* A relatively homogeneous group of customers to whom a company wishes to appeal.
- *Marketing mix.* A blending of controllable variables that a company puts together for the purpose of appealing to and satisfying its target markets.

tudes, patience, personnel, record keeping, investment, salesmanship, showmanship, decisiveness, timing and financial know-how, including accounting, cash flow, taxes, pricing, financial statements, and positioning.

Predict means to forecast and anticipate the future through use of efficient observation, attention and awareness, researched facts, business records, trade technology, government legislation, environment, changing social attitudes, and trends.

Plan means to develop strategies within each area of the business. It involves using ingenuity, psychology, and philosophy to determine the most appropriate course of action needed to achieve the stated "purpose." Plans should be in writing and should be monitored for performance. Planning cannot be done effectively without consideration of "probe" information, "perceived" findings, "performing" skills, and forecasted "predictions." The planning process requires attention to the skills of organizing, classifying, prioritizing, and policy making.

People means that marketing is "people oriented" and that heavy emphasis should be placed on communication (especially listening), training, and interaction among employees, suppliers, prospects, customers, other departments, the public, government, and industry. Stress is placed on human, employee, and customer relations, and on human behavior and motivation.

Professional means balancing the marketing mix effectively, carrying out the strategies and plans through constant monitoring, and following through to achieve goals and satisfaction among all parties involved. It requires individual commitment and dedication, progressive actions, and participation in professional associations to advance the state of the art of marketing. Above all, it means credibility.

Source: Allwyn A. Johnson, "Viewpoint," *Marketing News,* April 11, 1986, 2. Reprinted by permission from *Marketing News,* published by the American Marketing Association.

- *Marketing concept.* The philosophy that guides a marketing company in putting together its marketing mix so as to satisfy its customers and, as a result, make a profit. It stresses consumer satisfaction above profit and should be the basis for all retail strategy development.
- *Market potential.* The total number of possible opportunities for selling a product or service within target markets.
- *Market share.* The percentage of potential sales in markets that a firm achieves as a result of a successful marketing mix.
- *Marketing channel.* The route that a product or service takes from original developer to final consumer. As an example, the route of a Seiko watch begins at the manufacturing plant in Japan, then moves to a middleman (export-import wholesale firm), and ends up in one of a variety of retail stores worldwide, where it is purchased by the final customer. The customer may be the actual user (consumer) or only the final purchaser, because the watch may have been purchased as a gift for someone else.

With the Seiko example pointing out the retailer's place in the marketing channel, it is now time to consider some terms used in the retail industry.

- *Retailers.* Businesses or individuals that sell more than 50 percent of their goods and/or services to final consumers in small quantities.
- *Retailing.* The business of buying products or services from many resources and of reselling them to ultimate consumers in small quantities.
- *Retail mix.* A combination of activities: planning physical facilities, determining merchandise or services, pricing, promotional services, finance, and control engaged in by retailers in an attempt to satisfy their target markets.
- *Basic principle of retailing.* A guiding statement for the industry recommending that retailers have the right merchandise at the right time, in the right place, at the right price, and in the right quantity in order to satisfy their customers and to make a profit.

The basic principle of retailing should be thought of as the foundation for all retail decision making.

RETAILING IN THE CHANNEL OF DISTRIBUTION

Distribution is one of the most important marketing functions in modern society. There would be little **economic utility** and even less satisfaction if manufacturers created new items without giving any thought to their movement. In an industrial world where people are no longer self-sufficient, the key to success is having the goods in the right place at the right

Economic Utility
The power to
satisfy consumers'
needs and wants.
Utility created by
the movement of
goods results in
employment within
an economy.

time. If a marketing system works well, it also provides for the four basic utilities isolated by economists: time, place, possession, and form. In other words, the system arranges for producing and having goods available when and where they are wanted, that is, in retail stores. The completed retail sales transaction then provides possession utility.

Where does retailing belong in the vast marketing channel that brings California lettuce to Manhattan and Seventh Avenue fashion to San Jose? Are retailers always in the same channel position as goods move from manufacturer to user? There is no single answer to this question because retailers and others engaged in retailing exist at every level of the marketing channel and are therefore not always in the same place. For example, although the route traveled by Seiko watches is usually through the marketing channel, there is always the possibility of buying the product direct from a wholesaler or manufacturer. (See Figure 1.2.)

One does not have to be a retailer by definition in order to engage in retailing. Even though the largest percentage of consumer goods is marketed through the retail sector, many other firms throughout the channel engage in the functions traditionally performed by retailers.

Figure   1.2   Distributors of Consumer Goods in the Marketing Channel

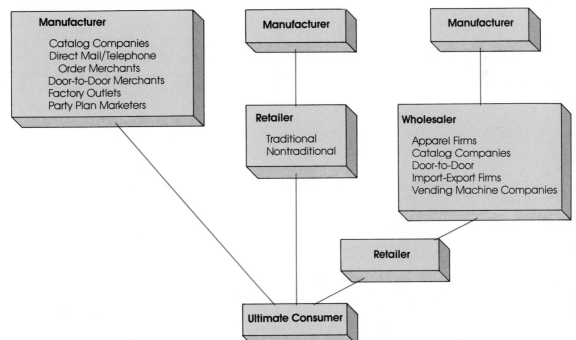

Manufacturer to Consumer

Manufacturers can play a number of retail roles. One example is the manufacturer of women's sweaters who opens an on-premise discount store to compete for the retail dollars of nearby consumers. Located in the lower level of the factory, it becomes a local outlet for seconds and irregulars. It also serves as a testing site for new merchandise, helping the manufacturer decide which designs in a forthcoming line have immediate customer acceptance and which do not. Through this operation, the manufacturer makes a larger profit on items sold through the outlet than if they had been sold in job lots to wholesalers or retail discounters and, at the same time, gathers valuable data that may become the basis for future merchandising strategies.

Manufacturer to consumer is the shortest, most direct channel, but one through which the smallest amount of merchandise is distributed. Because of this, it is relatively unimportant when compared to either of the other two routes. Included in this channel are such diverse direct sales organizations as:

1. French couture designers, who create and sell to individual customers as well as to retail accounts
2. Door-to-door companies, like Avon
3. Party plan firms
4. Mail order manufacturers
5. Factory outlet stores.

Factory Outlets
Stores that sell manufacturers' seconds, irregulars, overruns, and samples.

The marketing strategies of manufacturers operating as retailers are strictly consumer-oriented, because they are not selling to middlemen. Products are sold individually, not in lots, in cases, or by the dozen. In some instances, such as French couture clothes or Avon products, the name brand or label is extremely important. In other instances, such as suits made in Hong Kong or clothes sold in **factory outlets,** the emphasis is on price, and brand is of little importance.

Promotion strategies also vary. Direct mail may be the only medium employed, as in the case of Hong Kong clothes, whereas television may be the catalyst for inducing Avon sales. Personal selling is the promotion tool of the French couture, and factory outlets rely heavily on print media. No one marketing mix can serve all manufacturers who sell directly to the consumer, but whatever variations each selects, all the components are geared to the final market.

Manufacturer to Retailer to Consumer

A longer route, and one in which the retailer is the only middleman, is the one from manufacturer to retailer to consumer. Retailers are a very important link in the distribution chain, because most goods are marketed through some type of retail outlet. There are almost two million retail stores in the United States, with sales of over a trillion dollars annually. In spite of the large numbers, more than half of the nation's retailers sell less than $100,000 a year and account for less than 10 percent of total retail sales. At the same time, 4 or 5 percent of the retail stores sell over one million dollars in goods and services annually and account for more than half of all retail sales. The retail giants that do over one million dollars in business annually generally buy directly from producers.

Manufacturer to Wholesaler to Retailer to Consumer

The longest channel travels from manufacturer to wholesaler to retailer to consumer. Today it is hardly the most important one but under certain circumstances may be the only way for the retailer to get certain goods.

At one stage in history, wholesalers dominated the distribution channel. Before World War II, when retailers were located in city centers and the nation's transportation network was dominated by railroads, the wholesaler was the channel captain who brought goods from manufacturing centers to consumer centers. Here retailers from all over a region could converge and view, in one location, all of the various products brought from near and far.

After World War II the rapid expansion of retailing into the suburbs, plus the development of a nationwide highway network, made buying direct a more logical route. Retailers who needed more units for their additional stores were buying in quantity directly from the manufacturers, who then shipped to retailer-owned central distribution centers. So many retailers began taking over the distribution functions formerly performed by wholesalers that most wholesalers lost their dominant position in the channel. Yet, even in the 1980s, there are certain retailers and certain circumstances that call for the use of this longest channel. That is why it must be considered as a viable option for the distribution of merchandise.

Some middlemen also sell directly to consumers in small quantities. A typical example is sporting goods distributors that sell to a select group of consumers who know someone in management. Another example is central market apparel wholesalers who open their doors to the public on Saturday mornings and sell merchandise at prices slightly above wholesale.

At every point in the channel of distribution, channel members—large or small, manufacturer, wholesaler, or retailer—are willing to serve the consumer directly if it means added dollars. Competition exists at every level.

Retailer Classifications

This text focuses on firms that are classified as retailers rather than on manufacturers or wholesalers running retail operations as add-on functions. These marketers represent retailing in its truest sense and distribute the largest portion of our GNP. Some former manufacturers and wholesalers are now classified as retailers because once a company begins to realize more than 50 percent of its sales at retail it officially changes its channel position from manufacturing or wholesaling to retailing. The Firestone Tire & Rubber Company, which began as a tire manufacturer but now operates a nationwide chain of Firestone Automotive Centers selling all types of automotive accessories and equipment, is an example of this type of classification change.

Nonstore Retail
Mail order houses, vending machine operators, and other forms of direct selling.

In Chapters 6 and 7 the various types of retail operations are discussed in depth. Each type falls into one or two major retail classifications: (1) food based or (2) general merchandise. Each is vitally important to the economy as a whole. Most are traditional or in-store retailers, but the **nonstore retail** segment is growing. (Table 1.2 shows the different categories into which nearly all retailers fall.)

Table   1.2   Retail Stores by Category, 1982

Kind of Business	Number of Establishments[a]	Amount (in thousands)	Percent Change, 1977–1982
Retail Trade	1,322,058	1,033,727,988	48.3
Building Materials, Hardware, Garden Supply, and Mobile Home Dealers	66,033	49,940,393	32.0
Building Materials and Supply Stores	33,869	34,739,682	29.6
Lumber and Other Building Materials Dealers	24,940	31,430,439	28.4
Paint, Glass, and Wallpaper Stores	8,929	3,309,243	42.8
Hardware Stores	19,611	8,376,553	45.7
Retail Nurseries, Lawn and Garden Supply Stores	7,862	2,908,375	82.9
Mobile Home Dealers	4,691	3,915,783	5.6
General Merchandise Group Stores	34,022	119,301,044	36.6
Department Stores (including leased departments)[b,c]	10,035	107,082,582	39.2
Department Stores (excluding leased departments)[b]	10,035	99,109,432	39.5
Variety Stores	10,814	7,863,421	14.9
Miscellaneous General Merchandise Stores	13,173	12,328,191	30.6
Food Stores	176,212	240,408,494	56.9
Grocery Stores	128,128	225,671,016	56.4
Meat and Fish (seafood) Markets	11,029	5,599,958	60.3
Retail Bakeries	17,603	3,639,623	66.0
Retail Bakeries—Baking and Selling	15,676	3,206,523	68.6
Retail Bakeries—Selling Only	1,927	433,100	48.6

(*continued*)

Table 1.2 *(continued)*

Kind of Business	Number of Establishments[a]	Amount (in thousands)	Percent Change, 1977–1982
Other Food Stores	19,452	5,497,897	68.3
Fruit Stores and Vegetable Markets	2,950	1,406,440	62.5
Candy, Nut, and Confectionery Stores	5,060	853,960	73.2
Dairy Products Stores	4,968	1,491,760	35.9
Miscellaneous Food Stores	6,474	1,745,737	115.3
Automotive Dealers	89,207	187,843,499	27.5
Motor Vehicle Dealers—New and Used Cars	25,641	152,050,362	24.8
Motor Vehicle Dealers—Used Cars Only	11,551	6,391,861	23.3
Auto and Home Supply Stores	40,008	20,421,015	61.8
Tire, Battery, and Accessory Dealers	35,986	18,372,456	71.3
Other Auto and Home Supply Stores	4,022	2,048,559	7.9
Miscellaneous Automotive Dealers	12,007	8,980,261	16.0
Boat Dealers	4,122	2,869,835	14.3
Recreational and Utility Trailer Dealers	2,475	2,772,171	−0.2
Motorcycle Dealers	4,607	2,865,369	49.7
Automotive Dealers, n.e.c.	803	472,886	−12.4
Gasoline Service Stations	116,154	94,820,200	75.9
Apparel and Accessory Stores	133,920	57,180,275	57.4
Men's and Boy's Clothing and Furnishings Stores	17,426	7,685,752	10.8
Women's Clothing and Specialty Stores and Furriers	51,030	22,181,767	66.3
Women's Ready-to-Wear Stores	44,084	20,310,786	64.5
Women's Accessory and Specialty Stores and Furriers	6,946	1,870,981	88.7
Family Clothing Stores	17,899	13,471,427	72.7
Shoe Stores	36,031	11,320,406	63.5
Other Apparel and Accessory Stores	11,534	2,520,923	90.9
Children's and Infants' Wear Stores	5,323	1,367,858	93.2
Miscellaneous Apparel and Accessory Stores	6,211	1,153,065	88.2
Furniture, Home Furnishings, and Equipment Stores	93,355	45,098,193	42.2
Furniture Stores	29,575	17,183,597	26.1
Home Furnishing Stores	24,615	8,767,284	51.4
Floor Covering Stores	10,929	4,952,123	30.0
Drapery, Curtain, and Upholstery Stores	4,056	855,173	27.6
Miscellaneous Home Furnishing Stores	9,630	2,959,988	125.8
Household Appliance Stores	10,539	5,683,353	25.9
Radio, Television, and Music Stores	28,626	13,463,959	73.5
Radio and Television Stores	19,347	9,628,111	90.8
Music Stores	9,279	3,835,848	40.6
Eating and Drinking Places	318,765	100,794,030	64.2
Eating Places	257,577	92,232,439	69.2
Restaurants and Lunchrooms	122,773	46,993,188	64.9
Cafeterias	6,125	2,887,734	56.3
Refreshment Places	108,601	35,496,828	81.2
Other Eating Places	20,078	6,854,689	50.1
Drinking Places: Alcoholic Beverages	61,188	8,561,591	24.0

(continued)

Table   1.2   (continued)

Kind of Business	Number of Establishments[a]	Amount (in thousands)	Percent Change, 1977–1982
Drug and Proprietary Stores	48,637	35,777,064	53.9
Miscellaneous Retail Stores	245,753	102,564,796	58.9
Liquor Stores	34,071	17,143,733	39.9
Used Merchandise Stores	17,560	3,952,321	84.4
Miscellaneous Shopping Goods Stores	102,059	33,288,626	71.9
Sporting Goods Stores and Bicycle Shops	20,129	7,522,371	79.5
Bookstores	9,312	3,115,114	80.7
Stationery Stores	4,757	1,501,076	41.1
Jewelry Stores	22,240	8,261,676	56.1
Hobby, Toy, and Game Shops	7,680	3,246,135	112.9
Camera and Photographic Supply Stores	3,988	1,882,852	68.8
Gift, Novelty, and Souvenir Shops	22,302	4,667,644	108.8
Luggage and Leather Goods Stores	1,884	590,401	69.3
Sewing, Needlework, and Piece Goods Stores	9,767	2,501,357	33.9
Nonstore Retailers	20,764	19,418,474	37.9
Mail Order Houses	7,360	10,940,516	47.0
Automatic Merchandising Machine Operators	5,373	4,557,618	23.2
Direct Selling Establishments	8,031	3,920,340	33.4
Fuel and Ice Dealers	12,838	17,143,267	75.7
Fuel Oil Dealers	6,077	11,937,189	80.2
Liquefied Petroleum Gas (bottled gas) Dealers	5,919	4,801,646	62.8
Fuel and Ice dealers, n.e.c.	842	404,432	118.5
Florists	20,907	3,125,291	42.7
Cigar Stores and Stands	2,360	596,888	48.4
News Dealers and Newsstands	1,987	512,029	34.7
Miscellaneous Retail Stores, n.e.c.	33,207	7,384,167	85.1
Optical Goods Stores	10,551	1,716,498	55.9
Pet Stores	4,495	814,001	108.4
Typewriter Stores	902	208,969	33.3
Other Miscellaneous Retail Stores, n.e.c.	17,259	4,644,699	98.4

[a] Each kind-of-business classification includes leased departments classified in that kind of business as if they were separate establishments. Accordingly, data for leased departments are not consolidated with kind-of-business data for main stores in which they are located.

[b] Includes sales from catalog order desks.

[c] Includes data for leased departments operated within department stores. Data for this line not included in broader kind-of-business totals.

Source: *Census of Retail Trade,* Bureau of the Census, U.S. Department of Commerce, 1982.

RETAIL IMAGE IN RELATION TO MARKET POSITION

Today, regardless of their channel position or their classification, all retailers must find the right place in the minds of customers in order to prosper. This means that each must have a definite image, because image is as important to sell as are goods and services. A retailer's perceived image must coincide with the one sought by members of its target market or markets. (See Figure 1.3.)

In this context, positioning is another key to success. Shoppers want to feel comfortable, to belong. Neiman-Marcus attracts more Texas millionaires than ranch hands; K mart caters to more production workers than computer scientists; and more nonprofessionals than professionals buy homeowner's insurance from Allstate (Sears) than from local, independent brokers. The reason in each case is that consumers relate to the retailer's projected image and market position. They are comfortable shopping where they perceive that they fit.

Once retailers have found a successful image, they usually stay with it as they move along the wheel of retailing, changing only with corresponding changes in their customers' image. For example, the no-frills discount store gave way to the well-appointed mass merchant when the

Figure   1.3   Image Matched to Market: Macy's in Dallas

Source: Courtesy of Macy's New York.

city discount customer became the suburban homeowner, but the retailer's image was still being dictated by the same market (albeit one with a new image), not by potential new customers. Mass merchants now attract customers from every age and income class, more because of price consciousness than image; the primary market of the mass merchant is basically the same as it has always been. (See Figure 1.4.)

Some retailers do attempt to move into a new market. In this case, they make a conscious effort to change their existing image. J. C. Penney's $1 billion gamble in 1983 is a perfect example of a retailer's attempt to change its image without altering its basic channel position. Penney's purpose was to increase its market share by trading up.

Penney, in an attempt to shed its low-price, middle America image and to bolster its sluggish sales, signed an exclusive contract with Halston. The designer agreed, for what was rumored to be an eight-figure price, to produce a collection of men's and women's fashions, called Halston III, for Penney's 600 largest suburban mall locations.

The move toward such stylish but affordable fashions was a significant coup for the usually low-key and cost-conscious mass merchandiser and was part of Penney's bold new strategy for the 1980s. The company, which started in 1902 as a tiny country store in Kemmerer, Wyoming, began pushing hard to transform itself into the only truly national de-

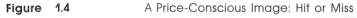

Figure   1.4   A Price-Conscious Image: Hit or Miss

Source: Photo by John Stapleton.

partment store chain in the country, one with big stores in major malls from coast-to-coast, all operating under the same corporate logo.

The company committed about $1 billion to remodeling several hundred of its largest stores. This was considered the most substantial investment of its kind ever in the retailing business. The company also carved out additional space for its more upscale, higher-margin clothing by dropping most of the things that made Penney Penney, including household durables, paint and hardware, and automotive and auto-service centers.

The stakes in Penney's push were big. And perhaps nothing indicated this more than the huge red banner with bold block lettering draped in front of its New York headquarters when the deal was made. It said simply: Halston III, J. C. Penney.[4] Maintaining a clear-cut image is never easy, and changing it is even more difficult, yet attention to image is vital for success in the marketplace.

RETAIL STRATEGY DEVELOPMENT

When planning strategies, it is necessary to keep size as well as function in mind. Although functions are generally uniform in all stores regardless of size, strategies guiding their execution must necessarily differ. Because the greatest retail dollar volume is attained by corporate giants (see Table 1.3), their strategies are usually studied and adopted by small retailers.

For every retailer, strategy development must precede creation of the retailing mix. During this stage decisions are made concerning controllable variables. These controllable elements—physical facilities/operations, merchandise/service offerings, pricing, promotion/image, and service—must be blended properly if retailers are to meet their dual goals of customer satisfaction and profit.

The creation of new strategies to help combat the tremendous wave of soft-goods discounters—who appeared in the retail scene in the early 1980s—illustrates the challenge traditional department store retailers face. Although **off-price retailers** such as Marshalls, Loehmann's, Burlington Coat Factory, Syms, and The Dress Barn represented only about 6 percent of the nation's overall retail apparel business then, they were expected to triple their market share to as much as 30 percent by 1990. Department store strategy development in 1984 required (1) increasing the variety of goods and services, (2) cutting prices, (3) eliminating suppliers that were becoming too broad in their distribution, (4) improving customer services, and (5) entering the off-price field themselves either by starting their own discount outlets or by acquiring existing discount chains. As examples, Dayton Hudson started Plum's; Zayre started Hit or

Off-Price Retailers Stores with turnover double that of traditional apparel shops, with prices as much as 60 percent lower on brand merchandise.

---

[4] "Penney's $1 Billion Gamble on Chic," *The New York Times*, July 10, 1983.

Miss; and Associated Dry Goods—operators of Lord & Taylor and Joseph Horne—acquired Caldor Inc. and Loehmann's.[5]

Strategic planning, according to Walter F. Loeb, vice president and senior retail analyst at Morgan Stanley and Company, involves a rational, focused determination of the answers to three simple questions: Where are we now? Where do we want to be? What is the best way to get there? Once these questions have been answered and a careful assessment made of the company's strengths, weaknesses, and optimum allocation of human and financial resources, a successful retail mix should result. Loeb cautions that "simply adding new units or merchandise lines does

---

[5] "A Revolution in American Shopping," *The New York Times*, October 23, 1983, Sec. 3, 28F.

Table 1.3   Twenty-Five Largest Retailing Companies

Rank 1985	1984	Company	Sales (in thousands)	Assets (in thousands) Amount	Rank	Net Income (in thousands) Amount	Rank
1	1	Sears Roebuck (Chicago)	$40,715,300	$66,416,900	1	$1,303,300	1
2	2	K mart (Troy, Mich.)	22,420,002	9,990,682	4	221,242	9
3	3	Safeway Stores (Oakland, Calif.)	19,650,542	4,840,611	7	231,300	8
4	4	Kroger (Cincinnati)	17,123,531	4,177,807	10	180,750	17
5	6	American Stores (Salt Lake City)	13,889,528	3,462,513	14	154,470	22
6	5	J.C. Penney (New York)	13,747,000	10,522,000	3	397,000	3
7	7	Southland (Dallas)	12,719,241	3,735,544	11	212,535	12
8	8	Federated Department Stores (Cincinnati)	9,978,027	5,353,643	5	286,626	5
9	9	Lucky Stores (Dublin, Calif.)	9,382,282	1,932,460	24	86,526	30
10	11	Dayton Hudson (Minneapolis)	8,793,372	4,417,514	9	283,620	6
11	10	Household International (Prospect Heights, Ill.)	8,685,500	11,928,500	2	210,900	13
12	13	Wal-Mart Stores (Bentonville, Ark.)	8,580,910	3,103,645	16	327,473	4
13	12	Winn-Dixie Stores (Jacksonville, Fla.)	7,774,480	1,238,738	32	107,895	26
14	15	F.W. Woolworth (New York)	5,958,000	2,535,000	19	177,000	18
15	16	BATUS (Louisville)	5,881,408	4,517,448	8	163,532	20
16	17	Great Atlantic & Pacific Tea (Montvale, N.J.)	5,878,286	1,363,101	29	215,779	11
17	14	Montgomery Ward (Chicago)	5,388,000	3,654,000	13	(290,000)	50
18	21	Supermarkets General (Woodbridge, N.J.)	5,122,633	1,103,841	38	63,712	37
19	18	May Department Stores (St. Louis)	5,079,900	3,442,300	15	235,400	7
20	19	Albertson's (Boise)	5,060,265	1,124,617	36	85,110	32
21	20	Melville (Harrison, N.Y.)	4,805,380	1,806,673	26	210,812	14
22	22	Associated Dry Goods (New York)	4,385,019	2,288,646	21	119,696	25
23	23	R.H. Macy (New York)	4,368,386	2,356,615	20	189,315	15
24	32	Wickes Companies (Santa Monica, Calif.)	4,362,454	2,648,298	18	76,130	33
25	26	Marriott (Bethesda, Md.)	4,317,900	3,663,800	12	167,400	19

Source: "The 50 Largest Retailing Companies Ranked by Sales," *Fortune*, June 9, 1986, 136. © 1986 Time Inc. All rights reserved.

not constitute strategic planning," and that "remodeling and refurbishing stores are merely a means for improvement, not ends in themselves."[6]

Retailers have control over location, management, operations, pricing policies, product and service offerings, store image, and promotional efforts. They have no control over competition; government laws; consumers; technology; or economic, political, social, and environmental conditions. These uncontrollables must also be taken into consideration during the strategic planning stage, because they greatly affect even the best-executed retail mix.

Both controllable and uncontrollable variables will be discussed in depth in later chapters. Our purpose here is simply to present a frame of reference so that the importance of these variables in developing specific retail strategies can be understood.

Summary

Retailing is educational, dynamic, and demanding. The cyclical pattern of retail evolution, according to the wheel of retailing theory, consists of (1) entry, (2) trading up, and (3) vulnerability. Retailing will be presented throughout this text in a marketing context. From trading posts to regional malls, retail stores in America have changed along with the society they serve. Trading posts and peddlers gave way to general stores, which in turn faded into history with the industrial revolution and birth of department and specialty stores. After World War II, city stores followed their customers to the suburbs, where many still remain.

Retailing exists throughout the marketing channel but, in order to be classified as a retailer, a company must sell more than 50 percent of its goods or services directly to individual consumers. In spite of this, many manufacturers and wholesalers engage in retailing and become direct competitors of their own retail customers. Today, retailers fall into two major classifications: (1) food based or (2) general merchandise.

To meet the competition for consumer dollars, retailers must constantly strive for excellence by developing new strategies geared to the changing environment in which they operate. This may include revamping or updating their retail mix to keep up with changing consumer demand and new competition and sometimes even changing their image completely.

Offering the right merchandise in the right quantity, in the right place, at the right price, and at the right time is no longer enough to guarantee success, although it is certainly the basis for success. Today's merchants must think, merchandise, and manage as marketers. Under-

---

[6] Samuel Feinberg, "From Where I Sit," *Women's Wear Daily*, February 21, 1984, 26.

standing both uncontrollable and controllable variables is the key to strategic planning both today and tomorrow.

Questions for Review

1. Explain what is meant by the qualitative dimensions of retailing.
2. What is the wheel of retailing theory?
3. Define the term *marketing concept* and explain its implication to retailers.
4. What are channels of distribution? Where in the channel does retailing occur?
5. Comment on the statement, "One does not have to be a retailer by definition in order to engage in retailing."
6. Explain what is meant by retail image and describe its relationship to market position.
7. Define the term *retail strategy* and comment on its importance to small, independent retailers as well as large chains.

CASE STUDY   K. F. Moore and Company

Problems in a Changing Economy

The article in the morning paper read:

> K. F. Moore reached the end of the line Thursday as its creditors'
> committee moved to have the company declared bankrupt and wind
> up one of the biggest liquidations in retailing history. Moore's is
> expected to close all of its remaining 450 stores today and reopen in
> five days, ready to hold going-out-of business sales over the next
> three to four weeks. The agonizing decision to liquidate was made
> after a day-long meeting of the committee Monday, according to
> Jonathan Baylor, attorney for the creditors' group. The decision
> boiled down to the conclusion that the company would not be viable
> after paying out money necessary to free secured claims and open up
> a flow of merchandise on normal credit terms.

Rose Gardner could not believe what she was reading. How could
something like this happen? K. F. Moore had always been a solid name in
retailing, one that had served the American people since 1910, and that
meant a great deal to her. Rose had been a salesgirl in the curtain department of the first Moore store from the time she graduated from high
school until her marriage five years later. Since that time she had remained a loyal customer, unaware that behind the scenes things were not
as ideal as they had seemed.

Why did Moore's fail? Other chains that had started in the golden era
of retailing were still operating successfully. In 1910, at the age of 21,
Kenneth F. Moore, a fabric salesman, had taken his entire life savings of
$950 and opened a store in Melrose, New York. He wanted to offer his
customers the same assortment of soft goods and convenience merchandise found in the typical five-and-ten store but of a somewhat better
quality and at a slightly higher price. His market fell somewhere between
that of the typical chain variety store and the more expensive department store.

Aimed at a definite target market and with a clear-cut image, Moore's
enjoyed a steady growth over the next two decades. During the 1930s, it
retained its image and continued to attract an increasing number of customers—people who were hard pressed for money and knew that they
could get real value for their dollar at Moore's. It was this basic philosophy, plus concentration on soft goods, that kept Moore's alive during the
Depression and World War II. Thus, in the 1950s, a healthy corporation
was ready for the postwar retail explosion.

Like many retailing organizations, Moore's caught expansion fever and opened new stores almost as fast as its real estate division could find suitable locations. Even though the market research that was performed often lacked depth, Moore's felt that following Mr. and Mrs. America to the suburbs would guarantee success. The company would join Sears, J. C. Penney, and Montgomery Ward as a national institution. It, too, would offer credit and carry a private-label line of appliances with a solid, American-sounding name—the Lincoln brand.

All the important economic indicators were right: a rapidly expanding economy, a growing population, more new households than ever before, and an escalating national income. What could go wrong? Did it matter that past success had been built on a foundation of soft rather than hard goods, that stores were proliferating faster than management expertise, that the credit business was much more expensive to operate than originally estimated, and not enough people were opening accounts?

Expansion was too rapid in terms of merchandise, stores, and services and a once clear-cut image was growing cloudy. Although Moore's had weathered these conditions during the 1960s and 1970s, things were different in the 1980s. Growth, slowing for a few years, had come to a virtual standstill. Phasing out the Lincoln brand of appliances was the first step. The chain's president, Robert B. Munroe, announced the formulation of an entirely new merchandising approach for K. F. Moore aimed at the female shopper, young marrieds, and first-time parents. The company was going to return to its traditional retailing roots, and major appliance marketing did not fit into its plans. Munroe cited unmistakable trends in consumer spending away from big-ticket appliance purchases sold through installment credit plans. Moore's management also decided to de-emphasize the Moore-operated credit program and private-label merchandise because these were unattractive retailing strategies to pursue.

Of the 1,000 stores operating in 40 states, 550 were closed and the reins were tightened in the three areas that had seen overexpansion: new store openings, hard-goods merchandising, and credit. As Christmas approached, Moore's, with $200 million in cash, initiated a big advertising campaign to draw as many shopping dollars as possible. However, bad became worse, and in February K. F. Moore declared bankruptcy. Even closing another 150 stores did not help. Poor management and merchandising, unsound credit practices, and a severely strained expansion plan in which more than 400 stores had been opened in five years had taken its toll and produced disastrous results.

As Rose Gardner put down the newspaper, she was more enlightened than before but still confused about how smart business people could get into such a situation. K. F. Moore, for so long an important part of the retailing scene and such a vital part of so many Americans' lives, would disappear as if it had never existed.

Questions

1. What lessons can be learned from the K. F. Moore experience? Explain.
2. Suggest a plan and strategies for retail expansion.
3. List the advantages and disadvantages of purchasing big-ticket appliances on installment credit.
4. List the advantages and disadvantages of purchasing big-ticket appliances for cash at a discount store.
5. How does the dynamic nature of retailing contribute to a bankruptcy such as that experienced by K. F. Moore?

The Retail Environment

Source: Courtesy of Urban
Investment and Development Co.

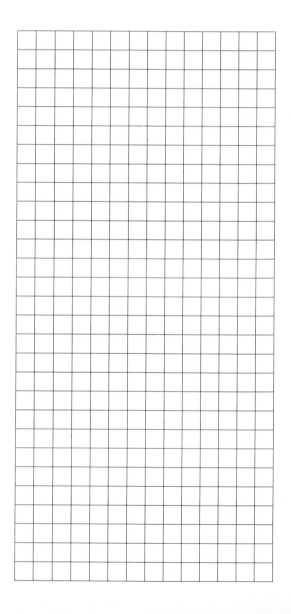

Herbert Landsman
Vice President, Merchandising
Brookstone Company

CARPE DIEM—
SEIZE THE DAY!

Specialty retailing is, by definition, a rapidly changing and evolving environment. The retailer who refuses to acknowledge or study those changes, who maintains the status quo, is destined to be at their mercy. Aggressively managing new business criteria on a regular basis can activate even greater opportunities than exist today.

And so it is true for Brookstone Company, a nationwide specialty retailer. The company entered the direct-to-consumer mail order arena in 1965 with a simple one-color brochure packed with hard-to-find tools that appealed to professionals, tool lovers, hobbyists, and weekend do-it-yourselfers. From the start, the primary focus was on treating the Brookstone customer with unusual care. This meant informative copy, immediate order fulfillment, a lifetime unconditional guarantee and, of course, the heart of the merchandising concept: unique, utilitarian, high-quality, fiendishly ingenious products.

The formula worked, and Brookstone never departed from it. The one-color mailer quickly became a 68-page catalog, expanding in both number and variety of products as well as in its appeal to a wider range of customers.

But the marketplace was changing. Consumers' mailboxes were becoming deluged with catalogs, all with the potential to share discretionary dollars. At this same time, Brookstone determined through focus group activity and market research that its core customer base tended to be affluent and older (in their mid-50s and 60s). Although neither issue posed insurmountable difficulties for a company that had developed such a well-defined niche, mail-order glut and a maturing target customer did limit the long-term growth and opportunity for an exciting, young concept. This provoked a search for alternative media to reach new or supplemental customers.

The specialty retail store concept emerged as the logical extension of the Brookstone business. The retail market offered a broader base of high-income, suburban, well-educated younger customers and could provide a natural synergy to the already established mail order business.

A total retail positioning was developed to reach this new audience. This involved defining merchandising assortments, formulating customer service requirements, even zero-basing product copy that reinforced the appropriate purchasing cues of the new consumers. In July 1973 the Brookstone retail store division was born. Store openings followed in rapid succession in Boston, Atlanta, Washington, Minneapolis, Chicago, New York, Hartford, Houston, Dallas, Los Angeles, Denver, St. Louis, Detroit, and Miami.

Each new store in each trading area has given an added dimension and complexity to the Brookstone business. Regional influences affect assortment mix, pricing, promotional timing, and store layout. Variations in market economies affect individual product trends as well as total store growth. The issues are diverse and demand consistent review through customer service questionnaires, focus groups, and mall interviews.

The awareness in the early 1970s of changing customer demographics and advancing mail-order saturation acted as a strong catalyst for Brookstone's decision to build a retail concept, national in scope. That foresighted decision gave Brookstone an early foothold in the marketplace, permitting it to outpace competitors and generate a total business that is greater than the sum of its parts.

Learning Objectives

Upon completing this chapter you should be able to:

1. Discuss consumer spending in an inflationary economy.
2. Understand the demographic changes that will affect retail strategy development in the decades ahead.
3. State why the 1980s will probably be remembered as the decade of the catalog retailer.
4. Describe the primary target market of off-price retailers and explain why it is the primary market.
5. Understand how retailers can develop their merchandise mix around political events.
6. Know why all retailers must have an understanding of federal, state, and local legislation.
7. Discuss positive effects of the technological revolution on retailing.

Chapter 1 introduced two sets of variables, controllable (the retail mix) and uncontrollable. This chapter will be devoted to the uncontrollables: environmental elements over which individual retailers have little control yet within whose framework they must develop their retail mix. Retailers must deal with inflation, recession, changing demographics, population shifts, new political alliances, advanced technology, social movements, and legal constraints. Students of retailing must also grapple with these problems because they will one day have to face them as practitioners.

RETAILING AND THE ECONOMY

Feel the pulse of retailing and you will feel the pulse of the economy. Depression, recession, war, peace, prosperity, and inflation are all reflected at the checkout counter. Retail strategies change in response to an oil embargo, an income tax hike, a state sales tax increase, or a lower textile quota. The everyday expression of economic theory is found in retailing. Retailers, in a broad sense, are therefore applied economists, using their special expertise to help advance the standard of living of those they serve.

How does the manager of a new branch store adjust to inflation? What happens to a local hardware store owner when wholesale prices continue to go up and there is direct competition from large, national chains? Can the costly service orientation of department stores allow them to survive the onslaught of off-price fashion merchants? These are only a few of the serious questions that retailers face day in and day out. Although specific problems may change from year to year, the need to work within a dynamic economy remains constant. Retailers must deal with, develop proper strategies for, and quickly adapt to economic changes by being constantly tuned in to current world, national, regional, and local economic indicators. Only in this way will they be able to create a proper retailing mix.

Income as an Economic Indicator

A retail company is an excellent laboratory in which to observe economic change. The dynamics of customers' decision making is a powerful stimulus to adaptability and, indeed, to survival. Purchase decisions reflect changes in **disposable income.** The more disposable income people have, the more they spend; the less they have, the less they spend.

Disposable Income Personal income after taxes are paid; income available for consumption or savings.

Consider the case of Mary and Peter Jones, who would like to own a self-cleaning oven. They cannot save enough money to purchase one however, because they live in a northern New England community in which the local shoe manufacturer, for whom Peter and most of the townspeople worked, had to close up shop because of competition from overseas. As a result of this industrial change, disposable income in the community dropped and the purchase of products like self-cleaning ovens had to be delayed.

Discretionary Income Money available after necessities are paid for; money available for optional spending.

Now let us look at a situation in which family purchase decision making is an indication of a change in **discretionary income.** Roger and Lynne Brown live in a booming Sunbelt town. They are both employed and thus have been able to enjoy many luxuries. Now their son is attending an expensive private college and their daughter a state university. Suddenly their substantial discretionary income has taken a nosedive. Like many middle-income families with college-age children, the Browns can no longer buy many of the things they desire. Choices must be made—a new car or a summer trip, tuition or a vacation home. As family expenses increase, retailers selling goods purchased from discretionary income find sales to this group dropping. Although based on personal rather than workplace factors, this particular change deserves attention from retailers in the community where the Browns are typical of half the population.

Studying a community's demographics can usually reveal reasons for changing expenditure patterns. This allows retailers to make adjustments in stock, prices, or promotion. Merchants must adapt if and when a large segment of their population undergoes significant economic change. (See Figure 2.1.)

Other Economic Influences

In addition to income, retailing reacts to other economic fluctuations. During a recession, for example, people generally spend less on goods and services than they do during prosperous times. Inflation cuts deeply into retail profit because the basic costs of doing business (wages, energy, credit) increase along with vendors' prices. Consumers, too, often change their buying patterns with inflation. As the cost of living increases, so does the sale of **generic goods** and private-label products. People eat at McDonald's more often than at Red Lobster.

Generic Goods
Plain-label goods, often priced much lower than advertised brands.

A change in the price of commodities such as oil has an immediate effect on supermarket shelves, especially if the supermarkets are chains that operate their own trucking fleets. In 1983, for example, oil was $28.55 a barrel, up from $4 a barrel in 1973. At least part of the increase in weekly grocery bills during that period of time could be blamed on this uncontrollable factor.

Successful retailers recognize that all changes in the economy eventually work their way through the system to individual operations. They know that when consumers speak, they must listen and adjust. The retailer who thoroughly studies economic trends will unquestionably be ahead of the one who waits to react when sales begin dropping off.

Figure   2.1   Married Couples, 1985: Who Brings Home the Bacon?

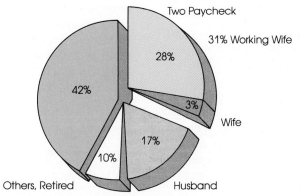

Source: "Marketers Must Cater to Women's Independence," *Marketing News,* June 6, 1986.

FROM THE FIELD

Promotions in the College Market

College state, a mythical 51st U.S. state consisting of 12.4 million students, actually constitutes the fourth largest U.S. population group, according to Chet Swenson, president of Marketing & Financial Management Enterprises Inc. (M&FM), Encino, California.

Citing statistics from Simmons Market Research Bureau Inc., New York, he said the average college student spends $175 to $200 per month on discretionary items—more than the average family of four. And the median age of U.S. college students (including graduates and undergraduates) is 23.8 years.

Simmons calls student dorm rooms and apartments "mini-households," where students first enter the world of independent decision making, purchasing goods and services, such as food, clothing, travel, banking, and sporting goods, Swenson said.

One commodity many students plan to buy is a new car. M&FM research found 38 percent of full-time college students with driver's licenses and active campus lives intend to buy a new car within the next three years. It also showed students have a deep-rooted distrust of some industries, including U.S. automakers.

Several automakers have run special promotions aimed at the college market, Swenson said, citing Nissan's amateur photography contest, advertised in college publications; campus fashion shows held by General Motors; and Ford's special sales offers for graduating seniors.

American Express modified its theme to "Don't leave campus without it," saturated the student market with ads in college newspapers, fliers in bookstore bags, and other promotions, and became involved in lifestyle events, such as campus festivals, talent shows, and commercial-writing competitions. Last year, an American Express talent show at the University of Miami (Florida) drew a crowd of 20,000.

These campus lifestyle promotions can be important for another reason: M&FM figures show that students watch only 7.5 hours of television per week on average, including noncommercial videocassettes and campus video.

College men and women are, however, heavily involved in activities such as movies (89 percent), concerts (76 percent), and intramural sports (61 percent). Swenson suggested that ongoing sponsorship and participation in these types of activities are one way for marketers to reach the large, but often elusive, college market.

———

Source: Excerpted from "Marketers Should Target the 51st U.S. State: The College Market," *Marketing News,* February 28, 1986, 28. Reprinted by permission from *Marketing News,* published by the American Marketing Association.

SOCIOLOGICAL VARIABLES IN RETAILING

Variables in society that bring about cultural lifestyle changes also bring about changes in retailing. Retailers who have moved with the population from rural towns to big cities to sprawling suburbs are a reflection of the society in which they operate. As societies change, retailers must change their merchandise mix, location strategies, pricing structure, promotion mix, and target markets. There is no room for good-old-days thinking in modern retail management. "The best of times is now . . . ," but only if retailers will recognize this fact, and change with the times.

The 1980s boom in new off-price fashion divisions at giants like Associated Dry Goods, Dayton Hudson, K mart, and Zayre attests that these merchants understood societal change. They knew that inflation-afflicted and recession-burdened shoppers were looking for greater values at the same time they were developing a taste for nationally recognized brands and designer-name merchandise. They realized that these consumers wanted goods that symbolized status as well as quality. Because they studied shopping habits, they opened their own off-price stores instead of ignoring the new growing segment of off-price specialty retailers. The success of off-price outlets is one illustration of how otherwise uncontrollable sociological variables can be harnessed and used by retailers to their advantage.

Demographic Changes

Statistics are important to retailers because they are directly related to strategy development and provide important information. Examples of **demographics**—statistical characteristics of human populations—are given in the next few paragraphs.

Demographics
Statistics on human populations: size, distribution, age mix, ethnic mix, education, income.

More households. There will be over 20 million more by 1990, but they will be smaller on average, declining from 2.8 persons to 2.4 persons by the end of the decade. Singles and "mingles" (unmarried couples who share a household) will account for a large share of these new households. In 1985 some 20.6 million Americans lived by themselves, a 90 percent jump in one-person households in 15 years. More households reflect dramatically changing family structure. The so-called "nuclear family" (working husband, nonworking wife at home raising children) now represents only 7 percent of all family structures. Single-parent families equal 19 percent, working women total 56 percent. (See Figure 2.2 on page 42.)

Shifting population. The migration from the Northeast and heartland states to the Sunbelt will continue, as will population shifts within geographic regions.

Figure   2.2   Breakdown of U.S. Households by Type, 1965–1985

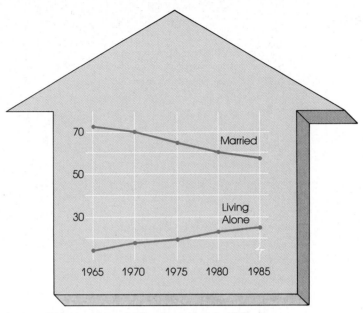

Source: "Solo Americans," *Time*, December 2, 1985, 41.

Changing age mix. Some extremely important shifts in population age distribution are underway as the post–World War II baby boom generation moves into middle age.

Baby Boom
The record 76 million Americans born between 1946 and 1964.

A new **baby boom** is anticipated that will peak about 1989. About 4 million births annually are expected that year.

There will be a short-term decline in the number of teenagers. This group should increase again by about 2.5 million in 1990.

The largest increase will be in the 25 to 44 age group, which will show a net gain of almost 20 million people. This group will be growing about three-and-a-half times as fast as the total population.

The number of persons age 65 and older will rise substantially, from approximately 25 million in 1984 to 31 million in 1990. For the first time, there will be more senior citizens than teenagers. Each *day* brings a net increase of 1,500 persons in the over 65 category. (See Figure 2.3.)

Higher educational levels. In 1970, only one adult in five had some college; by 1995, it will be one in two.

Higher incomes. Close to 40 percent of all households have more than one wage earner, and the number is increasing. By 1990, one of every three U.S. households will have incomes over $25,000, in constant dollars.

Changing ethnic mix. In 1984, about 9 percent of the U.S. population was Hispanic, and 12 percent black. Hispanics will probably pass blacks in the next decade and may account for nearly half of California's population by the end of the century. From 1970 to 1982, the U.S. population increased 11.2 percent: whites +6 percent, blacks +17 percent, Hispanics +71 percent, and Asians +126 percent. For the first time in the history of the U.S. census, homes where English was the second instead of the primary language spoken, increased.[1]

In summary, there will be (1) more working women; (2) more but smaller households; (3) changing family relationships; (4) greater population shifts to the South and West; (5) more babies, more 25-to-44's, more senior citizens, more Hispanics; (6) higher education levels; and (7) higher incomes.

---

[1] From a lecture by Peter A. Magowan, chairman of the board, Safeway Stores, Inc., Texas A&M Center for Retailing Studies Lecturer Series, March 5, 1984.

Figure 2.3

Number of Persons Aged 65 and Older, 1900–2030
Millions

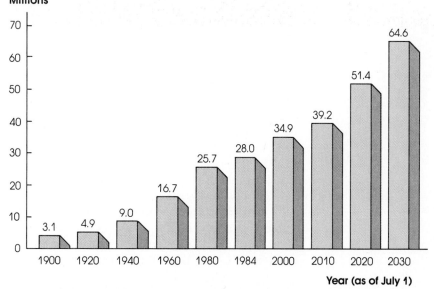

Note: Increments in years on horizontal scale are uneven. Source: "A Profile of Older Americans, 1985" (Washington: American Association of Retired Persons, 1985), 2.

**Zero Population
Growth (ZPG)**
The goal of
bringing to a halt
the growth of
world population.

Like economic elements, demographic variables greatly affect consumer lifestyles. Retailers must respond accordingly. If, for example, the population is shifting from the Northeast to the Sunbelt, **zero population growth (ZPG)** is already a fact of life for northeastern retailers, and their plans for new stores must reflect this. When Lord & Taylor goes to the drawing board, it may look at locations in the Southwest. Instead of building new stores in distant locations, other area retailers whose primary markets are regional may concentrate on strategic management in the existing ones. Even as competition moves south and west, certain retailers are electing to stay in the affluent suburbs of New Jersey and Connecticut. Their strategy centers around increasing services to a clientele with no intention of leaving the geographic area because their lives are ideal in their present location.

The changing age mix also has important implications for retailing. Because the baby boomlet is expected to peak about 1989, Lady Madonna Industries, a vertically integrated manufacturing-retailing-licensing maternity wear complex, expanded during the 1980s. The projected rise in births was the basis for its strategy.

Walk through any department store and you will see gray-haired shoppers buying tennis, golf, or ski clothes. The term *elderly* hardly applies to this rather large 50-plus group, who are active, vigorous, and full of unique wants and needs. The old adage "age is only a state of mind" has never had more meaning for retailers than it does now.

This mature market represents a largely untapped demographic pool, according to a health and age perception study conducted by Caldwell Davis Savage Advertising, a New York advertising agency, in 1986. The agency advised retailers to avoid pigeonholing people as arthritis sufferers, denture wearers, and so on. Nobody likes negative labels. Also, older people should be shown enjoying comfortable lifestyles because a lifetime of work often produces some affluence.

The study also found out that only 16 percent of the 50-plus segment suffers from health problems that interrupt normal activities and that a physically active image such as cross-country skiing is more attractive than sedate activities like bridge. People over 50 think of themselves as 15 years younger than they are, and they do not like to be characterized as retired.[2]

The huge increase in the number of working women over the past few decades means that most often no adult is home to answer the door when Avon calls. Today's Avon representative sells products to office coworkers instead of door-to-door. Because many working women have little time to shop during the day, more stores stay open during the evening. Still another response to the burgeoning female work force has been the increase in catalog retailing. Many a busy person who started out shop-

---

[2] "Guidelines for Ads Targeting Over-50 Market," *Marketing News,* February 28, 1986, 28.

ping by mail or telephone for convenience has adopted catalog shopping as a way of life.

One of the fastest growing market segments in the United States is the affluent **superclass.** This group is expected to grow at the rate of about 8.5 percent a year, doubling by 1990 to about 5 percent of the population.[3] Two reasons for this growth are the increasing numbers of working wives and the rising level of sophistication among the educated population of the United States. Many retailers have responded to this growing clientele by opening exclusive shops in such communities as Beverly Hills, California, and Scottsdale, Arizona. Boston's Copley Place is an entire center catering to a clientele who looks for quality and status before price. (See Figure 2.4.)

Superclass
Households earning more than $50,000 annually.

---

[3] Roger D. Blackwell and W. Wayne Talarzyk, "Lifestyle Retailing: Competitive Strategies for the 1980s," *Journal of Retailing* (Winter 1983): 7–27.

Figure   2.4   An Upscale Shopping Center: Copley Place in Boston

New multiuse center has office space, banks, hotels, theaters, restaurants, lounges, and more.

Source: Courtesy of Urban Investment and Development Co.

One extreme example of catering to the affluent occurred in October 1983, when Regent Air Corporation offered a first-class, one-way ticket on its inaugural flight between Los Angeles and Newark for $1,620. The first-class fare on other airlines was $650. The Regent in-flight menu included Maine lobster and Beluga caviar. The company's three 727s featured art deco interiors, plush swivel chairs as seats, and four private compartments for dining or sleeping. Each compartment had seating for four and sold for $4,320. This all-frills service was aimed at business tycoons and a select list of individuals who occasionally preferred to leave the private jet in the hangar.[4]

At the other extreme are retailers who have perceived opportunities among the growing price-conscious population. Some have opened off-price stores; others, warehouse-type grocery stores. Some manufacturers, such as Dansk and Bass Shoe, have opened retail outlets.

Cultural Changes

Statistics do not exist in a vacuum. Changes in quality of life go along with the numbers. Consumers today have a considerably different set of needs and preferences than they did just a few years ago, and most of them have a direct relationship to changing demographics: more working women, better educated consumers, a shifting population, changes in age mix, growing ethnic populations, and the changing family relationship cited previously.

---

[4]"New Airline Goes beyond First Class and Clients Pay for What They Get," *The New York Times*, October 16, 1983.

Table   2.1   Sampling of Current Retail Responses to Changing Behavioral Patterns, Values, and Attitudes

Behavioral Patterns	Values/Attitudes	Retail Responses
Most women working outside the home	Delay in starting families Less interest in preparing family meals Less time for shopping	Career shops in department stores Growth of fast-food restaurants More convenience foods Sale of prepared foods in supermarkets Longer store hours Growth of catalog shopping
Trend toward androgyny	Female adoption of male characteristics Male interest in cooking and home furnishing	Unisex clothing shops and beauty salons
More affluent, better educated consumers	Desire for higher education Desire for quality in life Desire for value for dollar	Growth of off-price fashion stores Availability of gourmet food in most supermarkets and growth of gourmet food shops Growth of off-price and ultra-price airlines

(continued)

Table 2.1   *(continued)*

Behavioral Patterns	Values/Attitudes	Retail Responses
Pride in ethnic differences	Recognition of and respect for differing origins	Availability of ethnic foods throughout United States Ethnic stores and malls
More single-parent households	Absence of stigma concerning divorce or the single state	Day-care centers in shopping malls and large department stores
Jogging, exercise craze	Concern with health and fitness	Growth of fitness centers Growth of jogging and running clothing Exercise clothing stores
Energy conservation	Concern with the environment	Sale of ecologically sound products
Emphasis on technology and information	Value on an information rather than an industrial society	Growth in teleshopping Experimentation with in-home computerized shopping Complete computerization in large stores Growth of retail management information system divisions in large stores

The cultural changes in any society are molded by the behavior, attitudes, and values of its members. These in turn become the guideposts that retailers must follow in order to meet the new needs and preferences within the culture. A sampling of the retail industry's responses to some changing cultural patterns is given in Table 2.1.

POLITICAL INFLUENCES ON RETAILING

Political events often bring about enormous changes that affect the day-to-day operations of all businesses. The emergence of new world powers, wars, and trade alliances between nations all result in change. A new regime in China or Russia, a new administration in Washington, terrorism in the Near East, and the emergence of women and black Americans as political groups have had ramifications that go far beyond the immediate political events.

Consumerism

Caveat Emptor
"Let the buyer beware." This is applied to merchandise sold without a warranty.

The consumer movement can be traced to medieval England, when an edict required certain products to be imprinted with an identification hallmark so that producers would bear the responsibility for defects. After World War II, consumerism became a significant social force in the United States. Consumers no longer accept a **caveat emptor** attitude from retailers. They demand quality in goods and services, and marketers have been forced to consider their demands. More informative labels and advertising have been one result of the consumer movement. (See Figure 2.5 on page 48.)

Consumerism as we know it today gained significance as a social movement in the 1960s. It soon became a political football as consumer legislators battled to support consumers' demands. Politicians who claimed they would keep marketers and retailers in line won the consumer's vote. The 1960s and 1970s saw many changes as the marketing concept took on new meaning for industry and customer satisfaction became a long-term retail goal. Today, consumer affairs in both public and private sectors is a multibillion-dollar operation.

The most dramatic evidence of the impact of the consumer movement

Figure   2.5   Examples of Good Labels

Labels should tell what the product is, the brand name, identification or model number (when needed), use and care instructions, manufacturer's trademark and name and address, and other pertinent information.

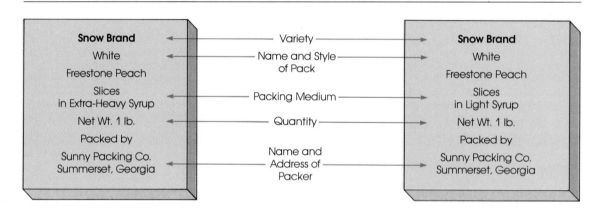

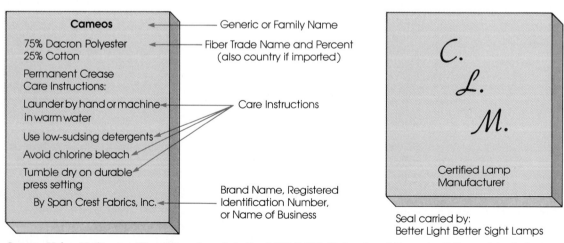

Source: Helen M. Stevens, "Bare Facts about Labeling," HE 5-157, University of Kentucky College of Agriculture, Cooperative Extension Service. Reprinted with permission.

is in existing and impending legislation. Product information and safety, consumer redress of grievances, and privacy of customers' records are all key areas of congressional activity. Many laws directly regulate retailing operations and functions. How credit is given, how customers are billed, how employees are hired and fired, how bills are collected, and how sales are run are all of federal concern, as are advertising, display, store hours, and merchandise offerings.

As we move into the 1990s, consumerism is obviously here to stay. More quality and price conscious than ever before, the American consumer will continue to force retailers to stay in line.

The Women's Movement

With the nomination of Geraldine Ferraro as the Democratic vice presidential candidate in 1984, the women's movement reached maturity. Women have won many victories since the 1960s and are now a major force in politics.

By 1990, more than 68 percent of all women from the ages of 18 to 64 will hold jobs outside the home. What does this mean for retailing? Among other things, a greater desire for one-stop shopping, fast food, and career clothing, but more importantly, it means more women in management positions. Now there are many women buyers in most retail establishments but few women merchandise managers. There are women in rank and file sales and advertising jobs but few in executive positions. Where are the women in the control division or the real estate division? A number have reached top jobs in human resource departments, but few can be found running growing management information system (MIS) divisions. This will change in retailing as in all businesses. After one woman has run for vice president of the United States, retailers cannot keep others out of the executive suite.

Ethnic and Minority Groups

Many retailers completely ignored both ethnic and minority markets until the 1960s. Since then marketers have recognized that these are viable market segments with specific needs. Demographics indicate this.

Many retailers still do not know how to serve ethnic markets. Special food sections in supermarkets are not enough nor do they bring in all the potential dollars these groups are willing to spend to satisfy their special needs. Ethnic products have also acquired a great deal of general appeal. For example, a Chinese Mall was opened in 1984 in Hinsdale, Illinois. It succeeded for these reasons: (1) many high-income Asian residents work in the high-tech industries nearby, (2) interest in China and its products has grown since the United States established diplomatic relations with mainland China in 1979, (3) an increasing number of Americans are traveling to China, and (4) U.S. trade with China has increased since 1980.

This example shows how international political events eventually trickle down to the retail scene. At the 1984 Canton Fair, U.S. importers avidly purchased goods despite their alleged high prices. The American consumer was willing to pay even higher prices because of the great interest in China. Those who could not afford a trip to Beijing, Shanghai, or Guangzhou could at least have a "Chinese experience" at the retail counter.[5]

International Politics

Because of increasing trade between Japan and the United States since World War II, young Japanese men and women have entered into a period of Western-style living, from clothing to music. Today, Japanese department stores spend a lot of yen on Seventh Avenue.

This is only one of many illustrations of the relationship that exists between international politics and retailing. Fluctuating oil prices, unstable leadership in many Near East countries, Vietnamese refugees pouring into the United States, and changes in immigration legislation are a few of the other variables that retailers have watched while selecting products, setting prices, and developing new markets.

Major store promotions are often built around political events. Since the late 1970s Bloomingdale's has created special promotions in its Manhattan store on behalf of the Italian, Indian, and Israeli fashion industries. Bloomingdale's is an example of how a retailer understands a country's political position in relation to the United States and uses this understanding and interest to promote sales.

In July 1979, Bloomingdale's sent a team of six buyers to China to explore the potential for apparel for the major China promotion the store planned to stage in the fall of 1980. The China promotion was to be another major Bloomingdale's event like the ones that had highlighted Israel, India, and Italy.

Bloomingdale's had begun carrying merchandise from China in 1971, when the trade embargo was lifted and the store opened its China Passage shop. The store's sales of Chinese merchandise in the decade that followed were said to total over $1 million a year, but the major promotion planned for 1980 was a direct result of the trade talks. In September 1980, Bloomingdale's opened a six-week promotion featuring down coats, sweaters, and luxury fabric lingerie. The total investment for the event was $10 million at retail in apparel, fashion accessories, and home furnishings.

---

[5]"At Canton Fair, Chinese Export Prices Leap," *Women's Wear Daily*, May 8, 1984, 13.

Political events can also have a negative affect on retailing. During the summer of 1986, European retailers lost hundreds of thousands of U.S. dollars because American tourists were afraid to leave the United States. International terrorism that year seriously hurt retail sales throughout the continent and in England.

LEGAL CONSTRAINTS

Legal issues are closely tied to political events and social movements. The legal framework within which retailers must operate is often determined by the country's political situation and social activism. Some of the current federal laws affecting retail operations are the direct result of consumer and civil rights movements.

The federal legislation that is most important to the retail industry is listed in Table 2.2. When retailers plan strategies and make decisions, they must pay close attention to this as well as to local, state, and international legislation. Buying goods for resale (domestic or foreign), hiring help, advertising services, and credit policies are all regulated in some way by the federal government agencies. Because consumers are

Table   2.2   Selected Legislation Important to the Retail Industry

Date	Act	Description
1890	Sherman Act	Prohibited monopoly or conspiracy in restraint of trade.
1914	Clayton Act	Made specific acts in restraint of trade unlawful.
1914	Federal Trade Commission Act	Established the enforcing agency for governing unfair methods of competition.
1931	Resale Price Agreement	Legalized resale price maintenance between manufacturers and retailers.
1935	Unfair Practices Acts	Prohibited sales below cost.
1936	Robinson-Patman Act	Prohibited unlawful price discrimination.
1937	Miller-Tydings Act	Legalized certain resale price maintenance contracts.
1938	Food, Drug, and Cosmetic Act	Expanded the responsibility of the Food and Drug Administration to include cosmetics and therapeutic devices, by amending the 1936 act.
1938	Wheeler-Lea Amendment to FTC Act	Expanded the FTC's responsibility to include unfair or deceptive acts or practices and gave it the power to take action whenever it is in the public interest, even when there is no proof of competitive injury.
1938	Fair Labor Standards Act	Established minimum wages.
1939	Wool Products Labeling Act	Required that products containing wool carry labels showing the fiber content.
1950	Antimerger Act	Regulated mergers that might substantially lessen competition.
1951	Fur Products Labeling Act	Required that all fur products carry labels correctly describing their contents.
1952	McGuire Act	Validated specific price maintenance contracts.

(continued)

Table   2.2   *(continued)*

Date	Act	Description
1953	Flammable Fabrics Acts	Prohibited the manufacture or sale of fabrics or wearing apparel that were dangerously flammable.
1958	Food Additives Amendment (Delaney Act)	As an amendment to the Food, Drug, and Cosmetic Act of 1938, required that food additives be limited to those that do not cause cancer in humans or animals.
1960	Hazardous Substances Labeling Act	Required proper labeling on packages of hazardous household products.
1960	Textile Fiber Identification Act	Required fiber content identification on all apparel.
1962	Kefauver-Harris Amendment to Food, Drug, and Cosmetic Act (1938)	Required that all drugs be tested for safety and efficacy.
1963	Equal Pay Act	Required compliance with regulations on child labor and employee health and safety.
1964	Civil Rights Act, Title VII	Required equal pay for similar work, regardless of sex, race, color, religion, or national origin.
1966	Fair Packaging and Labeling Act	Permitted the voluntary adoption of industry-accepted uniform packaging standards and required clearer labeling of consumer goods.
1966	Child Protection Act of 1966	Amended the Hazardous Substances Labeling Act (1960) to ban all hazardous substances and prohibit sales of potentially harmful toys and other articles used by children.
1967	Flammable Fabrics Act	Amended the 1953 act and expanded textile legislation to include the Department of Commerce Flammability Standards for additional products.
1968	Consumer Credit Protection Act (Truth in Lending)	Required full disclosure of the terms and rates charged for loans and credit.
1968	Age Discrimination in Employment Act	Prevented discrimination against employing anyone on basis of age; extended retirement age to 70.
1970	Fair Credit Reporting Act	Regulated credit information reporting and use.
1970	Poison Prevention Packaging Act	Provided for standards for child-resistant packaging of hazardous substances.
1971	Care Labeling Act	Stated that all apparel selling for over $3 carry labels with washing or dry-cleaning instructions.
1972	Consumer Product Safety Act	Established the Consumer Product Safety Commission and empowered it to set safety standards for a broad range of consumer products and to impose penalties for failure to meet these standards.
1974	Equal Credit Opportunity Act	Insured that the various financial institutions and other firms engaged in the extension of credit make credit available without discrimination on the basis of sex or marital status.
1975	Magnuson-Moss Act	Established disclosure requirements and minimum federal standards for written warranties.
1975	Consumer Goods Pricing Act	Outlawed legalized resale price maintenance.
1979	Trade Agreements Act	Regulated imports of certain textile and clothing products.
1980	Amendment to the Wool Products Labeling Act of 1939	Required that products containing recycled wool carry labels showing the content.
1986	Tax Reform Act	Eliminated deductions for sales tax and for interest payments on revolving or installment credit; also plugged many former tax loopholes for corporations as well as consumers.

becoming increasingly knowledgeable about retailing law and because the penalties for violation can be severe, no retailer can afford to engage in dubious merchandising or pricing practices.

Mergers are regulated by the FTC because the agency wants to foster the competitive prices and choices demanded by the public. A case in point is the 1982 FTC consent order requiring Batus, Inc. (then owner of Saks Fifth Avenue and Gimbels, among others) to reduce its Milwaukee-area department store space by some 200,000 square feet and its annual volume by at least $20 million. The reason for this order was the Batus acquisition of Marshall Field and Company. Because Batus already owned Gimbels department stores and Kohl's discount stores in Milwaukee and was the largest retailer in the metropolitan area, the addition of Field's (prior to the merger, the eighth largest retailer) greatly reduced department store competition in the city. This, according to the FTC, was an unfair trade practice.

Opening a new branch store in a state with a high sales tax might have a negative effect on company profits even though it opens up a new market. On the other hand, many Massachusetts-based stores are expanding over the border to southern New Hampshire, a state where there is no sales tax. A good interstate highway system makes it easy for Massachusetts residents to shop in New Hampshire for big-ticket items. This not only opens up a new market, but it also increases sales from within the existing one. Locating a store in a town that has a local ordinance against Sunday openings can hurt total sales, especially if there is no such law in surrounding communities. State and local legislation have an impact on retailers in each city and state.

In every retailing situation, the law is a determinant of strategy and imposes definite limits beyond which retailers cannot venture. Retailers claim that there are too many constraints, but consumers keep clamoring for more. Although every law has great meaning for retailers, three deserve special mention.

The Robinson-Patman Act

In 1936, the Robinson-Patman Act, which amended the Clayton Act, became law. It was intended primarily to help small businesses, especially retailers, and their customers by declaring price discrimination illegal. It set limits on brokerage allowances and quantity discounts offered by manufacturers and required that all promotional allowances be made available to all buyers on proportionately equal terms. In 1960, the act was amended to cover the granting of all promotional allowances to retailers whether goods were purchased directly from the manufacturer or through a wholesaler.[6]

---

[6] Dorothy S. Rogers and Lynda R. Gamans, *Fashion: A Marketing Approach* (New York: Holt, Rinehart and Winston, 1983), 59.

In spite of this law, many vendors still grant allowances to retailers according to size. They claim that they must give allowances where they will do the most good. The fact is that they do derive more sales from coupling their name with that of a well-known chain than from doing so with a local, little-known specialty shop.

The Consumer Goods Pricing Act

In 1975, the Consumer Goods Pricing Act was signed by President Gerald Ford. It officially eliminated fair trade laws. Thus, an era that began in 1937 with the Miller-Tydings Act was ended; the stormy, somewhat bitter controversy that surrounded fair trade became a thing of the past. No longer would manufacturers and retailers be able to use fair trade agreements as an excuse for uniformly high prices.

This act enabled the off-price retailer to become the newest entrant on the wheel of retailing. Once the act became law, brand-name merchandise could be sold at lower than the manufacturer's suggested retail price without fear of legal ramifications. This had not been the case prior to 1975. It is entirely possible that **resale price maintenance** may become an obsolete term to future generations of marketers.

Resale Price Maintenance
Supplier's control over selling price at various stages of distribution.

The Tax Reform Act of 1986

Passed by Congress in 1986, this was the most extensive restructuring of the federal income tax system in 40 years, consolidating 15 tax brackets into 2 and eliminating many tax breaks.

Because consumers can no longer deduct sales tax or interest payments on revolving or installment credit, retailers will undoubtedly lose some sales in the years ahead. Without this benefit, many customers, especially those who buy big-ticket items on credit, may think twice before making a purchase.

Like all corporations, retail firms must plan and implement strategies simply because they make good business sense, not because implementation means a tax break, as it did before 1987.

TECHNOLOGICAL CHANGES

Since the industrial revolution, no other phenomenon has had such far-reaching effects on business and industry as the technological revolution. Today it is almost impossible for a small business and virtually unthinkable for a large one to operate without technological aids ranging from copy machines to computers. The electronic revolution has given retailers the means for instant inventory update, on-the-spot credit checks, video training, competition analysis, customer profiling, and countless other techniques with which to make better decisions and more effective operating plans.

Retailing requires information in greater amounts and at higher speeds than ever before. Today, the computer is indispensible for success in this dynamic field. The computer can be programmed to give all the data needed for stock planning, human resources planning, and promotions. Point-of-sale equipment or optical scanners found in nearly all retail stores bring the marketing concept to life. These electronic analysts, tied to a mainframe computer, provide the kind of quick, accurate data on which both customer satisfaction and profit are built. (See "From the Field: Management Information System at Fisher Camuto.")

P.O.S. Systems

A number of different point-of-sale (P.O.S.) terminals are available. All operate in a similar fashion as modern-day replacements for sales registers. The amount and type of information processed depends on the computer program used and the sophistication of the terminal. Programs are available for specific types of stores—shoe stores, supermarkets, hardware stores, and so on. Any good P.O.S. system should at least be able to:

1. Verify entries
2. Take information from sales slips and merchandise tickets

FROM THE FIELD

Management Information System at Fisher Camuto

If sales skyrocket Tuesday in Des Moines for a given line of shoes, Fisher Camuto Corporation can boost production accordingly in Brazil on Wednesday, thanks to a management information system (MIS) the firm installed in late 1983.

When it was founded in 1977, Stamford, Connecticut–based Fisher Camuto manufactured shoes in Brazil and wholesaled them in the United States to a mix of department stores and independent shoe stores. But when the firm decided to open its own chain of retail outlets in 1983, it realized it would

need an MIS which could quickly and accurately report many kinds of sales data.

Fisher Camuto introduces six lines of shoes in a wide range of styles and fashion colors each year. It produces more than 15 million pairs of shoes each year in its facilities in Brazil, marketing them under the trade names 9 West, Gloria Vanderbilt, J. J. Calico, and Westies. It recently launched a fifth brand, Enzo Angiolini, which it designs and produces at a factory it leases in Italy.

When it decided to launch its 9 West retail chain, the company wanted to get maximum advantage from its vertical integration. Information had to flow

(continued)

FROM THE FIELD

Management Information System at Fisher Camuto (*continued*)

daily from the stores to corporate head-quarters and then to the manufacturing plants so production could be stepped up on hot sellers and slowed down on the poor performers. Information now is relayed overseas via teletext, but plans call for a satellite linkup.

Given the large number of colors and styles of shoes which it offers, the firm also needed a sophisticated system which could track a wide range of inventory variables. "Being able to align our production schedules to sales performance in the stores is a tremendous advantage," noted Ken Scharf, the firm's vice president and director of MIS.

"We could have written a software package for our IBM mainframe, but that would have taken at least a year, and we had to move fast. Instead, we bought a Quantel super-mini, which cost less than the software for the IBM would have."

Fisher Camuto has opened about 30 of its 9 West stores so far, and plans call for 200 units within the next three years. "Basically we purchased a standard package that we customized slightly," so information from the firm's mainframe computer could be downloaded directly into the Quantel. Sales data is fed nightly from IBM registers in the stores to the mainframe. The payoff is square footage sales which are well above the industry standard, the firm claims.

"We know right away what is selling, and we're able to test certain styles before going into full production," Scharf said. "We know how to optimally shift our inventory to regions of the country where a particular style is selling, and we can reduce out-of-stocks and quickly mark down poor performers by knowing what's hot and what isn't. We can tell what sales are during each hour of the day so that we have adequate staff on hand during peak times. The computer gives us a wealth of data."

"In most cases, the best you can get is once a week information by telephone," he said. "It's only as good as the accuracy of the two people on the phone. You have to transcribe it manually, it's prone to error, and you lose time and accuracy."

By contrast, the Quantel system lets management access key bits of information—such as styles, colors, material, department, class, type, size, width, and even heel height—without having to look at an entire report, as is the case with batch systems. "Our stores are all over the country, and as we open more units we will get more accurate data and a better idea of regional trends, and there are definite differences," Scharf said. (See Figure 2.6.)

Source: Excerpts from "MIS Lets Shoe Manufacturer Set Today's Production Schedule Based on Yesterday's Sales in Its Stores," *Marketing News*, February 1, 1985, 27. Reprinted by permission from *Marketing News*, published by the American Marketing Association.

3. Enter information into a perpetual inventory system
4. Check credit (store or bank cards)
5. Authorize credit transactions
6. Profile customers' shopping patterns
7. Keep track of sales staff's commission earnings.

Some type of computerized system is within the reach of almost every retailer today. More sizes, prices, and types will likely appear on the market each year as the technological age moves through its growth stage and on to maturity.

Optical Scanner
An electronic wand that picks up information from a product and enters it into a computer.

An alternative to a P.O.S. terminal is an **optical scanner.** This is an electronic wand that picks up information from a product and enters it into the computer. It works best when products are universally coded. Most packaged foods, including an estimated 80 percent of all supermarket products, are marked with a Universal Product Code (UPC). Department stores have their own code called optical character recognitions (OCRs). The use of optical scanners is currently not as widespread in department stores as in supermarkets.

Electronic funds transfer services (EFTS), devices through which customers can withdraw funds or charge purchases to their accounts, and automated teller machines (ATMs), which dispense cash and accept deposits, can now be found in many retail stores, particularly supermarkets.

Figure   2.6   Display Based on Computer Analysis of Consumer Needs

Source: Courtesy of Fisher Camuto Corporation (9 West™).

Teleshopping

Teleshopping
An electronic system for buying merchandise at home.

Some retailers are experimenting with **teleshopping (TS).** This is an electronic system through which customers can buy merchandise at home. A device that is either built into or attached to a television set enables a consumer to view products on the screen. Pictures indicate items, prices, and ordering information. When the customer makes a purchase decision, he or she inserts a card into the teleshopping equipment, which is connected to an EFTS at the store via telephone lines or cable television. Thus, a purchase can be made and delivered in a few days without the purchaser ever leaving the den or living room. (See "From the Field: Home Shopping Network," in Chapter 1.) Teleshopping will probably not be widely used by most traditional retail stores. It will, however, give a great boost in sales to the growing number of catalog retailers and to cable television companies.

The World Retailers Business and Equipment Exposition, held in April 1984 in Paris, brought together exhibits of sophisticated electronic and telecommunications technologies; efficient and creative store planning and marketing techniques; and equipment, systems, and services devoted to store inventory control, point-of-sale, credit management, handling and marking of merchandise, security, and engineering.[7] Retailers of all types are responding to the demands of the electronic age. Students preparing for a retailing career must therefore become thoroughly familiar with the various types of computer hardware and software used in retailing and also develop programming ability.

THE COMPETITIVE ENVIRONMENT

Competition comes from many directions, both domestic and international. As examples, U.S. firms compete against U.S. firms, while Sears operates stores in Europe and South America, and Al-Fayed Brothers—owners of Harrods in London and Illum in Copenhagen—hold stock in Carter Hawley Hale Stores. Department stores compete with other department stores, shoe stores with other shoe stores, grocery stores with other grocery stores. Department stores also compete with all the stores that sell merchandise contained in their assortment; shoe stores compete with discount stores; and grocery stores compete with fast-food chains. Because every retailer is eager to increase sales, none hesitates to invade anyone else's domain. Competition is now both horizontal (retailer against retailer) and vertical (retailer against wholesaler or manufacturer who engages in retailing).

The American consumer, with a fixed amount of money to spend, must choose carefully, especially when retailers offer numerous choices.

---

[7] "Expo Will Highlight Worldwide Advances in Retail Technology," *Marketing News,* February 3, 1984, 2.

Scrambled Merchandising
Carrying unrelated types of goods in the same store, where they can be sold profitably.

Conglomerate Merchandising
Carrying unrelated goods and offering unrelated services that can be sold profitably in the same store.

There are no sacred strategies. **Scrambled merchandising, conglomerate merchandising,** and one-stop shopping are universal.

Some retailers have tried to control their competition by purchasing rival firms, believing that if they own the competition, profits can be funneled into one corporate pocket. This may be a viable retail strategy, but it precludes a free market and thus limits consumers' choices. Moreover, such tactics are closely scrutinized by the Federal Trade Commission.

The competitive battle for market share is likely to escalate. The consensus of retail executives and analysts at the 1985 convention of the National Retail Merchants Association was that department stores and other traditional retailers may be pitted against one another rather than against off-pricers, manufacturers, wholesalers, and newcomers.

Competition will undoubtedly change in the years to come. From whatever direction it comes and whatever form it takes, however, it will continue to exist as long as free enterprise exists. Retailers can ignore neither one another nor marketers of consumer goods at different levels in the distribution channel. As the world becomes smaller and communication improves, competition may originate on distant shores as well as in our own backyard. Those who succeed will do so because they recognize the need for scientific study of competitive strategies and adapt to change.

Summary

The uncontrollable variables in a society guide retailing policy. Economic factors, changing demographics, population shifts, political events, social changes, and advancing technology all affect the retail mix of large and small retailers alike.

The retail marketing of goods and services is not an isolated process. Inflation, changes in tax laws, the two-income family, and the computer have all contributed to new retail strategies.

Retailers must be ready to respond to changes in disposable and discretionary income, and to the demands of the two-income family. They must be aware of new types of households as well as changes in age mix, population, and ethnic groups and must also be able to create strategies that reflect the behavioral patterns, values, and attitudes of their target markets. The desire for quality merchandise by a population segment with more taste than money sparked the off-price fashion industry, and catalog retailing grew because consumers became too busy to shop for all their needs.

Political events, both domestic and international, often become the basis for exciting merchandise promotional activities. Some events, like the terrorism of 1986, result in negative retail situations. Because there is a legal framework within which retailers must operate, all retailers should have an understanding of the legislation that affects their operations.

The new technological aids that include everything from P.O.S. systems to teleshopping are both a blessing and a hindrance. Competition becomes more difficult with available technology, and competition for the consumer's dollar has never been greater or from so many directions. In short, as this chapter makes clear, uncontrollable variables and the retail mix are very closely related where it counts—the bottom line!

Questions for Review

1. Comment on the statement, "Retailers are applied economists."
2. Differentiate between disposable income and discretionary income.
3. How have cultural lifestyle changes affected changes in retailing?
4. Describe the effect of political influences on retailing. How can retailers develop their merchandise mix around these political influences?
5. List two federal laws that have meaning for retailers and explain their effect on retailing.
6. What is meant by the technological revolution, and what has been its positive effect on retailing?
7. Explain the statement, "Competition is an uncontrollable variable."

CASE STUDY The Beauty Barn

Merchandising for a Clean Environment

In the late 1950s, Matthew Phillips opened a cosmetics and beauty aids shop in downtown Los Angeles. He had accumulated a little cash while working as the cosmetics buyer for a chain of drugstores in southern California and decided that it was time to try it on his own.

His shop, The Beauty Barn, was an immediate success, because Phillips understood his customers' needs. His stock was well selected, his prices were just below those of his competition, and turnover was excellent. Soon he opened a second store in Glendale. This too was immediately profitable, in spite of competition from department stores, drugstores, and other specialty shops. Phillips had hit on the right formula: in-depth assortments of popular items and brands, and only a smattering of the more prestigious lines. Markups just below those of his competition contributed to increased volume. Splashy promotional advertising and a self-service setup in each store were additional factors leading to a profitable operation. In short, Phillips knew his market.

During the 1960s, the sale of beauty aids flourished. Men as well as women were spending more dollars on them each year. The Beauty Barn was thriving with its chain buying power, its excellent management training program, and its choice locations. Problems of pricing, merchandise assortment, competition, and new locations had always been easy to solve for the excellent management group Phillips had put together as the chain grew.

In the 1970s, however, the environmental movement emerged and changed the entire nature of the cosmetics and beauty aids business. Environmentalists believed that any substance harmful to the environment should be eliminated from existing products and any ecologically detrimental item should be removed from retailers' shelves. The government became involved and established the Environmental Protection Agency. The Beauty Barn now had an entirely new set of problems. One of the major items on the agenda of the 1983 meeting at The Beauty Barn's national headquarters appeared under the title "Ecologically Unsound Products."

Matthew Phillips, still president, opened the meeting, reporting that it had been a good year. Sales had increased 17 percent over the previous year, and net profit was ahead by 7 percent. Ten new stores had been opened. The Beauty Barn now had 153 stores in 47 states offering discounted beauty aids and cosmetics to both men and women. Sales were up in all regions, and each store had contributed its share to the overall profit picture. Because store managers received a percentage of their stores' increase, they always stayed on top of customers' needs.

Rarely did a customer walk out of The Beauty Barn because of an out-of-stock item. Store managers watched the movement of stock to prevent it from dropping below a basic supply and to help keep track of changing consumer demand. They were requested to fill out a weekly report on consumer action in their stores in addition to sending to headquarters a rundown of sales by category. A computer then prepared the final report, indicating all fast- and slow-selling and out-of-stock merchandise. Matthew Phillips knew the value of consumer analysis.

It was this kind of reporting system and the resulting changes that had enabled The Beauty Barn to enjoy success year after year. Starting with the two stores in the Los Angeles area, Phillips had expertly piloted his chain through stormy years buffeted by heavy competition. At the merchandising planning meeting in the well-furnished boardroom overlooking the Pacific Ocean, he was still at the helm but, as always, ready to ask for help from the rest of The Beauty Barn crew.

As he glanced at "Ecologically Unsound Products" on the written agenda, Phillips recalled why he had insisted that more time be allotted to this item than to most of the others. In his managers' weekly reports there had been questions about the future of the large number of aerosol products carried by The Beauty Barn. Federal government bans already existed on many of the major ingredients used in cosmetics products; some states were establishing bans, and more were to come. The problem was becoming acute. Added to this was the fact that many ecology-conscious consumers were buying only biodegradable products.

Should The Beauty Barn continue to carry products that were possible pollutants even though they had not been officially banned? Was it ethical for a nationwide chain to promote items that might be spoiling the environment? Did all consumers actually want ecologically sound products? What percentage of them would stop buying at The Beauty Barn if the company did not change its policies? Perhaps an even more basic question was that concerning the role of the retailer in helping to ensure a cleaner environment.

The answer was to create the perfect blend: an assortment that would appease the environmentalists yet satisfy the group that considered personal comfort over universal well-being. Which was the larger group? Although Phillips felt that he already knew the answer, he could not make this decision alone. The Beauty Barn had always been a leader in offering new products when its only consideration had been profit. Here was an opportunity to be a leader again, when the major consideration was not immediate profit but ethics. He called for a discussion of "ecologically unsound" products.

Questions

1. How is the growth in the cosmetics and beauty aids industry related to economic conditions?
2. Should environmentalism be ignored by retailers when creating their marketing mix? Why or why not?
3. Discuss the question of ethics versus profit as it relates to "ecologically unsound" products. How do you feel about this issue? Why?
4. What advice would you give Matthew Phillips? Why?
5. List the changes in the cosmetics and beauty aids industry brought about by the Environmental Protection Agency since 1976 and the legislation responsible for them.

Chapter 3

The Retail Consumer

Source: Courtesy of Saks Fifth
Avenue.

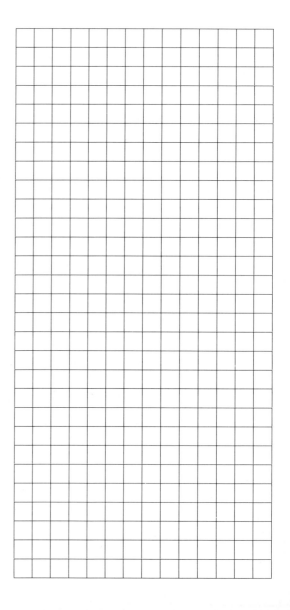

Laura Petronio
Assistant Buyer of Dresses

Debra Cavanaugh
Buyer of Image and Leather
Ann Taylor, Inc.

What makes Ann Taylor one of the most successful women's specialty store chains in the country? There are a number of contributing factors; however, the key component is continuing commitment to the customer.

The pioneers at Ann Taylor created an image. The present management is devoted to strengthening that image—in advertising, store design and displays, and most importantly, in the merchandising mix. Once the image is defined, it must remain consistent.

Who is the Ann Taylor customer? This is a question continually asked by the in-house design department. By zeroing in on the customer's needs and her many different lifestyles, management can analyze her purchasing decisions. She wants to be wardrobed; whether she's a professional, a housewife and mother, or a student, she looks to Ann Taylor for direction.

The formula for success has combined a sense of color, silhouette, and fine fabric with customers' personal styles. By offering the customer an image to identify with, merchandise that fills a want or need, a quality product at a reasonable price, and exclusivity and service she can't find anywhere else, management has ensured the continued growth of Ann Taylor.

Learning Objectives

Upon completing this chapter you should be able to:

1. Understand how demographic variables influence a consumer's store choice.
2. Describe a purchase situation for each step in Maslow's hierarchy of needs.
3. Understand how ethnic background plays a role in purchase behavior.
4. Relate G. P. Stone's category of shoppers to your customer groups, assuming that you own a women's fashion boutique.
5. Discuss the four traditional categories of goods and services.
6. Identify the steps in the consumer purchase decision-making process.
7. Understand the role of each step in the consumer's purchase decision.

Consumers are probably the most uncontrollable of all the variables retailers have to contend with. Fickle at best, consumers today have less stable purchasing habits than ever before. Why is that? Probably because our society is more dynamic than in any previous period. In this information age, luring the consumer is a far more intensive process than in the days when the printed media were the retailer's only promotional tools.

Retailers, along with the rest of industry, are serving people from increasingly varied roots. No longer does everyone want to be, look, think, eat, or dress alike. People throughout the world celebrate diversity. Wherever they live, consumers are interested both in their own roots and in the other cultures that make up the global economy.

Understanding consumers' motivations, buying habits, and lifestyles has always been a prerequisite to successful retailing. Now, in an age when great value is placed on instant communication, on ethnicity as well as diversity, and on participation, understanding consumer behavior is the key to retailing excellence. (See "From the Field: Sears Financial Network.") This chapter explores the many dimensions of consumer behavior from a number of vantage points.

FROM THE FIELD

Sears Financial Network

Sears built its financial network with the confidence that it knew what consumers wanted, according to Edward R. Kuby, vice president of marketing, Allstate Insurance Group, Sears, Roebuck and Company, Chicago.

The old marketing maxim that explains why people buy quarter-inch drill bits also pertains to financial services, Kuby said. "They don't really want quarter-inch drill bits; what they want is quarter-inch holes. And that's as true in financial services as it is in the hardware business. Consumers don't want insurance companies or banks or stock brokers. They want their financial affairs handled efficiently and professionally—and with full assurances of security.

"The consumer wants solutions, not institutions, and the Sears Financial Network is the delivery system we have created in response." This network is composed of Allstate for insurance, Dean Witter for investments, and Coldwell Banker for real estate. In California, it also includes the services of Sears Savings Bank.[a]

Sears Financial Services is not so much a revolutionary new direction as it is an evolutionary extension of well-established lines of business. In the 100 years since Richard Sears began his part-time mail-order watch business, Sears has developed the greatest consumer franchise in the history of American commerce. Three out of four American adults, or 128 million people, will visit Sears stores this year, Kuby estimated. More than 40 million households shop Sears stores and catalogs and about 60 million individuals carry a Sears credit card.

Sears' goal is to leverage this huge— and loyal—customer base, to build long-term financial relationships with the people who already know the company and feel comfortable in their stores. Common sense tells us that people move through income brackets as their lives change. It's essential to establish a relationship with consumers early in their spending and investment cycle, then continue serving them as their needs change.

By helping young adults obtain a credit card, open up their first savings account, or secure their first loan, Sears believes it can retain these customers when they decide to purchase insurance, obtain home mortgages, and plan for retirement.

Since 1911, generations of Americans have financed their purchases through Sears' credit operation. Sears started Allstate in 1931. Today, Allstate is the second largest property–casualty company in the nation and a leading life insurer. Since 1958, Sears has operated Sears Savings Bank, which today is the 21st largest savings and loan association in the country, with assets of nearly $6 billion. Contrary to early predictions, Kuby said Sears Financial Centers have gained widespread acceptance.

(continued)

FROM THE FIELD

Sears Financial Network (*continued*)

Consumers Digest honored Sears for outstanding service through the development of retail centers, and a poll conducted by *American Banker* found that consumers expect the quality of Sears' service to be as good as or better than that of other financial institutions.

The performance of Sears Financial Network seems to bear this out. Business is up for each of the member companies, and Dean Witter has found, for example, that 35 to 40 percent of its new accounts are opened through the centers. More than 80 percent of these accounts are either first-time brokerage accounts or reactivated dormant accounts. There is a vast middle market that is being overlooked by traditional financial services institutions. Sears is reaching this new investor and bringing new capital into the market.

Another financial services delivery vehicle Sears is pursuing is its Discover card, which provides consumers with a line of revolving credit at service establishments nationwide. The Discover card is more than just another vehicle for spending; it's "the glue that pulls together our banking, insurance, real estate, and investment products," Kuby said. "It offers the opportunity to save and invest. Card members can take advantage of a savings plan that pays tiered money market rates based on the level of their deposits. They also can earn real dollar dividends on their purchases."

---

[a] Sears Savings Bank was acquired by Citicorp early in 1987.
Source: Excerpted from "Knowing What Consumers Want Aids Sears' Financial Enterprises," *Marketing News*, April 11, 1986, 19. Reprinted by permission from *Marketing News*, published by the American Marketing Association.

FACTORS AFFECTING CONSUMER DECISIONS

Consumers make purchasing decisions on the basis of who they are, where they live, and how much they earn. These factors, along with consumers' motivations, family and personal relationships, and membership in ethnic, social, or age groups should become the basis for the retailer's selection of a target market, development of an effective image, and creation of a mix.

Demographics

Chapter 2 presented an in-depth look at changing demographics. Variables such as age, sex, income, education, and mobility are all involved in the retailer's attempt to understand and respond to the target market.

Demographic research will take on increasing importance as consumers' preferences, attitudes, and values continue to change. Six macro-demographic trends can be employed to guide a firm's retailing efforts. Each contributes greatly to shaping consumer demand.

The first five are (1) population growth and distribution, (2) family and household composition, (3) labor force participation trends, (4) educational attainment levels and (5) household income distribution. The population shift from North to South and from inner city to suburbs continues, changing the location and distribution of customers. The trend toward marriage at a later age, along with increasing numbers of single and divorced people, has created shifts in households and family lifestyles. Working women in the marketplace are becoming a powerful force and a specialized, lucrative market for firms producing apparel, special services, and products to reduce household chores. Two-earner households have more discretionary dollars to spend for goods but less time available to shop for them. Firms that can zero in on quality, time-saving devices will certainly meet with success.

The sixth trend concerns age structure. People age 55 and over continue to become a larger, more lucrative market to tap. In addition, baby boomers are moving through our nation's age groups like a pig in a python. Well-educated, well-heeled yuppie households already have influenced our markets in diet soft drinks, fashion apparel, exercise equipment, and time-saving quality goods and services.[1] (See "From the Field: Yuppies: A Retailer's Dream.") Age is, without a doubt, a powerful determinant of consumer behavior, affecting the individual's interests, tastes, purchasing ability, political preferences, and investment behavior. Thus, it matters greatly how people are distributed among different age groups in the future.

At a 1984 conference on attitude research, the editor of *American Demographics* forecast the following trends by age groups:

> *Children.* By 1990, there will be 17 percent more preschoolers than in 1980. However, as the baby boomers move out of their child-bearing years in the 1990s, growth of this age group will decline.

> *Youths.* The number of people aged 10 to 19 will drop by about 6 million during this decade, and there will be 3 million fewer in the 20 to 24 age group. Teenage unemployment may level off as entry-level workers come to be in greater demand. Thus, movie and record companies, jeans manufacturers, and others who depend on the teenage market mix face leaner times. Hundreds of colleges may have to close their doors, retailers will likely hire more older people to staff their checkout counters, and the military services may have trouble attracting volunteers.

---

[1] Craig E. Cina, "Six Demographic Variables Shape Consumer Demand," *Marketing News*, December 7, 1984, 11.

. By the turn of the century, the number of teenagers once again will grow rapidly as the children of the baby-boom generation enter that age group; however, the number of people in the 20 to 24 age group will continue to decline.

Young adults. In the years to come, America will no longer be a nation of young adults. In 1990, the number of people in the 25 to 29 age group will grow only at the national average, then decline rapidly during the rest of the 1990s. The 30 to 34 age group will decline even more sharply.

Middle age. The baby-boom generation is moving into the 35 to 49 age group, creating a lucrative market for manufacturers and service industries. In 1980, America had 26 million people aged 35 to 44; by 1990, there will be 38 million. The 45 to 49 age group will increase

FROM THE FIELD

Yuppies: A Retailer's Dream

Being a yuppie is more a state of mind than having a fat wallet, according to a study conducted by Market Facts Inc., a Chicago-based international market research and information organization.

Half of the baby boom generation (those born between 1945 and 1960) think and act like young, upwardly mobile professionals, but fewer than one in five of them meet the financial criteria, concluded the compilation of interviews conducted between mid-February and mid-March 1985, with a national sample of 1,385 consumers, including 412 baby boomers.

Yuppies, however, are an optimistic lot that expects much out of life and works hard to achieve its goals, states the study. "Yuppies are confident,

happy with their lives, and interested in financial success and its rewards," said Market Facts vice president Larry Labash, the study's director. "They view themselves as well organized, and tend to be socially liberal, but economically conservative."

Yuppies are a retailer's dream, Labash continued. They not only buy more consumer products, but they are willing to spend more for them than both the non-yuppies and the general population. For example, the study found, they would pay as much as 75 percent more for a watch than non-yuppies and nearly 50 percent more for a woman's cocktail dress.

Auto dealers—especially those selling foreign-made cars—are particularly fond of yuppies because they would pay

26 percent. This should create a lot of changes, such as older models in advertisements and a new interest in money and career.

The next decade should see a growing interest in travel, entertainment, and investments. The work force should become more productive as experienced workers will outnumber those in entry-level positions.

Empty nesters. The 50 to 64 age group will continue to decline until the turn of the century, at which time it will expand as the first members of the baby-boom generation reach their mid-50s. This group will enjoy a higher discretionary income and will likely swell the leadership ranks of business and government.

Retirees. In the 1990s, the number of people aged 65 to 74 will actually shrink while that of the 75 to 84 age group will increase. The

on an average of $11,680 for a new car, or better than $2,000 more than non-yuppies and $1,600 more than the general population. And more than 25 percent of yuppie families have Japanese or European models, twice the number owned by their age-group counterparts or the general population.

The products yuppies use, including the food they eat, also differ from the two other groups. "You won't find many yuppies savoring prosaic things like bologna, instant potatoes, or pre-sweetened cereals," maintained Labash. "Croissants, fresh coffee beans, and imported wines and beers are more their style."

The "hot" demographic darlings are further distinguished by their higher-than-average use of credit cards, automatic teller machines, personal computers, financial-planning services, and merchandise catalogs.

The study also confirmed segmentation within the yuppie market. Urban sophisticates are big-city oriented, have liberal ideals, and enjoy shopping; entrepreneurs are more interested in making money than spending it, but they still do.

These subgroups are further distinguished, the study found, by such things as the television shows they prefer; for urban sophisticates it's "Cheers," for entrepreneurs it's "Hill Street Blues."

The inclination of yuppies to buy more and better things, according to the study, reflects an average income of $30,070 compared to an average of $21,400 for other baby boomers and $26,900 for the general population.

Baby boomers are the nation's largest single age group, representing 26 million households, or 30 percent of the U.S. total, according to 1983 census data, Labash said.

Source: Excerpted from "Yuppies: The Big Boon of the Baby Boom," *Marketing News,* June 7, 1985, 10–11. Reprinted by permission from *Marketing News,* published by the American Marketing Association.

number of those aged 85 and over will have doubled by then, reflecting the improved health and incomes of the group as a whole. Women will likely continue to outlive men.[2]

These forecasts, along with predictions for changes in educational achievement and increases in discretionary income, should become the basis for retail change in the years ahead. The more educated and sophisticated consumers are, the more questions they ask and the more demands they place on marketers of goods and services.

Psychological Factors

Shoppers' Motivations

Hierarchy of Needs
Maslow's theory that people seek to satisfy needs in this order: biological, social, psychological.

Every consumer purchase is based on individual needs or wants. In the past, Maslow's **hierarchy of needs** made it fairly easy to pinpoint the buying motivations of one's market segments. (See Figure 3.1.)

[2] "The Year 2000: A Demographic Profile of Consumer Market," *Marketing News*, May 25, 1984, sec. I, 8019. From a presentation by Bryant Robey, editor of *American Demographics*, at the 15th Aptitude Research Conference of the American Marketing Association. Reprinted by permission from *Marketing News*, published by the American Marketing Association.

Figure   3.1   Maslow's Hierarchy of Needs

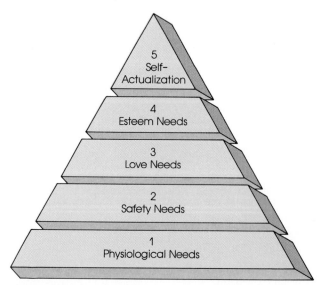

Source: Abraham H. Maslow, "A Theory of Human Motivation," *Psychological Review* 50 (July 1943): 370–396.

If you were a retailer during America's frontier days, and ran a trading post, all you had to worry about was selling basics: fur skins for bodily warmth, simple cooking utensils, and axes for cutting down trees for shelter and heat. If you were a retailer after World War II, when Americans for the first time had fists' full of disposable income, you would have found buying motivations to be generally representative of the next level on Maslow's scale. Women wanted attractive clothes, cosmetics, and new home furnishings because of their desire for attention and admiration. Men wanted sport clothes for newly found leisure-time activities. Parents lavished possessions on their children in what some psychologists and sociologists claim was one of the greatest attempts in history to buy love, substituting a new bike or dollhouse for an evening of shared activities.

Today, however, more consumers than ever are motivated to satisfy the higher-level need for self-esteem, and they have equally high levels of discretionary income with which to do so. Maslow's theory can no longer be the only basis for retail strategy development. Retailers must learn to deal with self-esteem as a customer need in the complex age of individualism.

In the 1950s and through much of the 1960s and 1970s, one measure of success was your car. If you drove a Cadillac, then you had a "Cadillac" home, wore "Cadillac" clothes, took "Cadillac" vacations, and so on. A single measure of success prevailed for all the world to see. In the 1980s, each individual's perception of success differs. There is no longer one mass expression for all. Some people buy the most expensive stereo equipment, yet drive compact cars, while others forgo lavishly furnished homes in favor of designer clothes and imported sports cars.

The few people who finally achieve **self-actualization** care little for status merchandise as a means of achieving self-fulfillment. They are totally secure and do not have the need to state their accomplishments through possessions. This group has always been and will continue to be the most difficult of all to serve. Obviously, Maslow's hierarchy of needs will not be sufficiently sophisticated to identify all buying motivations in the future.

Shoppers' motivations are important to retailers because they are factors in the purchase decision process. Understanding that Susie buys gifts for her friends because she has a need to be liked and that her daughter Liz wants Guess jeans to gain recognition from her peers is vital information when developing product and promotion strategies. The fact that Harry buys a Porsche to avoid feeling inferior in the eyes of wealthy friends can become the rationale behind a dealer's ad campaign.

Personality Types

Selling goods and services to a **want-driven society** rather than a need-driven society increases the necessity for retailers to understand consumer psychology and various personality types.

Self-Actualization
The desired result when a person sets out to become all that he or she is capable of becoming.

Want-Driven Society
Society in which consumers purchase goods/services because they satisfy the 3rd, 4th, and 5th levels of Maslow's hierarchy of needs, rather than levels 1 and 2.

Certain types respond to specific retail mixes. *Extroverts* enjoy attention. Because of this they usually enter into lengthy discussions during the sales presentation of the merchandise or service they intend to purchase. As long as the sale is open they have the attention of the salesperson. *Introverts,* on the other hand, prefer to make their own decisions. They respond negatively to high-pressure tactics because they do not enjoy directed personal attention.

Strategies that take into account the personalities of consumers in the target market have a good chance of succeeding. Like all marketers, retailers must know their targets inside and out and be able to see consumers as they perceive themselves. The consumer's self-image and not the retailer's image of the consumer is the determinant of the sale.

Sociological Influences

Reference Groups

Reference Group
Group such as family, social, or professional, which a person identifies with and looks to when forming opinions.

A person's self-image is developed from external as well as internal influences. The family, social groups, and professional colleagues, sometimes called **reference groups,** all offer input into an individual's decision-making process. Although these influences are often subconscious, they are extremely effective.

Mrs. B may not poll her family every time she goes to the supermarket, but because she knows that her family will not eat bran flakes, she does not buy them. Because Phil's fraternity brothers wear Polo sweaters, during his next trip to the local department store he will likely buy one for himself. Grace, following the custom of other young lawyers in her firm, chooses as her first car a small foreign compact.

These are specific examples of how reference groups in society influence individual purchases. Retailers must be aware of this as well as the broader implications of other social factors. Society sets certain norms of behavior to which its members are pressured to conform, and very little is bought at retail that does not reflect sociological influences. Who would buy items that put them out of sync with the rest of their world?

Cultural Variables

Chapter 2 discussed the cultural variables that affect retail strategy decisions. These same variables form the core of purchase behavior.

Russian people have a queue mentality—that is, they line up to make almost all purchases because availability rather than choice is the determinant. If only brown shoes are available, they buy brown shoes. If only plaid coats are available, they buy plaid coats. In Russia, almost everyone looks alike. This is changing somewhat under Mikhail Gorbachev's influence. Still, wearing brown shoes and plaid coats is very acceptable if that is the main fashion merchandise produced in a particular year. In contrast, Americans would never accept one color, one fabric, or one look. Purchase behavior in both countries reflects the values and attitudes of the culture.

Socioeconomic Class

Socioeconomic Class
Social situation of a person or group, indicated by a combination of social and economic factors.

People in the same **socioeconomic class** have similar attitudes, live in similar neighborhoods, and dress alike. They also shop for similar merchandise in similar stores. Informed retailers study the occupations, income, education, and influence of each group in their target markets before designing a retail mix. They also watch **opinion leaders** for clues to group behavior. By studying the similarities within each group, retailers have a better chance of attracting and keeping a large market share.

The Family Influence

Opinion Leaders
Trendsetters within a group.

The family probably exerts more influence on buying behavior than any other group within a given culture and socioeconomic class. Family structure deserves a great deal of attention from retailers for, as it changes, so must retail strategies change. A mix designed for a two-parent American family can fail dismally in a community made up of many single-parent households, or with many families in which children have two sets of parents (a mother and stepfather and a father and stepmother). In many such cases it is difficult to determine who makes the purchase decisions.

Psychographics
The study of combined demographic and psychological factors.

The life cycle purchase stages of the classical family are no longer an accurate measure of how families buy at each stage. The increasing number of single adults, single-parent families, multiparent families, childless couples, empty nesters, and retirees now have an impact on buying behavior at every stage. (See Table 3.1 on page 76.)

Lifestyle

Lifestyle
Network of possessions, affiliations, behavior, opinions, and attitudes: virtually everything a person owns or does.

The term lifestyle has been around for some time and, in fact, has almost replaced **psychographics** as the leading buzzword in consumer behavior literature. Both terms, however, are still important to retailers, because psychographics helps to define **lifestyle.** Those who have the same or similar values, are at the same general economic level, and have a similar educational background can be targeted as one market segment because they are thought to have the same lifestyle.

In a want-driven, affluent society, it is increasingly necessary to understand consumer psychographics and different lifestyles, because mass marketing techniques do not work as they did when most consumers had the same basic needs. Retailers who base their mix on lifestyle analysis find that they can readily pinpoint consumers' desires in each target market.

Consumers in affluent societies live life on the fast track. They want instant gratification, wide choices, and easy credit. Most are more sophisticated and more tuned in to the good life than those in nonaffluent societies, but different segments interpret the "good life" in different ways. Outdoor enthusiasts shop for clothes and equipment at L. L. Bean, Orvis, or Eddie Bauer. Others prefer Bloomingdale's for everything.

Table   3.1   Stages in the Family Purchase Life Cycle

Stage in Cycle	Classical Characteristics	Current Changes in Classical Characteristics
Single	Independent Young Early stage of career Low earnings Low discretionary income	Earnings often fairly high, resulting in moderate discretionary income
Newly Married	Two incomes Relative independence Present- and future-oriented	No major changes
Full Nest I	Youngest child over 6 One income Limited independence Future-oriented	One or two incomes Present and future-oriented
Full Nest II	Youngest child over 6, but dependent One-and-a-half incomes Husband established in career Limited independence Future-oriented	Two incomes usual Both husband and wife established in careers Less limited independence Present- and future-oriented
Full Nest III	Youngest child living at home, but independent Highest income level Independent Thoughts of retirement	Thoughts of retirement in some but not all members.
Empty Nest I	No children at home Independent Good incomes Thoughts of self and retirement	Thoughts of retirement in some but not all members
Empty Nest II	Retirement Limited income and expenses Present-oriented	Not all retired, thus some income not too limited
Sole Survivor I	Only one spouse alive Actively employed Present-oriented Good income	No major changes
Sole Survivor II	Only one spouse alive Retired Feeling of futility Poor income	No major changes

Members of each of these groups readily go to Toys 'R' Us when they look for children's toys. Stereotyping is not easy, which is why consumer research is growing in importance.

Today, profiling shoppers by lifestyle is far more difficult than it was in 1954 when G. P. Stone suggested the following four categories of shoppers:

1. *The economic shopper*, who selects a store based on economic factors such as price, quality, good selection, and efficiency of store personnel.
2. *The personalizing shopper*, who seeks out stores where a warm personal relationship with the personnel can be developed.
3. *The ethical shopper*, who favors small, local independents over large chains in the interest of furthering the community's prosperity.
4. *The apathetic shopper*, who sees shopping as a chore and thus tries to make it as painless as possible by selecting stores based on convenience.[3]

Some shoppers are still generally characterized as members of one of these groups, and most likely everyone at one time falls into each of them and at other times into none.

Retailers who capture large shares of the current markets realize that shopping habits have a direct link to varying lifestyles. Lifestyle is the reason some people spend a Saturday afternoon browsing through an upscale mall like Water Tower Place in Chicago while others spend a similar time period pouring over mail-order catalogs in order to save the little leisure time they have for tennis or golf. (See Figure 3.2.) Many retailers have lifted sagging sales through lifestyle merchandising; others, however, have found that in the long run it does not pay off.

In 1983, Shopwell Inc., a 65-year-old supermarket chain in New York and Connecticut, began to grow from a small regional chain into one of the industry's best examples of high-priced, targeted merchandising. At that time it had 17 premium groceries, known as Food Emporiums, in affluent urban and suburban neighborhoods in the New York metropolitan area and planned to transform as many as 20 of its 48 other stores into Food Emporiums. Shopwell bet on Perrier instead of Pepsi, catering to well-to-do shoppers more interested in specialty, high-quality goods than in price. Taking its understanding of lifestyle retailing one step further, Shopwell's management also decided to go after the price-conscious shopper and in 1983 opened a discount supermarket in Pelham, New York. The idea was to operate stores that fit opposite ends of the market and could capture both segments in the region.[4]

During that same period Foley's, one of Texas' leading department

---

[3] G. P. Stone, "City Shoppers and Urban Identification: Observations on the Social Psychology of City Life," *American Journal of Sociology* (July 1954): 35–45.
[4] Pamela G. Hollis, "The New Gourmet Shopwell," *The New York Times*, October 16, 1983, F4.

stores, decided to drop lifestyle merchandising, once hailed by its management as the panacea for fashion retailing. The reason, Foley's chairman said, was that too much emphasis had been placed on lifestyle merchandising or separating departments by vendor.

Often there were four or five departments carrying similar merchandise in different locations. Pulling merchandise together would not only make it easier for the customer to shop and find a complete assortment of the merchandise she wants to buy, but would also aid the store in reducing investments in duplicate merchandise.

Under the old structure, there was a buyer for updated and a buyer for traditional. These buyers could buy career clothes, active wear, anything they wanted to buy from the manufacturers we said were updated or traditional. We had a tremendous overlap of merchandise between the departments.

Consequently, classifications blurred. At each price level, a rounder of suits could be found next to a rounder of blouses, which could be found next to a rounder of jeans, all under traditional groupings and then the same thing could be found all over again as an updated grouping.

It's our belief that the customer who may dress traditional today

Figure   3.2   Lifestyle Merchandising: Saks Fifth Avenue Catalog

Source: Courtesy of Saks Fifth Avenue.

may dress very forward tomorrow. Women do not put themselves in packages.[5]

As these two examples show, retailers should consider lifestyle merchandising in developing their strategies but should pursue it only for as long as it works in their markets and with their merchandise mixes. (See "From the Field: Measuring Trends: Red Meat Sales.")

_____

[5] Melissa Turner, "Foley's Drops Lifestyle Merchandising," *Woman's Wear Daily*, June 15, 1983, 12, 14.

FROM THE FIELD

Measuring Trends: Red Meat Sales

Red meat sales in supermarkets in 1985 declined for the first time as income levels rose, reports the Food Marketing Institute, Washington, D.C. (See Figure 3.3 on page 80.)

"For the first time, the 1985 U.S.D.A. Nationwide Food Consumption Survey found that women shoppers at all economic levels have lowered their meat consumption—including beef, pork, luncheon meat, lamb, and veal," Robert Bartels, president of Martin's Super Markets Inc., South Bend, Indiana, recently told FMI's annual supermarket convention in Chicago.

The U.S.D.A. study, taken once each decade, measures long-term trends, Bartels noted, and those trends are "usually long lasting. In past surveys, higher income levels correlated with higher meat consumption. This is no longer true. In fact, in 1985 red meat consumption actually declined for the first time as income rose."

Beef still accounts for 37.6 percent of meat sales, but its share slipped almost 2 points, as reported in FMI's "Trends: Consumer Attitudes and the Supermarket, 1986."

Sales of processed and frozen meats plummeted 4.5 points to 16.6 percent; lamb was off slightly. Poultry (up 6.3 points to 19.2 percent), seafood, and pork registered gains.

Concern about preservatives, chemical additives, and "natural" foods has been declining steadily in recent years, but cholesterol and fat are a concern of 30 percent of shoppers, FMI has found.

To check lost sales, the meat trade and grocers are providing recipes, nutrition information, coupons, and educational materials to shoppers, including a Meat Nutri-Facts program that has reached 3,000 stores and is expected to be in 6,000 by year's end.

_____

Source: Excerpted from "Red Meat Sales Share Slipping," *Marketing News*, June 6, 1986, 19. Reprinted by permission from *Marketing News*, published by the American Marketing Association.

Engel's Laws
Theory of 19th-century German statistician offering basic view of how consumers spend their income on goods and services.

Convenience Goods
Products purchased with a minimum of effort or time.

Product/Service Classification

People shop for certain products and services at different stages of their lives. They also shop differently because of income, regardless of stage. The 19th-century German statistician Ernst Engel studied family expenditures and observed that:

1. As a family's income *increases,* the percentage of that income spent on food *decreases.*
2. As a family's income *increases,* the percentage of that income spent on clothing is *roughly constant.*
3. As a family's income *increases,* the percentage of that income spent on housing and household operations remains *roughly constant* (exception to this is a decrease in utilities).
4. As a family's income *increases,* the percentage of that income spent on all other goods *increases.*[6]

Although **Engel's Laws** do offer a basic view of how consumers spend their income on goods and services, they do not indicate where, when, or

---

[6]Note that the *percentage* of income, not the amount, changes. Generally, as a family's income increases, the *actual dollars* spent for all goods increase.

Figure 3.3   Decline in Red Meat Sales during 1985 as a Result of Lifestyle Changes

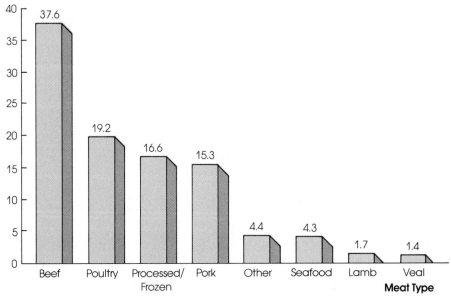

Source: "Red Meat Sales Share Slipping," *Marketing News,* June 1986, 19.

Shopping Goods
Consumer goods purchased only after the buyer compares the offerings of more than one retailer.

Specialty Goods
Consumer goods with special features for which buyers are willing to make a major purchasing effort.

Impulse Goods
Items that are likely to be purchased on the spur of the moment.

in what manner they do so. To help answer these questions, all goods and services have been broken down into four traditional categories:

1. **Convenience goods.** If you owned a convenience food store, customers would buy milk, bread, and soda because of your convenient location and hours, not because of their incomes, marital status, or number of children.
2. **Shopping goods.** If you sold automobiles or home appliances, you would need an effective sales staff. Consumers who are shopping around need to have product features pointed out to them regardless of how much they can afford to spend or whether they are interested in a small sports model or a family station wagon.
3. **Specialty goods.** If you sold imported cameras, your customers' decision to purchase would depend more on your selection and brands than on their income or age. They are camera buffs first and foremost.
4. **Impulse goods.** If you sold chewing gum, often an impulse item, you would have to display it so that shoppers could readily see it. Few people shop for chewing gum.

As these examples show, certain retailers can disregard such factors as income and life cycle stage and base their strategies on product categories alone. Because the goal of consumer buying behavior is to make a purchase, the categories of products and services must be thought of as yet another determinant of sales.

THE DECISION-MAKING PROCESS

At this point we will examine the actual decision-making process—the steps that usually lead consumers to purchase want-satisfying goods or services in the absence of any constraints, such as high prices or poor quality. By studying this process, retailers can develop strategies that not only will lead to sales and post-purchase goodwill but will also help overcome any objections along the way.

Steps in the Decision-Making Process

1. Stimulus

The decision to buy is not made in a vacuum; there must be some signal. This can come in a number of different ways, either from the external environment or from within.

Consider this simple example. You wake up at 7:00 a.m. and have breakfast at 8:00 a.m. At about noon, you begin to get a signal from within: your stomach tells you that you need to purchase lunch. Hunger is a basic stimulus that sets the purchasing process in motion.

2. Problem Awareness

The problem is that of an unfulfilled desire—you want to eat, but

a. With whom will you eat lunch? (social)
b. Can you afford to eat at the new French restaurant across town that specializes in nouvelle cuisine, or does your budget dictate the little Italian restaurant down the street with the $5 luncheon special? (economic)
c. How long is your lunch hour? (practical)
d. Is diet a consideration? (physical)

These are only some of the thoughts that lead to the next step, which involves searching for information that will help you make the final decision.

3. Information Search

At this point, you break down your problem as follows:

a. Who is available for lunch?
b. Is lunch on an expense account?
c. Which restaurant fits your time frame?
d. Does either restaurant have a dieter's lunch?

Assuming that your boss tells you to take a client who is on a diet to lunch, to use the company expense account, and to take as long as you need, the next step is to evaluate the above information.

4. Evaluation of Alternatives

Because of what you already know, it would seem that the new French restaurant is the better choice. After studying the criteria for your decision and ranking the two choices accordingly, you call and make a reservation for two for 1:00 p.m.

5. Purchase

At 1:00 p.m. you and your business guest arrive at Le Petit Cafe; you are seated immediately and order lunch. Although the restaurant is fairly expensive, the quality and variety of the food, the service, and the ambiance are all excellent. Lunch is a success, your client is impressed, and your American Express card is readily accepted.

6. Post-Purchase Behavior

Because of your satisfying experience, Le Petit Cafe will now become a regular stop for lunch whenever someone in your firm is entertaining a client. It will also be added to your list of dinner spots when you are out for a social evening. A good purchase leads to positive post-purchase behavior, as it reinforces the original purchase decision. Had the restaurant, the food, or the service been poor, the first lunch would probably have been the last.

Purchase Decision-Making Processes

Basically, consumers engage in three types of purchase decisions: (1) extended, (2) limited, and (3) routine.

Extended Decision Making

When a consumer goes through all six steps in the process, extended decision making occurs. Usually a major purchase is involved, such as a new home, a college education for a child, or an automobile. Because of the expense and risk, as much information as possible is needed in order to properly evaluate the alternatives.

Buying a personal computer for either home or business use is also a complex, risk-oriented decision and involves the extended decision-making process. Because marketers of big-ticket items know that consumers often stop before Step 5, they spend a great deal of time developing strategies for each step along the way. Television advertising can act as the catalyst by pointing out the need for a PC. Once this need is recognized, the potential buyer goes on an extensive search. Personal salesmanship is very important during this step, because the unknowledgeable consumer must rely on representatives who know the field, can analyze needs, and will help select the appropriate model. Computer marketers know this and therefore must hire expert sales help in all of their retail outlets. During the evaluation stage, often the recollection of one salesperson's presentation over all others leads to the purchase.

Post-purchase behavior is critical when buying a PC, because the purchase must be justified to oneself as well as to others. The buyer will feel pride in a correct choice but embarrassment, as well as a sense of having wasted money, in an incorrect one.

During the extended decision-making process, the consumer's lifestyle is an important influence, as are education, age, socioeconomic class, and professional status.

Limited Decision Making

The main difference between the limited decision-making process and the extended process is the amount of time spent on each of the six steps.

If Mr. Smith has been satisfied with his last three cars—all of them

Fords—and with the service he has received, when he is in the market for a new car he will likely go to the same Ford agency. His need (or problem) is still triggered by some stimulus (age of car, too much mileage, need for a second vehicle, and so on), and he still must have some information that he can use as a basis for making the final purchase. However, neither his search nor his evaluation need be as extensive as it would have to be if he were purchasing his first car. Previous postpurchase behavior (satisfaction with his previous Fords and the dealer's service) plays a great part in the limited decision-making process.

Routine Decision Making

When consumers buy items or services on a regular basis, routine decision making occurs. Although the steps are often unconscious, the consumer must have a problem that is triggered by some cue, must shop around to check the available alternatives, and must finally make the purchase. When the product is used up, he or she routinely buys again. Brand recognition and ease in shopping are important when making a routine purchase. Retailers rely heavily on brands that are well advertised by the producers of this type of merchandise.

Relationship of Categories of Goods/Services to Purchase Decision-Making Processes

When purchasing decisions are made, the category into which the product falls can be a determinant of the type of decision-making process employed. (See Table 3.2.)

Convenience goods are generally purchased routinely. Buying a quart of milk does not require extensive research on brands, quality, and so on. The brand carried at the most convenient store is usually the brand purchased.

Table 3.2   Relationship of Categories of Goods/Services to the Purchase Decision-Making Process

Categories of Goods/Services	Types of Purchase Decisions
Specialty	Extended
Shopping	Some extended, mostly limited
Convenience	Some limited, mostly routine
Impulse	Routine

Shopping goods are usually purchased with limited decision making. The selection of a dress for a special occasion requires shopping (or research). Styles, prices, labels, and material must all be considered and compared before the actual decision can be made. A woman seldom buys the first dress she sees, even though she has a preference for a certain designer and/or a certain fabric.

Specialty goods can be purchased with limited decision making, but generally the extended decision-making process is used when the product or service under consideration involves a major financial commitment or is being bought for the first time. Stored knowledge from the first purchase then makes the selection of a replacement easier. Less research is needed, especially if the next purchase is made within a year.

Impulse goods are purchased so quickly that a process is almost nonexistent. Buying your favorite newspaper is so routine that the decision is really subconscious.

Summary

As consumers change, so must retailing strategies. Retailers cannot use this year's successful mix next year in a society that is as dynamic as ours.

Understanding consumer behavior is more important today than ever before. Demographic, psychological, and socioeconomic influences—including Maslow's hierarchy of needs and G. B. Stone's category of shoppers—lifestyles, and even products and services themselves are factors that require constant study. They all affect the consumer's behavior in the marketplace. Desires change with age, income, education, and membership in business or professional and socioeconomic groups.

Retailers can never devote too much time to the study of consumer behavior. In addition to learning what motivates their customers, constant observation helps them understand the consumer decision-making process: the steps by which people become aware of and informed about products and services for which they shop. All consumers are problem solvers, and the first step in this process takes place when they become aware of a problem that needs solving. This is followed by a search for information, an evaluation of the alternatives, and the selection of a product or a service that will solve the problem. The final step is the evaluation of the purchase. This is used as input for future buying decisions.

When, where, what, and how consumers buy are also determined by the nature of the purchase. Some items classified as convenience or impulse goods are purchased routinely. Shopping for other goods involves a higher decision-making process and some type of research, whether limited or extended. Anything classified as a specialty item or service requires a lengthy decision-making process. This means an extended search and evaluation.

Whenever goods and services are sold, the final determinant of the sale is the consumer. No retailer can afford to ignore this principle. Constant study of consumers in a particular society is as important as study of world economics and the political scene. Consumer behavior is the basis for every retail mix.

Questions for Review

1. Name at least four macrodemographic trends and describe how they can be employed to guide a firm's retailing efforts.
2. Comment on the statement, "In the future, Maslow's hierarchy of needs will not be sufficiently sophisticated to identify all buying motivations."
3. What is meant by consumer reference groups? Give examples of how they can offer input into a consumer's decision-making process.
4. Explain how Ernst Engel's observations on family expenditures in the 19th century might account for the increase in discretionary income today.
5. Define and differentiate among the following:
   a. Convenience goods
   b. Shopping goods
   c. Specialty goods
   d. Impulse goods
6. What are the six steps in a consumer's decision-making process?
7. List the three basic types of consumer purchase decisions and give examples of products purchased on the basis of each type.

Chandler's

Reversing a Decline in the Cosmetics Department

Sales in the cosmetics department at Chandler's had been going steadily downhill for six months, and Bob Norton, the cosmetics buyer, was concerned. Why wasn't his merchandise moving? He seemed to be doing everything right.

Three years before, when he graduated from college with a B.S. degree in retailing, he had easily beaten out the other candidates for the position of assistant cosmetics buyer at Chandler's, Bedford's only full-line department store, an establishment with an annual volume of $4 million. When he was promoted to buyer 18 months later, he had been confident he could increase department volume to record levels; after all, he was bringing a lot more knowledge to the job than his predecessor had.

Elsie Collins, the previous buyer, had started at Chandler's as a salesgirl after graduating from high school. A devoted employee for 45 years, she had grown with the store and was rewarded during its expansion phase in the 1960s by being made buyer of the newly established cosmetics department. This was a logical decision, because she knew both the customers and the store policies and, as a mature woman, understood the place of cosmetics in the life of women. She was definitely right for the job and had proven her worth to management. Initially she had been able to buy most of the well-known lines and then increase sales in each of them year after year. As Bedford women became more educated and sophisticated, her sales soared along with cosmetic sales all over the country. Although it was becoming increasingly difficult to beat the previous year's figures, she was still holding her own.

When Bob Norton was hired as her assistant, there was a definite upturn in business. Norton had some computer background and was able to handle all of the inventory control, giving Collins more time to spend on the floor talking to customers and finding out what they really wanted. As it turned out, this was not always what communications from suppliers were indicating.

The cosmetics industry had been experiencing phenomenal growth for 20 years, leading cosmetics marketers to believe they were infallible and that women everywhere would buy whatever was earmarked as fashion-right. The promotional material that flooded every cosmetic buyer's office often did not take market differences into account; if a buyer bought without knowing firsthand the preferences of the market, the results could be disastrous. Because Collins now had the time to be on the floor, she was able to gather much of the information needed to do a better buying job. This greatly contributed to Chandler's increase in cosmetics sales, for she was able to buy merchandise specifically geared to her target market.

Every market is different. Bedford women were, for the most part, conservative, very value conscious, and preferred the out-of-doors suburban image to the more sophisticated look of the city dweller. Collins knew their buying preferences, their likes and dislikes, and their lifestyles.

When Collins retired, she passed on all of her market knowledge to Bob Norton. This, coupled with his academic training, seemed an ideal background with which to start the job.

The first year had been fine. Figures were far ahead of the previous year, and Norton looked forward to continued growth. But instead of growth, there was a decline—not a really serious one, but nevertheless a decline. What was he doing wrong?

Perhaps he wasn't doing anything wrong; he just wasn't doing enough that was right. Bedford, like many other outlying suburban areas, had become a mecca for many young families from the city. Apartment complexes and condos were also attracting career singles. This was a new population mix and one more difficult to serve than the customers for whom Elsie had bought in previous years. These thoughts, and thoughts about his competition, made Norton decide to put it all down on paper. Maybe with the facts in black and white he could come up with a solution.

He was carrying some of the most famous names in cosmetics: Revlon, which in Elsie's day had been the number-one international cosmetics house in sales, appealing to all age groups; Estée Lauder, a prestigious line with expensive products; Clinique, a special hypo-allergenic line; Elizabeth Arden, one of the oldest names in cosmetics; and Lancôme, a renowned French cosmetics name. All but Lancôme could be found in a number of other stores in the market area; in fact, for several years, Revlon had been stocked in nearly all of the discount chains. Although Chandler's benefited from the extensive national advertising being done in the cosmetics industry and the cooperative promotions of the companies from which it purchased, so did all of its competitors.

Prices were constantly increasing. Norton never raised his retail prices without worrying about customer rejection, yet it was impossible to operate without doing so. First, overhead was higher each year; second, the well-known companies frowned on individual store price cutting. Any retailer who cut price without approval risked losing the line.

Customer buying habits seemed to be changing too. Women no longer were spending as much time at the cosmetics counter as they had in the past. Most seemed to know what they wanted before entering the store and wanted no lengthy explanations or demonstrations; it was difficult to make a multiple sale unless it was initiated by the customer. Suddenly Norton found the key he had been looking for. The only way to achieve greater volume was to motivate the customer to buy not only what she had decided on before entering the store but items she had not even considered, once in the store. A working knowledge of consumer behavior would be essential for such strategy planning. Specific motives might change, but motivation would still be necessary if a sale were to take place. What motivated the typical Chandler customer?

Most of Chandler's current customers, whether married or single, were career oriented, well educated, and well traveled. They were more independent than any other generation before them but had the same basic needs as their mothers and grandmothers. This was the profile of the current Chandler customer.

Having identified what he felt sure was the basic problem, Norton outlined several alternative plans:

1. Eliminate all lines carried by discount stores; concentrate only on exclusive, franchised brands, and advertise Chandler's as the headquarters for them.
2. Discount lines sold at competing stores, and use promotional advertising to attract more business.
3. Offer free consultation with every purchase of $20 or more.
4. Engage in a direct-mail campaign, including in each month's bill a promotional brochure for a different line.
5. Have at least one cosmetologist employed by the manufacturer at each cosmetic counter on a regular, periodic basis.

The next thing for Norton to do was to carefully evaluate each of the alternatives.

Questions

1. Rate the five alternatives outlined by Bob Norton on a scale of 1 to 10, from best to worst.
2. Explain why you rated each alternative as you did.
3. Using the following consumer categories, analyze Chandler's current cosmetics market in terms of socioeconomic and behavior characteristics: (1) homemakers not working outside the home, (2) homemakers working outside the home, (3) college students, (4) high-school students, (5) nonprofessional single women, and (6) professional single women.
4. Which of the market segments described in Question 3 would most likely become Chandler's best cosmetics customers? Explain the reasons for your selections.
5. List some buying motives by sex that lead to the purchase of cosmetics.

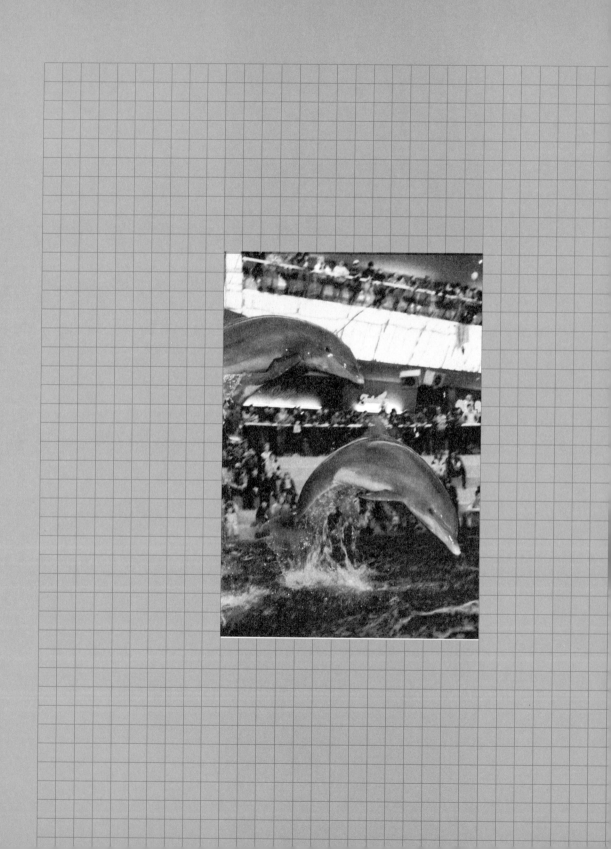

Part II

Human Resources

Chapter 4

Source: Jack Gifford, Professor of Marketing, Miami University of Ohio.

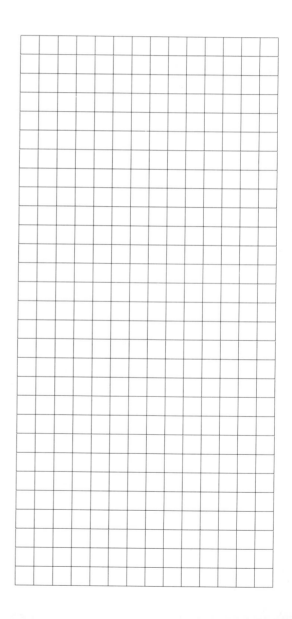

Industry Statement

Virginia Caillouette
Vice President, Employee Relations
R. H. Macy Inc.

Challenge, responsibility, accomplishment, and reward are all descriptive of the retail career experience.

The best retailers are the entrepreneurs who have initiative and imagination and are willing to take risks. New executives are given the opportunity to demonstrate that entrepreneurial spirit very early in a retail career. They are given responsibility for the management of a multifaceted business and the challenge of developing a success story.

The best personnel departments are able to identify potential executives with the necessary skills to become the future leaders of the business. They look for a good communicator, with an analytical mind, who can demonstrate the ability to gain the cooperation of others to achieve results.

Retailing is not only the buying and selling of goods. It is also operations, personnel management, sales promotion, finance, and a host of other support functions critical to the success of the business. Each of these areas typically works very closely with the merchandising line, and in some organizations career paths may crisscross. In this respect, retailing offers great breadth in career development opportunity.

The best way to evaluate your compatibility with this fast-paced, people-intensive industry is to work in it. A summer job, part-time work, or a college internship will provide a firsthand look at the business, at what it requires, and at the people who do well in it. It can be a good test of individual adaptability, energy level, and enjoyment.

Retailing is the right career choice if you have a sense of adventure and the desire and drive to see your ideas come to life.

Learning Objectives

Upon completing this chapter you should be able to:

1. Target the type of retail institutions in which there will be new job opportunities in the future.
2. Understand why a technological background can be important for a career in retailing.
3. Understand and discuss the benefits of a college internship experience.
4. Describe the personal characteristics important for success in retailing.
5. Describe the basic difference between a chronological and a functional résumé.
6. Develop a self-marketing plan for your job search.

If you enjoy diversity, new challenges, a fast pace, and geographic and career mobility, retailing *could* be the field for you. If you also enjoy being with people, being creative, and helping others to make decisions, retailing is *probably* for you. If, however, you want a 9-to-5 desk job where the functions at 10 o'clock each day are exactly like the functions at the same time the previous day, if you are not comfortable in a theatrical environment, and if you are put off by relatively low starting salaries, then retailing *may not* be for you. In any case, before making a decision, investigate all of the career options in retailing. The diversity of opportunities in this dynamic industry is enormous and could in some instances even satisfy a 9-to-5 type.

When thinking about a career in retailing you must consider your own qualifications as well as job opportunities. You should look into the various managerial positions open to you as an employee and also at ownership possibilities. Wherever you start, it is important to think about the **career path** from that first job. Where can you expect to be in five years, in ten years? Who are the growth merchants? Where are the growth locations?

In this chapter you will find answers to these questions and you will learn how to prepare yourself for a career search. This is presented early

Career Path
The planned sequence of jobs that leads to a career objective.

in the text so that, as you study the universal functions of retailing, you can relate your own ambitions and abilities to each job area.

CAREER OPTIONS

Retail employment in the United States should continue in an upward spiral, because it grows in direct proportion to consumer spending, and consumer spending is projected to be over $2 trillion by 1995.[1] In the future, as in the past, retailing will therefore offer a great many career opportunities, especially in the service sector. Retailers are everywhere and are found in every size and type: department stores, catalog merchants, computer product centers, automobile dealers, fashion chains, specialty food shops, and so on. There are careers for those who want to be in business for themselves and careers for those who prefer to work in large corporate organizations.

One of the great pluses in retailing is that experience is always transferable from one area to another because the basic functions are the same regardless of type of ownership. Once a retail employee is trained, it is easy to switch. The options are endless.

Opportunities with Traditional Retailers

In-Store Retailing
All types of retailing except direct marketing.

Traditional retailers, often referred to as the **in-store retailing** segment, include every type of store from supermarket to drive-in dry cleaner. A traditional retailer can be a large corporation where functions are divided by specialty. On the other hand, many merchants manage their own stores, performing all the functions themselves.

A career person in a very large chain may work in one division all of his or her life. Whether as specialists or generalists, however, careers in traditional retailing exist all over the world. Employees are needed for merchandising and real estate activities, in operations, in promotion, in personnel, to issue credit, run P.O.S. registers, design computerized inventory systems, or select new store sites. From C.E.O.s to sales associates, traditional retailers must have people with a variety of skills.

Merchants who sell services, even more than merchants who sell goods, are on the increase. They include fast food chains, travel agencies, hotels, and motels. Even a clerk at the front desk in a hotel can be thought of as a retail person. There will be 4,265,000 sales jobs in the United States alone by 1995.[2] This indicates an increase at the executive level also: the more salespeople employed, the more supervisors are needed.

---

[1] "The Economy in 1995," *Occupational Outlook Quarterly*, Spring–Summer 1984, 27.
[2] Ibid.

Opportunities with Nontraditional Retailers

A nontraditional retailer is one who does not sell through a store. Career opportunities are available in door-to-door operations, vending machine companies, catalog retail firms, telemarketing, and the newest entrant on the nontraditional wheel of retailing—the retailer who sells via television computer hookup in customers' homes. Although fewer in number, jobs are growing at all levels in this segment.

Amway gives generous rewards to its consultants who reach certain sales quotas through direct sales. Vending companies offer new ownership and/or franchise opportunities to those who are interested in dispensing fun and video games. L. L. Bean, one of the country's most successful catalog retailers, beckons young M.B.A. graduates to Freeport, Maine. (A few years ago, these same young executives could not find Freeport on the map.) Part-time jobs for students can be found in telemarketing firms, and retailing has finally found a use for computer engineers, who bring the new technology to in-home shopping.

College/University Support

In both traditional and nontraditional settings, men and women can climb the retail career ladder side by side. Today, management positions in retailing match and may even surpass salaries and benefits in other industries. Yet retailing suffers from a public perception that this is not so. The industry has not been able to put across the fact that people with ability can advance from assistant buyer to merchandise manager in ten years or less and achieve major compensation.

Retailing careers are finally getting a push on college and university campuses. The aim is to overcome the lingering negative image that hinders recruitment of many college graduates to retailing. Speaking to business students at Duke University, the Chairman and C.E.O. of Batus, Inc., said:

> The decade of the 1980s represents one of the most fertile periods of career opportunity in the history of my industry. Retailing is a stage for the expression of some of the most creative and theatrical ideas for the promotion of merchandise, providing some of the most exciting environments that any of us have experienced, and is the beneficiary of much of the disposable income of working women, two-income families, and retirees.[3]

In 1984, more than 70 U.S. colleges and universities offered retailing courses as an integral part of business curriculum leading to bachelor's, master's, or doctoral degrees. Many also sponsored one or more retail

---

[3] Samuel Feinberg, "From Where I Sit," *Women's Wear Daily*, December 11, 1984, 8.

executive seminars annually.[4] Academia, reinforced by the many opportunities for exciting retail careers and with help from the industry, finally began to boost retail education.

Technological Opportunities

Technology has had an impact on the retail industry—both traditional and nontraditional—as it has on every other growth industry. Today many jobs in retailing require the same type of expertise needed by manufacturers or computer firms.

Warehouses are mechanized and inventory is tracked by computer. Payrolls, credit systems, accounting, and financial controls are also on computer. Word processors and personal computers appear in the offices of department store merchandise managers and on the desks of chain store managers. Reports flow from branch to flagship store via electronic equipment. In-store videos promote the latest fashions, and scanners quickly pick up prices at supermarket and discount store checkout counters. Everywhere there are signs that retailing, along with the rest of business and industry, is in the electronic age.

Bytehead
Computer industry buzzword for those who create computer systems.

Computer scientists, systems experts, programmers, and technicians now have a chance to climb the retail career ladder. Even on the lowest rung, some technological know-how is important. Watch a salesperson entering a charge sale on a P.O.S. register and you will certainly agree. Because the entire industry is eager to make use of all that the technological age offers, there are even places for **"byteheads"** in retailing.

CAREER PATHS

Among the ways to start the climb up the retail career ladder are work experience programs, management training programs, promotion from within, and specialty store training.

Work Experience Programs

Internships

Interns
Students in a formal training program that allows them to learn on the job by working closely with professionals.

Many programs at two- or four-year colleges and universities offer students an opportunity to sample careers while still undergraduates. As **interns,** students work in selected jobs in their chosen field. They may work part-time during one semester, full-time for an entire semester, full-time for a portion of a semester, or either part- or full-time during a summer vacation period. Internships may be paid or unpaid. In either

---

[4] Ibid.

case, college credit is usually earned because the internship is treated as a learning experience.

A typical retail internship may take place on a department store selling floor or in a merchandise office. One student may work in Bloomingdale's Manhattan store during the busy Christmas season as an assistant to a floor section manager. Another may run the temporary Christmas decoration shop in one of the branch stores. A third may act as the second assistant manager in a national fashion chain store such as The Limited or Foxmoor. A fourth may learn from the owner how to completely merchandise a local hardware store.

Types of internships vary from one geographic location to another because jobs depend on the type and size of stores in the area. The value of an internship also varies because the training is only as good as the trainer and the demands of the academic supervisor. Most interns either follow a syllabus (see Figure 4.1) or complete workbook assignments while on the job.

A good internship is often the first step on the retail career ladder, and many retailers hire previous interns as management trainees. In some

Figure 4.1   Syllabus for a Retailing Internship

OBJECTIVES

The goal of this experience is to expose students to the real world of retailing so that they can learn how to function in a store environment. A written case analysis of a phase of the work program as each has experienced it, designed to aid the employer, will give the student an opportunity to truly relate academics and practice. In this way, the internship becomes a total learning experience for the intern.

PROCEDURE

Each intern is placed in a career-related workstation for a full semester (15-week minimum). As the intern is out of the classroom, the responsibility for all reports and correspondence rests completely on the student's shoulders. Noncompliance will lead to an Unsatisfactory grade and loss of 12 credits. While on the job, the following procedures must be adhered to:

I. Due in the Career Development Center two weeks after the internship begins are:
    A. *Detailed objectives* associated with the job. These should primarily be learning objectives and should be stated as such. Students must keep a copy of their original objectives. When the internship is completed, the final objective statement must relate to the original.
    B. An *employer information sheet* summarizing the historical and organizational background of the company. (This is to be filled out by the student.) Forms are provided.
    C. An *organization chart* for the company where the student is employed as an intern (references for this may be found in all introductory management texts). If working in a branch operation or a unit of a chain, please do this for the branch or unit where employed, indicating that it is a subsidiary of a major company.

(continued)

Figure   4.1   (*continued*)

II. *Monthly report forms* will be sent to each intern and must be returned to the Career Development Center within *one week* after being received by the intern.

III. An *on-site visit* with the intern's supervisor will be made by an officer of the Career Development Center whenever possible. If this is not possible, a midterm telephone or written evaluation will be requested from the employer by a CDC officer.

IV. *Career Exploration.* Each intern should take this opportunity to expand his or her knowledge of career options related to his or her major. This assignment should broaden knowledge of the work world and at the same time assist in appropriate career decision making. Three assignments are listed. You are to complete *all three.*

V. *Internship Project.* This is to be an original case study and is due the first day of the last week in the semester. Based on any problem or problems encountered while on the job, the case may depict a financial, managerial, or human relations problem, and must be written so that all the facts are clearly understood by the reader. The case analysis and possible solutions should accompany the narrative. The total number of typewritten pages should not exceed 15 nor be less than 8 (excluding exhibits).

VI. *Attainment of Objectives.* A statement concerning attainment of initial objectives is due the first day of the last week of the semester.

VII. *Assessment of the human relations aspects* of the experience, *an evaluation of the employer,* and a *job description* must be submitted by the student the first day of the last week of the semester. Forms are provided for the evaluation and an outline for the job description is given.

VIII. *Final evaluation by employer.* Each intern employer must submit a final evaluation of the student's performance before credit can be issued (forms provided to employer).

GRADING AND CREDIT

Upon successful completion of the internship experience, 12 credits will be given. Retailing interns may make arrangements for a business elective at the time of application. No intern is allowed to take more than 18 credits. Permission must be obtained from the Academic Dean's office for credit beyond 15.

The retailing internship will be graded Satisfactory/Unsatisfactory, the credit being based on the report of the on-site visit (or the employer's midterm report) and the employer's final report plus all reports, and the internship project. All reports must be accurate and received on time. If a student's job is terminated by the employer because of poor job performance on the part of the intern prior to completion of the internship, the resulting grade will be Unsatisfactory and no credit will be given.

Model for Developing a Case Study

Narrative

This section is an actual case and should be written in narrative form. Included must be basic facts about the company and its organization (historical and current), a statement of the problem or problems, plus any and all data (quantitative or qualitative) relating to the problem or problems.

Analysis

1. Define problem or problems (major problems as well as underlying problems contributing to the major one).
2. Present alternative courses of action (possible solutions).
3. Explore pros and cons of each alternative presented in 2, including their sensitivity to changes in internal and external environment of the company.
4. Make a decision and give rationale, recognizing strengths and weaknesses of the chosen course of action.
5. Suggest follow-up procedures.

(*continued*)

Figure   4.1   *(continued)*

Career Exploration Requirement

The Career Exploration component is a requirement for completion of your internship. It is hoped that the assignments will both broaden your knowledge of the work world and assist you in career decision making.

Assignment 1

Answer the question "What can I do with a major in _____?" (The blank is for you to fill in your declared major.) Identify at least three possible occupational choices for your major and write a report on each. You should be sure to include the following:
- Nature of the work
- Typical places of employment
- Training and educational requirements
- Employment outlook
- Earnings and working conditions
- A list of resources consulted for this information

Assignment 2

Identify at least three professional journals or periodicals in your broad career field: (a) describe the publication (its content, intent, readership, etc.); (b) choose one article from each of the three publications and summarize each article; and (c) list the article title, author, periodical, volume, and page numbers. Choose the articles on the basis of their dealing with current issues or innovations in your field or their relevance to your career interests.

Assignment 3

Select at least two persons in your career field to interview. The people must be *new* contacts to you. Do not interview friends, relatives, or coworkers. Write a report of the information gained from each of the two interviews. Also include the interviewee's name, title, organization, complete address, and phone number.

Guide to Arranging Interviews

Informational interviewing is the process of gathering facts about various career/work areas by talking to the people who actually do the work.

To help identify people to interview, you will find industrial and social service directories in the Career Development Center library or the reference section of most public libraries. Most directories provide names, addresses, and telephone numbers of people to contact. You may also pursue your own contacts by asking friends, family members, faculty, and alumni if they know people you might talk with. Finally, you may ask the Career Development Center staff for possible contacts.

When arranging the informational interview, explain to the person that you are a student doing career research. Indicate to him or her that you would like to set up an appointment to learn more about his or her job. Make it clear that you are not looking for a job but for information to assist you in making career decisions.

Before you go to the interview, prepare a list of questions to ask. These questions might include:

- What is a typical day or week like for you?
- How should an individual prepare himself or herself to enter this field?
- What do you like most about your job?
- What do you like least about your job?
- What skills would you say are most important for success in this area of work?
- How did you get into this field?
- What other career areas do you see as related to your work?
- Do you have any advice for me?

Before ending the discussion, always attempt to get the names of other people you might talk with to gather additional information. Always send a thank-you note to the person who agreed to meet with you. This is both good practice and common courtesy—it also leaves the interviewee with a favorable impression of you.

Source: New Hampshire College.

instances, former interns even start in management positions. Employers like to hire from this group, because its members are familiar with both the company image and retail work patterns. There are few surprises for the new management trainee who has had previous experience with his or her employer. Attrition is much lower, training is easier, and advancement is faster.

Cooperative Education

Cooperative Education
An educational methodology that employs alternate periods of formal study and successful work experience as a prerequisite for graduation.

The major difference between **cooperative education** and internship programs is in the number of work experiences. In a cooperative education program, students alternate between the classroom and the workplace. They may have as few as two work periods in a two-year community college or as many as five in a five-year bachelor's degree program. Because students often return to the same employer, it is possible to move from the lowest level during the first work term to a full-fledged managerial position by graduation. A few of the many possible cooperative education models are shown in Figure 4.2 on page 102. Cooperative education is an educational methodology practiced in over 1,000 colleges and universities in the United States and Canada. Programs also exist in the United Kingdom, Australia, and Europe.

Part-Time and/or Summer Jobs

Even if a college or university has no formal work program, students may still begin their retailing careers while in school. Many of the most successful retail executives began working part-time in retail while in high school and continued part-time and summers through college, committing themselves to a career in the field long before receiving their degrees.

Anyone who has experienced the late hours and low pay that are typical when starting out in retailing and still wants to pursue a retail career is an excellent candidate for success. If you enjoy the retail atmosphere as a part-timer, future commitment is easy.

Management Training Programs

Most large retail institutions have some sort of management training program. These programs, whether in merchandising or in store operations, offer college graduates their first real chance on the career ladder and are the fastest routes to junior executive positions.

Recruitment

Stores like Macy's, Bloomingdale's, Hecht's, Bullock's, Sears, J. C. Penney, B. Altman, Marshall Field's, and John Wanamaker, to name only a

Figure 4.2   Some Sample Cooperative Education Models

5-Year Alternating Plan

Fall	Spring	Summer	Fall	Spring	Summer
Academic Term	Academic Term	Academic Term	Academic Term	Academic Term	Work Term
Work Term	Academic Term	Work Term	Academic Term	Work Term	Academic Term
Academic Term	Work Term	Academic Term	Work Term	Academic Term	Work Term
Work Term	Academic Term	Work Term	Academic Term	Work Term	Academic Term
Academic Term	Work Term	Graduation	Work Term	Academic Term	Graduation

4-Year Alternating Plans

Fall	Spring	Summer	Fall	Spring	Summer
Academic Term	Academic Term	Free	Academic Term	Academic Term	Free
Academic Term	Academic Term	Work Term	Academic Term	Academic Term	Academic Term
Academic Term	Work Term	Academic Term	Work Term	Academic Term	Work Term
Academic Term	Academic Term	Graduation	Academic Term	Academic Term	Graduation

Fall	Spring	Summer	Fall	Spring	Summer
Academic Term	Academic Term	Free	Academic Term	Academic Term	Free
Academic Term	Academic Term	Academic Term	Academic Term	Academic Term	Academic Term
Work Term	Academic Term	Work Term	Academic Term	Work Term	Academic Term
Academic Term	Work Term	Academic Term	Work Term	Academic Term	Work Term
		Graduation			Graduation

few, recruit on selected college and university campuses. They also invite graduating students from all colleges to send them résumés.

Competition for slots in these programs is fierce, and it is not unusual for 800 students to be interviewed for 80 openings. Applicants who have had experience have a much better chance of being selected and of surviving the grueling first years.

Eaton's, Canada's leading department store, does no college recruiting. All of Eaton's trainees are former interns, coop students, or part-time or summer employees who, during their senior year, apply for full-time management positions at graduation. Not only does Eaton's save recruiting dollars this way, but the company is also ensuring a lower **attrition** rate. (Attrition is usually quite high in management training programs.) All Eaton's trainees are seasoned employees from either the main store or one of the branches.

Attrition
Shrinking of employee roles through resignation, retirement, or death.

Training

Most training programs produce both merchandising and management executives for all areas of the operation. Trainees tend to move ahead as quickly as their interests and skills develop. Programs usually combine intense work experience with structured seminars.

Management training programs vary in length from several months to three years, depending on the company. Starting salaries also vary according to the experience and educational background of the candidate and the geographic location of the employer.

Most companies conduct periodic reviews of trainees and award salary increases based on merit. Starting salaries for management trainees in retailing usually range from $18,000 to $20,000 per year. Although retailing salaries are notoriously low at the beginning, salaries for middle and upper management employees become comparable to, if not higher than, those in other fields. After five years of experience it is possible for executives to double their salary and make $36,000 to $40,000 per year.

Qualification for Selection

Recruiters differ on what academic degrees they prefer for candidates seeking entry into their management trainee programs. Some seek general business majors or those specializing in marketing, management, retailing, or finance. Others will consider liberal arts graduates. Most admit that they favor a business major over a humanities major, if all else is equal. Some recruiters will accept two-year program graduates. Candidates with an M.B.A. would certainly be viewed favorably because of the increasing role of business theories and computers in retailing. A degree in the computer sciences could also be useful.

Recruiters agree on the basic qualities they seek in candidates for the executive training program. Generally, individuals should be outgoing, should communicate effectively, and should show an interest in retailing. They must have intelligence and demonstrated leadership skills. Candidates with high levels of energy and the ability to think on their feet do best. Candidates should also be mature, assertive, and able to make decisions; have above-average communication skills and analytical abilities; and have some work experience.

Promotion from Within

Although executive training programs offer the fastest route to management positions, there are other alternatives. Selling has been a starting point for some executives in retailing. From sales clerk, individuals have moved to assistant department manager, group manager, assistant buyer, and even store manager. Some department store chains have special training programs for company personnel who show management potential. These programs generally take longer than executive training programs.

Because everyone who applies cannot possibly be selected for a firm's management training program, the sales route, although slower, is an alternative road to a top management job. Often a good person who is passed over by executive placement recruiters, and who is willing to start in sales, proves to be a more valuable executive in the long run than anyone in the training program.

Specialty Store Management

Another avenue to executive positions in retailing is working for a specialty store, such as a drug, shoe, furniture, or junior apparel shop. Many specialty stores offer management positions in which employees have a great deal of responsibility ranging from supervising the staff to accounting duties to total store operation. Besides store management, specialty chains also offer positions for buyers, district managers, division managers, and regional training directors.

Some Typical Career Paths

At Bradlees, one of the most successful discount department stores on the East Coast, clear paths of promotion begin with trainee positions in both sales (stores) and buying. (See Table 4.1.) The fact that promotion paths are not indicated for special departments does not mean that they do not exist. What it means is that employees are hired in these areas for a specific job, not as trainees. All of these departments consider their own people for promotion as openings occur. If an employee is qualified for the next level, then promotion is from within. In most of the corporate retail world, opportunities exist in every functional area.

▬▬ —

Table   4.1   Career Alternatives at Bradlees

Stores	Buying	Special Departments
Management Trainee	Assistant Buyer Trainee	Operations
Department Manager	Assistant Buyer	Advertising
Sales Manager	Associate Buyer	Human Resources
Store Manager	Buyer	Finance
Market Manager	Division Merchandise Manager	Management Information Systems
Regional Personnel Management	General Merchandise Manager	Inventory Management
Regional Trainer		Planning
Regional Manager		Distribution
		Other Areas

Source: Bradlees Recruiting Pamphlet, distributed by Bradlees, Braintree, Mass.

Figure 4.3 on page 106 illustrates the merchandising career path at Burdines in Florida. Figure 4.4 on page 107 shows both the merchandising and management paths at J. C. Penney.

PERSONAL QUALIFICATIONS FOR RETAIL EXECUTIVES

Generally speaking, the high-flying, free-wheeling executives of the past are giving way to managers trained in finance, asset management, and marketing. Yet discipline, finance, and planning must be balanced by an understanding of marketing strategy and an appreciation of the creative demands of a merchandise- and service-oriented business. Because of this, a very special kind of person is needed.

In its executive recruitment literature, Burdines of Florida presents a success profile that lists these qualities:

1. *Problem solving:* Ability to analyze facts, data for planning, managing, and controlling.
2. *Creativity:* To bring imaginative ideas to merchandising and be first in coming trends.
3. *Confidence:* To take action, seize opportunities, and make quick, confident decisions in the ever-changing retail world.
4. *Leadership:* Take the initiative, helping everyone work together to run a business smoothly.
5. *Flexibility:* Be receptive to changing trends in styles and attitudes, and be adaptable to the everyday surprises in retail.
6. *Energy:* Being able to handle the stress of the fast-paced, demanding job of a retailing executive.[5]

Not only the Burdines' executive but all retail executives need these

---

[5] Reprinted by permission of Burdines, a Division of Federated Department Stores, Inc.

characteristics. They must also understand the theatrics of the business. As a vice president of Associated Merchandising Corporation has said, "Retailing is showmanship with credibility."[6] There are a number of additional qualities that should be included on any list of criteria for success in retailing.

[6] Janine Linden, "Retailing: A Hard Sell Industry," in Business Week's *Careers*, December 1984–January 1985, 56.

Figure   4.3   Merchandising Career Path at Burdines

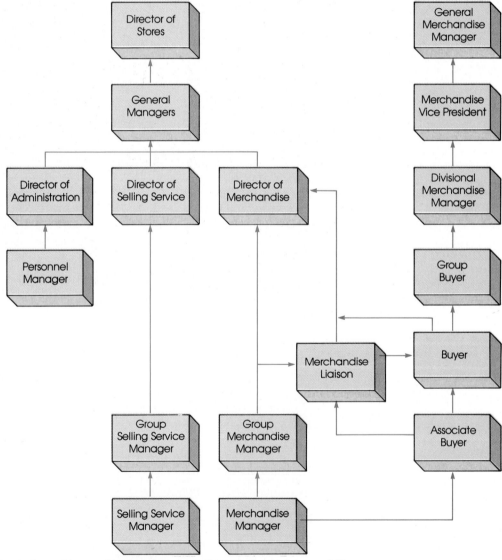

Note: The level of a position on this chart does not indicate the level of responsibility.
Source: Courtesy of Burdines—Florida.

Good Communication Skills

Written and oral skills are an absolute must in a people-oriented business. Because executives frequently give verbal instructions to those who work for them and send written reports to those for whom they work, misunderstanding because of incorrect English usage could have serious

Figure   4.4   Career Paths in Management and Merchandising at J. C. Penney

Opportunities for Promotion

Today's large store manager usually has a strong base of many store experiences, including operations and personnel assignments, as well as some experience in District or Regional staff work. Store manager jobs are highly prized for their degree of independence, responsibility, and level of compensation.

The key to advancement, of course, is job performance. As you advance, more and more opportunities open up.

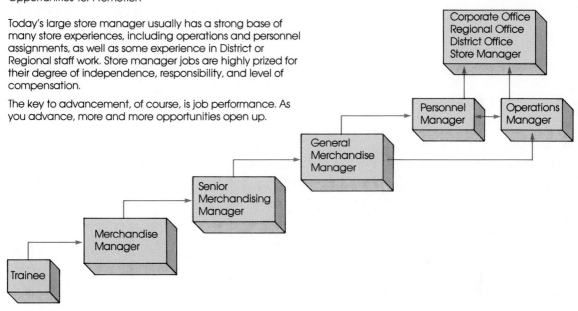

Opportunities for Promotion

Buyers serve their apprenticeships as assistant buyers. As part of JCPenney policy of "promotion from within," buyers are chosen from our staff of associate buyers.

Performance is the key idea in our buyer department process. Your future success and career will depend heavily on your performance as an assistant buyer.

The primary buying career looks like this:

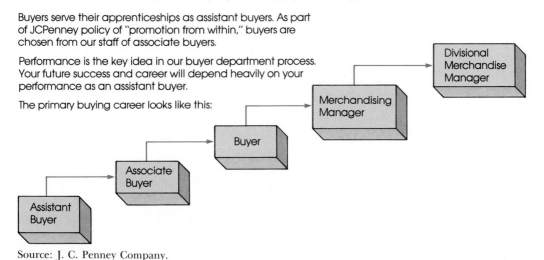

Source: J. C. Penney Company.

consequences for both the executive and the company. Students often tend to ignore the English professor who emphasizes the need for good communications skills in business. Listen well, future retailers; no lesson will ever be more important.

Human Relations Skills

As important as the ability to communicate with people is the ability to get along with them in a business setting. The human side of the market-place is often neglected in the rush for profits. Yet profits are sometimes lost because of this neglect.

An Ability to Function under Pressure

An ideal retail executive is a self-starter and a person who can do more than one thing at a time. The kind of person who thrives under pressure is perfect for the field.

An Optimistic Attitude

Because retailing is a dynamic business, there are often as many valleys as peaks. A good leader is optimistic at all times and acts as an inspiration to others.

Although possession of the right qualities does not guarantee success, without them a retail executive has much less chance for effective job performance.

THE CAREER SEARCH

Whatever your career choice, planning and preparation are essential in identifying jobs and employers. Without a plan you can easily end up in the wrong occupation, in the wrong location, and with the wrong firm. You must begin your search with your own special goals in mind and with a marketing plan that is based on those goals.

Even before setting goals, ask yourself three questions about the career field you are considering:

1. Does it have a future? Here trends in technology, economics, and politics must be considered.
2. Will it be financially rewarding?
3. Does it have enough potential growth to accommodate a reasonably large number of new entrants in the years ahead?

If retailing is your choice, then the answer to all three questions is definitely yes—provided that you make it past the trainee stage.

Strategic Career Search
Systematic job hunt matched to one's career plan.

Entry-Level Position
A job that requires little or no related work experience.

Goal Setting

As you start your **strategic career search,** you must ask yourself this question: "Where do I expect (or want) to be 5, 10, or 15 years from the time I enter the job market?" Growth potential is more important than the door through which you enter an industry or company. No one wants a dead-end job, but because too many people only think of the starting salary and job title, they miss the best opportunities. Thinking about your goals helps you stay on target as you develop, learn, and implement skills in your **entry-level position.**

Self-Analysis

Make an honest appraisal of your interests, abilities, and disabilities. Do they fit the picture you are painting of your future? If not, then before going any further, you must reappraise your goals. They have to be realistic in terms of who you are, your interests, and your aptitudes. Part of self-analysis is determining what knowledge or skills you have acquired through your educational and work experiences and judging how this knowledge will transfer to your desired career path.

If you have set goals and related them to who you are, what you desire, and how your capabilities and interests relate to the world of work, you are at least one step ahead of most of the competition for that first job. Most candidates only seek a job. They do not think about the long-range implications of planning for a career.

Job-Hunting Preliminaries

Now the real work begins. It is time to gather information from people in the field. Write to companies that interest you and ask about jobs, the company, and future opportunities. Call executives you know and ask if you can take a few minutes of their time to learn about careers with their firms. Most people are flattered to be asked, and if you do this in a polite way, you will almost always get an appointment. Talk to family friends, alumni of your college, and summer or part-time employers. Armed with information you will be better prepared to present yourself to potential employers.

Turning to friends, relatives, and business or personal acquaintances to learn about employment opportunities and to let people know you are in the job market is called **networking.** It is another excellent preliminary strategy. Often this type of communication leads to employment, because some of the people you speak to may be aware of actual job openings. A good tip when networking is never to leave one contact without getting the names of three more people. Because they know the

Networking
Creating an effective and organized system that helps in establishing support for job search activities.

first contact, they will be receptive to the idea of seeing you. This method can help build a wonderful resource file of potential employers.

Job Search Tools

Résumé
A brief history of education and experience that job applicants prepare for prospective employers to review.

Three basic tools are essential in getting the first job: (1) **résumés,** (2) letters, and (3) interviews. All three must be approached from a marketing point of view. The marketing concept should be your guide, just as it would be if you were selling a product or a service instead of yourself. Too, if you satisfy the need that exists, by targeting yourself (product) to the market, you will earn the kind of satisfaction (profit) you are seeking: financial, psychic, and lifestyle.

The Résumé

The two formats that can be followed when preparing a résumé are chronological and functional. (See Figures 4.5 and 4.6.) There is no overall consensus as to what constitutes the perfect résumé. However, one thing to keep in mind is that employers spend less than 20 seconds scanning a résumé to determine if a candidate is worth further consideration. Therefore, be certain your résumé is organized, attractive, brief, concise, complete, truthful, and clearly written with no misspellings. A good résumé opens interview doors.

Heading. The heading gives identifying information—name, address, and phone number.

Objective. The job or career objective may be a brief statement of short- and long-range goals. An option is a qualifications summary—a statement that indicates how your skills relate to your desired objective.

Educational Background. In giving your educational background, work backward from your most recent degree. Include your degree(s), major(s), minor(s), honors, date of graduation, and the name of your school. Courses are optional. Do not include your grade point average unless requested. Some companies may have a cutoff at 3.6 and your very respectable 3.5 would eliminate you as a candidate.

Work Experience. Again, work backward from your most recent job. Summer employment, part-time jobs, volunteer work, internships, and so on should be included. Use action verbs to describe your duties and responsibilities.

Interests and Activities. Your interests and activities indicate that you are a well-rounded person. Highlight the activities and identify interests that closely relate to your career goals or the needs of the employer.

Personal Background. Whether to include personal background information is optional. Although it is not important to state date of birth, marital status, and so forth, it might be important to mention that you are single if the job you want requires a great deal of travel.

References. On your résumé it is necessary only to write "References furnished upon request." References should be kept in your file in the college career center and can be forwarded as prospective employers request them.

A good résumé in itself does not guarantee that you will get the job, but a bad one can easily prevent you from being considered.

Letters

Effective letters are as important in the job search as an effective résumé. The following is a list of letters you should consider as part of your marketing campaign.

1. *Letter of application*
   Employers read the letter before they read the enclosed résumé. Make sure it is good. To keep the ball in your hands, you might end the letter with a sentence such as: "I will be calling you within a week or ten days in order to follow up this information and see if an interview might be arranged."
2. *Letter of appreciation*
   It is never wrong to say thank you after an interview. Such a letter shows that you are considerate and displays common business courtesy.
3. *Letter seeking additional information*
4. *Letter inquiring about status*
5. *Letter accepting a position*
6. *Letter rejecting an offer of employment*

The Interview

If a good résumé opens interview doors, a poor interview can quickly slam it shut, so be prepared. You will be judged on your grooming, the way you express yourself, your maturity, and personality. This is the time to sell yourself. Points to remember are discussed in "From the Field: The Interview." A good first interview leads to a second interview, and often the second interview leads to the job you want.

FROM THE FIELD

The Interview: Points to Remember

Analyze strengths and weaknesses. In preparing for interviews, start by doing some solid, honest self-assessment. Analyze your strengths and weaknesses, your background, your academic performance, your vocational interests, and your personal aspirations and values. In other words, begin to formulate, in your own mind, not only what you would like to do but also what you feel you are best prepared to do.

Read employer literature. Next, study your prospective employers. It is imperative that you have some knowledge about their policies, philosophies, products, and services. Failure to do your homework before an interview can be the kiss of death. Nothing turns recruiters off faster.

Dress in good taste. Although most employers are becoming more liberal in their standard of dress and appearance, let basic good taste be your guide. If a beard or Alice-in-wonderland look is going to jeopardize your chances for a job, that's your decision. With some employers, appearance could be the deciding factor. The question you have to ask yourself is "How important is it?"

Be yourself. Your attitude is going to influence the interviewer's evaluation. Don't try to be something you aren't . . . just be yourself. Emphasize your strong points and remember that the recruiter is looking for inherent personal energy and enthusiasm. The interview is your opportunity to sell a product and that product is *you!*

Dwell on the positive. Try always to dwell on the positive. While past failures and shortcomings need not be volunteered, don't try to cover them up or sidestep them. Should recruiters ask about them, try to explain the circumstances rather than give excuses or blame others. Remember, they're human, too . . . and probably have made a few mistakes. You'll create a better impression by being honest and candid.

Ask questions—when indicated. If appropriate, ask meaningful questions, particularly if you're not clear about the details of the job, the training program, or other job-related concerns. But don't ask questions just because you think that's what is expected.

Follow up. Finally, follow up on the interview. Provide whatever credentials, references, or transcripts are requested by the prospective employer as soon as possible. Be sure to write down the name, title, and address of the recruiter. You may want to consider a brief typed letter of appreciation for the interviewing opportunity.

Use your career planning and placement office. These are, of course, only general suggestions and observations. For more detailed and personalized advice, take advantage of the services of your college's career planning and placement office.

Source: "Career Planning and the Job Search," *1984–1985 Career Placement Council Annual,* Vol. I, "The Interview: Some Points to Remember." Reprinted by permission.

PROJECTIONS— WHERE THE JOBS WILL BE

One quick and easy way to research the retail job market is to read want ads. Scan both your local newspaper and the big-city publications, nearby as well as distant. Read trade papers, too. Even if no specific jobs seem right for you, you will get an idea of trends, growth companies, and booming geographic areas—places where the jobs will be.

The retail industry in general is expected to grow at about a 2 percent rate over the next decade. There will be a continuing need for well-trained and experienced people in retail merchandising and management positions. The need will be greatest for marketing, sales, and operations executives, especially those with some technological training.

Demand should be strong for specialty and department store executives, although the vice president for executive search at Walter K. Levy Associates does not quite agree. He claims that long-haul opportunities for younger people in discount and off-price chains will be greater than in traditional department stores. He thinks such retailers—represented by Zayre Corporation, Bradlees, and Target—as well as specialty chains such as The Limited and Toys 'R' Us, have more clearly defined, more exciting career paths and compensation packages, including bonus incentive plans. They have the allure and ability to attract high-ranking graduates.

He agrees that department stores do a much more effective job of recruitment on college campuses and of initial training. After the initial training stages, however, department stores lose a disturbing number of recruits to other firms in or out of the industry. Turnover at the buyer level is enormous. In an effort to retain young people, department stores move them up rapidly—too rapidly. Generally, buyers today lack the years of training that buyers had 10 or 15 years ago, when individual recognition, status, and clout were much greater. Career paths at department stores should be reevaluated and more meaningful training brought back. Discount and off-price buyers have a lower turnover rate than department store buyers, once line assignments are made.[7]

There will also be job prospects with direct mail houses and in the food/supermarket industry. If off-price merchants continue to proliferate, and they probably will, more executive recruitment activity will take place in this segment of retailing.

The future is bright for bright young graduates. They will be employed as executives for department, specialty, discount, supermarket, off-price, or general merchandising chains; as franchisers selling fast-food or services; and as store owners. There will be jobs in merchandising, promotion, finance, and control; in human resource management, operations, store location, and site selection; even in store construction. (See Figure 4.7.) The well-trained, realistic, energetic young executive will definitely be in great demand if an ad from *The New York Times* is any indication of things to come. (See Figure 4.8.)

[7] Samuel Feinberg, "From Where I Sit," *Women's Wear Daily*, December 1983.

The climb up the retail ladder should be even more exciting and rewarding in the years ahead than it has been in the past, as computer experts, managers, merchants, accountants, builders, and fashion coordinators all advance together.

Figure 4.7 Advertisement Seeking a Construction Supervisor for a Retail Chain

PROJECTS SUPERVISOR/ COORDINATOR

Store Construction

Zayre currently has an outstanding opportunity for an enthusiastic, detail-oriented individual to become chief administrative liaison responsible for the satisfactory completion of our many construction projects. Reporting to the Construction Manager, you will interact with architects, outside developers, and contractors to ensure compliance with contract specifications for multiple construction projects. Your responsibilities will include estimating and controlling costs, scheduling, and supervising construction, and representing projects to local planning/building boards.

The ideal candidate should have a college degree and 2-3 years of project management experience. The ability to deal with multiple projects simultaneously is essential. You should have strong mathematical aptitude, be a good communicator and willing to travel. Experience in a retail environment would be a strong asset.

Please forward your resume, with salary history, to: Executive Recruitment/Construction, Zayre Corporation, Speen Street, Framingham, MA 01701. An equal opportunity/affirmative action employer.

***Zayre**

Source: *Boston Globe*, January 3, 1985.

Figure   4.8   Advertisement Seeking a Bright Executive for an Upscale Retailer

Fifth Avenue, New York 10018

Dear Executive,

1   Are you kind, compassionate, people-oriented and motivated to succeed?

2   Do you strive for excellence in every area of your life?

3   Have you examined your career goals lately?

4   Do you have some experience in Management? Merchandising? Fashion? Operations? Marketing? Visual Presentation? Finance?

5   Are you an executive whose dreams have outgrown the reality of your present future?

Lord & Taylor would like to hear from you.

Our plans for expansion are immediate and know no boundaries.
To guide and implement that expansion, we want only the very best executive people.
If you believe you qualify to join the fastest-growing, brightest,
most motivated group of dynamic executives in this country—
and if you are ready for a future as bright and rewarding as your dreams
and your abilities can make it, then send your résumé in strictest confidence to
Mr. E. Keith Maloney II, Senior Vice President, Personnel
Lord & Taylor, 424 Fifth Avenue, New York, N.Y. 10018

We guarantee complete confidentiality.
Your résumé will be seen by no one but Mr. Maloney, The Chairman, The President
and The Vice Chairman.
This could be your turning point.
We hope so and we look forward to hearing from you.

Sincerely,

An Equal Opportunity Employer M/F

Source: *The New York Times*, Sunday, January 13, 1985.

Summary

Retailing offers many interesting and satisfying options to young people who want to use their skills in a people-oriented, profit-oriented business. The choices in retailing are so many that college students often find the field overwhelming. They may also misunderstand the job possibilities in retailing. Often, because of a bad part-time experience in a poorly run local store, they may never consider the industry when it comes time to plan a career.

Students must investigate the many and diverse jobs available in retailing, the many and diverse types of retail institutions, nontraditional as well as traditional, the many functions of retailing, and the different skills required to perform these functions. Even a technological background can lead to a career in retailing.

A retail career can be sampled through internship or cooperative education programs—or as a part-time or summer employee. A retail career can begin in a management training program or as an assistant specialty store manager. Once the climb begins, there are a number of routes to the top.

Whether you select merchandising, management, human resource management, operations, sales promotion, finance, management information systems, or real estate, the important thing is to match your interests, aptitudes, and abilities to your chosen career path. To do this you must understand your own qualifications. A successful retailer needs to have leadership and problem-solving skills; confidence, energy, creativity, flexibility, and courage; communications and human relations skills; and the ability to function under pressure.

Once a decision is made to pursue a career in retailing, the job search begins. The staff of college and university placement offices teaches the art of preparing résumés and letters that will open interview doors. These offices are also wonderful resource centers for career information on the retail industry in general and specific companies within the industry.

In these last years of the 20th century, as retailing continues to grow, it will offer a dynamic lifestyle to all who wish to climb the career ladder.

Questions for Review

1. List at least ten different job titles in retailing.
2. Do you agree that technological changes in the retail industry will result in the need for the same type of technological expertise needed by manufacturers or computer firms? Why or why not?
3. Describe the possible steps in a typical retail management training program.

4. List at least five personal qualifications of successful retail executives.
5. Enumerate the steps of a strategic career search plan. How does this resemble a typical business marketing plan?
6. What is the value of a retailing internship? Do you feel it is a necessary ingredient of a college retail training program? Why or why not?
7. Many of today's successful retailers do not have formal retail educational backgrounds. Some never attended college, yet have attained various degrees of success. Comment on this situation and give your views on the value of formal college education versus spending the time on the job.

CASE STUDY

A. B. Jackman

Hiring Candidates for Management Training

A notice at the university career center read as follows:

Tuesday, February 25
9 a.m.–4 p.m.
Mr. Richard Martin of A. B. Jackman
will interview all seniors
interested in the
Jackman Management Training Program

A. B. Jackman, one of the nation's largest general merchandise chains, with home offices in Cincinnati, was known as a progressive retail organization. Its management training program was highly regarded throughout the industry and it was known that Jackman had a policy of promotion from within. If you made it as a trainee, your future was secure. With 350 stores (mostly in the Midwest and South), this was an excellent opportunity for anyone interested in a retail career.

As Edith Andrews, the center director, looked over the names on the sign-up sheet, she wondered which of the students would be given serious consideration as candidates for the management training program.

She was certainly glad to see 15 names, for each year it became more difficult to find young people who wanted careers in retailing badly enough to put up with the long hours and relatively low starting salaries.

There were so many considerations when hiring. Having dealt with executive placement representatives for 20 years, she had seen criteria change over and over again. Whether because of the women's movement or antidiscrimination legislation, human resource people were definitely not making their decisions today in the same way they did a few years ago. What would be the basis for the decision this year?

For the past eight years, Jackman had hired at least one senior. Would Lynne Cohen be hired or would it be Oliver Brown or Maria Sanchez? Would Albert Johnson have an equal opportunity?

As she glanced over the résumés of those who were to be interviewed, she was glad that the decision was not hers to make. It would be difficult.

Richard Martin, A. B. Jackman's executive recruiter, had to take the first important step in the process. After interviewing, he narrowed the field to five seniors, each with different backgrounds. Each would be reviewed by the executive placement committee and then two would be invited to national headquarters for a final interview.

As Richard left the campus with complete information on each candidate tucked in his briefcase, he reviewed his impressions of the five he had selected:

Albert Johnson, aged 22. Four-year scholarship holder. Economics major. Highly recommended by professors, who stated he was intelligent and ambitious. President of campus NAACP chapter. Worked in college snack bar all four years; no other business experience. Father dead. Three younger sisters whom he would like to help educate. More concerned with opportunities for promotion than starting salary. Willing to work long hours. Would prefer urban location, preferably in the East.

Lynne Cohen, aged 21. Marketing major with minor in merchandising. Dean's list all four years. Worked part-time in father's dress shop during high school. Always interested in retailing and hopes someday to own a fashion shop. Good references from faculty, who stated that Lynne was industrious and creative. Not employed while in college. Engaged to pre-med student.

Maria Sanchez, aged 21. Oldest in family of eight. Born in Puerto Rico and brought up in New York City. College financed partly through scholarship and partly through work–study. Business administration major. Professors state that Maria is aggressive and hardworking. She has maintained a B average since her sophomore year. During her freshman year she had a C average. Popular with fellow students, she is vice president of the student government organization. Understands the work involved in a retail organization and is not outwardly bothered by the thought of long hours. Except for her years in college, Maria has lived in New York City.

Oliver Brown, Jr., aged 22. Only child of a successful surgeon. Attended prep school before entering college. No work experience other than three summers spent as a camp counselor in Michigan. Dean's List student majoring in political science with a minor in economics. Co-captain of tennis team. Thinks a career in retailing would be exciting. Willing to move anywhere in the United States. Asked questions concerning length of training period and time of first promotion. Good health.

Henry Henderson, aged 35. Veteran of Viet Nam. Henry stated that he would not have gone to college if he had not been a veteran. He was married at 20 to a Vietnamese. Wife works part-time as a packer in the local supermarket. Two children in elementary school. Henry holds a full-time job as a gas station attendant and goes to school nights. A business administration major, he has taken two courses in retailing and is fascinated with the field. Average grades (B/C) but his professors say he is a hard worker who asks penetrating questions and is never happy until he understands concepts as well as facts. Good health in spite of war-injured knee.

Questions

1. Develop a set of criteria that could be used as the basis for selecting candidates for A. B. Jackman's training program.
2. On a scale of 1 to 10, rate each candidate according to the criteria developed in Question 1. Give your reasons.
3. Based on your rating, which two candidates would you select? Why?
4. Do you think that the use of a rating scale is a good selection technique? Why or why not?
5. What other techniques could be used in selecting candidates? Explain.

Chapter 5

Human Resource Management

Source: Jack Gifford, Professor of Marketing, Miami University of Ohio.

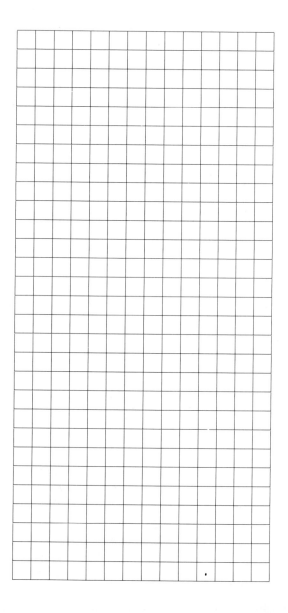

Industry Statement

Randolph C. Cox
Personnel Research Consultant
Ford Motor Company

The management of human resources plays a central role as companies deal with the changes buffeting the business world today. New legal and social requirements must be considered in dealing with employees. Employees themselves are more highly educated and often have different attitudes toward work than in the past. They are also less likely to remain with one company throughout their careers.

Human resources management must establish and monitor compensation and benefit systems so that a company can recruit and hire the best possible candidates for its work force. Effective human resources management strives to ensure that the corporate culture is one in which employees can flourish, where their ideas are respected and high performance is acknowledged and rewarded, where they can truly participate as a part of the corporate team and are encouraged to develop themselves and their careers.

In recent years, largely due to increased international competition, many companies have changed their approach to doing business. Many of these changes have been based on the belief that better management of human resources can lead to lower costs and higher productivity. The aim of employee involvement and participative management programs is to increase employee participation in the workplace on both an intellectual and a physical level. They and similar programs have been effective in changing the corporate culture of organizations to make human resources development a top priority.

Some companies encountered difficulties in making these changes, especially when management viewed the changes as separate programs that were not integrated into a comprehensive human resources management plan. In organizations that were really receptive to the programs, however, and made them integral to their human resources management systems, they have achieved significant improvement in productivity as well as in employee relations.

Learning Objectives

Upon completing this chapter you should be able to:

1. Discuss how a human resource manager develops the human resource budget.
2. Discuss the primary methods of hiring rank-and-file retail employees.
3. Understand the primary methods of hiring retail executives.
4. Explain what is meant by initial training.
5. Explain what is meant by continuous training.
6. Explain how job enrichment programs help employees.
7. Explain what is meant by a total compensation package.
8. Understand why the union movement has been slow to develop in retailing.

Every retailer in the world claims to be a "people person," but how many actually practice what they preach? Most are conscious of the people they serve—the customer. More often than not, they forget about the people who serve them—their employees. Yet the success of all retail organizations depends on the ability to attract, train, develop, and retain talented people at every level and in every function.

Why then have human resources always been singled out for the first budget cuts when business is down? Why, until recently, has the personnel division been treated like a poor second cousin to merchandising and promotion? One probable answer is that little time was left to consider the human factor during the scramble for new markets after World War II or during the rush for profits ever since.

This chapter will focus on human resource management as it should be practiced. Successful merchants in the future will recognize that carefully chosen merchandise, exciting promotions, good financial controls, or select locations cannot guarantee success unless there are also good people to perform every function.

HUMAN RESOURCE PLANNING

Human resources must be planned for, just like goods and services. People must be recruited and selected with an eye to the customer group served. Employees who do not understand target markets cannot be productive. Orientation and training should aid people in acquiring needed skills and behavior patterns, and supervision should reinforce what they have been taught.

Competition for good people is increasing. Government standards for pay, working conditions, and equal treatment continue to rise. Unions are attempting to create an additional partner for businesses. Thus, human resource management must provide a working environment that encourages personal growth along with company growth. This is one of the retailer's greatest challenges for the next decade.

One key to good human resource planning is support from top management. Human resource plans should be included in a company's overall strategic planning process—the process that lays out a firm's long-range objectives and ties them to its capabilities.

A senior vice president in human resources at Zayre Corporation once said, "Human resource planning is the capability to supply the right people at the right time—people who are properly trained to meet the objectives of the strategic plans."[1] Supplying the right people at the right time is not as easy as it sounds, because retail demand is irregular and seasonal, but it can be done.

The Human Resource Budget

Merchandise plans are made far in advance of need; the merchandise budget is based on an analysis of last year's figures and next year's trends. Staffing should be planned the same way. A human resource budget could be developed to take into consideration all of the peaks and valleys of the business on a yearly, monthly, weekly, and daily basis. Doing this would eliminate many of the problems retailers face and also ensure a greater return on wage/salary investment.

Pirating
Luring personnel from other firms.

Because most retailers do not hire enough entry-level people to provide for future growth, a human resource budget could build in future as well as immediate needs, to parallel overall expansion (or retrenchment) plans. The result would be short-term cost effectiveness and long-term productivity and savings. With a budget, the use of executive search firms or **pirating** would not be necessary when a sudden opening occurs. Staff cuts when business takes a downturn could also be avoided.

Budget Planning

The six steps for developing a human resource budget are as follows:

1. *Forecasting of personnel needs.* The forecast should begin at the lowest operating level and continue through to the highest level in the organization. It should include both the number and the skills of the people required.

---

[1] "Planning for Human Resources," *Stores*, February 1984, 42.

2. *Inventory of current employees.* A review of the personnel records of each employee helps identify the number, skills, and locations of current personnel. This indicates the type of training that is necessary for the current staff if they are to accomplish the store's objectives for the future.

3. *Modification of existing data.* Because both internal (rate of turnover) and external (automation) factors will affect the budget, they must be considered before going further. The condition of the economy also alters a firm's personnel requirements.

4. *Plan development.* The actual personnel plan is based on Steps 1 through 3 and annual employee losses. Improved selection and training methods may offset needs and employee promotions may result in other vacancies.

5. *Execution of the budget.* This should take place only after approval and support of top management. Without financing, facilities, and a staff to carry it out, the plan is bound to fail.

6. *Evaluation.* Continuous checking is essential. Without this, some executives could misuse the budget to satisfy their needs without considering the total organization.[2]

Employment Tools

Matching applicants and jobs is often the first step in cutting down high attrition figures. Three documents help in matching applicants to job requirements.

Job Analysis

A job analysis covers the specific tasks and requirements of a position. It focuses on job activities, required skills, working conditions, type of training required, previous experience required, educational level, supervision received, and supervision provided. The job analysis is accomplished through observation, questionnaires, and personal interviews. From the data gathered in a thorough job analysis, a meaningful job description can be written.

Job Description

A job description is a summary of the basic tasks of a position. The typical job description contains the following major sections: job identification, job duties, and job summary (see Figure 5.1). In an accurate job

---

[2] Adapted from Richard Israel, "Retail Manpower Planning," *Personnel News and Views* (National Retail Merchants Association, Fall 1978).

Figure   5.1   Brief Job Description for a Retail Salesperson

Job Title
Sales Associate, women's better sportswear department, at main store

Duties and Responsibilities

General:
To sell merchandise and maintain stock

Specific:
1. Meet customers and handle their requests
2. Process cash and credit sales
3. Set up displays
4. Stock shelves
5. Take inventory of stock

Reports to: Department Manager

Skills and Requirements
1. Selling skills
2. Clerical skills
3. Neat appearance
4. People skills

description, the section on job duties indicates what the employee does, how it is done, and why it is done. Through the job description, an employee becomes familiar with the job duties and also aware of the activities necessary for promotion. A job description can also serve as an evaluative tool. Standards can be established for each task in the job description so that a comparison of an employee's performance with the standard permits an objective evaluation of the employee.

Job Specification

A job specification identifies the personal qualifications necessary for the proper performance of a job. This is prepared from the information provided in a job description. The job specification is an important tool when recruiting because it indicates the education, experience, and personal characteristics needed for each position. Only those who meet the desired qualifications should be recruited for available positions.

RECRUITING

In retailing, the sources of employees are almost as varied as the jobs. An electronic help-wanted sign might attract the right kind of part-time employee to a local pizza shop, but would never bring the right part-timers to a department store. Different methods should also be used when seeking rank-and-file employees and management people. Regardless of level, however, the search method must be matched to (1) the job, (2) the type of retail establishment, and (3) the target market. This matching process cannot be stressed enough in an industry characterized by long hours, night and weekend hours, many part-time workers, low compensation, and a large labor pool of women and young people who often lack experience and training.

More than in almost any other business, staffing in retailing is critical because profit margins are so small. Both money and time are wasted if recruiting is done in a haphazard manner.

Methods for Recruiting Rank-and-File Employees

The *internal sources* for rank-and-file employees are:

1. *Current employees.* They are excellent for transfers or promotion, often on short notice.
2. *Past employees.* Former full or part-time help with good records can be productive with little training—good when business takes a sudden upward turn.
3. *Employee recommendations.* Friends or relatives of employees who are looking for work and have the needed skills and training must be carefully screened.

The *external sources* for rank-and-file employees are:

1. *Newspaper advertisements.* Ads are good for filling peak-season needs.
2. *Government employment agencies.* These are excellent places to post jobs for part- or full-time help at the entry level. The United States Training and Employment Service (USTES) has a national computerized **job bank** that lists nationwide job openings and attempts to match applicants to them. USTES also acts to control state agencies.
3. *Private employment agencies.* Of limited use for entry-level employees, they have some value in locating rank-and-file people in technical areas, such as accounting and computer work.
4. *Educational institutions.* Excellent sources for part-time or summer help are (a) high schools that offer distributive education programs and (b) two-year or four-year colleges and universities that have retailing, merchandising, or marketing majors with internship or cooperative education requirements.
5. *Unsolicited applicants.* Walk-in applicants often seek part-time or entry-level sales jobs.

Job Bank
Computer listing of job openings in private companies, developed by the U.S. Employment Service and updated daily.

Methods for Recruiting Managerial Employees

The *internal sources* for managerial employees are:

1. *Current employees.* Promotion from within is one of the best methods for securing new executives and has always had support from human resource professionals. The vice president for personnel at Associated Dry Goods Corporation once claimed that his objective was to fill all middle and upper level jobs in the corporation's 14 divisions on a ratio of 80 percent through internal promotion and 20 percent from outside the company.[3] The same ratio is still true today.
2. *Past employees.* Often a participant in a company's management training program will leave to work in a number of management positions in other firms and then return, years later, to fill a vice presidential slot. Keeping in touch with former executives who left in good standing is always a good idea.

The *external sources* for managerial employees are:

1. *Referrals.* When suppliers, customers, and even competitors suggest individuals as prospective executives, they are called **referrals.** Because the skills necessary in one retail organization are similar to those needed by other retailers, there is opportunity for movement within the industry. At conferences such as the National Retail Merchants Association, retail executives have the opportunity to get together and to examine the job market at least once a year.
2. *Advertisements.* When seeking middle and upper level managers, retailers often advertise in metropolitan and trade papers such as the Sunday edition of *The New York Times, Women's Wear Daily,* or *Chain Store Age.* Local papers are also used.
3. *Executive search firms.* These recruiters, often called **headhunters,** specialize in finding the right executives for their clients, usually on a fee basis. Pirating from other retailers is one of their techniques.
4. *College and university recruiting.* Four-year schools have long been a primary source for filling the ranks of retail management training programs. (See Table 5.1.) Now, two-year colleges are also considered excellent sources. Many national specialty chains, lacking structured programs, are beginning to recruit for entry-level management positions at colleges, as are local retailers. Some retailers, knowing how important it is to keep career planning and placement directors up to date, invite groups of them to their

Referrals
The names of an informed person's acquaintances who might be potential employees.

Headhunters
Individuals or agencies who are paid to find managers or executives for a client company.

---
[3] Samuel Feinberg, "From Where I Sit," *Women's Wear Daily,* March 14, 1984, 6.

Table 5.1   Schools Offering a Major in Retailing

Bernard Baruch College
  New York, N.Y.
	Philadelphia College of Textiles and
	Science
	  Philadelphia, Pa.

Bloomfield College
  Bloomfield, N.J.
	Rochester Institute of Technology
	  Rochester, N.Y.

Bowling Green State University
  Bowling Green, Ohio
	Simmons College
	  Boston, Mass.

Brigham Young University
  Provo, Utah
	Skidmore College
	  Saratoga Springs, N.Y.

Drexel University
  Philadelphia, Pa.
	Syracuse University
	  Syracuse, N.Y.

Drake University
  Des Moines, Iowa
	Virginia Intermont College
	  Bristol, Va.

Miami University
  Oxford, Ohio
	Western Michigan University
	  Kalamazoo, Mich.

New Hampshire College
  Manchester, N.H.
	Youngstown State University
	  Youngstown, Ohio

Source: American Collegiate Retailing Association.

stores to meet with executives. School directors can then relay the company's philosophy to their graduating students. Other retailers become involved in college and university internship or cooperative education programs, which allow them to bring potential trainees into the company while they are still in school. Still others become guest lecturers in retailing classes.

5. *Unsolicited applicants.* Graduating seniors often send résumés to retailers in geographic areas where they hope to locate. Large retail firms also attract recent M.B.A. graduates. Some retail managers who wish to relocate to another part of the country or the world send unsolicited résumés to firms in those locations.

THE SELECTION PROCESS

Blame for the high attrition rate in retailing can often be placed on the employment manager. Poor selection techniques are the number-one reason for high turnover. Careful selection and matching of potential employees to the existing openings will result in greater productivity and high company morale.

To select the best applicants, employment personnel must evaluate and rank each one on the basis of predetermined criteria. Here job descriptions and specifications are useful. Evaluation and selection techniques vary widely from one retailer to another; some rely on the "chemistry" that occurs during the personal interview. Others rely mainly on the résumé, application, and test scores. When the final choice is made, most firms use a combination of both objective and subjective measures.

Application Forms

Almost all retailers require prospective employees to complete an application form. (See Figure 5.2.) This gives them the type of preliminary information that helps determine further action. If, for example, the job for which the person is applying requires computer knowledge and the applicant indicates that he or she has no computer skills, action stops.

Application forms should contain only the type of questions that will aid an employer in distinguishing among qualified applicants. It is a violation of the Equal Employment Opportunity Act to ask questions that could be discriminatory, such as those concerning race, religion, or age. Even if no current openings match the applicant's skills, applications of good future prospects are always kept on file.

Résumés

The preparation of the résumé was discussed in Chapter 4. Unfortunately, this important document is often neglected by retail employment people, except as a screening device for executive management program candidates or management replacements. The résumé can indicate much about a person's organizational and communications skills, both of them important in retailing. Almost everyone who applies for full-time work, especially those who are looking for jobs that require customer contact, should be required to submit a résumé.

Interviews

Initial Interview
Preliminary or screening interview of a job applicant.

A job candidate may be interviewed several times before being hired. The **initial interview** usually takes place at the time the application is filled out. It is generally conducted by an employment interviewer and lasts only about 15 to 20 minutes. The purpose is threefold: (1) to obtain additional information from the applicant and to verify the information on the application, (2) to eliminate applicants who do not seem to qualify for the jobs available, and (3) to inform the applicant about the company. This is often the only interview, especially for rank-and-file employees.

Follow-Up Interview
In-depth interview of a job applicant who is being seriously considered for a position.

Candidates who are being given serious consideration, particularly for such jobs as managers or potential management trainees, are invited to return for a **follow-up interview.** This can be more formal than the initial interview. It can also take the form of a stress interview, in which more than one person representing the company asks "killer" questions in order to see how a person reacts under pressure.

An interesting interviewing technique called psycholinguistics was developed at Senseable Strategies, Roslyn, New York. It allows the interviewer to understand the direct correlation between language and behavior patterns. Awareness of how people talk and behave during an interview may help in selecting, motivating, and managing them effectively. Brooks Fashion Stores have used this interviewing technique and found that it enabled them to attract and hire people who fit the Brooks personality.[4] Psycholinguistics would be used only during follow-up interviews.

----

[4] *Women's Wear Daily,* January 15, 1985, 17.

Figure 5.2   An Employment Application Form

THE STOP & SHOP COMPANIES, INC.

The Stop & Shop Supermarket Co.
Bradlees Dept. Stores

EMPLOYMENT APPLICATION

PERSONAL HISTORY   **PLEASE PRINT**

People are our most important asset . . . . . .

Since people are the key to achievement of our business objectives, people constitute our most important asset. It is the policy of The Stop & Shop Companies, Inc. to seek and employ the best qualified people in all of our facilities and locations, to provide equal opportunities for the advancement of employees, including upgrading, promotion and training, and to administer these activities in a manner which will not discriminate against any person because of race, color, religion, sex, age, national origin, marital status, or physical handicap.

NAME (LAST)	(MIDDLE INITIAL)	(FIRST)	SOC. SECURITY NO.
ADDRESS (NO. & STREET)	(CITY)	(STATE) (ZIP CODE)	TELEPHONE NO AREA CODE ( )

IF YOU ARE NOT A U.S. CITIZEN, ENTER PERMANENT RESIDENCE VISA NUMBER:

INDICATE POSITION DESIRED/AREAS(S) OF INTEREST

FULL TIME PART TIME	DAY/HOURS AVAILABLE	DATE AVAILABLE FOR EMPLOYMENT	SALARY DESIRED

EDUCATION AND TRAINING

	SCHOOLS ATTENDED (INCLUDE CURRENT)	LOCATION	DID YOU GRADUATE?	COURSE(S) AND/OR DEGREES/CERTIFICATES
HIGH SCHOOL:				
COLLEGE:				
OTHER:				

EMPLOYMENT HISTORY-LIST MOST RECENT EMPLOYER FIRST

[1] CO. NAME	FROM: / TO:	BRIEFLY DESCRIBE YOUR RESPONSIBILITIES ON THE JOB
NO. & STREET	STARTING SALARY:	
CITY, STATE, ZIP CODE	FINAL SALARY:	
BUSINESS TELEPHONE AREA CODE ( )	BONUS:	REASON FOR LEAVING:
SUPERVISOR: NAME & TITLE		

[2] CO. NAME	FROM: / TO:	BRIEFLY DESCRIBE YOUR RESPONSIBILITIES ON THE JOB:
NO. & STREET	STARTING SALARY:	
CITY, STATE, ZIP CODE	FINAL SALARY:	
BUSINESS TELEPHONE AREA CODE ( )	BONUS:	REASON FOR LEAVING:
SUPERVISOR'S NAME & TITLE		

[3] CO. NAME	FROM: / TO:	BRIEFLY DESCRIBE YOUR RESPONSIBILITES ON THE JOB:
NO. & STREET	STARTING SALARY:	
CITY, STATE, ZIP CODE	FINAL SALARY:	
BUSINESS TELEPHONE AREA CODE ( )	BONUS:	REASON FOR LEAVING:
SUPERVISOR'S NAME & TITLE		

FORM NO. 80 1021 REV. 9/84

Testing

Tests are not as widely used in retailing as they were prior to the Civil Rights Act of 1964. Questions of discrimination gradually forced most large retailers to take a good look at their testing program. In doing so, many made the decision to eliminate tests except for those directly related to skills (typing, computer programming, and so on), because validity and usefulness are hard to prove. Small retailers have never used tests extensively.

OTHER WORK EXPERIENCES

PLEASE LIST ANY OTHER SPECIAL SKILLS OR AREAS OF KNOWLEDGE THAT MIGHT BE JOB RELATED,
e.g. PHOTOGRAPHY, OFFICE SKILLS, LANGUAGE PROFICIENCY, SPECIAL SEMINARS ATTENDED, ETC

HOW WERE YOU REFERRED TO THE STOP & SHOP CO'S., INC.?

WERE YOU EVER EMPLOYED BY THE STOP & SHOP CO'S. INC.? YES __ NO __ IF SO, WHERE? THE STOP & SHOP SUPERMARKET CO. ☐ BRADLEES DEPT. STORE ☐ MEDI-MART DRUG STORES ☐ CHARLES B. PERKINS ☐ THE STOP & SHOP MANUFACTURING CO. ☐ CORPORATE OFFICES ☐ WAREHOUSING & TRANSPORTATION	FROM MO./YR	TO MO./YR

HAVE YOU EVER BEEN CONVICTED OF A CRIMINAL OFFENSE WITHIN THE LAST FIVE (5) YEARS? **NOTE:** YOU MAY ANSWER "NO" IF ANY OF THE FOLLOWING CIRCUMSTANCES ARE APPLICABLE:

1. YOU HAVE A FIRST CONVICTION FOR ANY OF THE FOLLOWING MISDEMEANORS: DRUNKENNESS, SIMPLE ASSAULT, SPEEDING, MINOR TRAFFIC VIOLATIONS, AFFRAY, OR DISTURBANCE OF THE PEACE;

2. YOU HAVE FELONY OR MISDEMEANOR CONVICTIONS WHICH HAVE BEEN ANNULLED OR SEALED BY A COURT;

3. YOU HAVE JUVENILE DELINQUENCY OR CHILD IN NEED OF SERVICE COMPLAINTS WHICH WERE NOT TRANSFERRED TO SUPERIOR COURT FOR PROSECUTION.

__ YES __ NO

IF YES, PLEASE EXPLAIN. _____

PHARMACISTS ONLY

ARE YOU A REGISTERED PHARMACIST? __ YES __ NO	IF SO, LIST STATES AND CERTIFICATE NUMBERS
HAVE YOU EVER APPEARED BEFORE ANY PHARMACY BOARD FOR VIOLATION OF ANY PHARMACY CODES? __ YES __ NO DISPOSITION:	HAVE ALL REQUIRED CONTINUING EDUCATION CREDITS BEEN FULFILLED? __ YES __ NO

PHYSICAL EXAMINATION & REFERENCES:

I understand that I must meet the physical requirements for the position. If required, I agree to submit to a physical examination by a physician designated by the Company. I also understand that permanent employment is contingent upon satisfactory references from previous employers.

I further understand that the Company does not normally solicit the services of outside agencies to investigate and report on character, general reputation, personal characteristics and the like with respect to applications submitted by persons being considered for employment. However, I also understand that in individual cases the Company may elect to do so and that this statement has been included in my application for employment to inform me in this regard. I acknowledge that I have been advised that I have a right to request in writing information concerning the nature and scope of any such investigation. I hereby release all persons, firms, and/or corporations furnishing references or other information concerning me from liability.

I further understand that any misleading or incorrect information, misrepresentation, or omission of necessary facts may render this application void or may be cause for immediate dismissal and that the issuance of this application blank does not necessarily indicate that there are positions open at present.

I certify that the statements made on this application are true, complete, and correct and further agree that such statements may be investigated. I further agree to work safely and to abide by the rules and policies of the Company.

Applicant's Signature _____ Date _____

Comments by Interviewer: _____

Interviewer's Signature _____ Date _____

Source: Courtesy of The Stop & Shop Companies, Inc.

Some retail companies do make use of psychological tests to determine aptitudes. One test used to determine sales orientation and interpersonal skills is available from Career Development Resources, Inc., Chicago, Illinois. This kind of instrument could prove extremely useful in the retail selection process.[5]

Some companies ask applicants to submit to a polygraph or lie detector as a method of verifying their statements. Its preciseness is questionable and many states have restricted its use. Any applicant has the right to refuse to submit to this test.

Reference Checks

Toward the end of the selection process, the company checks references for the candidates they may wish to hire. A reference check can be conducted by mail, telephone, or personal contact. Checking references—professional, educational, or personal—gives the employer another opportunity to verify information that was obtained through the application and the interview. College placement centers keep files on graduating students and alumni that include references. One call to a placement officer allows an employment manager to do a thorough reference check. Credit bureaus are also excellent sources for checking on potential employees.

Physical Examination

Some retailers may require the best-qualified applicants for full-time jobs to take a physical examination. With the type of fringe benefit packages offered today, retailers want to avoid hiring anyone with a pre-existing condition that could cause their group insurance rates to skyrocket. Physical examinations are always required for those who handle food or drug products as part of their job.

Final Selection

Candidates who successfully pass all the steps in the selection process are hired. Human resource professionals do not make decisions lightly. They spend a great deal of time reviewing applications, résumés, and tests of the candidates who have made it to the final cut.

Yet even the best selection tools and judgment skills are not always enough. The story of a young specialty store management trainee, six

---

[5] Michael V. Mulligan, et al., *Career Search: A Personal Guide* (New York: Holt, Rinehart and Winston, 1985).

months on the job, illustrates this point. The regional buyer of the fashion department where the trainee was in charge of visual merchandising noticed that the entire department was merchandised without any consideration for color coordination. The trainee had to be terminated. He was color-blind. No one in personnel had thought of color blindness as a physical disability; therefore, there was no determining test, even though color recognition is important in fashion. A test would have prevented this situation and the financial loss to both the trainee and the company.

Just as excellent selection tools and judgment are not always enough, the best selection process cannot always produce perfect employees. All that human resource managers can do is try to improve methodologies. In some stores, candidates are asked to become involved in **role-playing exercises.** In others, a group decision is made by all who interview the candidate; usually this approach is limited to candidates for management jobs. In still others, a variety of assessment programs may be tried. Whatever the system, objective criteria and testing, human resource experience and good personal judgment all go into the final decision.

Role Playing
Exercise in which individuals experience a situation through a trainer's dramatization, often by participating as actors.

ORIENTATION AND TRAINING

Nothing is more anxiety producing than a beginning. Remember freshman orientation or the move to a new town? Starting a new job produces the same feelings even for those who have worked before. A new organization means new people, new regulations, and new duties. Because they are new, they are somewhat frightening. Even the most self-confident person needs to be eased into an organization.

Orientation

An orientation of some type should be offered to every new employee in a retail organization. This is true whether the new person is a full-time management trainee in a flagship store of a large department store group, a part-time salesperson in the unit of a specialty chain, or an assistant department manager in a supermarket.

Large department stores have orientation programs for all full-time employees—both rank and file and management—but do not bother with part-timers. This is one of the greatest mistakes retailers have made in the past. They tend to forget that profit can only be realized if *all* who serve the public are loyal members of the organization and have an understanding of how it meets consumer needs.

An **orientation program** is important for every new employee. It should start with an initial group meeting where company policy, organization, and history are discussed. If, as in many branch stores, a face-to-face meeting with top management representatives is not possible, a company film can be used. In all cases, new employees should be given

Orientation Program
Program that familiarizes new workers with their roles, the company, its policies, and other employees.

an orientation manual to use as a guide through the first critical weeks or months on the job.

Training

Training in all retail institutions has the same goal—to develop and retain employees' ability to the point where they can perform their job functions to the satisfaction of customers, supervisors, and themselves. Training is not for new employees only. Training programs should be made available on a continuous basis to all employees, because both knowledge and skills grow stale if not updated. Generally, new employees are trained in the basic skills required by their jobs. Other employees need sessions on new merchandising techniques, salesmanship, customer relations, promotional methods, and security.

Initial Training

Orientation and initial training are usually thought of as introductory. When new salespeople are hired, for example, they may spend a few hours of their first day on the job filling out various company and government forms, and then move on to an orientation session for the rest of the day. The next few days are spent learning the retail system. The exact amount of training depends on its complexity. It takes longer to learn to operate a P.O.S. register in a store like Bullock's than to write a sales slip in an owner-operated gourmet food shop. It takes longer to learn about the many different types of transactions in a Sears store than to learn how to handle cash-only sales in a convenience store. (See Figure 5.3.)

Figure   5.3   Training Sessions at Bullock's

Source: Courtesy of Bullock's Department Stores, Los Angeles.

On-the-Job Training (OJT)
Instructing employees during regular working hours while they are also doing productive work and are being paid normal wages.

After systems training, good retailers take time to offer the essential sales techniques course to those who will start as salespeople. This may be followed by a day or two of **on-the-job training (OJT),** which is the most prevalent type of initial training for nonsales help. Initial training techniques may also include (1) lectures, (2) role playing, (3) discussion, and (4) case studies. Perhaps the extremely high turnover rates in retailing could be lowered if existing initial training programs were improved and were offered to part- as well as full-time employees in every type of retail operation.

Continuous Training

Retailers often forget that employees need constant refresher courses if they are to maintain peak performance on a continuous basis and retain the company "high" that was felt after initial orientation. Continuous training indicates to employees that the company cares. It can take many forms, either on or off the premises.

Sending carpeting salespeople on a plant tour to the southern city where the carpeting is manufactured is a form of continuous training. Weekly department meetings with buyers, who bring the latest fashion news to their staffs, is a form of continuous training. A seminar in behavior modification for branch store managers is, also. Whatever form continuous training may take, the important point is that it must take place.

Management Training Programs

Management training programs are designed to develop managerial talent and are commonly found in large department store or chain store organizations. Some typical programs were discussed in Chapter 4, as they related to entry-level management jobs. College graduates enter a company as executive trainees and progress from lower to higher level management positions by interspersing study of policies and procedures with increasingly demanding work assignments. (See Figure 5.4.)

Today's executive trainee in almost all cases advances according to his or her ability and the needs of the company, not by a predetermined schedule. Training programs require both effort and an investment of time on the part of the trainee. For that reason, many who are unwilling to wait for the rewards leave in their first year. Statistics also indicate that 90 percent of people who enter beginning-level management from training programs move to positions with other retailers or other industries by the end of their fifth year.

One of the best-known management training programs in the United States is the R. H. Macy program. About 1,000 applicants a year are enrolled, 80 percent of whom are recent college graduates, some with advanced degrees. The formal training breaks down into 40 percent case study, 20 percent learner-controlled instruction, 15 percent lecture, 15

Figure 5.4

Example of Executive Progression in Retailing

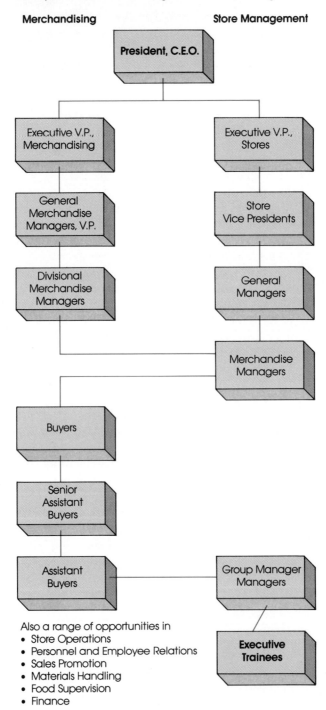

Merchandising

Store Management

President, C.E.O.

Executive V.P., Merchandising

Executive V.P., Stores

General Merchandise Managers, V.P.

Store Vice Presidents

Divisional Merchandise Managers

General Managers

Merchandise Managers

Buyers

Senior Assistant Buyers

Assistant Buyers

Group Manager Managers

Executive Trainees

Also a range of opportunities in
- Store Operations
- Personnel and Employee Relations
- Sales Promotion
- Materials Handling
- Food Supervision
- Finance

percent group discussion, and 10 percent role playing. In the New York division, the process begins with three weeks of formal classroom instruction and continues with six weeks of OJT, biweekly seminars in personnel-related as well as technical subjects, and a one-week assignment to a sales manager. Every major area—buying, selling, personnel, control, security, and sales support—has a career path.

Supervisory Training

Often retail employees who are promoted to supervisory positions are expert in their job functions but not in human relations. People they have been accustomed to dealing with as coworkers must be supervised, and they have difficulty handling this aspect of their new job. All new supervisors should be given a course in human relations. It is not easy to manage people effectively, to keep productivity up, and at the same time keep employees happy.

If you reprimand a salesperson in your department for being 15 minutes late the day of a big sale, more could be lost than 15 minutes. Feeling abused, the usually super salesperson might perform way below par. Reprimands, praise, and advice all have the proper time. Training is necessary in order to understand this—and not only for new supervisors. Everyone in management can benefit from seminars and workshops that explain new supervisory and human resource techniques.

JOB ENRICHMENT

Job Enrichment
A way to improve an employee's efficiency and satisfaction by increasing the challenges, opportunities, and rewards (non-monetary) provided by the job.

The finest training in the world cannot guarantee a good work force. Constant effort on the part of management is needed to keep (1) attrition down, (2) wage-cost ratios in line, and (3) employee productivity up. The best way to accomplish these three goals is through **job enrichment** programs that act as positive motivators.

Although job enrichment can take many forms, it must always fill the psychological void that exists when management offers only the expected monetary reward for expected performance. Job enrichment programs must encourage employees to take the extra step that will not only bring more profit to the company but will also offer more satisfaction to the employee. Programs should take the basic need for recognition into consideration.

Motivational Programs

Developing good motivational programs in retailing requires creativity in blending both cash and noncash incentives. Motivational programs must satisfy each person's need for achievement as well as recognition. Cash may swell the bank account of a manager whose department had the greatest increase in sales, but merchandise or a free trip will boost his or her ego.

Evaluation

Evaluation is a part of job enrichment because it guarantees job security to those who meet predetermined standards—and provides rewards to those who surpass these standards. The purpose of an evaluation is to assess an employee's performance and personal attributes for salary increases, promotions, or other rewards. Evaluations also point out areas where improvement is needed.

A good employee evaluation system should overcome the **Peter Principle** and keep morale high. Tough as it may seem, the problem people in a company must eventually be removed or reassigned. Too much time is wasted in many companies tolerating the repeated sins of omission or commission by employees at all levels.

Evaluation Methods

Retailers use a number of different methods to evaluate employees. Some are quite simple; others are not.

Performance records. These are a simple quantitative means of measuring things like (1) total dollar sales, (2) total number of sales transactions, (3) number of customer complaints, (4) number and dollar value of returns, (5) net sales per hour worked, and (6) number of days absent or late. Performance records are useful in identifying salespeople who are above, at, and below average.

Management by objective. This evaluation process sets measurable performance objectives that should match the description of the job being performed. Managers are often judged by how well they meet their job objectives and, because they are well aware of their goals from the moment they start the job, the **management by objectives process (MBO)** encourages self-development and self-evaluation.

Rating scales. Scales are used to identify and list performance criteria. Ratings may be a simple satisfactory/unsatisfactory, or the scale may provide for a poor, fair, average, good, or excellent rating. Supervisors find that this method is a quick and easy way to rate their employees. On the other hand, it is often too subjective to be of real value. Good rating scales provide space to explain the evaluation.

Shopping reports. These are frequently used by retailers to test either honesty or performance. Shopping reports involve having outside evalu-

---

Peter Principle
Principle that people in an organization tend to rise to their highest level of incompetence.

Management by Objectives
A process in which a superior and a subordinate jointly set job objectives for the subordinate and then meet periodically to evaluate progress.

ators come into stores as shoppers. Their evaluation is based on how they were treated as customers and their observation of the person under scrutiny.

Frequency of Evaluation

Evaluation should really be an ongoing process. Formal appraisals, however, are usually done once or twice a year—annually for managers and executives and semiannually for hourly employees. (See Figure 5.5.) Whenever a formal evaluation is to take place, the person being evaluated should be told. After the evaluation, feedback must be immediate. This avoids anxiety and promotes faith in the system.

Grievance Procedures

Grievance
A complaint that is handled formally through fixed procedures.

Ombudsperson
A person outside the normal chain of command who handles complaints and grievances.

Of all the positive employee reinforcement programs, the most important is a formal grievance process. Employees perform much better when they know that they have someone who will not only listen to their problems, but who is in a position to help with solutions. By just listening to a perceived **grievance,** a store manager can make a salesperson feel important, cared for, and an integral part of the organization.

Being able to air a grievance without fear of reprisal gives each employee a sense of belonging. The grapevine loses credibility when formal procedures exist. Company policy rather than company rumors become the basis for staff motivation.

Ironing out problems is usually quite easy when employees know that they can go to their immediate supervisors or, if necessary, to a human resource **ombudsperson.** Things remain simple if a formal program is in place; frustration is kept at a minimum. In an organization where the only outlet for a grievance is discussion with a peer who has no more authority to change things than the person experiencing the problem, frustration can be high.

Each retailer should develop a set of procedures that best suit the particular organization. In a small, owner–manager store, the procedure might be to go directly to the owner with any and all problems. Together, owner and employee will then assess the problem, the possible solutions, and finally select the one that is most acceptable to both parties. A large multistore retailer has a much more complex system. Rank-and-file employees first go to their immediate supervisor, who either solves the problem or takes it to his or her supervisor.

In the most serious cases, it might be necessary for a representative from corporate headquarters to visit the store where the grievance occurred. This ombudsperson or employee welfare manager would interview all involved parties and make a recommendation to the first-line supervisor, who would then discuss the recommendation with the disgruntled employee.

With a proper grievance process, retailers can go a long way toward keeping employees productive and happy.

Figure   5.5   A Performance Evaluation Form

RETAIL VENTURES, INC.

PERFORMANCE EVALUATION

NAME _____   DATE _____

POSITION _____   STORE
                                             NO. _____

DATE OF LAST REVIEW: _____

SCORING SCHEDULE:

1 = EXCELLENT   **Consistently** meets **all** minimum standards of performance and **exceeds all** of these performance standards on a regular basis.

2 = VERY GOOD   **Consistently** meets **all** minimum standards of performance and **exceeds most** of these performance standards on a regular basis.

3 = GOOD   **Consistently** meets **all** minimum standards of performance and **exceeds some** of these performance standards on a regular basis.

4 = FAIR   **Consistently** meets **all** minimum standards of performance.

5 = MARGINAL   **Not** consistently achieving **all** minimum standards of performance.

PERSONAL HABITS

A) **ATTENDANCE**   extremely punctual, dependable (1 2 3 4 5) tardy, unreliable

   AREAS OF IMPROVEMENT: _____
   _____

B) **APPEARANCE**   sharp, professional image   (1 2 3 4 5) unkempt, poor hygiene
                                                                           doesn't care attitude

   AREAS OF IMPROVEMENT: _____
   _____

C) **ATTITUDE**   enthusiastically takes   (1 2 3 4 5) "just a job" thinking
                               initiative

   AREAS OF IMPROVEMENT: _____
   _____

D) **COOPERATIVENESS**   understands and takes   (1 2 3 4 5) argumentative and
                               direction well   defensive

   AREAS OF IMPROVEMENT: _____
   _____

E) **CONGENIALITY**   helpful, courteous and gets along (1 2 3 4 5) disruptive and abrasive
                               well with fellow employees

   AREAS OF IMPROVEMENT: _____
   _____

F) **PROJECTION**   outgoing, sparkling, dynamic   (1 2 3 4 5) timid, reserved, in a shell
                               use of appropriate body language

   AREAS OF IMPROVEMENT: _____
   _____
   _____

COMPENSATION

Payroll is the largest single expense item for most retailers. It reflects costs of salary and wages as well as fringe benefits. Because a good compensation package is so costly, retailers are constantly looking for ways to trim this enormous expense without losing good employees, who are necessary for high productivity and a good public image.

VISUAL MERCHANDISING

A) LIGHTING   thorough working knowledge   (1 2 3 4 5) no concept of correct
                              of lighting guidelines   lighting

    AREAS OF IMPROVEMENT: _____

_____

_____

B) DISPLAYS   can put up sharp, professional (1 2 3 4 5) **throw** it together
                              displays per guidelines   approach

    AREAS OF IMPROVEMENT: _____

_____

_____

OVERALL APPRAISAL OF PERFORMANCE

☐ EXCELLENT   **Consistently** meets **all** minimum standards of performance and **exceeds all** of these performance standards on a regular basis.

☐ VERY GOOD   **Consistently** meets **all** minimum standards of performance and **exceeds most** of these performance standards on a regular basis.

☐ GOOD   **Consistently** meets **all** minimum standards of performance and **exceeds some** of these performance standards on a regular basis.

☐ FAIR   **Consistently** meets **all** minimum standards of performance.

☐ MARGINAL   **Not** consistently achieving **all** minimum standards of performance.

COMMENTS OF EMPLOYEE REVIEWED: _____

_____

_____

_____

I have discussed this evaluation   I have discussed this evaluation
with my supervisor.   with the employee.

_____   _____
Employee's Signature   Supervisor's Signature

_____   _____
Date   Date

    THE SIGNATURE INDICATES ONLY THAT THE REVIEW HAS BEEN DISCUSSED WITH THE EMPLOYEE AND IS NOT A SIGNED AGREEMENT OF SATISFACTION WITH THE REVIEW CONTENTS.

DISTRICT MANAGER - REVIEW

REVIEWED BY _____ TITLE _____

DATE _____

COMMENTS _____

_____

_____

_____

_____

Minimum Wage
Smallest hourly
rate that may be
paid to an
employee,
sometimes
established by a
union or others,
but usually the
federal minimum
wage law.

Today, 50 percent of all retail employees work part-time (usually no more than 20 hours a week) for very little more than **minimum wage.** This dispels the legend of long hours but not of low pay, because most part-time employees receive no fringe benefits. Hiring part-timers is a major strategy among retailers to keep payroll costs under control.

The best compensation packages directly relate reward to contribution to the organization. A satisfactory retail compensation plan should be:

1. Suitable for the functions being performed.
2. Fair to the employee and the owner, whether sole proprietor or corporation.
3. Easily calculated and understood.
4. Designed to provide relatively steady income and incentive for exceptional performance.
5. Related to performance without causing internal or external friction, such as fighting over customers for commission.

Nonexecutive Compensation Plans

Because of the many different types of jobs in retailing, there are a number of compensation plans. The plan for a salesperson in a furniture department will be different from that for a copywriter in the advertising department. Each plan should provide an employee with a sense of security, a desire to do his or her best, and a reward for outstanding performance.

Straight Salary Plan

Straight salary is a fixed amount of compensation for a specified work period such as an hour, a day, week, month, or year. For the retailer, the straight salary plan has the advantages of easy administration and a high level of employer control. Time can be spent in nonselling activities without penalty if the employee is in sales. At the same time, the retailer is assured that all the tasks of the job will get proper attention. For the employee, the straight salary (or hourly) plan has a known level of financial security and stability. One disadvantage of this plan for the retailer is a high ratio of wage costs to sales.

Retailers typically use straight salary plans when a sales job involves a considerable amount of customer service and nonselling time. They also use it for almost all rank-and-file positions in nonsales areas of the company.

Straight Commission Plan

Under this plan, sales employees receive a percentage of what they sell. Straight commission is usually offered for big-ticket products such as automobiles, jewelry, furs, furniture, and appliances. Salespeople who sell directly to the customer (door to door) are also paid straight commission.

The major advantage of a straight commission plan is monetary incentive. It can result in problems for the retailer, because commission salespeople sometimes ignore customers unless they indicate an interest in high-commission products. Other problems for retailers who use this plan can be customer "grabbing" and high-pressure selling.

The greatest weakness for employees in the straight commission plan is financial instability. Retail salespeople cannot control who enters the store nor can they influence a downturn in the economy. Because of this, some straight commission plans include a **drawing account** that allows employees to draw a fixed sum of money against future commissions at regular intervals.

Drawing Account
A regular allowance, available to salespeople working on straight commission, to be balanced at intervals against commissions earned.

Salary Plus Commission Plan

This plan combines the stability of the straight salary plan with the incentive of the straight commission plan. Generally, in the salary plus commission plan, the base salary constitutes the greatest share of the employee's total compensation; however, the employer does have the option of increasing the commission rate whenever additional monetary motivation is needed.

Quota Bonus Plan

Similar to the salary plus commission plan, the incentive pay in the quota bonus plan begins only after a certain sales quota has been reached. Quota bonus plans, if used, can vary from department to department within the same store depending on the product line and whether the department is a high- or low-traffic department.

Push Money

Push Money
A special bonus paid to a salesperson who is successful in selling a specified item.

Regardless of compensation plan, all sales employees may be offered **push money (P.M.)**—a form of incentive payment given to salespeople for selling certain items. This may be provided by the retailer or by the manufacturer of the item. As an example, an appliance manufacturer may offer $25 to $50 extra (above commission or bonus) to all salespeople who sell a refrigerator model that has been difficult to move. With P.M. the salesperson, retailer, and manufacturer all benefit.

Executive Compensation Plans

Most retail executives are amply rewarded for their hard work and long hours. In fact, good compensation packages begin on the first step of the executive ladder. Buyers, for example, earn anywhere from $20,000 to $75,000 a year depending on length of time on the job, type of store, department, volume, and bonus plan. At the other end of the scale, some store presidents earn over $1,000,000 a year. Owners of single stores usually take a salary each month and then, out of profits, award themselves a bonus at yearend. If the year has not been profitable, there is no bonus. Store managers on salary are also rewarded with a yearly bonus based either on net sales or net profit. The figure, of course, depends on the amount of control they have over store operations. Whether as a sole proprietor or a corporate manager, executives in retailing are paid as

FROM THE FIELD

Golden Era for Executive Compensation

The remaining years of the 1980s will be the golden age of the retail executive, with the opportunity to earn incredible rewards. Several trends in executive compensation are emerging.

There will be a continual move away from base salaries; more compensation will be put at risk with a move toward incentive pay. There will be a shift from annual incentives, with more incentives geared to three- to five-year plans and also geared to performance criteria.

Stock options will be geared to individual performance. And there will be continued use of restrictive stock, one of the best retention devices.

With the establishment of performance targets for incentive plans, there will be a move away from measurements. Because of current and impending legislation, supplemental executive excess plans will become more popular.

The success of women in the retail industry will also affect compensation. It will be necessary to consider their special needs. Perks that motivate men may not do so for women.

Rewards will be more performance related and less reactionary. Over the next years there will be a definite move toward tying rewards to longer performance periods.

Most retailers do not offer top performers in middle and lower level management the opportunity to earn performance-based incentive compensation, and thus the administration of base pay will be a major challenge. The challenge—because this level often looks at compensation as a birthright—is to put merit back into salary increases, the most striking new direction in executive compensation today.

Source: "Golden Era for Executive Compensation," *Stores* (February 1984).

well, if not better, than executives with comparable responsibilities in other industries. (See Table 5.2.)

Fringe Benefits

When one considers the fringe benefits offered to most retail employees—whether rank-and-file or executive—the total compensation package seems most appealing. The United States Chamber of Commerce re-

Table 5.2   Salaries of Chief Executive Officers at the Nation's Leading Retail Companies

Company	C.E.O.	Compensation			Profits			1984 Comp. as Percent of Net Earnings
		1984	1983	Percent Change	1984	1983	Percent Change	
Allied Stores	Thomas M. Macioce	$960,000	$850,000	+12.9	$140,773,000	$128,471,000	+ 9.5	0.7
Ames	Herbert Gilman	471,795	467,577	+ 0.9	28,516,000	19,886,000	+43.4	1.7
Associated Dry Goods	Joseph H. Johnson	509,887	607,524[1]	−16.1	120,657,000	115,520,000	+ 4.4	0.4
Carter Hawley Hale	Philip M. Hawley	770,547	677,500	+13.7	89,670,000	67,485,000	+32.9	0.9
Dayton Hudson	Kenneth A. Macke	842,539	794,239[2]	+ 6.1	259,346,000	245,457,000	+ 5.7	0.3
Dillard Department Stores	William Dillard	877,805	820,200	+ 7.0	49,558,000	34,139,000	+45.2	1.8
Dollar General	Cal Turner Jr.	162,077	131,598	+23.2	20,598,000	15,126,000	+36.2	0.8
Dress Barn[b]	Elliot S. Jaffe	360,000	300,000	+20	3,691,000	2,267,000	+74.7	9.7
Federated	Howard Goldfeder	714,500	600,000	+19.1	329,330,000	338,342,000	− 2.7	0.2
The Gap Stores	Donald G. Fisher	348,077	300,000	+16.0	12,230,000	21,607,000	−43.4	2.8
Jamesway	Herbert Fisher	868,856	802,707	+ 8.2	13,264,000	11,509,000	+15.2	6.6
J.C. Penney	W.R. Howell	500,593	497,663[3]	+ 0.6	453,000,000	467,000,000	− 6.8	0.1
K mart	Bernard M. Fauber	825,000	750,000	+10.0	499,100,000	492,300,000	+ 1.4	0.2
Limited	Leslie H. Wexner	596,372	690,980	−13.7	92,495,000	70,939,000	+30.4	0.6
R.H. Macy[b]	Edward S. Finkelstein	611,308	675,364	− 9.5	219,991,000	206,533,000	+ 6.5	0.3
May Department Stores	David C. Farrell	875,000	750,000	+16.7	214,100,000	187,000,000	+14.5	0.4
Melville	Francis C. Rooney	676,500	661,200	+ 2.3	190,386,000	176,260,000	+ 8.0	0.4
Mercantile	Leon F. Winbigler	653,600	628,500	+ 4.0	84,769,000	83,222,000	+ 1.9	0.8
Rapid-American	Meshulam Riklis	970,413	1,206,853	−24.8	(7,900,000)	12,900,000		
Sears, Roebuck	Edward R. Telling	1,481,250	1,425,000	+ 4.0	905,200,000	781,400,000	+15.8	0.2
Wal-Mart	Sam M. Walton	300,000	282,000	+ 6.4	270,767,000	196,244,000	+38.0	0.1
Woolworth	John W. Lynn	839,878	640,000	+31.2	141,000,000	118,000,000	+19.5	0.6
Zayre	Morris Segall	1,100,000	1,050,000	+ 4.8	80,316,000	61,462,000	+30.4	1.4
Total		16,252,997	15,608,905	+ 4.1	4,192,857,000	3,853,069,000	+ 8.8	
Average		706,652	678,648	+ 4.1	182,298,130	167,524,739	+ 8.8	

[a]Changes were as follows:
1. The late William Arnold, C.E.O. of Associated Dry Goods in 1983, was succeeded by Joseph Johnson.
2. William Andres, C.E.O. of Dayton Hudson in 1983, was succeeded by Kenneth Macke.
3. D. V. Seibert, C.E.O. of J. C. Penney in 1963, was succeeded by W. R. Howell.
[b]July fiscal year.

Source: *Women's Wear Daily*, August 16, 1985.

ports that the fringe benefits for department store employees amount to around 32 percent of their compensation. The tax-free aspect makes these benefits as important as actual dollars, and contributes greatly to high employee morale and a high level of performance. Low attrition also results when a good fringe benefit package is part of the compensation program. Employees may think twice before leaving a job that includes company-paid health insurance, discounts on merchandise, and profit sharing.

Some typical fringe benefits offered to retail employees are (1) insurance programs (health and accident, dental, life, and disability); (2) leisure-time programs; (3) pension plans; (4) profit-sharing plans; (5) tuition-refund plans; (6) stock options; (7) paid vacations; (8) sick leave, and (9) one of the most important of all, employee discounts on merchandise.

In 1984, the federal government, for the first time, instituted curbs on discriminatory fringe benefits. Thus, in 1985, there were tax consequences for highly compensated employees who received better discount rates than their subordinates. Because tax-free benefits are so important to employees, retailers must constantly study and reevaluate their discount system to make sure that it has maximum appeal and minimum risk. The 1980s have also seen an enormous rise in medical fees; retailers, along with the rest of corporate America, are being forced to pass some health-care costs along to employees. This, too, requires careful and constant reevaluation.

UNIONIZATION AND LABOR LAWS

After World War II, when retailers and all service industries were growing at a tremendous rate, they became perfect targets for union organizers. There were then (and now) many low-paid, unskilled workers in large stores who wanted and needed bargaining power. Unions seemed the perfect answer; yet great inroads were not made in the industry.

Labor Movement

Since the 1950s, the union movement has progressed in retailing, although more slowly than most labor organizers hoped or expected. The reason for the slow pace is retail management's gradual recognition of the important role human resources play in the struggle for profit. As compensation plans and enrichment programs increased, there was less need for employees to organize. Moreover, many full-time rank-and-file retail employees know that the possibility of promotion from within does exist and they therefore have a management attitude. A third reason for the slowdown in unionization is the extensive force of part-time help in most large retail organizations.

Some significant retail unions are the United Food and Commercial Workers (UF&CW), an affiliate of the UFL-CIO; the United Store Workers, an affiliate of the Retail, Wholesale Distributive Services Union; and the Retail, Wholesale, and Department Store Workers Union.

Labor Laws

Human resource policy in retailing depends on an understanding of federal legislation. Table 5.3 summarizes four federal acts that are concerned with labor.

Table   5.3   Some Federal Legislation Related to Labor Practices

Legislation/Agency	Date
1. Fair Labor Standards Act U.S. Department of Labor Wage and Hour Division This law requires payment of the minimum hourly wage and of time-and-a-half for working over 40 hours a week.	1938
2. Equal Pay Act Equal Employment Opportunity Commission This law requires compliance with regulations on child labor and employee health and safety.	1963
3. Civil Rights Act, Title VII Equal Employment Opportunity Commission This law requires equal pay for similar work, regardless of sex, race, color, religion, or national origin.	1964
4. Age Discrimination in Employment Act Equal Employment Opportunity Commission This law forbids discrimination on the basis of age. It extends the retirement age to 70.	1968

Summary

Proper management of human resources is essential in all organizations, retail or otherwise. In retailing, however, good human resource management has even greater meaning because profit and image are linked to it. In all retail institutions, the bottom line depends on employees' understanding of and service to consumers. If employees are poorly selected, trained, and compensated, the retailer's image reflects this.

A good human resource program starts with a plan that includes a personnel forecast, job analysis, job descriptions, and job specifications. A budget is then developed for people, just as it is for merchandise. After the planning stage, a recruiting system must be established so that the best employees can be attracted for all levels within the organization. The selection of new employees is based on applications, résumés, interviews, tests, physical exams, and reference checks.

Once hired, all new employees must be given some sort of orientation and training. The scope and length of this phase depend on the size and type of retail firm. Continuous training of employees is something all retailers should consider, especially for those in sales. A 1980s-trained salesperson cannot really understand the needs of the 1990 customer. Supervisory training is also important.

Job enrichment programs and good compensation packages are varied throughout the retail industry. The rationale for job enrichment is simply that a happy employee is a productive employee. Compensation alone is not the answer to productivity. A low wage/cost ratio is a goal of every retail human resource program.

Unionization is a fact of retail life today, and human resource managers must learn how to deal with all types of union contracts and grievances. They must also be experts in compensation and must understand salary and benefit administration as well as labor laws. Human resource management in retailing is complex and diverse. It requires a capable and knowledgeable staff that can accept and meet the challenge of people management in both a quantitative and qualitative context.

Questions for Review

1. List the six steps involved in developing a human resource budget.
2. Name at least three internal sources and three external sources useful in recruiting rank-and-file employees.
3. List at least five useful tools of the selection process.
4. Do you feel that orientation and training should be offered to every new employee, both full-time and part-time? Why or why not?
5. How can job enrichment programs benefit employees? Employers?
6. List at least three types of nonexecutive compensation plans.
7. Why has the union movement in retailing progressed more slowly than in some other industries?

CASE STUDY   Morgan's

Branch Store Training

A top management meeting was called for 10:00 a.m., and although it was only 9:30, Liz Carlton was extremely nervous. As Human Resource Director of Morgan's, she had the huge task before her of trying to convince top management not to cut the training budget for the 12 branch stores in the Morgan organization. Whenever money became a problem, her budget always seemed to be the first one to be slashed. Now, not long after winning the fight to hold onto her training staff in the flagship store, would she be able to keep at least one full-time training director in each branch?

Morgan's was a full-service department store organized along traditional lines with six major divisions: merchandising, operations, promotion, control, real estate, and human resources. Founded in 1908, Morgan's, along with all good center city retailers, flourished during the next two decades. The store survived the Depression and World War II and in the 1960s joined the exodus to the suburbs, opening 12 stores in 15 years. After 1976, there were 13 Morgan stores—12 branches and the original downtown store.

Liz had been Human Resource Director at Morgan's for ten years. She had previously worked as training director of a competing department store and was brought into the Morgan organization because of her expertise in this area. Morgan's emphasized training. The years had been rewarding and the department was successful under Liz Carlton's direction, as new employees, properly and efficiently trained, performed effectively on the job.

The memo that Liz had received from the executive vice president for store operations, along with the notice for the meeting, indicated that one of the major topics for discussion was "Budgetary Cuts—Human Resources."

Bottom-line thinking is the successful retailer's way of life, but Liz knew that the bottom line would suffer in the long run if all but the bare essentials were stripped from training. Morgan's had always been a service retailer and had to continue along these lines in order to compete in the current market. With the off-price merchant at one end of the scale and the specialty store at the other, the only way Morgan's could increase or at least maintain its share of the market was through service. Even brand names were no longer a reason to shop at Morgan's, because most of these could be purchased for less at catalog–warehouse showrooms, discount department stores, or through the mail.

Morgan's had built its reputation as the kind of store that cared—a store where salespeople, delivery people, and employees in service departments were all trained to believe that the customer was the most important item in the store. Concern for the customer was an important subject from the very first hour of every employee's orientation. The Morgan method of training—a special introduction to a special company—had always worked, and the Morgan attitude stayed with each and every employee until retirement. That, however, was another era. With 13 Morgan units, there were more employees in the branches than in the flagship store, and most were employed on a part-time basis.

Current management thinking was that it was not necessary to instill any special feeling in employees. Why should management bother to make the store a home away from home for help who worked only a few years while in college or while their children were in elementary school? Most worked a few hours each day, merely putting in their time in order to pick up a paycheck.

Liz was familiar with management's argument concerning the waste of extensive training in branch stores. She had heard often enough, "Give them systems training, that's enough; forget courtesy for the credit interviews." Or, "It doesn't matter if the girl behind the gift-wrapping desk is unpleasant. We don't pay her for her personality." They believed that training that went beyond the usual brief orientation and sales techniques was unnecessary and costly. Why wouldn't current management realize that the rising walkout statistics they so often worried about could be lowered with proper training of branch store personnel? This was a company that for years had believed in the training concept.

The department store shopper still wanted service. In fact, that was the major reason for shopping in a department store instead of a discount store, where price outweighed all other considerations. Morgan's was still the gathering place for customers searching for value rather than price, for personal attention, a friendly smile, and the offer of merchandise information. The only change was in the number of locations. Now customers were shopping in branch stores in regional centers, suburban centers, and free-standing areas more than in the main store, yet the only qualified training staff was in the main store.

It just didn't make sense! Even the suggestion of a roving training manager for the branches presented problems because Liz did not believe one person could cover all the stores within the required time period.

It was almost 10 o'clock. Liz would have to prove that she, too, was bottom-line oriented. She also had to prove that an orientation period, salesmanship training, and a brief course in human relations would pay off, if offered to all help in all stores. "But," Liz thought, as she entered the room, "am I right, will it? Is the cost worthwhile, or will customers return anyway? Maybe systems training is enough in this day and age. Maybe a roving training director is the answer." The president called the meeting to order.

Questions

1. List the benefits and the costs of offering a full training program in all branch stores as well as in a company's flagship store.
2. What are your views about the value of a roving training director in a retail firm such as Morgan's? Why?
3. Is training beyond basic systems really necessary in department stores today? Why?
4. What should be the goals of a carefully designed training program? Explain.
5. Relate branch store training to walkout statistics.
6. Do you agree or disagree with Liz Carlton? Why?

Part III

Retail Institutions

Chapter 6

The Store: A Traditional Approach to the Customer

Source: Photo by Pat Doty.

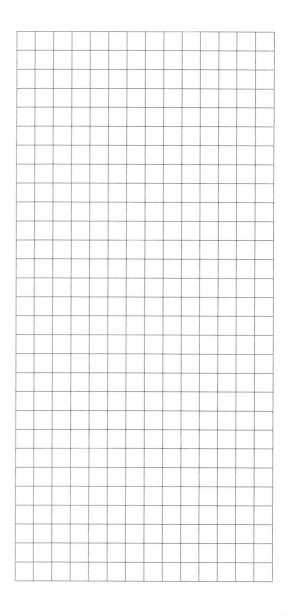

Industry Statement

Stanley Berkovitz
Vice President, Consumer and Community Affairs
Zayre Corporation

Many people think of retailing as a game of numbers—profit margins, rates of inventory turn, financial control—changing numbers in an environment demanding rapid response. The one constant in the retailer's equation, however, is the relationship with the consuming public. Because of that, the more things change, the more they stay the same. To the extent that the retailer has a finger on the pulse of the consumer, he or she can measure the health of his or her own business.

Zayre Corporation has built its success on sensitivity to the consumer. It now serves customers in 41 states. In 1956, Max and Morris Feldberg, experienced in traditional retailing, perceived a new need in the marketplace and created a new form of retail distribution to fill that need with one store. That was the beginning of modern discount retailing, as the Zayre neighborhood, self-service, general merchandise discount department stores caught on rapidly and spread into urban and suburban communities around the country. Zayre is one of the few discounters to enter many unserved urban areas with notable success. With Zayre stores now numbering about 400, the chain is recognized as one of the top in the discount retail business, serving America's urban and suburban families in 26 states.

In the mid-1960s, as more and more women entered the workplace, our Hit or Miss chain was conceptualized and came into being to provide one-stop specialty shopping of high-fashion, first-quality apparel at the lowest price, in convenient mall and urban settings. In 1984, Hit or Miss began to provide its busy customers catalog shopping with Chadwick's of Boston.

As economic forces led more segments of the population to seek out top quality, high fashion, and brand names at reduced prices, the time was ripe in 1977 for the entry of T. J. Maxx, now expanded to over 200 stores in 32 states. Selling large volumes of men's, women's, and children's lines at 20 to 60 percent off department and specialty store prices, the chain quickly became a recognized national leader in the off-price category of retailers.

In 1984, recognizing that its customers equated dollar value with high quality and time savings, as well as rock-bottom prices, Zayre Corporation introduced B.J.'s Wholesale Club. Soon after, we acquired Home Club. Both represented a brand-new thought in retailing—the wholesale warehouse—where limited-selection, rapid-turnover sales allowed broad categories of merchandise to be sold at or below usual wholesale prices. B.J.'s target market is small businesses, professional offices, selected institutions, and defined group members. Home Club's merchandising program is geared to do-it-yourselfers, trade professionals, and the general public. Both chains are expanding at a healthy pace.

The growth from one store in 1956 to a $5 billion operation appears to be a complex and monumental phenomenon. In reality, Zayre Corporation's development largely boils down to a relatively simple talent: listening to customers describe their evolving needs over time on a day-to-day basis—and caring enough to fill those needs.

Learning Objectives

Upon completing this chapter you should be able to:

1. Discuss how population change dictates changes in retailing.
2. Name the various classifications of stores.
3. Name the three types of branch store organization plans.
4. Discuss why there is more competition than ever before between department stores and general merchandise chains.
5. List the different types of stores classified as discount stores.
6. Name the types of franchised retail outlets that are currently in the growth stage.
7. Name the newest type of grocery retailer on the American scene.

The expression "you've come a long way, baby" could very easily apply to the present in-store retail scene. In spite of all the new and interesting nontraditional competitors that will be discussed in Chapter 7, in-store retailing—or conventional retailing, as some still refer to it—is very much alive and well throughout the United States and the rest of the industrialized world. This chapter, for the most part, will concentrate on retail store practices in the United States. Chapter 8 will open a window on the rest of the world.

There are almost as many types of retail stores as there are customer types. Each has its niche, each serves certain target markets, each has its own personality and image, and the same or similar functions are performed in each. Yet because there are similarities in organization, stores can be classified into a few major groups. The differences within each group are in specialization. Department and chain stores are the largest groups when measured by sales volume. (See Table 6.1 on page 162.) In terms of numbers, the largest group consists of single-store entrepreneurs.

Before discussing retail store practices for each of the groups, a summary description of the five universal functions of all retail businesses will be provided.

Table   6.1   The Top 12 Retail Companies in the United States

Company	1985 Sales[a]
1. Sears	$24.5
2. K mart	22.4
3. J. C. Penney	13.8
4. Dayton Hudson	8.8
5. Wal-Mart	8.5
6. Federated	8.2
7. F. W. Woolworth	6.0
8. Montgomery Ward	5.4
9. May Department Stores	5.1
10. Melville	4.8
11. Associated Dry Goods	4.4
12. R. H. Macy	4.4

[a] In billions.
Source: *Women's Wear Daily,* April 12, 1985, 30.

RETAIL STORE FUNCTIONS

The five universal functions of all retail businesses are merchandising, operations, promotion, finance, and human resource management.

Merchandising includes all buying and selling activities. Merchandising executives must coordinate their activities with those of finance, promotion, and operations. All of these activities will be discussed in Part V of this text.

Operations people are generally in charge of the physical plant. They oversee maintenance and housekeeping. Other operations activities are customer services; receiving, checking, marking, and warehousing of incoming merchandise; and store security. Some large chain stores have separate real estate divisions, but in all other stores, facilities development is part of operations.

Promotion includes advertising, visual merchandising (sometimes shared with merchandising), public relations, personal selling, and special events. Customer services, if not under operations, can fall under this division.

Finance involves control of the retailer's assets, responsibility for seeing that working capital is available, accounting and record-keeping systems, control of physical inventory, and merchandise and expense budgets. Financial officers or the financial staff prepare all of the financial reports for top management, various government agencies, and trade groups such as the NRMA (National Retail Merchants Association). A small entrepreneur might hire an outside accountant to perform financial functions because this requires special expertise above and beyond managerial or merchandising skills.

Human resource managers, as discussed in Chapter 5, oversee the recruiting, training, and evaluation of personnel. They administer the compensation and benefit packages and, if necessary, deal with unions. They also handle employee welfare.

These, very briefly, are the functions of retailing. Modifications, expansion, or concentration of some or all depends on the type and size of the retail store. Regardless of type or size, however, the computer has become one of the most important tools in all retail functions.

DEPARTMENT STORES

Multiunit Department Store
Department store organization consisting of a flagship store and two or more branch stores.

Mazur Plan
A plan for department store organization based on only four functions: finance, merchandising, promotions, and operations.

By definition, a department store carries a complete assortment of hard and soft goods and also offers a wide variety of services along with merchandise. From an organizational standpoint, each department is managed as a separate unit by either a buyer or a manager, and goods and/or services are grouped according to similarity. Table 6.2 lists the nation's top 100 department stores.

The functions are the same in large **multiunit department stores** and small single-unit department stores. The difference is that in a large, multiunit store like Macy's in New York, each function is performed by a specialist. In a small family-owned department store, one, two, or three generalists perform all the managerial functions.

In recent years the organizational structure of department stores and departmentalized specialty stores has changed from the basic, four-function **Mazur Plan** named in honor of Paul Mazur, an investment banker who had an interest in retailing.[1] (See Figure 6.1 on page 165.) The newer, more complex system accommodates the growth of branch stores and the separation of the buying and selling functions. Today most department stores have at least five major divisions and one of three branch store plans.

Branch Store Organization

Brood Hen and Chick

As the name indicates, in this plan the flagship store acts as the brood hen and oversees the merchandising, promotion, operational, and con-

---

[1] Paul M. Mazur, *Principles of Organization Applied to Modern Retailing* (New York: Harper & Row, 1927).

Table   6.2   The Top 100 Department Stores in the United States

Rank	Company/Division (headquarters)	Units	Sq. Ft. (000)	Volume (000,000)	Rank	Company/Division (headquarters)	Units	Sq. Ft. (000)	Volume (000,000)
1	Dillard's, Little Rock	101	13,551	$1,601.4	34	P. A. Bergner, Milwaukee	31	3,153	356
2	Dayton Hudson, Minneapolis	37	7,904	1447.9	35	Filene's, Boston	16	2,117	353.5
3	Macy's New York	21	7,454	1,383	36	Maas Brothers, Tampa	21	2,783	340
4	Bamberger's, New Jersey	23	6,399	1,297	37	Thalhimer's, Richmond	25	2,588	335
5	Macy's California	25	5,682	1,199	38	Hess's, Allentown, Pa.	39	2,935	330.7
6	The Broadway, Southern California	41	7,101	990	39	Gayler's, Mobile, Ala.	11	1,542	320
7	Bloomingdale's, New York	15	4,024	955.2	40	McAlpin, Cincinnati	9	1,394	300
8	Lazarus, Columbus	31	7,517	856.2	41	Higbee's, Cleveland	11	2,650	280.8
9	Marshall Field's, Chicago	21	6,425	805	42	D. H. Holmes, New Orleans	17	2,398	272.8
10	May Co. California	35	6,643	784.2	43	Jordan Marsh, Florida	16	2,872	260
11	Abraham & Straus, Brooklyn	15	5,538	767.5		Boscov's, Reading, Pa.	11	1,448	260
12	Lord & Taylor, New York	44	5,800	760	45	B. Altman, New York	7	2,105	250
13	Burdines, Miami	29	5,064	757.5	46	May Company, Cleveland	10	2,413	238.6
14	Bullock's, California	27	4,680	712.3	47	Frederick & Nelson, Seattle	15	2,365	230
15	Emporium-Capwell, San Francisco	22	5,146	690		Weinstock's, Sacramento	12	1,935	230
16	Foley's, Houston	17	4,380	680.3	49	Elder-Beerman, Dayton	24	2,839	220.9
17	Rich's, Atlanta	17	4,308	647.0	50	G. Fox & Co., Hartford	8	1,569	219.1
18	Macy's, Atlanta	26	4,700	625	51	Goudchaux/Maison Blanche, Louisiana	7	874	216.5
19	Hecht's, Washington, D.C.	23	3,847	567.8	52	Meier & Frank, Portland	7	1,819	212.2
20	J. W. Robinson's, Los Angeles	22	3,748	560	53	Castner-Knott, Nashville	11	1,270	205
21	Jordan Marsh, New England	18	3,964	550		Joslin's, Denver	9	1,065	205
22	The Bon, Seattle	39	4,538	490	55	Joseph Horne, Pittsburgh	13	2,474	200
23	Gimbels East, New York	20	4,875	480		Wieboldt's, Chicago	13	2,900	200
24	Woodward & Lothrop, Washington, D.C.	16	2,971	470.4	57	McRae's, Jackson, Mississippi	15	1,312	199.8
25	Famous-Barr, St. Louis	17	3,977	460.5	58	The Broadway Southwest, Phoenix	12	1,877	195
26	Sanger Harris, Dallas	18	3,274	450.7		Gimbels Midwest, Milwaukee	9	2,475	195
27	John Wanamaker, Philadelphia	16	4,356	450	60	Jones Store, Kansas City	7	1,430	190
28	Sterns, New Jersey	17	2,846	430	61	Younkers, Des Moines	26	1,821	181.0
	L.S. Ayres, Indianapolis	25	4,543	430	62	Sibley, Lindsay, Curr, Rochester	14	1,988	180
30	Kaufmann's, Pittsburgh	18	3,655	423.9	63	O'Neil's, Akron	10	1,398	175.4
31	Carson Pirie Scott, Chicago	20	3,584	406	64	May D & F, Denver	11	1,576	171.9
32	Joske's, Texas	27	5,029	400					
33	Strawbridge & Clothier, Philadelphia	12	3,190	380					

(continued)

Table   6.2   *(Continued)*

65	Goldsmith's, Memphis	6	1,338	169.1	83	Gottschalk's, Fresno	9	600	112.8
66	Gayfer's, Montgomery, Alabama	6	825	165	84	Buffums, Long Beach, California	15	N/A	111
67	ZCMI, Salt Lake	9	1,330	164.8	85	Reads, Bridgeport	6	865	110
68	Howland Steinbach, Hochschild, White Plains, N.Y.	28	1,109	162.6		Pizitz, Birmingham, Ala.	12	1,100	110
69	Donaldson's Minneapolis	15	1,888	160		Lion, Toledo, O.	3	610	110
70	Pomeroy's, Pennsylvania	15	1,997	150	88	Ivey's Florida, Winter Park, Florida	11	1,110	109
	Bacons/Roots, Louisville	7	770	150	89	Millers, Knoxville, Tennessee	13	1,379	100
	Liberty House, Honolulu	10	N/A	150		J. L. Brandeis, Omaha	11	729	100
73	Denver Dry Goods, Denver	12	1,400	145	91	Hutzler's, Baltimore	10	905	95
74	Miller & Rhoads, Richmond	21	1,882	140	92	Stone & Thomas, Wheeling, W. Va.	18	N/A	90
	Ivey's Carolinas, Charlotte	13	1,350	140		Block's, Indianapolis	11	1,542	90
	Hahne & Co., Newark	8	1,466	140	94	May-Cohen's, Jacksonville, Florida	6	643	73.5
	Goldwater's, Phoenix	9	1,029	140	95	Sage-Allen, Hartford	13	531	71.1
78	H. C. Prange, Sheboygan, Wis.	20	1,324	139	96	Hennessey's, Billings, Montana	5	N/A	65
79	J. B. White, Augusta, Ga.	7	N/A	135	97	Harris', San Bernadino	5	633	61
80	Gimbels, Pittsburgh	7	1,675	131	98	Cain Sloan, Nashville	4	769	60
81	Robinson's of Florida, St. Petersburg	9	1,298	120		McCurdy & Co., Rochester, N.Y.	7	710	60
82	Adam Meldrum Anderson, Buffalo	10	1,150	113	100	Petersen-Harned-Von Maur, Davenport, Iowa	10	N/A	55

Figure   6.1   The Mazur Plan for Department Store Organization

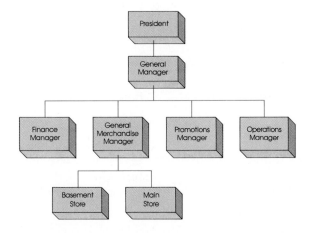

trol needs of its chicks. The flagship store is usually in its original downtown location, and the branches (chicks) are usually in the suburbs. Buyers in the main store purchase all the merchandise sold in the branches and work very closely with branch store managers who are responsible for selling it.

Brood-Hen-and-Chick Plan
Management plan under which the parent store organization operates the branches.

The **brood-hen-and-chick plan** works if there are only three or four branch stores, but beyond that it becomes too difficult for the buyers. Because of the problems that result when too many chicks demand equal attention from the brood hen, this organizational plan has limited acceptance even with today's technological communications tools.

Separate Store

Total branch store sales today usually exceed sales in the flagship store. When there are too many branches for the brood-hen-and-chick plan to work, department stores often adopt the separate store plan. Using this

FROM THE FIELD

Maximizing Department Store Sales

The key to maximizing department store sales and profits lies in three major approaches to market segmentation, according to Isaac (Ike) Lagnado, research director of Associated Merchandising Corp. These are: the career woman, particularly with a personal income of $25,000 a year or more, for apparel and accessories; the baby-boomer, notably in the 25-to-40 age range, for home furnishings; and the upscale mother, for children's wear. Lagnado thinks these customer segments will lead the way to performance. His explanation:

"The career woman market for apparel and accessories will be almost $30 billion by the end of the decade, as compared with $4 billion in 1977. This

woman spends over $3,600 annually for business and casual wear. Most of her purchases are at regular prices. Department stores gain over 60 percent of her business. She is brand-aware, leaning toward the Evan-Picone, Liz Claiborne, and Jones New York types of brands, although varying by classification."

In discussing the career woman, Lagnado said: "We at AMC research are stressing the $25,000 and over leadership core. It still comprises under 10 percent of the working woman population but is growing fast. The number is doubling every other year. The higher paid women are role models not only for the rest of the working woman population but also for nonworking females. Why else are career women featured in advertising, whether for apparel, toiletries, or home lines?

plan, each branch has its own buyers, who also supervise the sale of the goods they have purchased. An advantage of this plan is that carefully selected merchandise is geared to the branch's target market. A disadvantage is the cost of such targeted merchandising. Too many buyers, assistant buyers, and clerical people equal an enormous expense in salary and travel. Moreover, the discounts are lost that would be earned if one buyer were buying large quantities for many stores. As costs continue to go up, most department stores find that they cannot afford the luxury of the separate store plan.

Equal Store

This plan is borrowed from chain store organization. Buyers and other executives operate from a central headquarters. Every store is treated equally and buying and selling are separated as in the brood-hen-and-chick plan. This enables the economies of scale to be realized. Responsi-

---

"Half the business in career women's apparel is in better, bridge, and designer lines, with the major part in better lines. Most of these women wear Misses sizes. Slightly over one-quarter of the market is special sizes—petite, large, and some juniors.

"Career women spend substantial money on a wardrobe; they regard it as an investment. They're far more traditional, as opposed to updated or advanced, than manufacturers and retailers assume them to be."

On baby-boomers and home furnishings prospects: "This merchandise, typified by tabletop and furniture, demands enormous inventory dollars and doesn't turn very rapidly. It's crucial to survival in such goods to identify the fastest-turning customer niche—and that's baby-boomers, who are forming households and buy for fashion and design—and [buy] more frequently than their elders, who are mainly replacement customers. The implications for improving inventory turns are tremen-

dous. Although the baby boomers are more attuned to key brands for their formal lifestyle, they are very receptive to private label for the casual part of their lives. Exciting presentations and displays of home furnishings, as of apparel, are essential. Presentation is the most underutilized department store asset."

On the upscale mother: "The opportunity in catering to her is to offer a large selection of children's clothing basics and styles, depth of assortment, sharp value for the money, a couple of key brands as well as a private label, fashion, particularly as the child gets older, appealing merchandise presentation, and convenience of department location and method of payment." Each of these three opportunities is a business that could double in size in the next five years, if properly maximized.

Source: Samuel Feinberg, "From Where I Sit," *Women's Wear Daily*, March 15, 1985, 10.

Equal Store Plan
Plan for managing branch stores that separates the buying and selling functions, with buying done centrally and sales planning done by branch managers.

bility for selling lies with the branch manager, who can keep closer control over the salespeople than a buyer working in the flagship store miles away. Central control and the separation of the buying and selling functions characterize the **equal store plan.** This is currently the most popular of the three and should continue to be, as technological aids improve and proliferate.

Department Store Problems

When department stores were the royalty of retailing, there were few problems that could not be controlled through the implementation of well-planned management and merchandising techniques. Customers were easy to describe and target marketing strategies almost as easy to develop.

Times have changed, however, and the current department store market is being eroded by national chains and off-price merchants. By 1990, in apparel sales alone, department store sales could drop as much as 29 percent, as more stores selling off-price quality apparel brands enter department store markets. This trend began almost without notice while department stores were busy fighting one another, concentrating on high-margin apparel, and giving up such highly competitive merchandise as furniture, big-ticket appliances, piece goods, and sporting goods. Specialty stores along with the low-priced giants quickly filled the hard goods void and continue to become strong competitors—along with off-price merchants—for customers' dollars.

Another problem plaguing department stores is their sameness. This grew out of the common belt tightening that took place during the recession of the late 1970s when staffs were slashed, services reduced, and merchandise assortments and ads copied from each other. Where is the creative thinking, innovation, and originality that retailers always talk about? Department stores must stop trying to be all things to all people and match merchandise, layouts, and displays to selected markets with a particular lifestyle and/or geographic location. Marginal stores will probably fail during such a changeover, but those that remain will once more be recognized as truly exciting places in which to shop.

Merchants from all over the world can take a lesson in creativity from Bloomingdale's Manhattan store, which became a mecca for the yuppie generation before it had barely been born. "Bloomies" officers recognized a new city lifestyle and began to merchandise creatively for this group. Bloomingdale's understood that the key word in department store strategy now and in the future is *image.*

Some department stores may solve their market share problems through creativity. Others may do it through acquisition, as did Dayton Hudson Corporation in the early 1980s when it acquired Mervyn's and Target stores. Some department store ownership groups such as the Federated, Allied, and May companies are able to help their members tackle all sorts of problems because of size and power.

GENERAL MERCHANDISE CHAINS

Whenever national general merchandise chains are mentioned, the names that come to mind are Sears, J. C. Penney, Montgomery Ward, or K mart. There are also regional general merchandise chains with names that are familiar in different parts of the country. Merchants to millions, these stores sell a wide variety of hard and soft goods, mostly under their own label. Their customer segment might be classified as Mr. and Ms. America, although they now carry some upscale ready-to-wear for both men and women and have a few prestigious brands of their own, such as Penney's Halston III line and K mart's Jaclyn Smith fashions. Generally they deal in averages—average styles, prices, and sizes. The unusual is not considered when merchandise assortments are planned. Deviations from this policy would result in higher prices because there is always greater risk in assorting goods for a broader market than in staying with one segment.

The general merchandise chains are successful because they have researched their markets and created a merchandise mix geared to satisfy the needs of those markets. If customers from other segments occasionally shop in their stores they are grateful for the extra business but are not foolish enough to make the mistake of giving serious consideration to moving full force into these markets.

Some texts list Sears, J. C. Penney, and other national chains with department stores. We do not, because there were and are some basic differences in organizational structure, such as the addition of a real estate division, that are important to recognize. Because chains are constantly looking for sites in new growth areas, the real estate or site-locations function becomes an extremely important one, worthy of its own divisional status. Chain store companies may also have planning and research and MIS divisions. These are of major importance when units are located throughout the country or the world.

Central Headquarters

One difference between chain stores and most department stores is the centralization of all major functions in one location—a central headquarters, not a flagship store. Policies and procedures are determined at headquarters and merchandise is purchased by the central buying staff, even though the responsibility for selling and servicing the chain's customers lies with each store manager. Managers all receive equal treatment from headquarters.

As national chains grew over the past 20 years, corporate officers recognized the need to serve different regions in different ways and changed the balance of authority and decision making between central headquarters and newly opened regional offices. During the past decade, more and more buying power was given to buyers located in regional offices. They do a better job of purchasing goods for the stores in their regions than buyers at headquarters because they have a better understanding of the specific needs of the customers in the area.

Chain Decentralization
Transferring of certain functions from central headquarters to regional offices or individual stores.

To understand **chain decentralization,** one should think of headquarters as the clasp on a string of pearls. It is sufficiently strong to hold the necklace in place until more and more pearls are added to make a longer strand. Finally, the strand becomes too heavy for one clasp. Large gold links are then spaced every few inches to keep the clasp from breaking under the added weight. Changing of authority and responsibility for certain functions from headquarters to regional offices or certain stores (if the stores are extremely large) can also keep a chain of stores from "breaking" under the weight of too many units in diverse locations.

FROM THE FIELD

The K mart Image

Until this year [1986], it looked as if K mart Corporation Chairman Bernard Fauber's attempt to update K mart's merchandise had flopped.

Soon after he became chief executive in 1980, Fauber began to push through a program to improve the chain's image. "They decided to shed the polyester empire image, which had been theirs for the longest time," says Kurt Barnard, marketing consultant and publisher of the newsletter, *Barnard's Retail Marketing Report.*

But all the glitter added to K mart stores seemed to turn to lead instead of gold. Earnings sank in 1980 and again in 1981. After recovering in 1983, earn-

ings were flat through last year [1985]. Critics said K mart only muddied its reputation by trying to change it. After all, that's what happened when Sears, Roebuck and Montgomery Ward tried to upgrade their images.

Now, though, the changes at the world's second-largest retailer after Sears are beginning to pay off. (See Figure 6.2.) It's all a sweet reward for Fauber and his team of executives, who have been putting in extra-long hours at K mart's low-profile, honeycomb-shaped headquarters here. (Fauber sometimes gets in to work at 5:30 in the morning.) What they hoped to do was win over more quality-conscious consumers without driving away existing customers.

The Changing Chain Image

Sears is a perfect example of the changing image of chains. Sears is no longer frumpy, either in fashion or appearance. Stores now have a friendlier, welcoming look with more aisles, lower ceilings, and merchandise displayed at eye level with flair and style. Fashion labels with big names—Cheryl Tiegs, Arnold Palmer, Johnny Carson, and Yvonne Goolagong—attract the customer, and products have clearer, more informative labeling. The merchandise in Sears stores and catalogs constitutes a breathtaking array of products on which Americans are spending their money in the waning years of the 20th century. From gas barbecues to personal computers, lingerie to blood-pressure monitors, appliances to insurance policies, stocks and bonds to swimsuits and sleep sofas, Sears' new vitality is turning formerly dull goods and new services into big profits.[2]

[2]"Sears' Sizzling New Vitality," *Time*, August 20, 1984, 82–90.

Among the changes were the following:

- The stores began to carry more brand names. Today, you can pick up a Farberware pot in the Kitchen Korner and run down some Nikes, lined up in neat racks in the shoe section.
- K mart began to run advertising designed to improve its reputation for quality—including slick television commercials—along with its usual diet of price-dominated newspaper inserts.
- A line of clothes endorsed by actress Jaclyn Smith has been a great hit.

Executives also made sure they didn't monkey with the successful aspects: Inexpensive goods still are easy to find. And there are just as many blue-light specials as before—2.5 million of them every month at 2,183 K mart stores in the U.S.A. and Canada.

Now that the marketing strategy is in place, K mart can concentrate on improving operations and cutting costs at its stores. K mart can see the results in the form of changing consumer spending habits. The stores once lured customers by advertising bargains for items such as shampoo and tools, and then got them to buy items such as clothing that provide better profits. Now K mart persuades people through advertising and its improved image to head straight for clothing or kitchen supplies.

Don't be fooled, though; K mart stores still practice the fine art of sparking impulse purchases. The most popular departments are located at the back of the store. You need to walk past racks of clothes, cameras, and, of course, toys to get to auto parts or kitchen supplies.

Source: Excerpted from Jay McCormick, "C.E.O.'s Plan Adds Glitter to K mart," *USA Today*, July 16, 1986, 27–28. Copyright 1986 *USA Today*. Reprinted with permission.

Figure   6.2   Turnaround in Sales and Net Income at K mart

Fauber: Chief executive put marketing strategy in place.

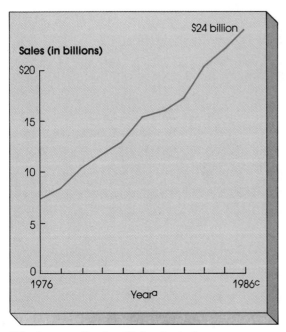

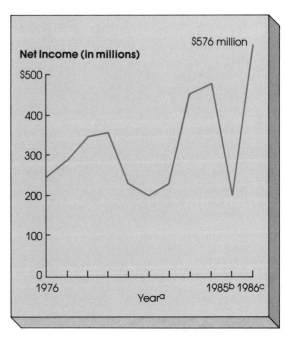

[a] Fiscal year ending last Wednesday in January.
[b] Includes write-off of Mexican operation.
[c] Estimate.
Source: Adapted from "Blue-Light Specials Still on at K mart," *USA Today,* July 16, 1986, 27. Photo of Mr. Fauber courtesy of K mart Corporation.

J. C. Penney, by repositioning its merchandise mix, has also worked hard in the past few years to overcome its old paint-and-hardware image. Soft lines now constitute about 75 percent of the mix. In a five-year period, more than $1 billion was spent to modernize the chain's metropolitan department stores. This included expansion, modernization, systems enhancement, and maintenance, with total capital expenditures for stores and catalog somewhere between $2 billion and $2½ billion. J. C. Penney also invested in regional malls because management wanted to be in the best environment for fashion apparel and home furnishings. Once J. C. Penney decided to catch up with department stores by creating a fashionable place to shop, it designed stores to respond to local market conditions.[3]

SPECIALTY STORES

Specialty stores can be found in urban, suburban, or regional settings, alongside department stores, chain store units, supermarkets, or mass merchants. Specialty stores are limited-line retail specialists that usually zero in on one particular market need instead of attempting to be all things to all people.

Because goods and/or services are concentrated in one area, specialty retailers attract many customers from their target markets. These customers know that by dealing with specialists rather than generalists, they have an excellent chance of finding just what they want. Functions in specialty stores are the same as they are in department stores, but again there is a difference, this time in degree of specialization. In department stores there are specialists in each division. In specialty stores all the major functions are performed by a few generalists. Buyers in these stores often spend more time on the selling floor than do buyers in department stores, who may be buying merchandise to be sold in a dozen or more locations.

There are specialty stores in almost all merchandise categories—clothing, food, appliances, automotive supplies, electronic equipment, furniture, home furnishings, jewelry, and pharmaceuticals. There are even shops that specialize in stuffed bears. The service sector also has its share of specialty retailers, such as dry cleaners, repair shops, and photo finishers. Ethnic restaurants, high-fashion boutiques, and florists are all specialty retailers. All deal in a limited line or lines of goods or services and all offer their customers more personal treatment than their large competitors.

Specialty stores have always been and will continue to be an important part of the retail scene, whether they stand alone as in San Francisco's Ghirardelli Square, Boston's Faneuil Hall Marketplace, or New York

---

[3] Samuel Feinberg, "From Where I Sit," *Women's Wear Daily,* November 29, 1983.

Specialty Store Chains
Chains that concentrate on a limited line of merchandise, such as groceries, automotive parts, hardware, or fashion apparel.

City's South Street Seaport, or are joined with branches of department stores, as in Toronto's Eton Center.

In the 1970s, **specialty store chains** began to proliferate throughout the United States, though a number had been around since before World War II. Pre–World War II stores like The Bell Shops and Lerner Stores were located in city centers and carried fashion merchandise that had already gained general acceptance in the marketplace. Their target markets were women in the medium-income range. The newer fashion chains (since 1960) cater primarily to an under-35 market and feature the very latest in youthful fashion. Examples of these are Foxmoor, The Gap, The Limited (which purchased Lerner Shops in 1985), Casual Corner, and Brooks. Automotive accessory stores and grocery and hardware chains are fewer in number now but do more in sales than they did in the 1950s and 1960s.

Concentration is probably one of the major reasons for the success of the specialty chains. It is easy to merchandise stores centrally, even in a variety of geographic locations, if market dimensions are similar and well defined and if the targeted customers have the same tastes and income. By concentrating on one kind of customer and one general merchandise classification, the new specialty chains plan their assortments with little risk. IBM Computer Product Centers illustrate this concept.

Specialty chains come in all sizes and types—health food stores; toy stores; apparel shops for women, men, or children; jewelry chains; fitness centers; fast food stands; and bookstores. Names like Toys 'R' Us, B. Dalton, Brooks Brothers, and Baskin-Robbins are as familiar west of the Mississippi as they are on the East Coast. When an easterner moves West and sees the familiar logo and layout of a store like The Limited, it is like seeing a welcome face from home, because specialty chains are home to their customers, regardless of location. Ask any teenager what Sam Goody means. Whether in New York or Los Angeles, the answer will be *music*.

OTHER MAJOR RETAIL STORE CATEGORIES

The Discount Segment

Discount Stores

Although there have always been retailers who practiced price cutting, the discount store as a major retail institution did not appear until after World War II, when a large suburban blue-collar market emerged with both the need and the money for home furnishings and appliances. Like other major retail store groups before it, the discount store group took its place on the lower spoke of the wheel of retailing to serve this new customer segment. The segment had not been targeted by any existing retail institution, especially not by the early suburban department store branches. Blue-collar shoppers wanted an environment in which they could feel at home, one similar to the department store basements they had left behind in the city. The discount store was the answer.

Discount stores multiplied quickly during the 1950s, 1960s, and 1970s. As their numbers increased, so did the sophistication of their original customers and, as a result, their merchandise mix. Fashion departments began to spring up in most establishments and soon customers began to think of the mass merchants to fill all of their needs, rather than only household and appliance needs. Customers from other market segments were attracted by the low prices. In Caldor or Wal-Mart stores one can find shoppers with varied demographic backgrounds. A bargain is a bargain and, even today, prices in discount stores are often lower than in the general merchandise chains and are usually lower than in department and specialty stores.

As discount stores moved on the wheel of retailing, their management and organization became more like that of department stores or chain stores. Wal-Mart is an excellent example of an astutely managed, highly profitable, and well positioned retail operation. Founded by Sam M. Walton in 1962, Wal-Mart dominates large rural communities of 5,000 to 15,000 people in an ever-widening tier of southern and southwestern stores. In the mid-1980s, it was the nation's fastest growing retailer, moving into medium-sized cities like Little Rock, Arkansas; Springfield, Missouri; and Shreveport, Louisiana; it was looking at Kansas City, Dallas, and St. Louis for the future.

Based in Bentonville, Arkansas, Wal-Mart combines an aggressive expansion program with a state-of-the-art computerized merchandising information system, a tight rein on expenses, a strong distribution network, and a progressive employee relations program. Wal-Mart executives perform the same retail functions all retailers perform, but under Sam Walton and his top team, they do it with the kind of zeal and competitive clout that hurts competitors.[4]

Off-Price Fashion Discounters

There are a number of different types of specialized discount stores, but fashion discounters, who came into their own during the 1970s, deserve special attention. These retailers have probably had a greater impact on both consumers and other retailers than any other group since the first department stores opened in the late 1800s.

The original store in this category was opened in 1920 by Frieda Loehmann in Brooklyn, New York. Today Loehmann's is a member of the May Department Stores Company. It still brings couture and designer clothes to consumers at amazingly low prices in stores that span the United States. (See Figure 6.3.)

---

[4] Isadore Barmash, "The Hot Ticket in Retailing," *The New York Times,* July 1, 1984, 4F.

Figure   6.3   Off-Price Fashion Advertisement

Source: Courtesy of Loehmann's, Inc.

Even earlier, in 1909, Filene's in Boston opened its automatic bargain basement as an outlet for fashion and general closeouts from manufacturers or other retailers. The store's basement was the first to effect a system of reducing prices 25 percent after 12 selling days, another 25 percent after 18 selling days, and still another 25 percent after 24 selling days. At the end of 30 days, the remaining merchandise was given to organized charities (and still is).

Loehmann's stores and Filene's Basement are no longer the only games in town. Competing with both are such stores as Marshalls, Cohoes, T. J. Maxx, Hit or Miss, Burlington Coat Factory, Syms, and The Dress Barn.

The philosophy of fashion discounting is based on high volume and bigger dollar (not percentage) profit, gained through lower markup and faster inventory turnover—12 or 13 times a year. This is a philosophy that many traditional retailers, especially department stores, are trying to emulate. It is not easy to do, however, when department store mentality aims at the highest gross margin possible and is historically tied to 4 or 5 turns a year.

Change is taking place and as the most aggressive department stores adapt themselves to the off-pricers' methods, they are learning. Department and big specialty stores are educating their customers to buy merchandise on sale through aggressive promotion techniques. This causes off-price fashion competitors to suffer because, when prices are comparable, consumers would much rather shop in the ambiance of a traditional department store and have charge and return privileges.

Like the full-line discounter, fashion discounters will continue to move up on the retail wheel, both to compete for profit and to carve out new niches in the marketplace. Like all new entrants to retailing, they too, after years of strong growth, may find their rate of sales and profit gains slackening. They will undoubtedly react by increasing margins to maintain profits while slowing expansion.

It is essential for off-pricers to attain high sales per square foot. Yet with every new entrant, this becomes more difficult. Some sort of shakedown is almost inevitable. Competition is now coming from all sides: traditional stores, full-line discounters, and the national chains. Those that have strong management and a clear image should still be around in the year 2000 and after.

Catalog/Warehouse/Showroom Merchants

Catalog/ Warehouse/ Showroom Merchant Discounter who sells through catalogs mailed to customers' homes or displayed in a showroom adjoining the warehouse.

In this type of discount operation, the consumer usually selects merchandise from a catalog that has either been mailed to his or her home or is prominently on display in the store. Whether at home or at the showroom, the customer usually writes selections on a sales order form. The order is then processed by clerks working in the warehouse area. **Catalog/warehouse/showroom merchants** purchase in large quantities, secure favorable terms, and need very little display space—except for jewelry. Because of this, branded hard goods such as cameras, tools, and small kitchen appliances are generally priced much lower than in competing stores.

The catalogs are usually prepared by large merchandising companies like Service Merchandisers, but individual merchants use their own logos on the ones they distribute and display. Although catalog/warehouse/showroom sales were $8.4 billion in 1980 and growing, costs often rise long after the prices have been printed in the catalogs, which come off the press far in advance of every selling season. This could cause problems in the future.

Factory Outlets

Factory outlets are used by manufacturers to sell their closeouts, seconds, and discontinued items. In the past they were located very near to production facilities. Currently, factory outlets are clustering together in outlet malls, often many miles from the factory. As long as they are easily accessible from the point of production, each store has much greater drawing power as a member of a mall than it did alone, located inside or close to the plant. Freeport, Maine, the home of L. L. Bean, has become

Figure   6.4   Walking Map of Freeport, Maine

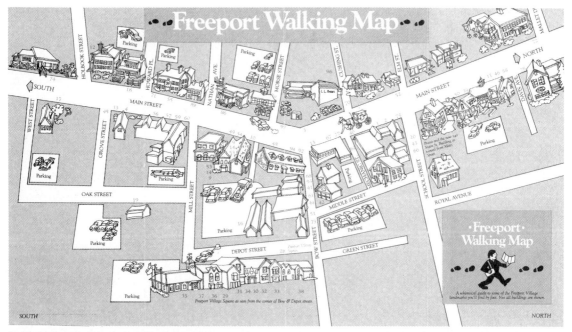

Source: "Some of the Best Things in Life Are in Freeport, Maine" (Freeport, Maine: Freeport Merchants Association).

Franchise Retailer
An independent store owner who sells branded items or service under licensed agreement with the franchise holder (franchisor).

Entrepreneurship
Capacity to organize, own, manage, promote, and assume the risks of an organization, usually a small business enterprise.

home to many factory outlets, among them: Barbizon (lingerie), Hathaway, Carter's (children's clothing), Anne Klein, Samuel Robert (leather fashions), Timberland (boots), and Polo/Ralph Lauren. (Figure 6.4 is a walking map of Freeport, Maine, where almost every store is a factory outlet.)

Franchised Retailers

Franchising, a method that involves franchisees handing over to the franchisor a set amount of cash for the right to distribute a product or service, has been and continues to be a popular form of contractual retailing. There are more and more **franchise retailers** of all types and sizes. (See Figure 6.5.) Sales and service franchise operations are booming. In 1984, they accounted for $456.7 billion in sales, a jump of more than 270 percent, from 1969, when only $112.8 billion came from franchising.

In 1984, nearly 1,800 companies franchised their wares to some extent. Franchising is one of the business world's most pervasive institutions, helping companies reduce costs of expansion and letting individuals reduce the risks of **entrepreneurship.** By the year 2000, it is predicted that franchising will account for more than half of all retail sales.[5]

[5] Phillip S. Gutis, "The Stunning Franchise Explosion," *The New York Times,* January 20, 1985, 4E. Copyright © 1985 by The New York Times Company. Reprinted by permission.

Figure   6.5   Total U.S. Franchised Units, 1969–1985

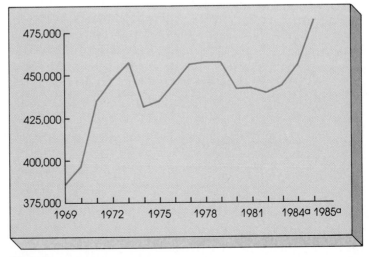

[a] Estimate.
Source: U.S. Department of Commerce.

In 1970, franchising seemed to have peaked. Charlatans abounded and some companies, spread too thin, faced lawsuits. In spite of the problems, however, growth did continue, especially after 1979, when the Federal Trade Commission stepped in and regulated the transactions. In 1985, Phillip S. Gutis had the following to say:

> The growth of franchising has brought with it a new diversity in types of franchise deals. For more than 100 years after the Singer Sewing Machine Company sold the first franchise in 1863, so-called trade name franchises, in which companies sold nothing more than the right to distribute their products to various mom-and-pop firms, were the only types of franchises around. But many trade name franchises are going out of business. In 1976, for example, there were more than 226,000 franchised gas service stations (one of the most popular types of trade name franchises). In 1984, the number had slipped to about 130,000.
>
> Today, the quickest growing form of franchise is the business format franchise, in which the franchisee gets access not only to the company's products or trademark, but also to its business plans and corporate support services. A typical franchise contract today would spell out the accounting, hiring, training, advertising, and marketing support that the franchisee can expect. The cost to the franchisee is a one-time fee of several thousand dollars and a continued percentage—generally varying from 3 to 20 percent of revenues.
>
> Although most franchises are still purchased directly from companies, franchising middlemen, or master franchisees, are growing more common. They purchase from a franchisor the right to develop franchises in an entire territory—or, in the case of companies expanding abroad, in an entire country—and then sell individual franchises themselves. Pop-Ins, the franchised maid service, sold 93 individual franchises for about $9,500 apiece, but has also sold 23 master franchises, at a price of $35,000 per million people included in the territory. The combined business plans of those master franchises call for 600 Pop-Ins across the country. Franchising will continue to grow for the foreseeable future.[6]

Grocery Retailers

In the United States today there are two basic types of grocery retailers. A third, a European innovation, has not made great inroads here but might be credited with being the inspiration for the new superstore.

---

[6] Ibid.

Convenience Stores

Convenience stores are characterized by their location, close to consumers' homes and places of business; long hours, often 24 hours a day; and limited food and nonfood items, from motor oil to milk. They are targeted at the fill-in or emergency market and generally carry major, recognizable national brands. Prices are higher than in supermarkets but customers accept this because the stores are in the right place at the right time with the right products.

Small in size when compared to other food retailers (1,000 to 4,000 square feet), this modern version of the corner mom-and-pop grocery store offers limited parking space, usually only a few cars at a time. Some convenience stores have even combined their services with gas stations so that fuel for the body and fuel for the car can be purchased in one stop.

Leading stores in this category are 7-Eleven, Arco, Circle K, and Jiffy. Because competition in the grocery business is so intense, many supermarkets are responding to convenience stores by staying open 24 hours a day. With lower prices as a draw, there can be no doubt about the results. They will offer even more competition in the years ahead.

The Supermarket

Supermarket
Self-service food store with minimum annual sales of $2 million.

A **supermarket** is a self-service food store with grocery, meat, and produce departments and minimum annual sales of $2 million.[7] Food stores with less than $2 million in volume are in the **superette** category.

Supermarkets as we know them began around 1920 when Clarence Saunders, sometimes referred to as the father of supermarket retailing, founded the *Piggly-Wiggly* stores in the South. He introduced self-service and customer checkout counters. Supermarkets offer a wide variety and assortment of dry groceries, fresh meats, produce, and dairy products. These are supplemented by frozen foods and household products.

Superette
Self-service food store with annual sales of less than $2 million.

Some of today's supermarkets stock almost as many nonfood lines as food lines. Customers can shop for health and beauty aids, housewares, prescription drugs, magazines, and even small appliances. Deli counters, bakeries, and ready-to-eat sections attract working women and men who, without such items, might spend a good percentage of their food dollars in restaurants. The supermarket of the 1990s will be a far cry from the A&P of yesterday. A&P, by the way, came back fast from obscurity under the able leadership of James Wood and during the 1980s took its place alongside Safeway, Kroger, American Stores, and the other thousands of regional chains that operate clean, modern, computerized facilities. Supermarkets operate on very low profit margins. In an attempt to increase their margins, many sell generic brands, their own brands, and national

---

[7]"FMI Redefines the Supermarket," *Progressive Grocer*, (April 1981): 44.

brands. This kind of internal competition keeps customers coming and sales up.

The Superstore

Superstore
Giant supermarket that carries a full line of food items plus hard and soft goods.

Some retailing experts point to the new giant operations (around 100,000 square feet) as American versions of the European hypermarket. Like the hypermarkets, **superstores** carry, in addition to a full line of food and grocery items, lines of hard and soft goods not found in most traditional supermarkets. Other experts claim that they are an extension of the American **combination store**—supermarket and discount store or supermarket and drugstore.

Either way, superstores have garden centers, television and appliance shops, clothing boutiques, wine cellars, bakeries, and prescription drugstores. They truly epitomize the conglomerate merchandising concept (unrelated goods and services sold under one roof). As a result, they have a much broader profit base than the supermarket. Because they require a substantial investment, they have not yet totally permeated the retail scene, although more and more are cropping up all over the country, especially in heavily populated urban or suburban areas. Wegmans in Rochester, New York, is a prime example. Although only 85,000 square feet, it meets the other criteria of a state-of-the-art American superstore.

Combination Store
Supermarket plus discount store or supermarket plus drugstore.

Summary

Retail stores compete with each other and at the same time complement one another. Although there are different classifications of retail stores, the functions in each group are basically the same. Goods or services must be planned for, purchased or created, priced, promoted, and distributed to markets that are preselected by those in top management. The view from the executive suite, be it hidden behind the stairs to the stockroom or located on the top floor of a Chicago skyscraper, is therefore very similar.

There are chain stores, department stores, specialty stores, supermarkets, and discount stores. Department stores have branches and chain stores have separate units. Supermarkets are becoming superstores, while discount stores are emulating department stores. Franchised names are seen from coast to coast and even overseas. There are mini-malls in small towns and mega-malls that serve entire regions. There are off-price malls, outlet malls, and specialty malls.

Retail stores are everywhere—some good, some not so good; some attractive, some not so attractive; some featuring high prices, some featuring low prices. All are tied together by a common purpose—to serve their target markets in the best possible manner, bringing satisfaction to their customers and profit to themselves.

The marketing concept must be practiced in-store just as it must be practiced throughout the marketing channel. For those that do, life will be long and rich. Those that don't will only be a memory as the wheel of retailing keeps turning.

Questions
for Review

1. Name the five universal functions of retailing.
2. List at least two activities involved with each of these functions.
3. Name at least five different classifications of general merchandise stores, and at least two types of grocery stores.
4. Explain the term *brood hen and chick* as it applies to store organization.
5. How do the national chain stores, such as Sears and J. C. Penney, differ in their organizational structures from traditional department stores?
6. Explain the growth and success of discount stores after World War II.
7. Comment on the following statement: "Although there are different classifications of retail stores, the functions in each group are basically the same."

CASE STUDY

Brookfield's

A Decision on Main Store/Branch Relationships

Brookfield's was considering opening a tenth branch, and management anticipated that, with the addition of this new unit, total sales would be somewhat in excess of $100,000,000. Brookfield's was growing in all respects as success followed success. Around every corner, however, new problems lurked that had to be dealt with if the success of the past 70-plus years was to continue.

Joseph P. Brookfield established Brookfield's in the early 1900s, when retailing was experiencing its first boom period in the cities. With the urban population increasing each year, more retailers were needed to serve the needs of the growing populace, and Brookfield's, a full-line department store, won immediate acclaim. Even during the Depression and World War II, the store thrived because it was a well-run, full-line department store. If one category of goods was not selling, others were; if one item was not available, a substitute could be found. As a result, Brookfield's was in fine shape when the war ended, and ready to open its first branch store in the newly developed suburban area outside the central city.

As the suburban population grew, so did Brookfield's branch store operation. One became two; two, four; and by the middle 1980s, Brookfield's consisted of the downtown flagship store and nine branches. Staffing was not a problem because each suburb had an adequate supply of housewives and students who were eager to work for 20 or 30 hours a week and, on a rotating basis, kept the store fully staffed. All personnel functions such as hiring, training, and employee welfare seemed to be easily handled by an on-site personnel director in each branch. Decisions, of course, came from the main personnel office in the flagship store. The merchandising and sales promotion functions also originated with the flagship store and were carried out in each branch by the department managers.

Each branch had a store manager and an assistant store manager. The assistants were primarily concerned with operations, while the store manager, in addition to being in charge, was the liaison between the department managers and the buyers at the flagship store.

Decisions were all made by the proper executive at the downtown store. Although the bulk of the sales was being realized in the nine branches, no branch had any autonomy or real authority to select merchandise, set store hours, or make promotion decisions. Even credit had to be checked through the main store, and total inventory figures were kept in one computer. Buyers gave printouts to department managers in each branch so that they could have information that pertained to their departments, but they did not know the total stock picture.

With the separation of the decision-making process from the point of execution, problems were increasing. The floor personnel who were meeting the public had very little knowledge of overall store policy. There was no flexibility at the point of sale, and customers at the branch stores were becoming dissatisfied when they did not find in-depth merchandise geared to their lifestyles. Only 50 miles could make a great difference in demand.

Although no Brookfield store was more than 50 miles from any other, what the buyers thought would be a top seller in all stores often did not move in one or two. Stock transfers were used, but they cost money and cut into gross margin. With each new store, the buyers' jobs became more demanding, and less time was available for branch visits. There were also advertising problems when one ad was used to cover the entire Brookfield market.

The realization that valuable selling space should be allocated to departments in each store according to the volume of department sales—and not simply because these departments existed in the main store—finally brought management to the brink of reorganization. Was the old brood-hen-and-chick concept the best or would another organizational relationship between the flagship store and the branches improve company sales and profits?

Before plans for new branches were drawn up, there had to be a decision on the organizational structure of the entire firm in terms of authority and responsibility within each major division and within each store, and the relationships between administration and branch management had to be clearly defined or redefined. In this way only would growth continue to result in profit.

What were the options? With somewhat similar yet differing consumer lifestyles in the 11 locations, it would seem as if each store should make its own merchandising, promotional, operational, personnel, and financial decisions. But was this logical or even feasible? Wouldn't the costs of staffing each store with highly paid executives far outweigh the benefits? Even if the costs were within reason, was it possible to find a pool of capable top-level people for 11 stores? Not likely! How would Brookfield's go about maintaining a single image under this plan? It was apparent that there was no easy solution.

Perhaps the answer was to maintain certain major divisions and chief executives at the main store while farming out other functions to the branches. Then the question arose as to which functions should have central control and which rightfully belonged in the branches where decisions could be made in light of customer needs.

Perhaps Brookfield's could establish a central office similar to a chain store where all policies, procedures, and controls would originate. Then each of the 11 stores would be treated exactly alike except that store managers would have greater input into all decisions affecting their market and greater authority and responsibility in terms of performance.

Perhaps the current system could work if it were revised so that department managers actually became buyers with responsibility for both the buying and selling functions instead of being charged, as they were at the present, with selling the possible mistakes of an absentee merchandising staff. All other major divisions could still remain at the flagship store with functions being carried out under the direction of the branch managers. There seemed to be an endless variety of possible solutions to the problems facing Brookfield's. The important thing was to choose the one that would work best within the current organizational frame without causing tremendous upheaval in the present ranks. One thing was certain: a new plan was needed.

Questions

1. Evaluate this alternative: Each branch store will make its own merchandising, promotional, operational, personnel, and financial decisions.
2. Evaluate this alternative: Functional responsibility will be divided between the flagship store and the branches.
3. Evaluate this alternative: The central office will control (chain-store style) all of the Brookfield stores.
4. Evaluate this alternative: Brookfield's will continue its current flagship–branch store relationship.
5. Compare the four alternatives.
6. Which would you select? Why?

Chapter 7

Direct Retail Marketing: A Nontraditional Approach

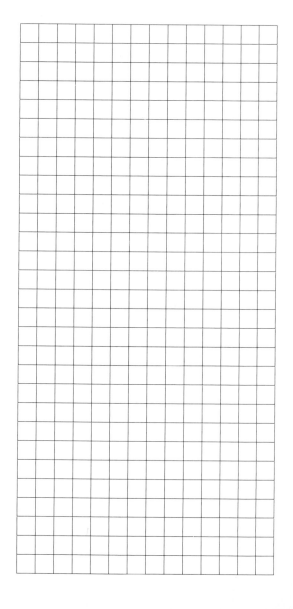

Industry Statement

Dinah Lin Cheng
Director, International Development
Telaction Corporation

Future trends in nontraditional retailing will continue to reflect the convergence of sociological, economic, and technological changes that began in the mid-1950s. Today's consumer demands better product and pricing information on a wide range of merchandise in order to comparison shop for the best value. Convenience and time savings are as important as dollar savings. The desire for products that meet individual requirements reflects the move away from a society of mass consumers. We are living in the age of electronic information. People will be able to choose and customize the information they need and the products they order to suit their schedule, their taste, and their budget.

New and emerging technologies are beginning to meet these consumer demands. At-home systems allow the consumer to shop with a modem-equipped computer or a television equipped with a special terminal and keyboard, the latter capable of producing computer graphics.

Interactive and transactional video disc terminals located in retail environments provide the shopper with the added benefit of superior television-quality motion video. At-home shopping systems now have full-motion color video. The demand exists, and the technology has been developed, but present costs are unattractive to the consumer. We need to recognize the growing desire for individualized choice and prepare to offer this to the public. If we fail to do this, we will find ourselves bypassed by those who do.

Learning Objectives

Upon completing this chapter you should be able to:

1. Understand why customers are now shopping in nonstore environments.
2. Explain direct marketing and its relationship to retail marketing.
3. Know the alternatives for a retailer who wishes to "sell direct."
4. Distinguish between the forms of electronic media.
5. Explain what future trends in shopping habits will bring for both consumer and retailer.

Chapter 6 stressed how retail stores have changed along with the society they serve. We will now examine the emergence of new communications technologies and marketers' discovery of how to use them. These developments coincide with deep cultural changes in the United States. The country is now experiencing a retailing evolution toward a partially non-retail society or a communications dominated society. Retailers will be moving from traditional in-store selling to an expanded arena of choice for the consumer. The choices include shopping from vending machines; through direct-to-home alternatives; and via telephones, mail, and cable.

WHY NONSTORE RETAILING IS GROWING

Direct Marketing
Nonstore retailing, including vending machines, door-to-door, and catalog sales.

The Physical Shopping Process

Whether a consumer is looking for a new pair of shoes or an office manager is investigating the purchase of a word processor, the physical process of shopping can be made easier by the direct marketing process. Frequently, salespeople in retail stores are less than helpful or the stores are not open at the moment of impulse to buy. In physical shopping, the process controls the buyer. In **direct marketing,** the buyer controls the process to a large degree. The flexibility of direct marketing is an attractive alternative to the relatively inflexible process of retail shopping.

Energy Consumption

Transporting the buyer or seller to the location of the sale will become increasingly wasteful as energy costs continue to rise out of proportion to communications costs. Because direct marketing is communications intensive, and because communications costs are inflation resistant, fundamental cost factors favor its use over other forms of retail selling.

Time and Convenience

Our society has changed its values associated with time. The two factors that have contributed most to this revolution in values are:

1. The demographic phenomenon of the dual-income household. The time previously spent by one family member in running the household is no longer available. Working couples must now fit all of the errands and tasks into their weekends or evenings.
2. The importance of leisure time. Even as more people are doing two jobs—one in the workplace and another at home—they are placing more emphasis on the need for recreation.

The reduced amount of time to shop, combined with the desire for more leisure, favors retailers offering convenience and service, both of which are provided by direct marketing.[1]

The Revolution in Communications Technology

The new media systems that are being perfected following breakthroughs in communications technology will not replace current media forms. Rather, they will add to the capability—and therefore to the growth—of direct marketing, which is a communications intensive process. (See Figure 7.1.)

ZIP Codes
Codes assigned by the postal service (to speed mail sorting) that enable marketers to reach specific market segments.

Direct marketing began with the publication of Montgomery Ward's first mail-order catalog in 1872. Since then it has grown in scope and sophistication. The Direct Mail Marketing Association, initially called the Direct Mail/Advertising Association, was founded in 1917.[2]

Several important developments occurred in the 1960s that acted as catalysts for the growth of direct marketing. The postal service introduced **ZIP codes,** which enabled direct marketers to reach specific

[1] Adapted from George S. Wiedemann, *Direct Marketing* (New York: The Direct Mail Marketing Association, Inc., 1981), 1–3.
[2] Kenneth C. Otis II, "Introduction to Direct Marketing," Manual Release: 100.1, April 1979.

Figure   7.1   Direct Marketing versus General Marketing

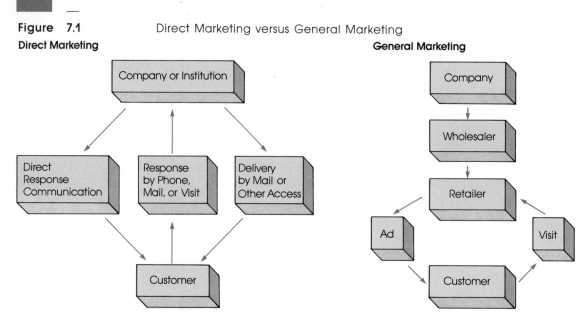

Source: Martin Baier, *Elements of Direct Marketing* (New York: McGraw-Hill Book Company, 1983), 18–19. Reprinted with permission.

groups of people through market segmentation. Computers were used to generate lists based on market segments. Detailed response analyses became feasible with the help of the computer. Credit cards were introduced in the 1960s, and the mailing lists of credit card companies were recognized as a potential source of affluent customers for direct marketing.

The future promises even more capability and convenience. Television capacity will be increased as more channels are made available through cable, satellite, or telephone technology, promising more interactive capability. At the same time, banking is likely to advance beyond the plastic credit card concept to a complete system of electronic money. In the future, one will be able to dial a shoestore, research the stock, investigate the prices, decide to buy, and transfer the money from bank account to store—all by means of a television screen and a touch-button device in the living room.

Tomorrow's shopping mall is apt to be the living room. Because the new media forms will not replace the old, one could just as easily mail in an order, of course. As more large corporations use direct marketing channels of distribution, professional marketing people are finding that the system is not competitive with retail, but complementary to it. (See Figure 7.2.)

Figure 7.2 Direct Marketing as an Aspect of Total Marketing

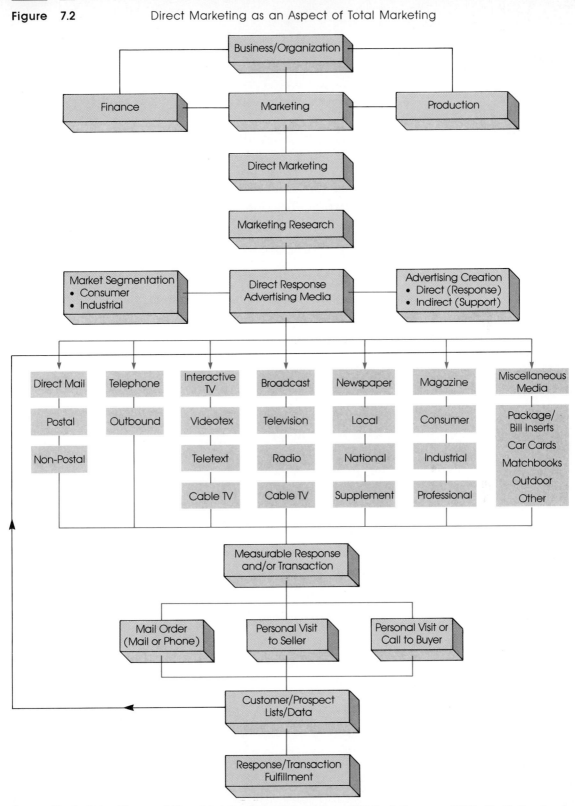

Source: Martin Baier, *Elements of Direct Marketing* (New York: McGraw-Hill Book Company, 1983), 18–19. Reprinted with permission.

**RETAILERS'
CHOICES IN
GOING DIRECT**

Direct marketing reflects the social and economic environment of a society together with the lifestyles of its members. For this reason, retailers need to recognize some basic facts:

1. All adult members in nearly 70 percent of U.S. households today are working. Between 1970 and 1980, women accounted for 60 percent of the growth in the U.S. labor force.
2. Although the number of credit cards issued by retailers exceeds the number of all other types of credit cards combined, retailer-issued cards account for less than 30 percent of credit card dollar volume. Bank cards account for about 35 percent and have, in effect, provided the American public with a universal credit system.
3. Specialty catalogs now account for 75 percent of mail-order volume. Mail order is no longer the exclusive domain of Sears, J. C. Penney, and Spiegel.

The specialty mail order business is not simply where the sales are; it is where the profits are. The return on stockholders' equity on publicly owned mail order business is about 60 percent greater than that of retail.[3]

Recognizing Alternatives

The comfortable old relationships are approximately as shown in Figure 7.3. In the consumer sector, over 90 percent of retailing has been and is being done in person at retail stores. Less than 10 percent is true mail

[3]"Caution: Retailing without Marketing May Be Dangerous to Your Health," *ZIP/Target Marketing* (May 1983): 23.

Figure   7.3   Traditional Retailing

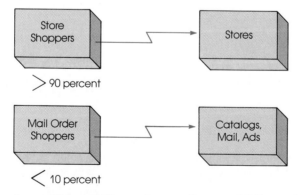

Source: "Adapt to Changes between Buyers and Sellers or Perish," *Direct Marketing*, June 1984, 71–76. Reprinted with permission.

order, meaning that people do not go to a store to shop, but order by mail or phone from catalogs, direct mail offerings, or magazine ads. An even smaller amount of business is done by sales representatives who visit the buyer at home or who have selling parties.

Stores are still at the top of the list. But more and more companies with stores are also issuing catalogs, taking orders over the phone, sending out direct mail packages, and putting inserts in newspapers that contain coupons and telephone numbers—so that people can order without going to the store. If retailers fail to notice these changes that have been taking place between buyers and sellers, they will begin to lose their share of the market.

Understanding the New Approach

What is new about the new retailing approach is not so much in the mail order techniques themselves. Catalogs, direct mail, and coupon ads have been around for some time. But in the past these techniques were used mostly by firms that concentrated on mail order as a method of selling. They were often looked down on by retailers, manufacturers, and even by some consumers.

What we see in Figure 7.4 is that more and more important and respectable retailers are using the techniques today in a consolidated, coordinated manner that has never existed before. Instead of assuming that most people shop in stores and some people shop from catalogs—creating two market segments—these retailers are saying, "Our customers will often want to shop at our stores. Sometimes, it will be more convenient for them to shop by mail or phone or videotex. We must be prepared to capture their business however they want to give it to us."

Changing with the Consumer

At the core of this new development in retailing is a changing consumer and a changing retail marketer. The expanded relationships now possi-

Figure   7.4   The New Retailing

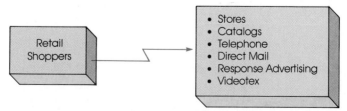

Source: "Adapt to Changes between Buyers and Sellers or Perish," *Direct Marketing*, June 1984, 71–76. Reprinted with permission.

Table   7.1   Shopping/Buying Options Offered to Retail Buyers

Customer or Prospect Situation	Traditional Option Go To Store	Expanded Options (Direct Marketing)					
		Look at . . .			Order by . . .		Both . . .
		Catalogs	Direct Mail	Print, TV	Telephone	Mail	Videotex
Want Demonstration	X						
Want Personal Help	X						
Want Social "Touch"	X						
Need Item *Now*	X						
Avoid Store and Sales Rep Problems		X	X	X	X	X	X
Order Outside Regular Business Hours		X	X	X	X	X	X
Just Looking Around	X	X	X	X	X	X	X

Source: "Adapt to Changes between Buyers and Sellers or Perish," *Direct Marketing,* June 1984, 71–76. Reprinted with permission.

ble between the new consumer and the new retail marketer are shown in Table 7.1. As you can see, depending on the situation, some of these shopper desires can best be filled by going to a store and some can best be filled by using mail order options. Note that the methods of selling evolve from people's needs and not because they say, "I am a store shopper" or "I am a mail order shopper." More and more consumers can regularly be both. Retailers must decide today whether they are going to serve all the changing shopping needs of their customers or only part of those needs.

THE VARIETY OF NONSTORE CHANNELS

Vending Machines
Automatic retailing via coin-operated machines that satisfies customers' need for convenience even at higher prices.

Vending Machines

The invention of vending machines helped retailers to minimize the problem of collecting money and recording transactions for the many impulse items they were adding to their stocks. Initially **vending machines** were placed near cashiers so that customers who needed change could get it. They dispensed small quantities of a single item, such as nuts, candy, or gum that sold for a penny. Enterprising retailers in tourist areas took advantage of developing technology and installed binoculars and pay telescopes. Soon advances in refrigeration made it possible to dispense cold soft drinks in bottles.

As the technology expanded, so did the lines of products sold in vending machines. Retailers installed machines in stores, transportation and entertainment centers, and eventually in hospitals, schools, offices, and factories. Today there are vending machines that sell a variety of products, such as panty hose, yogurt, photocopying, and rides for children.

Vending machines are open around the clock, eliminate the need for sales personnel, and may be located indoors or outdoors. The advantages, however, are offset by some disadvantages. Among the most important are theft, vandalism, high costs, breakdowns of machines, stockouts, and a low-quality image.

The future of vending machines is uncertain and will depend on developing technologies and new retailing techniques. A successful development, however, has been the recent proliferation of entertainment arcades, which are operating entirely on the vending concept.

Direct-to-Home Merchandising

Consultive Selling
In-home selling by specialists whose expertise is valued by the customer.

The **consultive selling** approach puts the consumer in a position of greater power than in many store environments, although the salesperson still controls the direction of the interaction. This kind of selling is used, for example, by decorator consultants who work for home furnishing businesses or department stores.

Party Plan
In-home selling to groups invited by the consumer/ hostess.

The **party plan** is a direct-to-home channel alternative in which a salesperson enlists the aid of one consumer in selling to others within a community. Usually a resident from the community becomes a sales representative or dealer for a party plan retailer. He or she then invites friends to an at-home gathering for refreshments and a presentation or demonstration of the products. Started by Stanley Home Products a half century ago, party plan selling accounts for something under 20 percent of direct sales.[4] Notable examples today are Tupperware, a division of Dart Industries, which uses party plan retailing to sell household plastic goods, and Mary Kay Cosmetics, which sells cosmetics and beauty aids.

Telephone Retailing

The telephone can provide retailers with a cost-effective means of generating incremental revenue and expanding market penetration. The telephone is a unique medium. A summary of its major characteristics will help to understand when to use the telephone and how to position it effectively.

1. *Person-to-person.* Experience indicates that, used correctly, the telephone will generate two and one-half to seven times the response achieved by mail alone.[5]

---

[4] Melvin Morgenstein and Harriet Strongin, *Modern Retailing: Principles and Practices* (New York: Wiley, 1983), 148–149.
[5] Ernan Roman, "Telephone Marketing: The Most Direct Response Medium," Manual Release: 250.1, April 1979.

2. *Totally flexible.* The phone can be used alone, but when used in tandem with other media it increases the overall effectiveness of both media.
3. *Immediately responsive.* Telemarketing, when tightly structured and controlled, permits immediate statistical feedback as well as meaningful market information from customers.
4. *Incremental.* When used in support of other media, the telephone can generate additional orders (for example, the two and one-half to seven multiple after mail). Heavily emphasizing a toll-free 800 number in mail may further improve the mail response. In terms of phone company billings, **800-number retailing** continues to be the hottest area of growth. The immediacy of response—the perfect medium for impulse buyers—is attractive to many retail marketers as a means of order taking, ticket upgrading, and cross-selling.
5. *Cost accountable.* Like mail, the telephone is a totally cost accountable medium, enabling the user to determine cost per name, cost per call, cost per lead, cost per order, and so on.

800-Number Retailing
Telemarketing that allows the potential customer to telephone the retailer toll free,

Convenience is the prime reason consumers prefer to shop by phone. Calls are usually toll free, can be placed any time of the day or night, and can cut delivery time because orders usually are processed immediately. Spurring the growth of teleshopping as well as catalog shopping are harried working women who have better uses for their free time than store shopping.

Catalog Retailing

At a time when most retailers are experiencing growth problems, two trends—the increasing numbers of working women and high energy costs—are contributing to a new source of growth: direct marketing via catalogs. The Direct Marketing Association estimates that consumers have been increasing mail purchases by 10 percent a year for the past decade, twice the growth rate in the rest of retailing.[6] About 6,500 catalogs were published in 1984, up from 4,000 in 1981. Never before have catalog shoppers had so many books and such a variety of mail order merchandise to choose from. Catalog companies are offering everything from exercise equipment and camping gear to gourmet food items and shoes for women with big feet.

Major department stores like Saks, Bloomingdale's, Lord & Taylor, and Neiman-Marcus have established thriving mail order operations. Large companies such as American Can, General Mills, R. J. Reynolds, and Quaker Oats have bought small catalog companies. Hanover House,

---

[6]"Growth Via Catalogs," *Stores* (February 1984): 3.

a subsidiary of Horn & Hardart (once the famous New York Automat cafeteria), issues more than 20 catalogs: Pennsylvania Station, New Hampton, Old Village Shop, and Adam York, to name a few. Disney, IBM, and Xerox are all planning mail order businesses.

Five Distinct Categories

The five distinct categories in catalog retailing are:

1. Direct mail (L. L. Bean, Hanover House, Spiegel)
2. Major chains (Sears, J. C. Penney)
3. Retailers who combine catalog and store business (Brookstone, Gump's)
4. Retailers who separate retail and catalog divisions (Lane Bryant, Talbot, Fredericks of Hollywood)
5. Upscale department stores (Bloomingdale's, Saks Fifth Avenue, Neiman-Marcus).

Catalog versus In-Store Retailing

A major difference between the two types of retailing is that the catalog business is long-term whereas item merchandising in stores is short-term. Another difference is that catalogs create a mood through design, layout, and paper quality, while retail stores rely on lighting, carpeting, music, and other elements to create an ambiance.

In terms of merchandising, the store sells to any customer who walks in, while direct marketers aim at repeat sales to a homogeneous audience. Stores depend on continuous input of new merchandise, while catalogs have periodic selling efforts with a significant percent of repeat items. Finally, catalog retailers analyze their sales per square inch on the page, while stores measure their sales per square foot.

In terms of inventory management, a store can sell comparable items or suggest a switch to another item when something is out of stock. Direct marketers must back order or cancel. In stores, inventory levels are planned in relation to overall sales and turn desired, while in direct marketing, commitments are made to fulfill each item's projected demand.

ELECTRONIC RETAILING

Utilizing home computers and home television, electronic retailing is finally leaving the realm of fantasy and entering the world of fact. More than two decades ago futurists predicted retailing methods that would allow the consumer to purchase all of his or her basic needs without leaving home. To date, only a few companies have ventured into electronic retailing—and with mixed results. By 1990, however, it will easily have matched printed catalogs as we know them.

FROM THE FIELD

New Image for Spiegel

Pursuing a daring strategy that some skeptics say is still loaded with risks, Spiegel, once the perennial Plain Jane in the catalog industry, has dramatically transformed its image. The company that once sold a decidedly homely line of goods on easy-credit terms to low-income shoppers in distant regions, has evolved in the past few years into a purveyor of quality goods to fashion-conscious career women.

By aggressively pursuing this upscale market, offering more select goods, and revamping its catalog, Spiegel has fulfilled the ambition of its chairman to make it a "fine department store in print."[a] In the process, it has propelled itself into the pace-setting position as trend maker in the booming catalog business.

Many loyal customers were forsaking Spiegel for the ubiquitous discount stores, such as K mart and Target, that have sprouted in the past 15 years. And the children of its bread-and-butter customers were growing up, becoming better educated, and moving on to more sophisticated shopping pastures.

The company revamped its personnel, bringing on board buyers and advertising specialists hired from leading department stores and trained in the mail order business.

The catalog started to feature the work of the country's most successful fashion photographers. The book is less cluttered and the presentations are slicker, with greater use of bold and imaginative graphics. The number of specialties—including books featuring seasonal and children's clothes, country themes (The Irish Catalog), Liz Claiborne fashions—has increased to over two dozen a year. The new Spiegel features toll-free telephone numbers for placing orders, and advertisements for the catalog in *Vogue* and other high-fashion magazines. (See Figure 7.5.)

Now [1984] 90 percent of its customers are in its new target group. Its average buyer is a 39-year-old working woman from a 2.8-member household with an annual family income of $38,000. Had the company continued its old ways, executives say, its average buyer today would be from a larger, less-educated, blue-collar household with income of $18,000. Spiegel's goal is to reach $1 billion in sales by 1988 and it has doubled its advertising budget to achieve it.

---

[a]Winston Williams, "The Metamorphosis of Spiegel," *The New York Times,* July 15, 1984, 6.
Source: Adapted from Frank E. James, "Spiegel Employs New Tactics to Fight Its Blue-Collar Past," *The Wall Street Journal,* March 29, 1984, 31.

Figure 7.5   Spiegel's New Catalog Image

Source: "Adapt to Changes between Buyers and Sellers or Perish," *Direct Marketing*, June 1984, 71–76.

Electronic Retailing
Space-age retailing that combines television for presentations with computers for order taking.

The presentation of merchandise in **electronic retailing** is via television.

Live Format. The live presentation is similar to a talk show. The host sits at a desk and demonstrates or displays merchandise, rather than just reading about it. This enables the viewer to see how the product works. Throughout this process a toll-free telephone number flashes across the bottom of the screen.

Computer Format. This presentation resembles a video-game screen with lots of bright graphics and color. Using a "black box," the viewer can call up thousands of catalogued items on the television screen. On the basis of a description and illustration, the viewer may decide to order the item through the black box.

These are the options for home shopping as they currently exist. Looking to the future, we know that consumers today are doing more shopping at home, because the growth of catalog sales continues. We also know their attitude regarding teleshopping. In a study by Dr. Jerry Thomas, "Psychographics of Teleshopping," some 83 percent of the sampled shoppers agreed that telephone shopping would enable them to expand their shopping area. Seventy-nine percent said that having greater telephone shopping capability would increase their purchases of items that did not warrant a trip to the store. Consumers liked the idea of being able to make a purchase decision after leaving the store. Eighty-seven percent said they would take advantage of such an option.[7]

Consumers today are also more aware of the need to learn to work with in-home computers. Children are becoming prime users, because they use computers in schools. Personal computer sales reached an all-time high of 3.5 million units in 1984.

Electronic Media Forms

Electronic media forms such as cable, videotex, teletext, and home information systems all compete for market share. Two of them—videotex and videodisc—will be examined here.

Videotex

Videotex
Subscription service that provides information and services (such as shopping and banking) via telephone or cable television hookups.

Subscribers can obtain information through existing telephone or cable television hookups via **videotex**. This includes text and graphic information such as news, weather, sports, or airline flight times, as well as interactive services such as shopping and banking. Systems are menu-driven,

---

[7] "New Technologies Changing Traditional Ways of Marketing," *Direct Marketing* (March 1984): 84.

listing all of the information categories available. If the consumer selects shopping, a menu lists the various types. The consumer need only identify the kind of merchandise or retail store in which he or she is interested. An array of brands, models, prices and stores is presented. The consumer continues to go deeper into the system until he or she has all the information needed. To order a particular item, the consumer enters a charge card number and the item number.

Videotex has a number of advantages over current mail order procedures. One is that videotex can be updated almost instantly. Cruise ship lines in Miami, for example, offer 50 to 70 percent off available staterooms the day before sailing rather than sail with empty rooms. Videotex can also be used for comparative shopping.

Videodisc

This is a means of storing digital information on a disc that looks much like a phonograph record. Text-type information, photographs, and videotapes, including sound, can all be stored on the same disc. **Videodiscs** will be used primarily in in-store and public-access terminals to assist customers in gaining product information. As much as 30 minutes of full motion video and audio can be stored digitally on discs.

Although production costs are high, they compare favorably with the cost of network-quality television commercials. Videodisc production may also be competitive with conventional print catalogs.

Using a push-button telephone and a cable television hookup, J. C. Penney has entered home shopping with a unique new service that emphasizes a new kind of interaction between the customer and store catalogs. Pictures and textual information are stored on laser videodiscs and transmitted via cable to the shopper's home television screen. Penney has formed a subsidiary, Telaction, for the project, which tested its first 125,000 cable homes in the northwest suburbs of Chicago in June 1987.

Another national video order company, Sky Merchant, Inc., expects to benefit from the effects of a burgeoning industry, according to its president and chief executive officer. "There are 42 million homes wired in now to single video merchandising systems. That is about 50 percent of the current capacity. Each home could have at least two systems, which would be like having access to two shopping centers at the same time. It should stimulate the industry."[8]

Major Markets for Electronic Shopping

The **at-home electronic market** requires a special terminal device that links a consumer's personal computer or videotex terminal to a com-

Videodisc
Sales tool designed for in-store and public-access terminals that conveys product information via text, photographs, and videotapes with sound.

At-Home Electronic Market
Potential customers reached at home through personal computers or videotex terminals linked by the telephone system to a computer center.

---

[8]Christopher Sharp, "TV Home Shopping," *Women's Wear Daily*, March 1987, 7.

**Public-Access
Electronic Market**
Potential customers
reached through
computer terminals
in shopping malls,
hotels, offices, and
other public places.

puter center via the telephone system. The at-home market will probably develop slowly over the next 10 years. Only 8.5 percent of American households now have a computer. The number will rise to more than 40 percent by 1989 and more than 75 percent by the mid-1990s.[9]

The **public-access electronic market** requires placing terminals in airports, hotel lobbies, offices, factories, and shopping malls. Consumers will have access to these terminals as they do to automated teller ma-

[9]"New Video Game: Shopping," *The New York Times,* April 26, 1984.

Figure   7.6

At-Home Shopping: The CompUcard System

Source: Copyright © B. E. White, 1987. All Rights Reserved.

FROM THE FIELD

CompUcard International

CompUcard International continues as the nation's leading electronic merchandising service. Indications are that it is well ahead of its competition.

CompUcard began in 1973 as a telephone-based home shopping service. Subscribers called a toll-free number to inquire about prices for a range of standard products—from television sets to cooking ranges.

When a subscriber phoned, a shopping consultant asked for the model and serial number of the items that the subscriber was interested in, checked the database for the lowest prices, and responded with an all-inclusive quote— a price for the product and shipping costs, as well as an estimated arrival time. With few rivals around, especially in discount shopping, CompUcard managed to attract more than one million subscribers at a fee of $25 per year.

Once CompUcard became successful, the company decided to venture into the computerized home shopping market. With the proliferation of microcomputers in the home, it felt confident that a service allowing home shoppers access to the CompUcard database through their computers could prove extremely successful. (See Figure 7.6.)

In 1979, CompUcard began marketing its Databucks service, which later evolved into its Comp-U-Store. Comp-U-Store provides direct access to the databases by computer terminals, either by calling CompUcard or through Dow Jones, The Source, or Compuserve. In addition to finding information on the manufacturer and model number, the user can browse the database and access items by features and by price. In 1986 the firm expanded this concept into Video Comp-U-Store, which was market tested in cooperation with J. P. Stevens (displaying the Bed and Bath Center). It is an interactive videodisc terminal equipped with either CompUcard's database or the customized database of a manufacturer or retailer. Thus shoppers can enter Hecht's in Washington or Jordan Marsh in Boston, for example, walk up to the product terminal, and call up information on an array of products.

A shopper also can order a product that is directly transmitted to a delivery center for pickup. Stores that display terminals that carry products other than their own will receive a commission for the products sold through the store.

The future for CompUcard is the electronic mall, a concept that will allow microcomputer users to shop from a variety of stores, including gourmet foods prepared by Neiman-Marcus and specialty meats by Omaha Steaks. The company is confident that it can add more and varied products to its mall, making the dream of armchair shopping a reality.

Source: Udayan Gupta, "CompUcard Has Head Start in Electronic Merchandising," *Electronic Media,* March 22, 1984.

chines. They will be able to obtain information about stores and merchandise and, if they choose, to place orders through the terminal.

Indeed, the field has so much potential that it has attracted the interest of three corporate giants—CBS, IBM, and Sears. They have begun a joint venture to develop a commercial videotex service for consumers with personal computers.

Summary

Because of dramatic breakthroughs in communications and technology, more and more retailers are choosing to sell directly to consumers. Because consumers are better educated, have less time for shopping but more for leisure activities, have more disposable income and demand better service, they are responding to these technological advances. They are shopping by mail, telephone, and in their homes through personal consultants or by using home computers hooked up to a variety of databases.

Traditional store retailers are entering the nonstore arena as a supplement to their existing business, but also as a future survival tactic. New kinds of retailers are becoming competitive because of the unlimited possibilities of selling directly to consumers. A new excitement is being generated for both the consumer and the businessperson involved in the retail buying and selling experience.

Questions for Review

1. Why is nonstore retailing growing?
2. Explain what direct marketing is and how it is related to retail marketing.
3. List at least three types of direct retail marketing.
4. Explain the advantages associated with each of the types you listed above.
5. Is direct marketing a new form of retailing? When did it begin?
6. Define electronic retailing.
7. Do you feel that electronic shopping will eventually replace the traditional retail store? Why or why not?

The Market Basket

Evaluating a New Retailing Concept

As John Larkin, president of The Market Basket supermarket chain, walked up and down the aisles of the new Sun City supermarket, one name kept running through his mind—Clarence Saunders, founder of the Piggly Wiggly food chain, and a man referred to as the "father of the supermarket concept." In the 1930s Saunders had visions of an automated grocery store, but he died long before he could realize his dream and before modern technology made it all possible. What if Saunders were alive today? How would he react to The Market Basket's venture into the future, the first completely automated supermarket in the Southeast? Would he be pleased, knowing that he had been prophetic and not entirely wacky (as his contemporaries had so often told him) or would he be more concerned with the problems that always accompany any new concept? In either case, he would most certainly be interested.

The Market Basket stores were in the enviable position of being in the Sunbelt, with several times the growth potential of the rest of the country. They were in the right place, and it seemed the right time, for this new venture. This new store was the result of a great deal of research, 20th-century technology, and advanced management thinking. A supermarket that incorporated all the best for today's consumer in a hurry. Here there would be no 20-minute checkout line, no out-of-stock classifications, and no need to cash checks. If the American consumer truly wanted fast and effective service above all else, as seemed to be the case, then The Market Basket could become the fastest-growing chain in the country, a supermarket whose policy would be to offer only quality packaged items. All depended on the success of this, the pilot store.

Automation was certainly not new. Many retail functions had been automated for years, and as the computer became more sophisticated, so did store operations in terms of its use.

Now, along with changing technology, retailers were faced with a changing customer—a customer who, in addition to one-stop shopping, wanted instant choice, instant checkout, and instant cash. Many people thought of food shopping as a chore, something that had to be done, often without pleasure. Patience frequently wore thin. With more women joining the work force, men were frequently assigned the task that formerly had been a female function, and on any given day at any given peak hour the head count was almost even.

How to satisfy the working family was a universal problem faced by all food retailers. John Larkin, president of The Market Basket, hoped he had the solution in the Sun City store. Fast, efficient, complete in terms of product and service mix, it was Clarence Saunders' dream come to life.

Upon entering the store, each customer pressed a button immediately inside the entrance. This released a punch card that then became the "shopping cart." As Mr. or Ms. Jones proceeded down the aisles, items were selected from the display samples that lined the shelves. This was accomplished by inserting the punch card in the slot immediately under the selection, where the number in stock and sizes available were listed. After each transaction, inventory amounts in the warehouse store were updated. In this way, daily records were kept accurately and merchandise flow was ensured.

Automation would eliminate out-of-stock conditions and sales would increase. Management had discussed the problem of meat and produce being sold only by sample, but had decided that the benefits of the total system outweighed the objections some people might have to not being able to "squeeze the tomatoes," and that the small percentage of lost sales would not be a significant factor in terms of storewide profit. As a matter of fact, profit should increase because damage and pilferage would be kept to a minimum. Moreover, as long as the store continued to sell quality meats, fruits, and vegetables, a firm reputation could be built. Management did decide to do away with special cuts of meat, however, and also to concentrate on specific weights. In this way, meat sales would be at the most desirable level and fruits and vegetables would sell at the same rate as packaged produce in most supermarkets.

Each customer approached a checkout area with only the punch card and a Market Basket credit card in hand. Here, a clerk took both items and recorded each purchase and the customer's credit identification number in one of the terminals that lined the front of the store. This transaction took an average of two minutes, eliminating the usual long, tedious line that was one of the worst problems in all self-service stores—a problem that at peak hour often resulted in disgusted customers. Inventory was checked again, at this time, when each customer's items were charged.

The customer carried out of the store only a perforated slip with a pickup number and a record of purchases. The number was given to an employee at the outside pickup area, where the groceries had already arrived via a conveyor belt from the warehouse built underneath the store. The computer record was kept by the customer.

The Market Basket saved time, space, and manpower, three things that were among the most costly on the expense side of any ledger. With land costs soaring, it was becoming less and less profitable to build supermarkets with the usual space requirements. A self-service supermarket needed at least 18,000 square feet for groceries, household products, meats, and produce, not to mention all the nonfood items now part of the normal market mix. The Market Basket had eliminated this need. With stock stored in the huge warehouse under the one-story building, the store itself, showing only samples, could be much smaller than usual, and more space could be allocated for parking.

Fewer employees were needed to stock the shelves and, with faster checkout, fewer cashiers were needed. Also, at the outside pickup area, a small number of minimum-wage, part-time employees could easily handle the placement of purchases in customers' vehicles. Shopping carts were not needed, thereby eliminating another expense. Therefore, in spite of the huge investment in electronic equipment, the long-range prediction was for profit and success. It looked as if the problems of rising wages and land costs and less shopping time had been solved, not to mention the greatest problem of them all—pilferage. The Market Basket could not fail! Clarence Saunders could rest in peace.

Questions

1. In your opinion, has The Market Basket eliminated the basic problems inherent in self-service? Why or why not?
2. List the advantages and disadvantages of selling grocery items by sample only.
3. Discuss the positive and negative factors in selling only prepackaged produce.
4. Discuss the positive and negative factors in selling only precut meat.
5. Is the concept behind The Market Basket a good one? A practical one? Why or why not?
6. What effect, if any, will automation have on impulse buying at the supermarket? Explain your answer.

Chapter 8

International Retailing

Source: Photographer David Cox ©
1985 Murjani.

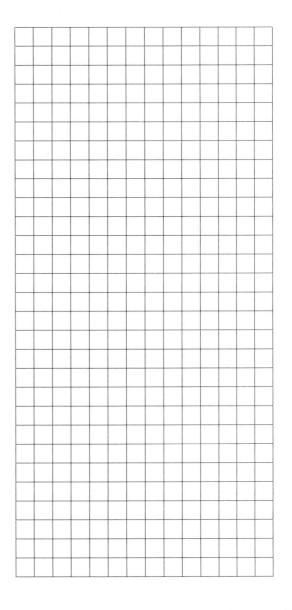

Industry Statement

Carla Fendi
Fendi, Rome

To enter the international market is no easy task; to keep your share of it and to increase it is the real "bravura." The peculiar quality of the fashion market is that it requires continuous renewal of the product, together with the maintenance of a quality and style standard. Therefore in fashion the key words are *creativity, quality,* and in our case, the special Italian touch that is *craftsmanship.*

I feel that the general objective for the future is to supply the demand from an ever-growing number of quality-conscious consumers, particularly young people, who are becoming more and more selective and quality oriented. To encourage their choice and develop their taste, we interpret the trends and moods of an ever-changing way of life through the experience and knowledge of many years in fashion.

Learning Objectives

Upon completing this chapter you should be able to:

1. Understand why it is important for the American retailer to think internationally.
2. Know how conducting business abroad differs from doing so in the United States.
3. Explain why the American retailer is importing.
4. Understand how private labeling, single-country promotions, product development, and licensing are affecting the American retailer.
5. Explain why we should be exporting American products abroad, and the impact that increased exports would have on our economy.
6. Know how to prepare for a career in international business.

In Chapter 7 we pointed out that consumers are becoming better educated, have improved their economic status, and have more leisure time. A large part of this leisure time is being spent on traveling abroad. This, combined with the fact that communication and transportation have made the world more accessible, requires today's retailer to consider all the possibilities of buying and selling abroad.

As the world's nations become increasingly interdependent, a critical need is arising for managers and executives who understand the dynamics and management techniques of foreign business. With home markets quickly becoming saturated because of foreign competition, American retailing is expanding to markets abroad, and other nations are marketing to the American consumer by opening or buying stores here. The result is a demand for global managers with insight into the problems and special issues that characterize international retailing.

AMERICA'S GROWING TASTE FOR FOREIGN GOODS

The Seiko alarm clock (made in Japan) awakens you. You slip from between T&J Vestor sheets (Italy) and into a Liberty silk robe (England). After showering with Crabtree & Evelyn soap (England) and drying your hair with a Norelco dryer (Holland), you pad down to the breakfast room in your Gucci loafers (Italy), switching on the Panasonic stereo (Japan) as you go. The aroma of Kilimanjaro coffee (Tanzania) in the Braun automatic coffee maker (West Germany) fills the room. The brew tastes rich and pure; it was made with bottled Evian water (France) and dripped through a Melitta filter (West Germany). With time for just a quick breakfast, you put orange juice in a Waterford glass (Ireland) on the teak dining table (Indonesia). On a Noritake plate (Japan) you put Dundee marmalade (Scotland), a bit of Black Diamond cheese (Canada), and an English muffin.

That is the way some Americans begin a day of the good life with products made in foreign countries. The exception is the English muffin, which is American, said to have been developed in an unsuccessful attempt to duplicate a British scone. (See "From the Field: Benetton—A Worldwide License.")

FROM THE FIELD

Benetton—A Worldwide License

Little green shops that thrive on fast-selling, trendy sportswear have sprouted across America. They are called Benetton and they are conspicuous not only in their growing numbers but for their simple storefronts, straightforward interiors, and fastidiously arranged shelves of bright and pastel T-shirts, vests, sweaters, and shorts.

Except for the two flagship stores near Rockefeller Center in Manhattan that are company owned, Benettons are owned and operated by licensees. Unlike franchisees, who generally have to pay out a percentage of sales, Benetton licensees pay between $100,000 and $400,000[a] for the customized Italian-made store fixtures and inventory. They can choose among 10 basic store designs. Even though they stock only Benetton-made goods, they have a wide selection in what they order and how they display it.

Despite Benetton's forays into far-flung exotic markets, the United States remains the focus for the company's growth. By 1989, the company hopes to have 1,000 shops under the Benetton name.

One of Benetton's many innovations was to produce garments in undyed fibers, leaving coloration as close to the selling time as possible. After all, who can predict what the hot colors of the season are until consumers start buying and wearing?

Benetton was also one of the first Italian designers to make extensive use of computer-aided design, another time-saving measure that cuts down on the guesswork about company styles. In 1986, the company opened a plant in Rocky Mount, N.C., which is expected

(continued)

Benetton—A Worldwide License (*continued*)

to ease problems with slow distribution in the U.S. markets.

Within retailing circles, Benetton's most important contribution is the degree to which it defines "specialty store." Instead of aspiring to be all things to all people, Benetton offers a limited selection targeted at a young, fashion-conscious clientele. Benetton stores sell *only* Benetton merchandise; Benetton merchandise can be purchased *only* at Benetton stores.

The company has started several types of stores with different lines: the children's stores, 012; the slightly fancier Sisley stores; the Benetton Uomo stores, which will sell a more rugged line of men's clothes; and shoe boutiques. Plans are under way to build bigger stores combining types of Benetton boutiques.

The product line has also moved beyond clothing. It has added a line of watches, Benetton-designed and Bulova-manufactured. There are Benetton sunglasses and Benetton teddy bears. The company unveiled a line of fragrances and cosmetics in the summer of 1987 called Colors de Benetton.

The company estimates that in 1986 $2.5 billion in Benetton items were sold at the retail level, although the figures are rough because of the loose licensee system. The Benetton Group itself reported net profits of $85 million on sales of $830 million.[a]

To keep the momentum going, Benetton executives will continue to push beyond apparel into related products. They are eyeing huge untapped markets such as the Soviet Union and China. They are even branching out into financial services, such as leasing and insurance, in part through a joint venture with another big Italian fashion producer, Gruppo GFT. This venture could also help the two firms exchange goods and know-how in developing countries. Since 1982, GFT has been doing turnkey construction of clothing factories in developing nations, including Nigeria, Iraq, and China. In addition to its own labels, GFT produces various collections under the designer labels of Valentino, Giorgio Armani, Emanuel Ungaro, Claude Montana, Andrew Fezza, and Chiari Boni.[b]

Benetton was founded in 1965 as a typical small Italian family enterprise, consisting of Luciano Benetton (see Figure 8.1), his sister Giuliana, and their younger brothers Gilberto and Carlo. The Benetton Group is now a complex of manufacturing companies. (Benetton controls, among others, Fiorucci, Inc., the Scottish cashmere company Hogg of Hawick, and the Italian shoe company Calzaturificio di Varese.)[c] It is now the world's largest manufacturer of knitwear and the world's largest consumer of virgin wool. A new Benetton license opens, somewhere, on the average of twice a day.

---

[a] Barbara Demick, "Benetton Is a Huge Success at Clothes Mass Marketing," *The Philadelphia Inquirer,* March 20, 1987, C11.
[b] Nadine Frey, "Benetton and GFT Form Financial Service Firm," *Women's Wear Daily,* March 9, 1987, 7.
[c] Andrea Lee, "Being Everywhere," *The New Yorker Magazine,* November 10, 1986, 53.

Figure   8.1   Luciano Benetton

The Price Paid by U.S. Business

Protectionism
Government policy
of using high
tariffs or other
import restrictions
to enable domestic
products to
compete with
imported ones.

Foreigners are selling more to Americans than U.S. companies are marketing abroad. Economists and business executives warn that the huge
gap between U.S. imports and exports, perhaps $150 billion, will not be
closed easily or soon.[1] The pressures to beat back the wave of foreign-
made products are probably the worst they have been since 1970 or
before.[2] If American businesses continue to seek **protectionism** instead
of finding ways to export their goods abroad, their products will not find
a welcome in foreign countries, which will likely retaliate by imposing
embargoes on U.S. goods. (See Figure 8.2.)

The Newest Foreign Invasion: Marketing Skill

Embargo
Government order
prohibiting the
handling of certain
goods.

Foreign producers have finally learned how to sell in the vast U.S. mar-
ket. Mostly they were taught by American retailers such as Sears and
Bloomingdale's. Sears' top-of-the-line bicycle, in fact, is now made in
China.[3]

[1] Craig Stock, "Trade Deficit: Worst May Well Be Over," *The Philadelphia Inquirer*, December 1, 1985, C1.
[2] Steven Greenhouse, "The Making of Fortress America," *The New York Times*, August 5,
1984, sec. 3, 1.
[3] "Is It an Import or Not? Only Maker Knows for Sure," *U.S. News & World Report*, October
11, 1982, 80.

Foreign companies are also becoming adept at American-style public relations using sports promotions for multimedia exposure. For example, Stolichnaya, made in the Soviet Union, was the official vodka of the 1982 U.S. Open tennis championships. Another entry on the sports scene is Brother Industries, maker of the official typewriter of the 1984 Olympics in Los Angeles. Its headquarters is in Nagoya, Japan.

Figure   8.2

American Designer Boutique in Florence, Italy

Ralph Lauren has reversed the normal trend of foreign designers seeking markets in the United States.

Source: Photo by John Stapleton.

Another factor contributing to the increase in imports is more efficient, less expensive worldwide transport. One flight by a specially outfitted cargo plane out of Taiwan can bring a year's supply of one brand of watches to the United States. In fact, four out of five watches sold in America are made abroad.[4]

Brand Names versus Product Origin

Actually, Americans would find it difficult to live on homegrown staples alone, even if they wanted to. The foreign connection of products in U.S. showrooms is often impossible to see. (See Figure 8.3.) Haagen-Däzs ice

[4] Ibid.

Figure   8.3   Coca-Cola Sportswear Made in the Far East

Source: Photographer David Cox © 1985 Murjani.

cream and Yoplait yogurt are American products; so are Amalfi shoes, Löwenbräu beer, and Pierre Cardin men's formalwear. Despite its oriental-sounding name, Atari, the video game giant, is an American institution, and Yves St. Laurent perfume comes from America's Squibb Corporation. Only one percent of the cosmetics sold in the United States is imported, despite their exotic names.[5] (See Table 8.1.)

On the other side of the coin, Tic Tac mints are made in Italy and Velamints in West Germany; Bridgestone tires and Pioneer electronic components are from Japan; Commodore computers are made in Asia; and most Timex watches are put together in Taiwan, as are Durango jeans. About 28 percent of the autos made by the Chrysler Corporation have engines made in Japan or Western Europe. Two small Chrysler cars are entirely Japanese made, as is Chevrolet's Luv truck. (See Table 8.2.)

Finding made-in-America versions of some items is virtually impossible. Nearly all hair dryers, radios, tape and videocassette players, single-lens reflex cameras, stuffed toys, Christmas ornaments, and balls for all sorts of U.S. sports are made abroad. Sixty percent of the athletic shoes worn in America are imports; for example, U.S. Keds are made in Korea. Other top brands, however, such as Nike and New Balance, are U.S. products.

Three out of five motorcycles and bicycles sold in the United States are imports. There are only three major motorcycle manufacturers left in

---

[5] Ibid.

Table   8.1   American Products with Foreign Names

Product	U.S. Company
Amalfi shoes	U.S. Shoe Corporation
Café au Chocolat coffee	R. C. Bigelow, Inc.
Smirnoff vodka, Dijon mustard	Heublein, Inc.
L'Hermitage cutlery	Towle Manufacturing Company
Cordoba automobile	Chrysler Corporation
Löwenbräu beer	Philip Morris, Inc.
Hai Karate after-shave	Pfizer, Inc.
L'Air du Temps perfume	American Cyanamid Company
Pierre Cardin men's formalwear	West Mill Clothes
Yves St. Laurent fragrances	Squibb Corporation
Fabergé cosmetics	Fabergé, Inc.
Rosarita Mexican foods, La Choy Chinese foods	Beatrice Foods Company
Tostito tortilla chips	PepsiCo, Inc.

Source: Copyright, 1982, *U.S. NEWS & WORLD REPORT.* Reprinted with permission from issue of October 11, 1982, p. 81.

Table   8.2   American Companies with Foreign Owners

U.S. Firm	Foreign Owner
Shell Oil	Royal Dutch/Shell Group (Netherlands and Britain)
Standard Oil of Ohio	British Petroleum (Britain)
Great Atlantic & Pacific Tea Company	Tengelmann Group (West Germany)
Marshall Field & Company	B.A.T. Industries (Britain)
Miles Laboratories, Inc.	Bayer AG (West Germany)
Lever Brothers Company	Unilever NV (Netherlands)
Crocker National Bank	Midland Bank, Ltd. (Britain)
Nestlé; Libby, McNeill & Libby; Stouffer; Beech-Nut	Nestlé SA (Switzerland)
Marine Midland Banks	Hongkong & Shanghai Banking Corp. (Hong Kong)
Howard Johnson Company	Imperial Group (Britain)
CertainTeed Corporation	Saint-Gobain-Pont-à-Mousson (France)
Keebler Company	United Biscuits, Ltd. (Britain)

Source: Copyright, 1982, *U.S. NEWS & WORLD REPORT.* Reprinted with permission from issue of October 11, 1982, p. 81.

this country, and two are subsidiaries of Japanese firms. Half of the china and three-fourths of good-quality earthenware are made abroad, as are three out of four pieces of stainless steel flatware. In recent years a dozen appliance manufacturers from Japan, Korea, and Italy have set up plants in this country to produce microwave ovens and small refrigerators.

To complicate matters, Americans cannot be sure of the country in which the profit from their spending will end up. Walk into an A&P and buy a package of Keebler crackers. On the surface, everything looks as American as grits and apple pie. But the supermarket chain is owned by a German company and Keebler by a British biscuit maker. Consume a frozen dinner from Stouffer, some cocoa from Nestlé, and some coffee from Beech-Nut and you are feeding the coffers of a Swiss company. Deal with Marine Midland Banks and the trail leads to the owner, Hongkong & Shanghai Banking Corporation. Buy a Bantam Book and contribute to the German economy. Flick your American-made Bic lighter and it adds to the bottom line of Société Bic in France.

FOREIGN-OWNED RETAILERS IN THE UNITED STATES

When you shop at Saks Fifth Avenue, Howard Johnson's, or Conran's (all British), at Ohrbach's (Dutch), or at Benetton (Italy), you become a customer of a foreign-owned retailer. By ordering an Anne Klein ensem-

ble from the Spiegel catalog, you are selecting a designer item manufactured by Japan's Takihyo, an apparel firm, and published in a West German retailer-owned (Otto-Vers G.m.b.H.) catalog.

FOREIGN RETAILERS IN THEIR OWN MARKET

Some of the most innovative concepts in retailing have come from outside the United States, particularly Europe, Canada, and Japan. This has
occurred because of the explosion of shopping space abroad. Retail
space in Europe alone increased more than 50 percent between 1962
and 1980.[6] On the average, in 1980 each person had eight times as much
shopping space to choose from as in 1952. Research at the Paris-based
International Association of Department Stores reveals that "the situation is greatly worsened when, as is happening in many countries, consumers spend less of their disposable income in the stores and more in
such leisure pursuits as vacations, cars, and other attributes of the good
life. In the United Kingdom, the proportion of disposable income spent
in stores fell from 50 percent in 1961 to 45 percent in 1971 and 41
percent in 1982."[7]

The plethora of large-scale retail facilities is being decreased by such
means as disposal of marginal stores or, failing that, alternative use of
unprofitable space: on-site parking, hotels and even nightclubs built into
stores, new forms of leased quarters, and elimination of central warehousing and dispersal of this function through stores.

Some examples of how stores in England, France, and Japan are cop-
ing with changes in consumer demand will round out this discussion of
foreign retailers in their own market.

Debenhams PLC

The British Debenhams Group is one of the largest retail groups in the
United Kingdom with 67 department stores throughout the country.[8]
More than 200 years old, it has been in the vanguard of changing traditional department store organization. Sixteen trading companies within
the organization each have their own selling staff and balance sheet. For
example, the toy department is not a toy department anymore—it is a
toy "company," paying rent to the managing director of store operations
for the floor space it occupies. Its managers are expected to generate
enough volume to pay that rent and to make a profit as well.

The experience has been positive in the sense that it forced Debenhams to identify its best management talent. When looking at this new

---

[6] Samuel Feinberg, "From Where I Sit," *Women's Wear Daily*, July 27, 1984, 20.
[7] Ibid.
[8] Camille Vickers, "International Retailing," *World* (April 1983): 32.

structure the group considered, "Is the person who is currently the head buyer in such-and-such a department the right managing director for that particular job?" Almost inevitably he or she was not. But hidden away in the recesses of its central management group, Debenhams found people of superior quality with the right entrepreneurial instincts to make the concept work.

Louis Vuitton

Louis Vuitton began handcrafting elegant luggage and handbags in a small Paris workshop in 1854. Long a favorite among the rich and prominent, Vuitton has gained a wider market over the past decade; today the *LV* monogram is a familiar sight on major shopping streets around the world.

In the early 1970s, Vuitton made a decision to expand. The demand for luxury goods was growing, particularly in the United States and Japan. More people had money and were willing to spend it on designer-name merchandise. Soft luggage, which the firm had been making since the turn of the century, was becoming popular again. The timing was right.

Vuitton reorganized the management of the company; began opening shops in the major cities of Europe, America, and the Far East; and increased its marketing efforts. It now has more than 60 stores around the world.

In fashion-conscious Japan, owning Vuitton luggage and handbags is a virtual mania. In late 1981, the company took over distribution from its wholesalers and set up 20 of its own leased departments in large Japanese stores.[9] The company's goal is to persuade all of the more than 100 U.S. stores selling Vuitton luggage to permit installation of replicas of its lavish Paris boutique inside their stores, as has been done in Japan. Vuitton's first such shop at San Francisco's I. Magnin has nearly doubled sales, and outlets in New York and Chicago are also booming.[10]

Japanese Department Stores

An orchestrated V.I.P. treatment for arriving customers is but one of many things that make the remarkable Japanese department stores very different from their Western counterparts. At New York's Saks Fifth Avenue, Dallas's Neiman-Marcus, or London's venerable Harrods, shoppers naturally expect to find a vast array of high-quality merchandise, departments, and services from the exotic to the simple. But how many

---

[9] "Vuitton: A U.S. Drive for Even More Status," *Business Week,* July 16, 1984, 41.
[10] Ibid.

would expect to find a dental clinic (at Tokyo's Odakyu), a rooftop beer garden (at Hankyu), a live dramatic theater (at Mitsukoshi), a fully equipped gymnasium (at Seibu), a golf driving range (at Keio), a wedding chapel (at Tokyu), an art gallery (at Matsuya), a school for ceramics (at Matsuzakaya), or a grilled eel restaurant (at Takashimaya)?

Depātos
Japanese department stores, which offer a mind-boggling array of goods and services.

Japanese department stores, or **depātos,** as they are conveniently called in westernized Japanese, boast a circus-like variety of goods and services seldom found in Western stores: basements filled with fancy foods and bakery items; pet shops; special soda fountains and restaurants; floors devoted to exotic silks, kimonos, and obi materials; beauty salons; travel and concert ticket agencies; and florists.

A customer can order a car, buy a prefabricated house, take a course in flower arranging or tea ceremony, learn all about kimonos, arrange special services in connection with the birth of a child, order his or her own Shinto tombstone, and even arrange a loan. "The accent is on service and quality, not only at Takashimaya but all major Japanese department stores," says Ichiko Ishihara, a Takashimaya managing director and the first female executive to sit on the board of a major depāto in Japan.[11] "It can be traced back to feudal times when the kimono shops had to be very careful about the quality of materials and services they provided the nobility and the imperial family. Their name and image were their only assets. It is still the same today."

Japanese depātos operate with a philosophy that in effect says the customer is not only always right—he is king. There are few places in the world where a customer will be treated with as much respect and attention.

THE U.S. RETAILER ABROAD

Why Retailers Import

With the cost of U.S. labor skyrocketing and the persistent poor quality of domestically manufactured goods, America has become noncompetitive in many types of consumer products. Through importing, U.S. retailers are able to bring in well-designed goods that their competitors will not have. They are also able to achieve a higher markup because the imported goods are exclusive and cost less than those produced domestically. Sears, Roebuck, the nation's largest retail company, buys about 11 percent of all its merchandise from foreign suppliers. At K mart, the second largest retailer, about 10,000 of the 80,000 items in all stores are made outside the country. J. C. Penney, the third largest chain, buys one fourth of its merchandise abroad.[12]

---

[11] "International Retailing," *World,* April 1983, 42.
[12] Jennifer Lin, "Retailers Take Up the Fight against Protectionism," *The Philadelphia Inquirer,* December 1, 1985, 1F.

An increasing percentage of the apparel business is imported clothing. In 1979, 22 percent of all clothes purchased by U.S. consumers were made overseas, according to the U.S. Department of Commerce. By 1984, 33 percent of the clothes came from abroad. (See Figure 8.4.)

Importing can be risky because of changes in international financing and politics. If the U.S. dollar is high against foreign currencies, it is

Figure   8.4A   U.S. Clothing Imports as a Percentage of Consumption, 1979—1984

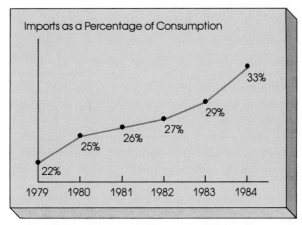

Source: Adapted from Jennifer Lin, "Retailers Take Up Fight against Protectionism," *The Philadelphia Inquirer,* December 1, 1985, F1. Data from the U.S. Department of Commerce.

Figure   8.4B   Five Sources Totaling More Than Half of All U.S. Clothing Imports

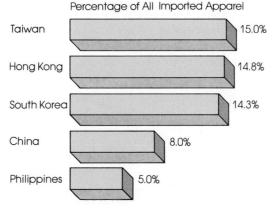

Source: Adapted from Jennifer Lin, "Retailers Take Up Fight against Protectionism," *The Philadelphia Inquirer,* December 1, 1985, F1. Data from the U.S. Department of Commerce.

cheaper for us to import than to buy domestically. If the United States is having a presidential election year, threats from organized trade unions often result in protective barriers being thrown up against certain product classifications, such as textiles. In order to get the union vote, the candidate will impose quotas and high tariffs on foreign goods to appease voters. Thus, retailers must be in constant search of new markets abroad that can produce quality goods at a low price and where the foreign manufacturers have ample quotas so that the retailers can receive their merchandise to offer for sale to the American consumer.

Private Labeling

Because so many stores are selling the same merchandise to the same customers in the same market, the trend in **private labeling** has affected today's merchandising. Private labeling occurs when a store contracts a manufacturer to produce an item that is exclusive to that store. The item will bear the store's name rather than the name of the manufacturer or a designer.

This is a very successful tactic when the store name carries an image of quality, fashion, or value. For instance, private label goods now account for 15 to 20 percent of ready-to-wear sales at Bloomingdale's in the moderate to upper through designer categories. At Saks Fifth Avenue, which sells its own brand of hand-knit sweaters for up to $600, private label goods reportedly are approaching 20 percent of the store's ready-to-wear volume. Two reasons for adopting private labels are that designer labels are too widely distributed and some designers are opening their own boutiques.

Bergdorf Goodman, which considers itself a fashion specialist, sees exclusivity as crucial. An increase in **designer licensing** activity has broadened the distribution of designer clothes. One solution is to use private labels, along with exclusive lines and confined items. The company considers the name Bergdorf Goodman to be as important in fashion as any other name. It has also introduced a color makeup collection and fragrance. Private labels combined with exclusives and confined items account for 40 percent of Bergdorf's apparel sales.[13] (See Figure 8.5.)

Product Development

The president of Business Careers, an executive search firm, reports that more and more manufacturing firms, as well as retailers, are looking for **product developers**—people with strong Far East or other overseas background or with 807 experience. (Congressional Bill 807 is a federal

---

Private Labeling
A way of differentiating and enhancing a store's image by offering exclusive items bearing the store's name.

Designer Licensing
Designer contracts a manufacturer to produce specific items for distribution to selected retail stores.

Product Developers
Buyers with expanded duties that involve generating ideas and specifications for new or replacement products and arranging for their manufacture.

---

[13] Steve Ginsberg and Pete Born, "Private Label Sharpens Its Fashion Image," *Women's Wear Daily*, May 15, 1984, 1.

statute under the Caribbean Basin Initiative permitting U.S. companies to enter such under-developed markets as Mexico, Haiti, and Jamaica.)

The product developer provides a set of specifications, and the foreign manufacturer produces a prototype for the store. After approval, the item is produced for that store alone. Product developers have to be much more knowledgeable than traditional buyers. They must be informed as to composition of fiber content and other materials, and they must be able to assess the production quality and capability of the factories with which they are dealing. They should also be able to speak the language of the country in which they are doing business. In many instances, they may have the assistance of a **resident buyer,** who may furnish a translating service. More will be said on the role of the resident buying office in Chapter 13.

The Far East is one of the prime sources for product development, especially Hong Kong, Taiwan, China, Sri Lanka, Singapore, Thailand, and South Korea. (See Figure 8.6.) Italy continues to be the most popu-

Resident Buyers
Individuals or members of a service firm employed by a group of noncompeting retailers to provide market coverage of the world's major markets.

Figure   8.5   Fendi, an Italian Name in American Stores

In Rome, Federica Fendi (left) instructs participants in a Drexel University International Marketing Seminar on the cutting and sewing of a fur coat. Fendi maintains both a fur salon and a leather-goods boutique at Bergdorf-Goodman, Bloomingdale's, and other upscale stores across the United States.

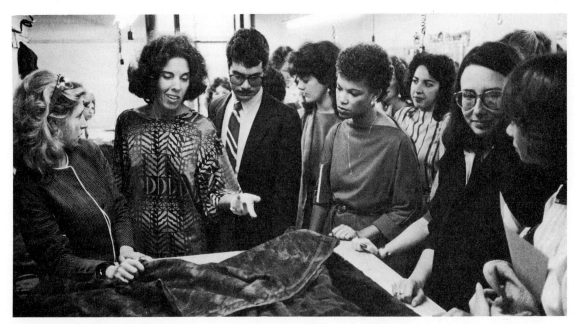

Source: Photo by John Stapleton.

lar source in Europe, and others are also being developed in France and Spain. The countries of South America and the Caribbean offer great potential for the future.

Return of the Single-Country Promotion

Single-Country Promotions
International merchandise promotions (in-store or catalog) featuring a single country's products and culture.

There appears to be a resurgence of **single-country promotions,** in which stores feature promotions based on one country, its goods, and culture. Such "happenings," so popular in the 1950s through the early 1970s, tapered off because the stores had run out of countries. Only a few nations can offer the wide assortment of merchandise needed for a truly interesting theme throughout an entire store. Italy is one country that can. As a result, Italy has been a theme at Bloomingdale's, John Wanamaker, Marshall Field's, Famous Barr, and J. C. Penney. The Penney campaign generated over $100 million in retail sales and was the largest single-country promotion ever held.[14] Japan and England are other countries rich in promotional possibilities. (See Figure 8.7.)

Some would credit Neiman-Marcus with being the catalyst for the renewed interest in international merchandise promotions; others would

---

[14]David Moin, "Penney's: Big Chain Reaction for Italy," *Women's Wear Daily*, April 2, 1984, 1.

Figure   8.6

Young American Buyers with Silver Craftsmen in Chiang-Mai, Thailand

Source: Photo by John Stapleton.

Figure   8.7   Single-Country Promotion

Source: Courtesy of Marshall Field's.

credit Bloomingdale's, whose spectacular promotions began in 1978 with an event celebrating India, followed by Israel, China, Ireland, Portugal, Great Britain, Japan, and Italy.

The first international promotion by Spiegel was a 40-page, full-color specialty catalog devoted to Ireland. Called *Ireland, the Magic Is Here,* the catalog featured Irish-made women's and men's apparel and home goods. Its target was to sell more than $1 million in volume. Home merchandise, such as Galway and Calvin crystal, woven tapestries, Dresden figurines, and linen tablecloths, comprised about 40 percent of the total volume; women's apparel totaled another 40 percent; and men's the remaining 20 percent.[15]

Licensing

A major development in the young trend toward big, exclusive tie-ins between designers and stores took place when The Limited unveiled its first Album by Kenzo collection. Under an agreement with the Japanese designer Kenzo, The Limited has responsibility for manufacturing the collection while the designer has approval of all production. All manufacturing is done by contractors in Europe, Hong Kong, and the United States, but may be produced by The Limited's own factories in the future. The Kenzo agreement is for the production of a full sportswear and accessories collection that The Limited has introduced in all of its more than 550 stores. The chain offers the designer total control of distribution and display as well as access to the entire U.S. market.

Why Retailers Export

Converting Business
Turning imported raw materials into finished goods before resale, instead of simply selling the raw materials, to increase the importer's profit margin.

For the present and future U.S. economy, it is vital that more American businesses export domestically made products. Because our balance of payments has been recording enormous deficits in recent years (we are importing three times more than we are exporting), U.S. firms must actively export to ensure their survival. The problem is that American firms are not internationally minded; for example, to sell in the Orient, you must have stock and samples over there before customers will buy.

"Americans are not export oriented. When the dollar is weak, they ship to English-speaking countries. The Japanese, on the other hand, have had to survive on exports," says Jack Shamash, president of the largest importer of Chinese ramie and silk fabrics in the United States. He has built his multimillion-dollar international importing, exporting, and **converting business** on his faith in one-world trade. He noted that few U.S. companies truly comprehend the working of international credit or what is required to ship goods quickly and efficiently from one

[15] Mark Sullivan, "The Limited: $44M in Kenzo Is Estimated," *Women's Wear Daily,* July 13, 1984, 1.

country to another.[16] China is the country in which he concentrates his trading efforts, and he still sees disparity in approaches: While the Chinese focus on long-term plans, Americans stress immediate results and the bottom line. When asked what will help the United States work more closely with China, Shamash replied, "Patience."

K mart

To take advantage of the growing international market, in 1983 K mart set up a subsidiary, K mart Trading Services, Inc., to sell U.S. goods—especially its own products—to retailers and wholesalers abroad. In addition, the subsidiary acts as a broker for U.S. companies that are looking for foreign products to expand their line or for foreign-made components that could be assembled in the United States. K mart officials hope

[16] Eileen B. Brill, "Shamash: Shuttling Textiles Around the World," *Women's Wear Daily*, June 25, 1984, 6.

FROM THE FIELD

Esprit de Corp

In 1969, Doug and Susie Tompkins pulled an amalgam of six divisions into the Esprit de Corp identification—borrowing the French word for "spirit" and its implied camaraderie—and calculated an image with mathematical precision. Total sales in 1984 were $613 million, with $335 million coming from their international division. International markets for Esprit clothing include Canada, Australia, the Benelux countries, the Far East, and Europe. West Germany alone did $100 million, making it by far the largest Esprit market after the United States.

Esprit designs a broad-based collection with a total classification approach. In addition to selling its collection to retailers, Esprit is opening its own retail stores. In 1983 it opened a store in Hong Kong. This was a bold experiment in retailing, commissioned by Esprit to the Hamano Institute of Japan and created by Shiro Kuramata, one of Japan's top designers. Susie Tompkins calls the selling technique "kind-to-kind;" that is, salespeople who wear the merchandise and enjoy the concept sell to the shoppers. "I love to see the boys and girls there shopping together," Susie says. "Men and women do a lot more things together today, not just because of the whole androgynous thing. I'd like to see shopping as a more social activity."

Source: Adapted from Jane F. Lane, "Esprit: Quietly Building $825M Empire," *Women's Wear Daily*, August 17, 1984, 1.

that the subsidiary will account for 10 percent of the company's revenue by 1988.

Fast Food Frenzy Overseas

Of the 500 or so new McDonald's restaurants built every year, about half are now going up outside the United States.[17] In 1984, the company had 1,527 units overseas that contributed 22 percent of revenues and 15 percent of pretax income.

McDonald's major strength in American suburbs comes from having the best locations. The company must continue to find good sites if it wants to keep expanding, and that is becoming increasingly more difficult. Moving overseas is the answer.

Miami-based Burger King, with only 69 outlets in Europe, primarily in Germany, was expected to expand that number by 1987.[18] Germany and England are due for 50 additional stores each, and an increased presence is also slated for Switzerland and Spain. Suddenly the market for U.S. fast food in Italy is opening up. While McDonald's and others have been expanding across Europe, they had bypassed Italy because of its tradition of inexpensive pizza, tough labor laws, red tape, and women who were content to stay home and cook for their families. Now the Italian market is changing, and U.S. fast food retailers are rushing in.

Wendy's International has stolen a march on its arch rivals, McDonald's and Burger King, by being the first U.S. hamburger chain to enter the Italian market. The Italian division of Dancer Fitzgerald Sample advertising agency created a U.S.-style newspaper ad featuring the stars and stripes and the legend "Eat just like they eat in Hollywood, on Fifth Avenue, in the Grand Canyon."

PREPARING FOR A CAREER IN INTERNATIONAL MARKETING

As a student, you can prepare yourself now for entry into the international business arena.

1. *Learn a foreign language.* Search out a teacher who is a native of the country whose language you are studying so that the accents and inflections will be correct. The language capabilities important today in the markets where you will be buying or selling are Chinese, Japanese, Russian, and Spanish. The last will serve you in South America.
2. *Study abroad.* Many colleges and universities offer diverse programs in which you can go abroad for as little as two weeks or as long as

---

[17] "Where's the Growth?" *Forbes,* April 23, 1984, 80.
[18] Scott Hume and Christy Marshall, "Burger King Arrives Abroad Just in Time," *Advertising Age,* November 28, 1983, 60.

a year. (See Figure 8.8.) The best study path would be to major in international business or marketing.

3. *Travel.* There are many inexpensive ways to travel outside the United States today, especially for students. Instead of spending your vacations at the sea or mountains, spend the same amount of money and learn another culture. When traveling, however, do not stay on the tourist routes. Look at the shops, supermarkets, advertisements, newspapers, television, and malls. Observe how people eat, spend their evenings and weekends, and so on. Compare prices and quality with U.S. merchandise. Notice how people are dressed. Speak with them about politics, art, music, and business so that you will learn their mentality and what they think of Americans. And before you go, read!

4. *Read.* American students tend to know little about their own geography and history and often find that when they travel abroad, foreigners know much more about the United States than

Figure 8.8   An American Student with a Craftsman in Volterra, Italy

Alabaster and marble products are featured in the giftware area of major American stores.

Source: Photo by John Stapleton.

they do. Become knowledgeable about not only your own country but the one in which you will be traveling. Read the international pages of the Sunday business section in *The New York Times* and the international section of *Business Week* and *The Wall Street Journal.*

5. *Watch television.* Certainly watch television—but not the serials and comedies. Tune into "Washington Week in Review" on your PBS station for a weekly half-hour roundup of world news. For a bit more depth on the issues, try the programs of David Brinkley, "Nightline," and the "McNeil-Lehrer Report."

Ministry of Trade
Foreign government office able to assist local businesses in their importing and exporting activities.

In preparing to go abroad, write for the free literature available from your destination country's **ministry of trade** office (usually located in New York). Another source is the U.S. Department of Commerce, which employs a staff of specialists in Washington for each foreign country. You can also try the larger international banks like Citibank, Mellon, Chase, and Barclays. They all prepare economic/marketing pamphlets for each of the foreign countries with which they do business.

Summary

It is increasingly important for the American retailer to think internationally. To satisfy American consumers' growing appetite for foreign goods, retailers are able to bring in specially designed goods that the competition will not have, at a higher markup than goods produced domestically. Import marketing methods currently employed by American retailers include private labeling, licensing, product development, and single-country promotions. At the same time, exporting American products abroad is one solution to the ever-growing deficit in the U.S. balance of payments. It is not too soon for the student to begin a five-point program in preparation for entry into the international business arena.

Questions for Review

1. Why is it important for the American retailer to think internationally?
2. Name at least five retail businesses that, although on the surface would appear to be American, are actually foreign owned. With each of the above, list the country of the owners.
3. Name at least five American products with foreign names, and list the U.S. company that produces each item.
4. Why do U.S. retailers import foreign goods?

5. List at least five American retailing chains that have expanded to foreign locations.
6. Why should American products be exported abroad? What impact does it have on our economy?
7. List at least four steps that a student can take to prepare for a career in the world of international retailing.

CASE STUDY | Galerie Boisvert

Differences in Foreign Purchasing

Store managers from all the stores in the Galerie Boisvert chain were gathered in the company's Paris offices to view the new line of sportswear that had been purchased by the buyers in the main office for distribution throughout the 157 stores in the chain.

Each season after the merchandise classifications had been selected, the managers gathered for a two-day meeting to see what they would now be responsible for selling. Although they had very little to say about buying, they did have the complete responsibility for sales. This was not an easy situation because customer taste varied from province to province but merchandise, purchased in bulk, did not. Often, items that sold well in the north of France became markdowns along the southern coast, and items that sold well in the cities did not sell in the more rural areas. Rarely, though, was there any one group that did not sell at all.

In recent years personnel in each store had been asked for ideas before selections were made; therefore, in general, the manager's sales job was becoming somewhat easier.

Galerie Boisvert had been founded in 1921 by the late Pierre Boisvert. His idea was to serve the customer in the provinces with quality merchandise that could be sold at somewhat lower prices than similar items found in the independent shops in each town.

Over the years he had been most successful. World War II brought a halt to expansion and almost to the business, but he managed to survive the war years and after the war he prospered with a policy of buying for all the stores through one central office. This allowed him to purchase in bulk. Bulk purchasing meant quantity discounts and retail prices that brought customers flocking to the new Galerie Boisvert store in each town.

The average French customer had always been fashion conscious and yet was very frugal. It was to these two needs that the Galerie Boisvert chain now catered. As business increased, more buyers were hired to work in the Paris office. Their function was to visit the various manufacturers throughout Europe, first viewing and then purchasing a variety of merchandise for distribution to the stores. Purchases were based on a carefully drawn assortment plan that they were also responsible for establishing. The sales forecast for each season was developed from the previous year's goals as reported by each store, each buyer's analysis of current market conditions, and projections for the future.

As far as quantitative analysis went, the buying staff had been doing and continued to do a magnificent job. Their ability in this direction, individually and as a group, seemed to improve each year. Yet even with

Awesome. Incomparable. What can be said about 5.2 million square feet of fashion and fun that has not been said before? West Edmonton Mall is more than exceptional retail. It represents a complete lifestyle with shopping, recreation, entertainment, amusements, and amenities that would be the envy of any community.

It all started as a mere glimmer in the eyes of former Iranian rug merchants and current Triple Five Corporation owners Nader, Raphael, Bahman, and Eskandar Ghermezian. The glimmer became a 110-acre bilevel mall offering dry goods, dresses, dining, and dreams. To the closely knit, Iranian-born Ghermezian brothers, it is a wondrous enclosed paradise. "It is education, it is entertainment, it is fun, it is fashion," crowed Nader, the images of incredible possibilities taking control. "It is a world within a world."

If nothing else, it is very, very big. More than 3 million cubic feet of concrete supported by 4,000 tons of steel house over 800 stores, a 2.5-acre lake, four $800,000 deep-sea submarines, a $3-million, 80-foot-long Spanish galleon, an 18-hole miniature golf course, four dolphins, 500 squawking yellow canaries, 40 lemon sharks, a 50,000-gallon aquarium, a fire-breathing fountain, 135 restaurants, and a five-acre water park— among other things. Construction took 5,000 tradesmen and 300 contractors 3,000 man–years.

Courtesy of Triple Five Corporation Ltd.

Shoppers browse in boutiques such as Ralph Lauren, Yves St. Laurent, and Cartier along magnificent 70-foot-wide Europa Boulevard.

Courtesy of Triple Five Corporation Ltd.

A marine theater in the 2.5-acre indoor lake features four trained dolphins performing throughout the day.

Courtesy of Triple Five Corporation Ltd.

Thousands line up at the five-acre water park for 22 water slides, a wave pool with six-foot waves, cable water skiing, and the tanning areas.

Courtesy of Triple Five Corporation Ltd.

The massive interior space of the mall is over five million square feet, making West Edmonton Mall the biggest in North America by more than a million square feet.

North America's Five Largest Malls

1. West Edmonton Mall, Edmonton, Alberta, Canada: 5.2 million square feet
2. Del Amo Fashion Center, Torrence, California: 2.6 million square feet
3. Lakewood Center Mall, Lakewood, California: 2.4 million square feet
4. Woodfield Shopping Mall, Schaumburg, Illinois: 2.3 million square feet
5. Roosevelt Field Mall, Garden City, New York: 2.2 million square feet

Courtesy of Triple Five Corporation Ltd.

An 80-foot replica of Columbus's Santa Maria is on view in the 438-foot-long indoor lake, along with a fleet of four submarines (larger in number than the Canadian Navy's).

Courtesy of Triple Five Corporation Ltd.

An ice skating rink National Hockey
League size provides mall visitors with
skating pleasure and the Edmonton Oilers
with a practice site.

Courtesy of Triple Five Corporation Ltd.

Rides at Canada Fantasyland, possibly the world's largest indoor park, include an old-fashioned merry-go-round and an indoor roller coaster a world-record 12 stories high. The name, style, and scale are Disney-like.

increasing sales figures yearly, there were problems. Markdown percentages were also increasing, and when a store-by-store cost analysis was done, it was found that a few stores whose sales were far ahead of plan were carrying the rest. In other words, in the majority of Galerie Boisvert stores the markdowns were increasing disproportionately to the increase in sales.

The problem seemed to be in the fashion categories. This was not a new problem; rather, it was a 20-year-old situation. Each year store managers tried to initiate a lengthy discussion of the problem at the biannual meeting in Paris. When they did this, the merchandising managers called them foolish, told them it was up to them to promote goods on the sales floor, and said it was not a buying problem but a selling problem.

The frustration levels grew among the managers, who knew that sooner or later the situation would become impossible. Yet nothing was done, and central buying of fashion goods continued in bulk from manufacturers who controlled the market with poor delivery and no-return policies.

In the mid-1980s, Galerie Boisvert management decided to look to American manufacturers for moderately priced fashion items. Even with tariffs, dealing with American firms offered greater selection, competitive prices, and better delivery. For the first time a group of buyers traveled to New York to buy merchandise that would go on sale in all 157 stores the following spring and summer.

One of the best buys they encountered was T-shirts. The French customer was beginning to adopt casual American fashion and T-shirts for men and boys were big sellers. A New York firm offered good-looking, short-sleeved T-shirts for men in a variety of solid colors and stripes, some with crew necks and others with button front and pointed collars. The fabric was a washable cotton, and the price per dozen was far lower than for similar shirts seen on the Continent. The deal was made. At last, they had found a staple fashion item that could be bought in bulk and easily sold in all the stores.

The T-shirt look had taken over in France the previous summer and, according to the trade papers, was to be even bigger in the coming season. Bulk buying would certainly pay off for all the stores this time, as each featured the lowest-priced T-shirts of quality fabric in town. The merchandising staff was elated. This would finally quiet the cries of the store managers who were constantly seeking the right of selection.

The T-shirts were delivered to the main warehouse and finally to the stores. Special promotions were built around them. Ads appeared in papers throughout France. The people came, they looked, they tried them on, but they did not buy. The price was right and the color and size assortment ideal, but they did not buy. The reason—French men did not like the wider cut of the American-made garment. Used to a body-hugging shirt, they found the looser fit unappealing in spite of the lower price.

As reports of "the great T-shirt markdown" poured into the Paris office, the message began to sink in. This complete failure forced the buying staff to realize what store managers had been trying to point out for years. Buying plans cannot be based on quantitative data alone; qualitative factors are of equal importance and sometimes even more important. Frenchmen vary from province to province and their tastes in clothes differ markedly. Sometimes the difference is very small and not discernible except to those who sell them their clothing.

This is what managers had been trying to get across for years. "Let us analyze our customer differences and pass this information on to you so that when you buy you can take it into consideration and select fashion goods, not in bulk, but according to regional differences." The answer had always been the same. This was not economically sound and would lead to higher retail prices in the stores and thus greater markdowns.

Finally, following the T-shirt failure, merchandising management realized that qualitative customer input, whether regional or national, was important for success. It took only one mistake in analysis to negate the profitability of a quantity purchase and point out the need at least to allow each store to offer an analysis of its particular market area.

Was this the beginning of a new era or would Galerie Boisvert continue to operate as it had in the past, refusing to accept the fact that bulk buying based on quantitative needs alone was not always the answer to profit when (1) fashion goods were involved and (2) the chain was not serving one market?

As plans for the forthcoming season were being discussed, the problem brought to a head by the T-shirts would have to be faced and somehow resolved if gross margin for the chain was to continue to move upward.

Questions

1. Indicate the similarities and differences between the buying motives of American and French consumers.
2. Discuss the differences listed in response to Question 1.
3. Discuss the similarities listed in response to Question 1.
4. What are the quantitative benefits of bulk buying? Why?
5. Discuss the quantitative costs of bulk buying.
6. How would you resolve the question of bulk buying of fashion goods for Galerie Boisvert? Explain.

Part IV

Marketing Approach to Location

C h a p t e r 9

Researching the Trading Area

Source: Courtesy of Urban Investment and Development Co.

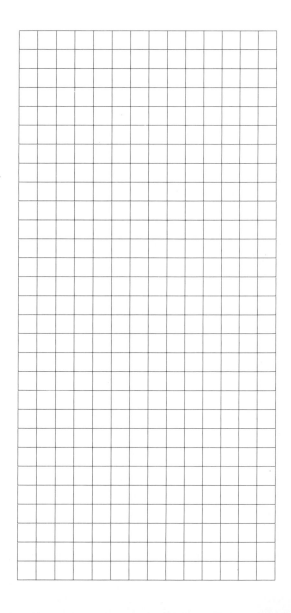

Industry Statement

Waldo Burnside
President
Carter, Hawley, Hale

The defining and analyzing of a trading area (or areas) is a most important initial step in the establishment of a retail business. Every trading area in retailing has a different makeup and therefore must be carefully assessed before a proper installation can be made. This applies regardless of the size of store or shopping center complex. There are a number of ways to approach analyzing a trading area using demographics and other measures. All of these have their merits, and no one is the single best guide.

The reevaluation of the makeup of trading areas is necessary from time to time because of changes in population movement. With the slowdown of growth in the suburbs, we are seeing the revival of urban areas. An example of this is downtown Los Angeles, where major relocations have taken place, including the combining of stores with hotel and office building projects.

Any effort to measure demographics of a trading area must be coupled with the marketing approach a particular company has chosen to pursue. Within any given trading area are a number of different types of customers. Certain types can be assessed through demographic measures. Others will require the application of nonstatistical data, including lifestyle and taste level measures.

Learning Objectives

Upon completing this chapter you should be able to:

1. Explain what a trading area is and how it should be analyzed by the retailer.
2. Determine the methods used to analyze the demographics of a location.
3. Understand how population changes in the United States affect the retailer.
4. Explain why downtown shopping areas are being revitalized.
5. See the effect that peripheral land development is having on the nation's retailers.
6. Understand how demographics are changing the use of shopping centers.

In Chapter 8 we emphasized that the retailer must know his or her customer in order to be successful as an international businessperson. The same holds true in the domestic environment, where stores are considering whether to expand on a small or nationwide scale.

The retail executive must take a marketing approach in order to understand this important element—place—and how it fits into the four Ps of marketing (product, price, place, and promotion). The explosion of retail expansion during the late 1960s and 1970s is over, and it is becoming more difficult to find new business sites that will provide a profitable return on investment.

This means that store managers must become more sophisticated in analyzing their customers, not merely by traditional demographics (sex, age, income, education), but by lifestyle—how they live and spend their money.

THE IMPORTANCE OF LOCATION

The choice of location is perhaps the single most important decision a retailer has to make. A good location is vital to success, because it allows ready access and attracts large numbers of customers. Further, the proliferation of retail outlets with nearly identical product offerings means

Trading Area
Area from which a location attracts its customers, usually determined by asking the owner, checking license plates, or checking competing locations.

Primary Trading Area
Area located closest to the store, containing 55 to 70 percent of the store's potential customers.

Secondary Trading Area
Area located just outside the primary trading area, containing 15 to 25 percent of the store's potential customers.

Fringe Trading Area
Wide area located outside the primary and secondary trading areas, containing 5 to 30 percent of the store's potential customers.

that even slight differences in location can have a significant impact on market share and profitability. Most important, because the location decision represents a long-term fixed investment, the disadvantages of a poor location are extremely difficult to overcome.

The Trading Area

The **trading area** is a term used to describe a store's customer potential. Once this is specified, a store can analyze the demographic and socioeconomic characteristics of its customers. The **primary trading area** encompasses 55 to 70 percent of a store's potential customers. It is the area closest to the store and possessing the highest density of customers to population and per capita sales. There is a minimum of overlap with other trading areas (intra- and interstore). The **secondary trading area** contains an additional 15 to 25 percent of a store's potential customers. It is located outside the primary area, and customers are more widely dispersed. Convenience stores draw poorly from this area. The **fringe trading area** includes all the remaining potential customers, who are most widely dispersed. For example, a discount store chain reported that its outlets have a primary trading area of four miles, a secondary trading area of four miles, and a fringe trading area of eight miles.[1]

Population Counts

Retailers must secure population counts from existing sources, such as chambers of commerce, local municipalities, and trade associations. More important, they must determine whether that population is expected to grow, decline, or remain constant. This will permit them to make short- and long-range business plans that will be more finely tuned to potential growth or decline in customer sales.

The occupations and income levels of potential customers within the trading area must be determined. Local banks and census reports can furnish these statistics. They will assist retailers in placing the right kind of store in a particular locale—for example, a designer furrier would probably not have success locating in an area inhabited by college students.

The potential customers' type of dwelling must be analyzed. What is the composition of homeowners versus apartment dwellers? A residential mix will indicate different needs for products and services.

Special consumer groups, such as ethnic, religious, or handicapped, will need particular kinds of merchandise. Sensitivity to differences in dress and dining requirements can be turned into meaningful profits.

---

[1] "Selecting a Store Site, the Computer Way," *Chain Store Executive*, March 1981, 47.

The sex composition of the trading area is important but must be further broken down by age and education. A 22-year-old college graduate will usually plan his or her expenditures very differently from a high school graduate of the same age.

METHODOLOGY FOR DEMOGRAPHIC ANALYSIS

A number of methods are available to evaluate a retail site. The retailer must understand which one best suits his or her needs.

Customer Identification

The first step is always to find out who the customer is and where he or she is in relation to the store. This is accomplished by conducting exit interviews with a random group of customers at existing stores. In order to delineate a trade area, it has been recommended that 1,000 customers per store should be interviewed.[2] For a macro, or basic, model, which offers a moderate degree of precision, 300 to 400 interviews per store should suffice. But if a solid demographic profit is all a chain is after, 150 to 200 customers per store—at a large number of stores—will be enough.[3]

The demographic items usually sought in an interview include family income, family size, age of respondent, number of children, education, occupation, and type of housing. The interviewer must also record the general area in which the customer lives and the amount spent during that particular visit to the store. Finally, he or she can gather information regarding the customer's attitude toward the store and its competition.

Analog Method
Method for obtaining a sales forecast by comparing potential new sites with existing sites.

By plotting the customer's home address on a map, the retailer's marketing analyst can determine how many sales dollars the store draws from that point. Taken in aggregate, this gives a picture of where the unit's total sales volume comes from. By drawing a circle around a percentage of those sales dollars—typically 70 percent—the analyst will have established that store's trading area. This method will also help the retailer obtain the basis for a model to which new sites can be compared. The retailer cannot determine whether a new site will work without a good idea of what has worked in existing units and what can be expected in terms of sales. This is the basis for the **analog method.** Using this approach, a retailer obtains a sales forecast by comparing potential store sites with existing store situations.

---

[2] John S. Thompson, *Site Selection.*
[3] "Methodology: The First Step in a Program for Self-Analysis," *Chain Store Age Executive,* January 1983.

Lifestyle Segmentation

Lifestyle Segmentation
Dividing of trading areas into segments on the basis of the way people live and how they spend their money.

Developers are starting to recognize opportunities in geographic regions they have bypassed before. Although they continue to use such traditional measurements of trading area potential as population growth trends, income, and number of households, they are becoming increasingly interested in **lifestyle segmentation.** This method begins with such basic market area statistics as age of population, occupation, and household size, but can be extended to include measurements of consumers' interests, activities, and life cycle stage.

Cluster Analysis

Cluster Analysis
Technique for analyzing markets that uses a computer to search among data for patterns and to group consumers according to attributes and behaviors.

To aid in analyzing such data, a number of marketing research firms are starting to use **cluster analysis** as a statistical technique. Donnelley Marketing Information Services[4] is offering Cluster-Plus, which displays 47 lifestyle classifications for any designated marketing area. These range from top-income, highly educated professionals to the lowest categories on the socioeconomic scale.

As an example of how Cluster-Plus data could be put to use, a study of an area might reveal that approximately 50 percent of the population fell into the category of younger, mobile professionals, homeowners, with children. With these results, a developer would need to produce a tenant mix to appeal to a younger, more active clientele—for example, toy and sporting goods stores. A totally different mix would be needed in an area that consists primarily of high-rise apartment buildings with no children.

ACORN

Cacci's classification system called "A Classification of Residential Neighborhoods" (ACORN) is based on geodemographics. It divides consumers into block groups averaging 250 to 300 households per group. Each group can be analyzed via more than 300 measurements applying cluster analysis and defining 44 lifestyle types that link it directly to geography.

PRIZM

Another lifestyle segmentation service based on geodemographics is Claritax's "Postal Residences in ZIP Markets" (PRIZM). It applies more than 1,000 U.S. Census demographic measures to each of the 35,600 residential ZIP code neighborhoods. Through analysis and classification

---

[4]"Developers Track the Data," *Chain Store Age Executive,* March 1984.

ZIP-Market Clusters
Segments (40) of the U.S. population determined by applying geodemographics to ZIP code neighborhoods.

of the results, these neighborhoods are assigned to one of the 40 **ZIP-Market Clusters.** Each is believed to represent a distinct neighborhood lifestyle and to indicate predictable patterns of buying behavior.

National Decision Systems' Model

A more thorough analysis of lifestyle and demographic data is provided by the demographic screening model from National Decision Systems. It can determine actual benchmarks for the success of any project. Developers are able to order printouts from the company that interpret data, indicating which types of tenants they will, or can, attract and which they will not, giving them a powerful tool when leasing a center.

CURRENT DEMOGRAPHIC CHANGES IN THE UNITED STATES

The U.S. population is in the process of restructuring, which is having an impact on retailers' expansion plans.

Resurgence of the Northeast

The new methods of site selection are making such detailed information available that we are able to observe the increase in development taking place in the Northeast. Interest in this particular region is a switch from the past few years, when most of the major development companies were passing it by. They were lured south by the strong population growth, the seemingly unlimited supply of land, and the relative ease of building in the Sunbelt states. But now, just as some of the glow of the Sunbelt is starting to dim (particularly in the Southwest), the Northeast is having a resurgence.

Restoration of the Economy

"When you look at New England, New York, and New Jersey, you see a fairly substantial restoration of the economy," according to James Newton, director of economic research for Management Horizons.[5] "In New England particularly, the economy has gotten out of heavy manufacturing, textiles, and other very cyclical industries and more into high-tech, service-related types of employment."

High-tech companies are also beginning to cluster around the headquarters of General Electric and IBM in New York's Hudson Valley and near Eastman Kodak's headquarters in Rochester, New York. Service-related companies are busy moving their headquarters to central New

---

[5] Ibid.

Jersey's business corridor, while firms in Connecticut, Massachusetts, and New Hampshire are all expected to benefit from increases in defense spending. The result of all this activity is that growth is coming from a relatively educated population with high income.

Retailers and developers are cautioned to look beyond simple growth rates and recognize that although growth rates may to a large degree be population driven, it may not necessarily be a highly employed, high-income population. Texas, one of the top three growth areas, is an example. Employment for new arrivals is becoming a growing problem, particularly with the collapse of oil and energy-related industries.

A more realistic view of market potential is available from per capita sales growth figures, which more accurately represent the true growth potential for such vital factors as sales per square foot. (See Figure 9.1.) When retail sales are examined on this basis—with the population veneer stripped away—projections show New England with an average per capita growth rate in total retail sales for the period 1983 to 1988 (based on 1972 dollars) of 2.8 percent. This compares to 2.2 percent for the

Figure 9.1   Average Annual Growth Rates in Per Capita Retail Sales, 1983–1988*

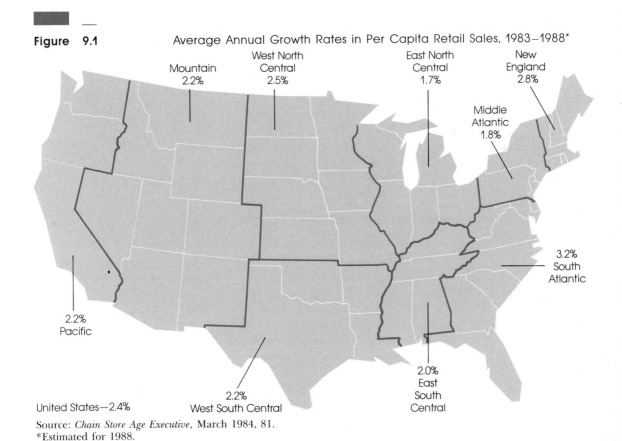

Source: *Chain Store Age Executive*, March 1984, 81.
*Estimated for 1988.

West South Central region and 1.8 percent for the Middle Atlantic states. The fastest growing region, at 3.2 percent, is expected to be the South Atlantic.

An indication of continuing strong growth is a forecast by Data Resources, Inc., indicating that real output in the Northeast region will grow 4.1 percent annually from 1983 to 1988. This compares favorably to the Sunbelt's expected 4.8 percent and is a clear-cut improvement on the region's 1.4 percent rate over the previous five years.

Opportunities in Suburban Regional Malls

The Northeast region holds still another attraction for the developer: there is simply less new competition. When a developer brings in a new center or renovates an old one, it is very likely to be the only project going on in town. While it is true that many market areas of the Northeast have been saturated, certain select areas of market opportunity still exist. Less than 10 miles outside of New York City, in Secaucus, New Jersey, the Harmon Cove regional mall is under construction.

Kravco has recently opened a large regional center 12 miles outside Atlantic City, New Jersey. (Atlantic City is reportedly one of the fastest growing markets for retail sales in the country.) Kravco also has in the works a possible new, full-scale regional center near Philadelphia.

Other examples include Pyramid's new Crossgates Mall; Fox Run Mall in Newington, New Hampshire; Crystal Mall in Connecticut; and the return of the big nationals like Ernest Hahn with its Bridgewater Commons, a regional center in Bridgewater, New Jersey. The Northeast is also characterized by a large number of aging but still viable downtown areas.

Continued Revitalization of Downtown Areas

For years, the phenomenal growth of outlying centers was widely interpreted as spelling the virtual demise of downtown, midtown, and neighborhood retail communities. In many instances, doleful predictions became self-fulfilling prophecies.

During the past decade, inner cities all over the country have been undergoing restorative measures as part of extensive rehabilitation programs by private developers and city, state, and federal governments.

The vice president for retail marketing of the Newspaper Advertising Bureau has commented, "Something very big and far-reaching is happening in retailing today—to department and specialty stores from Columbus Avenue in New York to Columbus, Indiana, and from Denver to Dallas and all points in between. . . . A major new dimension in American retailing has developed—a unique union of store concepts and design, goods and services, with the urban landscape.[6]

The in-town retail center serves a triple public—those who live in town, those who work there, and those who visit. Each is an important opportunity. Three different approaches are San Diego's Horton Plaza, Washington's Hecht metro center, and the specialty store areas on New York's Upper East and West Sides and in Greenwich Village. In-town retailing is not suburbia replanted. It has a character and identity all its own. At the same time, a strong population base in the suburbs will continue to fuel and support many centers there. (See Figure 9.2.)

Theatrical Merchandising

Tenants frequently are selected on the basis of their merchandising style and marketing sophistication, with mall developers and managers assuming responsibility for the theatrics—special events, entertainment, floral shows, and the like. All of this often occurs in a restored or renovated building or area that not too long ago was the victim of decay.

The excitement of the urban mall has spread to virtually every metropolis. There are Water Tower Place in Chicago; South Street Seaport, Citicorp, and Herald Center in New York; Portside in Toledo; Grand Avenue in Milwaukee; The Galleria in Dallas; Nicolet Mall in Minneapolis; and Waterside in Norfolk, Virginia, to name a few. (See Figure 9.3 on page 254.) More are in the planning stages for such cities as Albuquerque, Miami, Seattle, and Richmond.

In many instances, the rebirth of downtown shopping is simply a matter of good business sense. The city, after all, is where many urbanites as well as suburbanites work and, very often, play. More parking, better lighting, and more accessible expressways make it easier to return to the city for entertainment. There is also a return to city living among people from foreign countries, single people, and the affluent, all of whom have spawned a number of exclusive communities that will be better served with convenient, upscale retail centers. The Rouse Company, based in Columbia, Maryland, and the initiator of downtown revitalization for retailing with its Faneuil Hall Marketplace in Boston, sees the growth of the urban mall as part of a larger trend: the rebirth of the city.[7]

The Festival Marketplace

James Rouse, former chairman of the company bearing his name, refers to the projects of his newest company, Enterprise Development Com-

---

[6]"Developers Rediscovering that the Action Is Downtown," *Women's Wear Daily,* January 13, 1986, 1.
[7]"Malls Breathe New Life into Cities," *Advertising Age,* August 9, 1984, 13.

Figure   9.2   Denver Area Shopping Centers

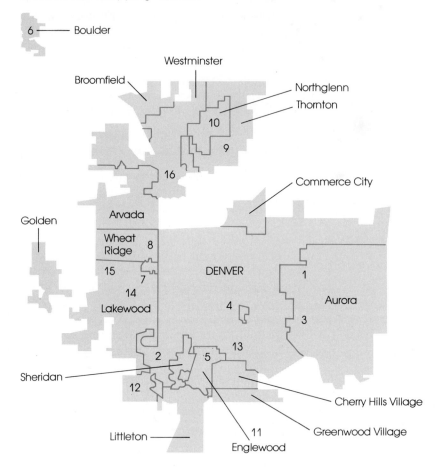

**Festival
Marketplace**
Specialty
marketplace in a
dramatic setting,
characterized by
excitement and
activity; also called
marketplace center.

pany, as **festival marketplaces.** Theatrical retailing at its best, Portside in Toledo, is a prime example. It is an attempt to create excitement and activity–a place where people of all ages and walks of life can come together to rub shoulders and interact.

To maintain a festive atmosphere, tenants are encouraged to be part of the Portside show. The pizza parlor owner, for example, sings opera, and the grocer hawks his wares. Meanwhile, EDC provides the special events—mimes, jugglers, and other entertainers. Tenants are chosen for their variety and include a year-round Christmas shop, a stuffed animal store, a fudgerie, a contemporary furniture operation, and a pottery and glass merchant. Seventy percent of the tenants are food establishments and the remaining 30 percent are retail shops and kiosks.

In addition to Portside, other festival marketplaces around the nation

Major Chain Stores

Map Code	Major Malls	J.C. Penney	Joslin's	May D&F	Montgomery Ward	Sears, Roebuck	Skaggs	Target	The Denver	Walgreen's	Woolworth	Broadway Southwest	Total Stores
1	Aurora Mall	●		●		●							135
2	Bear Valley			●									42
3	Buckingham Square				●	●						●	113
4	Cherry Creek							●	●			●	35
5	Cinderella City	●	●						●		●	●	220
6	Crossroads Mall	●		●	●				●				180
7	JCRS Shopping Center	●									●		32
8	Lakeside					●		●	●			●	65
9	North Valley				●	●							72
10	Northglenn	●						●	●	●		●	102
11	Southglenn				●			●	●			●	120
12	Southwest Plaza			●	●	●	●		●				192
13	University Hills				●	●						●	47
14	Villa Italia					●					●	●	60
15	Westland Mall				●	●							51
16	Westminster	●	●			●						●	80

Source: *Housewares*, April 1, 1986, 35–36.

Demographics note: The Denver market ranks fifth among the top 30 U.S. population leaders in projected population growth between 1983 and 1988. Over that span, the metropolitan area is expected to grow 13.4%.

With a per capita effective buying income of $13,224, Denver ranks eighth in the country's population leaders.

Denver ranks second in the nation in college graduates per capita. Half of the adults have some college education.

The Denver area ranks twelfth in the country in retail sales per household at $17,137.

In the state of Colorado, retail sales are projected at $33.7 billion by 1990.

The median age in Denver is 28.9, below the U.S. median age of 30.

are Harborplace in Baltimore, Pier 30 in San Francisco, Faneuil Hall in Boston, South Street Seaport in New York, and St. Louis's Union Station.

DEMOGRAPHIC ASSISTANCE IN DEVELOPING PERIPHERAL LAND

Demographic studies are assisting many developers in using a well-thought-out marketing and merchandising plan to profitably use land already owned on the fringes of their regional centers. (See Figure 9.4 on page 255.)

The Mixed-Use Development Approach in the Suburbs

Developers are now realizing that the development of peripheral land can add not only to the value of a new shopping center project but can add substantially to the worth of a newly acquired property where land has not been developed.

Peripheral Land
Land on the fringes of a shopping center, owned by the owner of the center.

Optimizing Land Use

The key to added value is optimizing land use to boost return on investment. Proper marketing and merchandising of **peripheral land** maximizes the investment by making the best use of it, which in turn enhances the value of the mall. May Company, for example, has established a separate department to handle peripheral land development.

FROM THE FIELD

Expansion at South Coast Plaza Mall

At South Coast Plaza Mall in southern California's Orange County, you'll find valet parking, a concierge desk, and a personal shopping service for customers who prefer to stay at home. There is also a Gentlemen's Agreement service for which customers pay $25 an hour to have somebody else do their shopping.

All of these services make South Coast *the* place for high-income shoppers in the area. The plaza already provides about one-fourth of total sales tax revenue for Costa Mesa, the city where the mall is located, and with a major expansion planned, it is expected to generate another $1 million annually by the year 2000.

Marketing the mall to the region's superaffluent has not dented its less well-heeled customer base. The blend of middle- to upper-end shoppers resulted in more than $300 million revenue in 1983 at the 200-plus stores in the 1.9 million-square-foot mall. A plan to gain more of the region's disposable income involves offering an exclusive charge card in conjunction with Bank of America.

South Coast has not always sought the ritzy customer. Its first store was May Company, which opened in 1966. The following year, a Sears store and more than 70 smaller stores opened. Over the years, the retail center has changed as the demographics of its customer base have matured. In 1981, South Coast bought out the remaining six years of a Woolworth Company lease. Several other leases, for a total of 100,000 square feet, were also bought

Homart's Willowbrook Mall project in Houston is one of the most massive projects in peripheral land development. It involves between 60 and 110 usable acres and will include, in addition to a regional mall with six department stores, a bank–office building, restaurants, a savings and loan, a 250,000-square-foot specialty retail center, a number of free-standing-type tenants, a fast food cluster, and an apartment complex.

Using Market Research

A market research study should be conducted in order to determine the needs of the particular market area. This will help clarify the specific demographics of the area as well as the services needed in the market-place. The cost of such studies can range from $2,000 to $25,000, depending on the methods used and the complexity of the study.[8]

---

[8] "Punching Up Profits on the Periphery," *Chain Store Age Executive,* May 1984, 69.

---

out and several new and upscale tenants were brought in.

It is now a combination of better-to-best stores, not just good stores. Anchors are Sears, Saks Fifth Avenue, Nordstrom, I. Magnin, May Company, and Bullock's. Tenant mix also includes some stores not often found in malls, such as Laura Ashley, Brookstone, Cartier, Courreges, Eddie Bauer, Custom Shop Shirtmakers, Descamps, and Yves St. Laurent.

With the center's allure extending to moderate-income shoppers, there are more than 30 restaurants spread throughout the complex. Reportedly, some 50 percent of shoppers eat while in the mall.

Industry sources report that several South Coast Plaza chain stores are the highest grossing stores of their respective chains. Average sales per square foot at the center are reported to be about $190, while the average cost of a tenant's lease is $24 per square foot. That is a hefty price tag, but it hasn't prevented South Coast from developing an extremely good reputation in the retail industry.

The pride of reputation is reflected in the management's approach to marketing the center. Shoppers are never called customers; they are patrons. The plaza is a retail center, not a mall. The strategy is to let the mall speak for itself.

The plaza never holds mall-wide promotions, such as automobile shows and art exhibits. Management feels that this would detract from the business of serious shopping.

In plaza image advertising, South Coast's upscale thrust is always emphasized. Ads in such consumer publications as *Architectural Digest* and *Vogue* promote the center's theme, "If you had one place to shop in America, this is the place."

Source: "South Coast Plaza: Thriving Center Caters to Affluent," *Chain Store Age Executive,* May 1984, 86. Reprinted by permission from *Chain Store Age Executive.* Copyright 1984 by Lebhar-Friedman, 425 Park Avenue, New York, NY 10022.

Figure   9.3   An Upscale Mall: Water Tower Place in Chicago

Source: Courtesy of Urban Investment and Development Co.

Possibilities for Land Use

Hotels and motels would use from three to six acres, depending on the land available and the location of the center. Recreational and entertainment facilities would include theaters, ice skating rinks, and bowling alleys. Restaurants with themes that are tablecloth operations would allow customers to eat and then stay in the complex and shop. Specialty retailers, such as eye care–vision centers, furniture showrooms, catalog showrooms, and toy stores, can be attractive because of the mall's drawing power. Office buildings provide a ready market for lunchtime business for both restaurants and shopping on the property. Approximate acreage needed would be between three and ten acres and could also include office–medical complexes. Financial institutions can provide a vital service and generally require from one to one and a half acres. Residential complexes can be an integral part of the periphery when there is sufficient land.

After the decision to launch a peripheral land marketing effort has been made and prime uses determined, the next step is to present this information to a professional land planner. The land planner will help determine where the various components should go for the maximum dollar return.

The planner still must deal with certain constraints that generally emanate from the reciprocal **easement agreements** drawn up between the

Easement Agreement
Agreement that allows limited use of land owned by someone else.

Figure   9.4   Profitable Use of Peripheral Land Owned by Shopping Centers

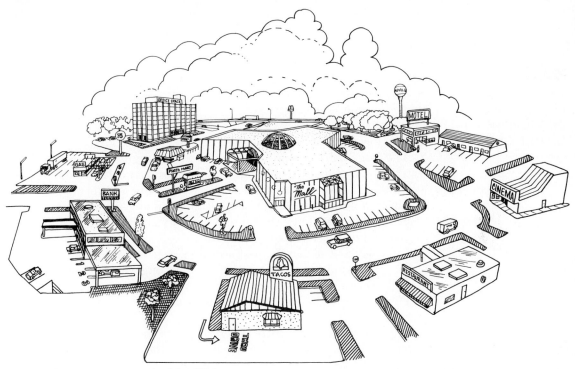

Source: *Chain Store Age Executive,* May 1984.

Anchor Tenant
Major mall tenant
occupying a large,
usually corner,
store.

developer and the major mall **anchor tenants.** These have a tremendous impact on what the developer can and cannot do on the peripheral land. This means that the developer is placed in the middle between the planner, who wants to put buildings in what he or she views as the proper locations, and the department stores, which want a varying degree of control over the land development.

Eastgate Mall in Cincinnati is a prime example of how peripheral land, well thought out and developed, can change an unwieldy site into a winner. Although extensive development had already been done on the site, the firm of Jacobs, Visconsi, and Jacobs and its partners in the project (Homart and J. C. Penney Realty) still found themselves with 110 vacant acres on the south side of the major street dividing the site and 60 vacant acres on the north side. They decided to undertake fringe land development to integrate the north and south parcels, including a new ramp system.[9] In addition to two restaurant operations, plans called for the

---

[9] Ibid.

construction of the first superstore in the United States plus the Eastgate South Shopping Center, a bank, and a medical office building.

With Eastgate and similar efforts, developers are finding that peripheral land development can make their investment more valuable today and even more valuable tomorrow.

DEMOGRAPHIC-BASED CHANGES IN SHOPPING CENTER USE

North America is undergoing convulsive population restructuring shaped by the following:

1. The low birthrate of the 1930s.
2. The huge baby boom of the late 1940s through the early 1960s.
3. The totally unanticipated fall in birthrates in the 1960s and 1970s, resulting in small categories of the very young and teenagers. Many of these are having a tough time gaining and holding jobs of their choice. They show great diversity and volatility in their tastes and choices in spending.
4. Improvement of health in almost every age bracket, which has led to a large and totally unexpected rise in longevity for both men and women.
5. Dramatic, unexpected halt of rural-to-urban flows in the 1970s.

At the same time, new forces are reshaping consumer buying patterns. Several trends are responsible for changing the way people buy:

1. The surge in single households as the young, the old, the separated, and the divorced have established their own residences.
2. The strong trend toward escalation of the number of income earners per household for continuing family formations.
3. Higher energy costs and energy conservation.
4. Swift technological change that has affected the profiles of merchandising and consumer spending procedures.
5. Steeply rising costs that have focused much greater attention on all aspects of retail management cost control systems.
6. Splintering and dispersion of consumer buying habits in turbulent times that have intensified the difficulties of judging consumer preference for the basic four store types:
   a. Comprehensive, modernized, widely inventoried department stores for truly one-stop shopping.
   b. Specialized, boutique-style stores operating with greater flexibility in accommodating changing interests and tastes.
   c. Off-price marketing with limited lines, small inventories, quick merchandise turnover, and the latest styles, with little or no service.

d. High-quality stores with highly personalized service, aimed at an affluent clientele.[10]

RETAIL SERVICE TENANTS IN SHOPPING CENTERS

Tenants who sell a service rather than a tangible item are providing a new way to round out a shopping center's array of goods and services. Insight into American lifestyles today affords a glimpse of the rapidly growing list of choices for the shopping center leasing specialist: tanning salons, health clubs, movie theaters, myriad financial institutions and services, and photo studios, to name a few.

Almost every type of shopping center, large and small, is jumping on the retail service bandwagon. One example is Herald Center, fashioned out of a vacant Korvette's unit in New York's Herald Square. The roster of the 140-store complex includes St. Mark W., a skin and hair care operation, and a United Airlines ticket and reservations office, offering domestic and international travel arrangements.

At Marina Pacifica Mall in Long Beach, California, a waterfront redevelopment, shoppers can arrive by land or by sea: one of the center's uses is a marina. Another is a six-screen American Multi Cinema theater.

Once linked as an ancillary function, hotels are avidly pursuing shopping center locations. Ramada Inns is openly advertising its availability as, if not a tenant, at least a shopping center functionary. Ramada is investing nearly $1.2 billion in developing its Ramada Renaissance Hotels chain as an alternative.[11]

At Boston's multiuse Copley Place project, two hotels—Westin and Marriott—provide not only a service adjacent to the shopping portion of the complex but avenues of access as well. Traditional retailing in Copley Place, headed by Neiman-Marcus, and the hospitality functionaries will feed off each other for traffic, with the hotels providing a way to get into the mall from various adjoining neighborhoods. (See Figure 2.4 in Chapter 2.) Other retail service tenants at Copley Place include Sack Theatres' multiscreen cinema and a bank.

Perhaps the consummate mix of service tenants is at the new Park Centre Shopping Plaza in Denver, which is almost all service. Its tenant roster includes the suburban office of a residential real estate broker, a dry cleaner, a hairstyling salon, a video rental store, a dance studio, a tanning salon, and a lounge–restaurant. The plaza management believes that these are the types of uses that are now needed in this area and that they will continue to grow extensively in the next several years along with the community.

---

[10] Samuel Feinberg, "From Where I Sit," *Women's Wear Daily,* July 31, 1984, 15.
[11] "How Change in Shopping Center Use Is Now Forcing Retailers to Live with New Neighbors," *Stores,* September 1984, 36.

A list of potential retail service tenants for shopping centers appears in Table 9.1. Originally a phenomenon of the strip center, such tenants are more often than not common to all centers—urban and suburban, enclosed or strip, large or small. The area of consumer services should be

Table 9.1   Potential Retail Service Tenants for Shopping Centers

Savings and Loan Association	Stereo Repair Service
Bank	Sewing Machine Repair Service
Finance Company	Vacuum Repair Service
Real Estate Brokerage	Pet Grooming
Insurance Agent	Key Shop
Title Company	Book Exchange
Escrow Office	Utilities Payment Office
Mortgage Broker	Print-Copy Center
Automatic Teller Machine	Pennysaver Office
Stock Broker	U.S. Post Office
Credit Union	Federal Express Office
Appraiser	Pre-School
Dentist	Game Arcade
Doctor	Radio Station
Optometrist	Dance Studio
Veterinarian	Educational Center—School
Emergency Medical Center	Health Spa
Chiropractor	Government Agencies
Counselor	Motor Vehicles
Accountant/CPA	Social Security
Bookkeeping Service	Interior Design Studio
Lawyer	Dressmaker
Employment Agency	Tailor
Business Consultant	Cobbler—Shoe Repair
Other Office Users	Appliance Rental–Repair
Food and Restaurant Users	Furniture Rental or Repair
Travel Agency	Costume–Uniform–Tuxedo Rental
Beauty Salon	Car Leasing Office
Skin Care Salon	Gift and Package Wrapping
Barber Shop	Library
Nail Salon	Community Room
Theater	Post Office Box Rental
Ticket Agency (like Ticketron)	Safety Deposit Box Rental
Dry Cleaner	Home Design Center for Residential Tract
Laundromat	
Portrait Studio	Diet Center
TV Repair Service	Phone Center

Source: *STORES* Magazine, September 1984. Reprinted with permission from *STORES* Magazine, © 1984 National Retail Merchants Association.

one of continuing growth, especially because such services are often yardsticks for changing lifestyles.

Summary

Store managers must become more sophisticated in the use of demographics when selecting a retailing location. Further, they must analyze trading areas by lifestyle as well as numbers. Several methods of analyzing demographics exist: lifestyle, segmentation, cluster analysis, ACORN, PRIZM, and National Decision Systems.

The restructuring of the U.S. population is having an impact on retailers' expansion plans. Because of a restored economy and less new competition, the Northeast is being viewed as an interesting alternative to the previous Sunbelt explosion for expansion.

The birth of festival marketplaces and theatrical merchandising has been important to the revitalization of downtown shopping. New trends toward developing land peripheral to shopping centers are changing the focus of the shopping center from an all-retail approach to one featuring retail service tenants.

Questions for Review

1. Define the terms *primary trading area, secondary trading area,* and *fringe trading area.* Why is it important for a retailer to be able to identify these areas?
2. List at least five customer demographics. How might each be of importance to a retailer?
3. Name at least three different methods used to analyze the demographics of a location. Explain what each is and of what use it could be to a retailer.
4. How can population shifts have an impact on retailers' expansion plans?
5. Why would developers consider revitalizing downtown shopping areas? Who would be served by this type of development?
6. What is meant by the term *peripheral land development?* What type of retailers might apply this concept?
7. Name at least three new forces that are responsible for reshaping consumer buying patterns and their effect on retailers.

CASE STUDY   **Charles**

Need for Marketing Research

Charles was a men's specialty store serving a localized market but with a fine national reputation. Located on one of the most fashionable shopping streets in Hub City, it attracted professional men who were looking for professional help in selecting a wardrobe.

Affluent shoppers came from many points within Hub City's trading area, and other fashion-conscious men traveled from as far away as 60 or 70 miles to satisfy their clothing needs at Charles.

This was a store capable of promoting intelligent fashion for a diverse audience. Charles Blaine was a successful merchant because he understood both the bodies and the lifestyles of his customers. From custom-tailored suits to casual sportswear, Charles kept abreast of the changing needs in the market. His customers were aware of the European shape long before the general menswear market had heard of it. Who were his customers? They were young lawyers and executives on their way up as well as senior men who had already become successful.

The younger Charles men often shopped on their lunch hour, on Wednesday evening, or Saturday. Some lived in apartments along the nearby streets and walked to the store. Others arrived in flashy sports cars, coming from the outskirts of the city or nearby suburbs where apartment complexes catering to the single set had mushroomed.

Most of Charles' older customers also lived in the suburbs, but in suburbs dominated by single homes on large lots. These were wealthy men who had demanding business lives and could not take the time from a busy day to look for a new topcoat or even a necktie. Sometimes their wives made the preliminary investigation, going from shop to shop to bird-dog a suit or a sweater and returning on Saturday with their husbands to make the actual purchase, provided there were no other social commitments. Some of these businessmen left the entire selection process to their wives and went to the store only if a suit had to be fitted.

An astute businessman himself, Charles was well aware that he was losing many sales from this older market. With all the new shopping malls beckoning to nonworking, over-35 wives looking for exciting places to shop, there was no reason to include the downtown Charles store in their selection process. Also, working wives and working girlfriends enjoyed the convenience and fun of shopping after work, together with the men. They looked first to the malls where they could dine, shop, and then attend a movie without having to worry about parking restrictions.

Charles thought it was time to open a branch store. The market was believed to be there. A branch in a well-selected location would therefore mean additional sales, not a diluted market. To analyze the market, surveys were taken and demographics studied. Finally, after months of deliberation, Cherryvale Plaza was selected.

The Cherryvale market area was made up of upper-income families. By opening a store, Charles could capture the entire Cherryvale market rather than the few who went to Hub City to shop. Some men living in Cherryvale had been Charles customers in the past but had not used their charge accounts for several years, according to the survey. They would return to the fold. After one look at the new store located in the center of the lower level of the two-story mall, they would offer no sales resistance. The store was not going to be the usual haberdashery. Even though prices would be high, this would not matter because the message to be transmitted was one of fashion and quality.

The store was planned to present a dramatic new shopping environment with individual areas for each category. It would offer the same basic assortments as the main store, broken down by concept rather than by item or size. Included would be:

- The London Corner: British look.
- Charles International: Collections from Europe's finest designers.
- Charles Domestic: American-made clothes.
- Young Sophistication: Fashions for the younger, adventurous man.
- The Custom Corner: Made-to-order clothing.

A complete assortment of suits, sport coats, slacks, outerwear, sportswear, and accessories would be available in each section.

Success seemed inevitable, but from day one it did not occur. Unexpected problems arose resulting from a lack of complete market analysis. Charles was amazed. He could not believe that he had lost his touch, his feel for the market. He would prove that a good-sized market existed.

The store in itself was a drawing card—a study in elegance—the customer seemed to be entering a magnificent home rather than a commercial establishment. Oriental rugs covered portions of the parquet floors. Crystal chandeliers hung from the ceiling, and beautiful furniture surrounded the huge stone fireplace in the center of the main room, a few steps down from entry level.

The staff, too, had been selected with the same care that had been taken with the fixtures. Salespeople must fit the surroundings. Many were interviewed, but only those who had the Charles image were hired.

At a conference held months before the opening, merchandise was also planned to match the total image created by the store. In the Hub City store the European cut had been causing much excitement among the younger customers. It was new, smart, and had a certain flare that appealed to men who wanted that special Continental look. Charles' customers liked high fashion, although some shopped at his store because of the quality and tailoring. Those customers really preferred the traditional styles that were also well-stocked in the main store.

All of these facts were considered when assortments were being planned, but traditional cuts were passed over. The decision was made to feature the slim, tapered European cut in all departments except Charles Domestic. Suits, pants, sport coats, and shirts were purchased with the look that was selling so well in the main store. It should sell even better in the suburb with its wealthy clientele, well aware of the latest in men's fashions.

After a few months of lagging sales and hours of analysis, the problem was finally clear. Charles had not been wrong, the market did exist. However, the suits were not selling, nor were the sport coats or slacks. Even the shirts, which had great eye appeal and had been quickly purchased by female shoppers, were being returned a week or so later. The reason was that wealthy executives and sophisticated professionals might have the taste and the money for the European cut, but at their age it was not right.

All the demographics in the world would not uncover this fact. Certainly no one was willing to list his waist measurement on a survey. Here was a problem that had never been considered when doing an analysis of the potential market. In-depth market analysis for a clothing retailer had to include some way of relating lifestyle characteristics to age and to physical types. Charles had not done this. He therefore had to make some changes at the Cherryvale store.

Questions

1. Design a questionnaire that would give a retailer of men's clothing the necessary information for current assortment planning.
2. Analyze the reaction of Cherryvale consumers to (a) the British look, (b) European designer clothes, and (c) American designer clothes.
3. Suggest ways of relating lifestyle characteristics to demographic data.
4. List any changes in merchandise assortments that, in your opinion, would lead to increased sales.
5. Suggest any changes in store design and layout that, in your opinion, might make a contribution to increased sales.

Chapter 10

Selecting the Site Location

Source: Courtesy of The Rouse Company.

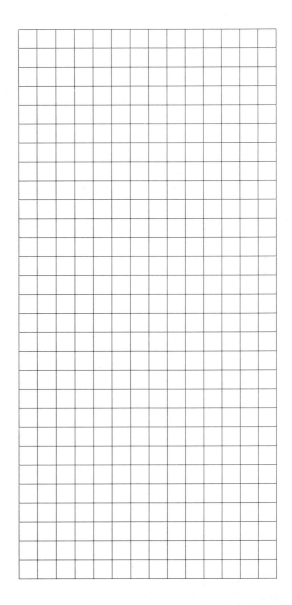

Industry Statement

Charles J. Cristella
Regional Real Estate Manager
The Gap

Location. Location. Location. These are the three ingredients most important to a successful retail operation.

Choosing a location has almost become a science. The initial step is a physical on-site review, noting visibility, access, vehicular and pedestrian traffic patterns, overall importance of the retail environment, and co-tenancy. The next step is to gain an overview of the marketplace through area maps identifying competition and/or complementary regional, community, and local shopping centers. Shopping surveys noting frequency of visits by the consumer and their favorite types of stores in various retail categories are valuable data. (This information may be compiled by developers and/or the Chamber of Commerce.)

Updated information on new retail developments and stores opening in the trade area should be secured. It is helpful to get the opinions of managers of established businesses, whether local or national, concerning their experience in the marketplace. Finally, evaluation of the demographic profile of a specific trade area is essential to determine the fit between your product and the potential customers in the trade area. This would include population, median and average household income, median age, and education levels.

With all of these ingredients as part of your evaluation, you will likely know more about the marketplace than do some merchants who have lived there a lifetime. This understanding of your business and how it fits into the environment, along with your "gut feeling" and observations, is the key to making your assessment an accurate one.

Learning Objectives

Upon completing this chapter you should be able to:

1. Understand why location is so important to retailers.
2. Determine the interdependent decisions that retailers must make in choosing a location strategy.
3. Identify the various types of locations and how they differ from one another.
4. Understand how location factors other than type of location affect the retailer's decision process.
5. Know why marketing plays a great part in the management strategies of major shopping center developers.

Even poorly merchandised stores can do well in spite of themselves—if they are located advantageously. Conversely, a bad location can drag down even the best merchandising team. Gut feelings no longer get a retailer good locations. The cost of development and operations has increased so dramatically that the price of a site mistake can be disastrous. Chapter 9 illustrated the importance of considering demographics in the choice of a location; this chapter will consider the impact of geographics on that choice.

CHOOSING A LOCATION STRATEGY

In the choice of a location, which is perhaps the single most important decision a retailer has to make, four interdependent decisions must be made. First is the selection of a region or market area in which new stores are to be located. This decision is followed by the identification of feasible sites for new stores based on land availability and zoning regulations. Next is the choice of a site or sites most likely to optimize the company's performance. Last is the determination of the optimal size and other design characteristics of the store or stores.

Types of Locations

After choosing a site, the retailer must next consider the type of location best suited to the store.

Freestanding Store

Freestanding Store
Store located away from any traditional commercial area.

Isolated from adjacent retailers, a **freestanding store** may be located on a highway or smaller street away from the traditional commercial area. Easy parking, flexible hours, low rent, and ease of one-stop shopping are some of its advantages. Because of the difficulty and expense of drawing clientele, small stores usually shy away from such locations. Larger retailers, such as supermarket chains and discounters, are often successful in such locations.

Figure 10.1

Forerunner of Today's Central Business District

The galleria concept originated in Milan, Italy, in the 19th century.

Source: Photo by John Stapleton.

Central Business District

Central Business District
Usually downtown; a grouping of stores that offers a broad range of products/services and prices.

Usually located in downtown areas, **central business districts (CBDs)** offer a broad grouping of convenience, specialty, and department stores with diversity in price points, products, services, location, and access to pedestrian and vehicular traffic.

Downtown development is one of the fastest growing areas of the shopping center industry. Whether in the form of downtown regional shopping malls, specialty–festival centers, mixed-use retail centers, or renovation of existing retail streets or pedestrian malls, downtown retail development is happening in cities both large and small throughout the country. Unlike the urban renewal movement of the 1960s and 1970s that caused massive destruction as it swept through many of the country's urban areas, this latest spate of downtown development is

FROM THE FIELD

Small Store Revival

While large and small retailers alike can effectively play the specialty game, smaller companies continue to dominate specialty market share. According to the government's latest figures, the market share held by smaller companies is considerably higher: 70 percent in sporting goods and bicycles, 60 percent in eating and drinking establishments, 78 percent in children's and infants' wear, to name a few. (See Figure 10.2 on page 270.)

When a major industry like retailing finds itself in the throes of a change like this, it is rather startling news. Big companies, after all, are supposed to muscle smaller ones out of the marketplace, not the other way around.

What is most surprising about the small store revival, though, is who the new shopkeepers are, and how they are going about their business. This isn't a trend that happened all by itself; rather, it is the work of a generation of entrepreneurs who are learning to run their companies in ways that would have astonished their five-and-dime-store predecessors. To survive, the new retailers have learned to pick and defend their niches with remarkable care; they have evolved sophisticated marketing and management techniques; and they have developed a healthy respect for the costs and benefits of growth.

The people engineering this transformation are an unlikely lot, and in many cases got into retailing for the most idiosyncratic of reasons.

Iqbal Ahmed, nearly blinded in an accident playing squash, abandoned his plans to become an economist and instead went to work in a friend's sport-

showing respect for the old, even when space must be made for new projects.

A study of downtown trends concluded that, although in many instances retail is serving as the anchor of CBD redevelopment, "Housing should be developed, there should be a ready market of office workers, and there should also be a visitor and tourist component. Developers are looking at this entire market, including the residential component, first."[1]

Shopping Centers

Before World War II, most of the population lived in urban and rural areas. After the war, returning veterans started new families and thus

---

[1] "Setting Sights on City Sites," *Chain Store Age Executive*, May 1984, 72.

---

ing goods store. Today he owns Athletic Experience, a gray-and-crimson-bedecked sports shop in Berkeley, California.

Gary Huffman, a national sales trainer with 3M Company, saw his father suddenly lose his job with a large corporation. Gary's wife, Dawn, watched her father suddenly quit his job as vice president of another large company. Worried about their own futures, Gary and Dawn opened a home-made ice cream store in St. Paul.

Lina Keeney, a toxicologist for a large pharmaceutical company, hated working with rats. She now owns a small franchised business in Haverford, Pennsylvania, called Mother's Work, which sells maternity clothes.

Kate Lynott, a probation officer by day, spent her evenings doing needle-work. Two and a half years later, she opened a needlework store with her sister in Philadelphia.

Because the new shops are typically clustered together, the shopping environment extends beyond the store's

walls, and an individual store can be only as successful as its neighborhood. When a bustling but financially unsuccessful Berkeley restaurant went out of business, neighborhood shopkeepers say their own sales dipped until the space was filled. "In the retail business, who is selling next to you is just as important as who you are," says Richard Bradley, president of the International Downtown Executive Association, in Washington, D.C. Shopkeepers, like first-time parents in search of similar friends, frequent one another's stores, use one another's services, and seek one another's advice. In New Haven, they organize street fairs and pool resources for joint advertising. In Philadelphia, they unite for affordable group health care. "Simply put," says Bradley, "it's a matter of survival."

Source: "A Nation of Small Shopkeepers," *INC.*, November 1985, 66. Reprinted with permission, *INC.* magazine, November 1985. Copyright © 1985 by INC. Publishing Company, 38 Commercial Wharf, Boston, MA 02110.

Strip Center
Relatively small group of stores in a trading area that serves 7,000 to 40,000 people; also called a neighborhood shopping center.

Community Shopping Center
Strip center expanded to serve a trading area of 40,000 to 150,000 people.

developed an intense need for new housing. This led to the exodus to the suburbs and the resulting new shopping areas designed to accommodate the new communities.

A neighborhood shopping center, sometimes called a **strip center,**[2] is usually constructed on main neighborhood roads that carry substantial traffic. The trading area serves between 7,000 and 40,000. The largest tenant is usually a supermarket, a drugstore, or a variety store within a relatively small group of stores located alongside one another.

A **community shopping center** is the basic strip center expanded to serve 40,000 to 150,000 people, anchored by a large tenant such as a supermarket or discounter. Centers contain a variety of convenience stores, parking, and planned competition.

A **regional shopping center** serves a minimum of 150,000 people in a dominant shopping area. It consists of at least two department stores and 50 to 60 small stores, with regional and national chain stores heavily represented. It is built either by a developer who rents the stores to retailers or by a large retailer, such as May Department Stores, that operates an anchor store in the center and rents the remaining stores to other retailers. The number and types of competitive outlets are controlled, business hours are regulated, and the stores share promotional and ad-

---

[2] Melvin Morgenstein and Harriet Strongin, *Modern Retailing* (New York: Wiley, 1983).

Figure   10.2   The Revival of Small Stores

Source: Photo by Pat Doty.

Regional Shopping Center
Center consisting of at least two department stores and 50 to 60 smaller stores, serving a minimum of 150,000 people.

Super Regional Mall
Shopping mall consisting of three to six department stores, hotels, office buildings, and recreation centers.

Traditional Shopping Center
Downtown grouping of stores.

Mixed-Use Center
Downtown center with two or more uses, such as an office building with retail promenade.

Marketplace Center
Center oriented toward entertainment as well as goods; also called festival marketplace.

vertising expenses. The center provides a management company, convenient parking, easy access, and, in many cases, enclosure.

The **super regional mall** is more than two and a half times the size of the regional mall's gross leasable area (GLA). It consists of three to six department stores, hotels, office buildings, and recreation centers on an average of 200 acres. Discounters like Bradlee's and Caldor are now beginning to enter these malls. Depending on how hot the property is, the developer may approach the large stores before actually signing to acquire the real estate. These malls often serve a population base of one million or more. They become almost a satellite city.

Classification of Shopping Centers

The Rouse Company of Columbia, Maryland, one of the nation's most creative developers, classifies shopping centers as traditional, mixed use, and marketplace.

Rouse's Grand Avenue in Milwaukee exemplifies the **traditional shopping center,** or normal downtown type. (See Figure 10.3.) Rouse stipulated that both Gimbels and Boston modernize their aging stores. Gimbels turned its basement into a chic food emporium and upgraded throughout the store, while its co-anchor updated its interior and selections to attract wealthy suburbanites who might otherwise drive 90 miles to Chicago for such goods. Boston reported its sales were up 50 percent as a result.[3]

Centers that include office space, hotels, and eateries in a downtown area are called **mixed-used centers.** This classification is typified by Evans Development Company's The Pavilion at the Old Post Office in Washington. (See Figure 10.4 on page 274.)

Centers oriented toward entertainment rather than the acquisition of goods are called **marketplace centers.** Faneuil Hall Marketplace, once an abandoned Boston landmark, is now a thriving 365,000-square-foot bazaar that attracts 12 million people a year. Harborplace, on Baltimore's long-neglected waterfront, is such a tourist attraction that out-of-towners account for 35 percent of business at the 140,000-square-foot center.[4] South Street Seaport, New York City, covers 240,000 square feet and is an ambitious venture with the South Street Seaport Museum on Manhattan's Lower East Side; it includes residential, office, hotel, and museum space, as well as the renovated Fulton Fish Market.

The secret of the specialty marketplace center is just that—special. Merchandise mixes, interesting architecture, and other amenities are necessary, but the center still must get people downtown by giving them something new, exciting, different, and exclusive. At Faneuil Hall the

---

[3] "The Shopping Mall Goes Urban," *Business Week,* December 13, 1982, 42.
[4] "Miles of Malls and More," *Restaurant Hospitality,* May 1982, 15.

attraction is the cacophony and color of the open-air food market. At Harborplace it is the oceanfront setting and the National Aquarium. (See Figure 10.5 on page 275.)

From the merchant's point of view, a marketplace center can rasp

Figure   10.3   The Victorian Arcade in Milwaukee's Grand Avenue Center

Source: Courtesy of The Rouse Company.

FROM THE FIELD

The Pavilion—Prototype for the Future

Located in a historical building on Pennsylvania Avenue midway between the White House and Capitol, The Pavilion combines 60,000 square feet of retail space on its first three floors with 140,000 square feet of federal government office space on the upper floors of a 10-story atrium.

Ushering in what its developers called "a new era in festival retail development," The Pavilion has created the greatest interest and received the most publicity for the developer.

As the first major undertaking made possible by the 1976 Cooperative Use Act, The Pavilion is expected to be a prototype for future projects throughout the country. The act allows for the involvement of private enterprise in opening government buildings for public use.

The concept, based on food, fashion, and the arts, creates an activity area for 50 specialty shops, restaurants, cafes, and food concessions, in addition to a performing arts center.

Performing arts events, which are scheduled at least five times a week, are the key. Wednesday features jazz; Thursday and Friday, popular music; Saturday, children's theater and special artists; and Sunday, live concerts. All events are free and open to the public.

Besides evening performances, noontime events are scheduled to attract the 150,000 office workers within a 15-minute walk of the project. Additionally, daytime and summertime evening traffic is augmented by the Smithsonian, situated directly behind the building.

Designed to appeal to residents and tourists alike, The Pavilion features a diversity of specialty shops, from stamp and toy collections to collections of domestic and imported apparel. In addition to four sit-down restaurants, numerous other food outlets are on Embassy Row, which features international cuisine, and Main Street USA, which offers American fare. Approximately 50 percent of the total gross leasable area (GLA) is devoted to food concessions.

The center is reaching sales levels that had been projected for its third year of operation. Current sales are over $450 per square foot, which the developers believe may not be valid as they do not encompass an adequate period of time. One food concession, Texas Cattle Company, is hitting sales per square foot of an astounding $2,000.

Source: "Back Downtown," *Stores*, May 1984, 58. Reprinted with permission from *STORES* Magazine, © 1984 National Retail Merchants Association.

Figure   10.4   A Mixed-Use Center: The Old Post Office in Washington

Source: Courtesy of The Pavilion at the Old Post Office.

away the rough spots in the historically uneven urban trade, where brisk lunch business usually means slow dinner trade or firm weekend traffic buoys soft weekdays. A marketplace center appeals to different markets at different times—office workers during the day, singles and suburbanites at night, and everybody on the weekends. The appeal stretches across the income spectrum as well—at Harborplace, you can eat 50-cent crabcakes from a stand or treat yourself to a $50 French dinner.

CHOOSING A SPECIFIC SITE

Now that the various decision strategies in locating a retail store have been examined and the choices of location types outlined, the factors important in choosing a specific site can be considered.

Pedestrian Traffic

The number and type of people passing by a location are the most important measure; however, these numbers must be qualified as to shoppers and nonshoppers. Traffic counts should be analyzed by time of day or night, age, and sex as well as by interviews that would shed light on actual potential shoppers for a particular store or stores.

Vehicular Traffic

For retailers who appeal to heavy vehicular traffic, an analysis of traffic patterns, congestion times, and road conditions is important. These would include convenience food stores, gasoline stations, fast food operations, and regional shopping centers.

Figure   10.5   Specialty Marketplace Center: Harborplace in Baltimore

Source: Courtesy of The Rouse Company.

Parking

The number and quality of parking spots, their distances from the store site, and the availability of employee parking should be evaluated. Even though most suburban shopping centers provide parking for customers, the parking area must be large enough to accommodate shoppers adequately at peak times. In urban stores, convenient and inexpensive parking should be available for customers who drive to the shopping area.

Some specialty stores in urban areas have recently instituted complimentary valet parking for all customers. This is a definite advantage if the store is located in the middle of a bustling city with less than adequate public parking facilities.

Access Roads and Transportation

Access Road
Approach road to a store or shopping center from a highway.

Both delivery trucks and customer vehicles require access from major highway networks via **access roads.** While many thoroughfares are able to absorb customer traffic, they often cannot bear truck traffic for deliveries. For stores located in downtown or secondary urban settings, proximity to mass transportation is essential. The convenience issue is joined by one of the safety of mass transportation—is it safe to ride the subway after a certain hour, and how well policed are the transit stops?

Placement and Visibility

The specific post on a street or in a shopping center needs to be carefully assessed. A corner location is important to major, high-volume retailers. Although the rent is higher, the larger sales volume more than covers it.

A smaller or exclusive store has other considerations. Should it locate near the corner spot or should it maintain a quieter, chic location? How visible is the storefront? Can it be seen from across the street or from the middle of the mall? If shoppers do not know the store is there, they will never become customers.

Retail Mix

What is the compatibility of the planned store with those already in the competitive shopping area? For a new retailer, the store must be able to attract shoppers from the existing stores. This is known as affinity, and means that the new store must be able to blend in and cooperate with its neighbors. As a group, all of the compatibly merchandised stores should generate more sales because they are located together than if they were situated apart. This group of stores would be highly compatible: department store; accessories shop; ready-to-wear for men, women, and children; and home fashion store. Another possible grouping might be supermarket, bakery, liquor–wine shop, butcher, drugstore, and card and gift shop.

Another aspect of the location mix is retail balance. This occurs when there is an optimal grouping of stores in a shopping area. A proper balance is achieved under a variety of conditions: a suitable tenant balance; equality of the location's market potential with the number of stores for each service or merchandise classification; and one-stop shopping provided by the wide assortment of product and service classifications.

BUYING VERSUS LEASING

In deciding whether to buy or lease a store, the retailer must assess the advantages and disadvantages of each option.

Buying

The retailer who buys a store has complete control over any physical changes, as long as they conform to the zoning laws. There are also the possibilities of financial appreciation over time and of renting the space to other merchants. In addition, the owner runs no risk of exorbitant rental increases or of the lease not being renewed.

Disadvantages are tax and maintenance increases, potential losses from fires and flood (although these should be covered under an insurance policy), and a possible decrease in the real estate value of the location.

Leasing

A retailer who leases often has a better chance to achieve maximization of funds. Monies can be more productive if put into inventories and advertising than if tied up long-term in land purchase. The disadvantage of leasing would be possible restrictions imposed on business hours, fixtures and displays, store alterations, or renewal potential.

SHOPPING CENTER MANAGEMENT TRENDS

Gone forever are the days when management had to be concerned with ensuring that the roof did not leak, that the parking lot was free of potholes, and the rents were collected on time. A growing professionalism in shopping center management now permeates the entire industry. Today the shopping center manager is likely to be involved in leasing negotiations, tenant relations, center and retail marketing, budgeting and income control, and other operational considerations. In all of this, the computer is proving to be an important tool.

The gain in sophistication has come primarily from a change in emphasis from the purely operational–physical aspects of a center to a concern for maximizing profit potential. One of the chief consequences of these changes is the considerably larger role that leasing is now playing in shopping center management. Today many of the leading firms realize that leasing, once mainly an unrelated area, is really the hub of their management efforts.[5]

Releasing

If one store goes out, you can increase the rent when you release the space, but you can also increase the pulling power of the entire center when it is leased to a better use. To properly manage any shopping center, first of all you must have a successful releasing program. You must begin by properly analyzing the existing tenants to make sure that they represent the tenant mix appropriate for the times. Then you must replace tenants who are not generating optimum revenues with others who will.

Sometimes this entails reclaiming some of the large older stores and subdividing or refiguring them into more efficient retail operations providing a wider variety of merchandise offerings. This has a direct impact on the bottom line.

Refurbishing

Many department store companies throughout the country have found themselves with units located in regional malls that may be as much as 15 to 20 years old. Shopping center developers discovered that refurbishing these older centers was probably the next best thing, when starting up new construction was hampered by the shortage of available money. It benefits everyone when the department store anchors—retailing giants like Sears and J.C. Penney—get in on the act.

One example is what happened at Montgomery Mall in Bethesda, Maryland. The owners, including May Centers, spent millions to expand and update the 15-year-old center. In response, two of its five anchor stores—Hecht's, a division of the May Company, and Garfinkel's, a division of Allied Stores—undertook massive remodeling programs. They were then joined by Sears, which selected Montgomery Mall as the first site to debut its store-of-the-future prototype in retrofit form in October 1983.[6]

---

[5] "Center Management: The Old Gray Mare," *Chain Store Age Executive,* June 1984, 46.
[6] Ibid.

Remerchandising

Remerchandising
Altering the tenant
mix of a
refurbished
shopping center.

Along with the refurbishing (and expansion) of existing centers has
come the extensive **remerchandising** of selected projects, altering the
tenant mix, and making previously leased spaces suddenly available.
This is when specialty stores come into the picture.

Leasing agents are particularly keen on going after "hot" retailing concepts. U.S. Shoe's Casual Corner, Caren Charles, and Ups N Downs
specialty stores and Melville's Thom McAn, Foxmoor, and Chess King
stores, are a few specialty operations of just two companies. Developers
like the near-stratospheric numbers generated by such concepts—sales
climbing up to $300, $400, and perhaps even $600 per square foot.[7]

As a result, the specialty store companies—U.S. Shoe and Melville in
particular—have added a great deal of new space over the past few
years. That is not the major reason why both companies are featured
prominently on the recent Big Builders roster, however; it is chiefly because of their commitment to their off-price divisions. Melville has Marshalls. U.S. Shoe has Front Row, T. H. Mandy, Outletters, Crackers, and
Merchants Linen Warehouse. Zayre also devoted a large percentage of
its capital expenditures budget to its off-price divisions, T. J. Maxx and
Hit or Miss.

Off-price stores are showing up everywhere—in regional malls, strip
centers, downtown mixed-use projects, freestanding units, and specifically designated off-price outlet centers. They are also finding a home in
some of the former Woolco units that, because of their mammoth size,
are being subdivided to house more than one retail tenant.

Discounters are resuming their expansion strategy. They did not cut
building programs to the extent that other retail segments did during the
recession of the early 1980s.[8] According to the results of a census survey
by *Chain Store Age Executive,* 43 percent of the department store operators queried and 50 percent of the home center retailers reported no new
building during that period. Only 23 percent of the discounters questioned said there was no new building at their chains during that period.
Moreover, some chains, such as T.G.&Y., Heck's, Wal-Mart, and Venture, plan to continue expansion.

K mart is refurbishing its stores, eliminating low-demand departments, and allocating the space to new ones such as home improvement,
computers, and kitchen shops. K mart has adopted a new strategy for
expansion that will increase its role as landlord as well as tenant. The
effort is designed to change its real estate involvement from overhead to
profit and to sharpen retail control in its stores.

---

[7]"Big Builders Draft 1983 Blueprint at $4.7 Billion," *Chain Store Age Executive,* November
1983, 21.
[8]"Center Management: The Old Gray Mare," *Chain Store Age Executive,* June 1984, 47.

Marketing Orientation

In addition to leasing, today's shopping center manager is more involved than ever before in working directly with individual tenants. This benefits both the retailer and the center owner. Increased professionalism of managers is also bringing about improvements in their relations with corporate leasing and construction departments, which in turn are granting them a great deal more respect.

At Taubman, management of shopping centers has been refined to the point where "management has become even more responsible to the customers and their needs. Everything we do in working with the stores is to present the best opportunities to our customers. Advertising and special events must benefit the customer. We work with retailers toward this end."[9]

Through working with tenants, managers are also becoming considerably more involved in the marketing function. The strongest trend in the industry is the more active role that managers are taking in marketing. This increased involvement has coincided with the increased professionalism in the marketing of centers. Marketing 10 or 15 years ago meant simply having an antiques show or a boat show.

Many companies are training their managers better by sending them to management and marketing conferences and by holding two to three meetings annually where industry trends and events are discussed and analyzed. Many managers receive monthly sales reports generated by computers. Using those reports, they are able to work with retailers in discussing why sales are good or why they need improvement. Most center managements today want their managers to be totally involved in the running of the centers, including preparing budgets, monitoring expenses, and understanding the income side.

Summary

Retailers have four interdependent decisions to make in choosing a location: selection of a region or market area, identification of feasible sites, optimization of the company's performance, and the determination of the optimal size and design characteristics of the store.

After selecting the strategy, they must next consider the type of location best suited to their stores. The three basic types are freestanding, central business district, and shopping center in all its various forms: neighborhood–strip, community, regional, and super regional mall. If a shopping center is chosen, further choices include marketplace center, mixed use, or traditional. Six factors involved in choosing a specific site

---

[9] Ibid.

are pedestrian and vehicular traffic, parking, access roads and transportation, placement and visibility, the retail mix, and whether to buy or lease.

As important as selecting the right site is determining how well it is managed. Trends to look for include releasing, refurbishing, remerchandising, and an orientation toward marketing. The marketing approach is being emphasized by major developer–managements throughout the country.

If developers are to be creative, they must explore other opportunities for growth. These include (1) participation in the development of mixed-use and multiuse projects, both downtown and in the suburbs; (2) entry into off-price center developments; (3) diversification into other areas of real estate development, including office buildings and residential complexes; and (4) the offering of management and related services to other shopping center owners.

Questions for Review

1. What are the four interdependent decisions a retailer must make in choosing a location?
2. List the characteristics of the various major types of locations the retailer must consider, as they are discussed in this chapter. What are the advantages and disadvantages of each of these types?
3. Why is the location decision such a critical one?
4. List the major factors important to a retailer in choosing a specific site.
5. Discuss the buying versus leasing decision. Explain advantages and disadvantages of each.
6. Discuss this statement: "Just as important as selecting the right site is how well it is managed." Do you agree with this statement? Why or why not?

CASE STUDY   **Harry's Hamburgers**

Deciding on a New Location

Harry's Hamburgers was a fast food restaurant chain. Founded by Harry Oliver in the early 1960s, the chain had spread out slowly from its home base in Indianapolis, Indiana, until it consisted of 260 company-owned stores throughout the Midwest. By concentrating on hamburgers, french fries, and beverages only, Harry's kept costs down and volume up.

Harry understood hamburgers. He was not familiar with the chicken, fish, or taco business. Moreover, if he expanded his menu, his costs would go up proportionately, and there was no guarantee that customer taste would make the increased expenditure worthwhile. All in all, an increased product mix did not appear to be a smart move. The American eating public was notorious for its fickle taste, but hamburgers were a sure thing, especially because Harry's offered 210 variations.

If new products were not the answer to growth, perhaps new locations would be. Location expansion was a serious undertaking and one that required extensive study before any decisions could be made. Most medium-sized chains in the past had decided to remain regional, recognizing that to compete with the major chains, with their huge advertising budgets and large number of units, was almost impossible. Only four companies—McDonald's (about 9,400 units), Kentucky Fried Chicken (over 6,000 units), Burger King (about 5,000 units), and Pizza Hut (nearly 5,300 units)—were truly national chains. Should Harry attempt to "go national" and compete with the giants or would success be easier to achieve if he stayed close to home and opened more units within his own region?

A second decision concerned site locations within each territory, whether regional or national. The method of expansion also had to be determined. Should it be through franchises or with company-owned stores? Finally, what type of construction would make Harry's Hamburgers restaurants unique in appearance and distinguish them from the competition? (Among the 260 there was little similarity in design and appearance.)

Harry Oliver and his corporate officers found no easy answers to any of these questions. Finally, they decided to bring in a management consultant with expertise in the fast food industry to study the situation and make a long-range plan. They hired Wylie Thomson, a consultant for Fast-Food Frontiers, Inc. At a meeting in the company offices in Indianapolis, he listened carefully to the facts and statistics. Then, indicating that his remarks were only preliminary to his final report, he shared some observations.

Concerning national versus regional expansion, he felt Harry's could expand nationally. This was because Harry's had a somewhat different approach to the hamburger business, offering depth—210 variations of the same product instead of a wide assortment of diverse products. They could fill a niche in the marketplace that giants such as McDonald's and Burger King had overlooked or chosen not to compete for. This void was nationwide, and it would therefore seem that national expansion was the route to take.

He had a unique idea for site location. Why not enter the urban market and capture the office worker trade? This could be done with modular-constructed buildings designed to look like railroad cars and placed on downtown corners leased by the month at a relatively low fee ($250 to $500). Reminiscent of old-time diners that dotted the American landscape for decades, they would cost in the vicinity of $35,000 to construct. The beauty of this scheme was that if the location did not work out, the car could be moved for less than $10,000.

In the suburbs a Kentucky Fried Chicken unit costs about $250,000 to open and a McDonald's about $450,000. Urban real estate prices limited their construction in the cities except, of course, for McDonald's Town Houses. Cities appeared to be the ideal locations for Harry's, especially if predictions that pointed to the revitalization of downtown areas proved correct. With lower construction costs than in the suburbs, profit would be greater. Was there enough market potential to justify a city location?

Ideally, all outlets would be company-owned because of the potentially greater earnings over franchising. But franchising is the quickest way to build a nationwide base. Because of the inexpensive construction, franchises could sell for about $6,000 plus a 6 percent royalty, for which the franchisee would receive the company's nationwide advertising support, company-produced regional ads, Harry's special recipes, and promotional visits from the originator of the 210 varieties of Harry's Hamburgers. The franchisee would also receive unannounced visits from someone who might not always be welcome—a company inspector.

The consultant's next suggestion was to concentrate on selling franchise territories rather than single-unit franchises, and primarily to experienced fast food operators who understood the numbers. This way Harry's would be assured of a group of mini-chains when the system matured, not a scattering of mom-and-pop stores. He said that it was particularly important to look for experience and financial strength when expanding nationwide. If franchising was the answer, then it should be implemented in a way that provided the best return on investment for all parties.

Harry and the corporate officers listened intently to all of the suggestions. At the next meeting he would return with data to back up his recommendations. At that time decisions could be made.

Questions

1. Rate five fast food restaurants in your area on a scale of 1 to 5 on the variables of product mix, product quality, price, cleanliness, convenience of location, and advertising.
2. What type of locations do you see as experiencing the largest growth in fast food restaurants? Why?
3. Analyze each of Wylie Thomson's recommendations.
4. What recommendations for ownership, location expansion, or location sites do you have for Harry's Hamburgers? Explain.
5. Do you agree that the revitalization of downtown areas will take place? Why?

Chapter 11

Store Layout and Design

Source: Courtesy of Sears, Roebuck and Co.

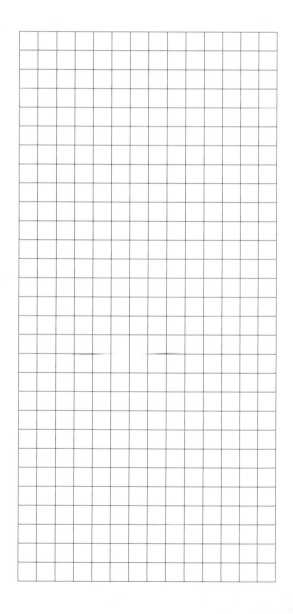

Industry Statement

Vilma Barr
Charles E. Broudy, AIA
Authors of *Designing to Sell*

The five trends related to the design and layout of retail stores that will be major influencing factors in coming years are:

1. The use of design themes for competitive differentiation.
2. Investment in design by chain stores.
3. Innovations in lighting and display.
4. The creation of smaller, targeted units.
5. The introduction of electronic and other visual selling aids.

Merchants are now seeking visual differentiation to give their stores individual appeal in look-alike shopping centers and malls. The importance of maximizing the customer draw of a store and of maximizing the yield from a site has never been greater.

Retailers have come to appreciate a professional, fully coordinated approach. Store design is one essential component of these new strategies. The external and internal appearance of the store and its overall ambience are a critical part of making a competitively differentiated appeal to potential customers.

Store atmospherics must then reinforce the investment of time in the store, reinforce the choice of merchandise, and reinforce the price-point choice—and they must subtly guide purchasing behavior.

Learning Objectives

Upon completing this chapter you should be able to:

1. Understand why the role of store designer is so important to the retailer.
2. Explain the basics of store design.
3. See how the elements of store design are currently being put to use by some of the nation's leading retail firms.
4. Explain how the roles of store designer and display designer differ.
5. Trace the factors that have led to today's trend toward reimaging and renovating.

Analyze what makes you go into a store. How do you feel when you approach it? When you are inside? Elegant? Thrifty? Inspired? Where would you rather buy a new soap dish? Bloomingdale's? The neighborhood 1930s hardware store? K mart? Imagine that you are the store itself. Do you want to say, "Stay out unless you want to spend a lot of money" or "I offer full service" or "I'm tasteful and conservative, solid and stable"? Chapter 10 stressed how important the choice of physical location is to a retailer. In this chapter we will concentrate on making the location an attractive one in which to shop.

Many stores in the same block or in the same shopping center carry the same or similar merchandise. How a store projects its image is often what gives it a competitive edge. Combined with advertising and other media promotional techniques, a unique or different visual image will help to identify the store with the goods it sells and to attract customers. The designer creates excitement in the space through lighting, traffic flow, materials, and the rhythm of the displays.[1]

RETAIL SPACE TRENDS

Until the year 2000 or beyond, emphasis will focus on redesigning existing buildings rather than constructing new ones. The high cost of land

---

[1] Vilma Barr and Charles E. Broudy, *Designing to Sell—A Complete Guide to Retail Store Planning and Design* (New York: McGraw-Hill, 1985).

and of new store construction and the need for more productive use of selling space are the governing factors. Regional malls will continue to be preferred locations. Department stores will survive only through an environment that conveys a blend of fashion, service, ambience, and value as well as promotional pricing. Macy's is a good example.[2]

With tens of thousands of mall leases coming due in the next few years, retailers must develop new design concepts that will result in the improved performance necessary to defray the rents being charged in the few new malls being built, and for leases that will have to be renegotiated. Retail consultant Howard L. Davidowitz has commented: "The preponderance of retailers committing themselves to huge remodeling, at costs that in some cases mount as high as for building a new store, don't own the technical talent in sufficient numbers to make these programs work in proper coordination with merchandising and marketing."[3]

Davidowitz takes the industry to task for its failure to develop in-house staffs. Expertise should be developed internally in the areas of architecture, store construction, fixtures, visual merchandising, color schemes, department and traffic layouts, lighting, floor coverings, special wall materials, photography and other graphics, hangtags, and carry bags.

Some specialty chains seeking to differentiate themselves are The Limited and its Limited Express, Casual Corner and Ups N Downs divisions of U.S. Shoe, Petrie Stores, Miller-Wohl, Brooks Fashion Stores, The Gap, Ikea, and Conran's.[4]

SHAPING THE RETAIL ENVIRONMENT

Suppose that a merchant needs a location in a particular market to sell jeans and pants. A space that is 12 feet wide by 75 feet long becomes available at a good rental. In less than three months the designer has to turn this bowling-alley interior into a busy specialty store. Where does the designer start?

This challenge was actually presented to Charles E. Broudy & Associates. Before beginning the project they had to answer the basic question, how do we best move the merchandise? Inventory and selection were primary, and fast turnover was needed. There was not room in the store for more than one theme, and this had to be functional. The solution was a series of revolving bins that resembled Ferris wheels that dispensed the merchandise. The designers called the entire vehicle a pantwheel. (See Figure 11.1.) It was manufactured to their design and specifications, and a patent application was applied for. The fixtures are operated by the

---

[2] Samuel Feinberg, "Retailing in 2004: The Look Should Be Different," *Women's Wear Daily*, December 4, 1984, 6.

[3] Samuel Feinberg, "Retailers' Remodeling Urge Called a Boost for Egos," *Women's Wear Daily*, August 8, 1984, 20.

[4] Ibid.

Figure 11.1   Pantwheel: Revolving Bins Operated by Customers

Source: Courtesy of Charles E. Broudy & Associates.

customer and fit the mood of the merchandise. They also help draw customers into the store's rear selling areas.[5]

Impossible Spaces

Impossible spaces are often the most exciting. A creative designer would rather work in a tough space like a narrow store, a triangle, or a space that wraps around a corner than a square with four matching corners and a flat ceiling. Difficult spaces invite designers to expand their design horizons.

The Theme

Supergraphics
Billboard-sized graphic shapes, usually brightly colored and of simple design.

A good jumping-off point for a retail design is a theme. It could be a movable merchandise wheel, as in the jeans store, or a pure geometric shape. As examples, a circular pattern could be effective in a store selling eyeglasses or shoes, while semicircular elements might be used for an art gallery. The theme could also be established through photographs and **supergraphics.**

Cubic Footage

Sight Line
Line of vision at eye level.

Think in terms of cubic footage, and take advantage of it. In dealing with a store-planning project, the designer has to treat areas like ceilings and walls above the typical **sight line.** These planes can be utilized to hang merchandise or displays so that every inch of space works to support merchandise presentation.

Creative Solutions

Be creative with colors, ceilings, texture, and surfaces. If a thorough search fails to turn up display cases or fixtures that relate to the merchandise and the design theme, create a special design.

Quality of Materials

Use quality materials when they enhance the merchandise, but do not put expensive materials in places where they do not mean anything to the customer or the items for sale.

---

[5] Vilma Barr and Charles E. Broudy, *Designing To Sell—A Complete Guide to Retail Store Planning and Design* (New York: McGraw-Hill, 1985).

Gondola
Hutch-type display
cabinet designed to
be placed against a
wall.

THE BASICS OF STORE DESIGN

Store Design
Design of exterior
features: interior
configuration; and
decoration,
fixtures, and
display elements.

Flexibility and Adaptability

Flexibility and adaptability comprise the creative core of successful retail plans. Display stands, racks, counters, **gondolas,** lighting, and everything else that is not critical to the structural support of the building will probably be moved. The original balance that was so carefully achieved may only be hinted at six months after the store opens. Little in retailing is inviolate, but a sensible traffic plan and a unifying theme that holds the space together should supply sufficient stability to uphold the design's integrity.

Store design is defined as the formulation of all aspects of the retail physical environment to achieve image, operational performance, and sales results.[6] It requires the coordination of all components—economic, merchandising, architectural, structural and mechanical engineering, and interior design. The role of the store designer is accordingly sophisticated and interdisciplinary, giving professional direction to a team whose decisions will create the multifaceted elements of the store.

Contemporary Influences on Store Design

Design and the design image in stores, as in all aspects of our culture, are the result of contemporary social influences. The move back to the natural as reflected in society's interest in ecology; pure fabrics like 100-percent wool, cotton, and silk; the rebirth of handicrafts; and the birth of the consumer movement have led to an upgrading of public taste.

The effects of the mass media, of product design, and of forms of marketing are omnipresent. The proliferation of lifestyles, of fashions, and of new forms has become a reality that forces store design to reflect these influences.

Achieving a store image must also be related to problems of economics. In the final analysis, a successful store is a planned environment for selling at profit. During the 1970s, construction costs in the United States escalated 10 to 15 percent per year.[7] In addition, the greater complexity and sophistication of new stores increase tangible costs. These two factors have led to serious tensions between the objectives of creating an attractive environment and of controlling feasibility costs. Designing a store therefore requires constant evaluation of new techniques, new planning ideas, new styles, new materials, and new methods of fabrication and installation. Only in this way will results meet objectives.

---

[6] Lawrence J. Israel, A.I.A., *Visual Merchandising* (New York: National Retail Merchants Association, 1979).
[7] Ibid.

A store image must be related to the market itself. The worst possible image is projected by an overdesigned store that does not reflect its own philosophy, price structure, and value systems. The fundamental responsibility of the store designer is to evaluate the interplay among image, merchandising, and values.

Many shoppers in regional malls go from one specialty shop to another without knowing the names of the particular retailers they visit. The overlap in merchandise is responsible for this failure to be able to differentiate among them—even though each company may seek to appeal to a slightly different segment of the total market. However, establishment of a distinct identity, whether in department stores, specialty stores, or supermarkets, is often more a matter of customer perception than actuality.

Elements of Store Design

Fixture

Fixture
Showcase, table, gondola, or rack used to house and display merchandise, usually with a useful life of about 20 years.

Designed to house, present, and display merchandise, the **fixture** is a carefully constructed component of the interior environment. It has a long-range life and is built within the standards of the store fixture industry. Because fixtures are built to last, both structurally and stylistically, the useful life of fixtures averages approximately 20 years.

Display Element

Display Element
Component with some functions of a fixture but more dramatic, less well constructed, and with about a five-year life.

Limited probably to a five-year life, the **display element** is generally designed to a more cyclical and fashion use than are fixtures. It is constructed of less substantial materials. More and more, the display element serves as a merchandising fixture, supplanting the standardized table, gondola, showcase, and rack. Most are imaginatively arranged, based on three-dimensional aesthetic forms that give the store fixturization plan a much more vivid, varied, and exciting character. (See Figure 11.2.)

Architecture

The exterior design of the building is the interface of the store's image and the community. Elements such as signing, window display, visual entrance conditions, protection from weather, a comfortable atmosphere, or distinctive character must be combined in an arresting architectural form. At the same time, the form is influenced by the configuration generated by the store's interior functional needs.

Opportunities for imaginative seasonal displays can be built into the exterior design. Variations will be based on location—whether in a

Figure   11.2   The Display Element Used as a Merchandising Fixture: Sears Food
Preparation Shops

Source: Courtesy Sears, Roebuck and Co.

downtown central business district, in a shopping mall, or freestanding store—and will depend on accepted regional standards of taste, use of materials, and construction techniques.

**CREATING THE
PROGRAM**

The first step in establishing a store design is initial programming. To define the store's philosophy of selling and to establish a comprehensive plan for the building space, there should be a serious meeting between the designer and top management.

Local community building codes will often establish the building–parking ratios. How the building will be layered is not only dependent on

Homogeneous Merchandising
Merchandising philosophy that limits goods presented to items similar in nature.

the site utilization but is also the result of an interior sales and merchandising objective. There could be a choice, for example, between a large floor sales area combining a heterogeneous mix of departments and a relatively small floor area presenting a **homogeneous merchandising** content. This decision would be made by the store's merchandising philosophy.

In programming the project, cost objectives must be established. These should encompass architectural, construction, and mechanical engineering systems; interiors and fixtures; display elements; and all

FROM THE FIELD

The Limited Approach

In the fall of 1985, The Limited opened its most ambitious store and its first major one on New York City's Madison Avenue. According to industry sources, executives at the company, based in Columbus, Ohio, think the Madison Avenue store could double the $5 million normally done at its comparable shopping center locations across the country.

The store, which reportedly cost more than $5 million to build, houses three Limited divisions—The Limited Stores, Limited Express, and Victoria's Secret. Each is merchandised independently of the other two within the structure, which has 19,500 square feet of total space.

A key element is the historic 1928 building at 62nd Street, originally designed by McKim, Mead & White, with its last major use as Porter's apparel store. (See Figure 11.3.) The Limited found the 1927 blueprints for the exterior and refurbished it accordingly, replacing the glass blocks with huge, clear

glass windows and outlining and decorating the granite and limestone facade with liberal amounts of bronze.

In sharp contrast, the interior is strikingly contemporary. The original two-story building was expanded to four full floors by capping the building with a greenhouse. A sweeping spiral staircase was cut from the basement level to the roof, under a large central skylight. Part of the upper stairwell is lined with narrow strips of mirrors, fitted edge-to-edge around the circumference. Between the four floors, three mezzanines were inserted, shooting off the staircase and bringing the number of merchandising levels to seven.

"The idea is you can stand on one level and see all the others," comments The Limited's presentation director.

"We wanted to draw customers up the stairs. Some of the most exciting merchandise is on the upper level," he continued. "It's very difficult to get people upstairs."

Source: Pete Born, "The Limited Set for a Big N.Y. Splash," *Women's Wear Daily*, November 6, 1985, 15.

Figure　11.3　A Historic Building Housing Contemporary Merchandise: The Limited

Source: Courtesy of The Limited, Inc.

operational equipment. Absolute candor is necessary to establish realistic cost control, and this cost must be hypothesized two or three years ahead to take into account the inflationary cost cycle during planning and construction. So that store management and the designer know when responsibility for decision-making events must be taken, it is essential that planning and construction time schedules be established.

BASIC STORE LAYOUTS

There are two basic planning guidelines for laying out a retail sales floor. Six basic plans can help the designer to carry them out. These are certainly not the only plans that can be developed, but they form the foundation on which others can be created. (See Figure 11.4.)

The Guidelines for Store Layout

1. Use 100 percent of the space allocated.
2. Do not sacrifice function for aesthetics. Successful plans combine both to the fullest.

Figure   11.4   Six Basic Plans for a Retail Sales Floor

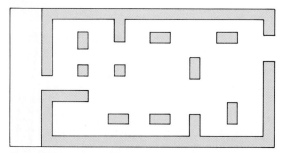

Straight Plan: Uses walls and projections to create smaller, economical spaces.

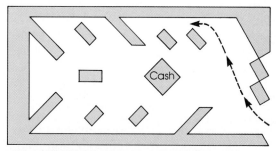

Diagonal Pattern: Permits angular traffic flow and creates perimeter design interest and excitement in movement. The central placement of the cash register permits security and vision.

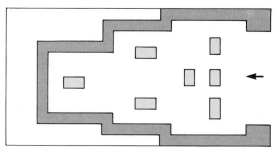

Varied Plan: Adds a variety of forms, which can work to a designer's advantage.

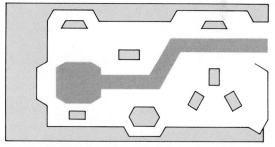

Pathway Plan: Pulls patrons through the store to the rear without interruption by floor fixtures. The path can take any shape, and it creates a design pattern.

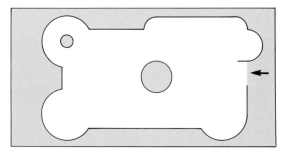

Circular and Curved Shapes: Soften the angular and square plan.

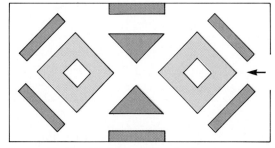

Geometric Plan: Establishes interest without excessive cost if appropriate to the store's product. Ceiling and floors can be lowered or raised to create zones and departments.

Source: Vilma Barr and Charles E. Broudy, *Designing to Sell—A Complete Guide to Retail Store Planning and Design* (New York: McGraw-Hill, 1986), 44. Adapted with permission.

Six Basic Plans

Straight Plan

The straight plan is a conventional form of layout that utilizes walls and projections to create smaller spaces. It is an economical plan to execute and can be adapted to any type of store, from gift shops to apparel outlets, from drug and grocery stores to department stores.

Pathway Plan

Applicable to virtually any type of store, the pathway plan is particularly suited to larger stores of over 5,000 square feet and on one level. The pathway plan, a good architectural organizer, gets shoppers smoothly from the front to the rear of the store.

Diagonal Plan

For self-service stores, a diagonal plan is optimal. The cashier is in a central location, with sight lines to all areas of the space. Soft goods or hard goods stores, including drug and food stores, can take advantage of the diagonal plan.

Curved Plan

For boutiques, salons, or other high quality stores, the curved plan creates an inviting, special environment for the customer. It also costs more to construct than angular or square plans.

Varied Plan

For products that require backup merchandise to be immediately adjacent (shoes and men's shirts, for example), the varied plan is highly functional. It is a variation of the straight-line plan with sufficient square footage allowed for box or carton storage off the main sales floor with perimeter wall stocking.

Geometric Plan

The designer creates forms with shapes derived from showcases, racks, or gondolas in a geometric plan. This plan is the most exotic of the six basic plans, and the designer can use wall angles to restate the shapes dominating the sales floor.[8]

---

[8] Vilma Barr and Charles E. Broudy, *Designing To Sell—A Complete Guide to Retail Store Planning and Design* (New York: McGraw-Hill, 1985).

Following the trend toward flashy displays that make maximum use of available space, Strawbridges, Philadelphia, houses merchandise in a colorful candy-filled castle.

The "Weekend People" theme adopted by this Philadelphia department store is enhanced through the effective use of mannequins and props on a stationary island area.

A product's wide variety of colors can be used to an advantage in designing a display area, as shown in this dynamic towel display for Shillitos.

Bright colors, powerful lighting, and the repeated patterns of giant Tinkertoys create a mood of activity and fun in the children's department at Hecht's, Washington, D.C.

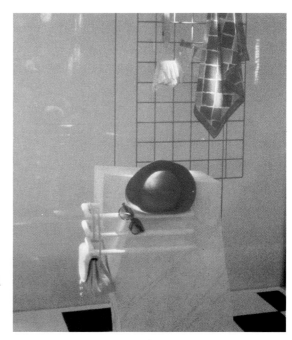

Macy's San Francisco uses a boldly colored hat as the focal point for this window display, drawing the customer's eye to an assortment of accessories.

Hardwood floors and elephant tusks entice shoppers into Banana Republic stores, where store design carries out the "safari" theme of the company's merchandise and mail order catalogs.

FIXTURIZATION

Fixturization is generally subdivided into wall systems and floor fixtures.

Wall Systems
Wall selling fixtures that include full-height perimeter partitions and high partitions between departments or zones.

Wall Systems

The **wall systems** include full-height perimeter partitions and high interior partitions between departments or zones of merchandise. High wall systems influence the requirements of all mechanical subsystems of the building: lighting, heating, ventilating, and air-conditioning. While a full-height partition background is attractive and creates a strong surface for identification and styling of a department, it structurally interferes with uniform spacing of the ceiling subsystems.

Floor Fixtures

The vast range of types of floor selling fixtures includes tables, gondolas, convertible units, showcases, island back fixtures, counters, self-selection counters, platforms, superstructures, garment racks, and a wealth of specially designed fixtures for impact at points of merchandise presentation. These are built as modules that can be interchanged and placed in different arrangements and clusters. Floor fixtures are generally prefabricated and prefinished. The designer must always bear in mind that floor fixtures are mobile by definition and that all possible combinations must be anticipated, because they are moved from time to time, seasonally, or as store selling techniques change. The forms, materials, and colors selected should be compatible with one another in any arrangement.

The selling fixture can be either custom designed or selected from manufacturers' stock catalogs. A third source is the display field. These are generally built of knockdown metal parts and are often designed to allow for simple on-site rearrangement of the parts.

Serious thought must be given to comparative costs of different fixture types based on resource, materials, form, size, and convertibility. The initial purchase can quickly become expensive if continuous service, maintenance, or replacement is required. Appropriate fixtures should be selected within budgets related to the pro forma sales plans and return on investment.

The Ceiling

Along with the development of the fixture layout and the determination of fixture types, a study is also made of the ceiling plane. One of the major elements of the interior, the ceiling contains lighting, air-condi-

Figure 11.5 Retail Store Lighting: Dos and Don'ts

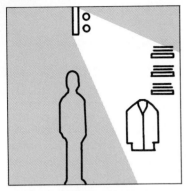

Don't illuminate the top of the merchandise; do illuminate the front.

Don't aim light at the customer; do use baffles or louvers.

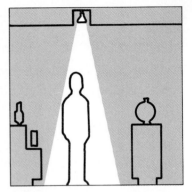

Don't illuminate the floor, unless it is a carpet store display.

Don't create glare on glass showcases. It hinders the customer's view of the merchandise inside.

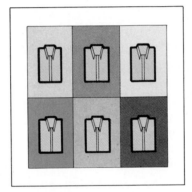

Do understand how fluorescent lamps affect color rendition. Refer to manufacturers' charts.

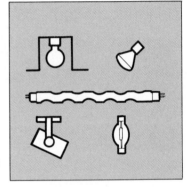

Do consider energy consumption when selecting fixtures.

Do conceal source lamps to prevent glare.

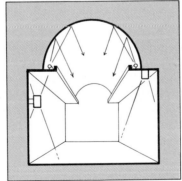

Do use lighting to sculpt or highlight important features of the space and the merchandise.

Source: Vilma Barr and Charles E. Broudy, *Designing to Sell—A Complete Guide to Retail Store Planning and Design* (New York: McGraw-Hill, 1986), 95. Adapted with permission.

Figure   11.6   Custom-Designed Lighting: Philadelphia Museum of Art

Source: Courtesy of Charles E. Broudy & Associates.

tioning, sprinklers, and acoustics. It is the most visual part of the store interior.

Lighting is a highly technical subdivision of store design. The basic dos and don'ts are illustrated in Figure 11.5. Custom-designed lighting can be used to visually tie together units of different heights, as shown in Figure 11.6.

DESIGN, DISPLAY, AND DECORATION

At this stage in the design development, it is important for the designer and the display person to meet in order to establish areas of mutual responsibility.

The designer is responsible for color and the selection of all materials. The selection of flooring can be used as an example. Like the ceiling, the floor is a large and important surface. Its design often controls the definition of sales departments by material, pattern, texture, and color. It also underlines public spaces and traffic circulation. The selection of exciting flooring must take into account merchandising, maintenance, and costs—and is therefore an important area for the designer to control.

Wall surfaces offer great variety of treatment beyond paint. The choice of coverings includes papers, woven rattans, and fabrics that add

Typographical Display
Type used to make a design statement.

dimension and textural interest to the partition systems. Artwork and graphics, including poster-like color, forms, and **typographical displays** are exciting sources for wall treatments. Art in the form of clever mural treatments, photo montages, blowups, and light sculpture can play a strategic role in highlighting, extending, and deepening the spectrum.

Construction

Construction Documents
Working drawings and specifications prepared by the store designer for use by contractors.

The store designer is now ready to prepare the **construction documents,** which are working drawings and specifications used by contractors for cost bidding and construction purposes. The specifications supplement detailed scale drawings and verbally describe the scope of work, quality of workmanship, and types of materials. They stipulate time limitations and contract completion dates.

Once contracts are awarded, fixture contractors customarily prepare a series of shop drawings that translate the design information of the contract documents to their own set of instructions and lists of materials. The shop drawings are then submitted to the designer for approval and comments before fabrication proceeds.

Installation

The store designer's responsibility for supervision and administration of the work includes: the review of shop drawings, communications and correspondence with contractors and representatives of the owner, and observation and field supervision of the installation. The extent of this supervision must be clearly explained to the owner, because there is a distinct difference in the architectural and store design field between observation and supervision of the work. Observation means a general review of the work as it progresses, assuring that major questions are answered and that the installation is progressing satisfactorily. Supervision means a complete on-site inspection and coordination, expediting, and checking daily of every phase of the installation to assure that the work is proceeding in strict conformance with the contract documents.

The final responsibility of the store designer is the approval of the installation by the contractors, the preparation of lists of deficiencies, and the certification that all parts of the installation are finally corrected and completed satisfactorily.

Store Designer as Team Leader

The store designer is the leader of a team involving merchants, architects, engineers, display and operations people, and contractors from the decorative and construction trades. It is his or her interdisciplinary responsibility to deliver an appropriate image within the limits set by time and cost controls but, at the same time, to demonstrate outstanding creativity.

REIMAGING AND RENOVATING

Image creation is critical. Michael Gade, president of RPA Enterprises, has pointed out: "Many shopping malls, particularly those built during the boom years of the 1960s, are already reaching economic senility. They don't pass the blink test. You could put yourself blindfolded in any of a dozen malls in a metropolitan area and when the blindfold came off, you wouldn't know where you were."[9]

A solution can be found in the observations of Anthony Belluschi, senior vice president at Charles Kober Associates. "I think of retail centers as being like theaters where shoppers like to be part of the audience but part of the play, too. The secret of the most successful spaces is never to let customers know if they are on stage or off."

The Trend toward Renovation

Belluschi believes that "doing renovations has become a trend because there are so many that can be done, ranging from centers that are 10 years old to some that are 30 years old. Whether successful or dying, they are decaying. But most often they still offer good prime locations. What we need to do with these projects is to create a totally fresh approach."[10]

He adds: "Studies have shown that at most centers 92 percent of the shoppers are repeat shoppers and they don't want to see the same old thing that they have been seeing all the time. We need to make the shopping places new and exciting."

His firm seeks to help center owners to maximize the return on investment by increasing spatial density, by providing for mixed use, and reducing the parking ratio. The firm also stresses making a strong architectural statement.[11]

New Images at Major Chains

In an effort to capture hearts, minds, and wallets, mass merchandisers today are spending millions of dollars to change their stores, product lines, and images.

---

[9] "Architects Translate Developers' Visions," *Chain Store Age Executive,* February 1984, 40.
[10] Ibid.
[11] Ibid.

"The influence of the major chains is felt throughout the industry," according to retail analyst Walter Loeb. "And all of the major merchandisers have made great strides in revamping their merchandise and updating the look of their stores."[12]

The United States has a store excess of about 47 percent. Mass merchandisers such as Sears, J. C. Penney, and Montgomery Ward are responding by cutting poorly performing lines, upgrading store presentation, and raising merchandise standards.[13] The decisions made independently by both J. C. Penney and Sears to implement full-scale changes in the physical images of their stores will result in a combined total investment of more than $4 billion. The monies will be spent on the largest remodeling programs in the history of either chain.

---

[12] Belinda Hulin-Salkin, "Mass Merchandisers Moving Up," *Advertising Age,* August 9, 1984, 12.
[13] Ibid.

Summary

The merchant–designer team gives the store its visual personality. A retail unit is born in their psyches. Before a line is drawn, they have to project themselves inside the store and act as the consumer. An honest answer to "What would make me interested in buying here?" provides the backbone of the program. Many subtle, unseen elements, like the senses of smell and hearing, play important roles in the overall theme.

The number of stock turns projected for the merchandise and the people who buy and sell it are the most important factors in organizing a retail design plan. Because the goal of store layout and design is to increase profits through turnover, each piece of merchandise should be approached as a modular component to be displayed. Retail store designers must visualize the space with its most important element, the merchandise, in place.

If they do not, they are running the risk of inviting the most devastating of all store design critiques: "The store looked great before we put the merchandise in it!"

Questions for Review

1. Define the term *store design.*
2. Keeping in mind the above definition, what is the role of the store designer?
3. What are the elements of store design?

4. Describe the six basic plans for a retail sales floor layout.
5. List at least five of the "dos and don'ts" of retail store lighting.
6. How does the store designer's responsibility differ from that of a display person?
7. What is meant by the phrase *reimaging and renovating*?

CASE STUDY   **Elkins Brothers**

Deciding on Interior Design

The Elkins brothers finally made the first decision. They were going to lease a store in the new regional mall that was soon to open in the White Pond trading area.

For months they had been dickering with the developers over rent and location within the mall and, once an agreement was reached, the remaining decisions concerned the store itself. The image had to be right to attract the many customers who would be patronizing the mall. In addition, with a total area of 20,000 square feet, they had to make the best use of the approximately 15,000 square feet of selling space if they wanted to pay off their investment and make a profit.

Should they open a full-service sportswear salon with spacious dressing rooms, expensive lighting, elegant fixtures of chrome and plexiglass, beautiful interior displays and thick carpeting, attracting the shopper to whom money was no object, or should they opt for wall-to-wall indoor-outdoor carpeting? The decision, of course, depended on their target market and the type of clothing they planned to carry.

Because they were starting from scratch, the only real limit on merchandising decisions would be set by the customer groups they wanted to attract. Was it to be a store for juniors, misses, or women? Was it to be full service or promotional? They decided on a complete sportswear shop because sportswear was the fastest selling category in all ready-to-wear, regardless of size or price line. They also decided to aim at the high school, college, and young career crowd and to stock all classifications in depth.

Other decisions had to follow. Elkins Brothers could resemble the best junior sportswear department of the biggest department store in the mall. Alternatively, they could carry slightly off-price junior and misses goods, still in depth but in a wider assortment than that available from the manufacturers on a predetermined classification plan. A third alternative was to carry only private-label goods made exclusively under the Elkins label. In any case, the store should have a look that made the proper statement and told the buying public what sort of merchandise to expect. The interior design and the windows make the fashion statement for any store.

Rob and Jay Elkins had been manufacturers' representatives for ten years, traveling throughout the Midwest with lines of pants, skirts, and tops carrying well-known brand names. They understood the women's wear business and, as a result, felt that they understood the needs of the consumer market, having listened to the hundreds of retailers who for years had made up their customer list. They now would have the opportunity to prove themselves as retailers in White Pond.

White Pond was a community of about 150,000 and White Pond Mall, the only regional mall in a 50-mile radius, was expected to have a drawing power double that number. With 300,000 people in the potential market, it was important to decide which customers to target and then plan for that particular group. In the diversified environment around White Pond were executive and professional families, career singles, and a large group of highly paid skilled workers employed at the electronics and computer plants in the area. Family income averaged about $20,000 annually. With three high schools in White Pond alone and five colleges in the vicinity, there was a large under-25 population. Many young people remained in White Pond after college because they were able to find good jobs in the industrial complexes that ringed the town. Besides, it was a nice place to live.

This was the information on which Rob and Jay had based their decision to open a sportswear shop and to merchandise a junior look for the 16- to 30-year-old market. All decisions had to be made as scientifically as possible. They could not afford to fail because of a simple mistake like the wrong layout, inappropriate fixtures or, for that matter, a store that presented a poorly conceived image.

What was the right image? The answer depended largely on their brand and price policies. Should they carry an assortment of well-known designer labels only, a mixture of American and European ready-to-wear brands, private label goods made exclusively for Elkins, or manufacturers' job lots and samples with the labels removed? If they decided to "go designer," the shop should have an exclusive air. On the other hand, if they sold only off-price goods purchased in lots, the store had to present a bargain atmosphere. If the merchandise was to carry a private Elkins label, the store would need a special Elkins look, starting at the entrance and carried throughout the entire shop.

Merchandising policies would thus dictate the interior layout of the store, the fixtures, lighting, display areas, fitting rooms, color, furniture, and flooring. No one would believe that Elkins prices were lower than the department or specialty stores in the mall if the store did not look promotional. No one would believe that Kenzo, Ann Klein, or St. Laurent clothes could be found at Elkins if it did not resemble a Paris boutique, with indirect lighting, a few soft sofas, and avant garde displays hanging from elegant ceiling fixtures. Would a mixture of butcher block and glass distinguish Elkins from all other junior specialty stores?

Tied in with the image as translated by the interior design was the question of service. A central checkout point and a bank of fitting rooms against the back of the store represented one extreme. The other would require strategically stationed salespeople dressed to convey the Elkins look and to be as much a part of the total atmosphere as the merchandise or the fixtures.

Neither Rob nor Jay, expert merchants, had ever thought about the importance of the physical plant. They were aware of construction and decorating costs, but the real hidden cost in building a store was the interior. If it did not complement the clothing, did not attract the right clientele, and did not allow maximum exposure of merchandise, the results could be disastrous. The greatest selection of merchandise in the world would not sell if no customers were attracted to the store. Rob and Jay Elkins listed the decisions already made and the remaining alternatives. In this way, they felt, the right interior layout could be determined.

Completed Decisions

1. To open a junior sportswear shop catering to the young female White Pond school and career crowd.
2. To stock all classifications of junior sportswear in depth.
3. To carry a small assortment of well-known U.S. designer clothes at regular markup and in-depth assortments under the Elkins label at a slightly lower markup.
4. To offer the following services: (a) sales help throughout the store, (b) acceptance of universal credit cards, and (c) individual fitting rooms.

Layout Possibilities

1. Self-service racks placed in rectangular fashion with very little attention to a beautiful atmosphere.
2. Elegant fixtures exposing all merchandise to the public, in a free-flow arrangement with a combination of direct, indirect, and strobe lighting.
3. A posh interior complete with elegant furniture and fixtures, hidden merchandise, and soft lights, all in a salon environment.
4. A combination of any of the above three basic plans.

The basic layout decision and the detailed plans would require a great deal of study.

Questions

1. Analyze the possible interior layouts as described in the case in terms of the completed decisions.
   a. Self-service
   b. Salon
   c. Self-selection
   d. Combination

2. Which plan would you select, based on your analysis in Question 1. Why?
3. Do you have any suggestions concerning lighting and music? Relate these to the plan selected for Question 2.
4. Draw a plan (to scale) of your suggestion for the Elkins store including all racks, fixtures, seating areas (if any), display areas, fitting rooms, and so on.

Part **V**

Merchandise Mix

Chapter 12

The Planning Phase

Source: Jack Gifford, Professor of
Marketing, Miami University of
Ohio.

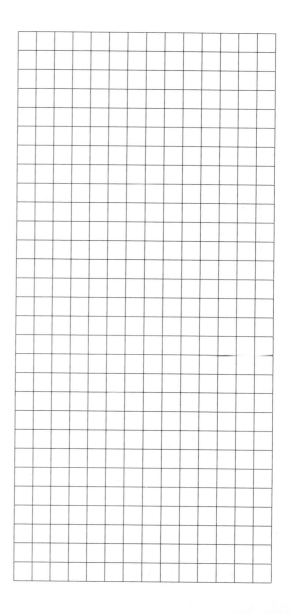

Industry Statement

Vice President, Marketing
Conair Corporation

A retailer's business is full of partnerships. It is these partnerships that dictate the success or failure of a retailer in achieving goals and objectives. They are the reason that planning is so important.

The partners are also called vendors, manufacturers, suppliers, and so on. They provide most of the merchandise that is sold through retail channels. It takes planning to make sure that the right merchandise is where it should be, when it is needed, and in the correct quantities. This planning is a partnership with input supplied by all partners. In recent years, planning has become more sophisticated at the retail level. It has also become more widespread. This has happened because planning improves merchandise turns and retail profits.

One of the more common planning elements used today is the *plan-o-gram.* This is a retailer's basic merchandise plan. It forces the vendor and the vendor's salesperson to take a more businesslike approach to presenting a product. The retailer is, in effect, saying to the vendor: "I have a certain amount of real estate. Come in and show me why I should assign you a certain amount of this real estate for your product."

The plan-o-gram also tells the vendor that, once he gets on the shelf, he is relatively likely to stay on for at least a year. Because of that, he can make investments—investments in merchandise and investments in the retailer himself, in the form of promotions, point-of-purchase fixtures, co-op advertising, and so on. He can also make investments in national advertising if he knows he has a place on the shelf for one year.

Once the basic merchandise plan is set, the balance of the planning follows. At this point a vendor can become a true partner to the retailer, as the three examples illustrate.

Advertising. The vendor knows the seasonality of his product—when it sells and when it does not. By using this information, the retailer can plan ads that offer the best use of his or her advertising dollars.

Promotion. Many vendors have sales tools such as coupons and rebates that can be structured and geared toward a specific time period and event. Without planning well in advance, a retailer could miss out on a great many opportunities.

Inventory. Retailers and vendors are concerned with maximizing their turns. With the use of the plan-o-gram, advertising planning, and promotion planning, a vendor can work with a retailer to plan an order/inventory cycle. This allows the retailer to take advantage of seasonal buy-in specials and quantity discounts while still maintaining solid control over inventory.

In short, planning at the retailer level is necessary so that the retailer can take full advantage of the various programs and opportunities presented by a vendor. The net result for the retailer will always be increased profits and merchandise turns.

Learning Objectives

Upon completing this chapter you should be able to:

1. List the goals of the merchandise budgeting process.
2. Describe the steps in a merchandise budget.
3. Detail the types of data that are helpful in planning future sales.
4. Determine when to use the weeks-of-supply method for figuring needed stock.
5. Use the basic stock method for determining needed stock.
6. Calculate an open-to-buy figure.
7. Explain the formula for figuring gross margin.
8. Understand the goals of classification merchandising.

Successful retailers can no longer belong to the seat-of-the-pants school of merchandising. A clear-cut plan of action for a specific period of time is necessary if, in this world of sophisticated marketing research methods and scientific management, assortments are to turn into sales. Retailing is big business, and retailers must make use of the same types of modern marketing and management techniques that their suppliers use. One weak link and the entire chain of distribution as we know it could fail. Proper assortment of the **merchandise/service mix** becomes more important for retailers each year. So does a proper merchandise budget—the focal point of this chapter.

Merchandise/Service Mix
Merchandise or service assortment.

PLANNING POLICIES AND GOALS

In all retail establishments, whether in-store or nonstore, the overall policies that govern the operation also govern the merchandise planning process. Sound policies are the foundation on which proper assortments are built.

Policies dictate the kinds of goods or services the store will sell, the quality of the goods or services, whether lines will be deep or shallow or broad or narrow, and whether goods or services will be limited to related items or expanded to include a variety of unrelated merchandise groupings. Policies become the basis for the actual merchandise/service mix. As an example, The Limited is a well-known national fashion chain that limits its merchandise to clothing geared to the middle-income woman under age 45 who wants the latest in smart fashion at moderate prices. The mix is described in the store name; the name and the merchandise policies are the same—limited! Price and quality are also governed by overall management policy. The Sears mix is based on a policy of conglomerate merchandising. Sears has everything from theater tickets to tennis equipment, computers to clothing, batteries to bonds. Policies provide a frame of reference that is preliminary to the actual budgeting process.

When setting policy and starting the planning process, merchandise/service planners must always keep in mind the wants and needs of their targeted customers, and their image. They must also give serious consideration to shifting economics and consumer attitudes.

The planning process begins with the merchandise budget, which must provide (1) a plan for future merchandising operations, (2) a guide for future purchasing, (3) a measuring device for evaluating current performance, (4) a measuring device for evaluating merchandising executives, and (5) a record of actual against planned figures.

Budget Terminology

Before the planning process is described, certain terms that are used in merchandise planning and budgeting must be defined.

- *Merchandise budget.* A forecast/plan generally expressed in dollars (although it can be expressed in units) for buying and controlling the amount of goods purchased to meet customers' needs during a specific period.
- *Merchandise assortment.* Related groups of items intended for the same general end use and usually placed together for customer convenience.
- *Assortment plan.* A detailed and complete list of all items making up an assortment by vendor, specific detail, and price.
- *Balanced assortment.* An assortment in which the items, amounts, and prices of the stock on hand during a certain period equal, as closely as possible, the items, amounts, and prices being demanded in the target market or markets.
- *Classification merchandising.* A technique that breaks down traditional merchandise categories into as many subclassifications as are manageable for purposes of pinpointing, to the most finite degree, emerging and declining areas of business.
- *Turnover.* Number of times the average stock for a period is sold and replaced.
- *Gross margin.* Best expressed as a formula:

$$\frac{\text{Gross}}{\text{Margin}} = \frac{\text{Cost of Doing}}{\text{Business}} + \frac{\text{Reasonable}}{\text{Profit}} - \text{Reductions}.$$

THE MERCHANDISE BUDGET

Because a balance between stock-on-hand and estimated needs must precede the actual assortment plan, a logical place to start the planning process is with the merchandise budget.[1] The five major segments in any merchandise budget are (1) estimated sales, (2) planned stock (inventory), (3) planned reductions (markdown plus shortages), (4) planned purchases, and (5) planned gross margin.

Estimated Sales

Estimating future sales (or income) is the starting point in any budgeting process. If future sales are not estimated as accurately as possible, inventory investment dollars will be spent incorrectly. When this happens, the four steps that follow will need constant adjustment throughout the period being planned, and the entire budget will be of little use.

Many retailers plan sales in dollars regardless of the economy. In an inflationary economy, however, some retailers estimate sales first in units and then in dollars, because future dollars will not always buy as many units as past or current dollars. In that case, if dollars were used as the base instead of units, the final figures might represent an insufficient number of planned items. Once units are planned, dollar amounts can easily be estimated by building in an inflation factor.

On the other hand, future dollars may buy more units than past or current dollars. When this happens, overstocking occurs. Buyers who purchase on the international market must be aware of this when foreign currency is in a deflationary period. A good example took place in 1985 with the deflation of the British pound. Because of the monetary situation, American retail buyers of fine British china or woolen goods could purchase much more than for the same dollar amount spent in 1984. As a result, they were careful when planning budgets for 1986 so as not to end up with too much inventory.

Although some merchants still plan sales by the beat-last-year's-figures method, most are much more scientific and use a number of aids, including the weeks-of-supply system, to be discussed later in the chapter.

P.O.S. electronic registers, primarily an inventory control tool, are also useful in providing information for sales planning. They can instantly record a wide variety of information that is useful in updating sales and inventory figures. P.O.S. registers enable buyers to compare actual figures to planned figures on a daily basis, even if buyers are located in a central office and not in the stores.

In addition to present facts and figures, research must delve into past records. Both past and present data are important when estimating sales.

---

[1] Although this is a planning tool for merchandise, more and more retailers will be using the same or a similar technique in planning for the sale of services (a growing classification in retailing). In studying the merchandise budget, this should be kept in mind.

In-Store Information

Sales. Past sales, broken down with the help of the computer into finite classifications, are a meaningful source of information for budget and assortment planning. Study of past sales, for example, lets the buyer know exactly which basic men's slacks were sold—in which colors, styles, and fabrics and from which vendors. Of course, this can be done only for items already in stock. Selection of new items is much more subjective.

Returned Goods and Adjustments. The unspoken message from consumers that accompanies the statistics on returned goods is, "Do not offer us this merchandise again." Retailers may use these figures to reject vendors, items, or entire classifications of goods.

Credit Department Data. Analysis of credit data results in two types of important information: (1) records of purchases and (2) charge customers' profiles. Because credit sales make up a large proportion of total sales, they are an excellent source of both quantitative and qualitative data. A study of computer records from the credit department not only indicates kinds and prices of merchandise purchased and returned but also shows who the charge account customers are, their income, and lifestyles.

Human Data. Both customer inquiries and suggestions made by salespeople and fashion coordinators—either staff or consultants—offer additional input to assortment planning. Customers do not ask about merchandise if they are not interested in it. Because fashion coordinators keep a constant watch on both the industry and the consumer, they know about items often still on the drawing board. Coordinators also know which customer groups are being targeted by which manufacturers and designers and can help retailers prepare future assortments in all fashion categories from clothing to home furnishings.

Out-of-Store Information

Other Successful Stores. A great deal of useful information may be obtained through a study of the competition, both in and out of one's market area. Small retailers who cannot afford costly market research should study store advertising in metropolitan areas. What sells in Macy's or Marshall Field's today will sell in small stores and on Main Street tomorrow.

When out-of-town retailers are on buying trips in central cities, they usually spend time visiting the area stores before finalizing their purchases. Retailers in the same cities send **comparison shoppers** to check on the direct competition. They report back to the merchandising staff on competitive items and prices.

A few retailers study the competition so they can avoid the same or

Comparison Shopper
A store employee sent to competitors' stores to determine goods carried and relative prices charged.

similar merchandise. Their strategy is to offer a unique selection that will draw customers just because it is different.

Studying other successful retail stores is therefore an excellent research method whether the goal is to meet, beat, or avoid the competition. Whether nearby or at a distance, what other stores are carrying is essential information when planning assortments.

Vendors. If listened to with caution, vendors' representatives can contribute valuable information, for they know what is selling, where it is selling, where demand is increasing, and where it is decreasing. Most vendors are completely reliable because lying to retail clients would serve little purpose in terms of long-term profit. This does not mean, however, that their suggestions should be taken as gospel. Vendors should be listened to carefully and their input considered in light of one's own market conditions.

Central Market Representatives. Central market firms (called resident buying offices in Chapter 13) study trends for their member clients and send them a constant flow of announcements, bulletins, and brochures interpreting market events and observations. Most retailers use their central market representative as a home away from home when on buying trips to the central market.

Publications. Daily newspapers are a great source of current data. Retailers in all locations, large and small, have this quick form of research available. A report on the president's State of the Union address becomes an immediate planning tool. Business strategies react to the national condition, to reports of new import quotas, to fighting in Central America, and civil strife in South Africa.

Trade papers are another information resource. Fairchild publications are one of the most important sources of data for merchandise planning. Many retailers consider *Women's Wear Daily, Footwear News,* and the *Daily News Record* to be their business bibles. These papers, in addition to offering all the latest merchandise news, discuss the effects of political, social, and economic events on retailing in general. Each major group in the retail industry has its own trade publication. *Supermarket News* and *Chain Store Age* carry articles to help specific retailers with their special needs. Reading general magazines like *Time* and *Newsweek* or business periodicals such as *Forbes* or *Business Week* also contributes to a retailer's bank of knowledge. Current information can be applied to current decision making in any industry.

Consulting Firms. Some consultants concentrate on retail clients and others are general marketing consultants. Firms from either group can be very helpful to a retailer in the merchandise planning phase. A small retail company might be wise to hire a consultant when planning the opening merchandise budget. A large retailer might need a consultant

Focus Group
Panel of a dozen or fewer people, typical of a target market, invited to discuss a product, service, or market situation.

Neilsen Reports
Reports to manufacturers on products sold through food stores, drugstores, and mass merchandisers, giving such information as brand shares, sales, and trends.

Underwriters Laboratories
Large, independent, not-for-profit testing group whose UL mark means the product has been safety tested against nationally recognized standards.

when a new market is being targeted or plans are being made to take on new lines.

The larger consulting firms are located in market centers. Walter K. Levy Associates in New York City is one of the best known. In smaller cities are experts like Nancy Hannah Huber in Minneapolis and R. G. Consultants in Manchester, New Hampshire. These regional firms are helpful because they understand their markets so well.

Customer Surveys. Probably almost everyone has received a telephone call at home asking about patronage of a particular retail store. These random surveys are useful to retailers in pinpointing patronage motives and/or customer merchandise/service preferences.

Even more helpful in gathering information on customer preferences are advisory groups, made up of representative customers from the store's total customer mix or from specific subgroups. These **focus groups** or panels are called on to pass judgment on the store's merchandise/service mix as well as judge advertising effectiveness and buying habits.

A few national organizations, such as A. C. Neilsen Company of Northbrook, Illinois, use customer surveys to develop valuable information for the industry. **Neilsen Reports** may be purchased by retailers.

Testing Laboratories. The offer of quality is something that customers have the right to expect from retailers. To ensure the quality of the goods they offer for sale, some retailers, if they are large enough—like Sears or J. C. Penney—do extensive testing in their own laboratories. If they are not in this position they can hire outside testing bureaus like **Underwriters Laboratories** to do it for them.

Vendors are an excellent source of product information and many seek product certification from publications such as *Consumer Reports* or *Good Housekeeping*. The *Good Housekeeping* Seal of Approval preceded many of today's better-known stamps of quality. Retailers like to purchase goods from vendors who have good reputations because they know how important this is to their customers.

After considering the present external and internal environments as well as past sales, retailers can begin to plan for the next year. Sales are usually planned first for the year, then for the season, and finally are broken down by month. Monthly sales estimates are not always uniform because of changing seasonal demand and fluctuating customer demand.

Planned Stock

The second step in the budgeting process is to plan the correct amount of merchandise to meet (1) sales expectations and (2) inventory requirements. Stock levels must be planned that take both of these needs into consideration.

New trends or changes in store locations or layout may affect plans, because the addition of more branches, new units in a chain, or an enlarged or renovated selling floor can change inventory requirements. During the 1970s, the growth of fashion boutiques within department stores resulted in the need for more merchandise in certain classifications. Because these were sold in the regular departments as well as the boutiques, stock levels had to be increased.

Stock plans must keep inventory investment at an acceptable level. Planners must remember that the end-of-period stock is just as important a figure as estimated sales. Two other things to remember are: (1) what is acceptable one year may change the next and (2) although it is difficult to create the perfect plan, some methods are very useful to retailers when planning this segment of the merchandise budget.

Weeks-of-Supply Method

Weeks-of-Supply Method
Inventory method in which stocks on hand are kept at a level representing projected sales for a predetermined number of weeks.

To determine the right amount of goods to have on hand, the **weeks-of-supply method** has been used successfully. Sales are planned on a weekly basis, and the goods on hand at any one time must be an amount equivalent to several weeks' sales estimates. This method is particularly successful when planning fashion stock.

Tables 12.1 and 12.2 illustrate weeks-of-supply mathematics. The first step is to deduct from beginning-of-month (B.O.M.) stock the current month's sales, keeping track of the number of weeks (4 or 5) represented. If the remainder is larger than the following month's sales, the month's sales are also deducted and the number of weeks (in that month) added to the first. The procedure is repeated until a point is arrived where the dollar value of the remainder stock is less than the dollar value of next month's sales total. At this point, the number of weeks in that month is divided into the month's sales to arrive at an average weekly sales total. The division of this average weekly sales figure into the remainder stock figure will result in the number of weeks and fractions thereof which, added to the previously accumulated number of weeks, extends the total weeks of supply at the beginning of the period.

The use of actual figures will help to illustrate the procedure. Calculations are based on the assumption that the months of March, June, September, and December have 5 weeks and all others have 4 weeks.

If stock at the beginning of February is $209.0 thousand and the projected sales for February are $71.0 thousand, the sales during the month of February (4 weeks) would leave a stock of $138.0 thousand. After the sales during the 5 weeks of March of $107.0 thousand are deducted, a difference remains of $31.0 thousand to be sold in April. Therefore, the $138.0 thousand for April is divided by 4 to arrive at weekly sales of $34.5 thousand. Dividing the weekly average into the $31.0 thousand

Table   12.1   Weeks-of-Supply Mathematics: Find February Beginning-of-Month Weeks of Supply (W/S)

Flow	Item		February (4)	March (5)	April (4)
Find	(A) →	W/S[a] B.O.M.[b] February → →		W/S	
Known	(B)	B.O.M. Stock	$209.0		
Known	(D)	Sales February	$ 71.0		
Known	(E)	Sales March		$107.0	
Known	(F)	Sales April			$138.0
B − D	(G)	E.O.M.[c] Stock February	$138.0		
Known	(E)	Sales March		$107.0	
G − E	(H)	E.O.M. Stock March		$ 31.0	
		Since March E.O.M. is less than April Sales (F)—April Average Weekly Sales must be calculated. Divide April Sales (F) by April weeks (4).			
F ÷ 4	(I)	April Average Weekly Sales			$ 34.5
H ÷ I	(J)	April W/S			0.9 weeks
		Solution			
		No. Weeks February	4.0 weeks +		
		(+)No. Weeks March		5.0 weeks +	
		(+)No. Weeks April			0.9 weeks
			↑		
Solution	(A) →	W/S B.O.M. February → =	9.9 W/S		

[a] W/S: weeks of supply.
[b] B.O.M.: beginning-of-month.
[c] E.O.M.: end-of-month.
Source: From Merchandata, 33 Dover Street, Brockton, MA 02401. Reprinted by permission of the Merchandata Group.

figure results in approximately 0.9 weeks. Adding this to the previously accumulated 9 weeks, stock on February 1 represents 9.9 weeks of supply.

The same logic can be applied when the problem is to determine what stock *should* be, if plans are made to maintain a predetermined supply available for sales. Assume that the month of December is to begin with 10.9 weeks of supply, and sales for December are planned at $250.0 thousand, January $100.0 thousand, and February $80.0 thousand. The B.O.M. stock for December would be calculated as follows: Cover the 5 weeks of December with $250.0 thousand worth of stock. Add to this the $100.0 thousand planned to be sold in January and add further 1.9 weeks' sales for February of $20.0 thousand ($80.0 ÷ 4 = $20.0 × 1.9 weeks) for a total of $38.0 thousand. This equals 10.9 weeks' supply.

Basic Stock Method

Just as the weeks-of-supply method is good for calculating fashion inventory levels, use of a basic stock list is good when determining inventory

▄▄▄ ___

Table 12.2 Weeks-of-Supply Mathematics: Find December Beginning-of-Month Stock

Flow	Item		December (5)	January (4)	February (4)
Known	(A) →	W/Sª Goal → →	10.9 W/S		
Find	(B)	B.O.M.ᵇ Stock December →			
Known	(C)	Sales December	$250.0		
Known	(D)	Sales January		$100.0	
Known	(E)	Sales February			$80.0
		Since 10.9 W/S goal must extend into February—calculate February Average Weekly Sales. Divide February Sales by February weeks (4).			
E ÷ 4	(F)	February Average Weekly Sales			$20.0
10.9 − 9.0	(H)	February W/S Balance			1.9 weeks
F × H	(I)	February Average Sales × February Weeks Balance			$38.0
		Solution . . . ⟍			
		5.0 Weeks December Sales	$250.0 +		
		+4.0 Weeks January Sales		$100.0 +	
		+1.9 Weeks February Sales			$38.0
Solution	(B) →	B.O.M. Stock December → → =	$388.0 ↑		

ªW/S: weeks of supply.
ᵇB.O.M.: beginning-of-month.
Source: From Merchandata, 33 Dover Street, Brockton, MA 02401. Reprinted by permission of the Merchandata Group.

▄▄▄

Staple Goods
Goods bought because of an actual need.

Basic Stock Method
Inventory method in which estimated sales for the month are added to a basic minimum stock to determine the beginning-of-month stock.

levels for **staple goods.** Staple goods are those items that sell fairly steadily from year to year, generally in the same form.

Today, staple items are not as easy to define as they were years ago before the tremendous competition for consumer dollars caused manufacturers to differentiate even the simplest products. Items that formerly could be tracked through one basic stock list no longer fall into one category. Coca-Cola, for example, now comes in a number of different varieties—Classic Coke, New Coke, Diet Coke, Decaffeinated Coke, Diet Decaffeinated Coke, Cherry Coke, and Diet Cherry Coke. For each classification a different stock list is required and, as demand changes, each basic list must be revised.

In spite of fluctuations in demand, the **basic stock method** helps meet sales expectations and avoid out-of-stock conditions by beginning each month with stock levels that equal the estimated sales for that month plus an additional basic stock amount which serves as a "cushion" in case actual sales exceed estimated sales. The cushion also protects against stockouts if future shipments of merchandise are delayed or have to be returned to the vendor because of damage.

As good as the basic stock method is for staple goods, there is danger in using it. Building in a cushion increases the inventory investment and thus costs. Because margins are small on most staple items, this could cut into a retailer's profit.

The basic stock method involves calculating the B.O.M. stock for each month of the sales period. The B.O.M. stock is arrived at by adding a basic stock amount to the planned monthly sales figures. The basic stock method allows retailers to plan B.O.M. stock for each month in the sales period.

Calculations for the basic stock method can be expressed in these equations:

$$\text{B.O.M. Stock for Month X} = \text{Planned Monthly Sales for Month X} + \text{Basic Stock}$$

$$\text{Basic Stock} = \text{Average Stock for Sales Period} - \text{Average Monthly Sales for Sales Period}$$

$$\text{Average Stock for Sales Period} = \text{Total Planned Sales for Sales Period} \div \text{Estimated Inventory Turnover Rate for Sales Period}$$

$$\text{Average Monthly Sales for Sales Period} = \text{Total Planned Sales for Sales Period} \div \text{Number of Months in Sales Period}$$

Model Stock Method

Model Stock Plan
Inventory method based on model stock lists that show different assortments needed at specific dates during a budget period.

Model stock lists can be used to show the different assortments needed at different specific dates during the budget period. The **model stock method** for planning inventory levels is used for fashion goods because it takes into consideration the variations that occur not only from season to season but also during a season.

In preparing a model stock list, the amount of goods needed in each classification is determined by past sales and current trends. Three steps must be taken:

1. A decision must be made about the selection factors to be provided: classifications, types, prices, colors, sizes, and so on.
2. Important dates in the season for which model stocks are to be constructed must be determined.
3. Estimates for sales for the months preceding and following the date for which the model stock is set in units have to be calculated and the total translated into dollars and then checked against the dollar departmental classification plan.[2]

Planned Reductions

Because reductions are inevitable, smart merchants build a planned figure into their merchandise budget. Markdowns, stock shortages result-

[2]John W. Wingate and Joseph S. Friedlander, *The Management of Retail Buying*, 2nd ed. (Englewood Cliffs, N.J.: Prentice-Hall, 1978), 196, 198.

ing from pilferage, damaged or misplaced goods, discounts, and human error all contribute to this budget item.

Assortments can easily be out of balance when reductions are not planned for. Retailers who do not allocate a reasonable percentage of sales for reductions when putting budgets together could end up with loss of sales and a dent in their gross margin, having underestimated needed stock. For example, a retailer of trendy women's ready-to-wear could purchase a group of handsome new skirts only to find that at delivery they were already appearing in the fashion discount stores. This set of circumstances dictates a markdown. If a number of big-city shoplifters find that a new supermarket is particularly vulnerable, the result will be stock shortages. If there are many errors in sales information gathered manually during a three-hour computer breakdown in a major department store, the result will be incorrect inventory amounts—either short or over.

Because such occurrences are common in retailing, a logical percentage for reductions, based on past performance and current trends for each merchandise group, must be assigned in advance. Planning for reductions makes good budgetary sense.

Planned Purchases

Planned purchases can be computed by using a very simple formula:

$$\text{Planned Purchases} = \text{Planned Ending Inventory} + \text{Planned Sales} + \text{Planned Reductions} - \text{Beginning Inventory}$$

The following example shows how the formula works. Harry Henderson is the owner of a men's shop in a Colorado college town. The shop features better casual wear for men between the ages of 18 and 38. Henderson is planning his corduroy pant budget for the fall season. Because of both his geographic location and the demographics in his market, he figures that he should be able to sell a total of $200,000 in three different corduroy classifications. His estimate looks like this:

Planned Sales	$200,000.00
Beginning Inventory	83,000.00
Planned Reductions	20,800.00
Planned Ending Inventory	58,000.00

Using the formula, planned purchases equals $195,800.00 and is Harry's open-to-buy figure for the fall season. For a new store, department, or classification, there is no beginning inventory to subtract. The formula must therefore be modified:

$$\text{Planned Purchases} = \text{Planned Ending Inventory} + \text{Planned Sales} + \text{Planned Reductions}$$

If Harry's store had been new, his open-to-buy figure would be $278,800.00.

Open-to-Buy (O.T.B.)

Open-to-buy is the term used to refer to that amount of money a buyer has allocated for purchasing merchandise for a designated period of time. The O.T.B. figure should always be thought of as a guide, not an absolute.

As noted in the examples, planned purchases become the **open-to-buy position** for the period under consideration. The planned purchase and open-to-buy figure are the same when the season or month being planned is not yet underway. Once either is underway, the situation changes. Buyers must be able to calculate an open-to-buy figure at any time during a season or month. The following, again using Harry's store as an example, is an easy-to-follow method.

October 1 Data

Actual Sales	$82,000
Merchandise Purchased but Not Delivered	10,000
Merchandise Purchased and Delivered	115,000
Actual Reductions	5,000

(All other figures the same)

To find the open-to-buy figure, it is necessary to estimate how much merchandise is needed, then determine how much of it is already available. The mid-season open-to-buy figure is found by subtracting available goods from needed goods.

To determine what is needed, sales to date are subtracted from planned sales, and this figure is added to planned ending inventory and remaining reductions.

Planned Sales	$200,000
−Sales to Date	82,000
Planned Remaining Sales	$118,000
+Planned Ending Inventory	58,000
+Remaining Planned Reductions	15,800

Now let us look at what is available. The period started with an inventory of $83,000. During the period, $115,000 was purchased and delivered. Moreover, $10,000 worth of goods was purchased but not delivered. During the period, therefore, a total of $208,000 was available. Sales to date equal $82,000, and reductions for the same period are $5,000. Still available is $121,000 in merchandise.

If there is $121,000 worth of merchandise available, what is needed for the remainder of the period? This is determined by adding together the planned ending inventory of $58,000, the remaining expected sales

Open-to-Buy Position
Amount a buyer is in a position to spend on merchandise to replenish supplies for a period.

of $118,000, and the remaining planned reductions of $15,800. Thus, $191,800 worth of goods is needed for the remainder of the fall season if Harry is to meet his budget plan. Because he has $121,000 in merchandise available, his open-to-buy figure as of October 1 is $70,800 at retail, arrived at in this way: $191,800 needed − $121,000 available = $70,800 O.T.B. at retail. If the amount of goods on hand had exceeded the amount needed, the store would have been in an overbought position. (See Table 12.3.)

Because budgets are always planned using retail values for all categories, the open-to-buy figure is usually computed at retail, but actual purchases are made at cost. Conversion is necessary. If the margin is 55 percent, cost is 100 percent less 55 percent, or 45 percent. In the example given earlier, the open-to-buy figure at retail is converted to cost in this way: 45% × $70,800 = $31,840.

As already mentioned, an important fact about open-to-buy that must be considered is that the open-to-buy figure should be thought of as a guide (albeit a strict guide) rather than as an absolute. Conditions often change, even during one period. If, for example, inflation forces prices up to new levels, it would not be possible to purchase the number of units needed to satisfy consumer demand with the exact open-to-buy amount stated in the budget. If this happens and all other market conditions remain equal, sales could be lost unless the O.T.B. has been adjusted.

Planned Gross Margin

Selling price is the cost price of the item plus the cost of doing business plus a reasonable profit. Gross margin is the final amount by which the actual selling price exceeds the cost price of the item. It must cover the

Table   12.3   Calculation of Open-to-Buy

Available Merchandise		Needed Merchandise	
Beginning Inventory	$ 83,000	Ending Inventory	$ 58,000
Purchased and Delivered	115,000	Remaining Expected Sales	118,000
Purchased, Not Delivered	10,000	Remaining Planned Reductions	15,800
Total	$208,000	Needed	$191,800
Less Sales for Period	82,000		
	$126,000		
Less Reductions Taken	5,000		
Available	$121,000		

Maintained Markup
Gross margin.

cost of doing business, plus profit, less reductions. Gross margin is sometimes called **maintained markup.** The gross margin, or maintained markup, is an extremely important figure that should be planned for in the overall budget and in each classification:

$$\frac{\text{Gross}}{\text{Margin}} = \frac{\text{Cost of Doing}}{\text{Business}} + \frac{\text{Reasonable}}{\text{Profit}} - \text{Reductions}$$

If the initial markup (when goods are first put on sale) is not high enough, gross margin, because of reductions and the rising costs of doing business, may fall. This affects profits. If, on the other hand, the initial markup is too high, it might price items right out of the market, and profit will again be affected. When planning, consideration must be given to the contribution to gross margin from each planned category.

Careful planning of the merchandise budget as well as careful assortment planning assures retailers of a much better chance for profit than if buying were done by the old seat-of-the-pants method. With so many uncontrollable factors affecting profit, it would be disastrous to attempt to buy assortments without advance planning. (Figure 12.1 is an illustration of a merchandise plan.)

CLASSIFICATION PLANNING

Classification Planning
A system that breaks major categories of merchandise into smaller, manageable classifications for the purpose of inventory control.

Once the merchandise budget for a major category is completed, most buyers begin to break down the total into manageable classifications, whether for fashion or for basic goods. Some buyers start with classification plans and build up to the major category. With either method, the budget or guide is even more definitive when there is a classification plan and specific dollars can be allocated to specific groups or items. With classification plans, dollars can be placed to give the best possible return on investment. For example, if naturally decaffeinated instant coffee is selling better than regularly decaffeinated instant coffee, this should be considered when determining stock levels. If instant coffee is not broken down into naturally and regularly decaffeinated classifications, this statistic might not be known. Without **classification planning** there is a greater chance of understocking one item and overstocking the other.

In 1970, Charles G. Taylor listed a number of basic objectives that should be achieved when planning a merchandise budget by classification. These objectives have as much meaning in today's computerized retail world as they did almost 20 years ago, when budgets were planned without advanced technological aids. A well-conceived classification plan should:

1. Enable dollar sales and stocks to be planned with reasonable precision.
2. Permit the development of a realistic dollar open-to-buy figure.
3. Allow the buyer to evaluate each segment of his or her business

Figure   12.1   A Six-Month Merchandise Plan

SIX-MONTH MERCHANDISE PLAN (BUDGET)

☐ TOTAL STORE

☐ DEPARTMENT_____ DEPARTMENT NO._____

☐ CLASSIFICATION_____ CLASSIFICATION NO._____

☐ SPRING, 19 ☐ FALL, 19	FEB. AUG.	MAR. SEPT.	APR. OCT.	MAY NOV.	JUNE DEC.	JULY JAN.	TOTAL
Net Sales Last year							
Plan							
Revision							
Actual							
Beginning-of-Month Stock (At Retail) Last year							(End-of-Season Stock)
Plan							
Revision							
Actual							
Markdowns + Shortages + Discounts Last year							
Plan							
Revision							
Actual							
Purchases (At Retail) Last year							
Plan							
Revision							
Actual							
Purchases (At Cost) Last year							
Plan							
Revision							
Actual							

in order to locate areas for sales growth, greater profitability, and expense reduction.

4. Permit all levels of supervision in each selling location to understand what merchandise is to be stocked and at what prices.
5. Allow store supervisors (especially when there is more than one location as in department/branch store operations) to point out merchandise areas for which they have an unfulfilled demand and price lines and classifications carried for which there appears to be insufficient request.
6. Prevent unplanned duplication of merchandise.
7. Focus attention on the optimum timing—beginning, peak, fall-off, end—for each classification.
8. Call attention to exceptions in seasonal timing.
9. Make sure that adequate plans exist to house each needed classification at each location (if more than one).
10. Highlight the classifications producing exceptional volume and/or better markup.

Budgeting by classification should assure coverage of each segment of observable consumer demand. In addition, it guarantees proper representation of items at planned prices and prevents unnecessary duplication. Ideally, it channels purchases into preferred resources and, if carefully conceived, places a floor—and, for discount merchants, perhaps a ceiling—on an initial markup.[3]

As already mentioned, in times of rising costs some distributors start their plan for each subclassification by units rather than dollars. Under such conditions it is better to translate units into dollars at the current market value than to translate dollars into units, because dollars may actually represent fewer units and a potential loss of sales. Classification planning helps ensure well-balanced assortments geared to the market.

A PLANNING AID: THE 4–5–4 CALENDAR

Merchants plan by the season, the month, the week, and finally the day. Figures are a way of life in retailing because turnover represents dollars— dollars for future investment or profit. When planning is done by the calendar, turnover can be anticipated. The best way to do this is to use a calendar that offers some uniformity. The 4–5–4 accounting calendar is such an instrument and aids in assortment planning. (See Figure 12.2.)

With this calendar, each season has the same number of weeks and days for two consecutive years. In the third year the last season has an extra week the last month, and so it is a 4–5–5 rather than a 4–5–4 quarter. When preparing assortment plans and budgets, merchants like

---

[3] Charles G. Taylor, *Merchandise Assortment Planning* (New York: National Retail Merchants Association, 1970), 12.

Figure 12.2 Fiscal 4-5-4 Accounting Calendar

Fiscal 4-5-4 Calendar AMC 1987 — 52 Weeks

Feb. 12 .... Lincoln's Birthday
Feb. 14 .... Valentine's Day
Feb. 16 ... Washington's Birthday
April 19 .... Easter Sunday
May 10 .... Mother's Day
May 25 .... Memorial Day
June 21 .... Father's Day
July 4 .... Independence Day
Sept. 7 .... Labor Day
Oct. 12 .... Columbus Day
Nov. 3 .... Election Day
Nov. 11 .... Veteran's Day
Nov. 26 .... Thanksgiving
Dec. 25 .... Christmas Day
Jan. 1 .... New Year's Day
Jan. 18 ... M.L. King's Birthday

FEBRUARY–4 WEEKS

WEEK	SUN	MON	TUE	WED	THU	FRI	SAT
1	1	2	3	4	5	6	7
2	8	9	10	11	12	13	14
3	15	16	17	18	19	20	21
4	22	23	24	25	26	27	28

MARCH–5 WEEKS

WEEK	SUN	MON	TUE	WED	THU	FRI	SAT
1	1	2	3	4	5	6	7
2	8	9	10	11	12	13	14
3	15	16	17	18	19	20	21
4	22	23	24	25	26	27	28
5	29	30	31	1	2	3	4

APRIL–4 WEEKS

WEEK	SUN	MON	TUE	WED	THU	FRI	SAT
1	5	6	7	8	9	10	11
2	12	13	14	15	16	17	18
3	19	20	21	22	23	24	25
4	26	27	28	29	30	1	2

MAY–4 WEEKS

WEEK	SUN	MON	TUE	WED	THU	FRI	SAT
1	3	4	5	6	7	8	9
2	10	11	12	13	14	15	16
3	17	18	19	20	21	22	23
4	24	25	26	27	28	29	30

JUNE–5 WEEKS

WEEK	SUN	MON	TUE	WED	THU	FRI	SAT
1	31	1	2	3	4	5	6
2	7	8	9	10	11	12	13
3	14	15	16	17	18	19	20
4	21	22	23	24	25	26	27
5	28	29	30	1	2	3	4

JULY–4 WEEKS

WEEK	SUN	MON	TUE	WED	THU	FRI	SAT
1	5	6	7	8	9	10	11
2	12	13	14	15	16	17	18
3	19	20	21	22	23	24	25
4	26	27	28	29	30	31	1

AUGUST–4 WEEKS

WEEK	SUN	MON	TUE	WED	THU	FRI	SAT
1	2	3	4	5	6	7	8
2	9	10	11	12	13	14	15
3	16	17	18	19	20	21	22
4	23	24	25	26	27	28	29

SEPTEMBER–5 WEEKS

WEEK	SUN	MON	TUE	WED	THU	FRI	SAT
1	30	31	1	2	3	4	5
2	6	7	8	9	10	11	12
3	13	14	15	16	17	18	19
4	20	21	22	23	24	25	26
5	27	28	29	30	1	2	3

OCTOBER–4 WEEKS

WEEK	SUN	MON	TUE	WED	THU	FRI	SAT
1	4	5	6	7	8	9	10
2	11	12	13	14	15	16	17
3	18	19	20	21	22	23	24
4	25	26	27	28	29	30	31

NOVEMBER–4 WEEKS

WEEK	SUN	MON	TUE	WED	THU	FRI	SAT
1	1	2	3	4	5	6	7
2	8	9	10	11	12	13	14
3	15	16	17	18	19	20	21
4	22	23	24	25	26	27	28

DECEMBER–5 WEEKS

WEEK	SUN	MON	TUE	WED	THU	FRI	SAT
1	29	30	1	2	3	4	5
2	6	7	8	9	10	11	12
3	13	14	15	16	17	18	19
4	20	21	22	23	24	25	26
5	27	28	29	30	31	1	2

JANUARY–4 WEEKS

WEEK	SUN	MON	TUE	WED	THU	FRI	SAT
1	3	4	5	6	7	8	9
2	10	11	12	13	14	15	16
3	17	18	19	20	21	22	23
4	24	25	26	27	28	29	30

Fiscal 4-5-4 Calendar AMC 1988 — 52 Weeks

Feb. 12 .... Lincoln's Birthday
Feb. 14 .... Valentine's Day
Feb. 15 ... Washington's Birthday
April 3 .... Easter Sunday
May 8 .... Mother's Day
May 30 .... Memorial Day
June 19 .... Father's Day
July 4 .... Independence Day
Sept. 5 .... Labor Day
Oct. 10 .... Columbus Day
Nov. 8 .... Election Day
Nov. 11 .... Veteran's Day
Nov. 24 .... Thanksgiving
Dec. 25 .... Christmas Day
Jan. 1 .... New Year's Day
Jan. 16 ... M.L. King's Birthday

FEBRUARY–4 WEEKS

WEEK	SUN	MON	TUE	WED	THU	FRI	SAT
1	31	1	2	3	4	5	6
2	7	8	9	10	11	12	13
3	14	15	16	17	18	19	20
4	21	22	23	24	25	26	27

MARCH–5 WEEKS

WEEK	SUN	MON	TUE	WED	THU	FRI	SAT
1	28	29	1	2	3	4	5
2	6	7	8	9	10	11	12
3	13	14	15	16	17	18	19
4	20	21	22	23	24	25	26
5	27	28	29	30	31	1	2

APRIL–4 WEEKS

WEEK	SUN	MON	TUE	WED	THU	FRI	SAT
1	3	4	5	6	7	8	9
2	10	11	12	13	14	15	16
3	17	18	19	20	21	22	23
4	24	25	26	27	28	29	30

MAY–4 WEEKS

WEEK	SUN	MON	TUE	WED	THU	FRI	SAT
1	1	2	3	4	5	6	7
2	8	9	10	11	12	13	14
3	15	16	17	18	19	20	21
4	22	23	24	25	26	27	28

JUNE–5 WEEKS

WEEK	SUN	MON	TUE	WED	THU	FRI	SAT
1	29	30	31	1	2	3	4
2	5	6	7	8	9	10	11
3	12	13	14	15	16	17	18
4	19	20	21	22	23	24	25
5	26	27	28	29	30	1	2

JULY–4 WEEKS

WEEK	SUN	MON	TUE	WED	THU	FRI	SAT
1	3	4	5	6	7	8	9
2	10	11	12	13	14	15	16
3	17	18	19	20	21	22	23
4	24	25	26	27	28	29	30

AUGUST–4 WEEKS

WEEK	SUN	MON	TUE	WED	THU	FRI	SAT
1	31	1	2	3	4	5	6
2	7	8	9	10	11	12	13
3	14	15	16	17	18	19	20
4	21	22	23	24	25	26	27

SEPTEMBER–5 WEEKS

WEEK	SUN	MON	TUE	WED	THU	FRI	SAT
1	28	29	30	31	1	2	3
2	4	5	6	7	8	9	10
3	11	12	13	14	15	16	17
4	18	19	20	21	22	23	24
5	25	26	27	28	29	30	1

OCTOBER–4 WEEKS

WEEK	SUN	MON	TUE	WED	THU	FRI	SAT
1	2	3	4	5	6	7	8
2	9	10	11	12	13	14	15
3	16	17	18	19	20	21	22
4	23	24	25	26	27	28	29

NOVEMBER–4 WEEKS

WEEK	SUN	MON	TUE	WED	THU	FRI	SAT
1	30	31	1	2	3	4	5
2	6	7	8	9	10	11	12
3	13	14	15	16	17	18	19
4	20	21	22	23	24	25	26

DECEMBER–5 WEEKS

WEEK	SUN	MON	TUE	WED	THU	FRI	SAT
1	27	28	29	30	1	2	3
2	4	5	6	7	8	9	10
3	11	12	13	14	15	16	17
4	18	19	20	21	22	23	24
5	25	26	27	28	29	30	31

JANUARY–4 WEEKS

WEEK	SUN	MON	TUE	WED	THU	FRI	SAT
1	1	2	3	4	5	6	7
2	8	9	10	11	12	13	14
3	15	16	17	18	19	20	21
4	22	23	24	25	26	27	28

Source: Courtesy of Associated Merchandising Corporation.

Figure   12.3   A Month-to-Month Calendar

FEBRUARY 1984						
			1	2	3	4
5	6	7	8	9	10	11
12	13	14	15	16	17	18
19	20	21	22	23	24	25
26	27	28	29			

FEBRUARY 1985						
					1	2
3	4	5	6	7	8	9
10	11	12	13	14	15	16
17	18	19	20	21	22	23
24	25	26	27	28		

to be able to compare planned sales to past sales for equal periods of time. On a regular monthly calendar this is not always possible because months may end or begin in the middle of a week.

As an example, if February 1985 was compared directly to February 1984, the sales for 1984 might be difficult to match or exceed. Not only was 1984 a leap year, with an extra day, but the extra selling day was Wednesday, usually a very active shopping day. Using a month-to-month calendar for comparison, as illustrated in Figure 12.3, it is possible that certain classifications, if not all, could be overbought in anticipation of sales that would not be realized the second year.

An uncontrollable factor becomes controllable by using the 4–5–4 calendar. This calendar was used in the example for planning stock according to the weeks-of-supply method.

Summary

The retailer's primary function is to generate a profit by buying and selling merchandise and services. This can only be accomplished by the proper planning, controlling, and managing of merchandise assortments. Because inventory represents the dominant portion of a retailer's current assets, planning of inventory investment must be a dominant concern. Effective management and control demands an intelligent merchandise plan for each category and classification of goods or services.

The merchandise mix in any store is determined by the store's policies that spell out the kind of goods or services the store will sell, the quality of those goods and services, and the price lines. Using these policies as guideposts, retailers then begin the actual inventory planning process, which involves analysis of past and current information from both internal and external sources and the creation of the merchandise budget. This is a financial plan that requires consideration of sales, stock levels, reductions, purchases, and gross margin.

Merchandise budgets are based on all kinds of computer reports from daily sales to sales–stock analysis. Budgets are more and more accurate each year because of the computer.

   Inventory planning is truly the most critical problem faced by all retailers from the giant chains to the smallest shopkeepers. No formula guarantees having the optimum number of items on hand to meet the demands of the market, but adherence to a planning process and using methods like the weeks-of-supply, basic, or model stock plans can help in calculating open-to-buy figures and gross margin. A budget by classification does guarantee that the buying function will be performed as scientifically as possible even in a world with shifting economics, changing consumer attitudes, and constant competition.

Questions for Review

1. Why is it necessary for retailers to use a formal budget?
2. What does a proper budget provide the retailer?
3. Define the following terms:
   a. Merchandise budget
   b. Merchandise assortment
   c. Assortment plan
   d. Balanced assortment
   e. Classification merchandising
   f. Turnover
   g. Gross margin
4. List the five major segments of a merchandise budget.
5. What is meant by the term *open-to-buy (O.T.B.),* and what is its relationship to planned purchases?
6. Explain the term *classification planning.*
7. Comment on the statement, "Inventory planning is truly the most critical problem faced by all retailers, from the giants to the smallest shopkeepers."

Mitchell's Gift Emporium

Forecasting Sales for the Purpose of Stock Planning

Alexandra St. Claire had just purchased Mitchell's Gift Emporium, Mt. Vernon's only gift shop. Mitchell's was located in the newly renovated central business district. Alexandra was excited about the prospect of running her own store and, although it was only November, was looking forward to the summer season.

Mt. Vernon was a small resort community and Mitchell's had been the focal point for gift items purchased by the many summer residents and tourists as well as the year-round residents from the time it opened in 1948. During June, July, and August, Mitchell's carried a wide assortment of fine crafts and pottery in addition to its usual lines. These always drew many customers who returned year after year to view and to buy the new creations of the well-known artists whose wares were on display. Nearly everyone who came to enjoy the lake on which the town was situated visited Mitchell's during the summer. Often the townspeople themselves, anticipating their Christmas needs, purchased gifts in advance when Mitchell's stock in crafts and pottery was at its peak.

Even with this positive history, the two product categories that worried Alexandra were crafts and pottery. She knew that the entire year's profit often depended on how well these items sold during June, July, and August. Although she had three years of experience as assistant buyer for the gift shop in Holt's department store in nearby Cottersville, this was the first time that all of the planning rested completely on her shoulders. Much depended on her ability to forecast sales correctly for those three important months.

Over the preceding ten years, Mitchell's sales volume had increased at an average annual rate of 5 percent, and last year total sales had reached the $500,000 mark. Over 60 percent of yearly sales were realized in the three summer months and 40 percent of that figure came from crafts and pottery.

Alexandra had been involved in the planning of the merchandise budget at Holt's and knew the importance of such a budget. Anticipated sales were estimated first. These were broken down monthly for each category in stock. Then, with these figures, it was possible to plan proper stock levels. Nothing was more important than keeping a balance between stock and sales.

Because of the growing interest in handcrafted merchandise, Alexandra felt that she could increase sales in these categories even more this coming summer if she planned correctly. No complicated or sophisticated forecasting techniques were required. What was needed was application of sound judgment based on knowledge of Mitchell's summer customers, the general business outlook, in-store conditions, and past sales.

She felt that on the basis of expected business conditions, price trends, and the planned promotional efforts, sales for June, July, and August could increase as much as 7 or 8 percent. National gift-industry figures indicated that sales in both crafts and pottery were increasing faster than sales in any other gift category. Because these were name or signature items, prices in these classifications were higher each year. Alexandra also intended to increase the advertising allotment. She prepared the data shown in Table 12.4, and from this expected to prepare a sales forecast for crafts and pottery for the coming year.

There were other factors, in addition to past sales, that had to be taken into consideration when forecasting future sales. Fortunately, Alexandra understood the need to include them in her analysis.

She did not expect to change the amount of floor space devoted to sales, but she did plan to rearrange the merchandise, placing hand-crafted goods in one area to the right of the entrance in a special boutique.

During her last few years at Holt's, sales of items made by well-known artisans had increased each year. Alexandra recognized this trend and

Table 12.4   Crafts and Pottery Sales and Transactions: June 1, 1984–September 1, 1986

Month	1984		1985		1986	
	Sales	Transactions	Sales	Transactions	Sales	Transactions
June						
Crafts	$20,000	1,360	$21,312	1,300	$21,630	1,328
Pottery	12,000	790	12,188	852	12,670	873
	$32,000	2,150	$33,500	2,152	$34,300	2,201
July						
Crafts	$31,000	2,912	$32,600	3,003	$33,000	3,005
Pottery	17,000	1,838	18,400	1,813	21,200	1,905
	$48,000	4,750	$51,000	4,816	$54,200	4,910
August						
Crafts	$18,000	1,480	$18,100	1,510	$18,215	1,548
Pottery	22,000	1,620	23,400	1,625	25,585	1,657
	$40,000	3,100	$41,500	3,135	$43,800	3,205
Total	$120,000	10,000	$126,000	10,103	$132,300	10,316

intended to concentrate a large percentage of her open-to-buy on these categories when she bought for Mitchell's. Her merchandise plan would reflect this intention.

Each year Mt. Vernon still attracted as many summer visitors as the previous year, if not more, and all the local retailers were optimistic about the summer ahead. Moreover, it did not appear that any appreciable shift would occur in the local competitive situation that might affect Mitchell's sales one way or the other. No new gift outlets were expected to open, and Mitchell's could plan to virtually corner the growing craft market.

Alexandra was ready to prepare her sales forecast for crafts and pottery. She listed all the data she had collected.

1. Craft and pottery sales and transaction figures for the past three years. (See Table 12.4.)
2. Trends in the sales of handcrafted gift items.
3. General business conditions in Mt. Vernon.
4. Planned changes in the layout of Mitchell's.
5. Price trends in the craft and pottery trade. Table 12.4 shows that transactions did not increase at the same rate as dollar sales, thus indicating higher unit prices each year.
6. Local competition.

The task was to come up with the proper sales figures.

Questions

1. Project the next year's sales figures for crafts and pottery for the months of June, July, and August.
2. Based on your projections in Question 1, plan for the dollar investment in stock in each category.
3. List external conditions (general and specific) that must be considered when planning future sales.
4. What important factors (within Mitchell's Gift Emporium) will affect future sales? Explain.
   a. Factors pointing to an increase in sales.
   b. Factors pointing to a decrease in sales.
5. Develop a merchandise budget for craft and pottery classifications for the months of June, July, and August.

The Selection Process

Source: Photo by John Stapleton.

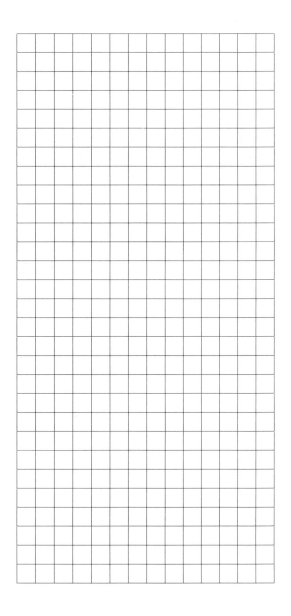

Industry Statement

Marvin Traub,
Chairman,
Bloomingdale's

The trends of the 1990s are in formation now. The nature of a trend is that it is, by definition, flexible and subject to change. However, the broad outlines are apparent:

- The return to urban communities
- The smaller family unit
- The redefinition of leisure time with emphasis on its use for physical fitness and active sports
- The growth of direct marketing
- The broadened application of electronic media
- The redivision of the consumer dollar

All of these present obvious challenges and opportunities to retailers. Creative marketing forces in the 1990s will have to anticipate the desires of consumers and meet their needs.

The strongest consumer force is a desire for the special, the unique. Decades of safety in uniformity ended in the 1960s. The role of product development is now vital. The edge of difference on the store floor is that the product cannot be found elsewhere, and that it is fulfilling a desire, even an unanticipated desire. Product development necessitates a coverage of broad international markets to seek new sources, new crafts people, new techniques.

The final step in the marketing process is presentation. Whether it is the clutter of a bazaar or the starkness of folded oriental merchandise, presentation is the final enticement to the customer, involving him or her in the process of shopping.

Shopping is a human desire. It will always exist. Our challenge is to know the patterns of their desires even before consumers realize them.

Learning Objectives

Upon completing this chapter you should be able to:

1. Know how patterns of consumer preferences are changing the competition for customer dollars among retailers.
2. Discuss the various sources of buying information.
3. Understand the actual process of buying merchandise.
4. Assess the skills that a buyer must develop in order to successfully negotiate a purchase.
5. Explain the importance of product development and private label to today's retailers.

Survival of the smartest—the smartest marketers and merchandisers, that is—is the name of the retail game for now and the future. The smartest are those who understand how best to serve their customers and how to market themselves to appeal to an even broader buying segment. The key is to be fully aware of who the competition really is and why customers shop where they do.

Until 1980, retailers needed only to build another store in order to increase sales, but with the shift in the economy, the focus itself shifted from new site development to increased productivity in existing stores. It became necessary to maintain market share.

In Chapter 12 we saw why an efficient system of planning budgets and inventory is vital to profits. Equally important is examining customer bases in order to make intelligent and market-right buying decisions. In the strategic planning necessary to ensure that merchandise assortments will reflect the desires of the customer, three questions must be answered: Where are we now? Where do we want to be? What is the best way to get there?

SELECTION TECHNIQUES

Retailers are beginning to use research techniques to gain a better reading of who their customers are—and the kind of shopping environment they seek. These techniques include becoming more introspective, positioning merchandise, developing a competitive positioning strategy, and specifying a marketing plan.

Introspection

Retailers will have to become more introspective in examining their internal share of market. Is the customer who is buying the store's dresses also buying its shoes? How will the retailer get customers to spend more in his or her store?

Positioning of Merchandise

Customer Segmentation
Dividing customers into segments by social, psychological, demographic, economic, geographic, and lifestyle characteristics.

Marketing stresses **customer segmentation** by seeking to draw selected groups into a store as loyal customers. More and more stores are overhauling their merchandise mix and even their physical makeup to better target their desired market. Mass merchandisers, in particular, are aggressively pursuing a more affluent shopper with upgraded private label and name brand products while weeding out the lower end lines. As examples, Federated Department Stores entered the low-margin business, Wal-Mart developed the Sam Wholesale Club format, Toys 'R' Us opened Kids 'R' Us stores, Dayton Hudson started Plum's, and J. C. Penney repositioned its merchandise.

Competitive Strategy

Most retailers tend to react to all competitive pressures. They try to be all things to all people instead of developing a specific marketing strategy and merchandising strategy. Identifying customers is only half of the puzzle for retailers; the other half is to find out why they also shop the competition. An example of a competition shopping report is illustrated in Figure 13.1.

The Marketing Plan

Management sets the direction of the marketing plan, establishes the process and priorities, allocates resources, and determines the time frame. Buyers assemble the merchandise assortments to achieve marketing objectives that project the company's viewpoint on themes that embody current trends endorsed by targeted customers.

Figure   13.1   Competition Shopping Report

Store No. _____   Date _____

Dept. No. _____   Qualified Competition Shopped:

1. _____

2. _____

I.B.M. Style No.	Mfr. Model or Style	Description	Barkers Price	1st Compet. Price	2nd Compet. Price	Store's Recom. Price	Buyer's Recom. Price

Item seen at our competitor's store which we should carry:

Manufacturer	Mfr. Model or Style	Description	List Price	Sale Price	Buyer's Comments

_____   _____

Signature of Shopper   *Store Manager*

SOURCES OF BUYING INFORMATION

Assistance in the actual buying process is available to buyers from several sources.

Resident Buying Office
Link between a buyer and distant manufacturers, paid by the retailer to provide market coverage.

Resident Buying Offices

Few stores are able to support a permanent staff in all of the world's merchandise markets. Most department and specialty stores therefore use the services and facilities of **resident buying offices,** which provide their services to a group of noncompeting stores. Most of these offices are headquartered in New York City—with branches located in secondary market centers such as California—and in the capital cities of Europe, South America, and the Far East.

The offices are organized so that all the members of the merchandising staff work on behalf of and with their counterparts in the stores. The offices are organized to parallel the stores they serve, with a senior merchandising executive (or more than one) who is equivalent to the store's general merchandise manager. Divisional merchandise managers, responsible for the supervision of a number of market representatives, are on the next level. The **market representative,** counterpart to the store buyer, is responsible for a department or classification of merchandise. It is important that market representatives understand the store, its philosophy, its customers, and the objectives of the store and the buyer.

Market Representative
The person in a resident buying office who concentrates on a particular grouping of goods.

Functions of a Buying Office

The primary service of the buying office is market coverage. The market representative spends most of the time visiting vendors in the market to gather information on trends, color and fabrications, fashion, new resources, hot items, best sellers, prices, and delivery dates. This information is then made available to store buyers through a variety of reports, such as flashagrams, pre- and post-market reports, catalogs of market offerings, or special reports on special topics.

Another important function of a buying office is to alert buyers to potential best sellers, known in today's competitive trade as **items.** In some offices, the market representative is empowered to place sample orders of new merchandise in stores, which has the advantage of allowing a store located far from the market to test the latest items immediately without the buyer having to travel to the market.

Items
Hot items; any goods that exhibit quick salability.

Changes in attitudes, lifestyles, and patterns of consumption tend to move across the country in uneven cycles. A buyer may learn of an advancing demographic or psychographic trend from a market representative and can be better prepared when it reaches his or her market.

Types of Buying Offices

The independent buying office is the most common type. In this arrangement, a group of noncompeting client stores purchase professional services as they would those of any other consultant. The buying office and the stores have no voice in controlling or setting policy for one another. They are entirely separate entities, such as Independent Retailers Syndicate or Felix Lilienthal & Co.

A cooperative buying office is owned by the stores that are its members. A board of directors, made up of store executives, sets policy and specifies services that are to be provided. Examples are Frederick Atkins, Inc., and Associated Merchandising Corporation.

A division of a corporation that operates a group of retail companies is a third type of buying office. Only the members of that corporation are served by the office. Macy's Corporate Buying Division and May Company would be examples.

An office that is owned by and serves only one company is the fourth type, exemplified by Sears and J. C. Penney.

A **commission buying office** is a special type that receives its income from manufacturers rather than retailers. Manufacturers pay a commission on orders placed by the buying office.

Commission Buying Office
A resident buying office that is paid by manufacturers for placing orders with them.

Publications

A variety of publications in the trade carry information on trends in fashion and demographics as well as on new resources. Some of them are daily, such as the Fairchild publications: *Women's Wear Daily, Daily News Record,* and *Home Furnishings Daily.* Others are monthly or bimonthly; for example, *Stores, Chain Store Age Executive,* and *Visual Merchandising.* In addition, *Business Week, Forbes, The Wall Street Journal,* and *The New York Sunday Times* offer invaluable business information on a continuing basis.

Trade Shows and Market Weeks

Manufacturers, foreign countries, and fabric houses present their new merchandise at trade shows in New York and in regional markets like Dallas, Atlanta, Miami, and Chicago. Many trade publications carry ads and registration forms well in advance. These shows not only indicate trends but enable a buyer to book actual orders at the vendors' booths. (See Figure 13.2.)

Specific lines of merchandise like shoes, accessories, or sportswear can

Figure   13.2   Trade Show Registration Form

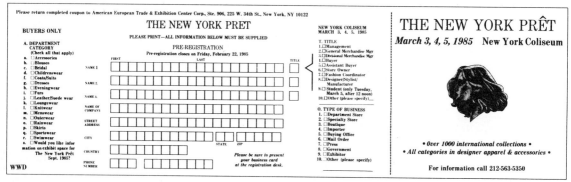

Source: *Women's Wear Daily,* February 12, 1985.

Market Week
Scheduled showing
of merchandise by
manufacturers in
one area; unlike
trade shows, for
which merchandise
is brought together
from many areas.

be viewed several months in advance of a new season during **market weeks.** There is plenty of notice so that buyers can schedule the trips to coincide with other business they need to do in the market.

Movies, Television, and Travel

The buyer must be aware of every inkling of a trend. Often trends are picked up by watching one of the BBC series on public television—for example, "Jewel in the Crown" or "Brideshead Revisited," which influenced an entire season of spring and summer ready-to-wear clothes for men, women, and children. Equally important are period movies like "Out of Africa," "Passage to India," or "Saturday Night Fever," which set trends in home furnishings as well as clothing.

Travel is essential in order to spot trends on the streets of London or the beaches of the French Riviera or the cafes of Milan. Because so much fashion today comes up from the streets, being there is important. Of course, there is the added dimension of discovering new designers, handcraftsmen, and fabrics if one explores the offbeat tourist areas of foreign towns and cities.

THE MECHANICS OF BUYING

Not long ago, Stanley Marcus and Andrew Goodman ran two of America's most successful specialty store operations, Neiman-Marcus and Bergdorf Goodman. Although they are no longer active at their stores, their observations on buying and merchandising are as pertinent as ever.

On Marcus's desk is a sign, "Quality is remembered long after price is forgotten." He recalls having purchased the sign from Aldo Gucci for "possibly $15." Some of Marcus's own provocative observations are these:

> For many years, retailers have set themselves up as targets of off-price selling. It was inevitable that new retailers would come along and say: "I don't want advertising or markdown money and will not make unjustified returns. I won't pretend to lose invoices so as to get an extra 30 days on terms. I will pay cash." On the other hand, if I were still in business, I would see to it that manufacturers who sell to off-price retailers were crossed off our list. Private labels are another strong countermeasure. I don't think there are any one or two lines that are essential.
>
> If Neiman's, Bergdorf's, or I. Magnin shows the identical dress carried by an off-price retailer, it will eventually lose the prospective customer. To justify its markup, the conventional department or specialty store must place greater emphasis on added value— superior breadth and depth of edited selections. Too many retailers have become commodity traders, not merchants.

I'm not sure what buyers know about fiber content and fabric structure. Too many buyers have been taught merchandising, not merchandise. It's like a withered arm that has atrophied when it fails to do what it's supposed to do. It is up to management to decide not whether the article will sell, but whether it should be sold in the first place.

I see only limited evidence that the taste of the American public has improved. How many well-dressed people do you see at airports, or any other place? Personally, to quote Oscar Wilde, I have the simplest taste, I am easily satisfied with the best.[1]

Responsibilities of the Buyer and Merchandising Team

The levels of merchandise management at Woodward & Lothrop, a department store in Washington, D.C., are shown in Figure 13.3. The titles, other than buyer and assistant buyer, may change from store to store, but the same functions and responsibilities are performed by all retailers.

Buyers. Buyers select and purchase merchandise according to current fashion trends, their planned merchandising strategies, and the needs of

---

[1] Samuel Feinberg, "Stanley Marcus," *Women's Wear Daily*, May 9, 1984, 6.

Figure   13.3   Levels of Merchandise Management at Woodward & Lothrop

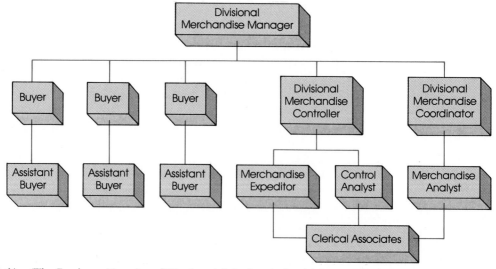

Source: *Woodlothian* (The Employee Magazine of Woodward & Lothrop), Special Issue, Fall 1983.

the customers. They will visit the market, establish and maintain relations with vendors, develop departmental business through advertising, and monitor the competition. The buyer reports to the divisional merchandise manager.

Assistant Buyers. Assistant buyers provide merchandising and administrative support. They will set up market trips for buyers, assist in planning purchases, monitor delivery of merchandise, initiate markdowns, work with advertising, and see that merchandise controllers and coordinators have all the information they need. The assistant buyer reports to a buyer.

Divisional Merchandise Controllers. Divisional merchandise controllers maintain the financial, budgetary, and inventory records and systems necessary to support the buying function. They work closely with accounts payable and statistical departments and are responsible for the accuracy of the purchase and markdown journals and the fashion information system. Their function will enable more effective planning and implementation of a profitable business strategy. The divisional merchandise controller reports to a divisional merchandise manager.

Divisional Merchandise Coordinators. Divisional merchandise coordinators ensure that each store has the optimal assortment of merchandise to maximize sales, profit, and customer satisfaction. They make distribution recommendations to buyers based on their close monitoring of stock levels, regional needs, and local competition. They also communicate presentation and merchandise information to the stores. The divisional merchandise coordinator reports to the divisional merchandise manager.

Merchandise Expeditors. Merchandise expeditors assist the divisional merchandise controller in monitoring the flow of merchandise from the vendor through the warehouse to the stores. They work closely with the warehouse to forestall problems and handle them as they occur. The merchandise expeditor reports to the divisional merchandise controller.

Control Analysts. Control analysts assist the divisional merchandise controller in making plans and maintaining financial controls for a buying office. The control analyst reports to the divisional merchandise controller.

Merchandise Analysts. Merchandise analysts assist merchandise coordinators in planning stock levels, communicating information, and distributing retail merchandise to the stores. The merchandise analyst reports to the divisional merchandise coordinator.

Clerical Associates. Clerical associates contribute to the overall efficiency of their respective offices through their administrative support.

Where to Buy

To determine the value of a resource, the retailer should consider the following factors: quality of merchandise, the location and reputation of the vendor, brand policy, terms of purchase, resale aid, and sales and profit experience.

Buying at the Market

Going directly to the market offers an opportunity to see many different lines. This can have several effects. The buyer may see a line that appears stronger than a line presently carried, and therefore reduce the quantity of one line to make room for a new line. On the other hand, the buyer may find that a currently used resource has increased its product mix or extended its range, and realize that the store should go along with this expansion and extension.

Buyers should study all their resources to ensure that each serves a purpose and is the best available for that need. Good vendor relations are of prime importance. Building key resource or "partner" relationships helps increase bargaining power and gains many advantages for the store. Being important to a few key resources is an objective that should always be kept in mind.

Buying at the Store

Buying near the store, whether from representatives on the road coming into the store or from a trade show, has both advantages and disadvantages. The biggest advantage is convenience. The buyer does not need to take time away from the store to travel to a market area, the buyer's normal work can continue, and the buyer may well feel more in tune with the likes and dislikes of the community than when away from the store on a market trip.

The disadvantages of buying in or near the store are almost as convincing. Buying away from the store means that the buyer can concentrate on one thing—buying—without having to worry about floor responsibilities and other duties. Buying away from the store also means that a buyer can, in most cases, see many more lines than would be possible by relying on representatives' visits. Also, the thinking of buyers is more focused during peak market periods and may lead to wiser decisions than would be made at other times.

Buyers should post exact days and times during the week when they will see representatives. This avoids lost time for both of them.

Buying Abroad

With today's emphasis on private labeling and exclusives, buyers are turning to sources abroad. Two directions are important: Europe for the greatest influence on design, especially Italy, and the Far East for production of volume merchandise. (See Figure 13.4.)

Other sources are important for particular classifications of merchandise—Brazil, Argentina, Peru, Haiti, and some of the African countries. These countries are known for furniture, sweaters and knits, and home accessories such as hand-carved mahogany and soapstone figures. Interesting fabrications are still undiscovered in Africa and South America, but the buyer must have the patience and time to work closely with the

Figure   13.4   Market Week in Florence, Italy

A buyer selects an assortment from a showing of sportswear in Emilio Pucci's palace during market week. Following the show, she will return to write the actual order with the designer's sales staff.

Source: Photo by John Stapleton.

manufacturers. These, in many cases, are craftsmen or cooperatives of skilled labor.

The buyer must be aware of the latest U.S. Customs regulations, especially in fabrics, before negotiating a deal abroad. Many developing countries are granted **preferred nation status;** this means that most items can be imported duty-free to the United States.

Preferred Nation Status
Situation of developing countries that are granted special trade privileges by the United States, including lower tariffs on their goods.

The resident buying office can be useful in guiding and planning the store buyer's visit to foreign countries. This trip is most important because no one can buy for the buyer. If foreign purchases are to be a success and if continuity is to develop, the buyer must do the buying personally. Until fairly recently the buyer shopped alone and exerted his or her own taste and knowledge and planned the promotions. Now the trend is for buyers to travel in groups, accompanied by a merchandise manager or fashion director. Their purchases are planned to arrive at specific times for specific promotions.

Overseas buying offices are the key to the best merchandise produced in a country. Knowledge of the market and what is new can mean the success or failure of a buyer. If the office is important in its country and a force in the market, it will be important to the buyer because it will be able to arrange exclusives, introductions, and promotions. Among the most progressive of the buying offices abroad are those of Associated Merchandising Corporation.

Commissionaire
A purchasing agent in a foreign market acting on commission for retailers or others importing from that country or area.

If a store is not represented by a domestic buying organization, a buyer can work through a **commissionaire.** The commissionaire serves as a general representative of the buyer's company in a foreign market, in very much the same manner that a resident buying office serves out-of-town stores in the U.S. market. Normally commissionaires operate on a straight commission basis, although sometimes a minimum volume is required. Further, the rate or rates of commissions, aside from being negotiable, vary considerably, depending on the nature of the market and the types of merchandise being purchased.

NEGOTIATING THE SALE

Terms of purchase vary according to the trade. In the food trade, for example, the terms of purchase are not as liberal as in the apparel trade.

Terms vary from one resource to another and change as business conditions change. As a rule, the faster the merchandise is sold, the shorter the terms and the smaller the discount. Discounts alone, however, should not lure a buyer into a purchase that is not suitable for the store's clientele.

The purchase terms to be considered by a buyer include: discounts, date of delivery, form of delivery, price, point of transfer of title, exclusivity, advertising, returns, and special cuttings.

Discounts and Dating

Almost all lines of merchandise carried by a store are purchased with cash discount terms, commonly ranging from 2 to 8 or 10 percent. Consequently, obtaining cash discounts is of great importance to a store's operating success.

The discounts are listed in percentages of total purchase price and are offered in return for prompt payment. A cash discount has three elements: a percentage figure, a discount period consisting of a certain number of days, and a net period.

An example of terms is 2/10 net 30. The first numeral gives the discount rate. The second stipulates the number of days that the rate is available: "2/10" means that 2 percent of the total amount of the invoice may be deducted if payment is made within 10 days. After 10 days, the full amount of the invoice is due. "Net 30" means that the invoice must be paid not later than 30 days from the date of the invoice. It will be past due if not paid by that time and may be subject to an interest charge.

If retailers pay their bills before the expiration of the cash discount period, they ask for an extra discount called **anticipation.** In periods of rising interest rates, it is not uncommon for retailers to request rates as high as one percent monthly, or 12 percent a year. Anticipation is deducted from the invoice price.

A reduction allowed by manufacturers to wholesalers and jobbers, but not normally allowed to retailers, on a few lines of merchandise quoted at catalog prices, is called a **trade discount.** Trade discounts are commonly quoted in a series. The amount of the discounts varies with the market prices at the time and with the size of the order. If an invoice for $1,200 carried trade discounts of "less 25%, less 10%, less 5%," the computation would be as follows:

Invoice	$1,200.00
Less: 25% discount	300.00
	$ 900.00
Less: 10% discount	90.00
	$ 810.00
Less: 5% discount	40.50
	$ 769.50

When large chains and department stores buy much larger quantities than some wholesalers, they too are able to secure trade discounts.

Retailers buying seasonal products—such as bathing suits, winter outerwear, or toys—can benefit from **advance dating.** Here, the merchant arranges to have the credit date based on a date later than the invoice date. Thus, an invoice could be dated July 1, effective November 10. If a

Anticipation
Payment of an account before the due date; also, the resulting discount.

Trade Discount
A deduction from the agreed price, normally granted by manufacturers to wholesalers but sometimes also to large retailers.

Advance Dating
Added time allowed to pay for goods after the invoice date when the ordinary dating period begins, resulting in a discount for the purchaser.

cash discount of 2/10 were in order, the two percent could be deducted through November 20.

Delivery

Free on Board (FOB)
Term identifying the point from which the retailer is to pay transportation charges for merchandise purchased; also called freight on board.

Because the retailer can cancel the order if either the date of delivery or the quantity purchased is not clearly stated on the invoice, the price and terms must be very specific as to mode of delivery (air freight, air parcel post, water, rail, truck, Federal Express). In addition, the party responsible for shipping charges must be spelled out. The term FOB in shipping instructions means **free on board** and is applied to the point to which the vendor will pay transportation charges.

FOB destination means that the manufacturer pays shipping charges from the moment goods leave the factory. FOB factory means that the manufacturer will pay no transportation charges. These two types of shipping agreement are not the only ones possible, however. A manufacturer might, for instance, pay trucking costs from the factory to a railroad shipping point while the retailer agreed to pay the remainder of the shipping costs.

To illustrate, an invoice for $650 was dated June 10. The cash discount terms were 3/10 net 30. The shipping agreement called for sending the goods FOB destination but the vendor let them go collect. The freight charges, paid by the retailer, were $7.00. Remittance was made on June 20. The amount of payment would then be:

Invoice	$650.00
Less: 3% discount	19.50
Discounted bill	630.50
Less: freight	7.00
Amount of payment	$623.50

Transfer of Title

On Consignment
Turned over by an owner to a retailer. The retailer pays only when and if the goods are sold.

Because there are several alternatives for transfer of title, the buyer must understand the differences in responsibility for each one. The retailer may assume ownership at various points in the purchase process: upon purchase, when the merchandise is loaded for delivery, when the shipment is received, or at the end of the billing cycle. Another possibility is that the retailer does not own the goods at all, but accepts them **on consignment.** In this arrangement the seller retains ownership, requiring the retailer to pay only for the goods that are sold. This might occur when the manufacturer needs the retailer as an account, or in the case of unusually high-priced merchandise, such as furs or fine gems.

Exclusivity and Special Cuttings

In order to gain a competitive edge in the marketplace, the buyer can confine a line or items in a line to his or her store only, within the geographic selling area. Alternately, a manufacturer may agree to cut a specific style, perhaps with an alteration to the collar or sleeve interest, especially for one retailer or a retail chain. Saks Fifth Avenue demands this frequently.

Advertising

Vendors often make cooperative advertising part of their offer. Here, the manufacturer might pay all or part of the media bills for promoting a particular item or designer name in a store ad.

Returns

A buyer might negotiate to return to the vendor all items in a particular buy that did not sell after a specific date. Often, the buyer can also negotiate for markdown money to promote the buy, if it is not moving well from the store.

TRENDS IN THE SELECTION PROCESS

New Roles for the Fashion Director

The fashion director's job has definitely changed since the time when it was primarily doing fashion shows and charity luncheons. What was important then were social connections. Now the fashion director is more a merchant than a member of the social set. The role of the fashion office is to understand customers' needs, get an overview of the entire market, and then transfer this information to buyers and manufacturers.

At Sanger Harris, Dallas, there are two fashion directors. The corporate fashion director covers ready-to-wear in both foreign and domestic markets. This person works with buyers and division managers and is the forecaster of ready-to-wear. The other fashion director works with store display people and store managers to make sure that the corporate fashion director's predictions actually happen. An additional responsibility is to work with salespeople to make sure they understand the merchandise and the trends.[2]

[2] "New Roles for the Fashion Director," *Stores,* January 1983, 68.

Product Development/Private Label

Retailers are plunging into manufacturing in response to manufacturers' getting into retailing with their factory outlet stores. Traditional retailers, in competition with off-pricers and often each other, are wheeling product development programs on line to an extent that may make PD (product development) as much a part of retail parlance as OTB (open-to-buy), RTW (ready-to-wear) or DMM (divisional merchandise manager).

Intensely price concerned, most of these PD programs are, of course, linked to PL (private label). Typically, they are not aimed for sky-high initial markup, but rather for first-off-sell-through and repeat sales. (See Figures 13.5, 13.6, and 13.7.)

A major store president has commented, "Expectations for substantial selling at an inflated first price are not high today. So the end result of our product development programs is a host of items—family apparel, accessories, and home goods—put out at everyday good prices that are somewhat less than what equal quality would sell for competitively."[3]

[3] "Strategies for Product Development Programs: More Than Merely Private Label," *Stores*, September 1983, 16.

Figure   13.5   Private Label as a Percentage of Total Women's Wear Sales and Inventory, 1984–1986[a]

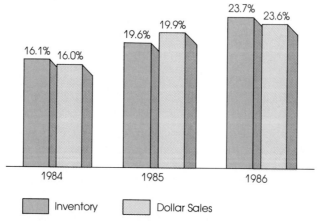

[a] Figures reflect mean percentages; 1986 figures were estimated.
Source: *APPAREL Merchandising Magazine*, December 1985, 14. Reprinted with permission.

Figure   13.6   Private Label Women's Wear Broken Down between Fashion and Basic Merchandise, 1984–1986[a]

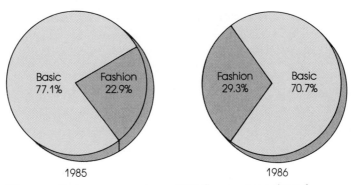

1985   1986

[a] Figures reflect mean percentages; 1986 figures were estimated.
Source: *APPAREL Merchandising Magazine*, December 1985, 16. Reprinted with permission.

Figure   13.7   Private Label Women's Wear Broken Down by Price Range, 1984–1986[a]

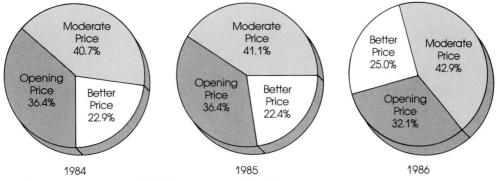

1984   1985   1986

[a] Figures reflect mean percentages; 1986 figures were estimated.
Source: *APPAREL Merchandising Magazine*, December 1985, 16. Reprinted with permission.

At Carter Hawley Hale Stores, an office for product development was set up in the New York corporate offices in 1980 with a staff of nine. That number had escalated to 85 by 1984. A successful result of that collaboration is the Cradle Crowd private label developed for their infants' wear department. (See Figure 13.8.) In addition, nearly every store company has its own private labels—for example, Neiman Marcus's Red River and Wanamaker's John Wanamaker.

Figure 13.8   Brochure for a Private Label

CRADLE CROWD®

Introduce yourself
to the very special world
of Cradle Crowd. It's a
wonderful place filled with
extra softness, where luxury
begins with pure cotton fabrics
that are easy to care for, yet
never shrink or fade. And
everything is fully sized for
the most comfortable fit.
There are so many nice ways
to join the Cradle Crowd...
Come in and see for yourself.

SIZE CHART
3	MONTHS	UP TO	13 LBS
6	MONTHS	14 TO	18 LBS
12	MONTHS	19 TO	22 LBS
18	MONTHS	23 TO	26 LBS
24	MONTHS	27 TO	29 LBS

Summary

Retailers must position themselves in the marketplace and then follow through with merchandising and promotion strategies that are targeted to that position. Definite patterns in consumer preferences are demanding more creativity on the part of the retail executive. Competition is coming from all levels: other retailers, manufacturers and designers who now own their own stores, and foreign firms. As a result, retailers must become more knowledgeable and decisive than ever.

Sources of information for the buyer include the services of various types of resident buying offices, trade and consumer publications, market weeks, trade shows, movies, television, and travel.

The responsibilities of the buyer and the merchandising team are changing, and the choices of where to buy are expanding both domestically and abroad. Not only does the buyer have to be competent in planning and selecting merchandise, but he or she must be extremely bright in negotiating the sale. At this point in the buying process dollars can be added to profit through skilled negotiations on discounts, dating, and delivery.

Figure 13.8
(continued)

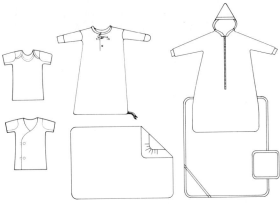

SIDE SNAP SHIRT
100% COTTON

SLIP ON SHIRT
100% COTTON

BODY SUIT (NOT PICTURED)
100% COTTON
SNAP CROTCH
LAP SHOULDER

KNIT SACQUE SET
100% POLYESTER

DRAWSTRING GOWN
100% POLYESTER
MITTEN CUFFS
SNAP FRONT CLOSURE

FITTED CRIB SHEET
100% COTTON
STRETCH FOR EASY
SLIP ON AND SNUG FIT
FITS STANDARD CRIB (28 × 52)

TERRY AFTER BATH BAG
75/25 COTTON/POLYESTER

TERRY HOODED TOWEL
30 × 40 PLUSH TERRY
75/25 COTTON/POLYESTER

TERRY WASHCLOTHS
75/25 COTTON/POLYESTER

TERRY STRETCH COVERALL
100% POLYESTER
2 WAY STRETCH TERRY
DOUBLE SNAP CROTCH
AND LEGS

TERRY BIB
75/25 COTTON/POLYESTER

RECEIVING BLANKET (NOT PICTURED)
100% COTTON FLANNEL
36 × 36 LARGE SIZE

Source: Courtesy of Carter Hawley Hale Stores, Inc.

New directions are important, such as the changing role of the fashion director and the strong emergence of product development and private labeling. These trends will continue to gain strength and offer an interesting alternative career path to those who aspire to the title of buyer.

Questions for Review

1. What is meant by positioning merchandise?
2. What is a resident buying office and what is its major function?
3. Explain the responsibilities of a retail buyer.
4. Discuss the advantages and disadvantages of buying merchandise in a store as compared to buying away from the store.
5. Define the terms *cash discount, anticipation, trade discounts,* and *advance dating.*
6. How has the role of the fashion director changed?
7. Explain why retailers are getting into manufacturing and private labels.

CASE STUDY

Mercer's Tennis Shop

Evaluation of Supply Resources

Ted Hickox had been working as the sporting goods buyer at Peters Department Store for a year. Two years earlier, when he completed the executive training program at Peters, he was assigned to the sporting goods department as assistant buyer. During his year as assistant buyer he had the opportunity to practice many of the merchandising principles he had learned during his training. When the buyer, Dwight Pearson, was transferred to the appliance department, Ted was made buyer.

Sales increased in his first year and he was looking forward to an even better second year when an unusual opportunity came his way. Red Mercer, an old friend of Ted's family and the owner of Mercer's Tennis Shop, suffered a mild heart attack. He did not want to give up his lucrative business, but felt that he could no longer bear the pressures of one-man management. And he did not want to see his efforts come to an end.

One day he discussed his dilemma with Ted's father. Mr. Hickox suggested that perhaps Red should talk to his son. Although Ted seemed to have a good future with Peters, his father knew that he would be most interested in the possibility Red Mercer offered. Red was looking for a bright young person to take over all the merchandising and promotional activities and share in the store management. He would pay an excellent salary plus a yearly bonus on sales and, in addition, he wanted to sell the store to this new employee over a five-year period. Therefore, there was no need for any immediate investment. All Ted had to contribute at first was his ability as a merchant and his willingness to work hard and continue to build the business.

Projections showed that tennis would be an "in" sport for some years to come, and both tennis clothes and equipment would sell at a record pace if merchandised correctly. How could Ted lose? He gave his notice to Peters' management and one month later found himself running Mercer's Tennis Shop.

There was a great deal of competition in the tennis business, and although Red Mercer had a successful operation, there was no guarantee that sales would continue to increase at the same rate as over the previous four or five years.

Almost anything had sold during that period, when everyone was getting into tennis, regardless of age, sex, income, or lifestyle. No longer was tennis a sport limited to young men and women or the jet set or wealthy Ivy Leaguers. Like golf, tennis had become an everyman's activity, and like other retailers who opened shops at the beginning of the boom, Mercer's experienced phenomenal success just by existing.

The big growth years for the small tennis shop, however, were over. The merchant who would remain on the scene was the one who not only understood the market but who also knew which supply resources were the best for that market.

This was the kind of expertise that Ted brought with him. He knew how to select the proper supply resources for a specific market—he had learned this from Dwight Pearson, who was constantly evaluating and reevaluating the sporting goods manufacturers and wholesalers Peters bought from. He had specific criteria, and any seller who did not measure up was soon off the list.

Ted found that Red Mercer had kept very few merchandising records since he had opened the shop, and this caused unnecessary problems. Red recognized this, too. He had been concerned about which suppliers he should buy from even before he became ill. He knew that he should keep records, but really did not know where to begin. He was fortunate to have found a person with Ted's capabilities.

Ted's first task in his new position was that of devising an adequate system of records for all classifications of merchandise in the two major categories—tennis equipment and tennis clothes. His previous experience proved valuable in this project and he developed a system that he believed not only provided for needed control of the buying function, but also one that would serve as a valuable guide in buying.

Ted believed that a good resource file was a must. It should include the names and addresses of all firms with which orders were placed, together with pertinent information concerning their offerings and business practices. Also, a vendor evaluation form should be developed and maintained for each. This would provide a complete record of all items bought, sold, and on hand in both units and dollars; cost of goods sold; and gross margin realized both in dollars and as a percentage of sales.

In addition, notations were to be made in each vendor's files relating to the reasons for returns and adjustment, customer complaints, and failures to comply with order specifications and shipment promises. Other items of information or importance used in judging the value of each particular resource would also be entered for each supplier. Ted was amazed at the tennis shop's success despite the absence of such record keeping.

Although the maintenance of this resource file would be time consuming and costly, Ted considered it essential if maximum buying efficiency were to be achieved, especially because tennis department buyers in department and chain stores had access to daily computer records with similar information. Mercer's might be small, and might not have the aid of a computer, but a manual resource file, kept up to date, would certainly help in the battle against competition, both large and small. Even if Mercer's should seek the services of a buying office some day, this type of file geared to the store's special needs was invaluable. No buying office could do this kind of study for a client. Ted decided to experiment with information for a resource file.

As far as Ted could tell, Red Mercer had been buying most of his tennis dresses from three major resources—Tennis Girl, Clay Court Casuals, and Leisure Lady. Ted looked over the previous year's records, such as they were, to see which of these three might be developed as a key resource and which, if any, should be discontinued. Then he summarized information that he felt would be helpful in the decision-making process and could be placed in the newly created file for each of these resources. This information was as follows:

Tennis Girl. Relatively new division of major sportswear manufacturer. Rigid quality control program. Fewer than average returns necessary. No substitutes without prior authorization. Shipments on time. No special services except some advertising in tennis magazines. Usual terms and datings. Minimum order, one-quarter dozen.

Clay Court Casuals. A small producer with backing from one of the country's leading professional tennis players. Excellent styling and quality for the price. Distribution on a limited basis, usually to small tennis shops rather than department stores. Mercer's was only outlet in area carrying this name. Well-fitting garments with suggested retail price placed on hang tags by the manufacturer. Limited advertising. Few customer complaints and no returns to vendor. Substitutes only on authorization. Customary terms and datings. No minimum order required.

Leisure Lady. A large sportswear firm and a leader in national advertising. Golf dresses have had wide consumer acceptance since 1950. Intensive distribution policy; three competitors carry this brand in the immediate area. Quality control program, but inspection seems to be deteriorating. Substitutions frequent, but generally satisfactory. Delivery sometimes uncertain. Customer complaints high. Often slow in making adjustments on returns. Wide line of special services. Customary terms and datings with minimum order of one-quarter dozen specified.

Questions

1. Develop criteria by which to judge resources.
2. From the criteria developed for Question 1, set up a resource file for Mercer's Tennis Shop.
3. Evaluate and rate Mercer's three major resources.
4. Based on the evaluation in Question 3, decide which one or ones Mercer's should continue to use. Why?
5. How many different resources should a shop like Mercer's buy from on a regular basis? Why?
6. Is a resource file really necessary for Mercer's? Why?

Chapter 14

Pricing for Profit

Source: *Apparel Merchandising,*
December 10, 1984, 29.

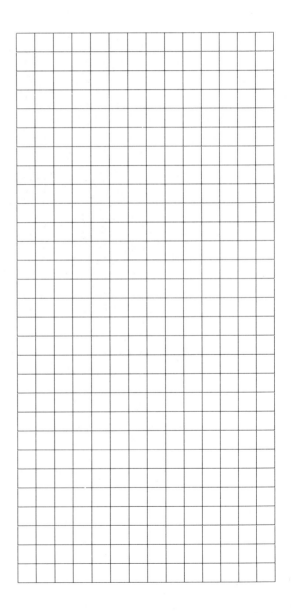

Industry Statement

Michael J. Edwards
Housewares Buyer
May Company, Denver

The most important trend in retail pricing is combining value and promotional pricing within the merchandise mix. Traditionally, department stores have brought merchandise into the distribution center and ticketed it 25 percent higher than its normal 50 percent markup. The merchandise has then been on the floor at this high price for about three weeks.

After the promotional date was reached, the merchandise was retailed at the lower price—the 50 percent markup price—and promoted as being on sale. When customers became aware of these practices, they shopped only on sale days. Thus, the department store lost its day-in, day-out business to discounters and warehouse clubs that use value pricing.

Value pricing originated with discounters like Target, Bradlees, and Caldor, where the initial ticketing of the merchandise is at a sharp price. The discount buyer negotiates the terms, freight allowance, and price—not advertising markdowns or rebates. The goods are priced to generate volume without the expense of advertising. Today, with the emphasis on profit rather than on gross margin, value pricing builds customer loyalty, asset turnover, and net advertising expense savings.

In summary, department stores need day-in, day-out sales increases as well as volume promotions in the form of one-day sales. They must identify key items and value price them to build a large business that is not fueled by advertising or markdowns. In addition, the customer must have confidence that, on a basic item, he or she can shop at a department store and get a needed item at true value. Department stores must also promote merchandise on sale to help create a sense of urgency and excitement around a major event. Thus, promotional pricing is an important tool in adding credibility to this type of event.

A good pricing strategy will implement the exploiting of the opportunities created by both value and promotional pricing in the merchandise mix.

Learning Objectives

Upon completing this chapter you should be able to:

1. Understand how pricing fits into the overall retail marketing system.
2. Describe the component parts of a retail pricing strategy.
3. Know why current price competition is forcing retailers to intensify their market-share battles.
4. Assess pricing strategies being used by retailers to meet intense competition.
5. Determine how retailers choose a pricing strategy and how they implement it, once it is chosen.

The retailer must be as concerned with the selling price of goods as with their cost, because each of these functions affects profits equally.

Customers perceive price as representing many factors—quality, value, ambience, convenience, and service. They can more easily make price comparisons between department stores and off-pricers now that department stores are eliminating or charging for services that once were free. In the past customers did not know how much it cost to deliver or alter a garment or provide extended 30-day credit. As department stores charge for these services and cut the sales staff drastically, they have few reasons to justify a price differential.

It is essential that a store portray a true and consistent pricing policy to its clientele, because increased sales and profits potential often lie within its own customer base. At most stores about 75 percent of volume comes from only 25 percent of the customers. The largest potential for expansion is among the 75 percent of repeat-shopping customers who contribute only one-quarter of the sales.

FACTORS AFFECTING A RETAIL PRICING STRATEGY

Before choosing a retail pricing strategy, store executives must consider several factors that may have an impact on their decisions—customers, competition, and government.

The Customer

Unless the retailer knows the economic status of the store's consumers, he or she cannot make proper decisions on price levels. Paired with income should be a study of lifestyle. A blue-collar worker earning $35,000 a year would probably differ in spending patterns from a college professor earning the same salary.

Atmospherics
Interior design
intended to create
or suggest a
particular mood.

Not all customers buy with price as their first priority. The **atmospherics** of the store, such as the visual presentation of merchandise and general ambience, have a strong influence. Image can be as important as price. When Sears first experimented with a fur coat salon in the 1970s, it did not meet with much success. Even though the mink coats were priced well under competitive stores in the Main Line area of Philadelphia, few people were willing to buy a mink at Sears.

Competition—Other Retailers and Suppliers

Too many retailers are chasing the same customer. The problem has been building since the late 1970s, when the big national chains emerged from a 20-year expansion trend to find most major retail markets saturated. Nevertheless, retailers continued to expand aggressively, triggering a struggle for market share.

Retailing is beginning to be characterized by a smaller number of large players, with a lot of squeeze on smaller companies with limited resources. Associated Dry Goods Corporation of New York acquired two large discount chains—Caldor Inc. and Loehmann's Inc.—in order to reduce reliance on its slower growing regional department store chains. They, in turn, were acquired by May Company in 1987. F. W. Woolworth Company, best known for its variety stores, now operates more than 20 businesses, including children's wear stores and fast food hamburger franchises. Federated started MainStreet in 1984, aimed at young, middle-income families in locations where there was not much to buy in that market segment.

Discounters

Today's generation of discounters is different from its predecessors, who sold a wide variety of lower-priced—and often lower-quality—merchandise in one store. The new discounters specialize in one category—such as clothing, toys, or health and beauty aids.

The philosophy of discounting is based on high volume and bigger dollar profit—not percentage profit—gained through lower markups and inventory turns of 12 or 13 times. On the other hand, the department store mentality aims at the highest gross margin as the number-one priority. Historically, turns have been four or five times a year. That will change as the most aggressive department stores, such as Macy's and Nordstrom, adapt themselves to the methods of off-pricers.

FROM THE FIELD

Dayton Hudson Pricing Strategies

Dayton Hudson is generally conceded to be the best-managed company in retailing. Since 1979 the department store chain's sales have climbed 100 percent, while earnings from continuing operations have almost doubled, too, to $243 million.

What next? It will not be hot pursuit of the trendy crowd as, for example, Macy's New York has happily chosen. Dayton Hudson, based in Minneapolis, is taking a lower road. It is putting growth money in low-priced, discount-type stores similar to K marts and in a separate chain of clothing stores stocking wares a little better and a little higher priced than those at discount stores.

The Target store discount chain is heavy on hard goods, electronics, and the like. The clothing stores, called Mervyn's, are the kind of store where a man's three-piece suit costs under $100. People who shop there typically earn $20,000 to $40,000 a year. (See Figure 14.1.)

The strategy works. The proof is that Dayton Hudson, which also runs first-rate department stores and suburban mall stores in Michigan and Minnesota, has had average earnings-per-share growth of 17 percent since 1979 and sports a five-year return-on-equity average of 17.9 per cent, second only to R. H. Macy.

Dayton Hudson founded its Target stores in 1962 and acquired Mervyn's in 1978, convinced that its own low-priced retailing was the way to meet the relentless rise of discounter competition. Expansion for Mervyn's will be 142 new stores, bringing the total by 1990 to 268 in at least 12 states. For Target, 72 new units are planned, bringing the total to 288 in 22 states.

Mervyn's and Target have done well because, clearly, customers are getting wise to the ways of big department store merchandising. Maybe 70 percent of the dollar volume in clothes in a department store comes in at some "sale" price. Says one sweater manufacturer, "Today the real price is 'off-price,' and the department store real price is the wrong price. To make matters worse, the department stores have winter goods in the summer and summer goods in winter. Have you ever tried to buy a bathing suit at a department store in July?"

Source: "Never Mind the High Road," *Forbes*, December 3, 1984, 174–177.

Led by Dayton Hudson, big department store chains are beginning to become involved in discount or off-price merchandising. Federated Department Stores, for example, opened three stores called MainStreet (Figure 14.2) in the Chicago suburbs as a first step toward taking the chain national.

Figure   14.1   Two Pricing Strategies from the Dayton Hudson Department Store Chain

Source: Courtesy of Dayton Hudson Corporation.

Figure   14.2   Discount Store Owned by Federated Department Stores: MainStreet

Source: Copyright © B. E. White, 1987. All Rights Reserved.

MainStreet's affiliation with Federated gives the stores the advantage of increased buying clout coupled with substantial cost-cutting opportunities. For example, Gold Circle, another Federated discount chain, will do all of MainStreet's data processing. MainStreet will also draw from the latest retailing technology, helping to keep productivity high. Sources close to the company peg MainStreet's goals for sales per square foot of selling space at about $200, more than the department store average of $135, but realistic when compared with the $295 per square foot that Mervyn's achieves.

Dayton Hudson is wedded to an economic function, not a retailing style. "Words like discounter, off-price, and highly promotional don't mean anything to the customer," the company's chief officer has said. "What she cares about is value and consistency of product. You abandon that customer, and you pay for it."[1]

Off-pricers

The off-pricer is like a specialty store that sells merchandise of moderate to better quality, including designer-name apparel. Services are minimal and the ambience is no-frill, often with pipe racks as fixtures. Turnover usually runs double that of traditional apparel stores. These stores are capitalizing on the fact that approximately half of retail business across price lines is done at off-price—60 to 70 percent in some classifications.

Part of the growth in sales volume comes from the sharp increase in the number of off-price outlet centers across the country. Lower operating costs—usually about 25 percent—have also helped make off-price merchants competitive. They pay lower rents by taking over shuttered supermarkets or stores in less than prime locations. In addition, they are mostly self-service operations, with few salespeople and central checkouts.

Once strictly a general merchandise discounter, the Zayre Corporation started T. J. Maxx and Hit or Miss apparel chains a few years ago. Unlike Marshalls, these off-price chains sell only first-quality, in-season apparel. They are producing more than double the profit margin of the regular Zayre discount stores.[2] (See Figure 14.3 and Table 14.1 on page 370.) Management Horizons, Inc., a Columbus, Ohio, consulting firm, estimates that by 1990 off-price will represent 10 percent or more of all apparel and footwear sales, or at least $19 billion.

Membership Retailing
Discounting operations that require payment of a membership fee in order to shop in a warehouse.

Warehousing/Membership Retailing

Warehousing, or **membership retailing,** is a combination wholesale/retail general merchandise market expected to expand to at least $20 billion in the final years of the 1980s.[3]

---

[1] "Never Mind the High Road," *Forbes*, December 3, 1984, 174.
[2] Isadore Barmish, "A Revolution in American Shopping," *The New York Times*, October 20, 1983, G1.
[3] "Membership Retailing Trend Taking Off," *Chain Store Age Executive*, November 1984, 17.

Figure   14.3   Index of Sales Growth for Leading Clothing Chains in Three Categories, 1978–1982[a]

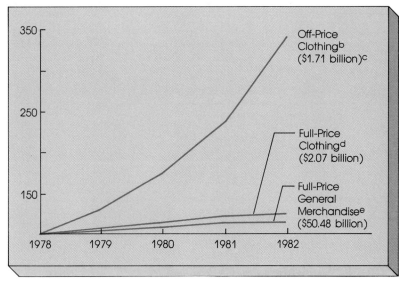

[a] 1978 = 100.
[b] Marshalls, T. J. Maxx/Hit or Miss, J. Brannan, Burlington Coat Factory, Syms.
[c] Dollar amounts are total 1982 sales.
[d] Petrie Stores, Miller-Wohl, Charming Shoppes, Lerner Stores, The Limited (excluding Lane Bryant division).
[e] Sears, Roebuck (merchandising group only), J. C. Penney, F. W. Woolworth (excluding J. Brannan division), Federated Stores, Dayton Hudson.
Source: *The New York Times*, October 23, 1983, 350.

The stores are drafty when the weather is cold and stuffy when it is hot. Customers have to find dollies and grappling hooks and then wrestle refrigerators, desks, and other heavy items to the checkout line themselves. There are no home deliveries. Credit cards are not accepted, and shoppers even pay a membership fee for the privilege of spending their money. But no one seems to mind because everything is so inexpensive. Merchandise is typically sold at 20 to 40 percent below supermarket and discount-store prices.

Warehouse clubs could be found by the mid-1980s in about half of the 100 largest markets in the country, and even faster growth is projected.[4] (See Figure 14.4 on page 371.)

Private Label

Retailers who are traditional pricing stores are developing their own lines of merchandise with their store label as a way of competing with

---

[4] "Boom Times in a Bargain-Hunter's Paradise," *Business Week*, March 11, 1985, 116.

Table   14.1   The Leading Off-Price Clothing Chains

Chain (Parent Company)	Sales[a] (in millions)		Number of Outlets	
	1982	1983[b]	1982	1983[b]
Marshalls (Melville Corporation)	$830	$1,100	137	175
T. J. Maxx, Hit or Miss (Zayre Corporation)	525	755	353	471
Loehmann's, Inc. (Associated Dry Goods)	260	275	61	70
Pic-A-Dilly (Lucky Stores)	165	210	250	271
Syms, Inc.	147	185	8	11
Burlington Coat Factory	128	200	31	46
J. Brannan (F. W. Woolworth)	85	75	30	38
T. H. Mandy (U. S. Shoe)	80	200	52	122
Dress Barn, Inc.	32	44	49	70
Ross Stores[c]	15	80	6	26

[a]Some sales figures are analysts' estimates.
[b]Estimated.
[c]Began operations in June 1982.

stores who are selling national brands at discounted prices. This was discussed in Chapter 13.

Bridge Lines

One department store executive calls them "designer II," another, "bridge," while a third refers to them as the "sons and daughters" of the designers. Whatever they are called, retailers agree that Anne Klein II, Calvin Klein Classifications, Perry Ellis Portfolio (see Figure 14.5 on page 372), and Ralph Lauren Classifications, by virtue of strong consumer acceptance, have earned permanent positions in their merchandising mix and are forming the core of the developing bridge sportswear category. **Bridge lines** have a price range several hundred dollars below the regular designer lines. For example, Anne Klein II retail prices range from $35 for a T-shirt to $250 for a wool blazer.[5] (See Figure 14.6 on page 373.)

Bridge Line
A line of apparel by a name designer that is priced considerably lower than usual designer fashions.

Government

In the 19th century a need existed to protect small retailers that were being hurt by larger firms with greater purchasing power; the Sherman

[5]"Bridge Lines Span the Gap," *Apparel Merchandising*, December 1984, 29.

Figure   14.4   Sales of the Largest Warehouse Clubs, 1984–1985[a]

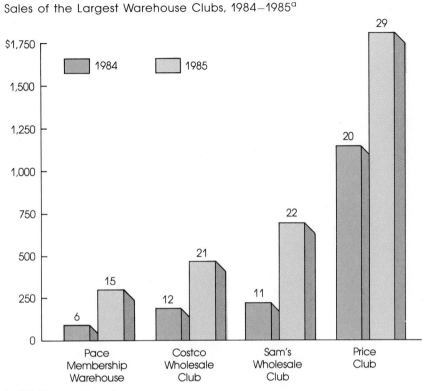

[a] 1985 figure projected.
Source: *Business Week*, March 11, 1985, 116. Data from Goldman, Sachs & Co.

Antitrust Act was passed in 1890 to prevent horizontal price fixing that might take place in any kind of business. The law, aimed at keeping competition open, makes it illegal for manufacturers, wholesalers, or retailers to fix prices.

Individual states have enacted a number of unfair trade practice laws in efforts to protect the smaller retailer. These laws require that the retailer charge a minimum price for goods based on the merchandise cost plus an overhead percentage.

Manufacturers are prevented from price discrimination in the sale of goods of like quality by the Robinson-Patman Act. However, the act does permit manufacturers to establish price differentials based on cost differences when selling to retailers. They must prove, however, that these specific price agreements do not hinder competition.

CHOOSING A RETAIL PRICE STRATEGY

A store must choose one or more market segments and then target its marketing to these customers. The retail price decision is therefore tied to target market decisions.

Figure   14.5   Bridge Line: Perry Ellis Portfolio

Source: *Apparel Merchandising,* December 10, 1984, 29.

Unit Pricing
The quotation of
prices in terms of a
standard measure
such as ounces,
feet, or dozens.

Single Versus Flexible Pricing

When all customers pay the same price and purchase an item under
similar conditions, a single pricing/one-price policy occurs. John Wanamaker was the first merchant to mark each piece of merchandise with its
own price, which eliminated bargaining and led to the newer policy of
unit pricing. This concept has been adopted by many supermarkets.
The exact cost per pound or pint is computed for every item in grocery

Figure   14.6   Bridge Sportswear Design: Anne Klein II

Source: Courtesy of Anne Klein II.

Flexible Pricing
The setting of
prices that are
open to
bargaining.

and dairy departments. Labels with unit prices are often attached to the shelf where the merchandise is displayed.

In contrast to single pricing, **flexible pricing** often occurs in automobile showrooms, jewelry shops, and in real estate transactions. This permits the customer to bargain. In order to do so successfully, he or she should be knowledgeable about the merchandise and the competitive selling situation.

Multiple Pricing
The offering of a
discount for
buying in a preset
quantity, such as
12 for $1.

Multiple Pricing

Using a form of psychological pricing, **multiple pricing,** the retailer offers customers discounts for buying in quantity. As an example, six packs of bubble gum may be offered for $1.15, making the unit price 19 cents, while a package purchased separately might sell for 20 cents. The customer must then choose between a larger quantity at a lower price and a smaller quantity at a higher price. The retailer can expect to achieve an increase in overall profit on sales, although the profit per unit is reduced.

Odd Pricing

Odd Pricing
The setting of prices that end in an odd number, often a 9, as in $1.99.

Another form of psychological pricing, **odd pricing,** occurs when the retailer sets prices at points that are below even dollar values, such as $.79, $9.95, and $999. This strategy is aimed at the customer who might, for example, have set a maximum of $1,000 for a mink jacket, and so a price of $999 has immediate drawing power. The retailer hopes the customer will feel that she has found a bargain.

Leader Pricing

The retailer who sells a key item in the product assortment at a lower than usual price, with reduced profits, is using a leader pricing strategy. It is intended to induce customers to shop for these specially priced items, but with the hope that additional purchases will be made by that same customer at regular price, thereby increasing total sales volume and profits. This happens often in advertising nationally branded, high-volume merchandise. For example, Scott Towels or Coca-Cola may be used by a supermarket chain to generate traffic if they are offered at 20 cents off for one week. The market may gain additional customers who will shop for their entire weekly food order because of the prices of those two items.

Loss Leaders
Items sold below cost to pull customers into the store. This practice is forbidden in some states.

Items that are priced below cost for the purpose of generating increased traffic are called **loss leaders.** They are restricted by minimum price laws in some states. Loss leaders are used by both supermarket and drug chains to draw additional customers.

Value Pricing

Merchandise priced at an everyday low price is value priced. Generally, the store will not advertise merchandise at a price lower than its ticketed price. Most department stores are applying value pricing to basics and key items to build a day-in, day-out business.

Promotional Markup (PMU)
A higher price used during a short, initial sell-off period and then later in comparative advertising.

Promotional Pricing

Most stores use a system called **promotional markup (PMU)** to establish a comparative price for advertising purposes. After the item has been on the selling floor for perhaps ten days and has a 10 to 20 percent sell-off, it is permanently ticketed at a low, or sale, price.

Price Lining

The first consideration of a buyer in the market must be the selection of style, quality, and price that answer the demand of his or her customers. Before an order is placed, however, the buyer must be convinced that customers will be willing to pay the price that must be asked in order to cover expenses and make a profit. A buyer usually has only a limited choice of prices to place on any item, because store policy sets **price lines** for the various departments.

Price lines are retail prices, set by policy, at which merchandise may be offered for sale to consumers. For instance, if store policy establishes price lines at $16.50, $26.50, $32.00, and $39.00 for a moderate blouse department, the buyer for that department will not have authority to mark any blouse with a price of $29.00 or any other price not included in the established lines. Merchandise assortments should be intensified at the price point for highest volume.

If price lines are wisely established, they are close enough together to afford some range of choice for a customer at any income level, and far enough apart to make differences of quality and style distinguishable. A customer who is prepared to pay $32.00 for a blouse may be interested in looking for blouses at $39.00 or $26.50, the next higher and next lower price lines; having examined them, she should be able to make her choice knowing that clearly distinguishable differences exist among them. If blouses were permitted to be offered at random prices, the buyer could not give clear-cut justification for differences in price and the customer might lose confidence. Among the advantages of limiting price lines is the possibility of recording past sales by price lines, which will help in planning future assortments more intelligently.

Price Lines
Distinguishable price levels, set by store policy, that must be applied to all merchandise.

MARK-ON

A buyer goes to market with the clearly defined purpose of finding an article that he or she can offer with confidence at a given price line. Another requirement is that a certain cumulative mark-on percentage must be obtained.

Mark-on
The difference between the gross delivered price of merchandise and the original retail price.

Cumulative Mark-on

Cumulative **mark-on** is the difference between the gross delivered cost of the merchandise and the original retail price. Gross delivered cost of merchandise is the cost listed on the invoice, plus transportation charges, without deduction of cash discount or anticipation. It is to be distinguished from net delivered cost of merchandise. Cash discounts and anticipation do not affect the initial mark-on. The total amount of discount accumulated during a given period is eventually taken into account in connection with the preparation of the operating results of the store as a whole as well as for its individual departments. The word *cumulative* is applied to the mark-on percentage after cost and retail figures for opening inventory, various purchases, inward freight, and additional mark-on have been accumulated over a period of time.

The first markup on a single purchase or a single article among the purchases is called **initial mark-on** or purchase mark-on. As an example, if the invoice cost of an article is 58 cents and the transportation cost 2 cents, the delivered cost is 60 cents; then, if the buyer places an **original retail price** of $1.00 on the article, its initial mark-on is 40 cents; and the initial mark-on percentage is 40 percent.

A buyer is allowed latitude in deciding what initial mark-on to place on any given item, but a goal is generally fixed for the average mark-on for all purchases during a given period. The goal is defined by the control and merchandising divisions, after they have analyzed past records and considered the outlook for the coming period. If the buyer in a dress department is told to reach an average mark-on of 47 percent on accumulated purchases for six months, the buyer knows that if he or she takes less than 47 percent on some articles, it is necessary to take more than 47 percent on others.

Calculation of Initial Mark-on

The buyer should understand how to figure initial mark-on in two situations. The first arises when original retail in dollars and initial mark-on in percent are known, and it is necessary to determine cost in dollars. As an example, the buyer for a dress department is ready to buy blouses for a $19.50 price line. The cumulative mark-on toward which he is aiming is 40 percent. What is the highest amount that he can afford to pay the vendor as a gross cost, delivered?

Original retail in dollars multiplied by initial mark-on percentage gives initial mark-on in dollars. Initial mark-on in dollars subtracted from original retail in dollars gives cost in dollars. This relationship is expressed in these two formulas:

$$\begin{matrix} \text{Original Retail} \\ \text{(Dollars)} \end{matrix} \times \begin{matrix} \text{Initial Mark-on} \\ \text{(Percentage)} \end{matrix} = \begin{matrix} \text{Initial Mark-on} \\ \text{(Dollars)} \end{matrix}$$

$$\begin{matrix} \text{Original Retail} \\ \text{(Dollars)} \end{matrix} - \begin{matrix} \text{Initial Mark-on} \\ \text{(Dollars)} \end{matrix} = \begin{matrix} \text{Cost} \\ \text{(Dollars)} \end{matrix}$$

The original retail in dollars may also be multiplied by the percentage of original retail that represents cost of merchandise. The cost percent-

Initial Mark-on
The first markup on a single purchase or a single article among the purchases.

Original Retail Price
The first retail price placed on merchandise; must be distinguished from prices that are reduced by taking markdowns.

age of original retail is the complement of the initial mark-on percentage, namely 100 percent minus the initial mark-on percentage. Translating this into a formula, cost in dollars is found thus:

$$\underset{\text{(Dollars)}}{\text{Original Retail}} \times \left(100\% - \underset{\text{[Percentage]}}{\text{Initial Mark-on}}\right) = \underset{\text{(Dollars)}}{\text{Cost}}.$$

Suppose the buyer is purchasing for the $19.50 price line and is aiming for a 40 percent cumulative mark-on. The required cost can be determined by the following calculation:

$$\$19.50 \times .40 = \$7.80 \text{ Mark-on}$$
$$\$19.50 - \$7.80 = \$11.70 \text{ Cost,}$$

or by the following alternate method:

$$\$19.50 \times (100\% - 40\%) = \$11.70 \text{ Cost.}$$

The buyer can afford to pay no more than $11.70 for a garment to be retailed at $19.50, if an initial mark-on of 40 percent[6] is to be obtained.

The second situation in which the buyer should understand the figuring of initial mark-on requires another example. Suppose that the buyer, having gone to the market to purchase blouses for the $19.50 price line, sees a good model quoted at $12.50, delivered. If the buyer should purchase the garment at that cost, how much would the mark-on fall below the desired 40 percent?

In this situation the original mark-on percentage is to be found. The original retail minus the gross cost in dollars equals initial mark-on in dollars; initial mark-on in dollars divided by original retail equals initial mark-on percentage. The calculation can be expressed in these two formulas:

$$\text{Original Retail Dollars} - \text{Cost Dollars} = \text{Initial Mark-on (Dollars)}$$

$$\frac{\text{Initial Mark-on (Dollars)}}{\text{Original Retail (Dollars)}} = \text{Initial Mark-on (Percentage)}$$

The solution of the case is as follows:

$$\$19.50 - \$12.50 = \$7.00$$
$$\frac{\$7.00}{\$19.50} = 35.8\%$$

---

[6] Any mark-on stated as a percentage of retail can be readily converted into its equivalent percentage of cost. Divide the mark-on percentage by the corresponding cost (100 percent minus mark-on percent) also stated as a percentage of retail. If the mark-on is 40 percent, the corresponding cost is 60 percent (100 − 40).

$$\frac{40}{60} = \text{Mark-on as a Percentage of Cost} = 66\frac{2}{3}$$

If this buyer had no price lines and determined the original retail solely on the amount of desired initial mark-on, the blouse would have retailed at $20.83. The gross cost in dollars was $12.50. The desired initial mark-on percentage of 40 subtracted from the original retail percentage of 100 gives a cost percentage of 60. The cost percentage of 60 is equivalent to a cost in dollars of $12.50. If 60 percent equals $12.50, then 1 percent equals .2083 ($12.50 ÷ 60) and 100 percent equals $20.83.

A shortcut may be taken by dividing the gross cost stated in dollars by 100 percent minus the initial mark-on percent. Reduced to a formula the process is this:

$$\frac{\text{Cost (Dollars)}}{100\% - \text{Initial Mark-on (Percentage)}} = \text{Original Retail (Dollars)}$$

MARKDOWN

Every retailer's budget includes a fixed percentage of sales for markdowns. Markdowns should be spent in the way that best helps the store to achieve a sales plan without hurting the gross margin. They can be used for sharpening the price of advertised merchandise, to help clear stocks of obsolete or slow-selling goods, and to clear stocks of damaged goods that vendors will not take back. Finally, markdowns should be spent only after a complete analysis of business has been made.

Summary

Factors to be considered when deciding on a retail price strategy are the customer, competition from other retailers and suppliers, and the government. Not all customers buy with price as their first priority; they also consider the decor of the store, personal services, and merchandise assortments.

Current competition has forced retailers to further intensify their market-share battles. This has led to diversified pricing strategies, such as discounting, off-pricing, warehousing, membership retailing, and private labeling.

In choosing a pricing strategy, a retailer may opt for single pricing, multiple-unit pricing, odd pricing, leader pricing, or price lining. After choosing a strategy or a combination of strategies, the retailer must figure out a markup policy based on the cost of the item, the cost of operating his business, and the profit goal.

Finally, a markdown system must be adopted so that the retailer will constantly be moving goods out, replenishing inventory, and turning over the cash investment to produce fresh merchandise for customers and profit for the retailer.

Questions
for Review

1. List three major factors that may have an impact on a retailer's pricing strategy.
2. What factors, other than price, can influence a customer's decision to buy?
3. How does the basic pricing philosophy of a traditional department store differ from that of a discount store?
4. What, in your opinion, is contributing to the growth of off-price retail stores?
5. Define the terms *single pricing, multiple-unit pricing, odd pricing, leader pricing,* and *price lining.*
6. Explain two situations a buyer could face in figuring initial mark-on.
7. Why does a retailer use markdowns?

CASE STUDY

Betty's Boutique

A Pricing Decision

Elizabeth Whiting, proprietor of Betty's Boutique, Ocean Bluffs' most exclusive dress shop, was concerned about sales for the first time since she opened the boutique ten years earlier. The empty store across the street had just been rented to the Hillman Company, a firm that operated a number of off-price fashion stores throughout the state.

Hillman's had started five years before with one store in Port Charles. When the store in Ocean Bluffs opened it would make the seventh. The company's strategy was to buy fashion goods in job lots from well-known manufacturers whose names would attract the fashion-conscious shopper and to price these items 20 percent lower than the same goods in department and specialty stores. The Hillman management knew that many women have "champagne taste and beer wallets."

Not only had they done a great deal of research, they were also well aware of the effects of modern communications on every stratum of society. In today's world, awareness is immediate. Mary Jones does not want to wait for the newest "look" until it is copied in a lower price range. Her mother, after spending most of the family clothing allowance on her daughters, also wants some designer clothes in her wardrobe. The Hillman concept was the answer: Buy clothing from the same resources as the finest specialty and department stores, but not as far in advance of each season as these stores do. Closer to the actual selling period suppliers are willing to sell in lots priced as a package rather than per garment.

At the peak of each selling season, Hillman's would therefore have an assortment of the same lines found in the expensive shops and fashion departments of Port Charles stores but for much less money. Because sizes, colors, and styles cannot be selected according to a predetermined classification plan when purchased the Hillman way, customers who want to be assured of a certain style, color, or size would never become Hillman devotees, nor would those who prefer to get exactly what they want preseason. Yet, while many shop only in the better boutiques and department stores because of the assortments and services provided—such as credit, alterations, and delivery—Hillman's and other stores like it with their off-price fashion concept are definitely capturing a niche in the fashion marketplace.

Competition has always been rough in the fashion business, but at least price had not been a major factor to contend with. Retailers like Elizabeth Whiting all worked on an approximate 50 percent initial markup based on retail, and differences in prices for identical garments were never more than a dollar or two, at the most, in competitive stores within one trading area.

Now Betty's Boutique was faced with the same problem plaguing fashion merchants all over the country. An off-price fashion store was about to show its ugly head in Ocean Bluffs. The problem was compounded by the fact that its ugly-head image was seen only by merchants. Consumers seemed to be eagerly awaiting Hillman's opening day.

It could be expected that even loyal customers of Betty's Boutique, those who loved the one-day alteration service, intended to buy whatever they could at Hillman's. Price was price and, with income having to be stretched further each year, everyone was looking for a bargain.

Elizabeth was an expert on customer services. Her displays were among the most creative in town. Her staff was known for its courteous treatment of all customers, whether or not they were regulars. Competitive price strategies, however, were not her forte. How was she to meet this latest challenge?

She felt she had a number of viable alternatives. Elizabeth knew that she had to give serious consideration to each one, for her decision would be crucial to the future of Betty's Boutique. She would no longer be able to rely on designer names or brand names when the same merchandise was being sold for less money across the street. No longer would she draw new customers because of her special services. Price was the question and price was the answer.

She had long been aware of the Filene's Basement approach to pricing fashion goods, but had never considered it as a possibility for her shop. Perhaps she could adapt this method to her needs by setting aside half of the shop as a mini basement, and use it to sell her own markdowns as well as job lots and end-of-season goods purchased from other high-priced retailers in the region.

This was basically how Filene's Basement in Boston operated. The entire stock was made up of merchandise bought in lots from the finest retailers and manufacturers in the world as well as, a few times a year, from Filene's own store and branches. Because buyers for Filene's Basement took the entire group from each source without regard for quality and assortment, they were able to buy everything at lower prices than if they had been selective.

The differences between the methods of Filene's Basement and Hillman's were primarily differences in resources, timing, and selling strategies. The buyers for Filene's Basement were even less selective and, therefore, eligible for better buys. Their resources were eager to do business with them. Manufacturers were glad for the opportunity to sell stock that had done poorly during their season plus all other odd sizes and colors in their line. Retailers knew that they could count on Filene's Basement to buy out their entire stock or any portion of it that they were not able to sell as long as it was priced right.

Many fashion shops in small cities had been dealing with Filene's for years. Rather than planning and running their own sales, they rid their racks in one fell swoop by selling everything to Filene's Basement. Perhaps by running their own sales they might realize a better return on some units, but the costs involved, plus losses on those numbers that had to be almost given away, made dealing with Filene's a better deal.

Famous fashion stores like Neiman-Marcus in Texas and Bergdorf Goodman in New York were regular suppliers, and Filene's Basement customers counted on being able to buy $300 designer dresses and $350 designer suits for half price. The rich and the not-so-rich rubbed shoulders while looking over the vast assortments brought together by the management of this famous bargain basement.

The buying methods made Filene's Basement unique, but sales strategies were also a bit unusual. When merchandise was first placed on the selling floor, it was given prime space. Expert promotion ensured management of a maximum market for all new stock. Merchandise that was left after 12 days was moved to a less desirable location on the floor while new arrivals took over the prime spot. From this second location the leftovers were moved again to a third area. With each move, prices were reduced until finally the items that remained were given to charitable organizations.

A most unusual and successful retail institution, Filene's Basement attracted customers in droves and the concept had been well known for years to practitioners and students of retailing alike. Elizabeth had always been fascinated with the operation, and visited the basement whenever she was in the Boston area. Why couldn't she do something similar? She could limit her sources and buy only from retailers in her geographic region, eliminating manufacturers completely. Once it acquired a reputation as an outlet, Betty's Boutique could become the one clearinghouse for top-flight fashion in the region and customers would flock to the "Filene's Basement of Ocean Bluffs." One question to be answered was whether she could operate half of the store as an exclusive dress shop or should use all of the space for bargain items from other exclusive shops.

Advertising would have to be quite intensive, especially in the beginning, but Elizabeth was not worried about this. She was confident that the increased income would support an increased promotion budget.

If this was not the best direction to take, either in part or totally, could she become another Hillman's instead? Could she afford to wait and invest her entire open-to-buy just as the season was starting in whatever the resources had available? Should she forget the merchandise plan that had been the basis for success for many years? Where would customers go who wanted selection and service? Would she lose or gain in trying to compete directly with Hillman's? Hillman's had the ability to take advantage of manufacturers' lots on a much larger scale than Betty's Boutique, for they had seven distribution points. With only one store Elizabeth was sure to pay more for the same group of merchandise, and paying more meant either higher prices or a lower markup.

Of course, Betty's Boutique could ignore the new competitor in town and continue offering a fine selection of designer clothes at full price.

Selection and service still had value. The question was, how many in the Ocean Bluffs market wanted value over price?

Questions

1. Relate the Hillman concept to today's communications revolution.
2. Visit a local specialty shop and an off-price fashion store and describe the customers you find shopping in each.
3. Should Elizabeth adopt the Filene's Basement plan? Why?
4. What are the chances of survival for Betty's Boutique once Hillman's opens its doors? Give reasons for your answer.
5. In your opinion, is there still a sizable market for stores like Betty's Boutique? Explain.
6. What are the advantages and disadvantages of buying according to plan rather than by lot? Explain.

Appendix 14A **Retail Math**

The accounting department of any business continuously makes a record of transactions as they occur. At the end of a fiscal year, if not more often, a statement is compiled that summarizes the results of the transactions for the period. This summary is called a *profit and loss statement*.

Expressed in simplest terms, a profit and loss statement shows the difference between income and expenses. If income is greater than expenses, the result is a *net profit*. If expenses exceed income, the result is a *net loss*. A business that sells goods—such as a store or manufacturer—receives its income from sales. We will use, as an example, the profit and loss statement of a retail business that buys merchandise at wholesale for resale to consumers.

For a retail business, the first expansion of the following equation breaks expenses down into two broad, basic types:

$$\text{Income} - \text{Expenses} = \text{Net Profit or Loss}$$

These are expenses of merchandise bought and resold (hereinafter called *cost of merchandise*) and expense of all other kinds incurred in operating the business (called *operating expenses*). The use of different words, cost and expense, is evidence of the importance of accounting separately for merchandise and for all other expenditures made in operating a retail business. First the cost of merchandise sold is subtracted from the income derived from net sales to arrive at a figure called *gross margin*. From the gross margin, operating expenses are subtracted to determine net profit or loss. Table 14A.1 shows such a computation.

In the skeleton form of profit and loss statement shown in Table 14A.1, there are three kinds of dollar amounts: retail, cost, and margin. The nature of these should be noted. *Cost* is an amount paid by the merchant for goods bought for resale. *Sales* are a retail figure, which normally is higher than the cost figure on any given article or lot of merchandise. *Margin* is the difference between cost and retail. *Profit* is the part of the margin that remains after operating expenses have been paid.

Table   14A.1   Skeleton Form of Profit and Loss Statement

Income from Net Sales	$10,000
Cost of Merchandise Sold	6,000
Gross Margin	$ 4,000
Operating Expenses	3,500
Net Profit	$ 500

COMPUTATION OF COST OF MERCHANDISE SOLD

In the skeleton form of profit and loss statement shown in Table 14A.1, the cost of merchandise sold was not computed, but was set forth as if known without computation. However, this figure must always be computed if the life of the business extends beyond the period covered by the profit and loss statement. The reason is that merchandise was on hand at the beginning of the period and at the end.

Management must set up a limit of time, such as the fiscal year, for which net profit or loss is computed. Only in this way can profit trends be seen and one business compared with another. Moreover, income tax returns must be filed annually.

The flow of merchandise into and out of a prosperous store cannot be broken off on the dates that end accounting periods. The store must have merchandise on hand sufficient to meet the demand at all times. However, no reasonable figure for net profit could be arrived at, if from the sales of this year were deducted cost of merchandise not intended for sale until the next year. Real profit is measured by goods sold, not goods in stock. It is therefore necessary to compute the cost of merchandise sold. Table 14A.2 expands the skeleton form of Table 14A.1 to show the computation.

To the opening inventory, or goods on hand at cost price at the beginning of the fiscal period, is added the cost of all purchases of goods during that period. The sum is the *total merchandise handled,* which is really the total merchandise available for sale. From this is subtracted the inventory of merchandise on hand at the end of the period, and the result is the *cost of merchandise sold.* The foregoing statements may be expressed in the form of equations as follows:

$$\text{Opening Inventory} + \text{Purchases} = \text{Total Merchandise Handled}$$

$$\text{Total Merchandise Handled} - \text{Closing Inventory} = \text{Cost of Merchandise Sold}$$

One more expansion of the profit and loss statement adds inward freight to merchandise costs. Table 14A.3 shows the handling of this

Table   14A.2   Computation of Cost of Merchandise Sold

Income from Net Sales		$10,000
Cost of Merchandise Sold:		
Opening Inventory	$1,200	
Purchases	6,200	
Total Merchandise Handled	$7,400	
Closing Inventory	1,400	
Cost of Merchandise Sold		6,000
Gross Margin		$ 4,000
Operating Expenses		3,500
Net Profit		$ 500

Table   14A.3   Inclusion of Inward Freight with Merchandise Cost

Income from Net Sales			$10,000
Cost of Merchandise Sold:			
Opening Inventory		$1,200	
Purchases	$5,500		
Inward Freight	700	6,200	
Total Merchandise Handled		$7,400	
Closing Inventory		1,400	
Cost of Merchandise Sold			6,000
Gross Margin			$ 4,000
Operating Expenses			3,500
Net Profit			$ 500

item. Inward freight is merely added to the cost of purchases. The item *inward freight* covers all transportation costs paid by the retailer in bringing the merchandise into the store whether by rail, express, truck, water, or air. The word *inward* distinguishes this item from expense of delivery of merchandise from store to customer, which is classified among operating expenses.

ANALYSIS OF PROFIT AND LOSS STATEMENT: FIRST STEP

Two equations used in analyzing a profit and loss statement are repeated here:

$$\text{Net Sales} - \text{Cost of Merchandise Sold} = \text{Gross Margin}$$
$$\text{Gross Margin} - \text{Operating Expenses} = \text{Profit or Loss}$$

An examination of the two equations reveals that the amount of all other items is contained in the amount of net sales. The one exception to this occurs when there is a net loss. Because net sales cover cost of merchandise sold, operating expenses, and net profit, it is natural in making an analysis to let net sales equal 100 percent. The items in Table 14A.1 expressed in percentages of net sales appear in Table 14A.4.

The equations must, obviously, hold good for the percentages as for the dollar amounts. Net sales, 100 percent, minus cost of merchandise sold, 60 percent, equals gross margin, 40 percent. And gross margin, 40 percent, minus operating expenses, 35 percent, equals net profit, 5 percent.

Even in a single, isolated statement, percentages have more meaning for purposes of analysis than do dollar amounts. However, for purposes of comparison percentages are especially important. Table 14A.5 shows dollar and percentage amounts for three stores. If the first three columns stood alone, the reader would not have a clear idea of the comparative performance of these three stores.

The percentage figures make possible a clear-cut comparison. From them the reader can see at a glance what, on the average, became of each dollar of sales. For instance, at Store A, 61 cents of each dollar of sales

Table 14A.4   Items of Profit and Loss Statement Expressed as Percentages

Income from Net Sales	$10,000	100%
Cost of Merchandise Sold	6,000	60
Gross Margin	$ 4,000	40
Operating Expenses	3,500	35
Net Profit	$ 500	5

Table 14A.5   Use of Percentages in Analysis

Items from Profit and Loss Statement	Stores			Stores		
	A	B	C	A	B	C
Net Sales	$8,550[a]	25[a]	$12,905[a]	100%	100%	100%
Cost of Merchandise Sold	5,216	68	7,614	61	54	59
Gross Margin	3,334	57	5,291	39	46	41
Operating Expenses	2,308	51	3,613	27	41	28
Net Profit	1,026	6	1,678	12	5	13

[a] Dollar amounts are in thousands.

went into the purchase of merchandise sold. Stores B and C spent 54 cents and 59 cents, respectively, of the sales dollar on this item. Gross margin, operating expenses, and net profit for the three stores also become comparable.

Expansion of Income Section

Table 14A.6 presents a profit and loss statement in amplified form. Because most retail stores will have returns of some of their sales, these must be deducted from the gross sales figure to find the amount of net sales. Sales checks, cash register tapes, and computerized sales reports provide original records. Credit slips on charge sales returned and cash

Table   14A.6   BROWN'S HOME FURNISHINGS
Profit and Loss Statement for Year Ending January 31, 19XX

Income from Sales:				
Gross Sales		$3,041,367		
Customer Returns and Allowances		144,827		
Net Sales			$2,896,540	100%
Cost of Merchandise Sold:				
Opening Inventory		$ 604,088		
Gross Purchases	$1,905,110			
Purchase Returns and Allowances	9,478			
Net Purchases	$1,895,632			
Inward Freight	28,868	$1,924,500		
Total Merchandise Handled		$2,528,588		
Closing Inventory		619,768		
Gross Cost of Merchandise Sold		$1,908,820		
Cash Discounts		75,310		
Net Cost of Merchandise Sold		$1,833,510		
Alteration Costs		14,483		
Total Merchandise Cost of Sales			1,847,993	63.8
Gross Margin			$1,048,547	36.2
Operating Expenses:				
Administrative		$ 231,723		8.0
Occupancy		139,034		4.8
Publicity		176,689		6.1
Buying		112,965		3.9
Selling		251,999		8.7
Total Operating Expenses			912,410	31.5
Net Profit			$ 136,137	4.7

refund slips on cash sales returned are accumulated, to arrive at total customer returns. Sometimes an allowance is made by the store in an adjustment when merchandise is not returned. The sum of amounts involved in such adjustments accounts for the word *allowances* on the profit and loss statement.

Further Expansion of the Section on Cost of Merchandise Sold

Table 14A.6 shows the handling of three additional items in the cost of merchandise sold: purchase returns and allowances, cash discounts, and alteration costs.

The retailer may occasionally have to return goods to the manufacturer or wholesaler who supplied them. They may arrive different from the samples, for example. Again, a defect in merchandise may result in an adjustment through which an allowance is given to the retailer. The accumulated amount of such adjustments constitutes the item called *purchase returns and allowances*. This item is subtracted from gross purchases to determine net purchases. In Table 14A.6, purchase returns and allowances in the amount of $9,478 were subtracted from gross purchases of $1,905,110 to find net purchases.

The next item to be considered is cash discounts. Table 14A.6 shows cash discounts of $75,310 listed under gross cost of merchandise sold and subtracted from it to obtain net cost of merchandise sold. The earlier illustrations assumed that there were no cash discounts. Consequently, there was no occasion to distinguish between gross cost and net cost. With the introduction of cash discounts into the accounts, the need for the terms *gross* and *net* arises.

Cash discounts are reductions from the purchase price of merchandise allowed by manufacturers or wholesalers as an incentive to prompt payment by the retailers.

The third item introduced is *alteration costs*. Apparel stores or departments often have alteration workrooms, for which records of income and expense are kept. A net loss shown by an alteration workroom is transferred to the profit and loss statement of the department or store as a factor among its merchandise costs. The item of $14,483 found in Table 14A.6 is the accumulated alteration workroom costs for the whole store. This item is added to net cost of merchandise sold to arrive at a new total called *total merchandise cost of sales*.

Expansion of the Section on Operating Expenses

Every profit and loss statement must show an operating expense total. No matter how few or many the classifications of operating expenses recognized by any given store, the profit and loss statement has only to add them to arrive at a total.

The classification shown in Table 14A.6 is one suggested by the National Merchants Association and is called a *functional classification*. It includes such items as payroll, rentals, advertising, taxes, interest, and supplies. From a glance at the nature of these classifications, it is evident that every item of expense belongs somewhere in each of the classifications. The payment of any salary, for instance, belongs in payroll, and it also will come under some one of five functional classifications that are all-inclusive. The salary of an executive will be classified under the administrative function, whereas the salary of a salesperson will belong under the selling function.

The purpose of any classification of expense is to facilitate comparisons, budgeting, and control. Table 14A.6 shows the functional classifications as percentages of net sales.

Distribution Systems and Inventory Control

Source: Courtesy of Babcock
Industries, Inc.

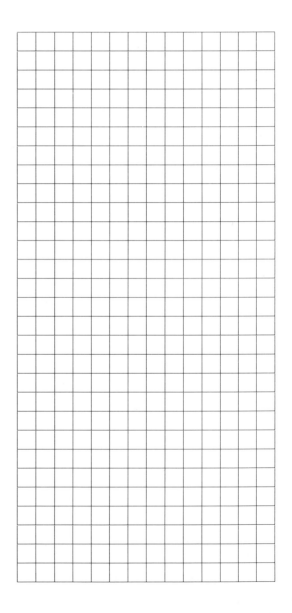

Industry Statement

Jane V. Holdsworth
Director of Material Handling
Fortunoff's

The scope of retail distribution involves the movement of merchandise from the vendor to the retail selling floor. It encompasses the responsibilities of the traffic department, distribution and marking operations, and store line personnel.

The major consideration from an operational standpoint is always cost. Is it cost effective to:

- Buy large quantities in bulk and pick merchandise to fill stock levels over a period of months?
- Have vendors provide ticketing services rather than doing ticketing in-house?
- Take markdowns on slow-selling items or transfer stock to fill potential demands in other store locations?

Timing is also an extremely important aspect in distribution. Often the success of an item depends not only on the selection made, but whether the shipment can be delivered and placed on the selling floor at the point of highest demand and before the competition.

As retailing corporations become larger, more emphasis is placed on economies of scale. Distribution and marking facilities are becoming larger and are located closer to the major markets. This trend will continue as distribution facilities become more sophisticated in processing merchandise and controlling paper.

The future will see manufacturers and retailers working more closely than ever, enabling the retailer to reduce distribution costs and the manufacturer to more accurately plan production levels.

Learning Objectives

Upon completing this chapter you should be able to:

1. Understand why the concept of physical distribution is important to today's retail executives.
2. Know the goals of a physical distribution system that is functioning well.
3. Describe how the components of an efficient distribution and control system will work in tandem in the 1990s.
4. See the relationship of customer service to the physical distribution system of a store.
5. Explain why retail managers will be assessing the tradeoffs within the physical distribution during the next decade.

Physical distribution represents a large part of every dollar the consumer spends, although few of them realize it. Physical distribution costs account for over half of all marketing costs. They amount to approximately 14 percent of sales for manufacturing companies and 26 percent for other channel members.[1] Thus, physical distribution represents such a huge cost center for a retailer that small increases in efficiency often result in large dollar savings.

Physical distribution also represents a potential profit-generating area. If a company can deliver products faster and more consistently than its competitors, it will have a differential advantage. Similarly, a company whose product is always on the retail shelf when the consumer wants it will be at an advantage over a company whose product is often out of stock. As one retailing executive wrote,

> Profits will hinge on how easily, how inexpensively, one is able to bring goods into the store. I see five critical points where substantial change can occur: (1) the vendor, (2) our own delivery system, (3) import transportation, (4) distribution from the warehouse to the store, (5) the store.[2]

---

[1] John T. Mentzer and David J. Schwartz, *Marketing Today* (New York: Harcourt Brace Jovanovich, 1985).
[2] Stephen L. Pistner, "Retailing in 2004: The Look Should Be Different," *Women's Wear Daily,* December 4, 1984, 6.

THE IMPORTANCE OF PHYSICAL DISTRIBUTION

The National Council on Physical Distribution Management defines physical distribution as:

> the integration of two or more activities for the purpose of planning, implementing, and controlling the efficient flow of raw materials, in-process inventory, and finished goods from point of origin to point of consumption. These activities may include, but are not limited to, customer service, demand forecasting, distribution communications, inventory control, materials handling, order processing, parts and service support, plant and warehouse site selection, procurement, packaging, return goods handling, salvage and scrap disposal, traffic and transportation, warehousing, and storage.
>
> Note that this definition includes inbound, outbound, internal, and external movements.[3]

For our purposes we will define physical distribution as all the activities required to physically move the product from the manufacturer to the final customer. They include transportation, warehousing, inventory control, order processing, and customer service. (See Figure 15.1.)

Mass merchants today have three basic problems: the great distance between stores in a chain, the difficulty of getting the merchandise quickly from the supplier to the customer, and the problem of making sure that the merchandise is sold in great quantities.

To solve these problems, they need a high degree of planning, a high level of orderliness, a considerable amount of merchandise information, and enough flexibility in the organization to allow two almost mutually exclusive conditions to exist. These two conditions are budgeted space in every store for every item and the opportunity for local managements to respond quickly to local needs.

Throughout the retail industry there is growing recognition that strategists are as necessary as the people who determine what goods to offer customers. As chains continue to expand, the planning and distribution functions have been segregated from the buying staff. Distributors are not simply repositories of information, but actually break down point-of-sale information, replenish, and have functions and responsibilities of their own.

Federated Department Stores is launching huge expansion plans in several divisions, with units that are far-flung from the headquarters operation. Their Children's Place, which was acquired in 1982 and is based in Pine Brook, N.J., opened 19 stores in 1985, bringing the total to 158 units in 27 states. Plans call for the chain to grow to at least 300 units by the end of the decade. The quality of the division's distribution system

---

[3]"What It's All About" (Chicago: National Council of Physical Distribution Management), 1–2.

Figure   15.1   Overview of Channel Institutions

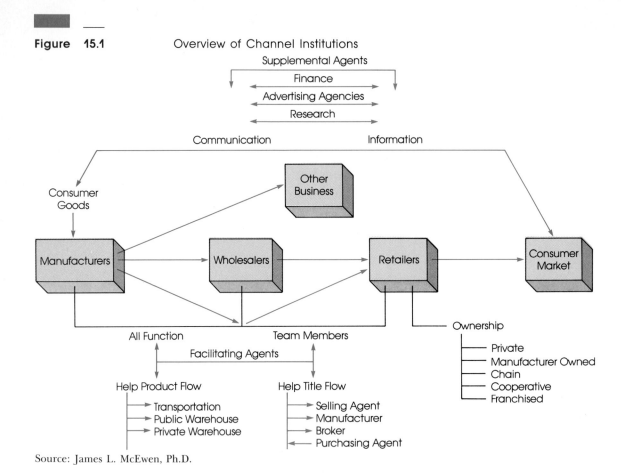

Source: James L. McEwen, Ph.D.

and supervisory staff is so high that management believes they could launch a totally different kind of specialty chain in the future at a very low additional investment. (See Figure 15.2.)

To hold down distribution costs, Liz Claiborne, Inc., designer and one of the largest makers of women's sportswear and apparel, concentrates on large department stores. There is no need then to spend heavily to woo the hordes of small store buyers, detail men, and road men. Today, almost a quarter of Claiborne's sales are to ten large stores.[4]

In the years to come, mass merchants and chains, in particular, will use their purchasing power to persuade vendors to make substantial contributions in terms of case pack and price-marking of merchandise. Because retailers will no longer be able to afford to carry excessive invento-

---

[4]"What's in a Name?," *Forbes*, March 12, 1984, 43.

Figure   15.2   Increased Expansion Capability of Federated Department Stores Made Possible by Strong Distribution System

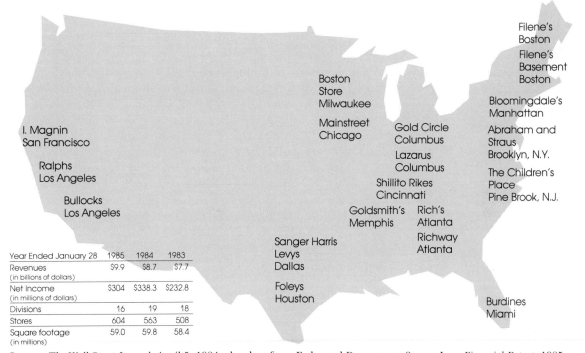

| Filene's Boston |
| Filene's Basement Boston |
| Bloomingdale's Manhattan |
| Abraham and Straus Brooklyn, N.Y. |
| The Children's Place Pine Brook, N.J. |

Boston Store Milwaukee

Mainstreet Chicago

Gold Circle Columbus

Lazarus Columbus

Shillito Rikes Cincinnati

Goldsmith's   Rich's
Memphis   Atlanta

Richway Atlanta

Sanger Harris Levys Dallas

Foleys Houston

Burdines Miami

I. Magnin San Francisco

Ralphs Los Angeles

Bullocks Los Angeles

Year Ended January 28	1985	1984	1983
Revenues (in billions of dollars)	$9.9	$8.7	$7.7
Net Income (in millions of dollars)	$304	$338.3	$232.8
Divisions	16	19	18
Stores	604	563	508
Square footage (in millions)	59.0	59.8	58.4

Source: *The Wall Street Journal,* April 5, 1984, also data from Federated Department Stores, Inc., *Financial Report,* 1985.

ries or provide needless warehouse space, resources must afford the right quantity at the right store at the right time. In return, the retailer will transfer payment through electronic funds transfer, not in 30 days, but in 30 seconds.[5]

In domestic transportation of goods, there will be fewer rail and more truck deliveries—larger trucks on the road and specialized vehicles to handle all types of merchandise most effectively.

An increasing volume of imported merchandise of high quality and value may be expected. New markets will open in Third World countries. New consolidation techniques and transportation logistics will be needed.

Efficient physical distribution allows geographic regions to specialize in products that best fit natural resources, climate, and other local char-

---

[5] Stephen L. Pistner, "Retailing in 2004: The Look Should Be Different," *Women's Wear Daily,* December 4, 1984, 6.

acteristics. Orange growing can be concentrated in Florida and California, because our efficient physical distribution system provides the means for delivering fresh oranges anywhere in the country. Without the system, each region could consume only what it produced and no product could be marketed nationally.

PHYSICAL DISTRIBUTION OBJECTIVES

As recently as the 1960s little time and effort were required to deal with distribution. Fuel was cheap, markets were growing, and the distribution assets of most firms were not highly visible. The situation changed in the 1970s. Markets no longer grew at the same rate; many decreased. The energy crisis forced reevaluation of various fuel forms. Labor costs reflected high inflation rates. A new pressure on profitability emerged as sales growth was seen clearly as a phenomenon of the past.

By the early 1970s, many firms had squeezed major inefficiencies out of their production process. Within a short time, management found that distribution could be better organized for increased profit.

The Broad Objective

The broad objective of a physical distribution system is to move products to other channel members and to consumers in the most efficient way possible that is consistent with the level of service that customers require.

The Key Goals

The key goals of physical distribution are efficiency and satisfactory service. They may, however, conflict. For example, it may be more efficient in terms of cost to ship products by rail; in terms of service the customer may demand extra-fast delivery, which may dictate the use of air freight.

In practice, managers must make frequent trade-offs between efficiency and service to achieve the best end result—profitable sales and a satisfied customer. To achieve this end result, physical distribution managers must aim for improved cost efficiency, better physical distribution service, and increased profitability.

Cost Efficiency

Many opportunities exist for cost reduction in physical distribution systems. Physical distribution managers can reduce costs by, for example, determining the optimum number and location of warehouses, improving materials handling to speed movement of products inside warehouses, increasing stock turnover through better inventory management, and using sealed containers to ship products.

Physical Distribution Service

Buyers often base purchasing decisions on which supplier provides the "best" physical distribution service (PDS). When other retail marketing controllable variables are equal, buyers will normally buy from the supplier who can consistently deliver undamaged products the fastest. Consumers are also more likely to develop brand loyalty for products that are consistently available in retail stores than for products that are often out of stock. For example, a survey of shoppers showed that 64 percent switched brands and 14 percent switched stores when faced with a stock-out (the product desired was not on the shelf).[6]

The goal of the physical distribution system is to provide three aspects of service to customers: availability, timeliness, and quality. Availability is having the right product in the right place at the right time. Is the product available when the customer wants it? Availability is often measured as the percentage of times a product is out of stock.

Timeliness implies the ability to fill orders as quickly as the customer desires them. Consider your own experience with mail order purchases. If you expected your purchase within two weeks after placing an order, but delivery took two months, you would not be satisfied with the company's physical distribution service. You might even stop buying from it. In that case, lack of timeliness would lose the company a customer.

Quality means delivering the product in the condition desired. Quality of PDS is lost if the product is damaged, if the size or color is wrong or if the wrong product is delivered. A company that designs a good product and promotes and prices it correctly cannot afford to deliver it late or damaged.

Increased Profitability

You may have noticed that the first two objectives are somewhat at odds with each other. How can physical distribution keep products on the shelf (which requires money tied up in inventory), make timely deliveries (which requires faster, more expensive transportation and order processing), and protect the product from damage, but still hold costs down? The answer lies in a trade-off between the best physical distribution service possible and the costs incurred. To find the trade-off point, we need to look at the total costs of the PDS decision.

Every time a customer tries to buy a product that is not available and buys a competitor's product, the company has lost a sale. The cost of that lost sale is the profit the company would have made. Therefore, the worse a company's PDS, the more sales will be lost, and the higher the total cost of lost sales. By improving PDS the company can lower this

---

[6]Clyde K. Walter and Bernard J. LaLonde, "Development and Test of Two Stockout Cost Models," *International Journal of Physical Distribution* 5, (1975).

Figure   15.3   Total Costs of Physical Distribution Service (PDS)

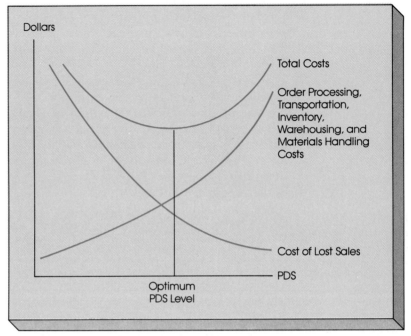

Source: From *Marketing Today,* Fourth Edition, by John T. Mentzer and David J. Schwartz, copyright © 1985 by Harcourt Brace Jovanovich, Inc. Reprinted by permission of the publisher.

cost, but it will have to spend more on order processing, transportation, inventory warehousing, and materials handling. Figure 15.3 illustrates this situation. The physical distribution manager is constantly striving for the best trade-off between maximizing PDS and minimizing the costs of obtaining that service. That point exists where the total costs are minimized.

How physical distribution minimizes costs and maximizes services through the activities of transportation, warehousing, inventory control, order processing, and customer service is the subject of the rest of this chapter.

THE COMPONENTS OF DISTRIBUTION AND CONTROL

Transportation

Transportation involves the movement of goods in a number of ways: raw materials to the plant, finished goods to warehousing, and goods from warehouses to customers. The two major categories of transportation are line haul and local delivery. The movement of raw materials to the plant and finished goods to the warehouse fits typically into the line

Line Haul
Movement of goods between cities and towns, as opposed to local delivery.

Freight Forwarder
A firm that groups small shipments of several manufacturers into truckload or carload shipments.

haul category. Moving goods from warehouses to customers is usually local delivery.

Line haul normally involves large trucks, usually tractors with trailers that use open highways for delivery of large quantities to major drop-off points. Until the fuel crisis, line haul routes were established but seldom reviewed. Today line haul managers increasingly spend time looking at routes in an effort to find better ways to dispatch and reduce mileage. They are reluctant to dispatch less than full truckloads and attempt to back-haul goods. This trend is exemplified by the cooperation among divisions of large corporations. As an example, a division with production facilities in Los Angeles and warehousing in San Diego can work with another division with production in San Diego and warehousing in Los Angeles. The line haul vehicle leaves the plant in Los Angeles, delivers its goods to the San Diego warehouse of the first division, picks up finished product from the plant of the second division and line hauls it to the Los Angeles warehouse. Both divisions have reduced their line haul costs by half, and the corporation has benefited as well.

Another example of the infrastructure of distribution is the consolidation of shipments. Small shipments are much more expensive than a single large one consisting of smaller components. The independent trucking industry, mainly **freight forwarders** and consolidators, now provide this service. In Montreal, for instance, a firm has been established to bring together shipments of garments being manufactured by many small firms and transport them as one shipment to major retail chains in Toronto. The service saves the shipper considerable freight costs and the chains benefit as well. The trucks used by the transporter are specialized vehicles, with appropriate in-truck fittings. Product is hung on racks, and this cuts the freight costs because charges are invoiced by the inch. When received, the garments are handled automatically by the chains, a process that eliminates the old manual process of taking each garment out of the box, putting it on a hanger, and then placing it in inventory. However, it is in the area of local delivery that the greatest advances in distribution have been made.

The number and diversity of trucks in any major city provide visual evidence of the size of the operating and capital investment involved. As with line haul operations, local delivery routes were established based on criteria such as miles driven or commissions earned. Little attempt was made to measure the effectiveness of these control devices. Little was known about whether the people on the trucks actually worked eight hours a day or if the routes were the most efficient from the viewpoint of mileage, waiting at the customer's place of business, or delivery. There was no mechanism to find the answers.

It appears inevitable that as labor and fuel become more expensive, more companies will have to turn to computer assistance for better input to decision making in managing local delivery distribution. (See Table 15.1.)

Table   15.1

Vendor-to-Sales-Floor Transportation Costs, Stated as Percentage of Sales[a]

Annual Volume	Inward Transportation	Internal Costs[b]	Total
Department Stores:			
$2 to $5 million	1.41%	.90%	2.31%
$5 to $10 million	.62	1.13	1.75
$10 to $20 million	.68	1.25	1.93
$20 to $50 million	.93	1.55	2.48
$50 to $100 million	.71	1.79	2.50
Over $100 million	.74	1.95	2.69
Specialty Stores:			
$1 to $5 million	.56	1.17	1.73
Over $5 million	.67	1.46	2.13

[a]Calculations derived from NRMA Financial and Operating Results, 1983 edition.
[b]Receiving, marking, storage, and distribution.
Source: *Stores*, April 1984, 59. Data from NRMA Financial and Operational Results, 1983 edition.

Warehousing

Major questions asked about warehousing during the past decade have included:

- How many warehouses do I need?
- Where should they be located?
- How big should they be?
- What level of automation should I have?

Trade-Off Analysis
A study of the gains and losses when one option is exchanged for another.

The first three questions can be answered through rigorous **trade-off analysis.** An understanding is needed of customer service requirements in terms of **turnaround time** for delivery and minimum acceptable order fill rates. When these variables are known, location of warehouses is a trade-off against additional transportation costs to reach customers from some other stocking point. There is a least-cost solution that meets the service level constraints, and it can be readily computed.

Turnaround Time
Response time; the time that passes between an action and the response to it.

A number of computer models have been developed to help in this type of analysis. **Random storage,** for example, in which warehouse space is not assigned needlessly to product that does not occupy it on a particular day while another product requires additional space, has served to free up warehouse space and defer expensive expansion plans. **Automated storage and retrieval** systems reduce both the aisle space and manpower required.

Random Storage
Computer model for optimal use of stock storage space.

The feasibility of these systems, as might be expected, relies on trade-

Figure   15.4   Trade-Off Analysis of the Distribution Process

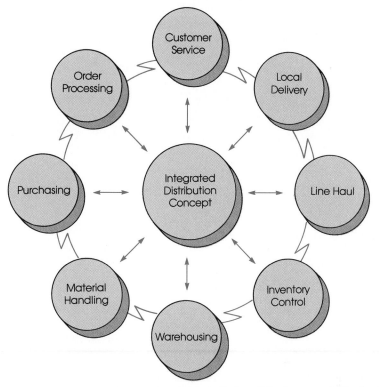

Source: F. Ronald Denham and Gabriel C. Shelley, "The Integrated Distribution Concept: Management's New Approach for the 1980s," *The Business Quarterly* (Winter 1979). Reprinted with permission.

Automated Storage and Retrieval
Warehousing system that combines the use of computer control of stock records with mechanical handling.

off analysis. (See Figure 15.4.) The capital cost of automation can be traded off against labor savings, better inventory control, and better customer service.

More and more companies are performing trade-off analyses in distribution, and especially warehousing. The question of developing the best network of warehouses is inevitably critical to assure the competitive survival of most firms.

Inventory Control

The single area where the computer has made the greatest contribution to physical distribution is inventory control. The days of the manual card system for controlling in and out movements of inventory are over. The manual system had serious deficiencies. Response time was too slow,

FROM THE FIELD

State-of-the-Art Computer Systems

Computerized state-of-the-art systems can read labels, pick inventory, transport it through the warehouse, load it, and ship it to the correct store.

Revco, for example, a drug chain based in Twinsburg, Ohio, has equipped its newest facilities with a state-of-the-art computer system. Warehouses in Kansas and Alabama have computers that print labels to expedite picking of merchandise.

Lane-designator labels, attached to completed orders, are keypunched into a terminal located near shipping docks and this, in turn, triggers high-speed rollers that divert merchandise to the proper truck for loading.

The Revco chain, which invested an estimated $25 million in the computer system and expansion of a warehouse in North Carolina, uses IBM 38 hardware with customized software. On completion of the installation, the chain added over 2 million square feet of warehouse capacity.

Another example is Waldenbooks, with a 168,000-square-foot central distribution center in Central Valley, N.Y. The warehouse is tied into the P.O.S. system. Each evening all stores are polled by a computer in Los Angeles and data is then relayed over phone lines to the distribution center. Hand picks are made to replenish stock. A one-week shipping cycle is in effect.

Waldenbooks' public relations director said that the automatic re-ordering system permits the chain to carry more titles and still control inventory: "We've expanded our assortment while reducing our inventory investment." Applied to the backlist—books in print for at least a year—the system includes almost 20,000 titles. Despite the success of the facility, high transportation costs have caused the chain to consider a second distribution center.

A third pioneer in computerized warehousing is Kobacker Stores, a company based in Columbus, Ohio, that operates almost 300 shoe stores under the names of PicWay, Koby's, Pix, and Shoe Works. The company installed a computerized system designed to handle individual pairs of shoes. Called Sortrac Sortation System, it was installed at a cost of $1.5 million. (See Figure 15.5.) It permits the company to pick about 20,000 pairs of shoes per day. Sortrac Sortation is made by Babcock Industries, Inc., Acco Material Handling Group, Warren, Michigan.

Using the system, Kobacker picks shoes manually by size, and scannable labels are then applied to the boxes. The computer scans the labels and automatically expedites the boxes to the correct store.

Source: "Punching Up Distribution," *Chain Store Age Executive,* July 1983, 66. Reprinted by permission from *Chain Store Age Executive.* Copyright 1983 Lebhar-Friedman, 425 Park Avenue, New York, NY 10022.

Figure 15.5   State-of-the-Art Distribution System

Sortrac's computer scans the labels on boxes and automatically assigns the merchandise to the designated location. It can handle 20,000 pairs of shoes per day.

Source: Courtesy of Babcock Industries Inc.

Return on Investment (ROI)
Net profit in relation to total costs, given as a percentage.

counts were frequently wrong, measures of customer service were difficult, reorder points were approximate, follow-up systems were poor, and few buyers believed the figures.

Computer assistance for inventory control came early for reasons that are quite clear. Management directives for better **return on investment (ROI)** performance inevitably resulted in reductions of inventory. To be most effective, buyers slowed buying of highest-demand items. As the volumes ordered decreased, safety stock levels plummeted and out-of-stock items soared.

In the 1980s, computer control of inventory extended to statistical forecasting of product classifications to the **stockkeeping unit (SKU)** level, calculation of reorder points, and reorder quantities.

Stockkeeping Unit (SKU)
A unit controlled by the inventory control system; generally an item with a specific description, such as No. 327 shoe, black, size 7½D.

Order Processing

Order processing has been the bane of retail distribution systems for years. The best-designed distribution network will not work if the order processing system does not operate as planned. In many stores, it is simple to improve the customer turnaround time on orders merely by improving order processing procedures. Frequently the use of data

On Line
Under the control
of the central
processing unit
of a computer.

transmission equipment, small-computer assistance, and reduced paper-work can reduce internal time significantly.

The cost of **on-line** order processing devices was prohibitive at the beginning of the 1970s. A dozen years later the simplest of mini computers were available for less than $5,000. Tied to the inventory systems, order processing can be a most effective retail marketing tool in the following areas:

- Order cycle: When customers order store merchandise, how long will they wait for delivery?
- Order fill: When customers order, what level of merchandise availability will they expect? To what extent will they tolerate incomplete orders, and how long will they be willing to wait for back orders to be filled?
- Competition: To what extent will the store be required to meet or exceed competitive retailers' levels of order cycle and order fill?

Department stores have moved quickly to this system for big-ticket items and are now adapting it for their catalog businesses, which are separate divisions from the stores. A piece of merchandise can be reserved as soon as it is purchased. Only the computer can release the product, and this control ensures that it will be delivered to the appropriate customer. Abraham & Straus has made significant strides in this area with its catalog business. A customer who phones in an order to an 800-number is immediately told if the item is in stock, given a delivery verification code number, and told what the delivery period will be.

Implementation of such systems can usually be justified on the sole basis of the amount of clerical paperwork that will be eliminated. Just how effectively a total system may be used for a large department store was outlined in a speech given by an executive of May D&F, of which Hecht's is a division.

Hecht's has developed a system called purchase order management (P.O.M.), an on-line and fully integrated system, which will eventually be adopted by all May Company stores.

Starting with the order, a clerk enters the Dun number of the vendor into a CRT (giving terms, name of vendor, address, and delivery terms). Additional data can be input (sizes, quantity, color, classification, price, and store). The system will also extend prices. A merchant can develop a one-time model . . . or use an existing model. The system will give the merchant the total markup on the total order, and it will also flag an order if it's below the planned markup. At that point, the DMM will review the order and approve it on the system, with a copy going to the vendor and one copy being entered into the "store approved memory."

In distribution . . . at the time of the arrival of the merchandise to the warehouse, by entering the same vendor number as above, the entire order can be brought up on the screen.

In the checking and marking area, they can see the order information by style/quantity and will generate the tickets against the information. It will immediately verify overages and shortages, since the number of tickets below or above items will tell them.

In fashion reporting system/control . . . this data is automatically fed into the fashion system, which shows merchandise on hand. The data is then transmitted to Accounts Payable's system, where the invoice is waiting to be paid. With a record of receipt of merchandise, they can match the invoice with the receipt of goods, and authorize the cutting of a check (only about 50 percent of the transactions are an automatic match).

This system eliminates many separate operations, which cuts down on error, since most vendor numbers are 7-digit ones.

The buyer can also track at what point a shipment is, thereby eliminating 75 percent of phone calls to ascertain the same information. This is very important, because the average number of classifications in a store is 12,000.

In the merchandising division, the P.O.M. system can generate additional kinds of "reporting" for hands-on control:

- Corporate Class Report.
- Weekly Class Sales Report by store to spot trends.
- Sales/Inventory/On-Order Report by store, which is accessed to all divisions of May Company across the country. This gives a continuity of information to all levels of merchandising so that they can hop onto a hot trend . . . or get out of a "bummer."
- On-Line Sales Reporting. A new system that gives sales by store, by department, by classification, by 6 a.m. the following morning. At the moment, only two executives have that data in their homes: the store president and the vice president of stores, through their own CRTs.
- Merchandise Planning. The system allows the "what if" capabilities, by changing markup or gross margin numbers, to plan the merchant's open-to-buy. Information can be generated by month, department, classification, and store.
- Planning for a Total Store Merchandise System. Information can be generated which allows the gross margin and all of its components to be known at all times by total company, division, and departments. It tracks markdowns and markups on an ongoing basis.
- Merchandise Communication System. Keeps tabs on all transfers of merchandise: inter- and intra-store and between store and vendor.
- Manifesting. When the merchandise is loaded at the warehouse for delivery to individual stores, the system will spot exactly where the truck actually arrived.[7]

---

[7] Gerald A. Sampson, "Technological Advances," speech delivered November 1, 1984, at Tyson's Corner, Virginia.

Customer Service

Although it does not properly belong to physical distribution, customer service is discussed here because it has a direct impact on the customer. It is the final point in the purchase process. If the customer does not receive good service, the distribution system stands accused.

In any distribution work, whether on a project or line operating basis, the setting of customer service levels is the single most crucial step in the distribution process. It is difficult for two reasons. First, what level of service do customers really expect from stores? Second, what real level should be provided? The distribution process can be seriously affected by wrongly defining the service level needed.

Summary

The objective of physical distribution is to move products to other channel members and to retail consumers in the most efficient way possible that is consistent with the level of service that customers require. The goal of the physical distribution is to provide three aspects of service to customers—availability, timeliness, and quality—all with increased profitability to the retailer.

The components of a physical distribution system that is functioning well are transportation, warehousing, inventory control, order processing, and customer service. They cannot be addressed individually, but must be examined together. No decision can be reached in any area without an impact on the others.

In the 1990s, changes will be more in intensity than in substance. Retailers will look for rationalization of total systems rather than remote improvements. These moves will take the form of trade-off analysis, service levels versus profitability, and warehouses against transportation.

There will be greater need to understand true service levels required by the marketplace. As markets mature, retailers will become more competitive in their attempts to increase business. It will be less effective to pursue the targets that each of the other competitors seek at random. By studying and understanding the service levels expected by each segment of the market, more retail firms will adapt distribution strategies to meet those requirements.

Questions for Review

1. What is meant by the term *physical distribution*?
2. What are the two key goals of a physical distribution system that is functioning well?
3. Give at least three examples of how a physical distribution

manager might address the issue of cost efficiency and thus reduce costs.

4. List three aspects of service to customers that a good physical distribution system should provide.

5. Name the distribution system components that are presented in this chapter.

6. Which distribution system components have benefited most from the use of the computer? How?

7. How is customer service related to a physical distribution system?

CASE STUDY

Stanton's Luggage Shop

Installing a P.O.S. System

The time had come for Bob Stanton, proprietor of Stanton's Luggage Shop, to make a major decision. He was not sure he wanted to become part of the age of technology or that he really needed to. If he did, it would involve purchasing modern electronic equipment to handle the sales transactions in each of his 10 locations.

Even though it was becoming more difficult each year to operate with old-fashioned cash registers, would the benefits of a point-of-sale (P.O.S.) system outweigh the costs? A great deal of study was needed so that the right decision could be made.

Over the years, most of the major decisions Bob made had turned out to be the right ones. A man who thought for himself, he rarely consulted with outsiders, except his accountant and lawyer. In the past he had relied on his own knowledge of retailing and his own judgment whenever problems arose or changes were being considered. This time, however, he did not feel secure. He had very little technical background and felt threatened by the electronic monsters he had viewed at a national retailers meeting.

The one thing he knew for certain was that he must be in control in order to function. Even though several sales representatives had assured him that an electronic P.O.S. system would give him more information more accurately and more quickly than before, and thus enable him to have more control, he was skeptical. He was accustomed to stepping into any one of his stores any time of any working day, opening the cash register, and counting the daily receipts. Could he adjust to having this done mechanically? He was not convinced that he would have better access to daily sales as well as to all kinds of additional information that, in the long run, would make control easier. For one of the few times in his long retail career, Bob needed advice.

Twenty years earlier he had opened a small luggage shop in the central business district of Pelham City, a shopping location that served about 75,000 people, most of whom lived within the city limits. Because no other store offered quality luggage, Bob was able to corner the market. He acquired two well-known national brands and carried each in depth. He also stocked a variety of lesser known labels.

Luggage sales rose sharply. It seemed as if everyone was traveling, whether for business or for pleasure. Stanton's also did an enormous gift business, especially during the graduation season. Soon Bob began to carry a wide assortment of travel accessories as well as luggage and, before long, Stanton's was a full-line luggage shop with leather luggage, canvas luggage, attaché cases, briefcases, cosmetic kits, travel clocks, wallets, key cases, card cases, and passport cases.

With the Pelham City store operating successfully, Bob opened another in North Pelham and then another in a nearby suburban shopping mall. He eventually owned 10 stores, all of which were profitable. He was an astute merchant, dealing in quality, and thus was not seriously affected by the discount stores all around him that were selling luggage and leather goods at low prices.

Because Bob served a quality-conscious market, his strategy over the years had been to trade up rather than try to compete with mass merchandisers. He had a high-class operation. However, his customers no longer seemed to have time to wait for lengthy transactions to be completed by his salespeople, who had to wait for access to the single register located in each store. The new philosophy seemed to be to make a purchase and leave as quickly as possible. This philosophy required new and faster methods to accommodate customers. The P.O.S. system Bob had observed in most of the large department stores, discount stores, fast food service chains, and supermarkets might be just what was needed.

From what he had seen at the national retail meeting, the initial equipment cost was enormous—$4,000 for each terminal plus $100,000 backroom investment. Additional costs were involved in changeover, training, and upkeep. Was speed worth the cost? Must he finally enter the computer age or could he still operate profitably using the system that had served retailers like himself for generations?

The first thing to do was analyze his needs, the available space, and the viable alternatives. He had to check on the various systems available to a merchant with his particular needs. He had to determine the other possibilities if he decided not to go electronic. Then he would have to consider the benefits in relation to the costs, both initial and long-term.

Bob had already talked to representatives of NCR and Singer, both of which had excellent systems. A number of smaller firms had also indicated they had the capability of tailoring a P.O.S. system to individual needs but, regardless of whose equipment he purchased, the fundamental consideration was the same—cost versus benefits.

At all 10 stores, all sales transactions were tallied at the end of the day. On the cash register in each store were two keys, one for luggage and one for accessories. Thus, daily records reflected totals in only the two major classifications. At the end of the week, there was no way of knowing which items were the fast sellers and which were not moving. Each store manager updated his inventory by checking out manually those items that had been sold during the week. This information was not relayed to the Pelham City store until the following Monday. Problems of poor mail delivery and slow entry of the data in the master control records by unit control clerks often resulted in out-of-stock conditions.

Bob and his merchandise manager often did not review the previous week's sales until Wednesday or Thursday. If a yellow American Tourister garment bag had been sold out the previous Tuesday in any one of the stores, and none of the other nine had extra stock to transfer to the one in need, sales were lost. Because this information was not known, a reorder was not placed until the following week, and total sales suffered.

With a P.O.S. system, there would be immediate inventory update as information went directly from store terminal to central control in the Pelham City office. Also, the daily update could be broken down by category of goods, color, size, price, brand, and so on. Each day Bob Stanton and his staff would know in detail what was selling. This had to be better than receiving weekly reports in only two major categories. Here then was a definite benefit. The risk of human error was eliminated, not to mention the delay factor. Immediate reordering could cut back on lost sales.

Bob would also have a record at the end of each day of every salesperson's production, as well as total store sales. Sales quotas could be established more realistically and peak selling periods could be isolated. With this information there would be better control of wage costs in each of the 10 stores. If any one store were experiencing a problem, it would show up immediately rather than at the end of the year, when it would be too late to do anything about it in relation to that year's profits.

Stanton's sales were 40 percent cash and 60 percent charge (two universal credit cards were accepted), requiring two different types of sales transactions. With an electronic terminal in each store, all sales could be entered in one system. This was another positive factor.

Would the cost of a P.O.S. system for a 10-store chain of specialty stores doing a volume of $1,000,000 annually outweigh the long-term savings? Bob had never faced a more difficult question.

Questions

1. What would you do if you were Bob Stanton? Why?
2. Are there any advantages to using old-fashioned cash registers? Explain.
3. List the advantages and disadvantages of a P.O.S. system.
4. Compare two major P.O.S. cash register systems.
5. Weigh the costs versus the benefits of installing a P.O.S. system in a 10-store chain such as Stanton's.
6. Will a P.O.S. system improve Bob Stanton's decision making in the following areas? Why or why not?
   a. Selection of personnel.

   b. Inventory control.
   c. Selection of new store sites.
   d. Future buying.
   e. Reordering.
   f. Markdowns.

Part **VI**

Retail Promotion

Chapter 16

Retail Advertising

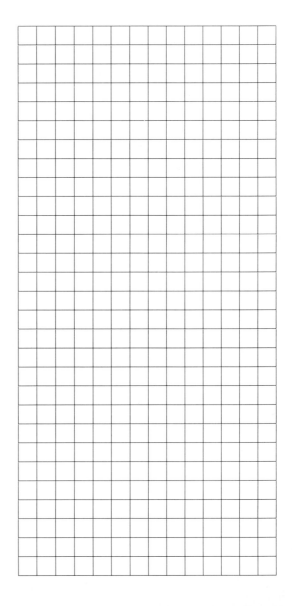

Industry Statement

Douglas R. Tompkins
Esprit de Corp

As we move further into an information age, products will have to contain more and more information. In the fashion apparel field, services previously unthought of or considered unnecessary will have to be provided. Certainly the ability to identify a target audience and thus market directly, and therefore effectively, will be first and foremost; but it will also be essential to produce value in workmanship, materials, and design.

Each product will have to include *ad valorem* information that will make the product attractive beyond its use. In postwar America and Europe (and now Japan) there is no real need for mere products. Reasons must be invented to justify consumers' purchases. In short, we have all that we need and consumption will be more for status, satisfaction, pleasure, or security. Information must be provided that informs the potential buyer about the use, the look, and the social–political positioning of the product. Display and presentation, the inference of status by label identification will become the paramount features of future marketing. How one wears, styles, and puts together well-known brands that reflect images of different lifestyles will be the foundation of the value-plus (*ad valorem*) of successful products.

There will be a large increase in vertical vendors, either existing retailers producing their own products or designer–manufacturers selling their products with very specific points of view—directly or through carefully managed image shops of large retailers.

Learning Objectives

Upon completing this chapter you should be able to:

1. Understand how advertising differs from other promotional vehicles used by the retailer.
2. Explain the purposes of retail advertising and how it differs from national advertising.
3. Know why the choice of a proper media mix is essential to the success of advertising.
4. Compare the advantages and disadvantages of the various media.
5. Know why it is important to formulate an advertising plan and budget and then evaluate the results.

Marketplace control has shifted from the manufacturer to the retailer. This is clearly evident in the consumer's shift in allegiance from national brands to private labels and generic products over the past few years. The consumer puts his or her faith in Kroger or Walgreen or Macy's rather than in General Foods, General Mills, Levi Strauss, or other manufacturers of national brands.

In most local markets today, the retail trade now dictates what the manufacturer must provide in the way of price and promotion simply to get the product stocked in the retail store. As the retailer's power increases, there will be additional pressure on the manufacturer to provide more trade deals, trade coupons, co-op advertising allowances, and the like.

Although the retail trade recognizes the need for the manufacturer to presell and gain acceptance with the consumer through advertising, the retailer's primary concern is quite different. The retailer is really interested in differentiating himself or herself from the local competition. That is generally accomplished through various forms of pricing and selection differentiation, along with advertising.

THE IMPORTANCE OF ADVERTISING TO THE RETAILER

Advertising plays a vital role in the day-to-day and week-to-week business of retailing. It is the voice of retail merchandising, using print or broadcast media. Because few merchants can rely on their location alone to create customers, they must communicate their image and merchandise to a wide-ranging audience. Advertising is the vehicle for this communication.

Advertising Differentiated from Other Promotional Vehicles

Advertising has been defined as "any paid-for form of nonpersonal presentation of the facts about goods, services, or ideas to a group."[1] This definition provides the basis for differentiating advertising from other promotional vehicles in marketing.

In contrast to publicity, which is free, advertising is *paid for* and always designates the sponsor of the information. Unlike salesmanship, which is personal, advertising involves only *nonpersonal* methods of disseminating information. Unlike display, which presents the merchandise itself, advertising presents facts or information *about* the merchandise. Advertising addresses hundreds or thousands of people as a *group,* in contrast to salesmanship, which involves interacting with customers through personal contact.

The Purposes of Retail Advertising

Advertising is a business, not a form of self-expression.

Every ad must sell. It can sell an idea, a service, an item, or the store. Advertising is deliberately planned and created to elicit a specific reaction. The reaction may be an immediate one, like picking up the phone to order, or it may be an emotional response, like thinking that the store is a comfortable or exciting place to shop.

Every ad must attract an audience. It must say, "Stop! Look at me!" The customer must notice the ad through its layout or copy or illustration. Studies have shown that an advertisement has exactly three seconds to stop viewers or readers before they go on to something else.[2] The customer who does not notice an ad cannot react to it.

Every ad must answer the customer's unspoken questions. The most important one concerns customer benefit. All the facts necessary to make a buying decision—such as sizes, prices, fabrication, and colors—should be presented clearly. The customer must be able to recognize the

---

[1] Charles M. Edwards, Jr., and Carl F. Lebowitz, *Retail Advertising and Sales Promotion* (Englewood Cliffs, N.J.: Prentice-Hall, 1981), 3.
[2] Judy Young Ocko and M. L. Rosenblum, *How to Be a Retail Advertising Pro* (New York: National Retail Merchants Association, 1977), 2.

article from the description and illustration when he or she enters the store.

Every ad must give the news. News can be fashion, price, assortments, sizes, or ideas. Merchants would not spend money to advertise merchandise if it did not have some kind of news.

Every ad must give a reason to shop in the store. Customers must have a reason why they should go to one store rather than any other for a Proctor iron or Estée Lauder perfume. The reason could be that one store has the merchandise exclusively or has the best price, the best taste, or greatest convenience. If the store is stressing fashion in ready-to-wear or home furnishings, an advertisement with the right fashion and artwork is enough to establish superiority.

Every ad must reflect the store's personality. If the reader can cover the store logotype (name and trademark of the store) and can still recognize whose store it is, the ad has achieved individual style and personality. The ad tells the reader a lot about the store and its merchandise. If merchandise is newsy, exciting, and full of ideas, the customer will get the message from the ad. The best ads today talk *to* the customer, not *at* her or him.

KINDS OF RETAIL ADVERTISING

Retail differs in several pertinent ways from national advertising.

- Territory covered: Retail advertising is confined to the territory from which the store draws its trade.
- Relationship to customers: The retailer can direct advertising to relatively homogeneous groups of people because the average store draws business from a limited area, such as a city or nearby suburbs.
- Reader interest: Because most customers expect to make their purchases in local stores, they tend to read retail advertising more intently than national ads.
- Response expected: Retail advertising is aimed at a buy-now audience as it induces the customer to promptly purchase the item.
- Use of price: Because the retail ad is immediate, price is a key element and must be included in the ad.

Image Advertising Advertising intended to convey positive mental pictures of the advertiser; institutional advertising.

Institutional Advertising

Institutional advertising is designed to sell the entire concept of the store and its image rather than a particular type of merchandise. Sometimes it is referred to as idea or **image advertising.** (See Figure 16.1.)

Used by retailers to aim for long-range sales results as opposed to

Figure   16.1   An Institutional Ad

Source: Courtesy of Neiman-Marcus.

immediate sales, these advertisements concentrate on building the reputation of the store by focusing on unique qualities and services. Some advertisements attempt to build an image of fashion leadership; others stress unique services. In any case, marketing the total store is as important as advertising certain items.

Promotional Advertising

Promotional advertising is day-to-day advertising that attempts to sell specific items or services and is designed to bring customers to a store for

Figure   16.2   A Promotional Ad

immediate action. The three types of promotional advertising are regular price line, special promotion or sale, and clearance. Most retail advertising is promotional in nature. (See Figure 16.2.)

Vertical Cooperative Advertising
Retailer advertising of a specific product for which wholesaler or manufacturer agrees to share costs; also, ready-made advertising furnished to retailers.

Cooperative Advertising

Manufacturers, suppliers, or other retailers often share with merchants the costs of advertising. These arrangements for cooperative advertising can be either vertical or horizontal.

Under a **vertical cooperative advertising** agreement, manufacturers or suppliers pay part of the costs for featuring specified items or brands. Retailers are reimbursed after the ads have been printed or aired. Invoices or documents from the media, such as **tearsheets,** are required as proof that the advertisements appeared. In some cases the manufacturer supplies a variety of aids to the retailer, such as completed artwork and advertising copy containing open space for the retailer's name.

Tearsheet
Page torn from a
publication and
sent to an
advertiser or
agency to prove
that an ad is in the
publication.

**Horizontal
Cooperative
Advertising**
Joint advertising by
a group of retailers
for their mutual
benefit, usually to
increase store
traffic or interest
in a product.

Case Allowance
Rebate offered by
a manufacturer or
wholesaler to
retailers who
advertise and sell a
specific product at
a reduced price.

**Supplier-
Controlled
Cooperative
Advertising**
Advertising
initiated and
controlled by a
supplier or
manufacturer,
often for a type of
product or service
not sold by major
retailers.

In a **horizontal cooperative advertising** agreement, several retailers sponsor and pay for the costs of advertising to increase traffic to an area or increase the demand for a product. Groups of merchants in shopping centers often sponsor ads jointly in order to draw people to the center. To stimulate demand for certain items, merchants carrying the same product lines in noncompeting areas frequently sponsor ads jointly in order to spread product awareness.

Small merchants are often unaware of cooperative funds and do not know how to apply for them. Manufacturers often push large retailers into joint advertising but not small merchants, partly because it is more costly to administer programs involving many small merchants. The Robinson-Patman Act, however, requires sellers to give the same allowance for promotion to all buyers on a proportionately equal basis. Therefore, if a seller gives a large department store chain a 5 percent advertising allowance, all other buyers (large and small) are entitled to the same arrangements.

New Entrants

Suddenly and quietly, co-op advertising has burgeoned from a $3 billion industry to an estimated $8 billion industry.[3] Much of the new co-op money has come from industries not traditionally associated with the system. In the past, grocery products were promoted on the retail level through an established form of **case allowances**—a rebate on each case sold when the retailer proves he has cut the price on the product.

More recently, expansion of the larger retail chains has been accompanied by increases in product variety. As a result, co-op advertising has slowly been replacing the case allowance system because many of the added products have existing programs, and the retailer has found it easier to unify his advertising under one co-op umbrella.

Some of the products enjoying traditional co-op programs within diversified retail outlets include auto parts and accessories, such as oil, filters, or spark plugs. These are now sold in many grocery chains as a partial reflection of the permanence of the do-it-yourself market. Such products come to the grocery chains with established co-op allowances because they are also sold in other outlets.

New Form

Computer firms are but one new industry involved in a relatively new co-op form: supplier- or manufacturer-controlled cooperative advertising. Along with insurance and travel companies, these firms are initiating co-op programs that they control.

Fundamentally, **supplier-controlled cooperative advertising** tends to

---

[3] "Co-op's Quiet Revolution," *Marketing and Media Decisions,* November 1983, 139.

work best in highly centralized industries, like the lawn and garden market, where no major retailers are involved, and the manufacturer exerts more pressure on the market than the sum of the retailers.

One of the features of supplier-controlled co-op is agency involvement. Agencies have traditionally kept a low profile but now deal directly with the manufacturer creating the program. They must know how to create retailer-oriented campaigns for the manufacturer to present to retailers. Media people at the agency must know how to buy the kind of time or space the retailer needs at the rates offered on the local level.

The manufacturer's benefits are numerous. The primary one is that the manufacturer maintains control over media selection. This is important because uncontrolled retailers tend to place advertising in low-efficiency media such as free-circulation weekly papers. At the same time, the manufacturer's money can get placements individual retailers would not be able to afford. Broadcast and magazines are two of the more popular media used in such co-op programs.

Retailers benefit because the manufacturer picks up the cost of customized advertising, produced by the manufacturer's agency. An insert in the metropolitan edition of a news weekly will be tailored to the retailer's market. The retailer will also profit from the selectivity of the environment.

MEDIA

Media are vehicles by which the advertiser's selling message is carried to the customer. In order for retail advertising to make an impact, the store's message must reach the correct target market. Some of the media options offered to retailers are magazines, newspapers, radio, television, outdoor transit, and the newer forms—especially cable and satellite communications systems, low-power television, and teletext. (Chapter 7 describes these media as well as direct mail.)

Kinds of Media

Internal Media
Various means of communicating ideas to customers inside the store.

Methods of communication to customers inside the store include signs and posters, handbills, sound systems, slide and film projection, internal telephone systems, and displays. These are called **internal media.**

External Media
Various means of communicating ideas to potential customers not in the store.

Ways to entice customers into the store include newspapers (run of paper, sections, inserts), broadcast (radio, television, cable television), magazines, telephone, and outdoor signs (including spectaculars like sky and rock writing). These are called **external media.** Shopping bags, matchbooks, business cards, and some other specialties are both internal and external.

Media Mix
All of the media
chosen by an
advertiser for a
particular message
or campaign.

Media Mix

Several different media used to reach a total market make up the **media mix.** Unfortunately, there is no one successful formula, because stores, markets, and customers differ. Media availability and circulation also vary.

Questions the retailer must consider before making media mix decisions are:

FROM THE FIELD

Superclock

Superclock, an in-store marketing tool that includes a backlit advertising sign, highly visible clock, store logo, and "thank you for shopping" message, has been available for several years through Van Wagner Advertising, New York. (See Figure 16.3.)

Made of aluminum, the 2-foot by 7-foot device is mounted 8 feet off the floor so it does not take up shelf or floor space. Wagner said its research shows the average shopper sees Superclock six times during a supermarket visit. Because nearly two-thirds of shoppers' buying decisions are made in the store, Wagner believes Superclock can increase sales of products advertised on the medium.

A "Superclock network" of national and regional supermarket chains offers nonoperating profits to a retail operation. The individual units are available to any supermarket with at least $3 million in annual sales or five checkout counters. Each installation guarantees a minimum income of $50 per month, or 25 percent of net ad revenue, which-

ever is greater. And this is at no cost to the supermarket.

Advertisers usually purchase the Superclock network on a rotation basis, choosing to saturate a market for two to four months. Van Wagner handles the installation and rotation of advertising.

A two-year contract with two renewal terms is offered. Supermarkets are granted the right of "reasonable approval" over the product or service being advertised. Van Wagner provides the advertisers with maintenance and insurance on the units.

Advertisers are guarantees that Superclock's line of sight will never be blocked by any other store signage or promotional device and so their messages are always visible.

In 20 supermarkets in the Boston area, an independent research study showed a 25 percent increase in sales for Campbell's Le Menu frozen entrees featured during a 12-week period.

Source: Adapted from "Shoppers Find Time for Superclock," *Marketing News,* November 9, 1984, 43.

Figure   16.3   An In-Store Advertising Medium—Superclock

Source: "Shoppers Find Time for Superclock," *Marketing News*, November 9, 1984, 43. Reprinted courtesy of *Marketing News*, published by the American Marketing Association.

- Which media can best reach the greatest number and kinds of people at the time you want to reach them?
- Which media or combination of media can you afford?
- If one medium does not reach a large share of your market, what other medium will? At what cost?
- Will a greater expenditure in the *present media* generate a bigger dollar share of the market?
- Will a greater expenditure in *additional media* in the same market area bring extra business? At what cost?

Media Selection

A sound principle for buying media is to avoid spreading advertising dollars too thin. Instead of using a number of media, make a maximum impression in one medium before considering others.

Standard Rate and Data Service is the recognized authoritative publication on media in this country.[4] Its volumes include maps of marketing areas; circulation; and space and time costs for almost every newspaper, magazine, and broadcast station in the United States.

Media options are so varied that the advertising representative of the newspaper, the magazine, or the station should be invited to explain them. You can then relate the information to your marketing needs and your budget. Study it piece by piece, eliminating what is not right for you. The end result should be a suitable and business-like decision.

Recently an interesting new option for the retailer has emerged—the **media buying service.** A media buying service basically pools its clients' money and buys time and space in volume. In contrast, an ad agency media department works in a brand-specific setting, generally buying time and space when and where it is needed for a client's specific product. The media buying service can wield considerable clout and leverage even though the volume of space or time used by a specific client may be the same as if it had been bought by an agency media department.

Media Buying Service
Organization of media specialists that buys blocks of advertising time and space on behalf of a group of retailers.

Major Media Categories

In the assessment of each medium, reach and coverage are important considerations, but the advantages and disadvantages must also be taken into account. (See Table 16.1.)

Print Media

Print media include newspapers, magazines, direct mail, telephone directories, and flyers. Newspapers offer a choice of editions—morning, evening, weekly, and Sunday—as well as weekly shoppers and inserts. (See Figure 16.4.) Newspapers are the most-used medium for retail advertising and the volume continues to increase, with department stores leading the way, according to the Flash Report of Newspaper Advertising Investments. This report, prepared for *Advertising Age* by Media Records, tracks newspaper retail advertising in 15 markets.

The use of magazines was limited in the past to large retailers like J. C. Penney and Sears, because consumer magazines were generally too expensive for local merchants. In recent years, however, many national magazines have introduced regional and local editions in an attempt to increase their share of the local retailer's advertising dollar. This practice is known as offering a **split run.** The publisher divides the national circulation into smaller sections, and merchants pay only for the geographic areas that carry their ads.

Split Run
Practice of national magazines selling advertising space at reduced prices to regional retailers; the ads appear only in magazines sold in their region.

---

[4]Judy Young Ocko and M. L. Rosenblum, *How to Be a Retail Advertising Pro* (New York: National Retail Merchants Association, 1977), 207.

Table 16.1   Comparison of Major Media Categories

Advantages	Disadvantages
Newspaper	
■ Recall potential. The reader can go back and look at the ad or cut it out.	■ Possibly inferior quality of reproduction and color compared to direct mail and magazines.
■ Space in which to sell.	■ Missed customers. Some potential customers may be located outside the circulation area.
■ Format control. Photos or drawings in any style can be used. Ideas can be emphasized by adjusting size of art or type and length of copy.	■ Waste circulation. Some readers are not geographically or economically potential customers.
■ Acceptance of newspapers as a kind of people's trade journal that provides news in both editorial content and ads.	
Magazines	
■ Specific audiences. The retailer can reach audiences based on interests, sex, age, and ethnic background.	■ Added costs for the retailer because ads must be ready for printing.
■ Long life and fine-quality color.	■ Generally long lead time (two to three months). This limits effectiveness for retailers, who generally use more immediate media.
Direct Mail	
■ No competition. Direct mail is personal.	■ Long lead time to prepare.
■ Long life. Direct mail stays around the house.	■ High cost of printing and mailing— and becoming higher.
■ Something for everyone. Direct mail permits the offering of diverse merchandise in one advertisement.	■ Growing clutter of mailings reaching customers.
■ Fine reproduction and color.	
Radio	
■ Flexibility. Radio advertisements can be changed quickly. Different approaches can be taken on different stations.	■ No picture. Radio is not suitable for merchandise that cannot be described in words.
■ Coverage. Radio goes into most homes.	■ No listener recall.
■ Immediacy and urgency. These impressions result from the nature of the medium.	■ Need for constant identification.
■ Low cost to produce.	
Television	
■ More dimensions than other media— motion, words, pictures, sound.	■ Cost. Television can be very expensive.
■ Merchandise shown in action.	■ Staff skills. Special techniques and skills are required to produce television.
■ Glamor and prestige medium.	■ No viewer recall—off the tube, out of mind.
	■ Merchandise limitation. A limited number of items can be shown in a single commercial.

Figure   16.4   An External Advertising Medium—Newspaper Insert

Source: Courtesy of Caldor, Inc.

Broadcast Media

Broadcast media include radio and television advertising, cable television, and video. Radio is increasing its advertising revenue from retailers but still has a long way to go before it commands the amount being spent in newspapers and television. Only 9.1 percent of retailers believe that television is the best medium to reach their overall target audience, according to research done by ADVO-Systems, Inc.[5] But when trying to reach a specific target audience like youth, which has been weaned on television, the use of television increases.

Rock/fashion videos are becoming the designers' new runways. The fashion industry has discovered a new world for inspiration that is far more exotic than Japan and far more colorful than the street scene in London. Rock/fashion video is influencing what young people wear and how they like to receive their messages, and it is just beginning.

Seventh Avenue is going to a still more sophisticated format—videos that entertain with songs and stories and attempt to dazzle with images. In addition to their use in stores, these videos are finding their way into the homes of potential customers, as a growing number of television shows turn to them to fill air time.

Videodiscs

Videodiscs and computers are fusing into one system that will give shoppers and retailers a new information aid. Travel agencies now have computerized systems that show customers videodisc pictures of what an intended vacation spot looks like. At the same time, the computer displays room rates, airline schedules, or other computer text information over the video image. The system is only one of the new products emerging as manufacturers tap the power of the so-called smart videodisc.

One of the most exciting applications for consumers will be freestanding, kiosk-like terminals in shopping arcades. Units dedicated to selling a particular item will broadcast a recorded sales message when approached. Others will respond to a touch on the video screen. A company launched by video game inventor Nolan Bushnell built a prototype of a remote shopping terminal that would allow a customer to insert a credit card, receive a video presentation of selected items, and, using the computer keyboard, order a product that would be delivered to the buyer's home and charged to the card.

The company, ByVideo, began marketing a system suitable for hotel lobbies and airports in 1983. There are still a lot of variables—for instance, which merchandisers' products or catalogs will be stored on the 54,000-frame discs, who will own and operate the machines, and how much they will cost.

---

[5] "Medium Gets the Message to Youth Market," *Chain Store Age Executive*, April 1985, 23.

FROM THE FIELD

The Video Age

Seventh Avenue executives report they are spending much time researching the video industry, screening production firms, and eyeing their competitors' videos almost as carefully as they scrutinize their collections.

Although there is no limit, the cost of producing a typical video ranges from $15,000 to $50,000. Many firms have already seen a higher return on their investment as a result of the exposure they have been able to get via the syndication of documentary videos to television shows, such as the magazine-format programs or local new shows.

For example, on six videos documenting fashion trends, which cost $20,000 apiece to produce and distribute, Ann Klein II got air play equivalent to an estimated $80,000 advertising time each. They aired on local news shows in the top 30 markets.

Although the television market for documentaries remains strong, more and more Seventh Avenue firms are producing the newer format fashion videos in addition to the runway variety, and instead of or in addition to documentary ones.

A runway video does for a collection what the dictionary does for language. It records it. It is a rare designer or volume manufacturer who does not videotape his runway show, but these tapes, generally 15 to 30 minutes long, are kept mainly in the showroom for educational and reference purposes.

An instructional video teaches salespeople how to present a line or teaches a customer how to put it together. The field of documentary videos is a wider one, but typical documentaries focus on market trends, interview the designer, or give a behind-the-scenes look at the company.

Fashion videos entertain rather than inform. Called by some "MTV-style" because of their similarity to music videos played on that cable channel, fashion videos have a story line, with lots of fast editing, and are set to music. (See Figure 16.5.)

While most executives said their main use of video would be to bolster consumer interest at point of purchase, they are all keeping an eye on the cable and local television markets opening up for fashion videos.

Source: "SA—Deep in the Video Age," *Women's Wear Daily*, November 27, 1984, 10.

Outdoor Advertising

Designed to appeal to general audiences but more permanent in nature, billboards and signs are generally located along highways and in strategic metro areas leading to the store. (See Figure 16.6.) An interesting development has been phone booth advertising. Some of the most sophisti-

Figure   16.5   In-Store Video Advertising

Source: © 1987 Phyllis Woloshin.

cated is being sold through New York's Phone Kiosk Advertising. The ads are 48 inches by 27 inches in backlit panels that increase illumination and safety for phone users inside the booths and also make the booths more attractive. (See Figure 16.7.)

Ad panels are planned at a minimum of 400 booths from Manhattan's Battery Park to East and West 96th Streets. The city was divided into districts, or grids, and was sold to advertisers on a monthly basis. Minimum buy has been 10 booths for $4,000 a month, up to 100 booths for $24,000 a month.

Figure   16.6   Traditional Outdoor Advertising—Billboard

Transit Advertising

Transit advertising exploits the commuter's boredom in order to gain readership. It can be seen in and around bus and train stations and also includes the cards and posters seen in trains, buses, and taxis and on platforms. A recent addition is Taxi Grams positioned above and in full vision of the riders in cabs. Crawling red lights carry 20-word ad messages and public service announcements in repeating, four-minute units.

THE ADVERTISING PLAN AND BUDGET

The advertising plan consists of the overall objectives, the budget, and the types of media selected. Desired objectives include increasing sales and profits, maintaining loyal customers, and attracting additional customers with appropriate offerings. In a small store, when money is spent for advertising space and production, the owner feels that it is coming out of his pocket. It probably is. In large stores, advertising space, production, and supplies come out of a budget that is planned by upper-level executives, merchandising personnel such as buyers and merchandise managers, and advertising executives. Their decisions include the planned cost of the advertising and the amounts needed to help sales grow.

Figure   16.7   Innovative Outdoor Advertising—Phone Booths

Source: Courtesy of American Media Network, Inc.

The unit-of-sales method for establishing a budget is based on the unit (number) of sales rather than on dollar amounts. A fixed sum is set aside for each unit the merchant expects to sell. For instance, if it takes 10 cents worth of advertising to sell a bottle of perfume and the retailer plans to sell 15,000 bottles, the store must plan to spend 15,000 times 10 cents, or $1,500, on advertising. The key to unit-of-sales planning is past experience, because the amount of advertising needed to sell a particular unit must be known. This method is especially effective for retailers of specialty goods like fine jewelry, furs, rugs, and cars.

The percentage-of-sales method for establishing a budget is based on a percentage of anticipated sales, past sales, or a combination of both. Anticipated sales are estimates. Past sales are the figures for the previous year or an average of several years. A combination of the two is preferred for establishing a budget during periods of fluctuation or changing economic conditions, because it permits input from studies of trends and business in general.

The objective-and-task method relates the advertising budget to sales objectives for the coming year. It is considered the most accurate method. The merchant must look at the total marketing program and consider store image, size, location, and so on. The task method stipulates exactly what the merchant must accomplish and what must be done to meet the objectives. The level of advertising expenditure is then directly related to how much it will cost to do the job. This method can be effective where new business is to be developed—for example, establishing a new designer boutique or focusing on petite women's sizes.

MEASURING ADVERTISING RESULTS

Even though every ad is planned to sell, not every ad has an immediate and measurable response. Each of the three broad classifications of ads has its own measurement of results, from immediate to long-range.

Institutional Advertising

Through institutional advertising a store creates and maintains its personality. This advertising is usually measured in decades. The results measured are (1) continuing respect for the store by its customers, suppliers, and stockholders and (2) the way the store profits and grows over the years.

Regular Price Advertising

Regular price advertising creates and maintains the store's reputation through its merchandise, bringing a response that should be measured over a period of a week or a season, not the next day after the advertising appears.

Promotional Advertising

Sale, off-price, clearance, and special purchase are all promotional advertising. This advertising is planned for immediate response and is measured by the increase over normal business. Normal is considered to be the amount of business a department would do without the ad. Promotional advertising can be measured the next day or the next week, depending on the length of the event.

If measuring ad results, the retail trade expects that, for each ad dollar invested, ten dollars in sales will be generated. This will vary from store to store, depending on whether it is in a highly promotional period with lots of sale ads or is a specialty store in a remote location. Factors that contribute to the success or failure of an ad can include a weather change, the economic climate, or an unexpected occurrence in the news. These must be taken into account when measuring ad results.

Summary

The primary purpose of retail advertising is to sell something: an idea, a service, or merchandise. Retail advertising differs from national advertising in the territory covered, its relationship to the customer, reader interest, response expected, and the use of price. Three broad classifications of advertising are institutional, promotional, and cooperative.

Internal media are methods of communication inside the store; external media are ways to entice customers into the store. The media mix is comprised of several media used to reach a total market. Major media categories in both print and broadcast can be evaluated according to reach, coverage, advantages, and disadvantages. Emerging media include rock/fashion videos and videodiscs.

After examining media options, the retailer must formulate an advertising plan and budget that will return a projected sales volume for the advertising dollars invested. Budgets may be established on the basis of the unit-of-sales method, the percentage-of-sales method, or the objective-and-task method. Finally, the retailer should measure the results from the advertising in each of its broad classifications: institutional, regular price, and promotional.

Questions
for Review

1. What is advertising and how does it differ from other promotional vehicles?
2. How does retail advertising differ from national advertising?
3. Differentiate between institutional advertising and promotional advertising.
4. Define cooperative advertising and differentiate between the two types—vertical and horizontal.
5. What is meant by the term *media mix* and what are the choices available to a retailer?
6. List advantages and disadvantages of the various major media categories—newspaper, magazine, direct mail, radio, and television.
7. Explain the various methods used to establish an advertising budget.

CASE STUDY

Mickey's Sporting Goods

An Advertising Decision—Print versus Television

Mickey's Sporting Goods was a well-known landmark in downtown New-bury, having occupied the same location on South Main Street for 29 years. Virtually everyone in Newbury patronized Mickey's at one time or another for work clothes, fishing equipment, sneakers, rifles, skis, or camping equipment. Mickey's also carried a complete line of sportswear for men and boys and, in addition, was headquarters in Newbury for Levi's.

As consumer interest in the great out-of-doors grew, so did Mickey's sales. Business was fantastic even though Mickey spent very little money on advertising. He was a marvelous salesman and had trained his staff to treat every customer with courtesy. Mickey's offered prompt service and the word spread, so that new customers came to shop even though they had not seen newspaper ads or heard radio commercials.

Mickey was also an astute businessman, and he knew that the kind of growth he had been enjoying could not go on forever, especially because competition was increasing. Two new discount houses had opened in Newbury and one of the country's biggest sporting goods chains was soon to move into the Newbury Mall.

The mall had been open a year and most of the other old-time mer-chants, feeling its presence, had already increased their advertising bud-gets. People no longer checked out the downtown stores first. Many went directly to the mall when they had need for clothing, furniture, or appli-ances, and then they shopped downtown later, if at all. Often they were able to make all of their purchases in one of the 60 mall stores.

Many of the downtown retailers began to advertise heavily, as a result, both in the daily newspaper and on local radio stations. Although the anchor store in the mall did some television advertising, none of the downtown merchants had yet made a decision to use this medium.

In addition to carrying the right merchandise and offering the ex-pected services, the key to continued success for downtown stores was to reach customers while they were still in the thinking stage, before they actually got to the point of purchase. If the interest of a potential cus-tomer was aroused through effective advertising, most likely he or she would go to the store that ran the advertisement before starting on a random shopping trip.

Mickey realized that the time had come for him to make a major adver-tising commitment. He needed to know which of the available media would offer him the best return on his advertising dollar. Should he use the daily newspaper or try spot announcements on one or both of the local radio stations? Maybe he should be the first downtown merchant to advertise on television. Perhaps some combination of media would be best.

Mickey also knew that he would have to approach the problem in as scientific a manner as possible in order to make the correct decision. Advertising is costly, and good money would be wasted if he did not reach his market. His first step, therefore, would be to isolate his markets. His next step would be to analyze his customers' prepurchase behavior.

Were his customers avid television viewers and, if so, did they watch the local channel? If they did watch the local channel, at what time of day was there a sizable audience interested in Mickey's type of merchandise? Would newspaper ads be more effective because they could be kept as reference after initially attracting attention? What percentage of his market read the *Newbury News* daily? He knew that many Newbury residents received metropolitan papers through the mail and did not subscribe to the *Newbury News*. Were these his customers? If so, why waste money on ads in the local paper? Was radio a meaningful alternative for him and, if so, which station and what times?

He ruled out the use of direct mail because of his personal distate for the method as well as the fact that it had been overworked by supermarkets and discount stores. Of all the direct-mail techniques, bill enclosures appealed to him most. He could not use this type of direct-mail advertising, however, because he did not offer charge accounts and had no monthly billings.

Once his customers' habits were known, Mickey could decide on the best media combination for his first major advertising venture. Even though retailers, both large and small, in cities throughout the United States were turning to television, was it right for him or was television a tool for giants like Sears or J. C. Penney? Were small-town merchants better off concentrating on print media because local newspapers seemed to produce more professional ads than local television stations? (Newbury's trading area drew approximately 150,000 potential shoppers from a radius of about 50 miles.) These questions would have to be thoroughly investigated. If he found that his customers watched little local television, the questions would be rhetorical, of course.

Mickey believed that some type of intensive advertising was the answer to increased sales. He felt he could go no further through word of mouth alone. Too many other retailers were reaching out for the same customer dollars, and although his excellent reputation was enough in the past, times were changing. If he did not attract new people who would be exposed to his good service and fair prices, he would not be able to build on this reputation for repeat sales.

The time had come for Mickey's Sporting Goods to launch a full-fledged advertising campaign, but before an ad budget could be drawn up, Mickey had to decide on his media mix. Mickey started his exercise in scientific problem solving by listing the tasks to be performed and the order of performance.

1. Isolation of target market(s).
2. Research into buyer behavior of potential market(s) isolated in Task 1.
3. Listing of available media and cost of each.
4. Development of matrix showing market(s)–media relationship in order of importance.
5. Selection of media mix for first advertising campaign.
6. Establishment of advertisement budget.
7. Creation of a yearly ad calendar.

Once these tasks were completed, work could begin on the ads themselves. Mickey's Sporting Goods would enter the second phase in its history as a successful small town merchant.

Questions

1. Design a plan that will give Mickey the market information necessary to make a media decision.
2. How valuable do you consider television advertising to be for Mickey's Sporting Goods? Explain.
3. What is the value of local newspaper advertising for a store like Mickey's Sporting Goods? Discuss.
4. List the benefits of radio and direct-mail advertising for the small-town merchant.
5. Create a yearly advertising calendar for Mickey's Sporting Goods.

Chapter 17

Visual Presentation of Merchandise

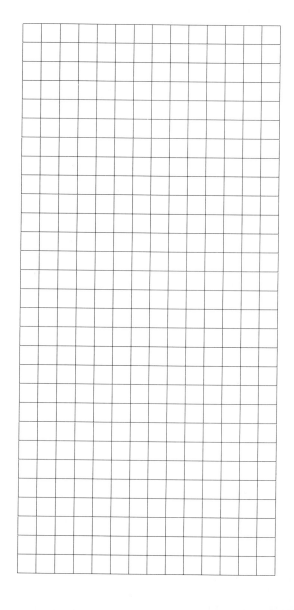

Industry Statement

Andrew J. Markopoulos
Vice President–Central Director, Visual
Merchandising and Design
Dayton Hudson Department Store Company

Mediocrity is expensive! Today many stores tend to bore their customers with mediocre presentations that, in turn, force the customer to seek alternatives. Not only is mediocrity boring, but it is therefore nonproductive in terms of the bottom line.

Creativity in its truest form allows the customer to view collections of merchandise, in both dominant assortments and segments, in a way that immediately relates it to the customer's lifestyle. To be successful, stores must be innovative and respond positively to the customer's needs.

In today's competitive environment, customers lead busy and varied lives. They want and expect stores that are exciting and attractive, in terms of both design and store layout. Stores must allow efficient use of customers' time and have an atmosphere that is conducive to return visits.

Change is part of the formula that creates excitement. Moreover, as demographic changes profoundly affect our society, change is necessary on an ongoing basis. The major challenge to visual merchandising is to manage change, to anticipate change, to understand and adapt to change and, finally, to respond to change in presentations.

Learning Objectives

Upon completing this chapter you should be able to:

1. Illustrate how the role of the visual merchandiser has evolved from window trimmer to top executive.
2. Explain the phrase "the store as theater" in terms of profitability.
3. Understand why the elements of display must work in tandem with the principles of visual merchandising.
4. Distinguish the options available to the visual merchandiser for use in both exterior and interior display.
5. Know why self-service displays are growing in importance.

Throughout the centuries, the most advantageous method for selling wares has been to exhibit them so that the prospective buyer is permitted a visual and tactile inspection of them. This elementary principle of merchandise presentation has persisted, intact, in Mexico, Africa, and India. In our society merchandise presentation has experienced a dynamic evolution because of changes in the culture, changes in the merchandise itself, and new merchandising philosophy as well as increased demands and sophistication on the part of the consumer.

In this century we have seen the window trimmer give way to the visual merchandiser, who today occupies major executive status in most large retail companies. Chapter 16 illustrated the importance of advertising to the success of the retailer. Here we will focus on the role of visual merchandising in the retail selling environment.

VISUAL MERCHANDISING— THE STORE AS THEATER

The best theater and the best stores relate to the widest possible audience. The ability of the theater producer or the retailer to convey a message to the audience contributes to his or her continuing success. Customers want to see activity. They want assurances that they are seeing the best show around so that their peers will judge them to be the smartest shopper.

Communicating through Merchandise Presentation

Subliminal Cues
Messages below receivers' awareness level intended by the sender to register subconsciously.

What kind of visual picture does the merchandise present and what is it actually saying to the customer? Merchandise presentation should communicate to the customer through **subliminal cues** and messages—whether service, quality, or prestige. It should also target specific merchandise and areas in the store.

Retailers should not overlook other senses, in addition to the visual, in merchandise presentation. Touch, for example, communicates important sensations, and a customer's buying juices can be turned on by aroma. An example is Macy's lingerie floor, which includes a central fragrance area.

Statistically, market research shows that 50 percent of the most loyal customers will visit a store once every two weeks, and they are generally responsible for 70 percent of the purchases.[1] Retailers who do not merchandise toward these customers will bore them, and when key customers are bored, they will not come back.

Change, the Key to Merchandise Presentation

The ongoing change in merchandise presentation that will hold the interest of loyal customers requires the visual merchandiser to balance flexibility against some basic tenets. When a customer approaches a department, the first thing he or she should see is a feature presentation, followed by the presentation on the back wall, which is the highest point of merchandise presentation in the department. There should be a relationship between the two in the merchandise presented. In effect, the customer is attracted into the department by groupings of merchandise that influence traffic patterns.

Theatrical Elements

Retailers must bring theater into the store and then into the merchandise. The customer should be entertained, excited, and educated. Theatrical elements can be used to lead customers to the merchandise and to purchases. (See Figure 17.1.)

Use repeat patterns, angles that make eyes focus on selected areas, triangles, hot colors, incongruities. Create action and you will measure the success of your store in sales.

---

[1] "The Store As Theater," *Stores*, February 1984, 43.

Figure   17.1   A Theatrical Entrance: Parisian, Inc., Birmingham, Alabama

EVOLUTION OF THE VISUAL MERCHANDISER

In the 20th century we have seen the window trimmer added to the retail staff and then evolve in large multiunit stores into a manager with a title such as vice president for merchandise presentation or vice president for sales promotion and visual merchandising. Visual merchandisers have large staffs that encompass many types of people in both supportive and work functions. He or she is part of the executive team. A good display person has come to be regarded as an artist who practices a legitimate art form.

Visual merchandising has long since taken the place of display in most stores. Phyllis Tama, executive search consultant for the Thorndike Deland placement office, and with a record of high-level service with May Company, Saks Fifth Avenue, and Associated Merchandising Corporation, has said:

> This visual-whatever-you-want-to-call-it position is one of our most active categories today on both the seek and supply sides. It is no longer considered to be just a glorification of the display manager's job, with titles awarded in lieu of or to sweeten a relatively modest pay raise. Stores with openings have some very broad and stiff requirements:
> - An intimate knowledge of store planning, fixturing, and installation
> - A driving, coordinative sense of sales promotion
> - Administrative strength
> - Knack for enthusiastic collaboration with everyone from top management to sales floor employees.[2]

About 80 percent of the merchandise in any directly competing stores is virtually identical. Further, much of the selling is done where stores are clustered, so that a customer's first contact may depend largely on where a parking slot can be found. Finally, there is an overabundance of retail floor space, just as there is an oversupply of goods. Any given store must therefore create a general atmosphere and countless specific presentations that will trigger buying decisions on its own sales floor while precluding purchases at a competitor's store.

Call this theater or what you will, it is an art expressed with color, lighting, signing, mannequins, fixturing, and positioning. Visual merchandising conveys attitude up to the point where employees take over with alert and courteous service.

Visual merchandising thus creates interest and excitement in the merchandise and provides the customer with the impetus to buy. The visual merchandising department is an important part of the selling team, for it presents the image of the store to the customer and issues an invitation to come in and shop. Like nothing else, it can maximize a traditional store's assets vis-à-vis discounters and off-pricers. Because of various economic and competitive factors, it will continue to grow for the rest of this century.

---

[2] "Looking In," *Stores*, June 1984, 22.

Figure   17.2   A Specific Purpose Display: Wooden Figures for Knitwear

Source: © 1987 Phyllis Woloshin.

THE PRINCIPLES AND ELEMENTS OF VISUAL MERCHANDISING

The visual merchandiser is the last link between the product and the customer. Visual merchandising represents a marriage between merchandise managers, department managers, and visual managers. It employs the same basic principles and elements of design as do all recognized art forms. The main difference is that visual merchandising creations are temporary in nature and have a merchandising purpose rather than a purely aesthetic one. (See Figure 17.2.) The success of any display can be measured (1) by the resulting sales and (2) by the artistic merit of the display itself.

Display Formats

The format of the display must be consistent with the merchandise and the area in which the display is used. The three most common formats in use today are the step format, the pyramid format, and the zigzag format. These can be used with almost any classification of merchandise and in any type of display.

The **step format** is a graduation in levels from lowest to highest with all the levels parallel. If looked at from the side, the display would approximate a series of steps. (See Figure 17.3.) With this format the display may be either symmetrically or asymmetrically balanced, depending on the impact desired and the merchandise used.

Step Format
Display that begins at a low point on one side and climbs smoothly to a higher point; sometimes called diagonal arrangement.

Figure   17.3   Step Format

Pyramid Format
Display that is
geometric and
often follows the
lines of a perfect
triangle, beginning
at a broad base
and progressing to
an apex.

Zigzag Format
Display resembling
a modified
pyramid that
begins at a broad
base and zigzags to
the top, with no
two heights the
same.

The **pyramid format** approximates the shape of a three-sided figure. If the top of the form is used as the apex and a line is drawn down to the left and down to the right of the display, the pyramid shape can be seen. Whether the pyramid is in a horizontal or a vertical position, the merchandise at the base of the pyramid will be larger and more spread out, and the items will be smaller and more compact as they near the top. The pyramid format is more static than the step arrangement.

The **zigzag format** is a combination of the step format and the pyramid format. (See Figure 17.4.) This type of display is alive, has a lot of movement within it, and directs the viewer's eye because of the various heights. The merchandise is usually arranged in steps designed to move the customer's eye from lower right to upper left. The steps are not uniform in height, and this increases the areas in the display that can be used as focal points.

Display Elements

Certain elements of visual merchandising must be considered if the display is to work. These elements are line, texture, weight, lighting, and

Figure 17.4 Zigzag Format

color. They can bring the merchandise to life and create mood, movement, and direction.

Line

The merchandise itself dictates the line and imparts specific meaning to the customer. A straight line produces a feeling of precision, rigidity, directness. A curved line gives a feeling of flexibility, action, and a flowing continuity. The horizontal line represents calm, quiet, and restfulness, and may also give the impression of width.

Lines join together to form two- and three-dimensional shapes that may be of any geometric configuration. The most common shapes utilized in visual merchandising are squares, circles, rectangles, triangles, cubes, spheres, boxes, and pyramids. All display areas are specific shapes. The differing shapes of the merchandise have importance in their relationship with each other and to the total display.

Texture

Texture is the look or feel of an object's surface. Texture may be real or artificial. The element of texture is vital in a display, for it creates either harmony or contrast. Real texture is inherent in the merchandise itself; examples are the smoothness of marble or the roughness of straw. The

Artificial Texture
An illusion of
surface feel created
by the design artist
to enhance a
display.

Optical Weight
The amount an
object appears to
weigh rather than
what it actually
weighs.

Track Lighting
Display lighting
that consists of
movable units
mounted on
vertical or
horizontal tracks.

Art Deco
Style from the
1920s and 1930s
that combines
exotic (1920s) or
sleek (1930s)
design with new
materials.

customer can easily detect real texture by touch. **Artificial texture** is created through techniques that make something appear different from what it really is, such as the painting of bricks on a smooth wall.

Weight

Every piece of merchandise has an actual weight and an **optical weight.** A foam pillow covered with dark fur may look heavy because of the texture and color, for example, but in reality it is very lightweight because of the materials. The optical weight of an object is the more important in terms of visual merchandising and balance in a display. The shape, color, and texture will determine the optical weight of an object, and this will determine its placement in a display. Lighting can also affect the optical weight of an object.

Lighting

To underlight is better than to overlight. With the vast array of lighting options in today's market, care should be taken when deciding whether to light floors or individual displays. For installation in ceilings and cases, long fluorescent tubes are usually the choice. Spotlights are concentrated on specific parts of a display or to create mood lighting.

The most popular form of window lighting is **track lighting.** It is today's mass version of theatrical lighting. Tracks can be mounted horizontally or vertically. High-intensity discharge (HID) systems are both energy efficient and design effective. The reason is their high output of light relative to wattage. Another advantage is their compact size.

Color

Color is a dramatic and powerful tool both in displays and in general store design. Color can be used to identify areas or shops within the store itself. (See "From the Field: Accessories Presentation at Bradlees.")

Color can be used as a theme to register a promotion or can be used to provide impact for normally dull merchandise. It can also be used to create a specific mood—black and silver for **art deco** or oranges, yellows, and bright greens for a summer atmosphere. Display artists must first consider the colorations of the merchandise and the packaging that is to be used. From this point, they can build a color story that will register with the customer.

Colors have psychological overtones and personal associations. Consumer preference for colors, from most to least preferred, is blue, red, green, violet, orange, yellow.[3] Blue is considered a restful color and is

---

[3] Richard Carty, *Visual Merchandising* (New York: Milady Publishing, 1978), 84.

associated with the sky and the ocean. Red is the most vibrant color. Associated with Christmas and Valentine's Day, it can provide a vibrant accent for otherwise dull displays. The earth tones of beiges, browns, and russet–oranges are popular because people are oriented to the colors found in nature. They are used frequently in the home division of stores. (See Figure 17.5.)

Color is probably the most important element of visual merchandising because it is inherent in each piece of merchandise, each prop, and each fixture. The visual merchandiser must elicit the correct psychological reaction from the consumer through an understanding and manipulation of color.

Figure   17.5   A Home Division Display

Source: © 1987 Phyllis Woloshin.

Display Principles

Both merchandise and display elements must be worked into the display according to the principles of visual merchandising design—balance, repetition, proportion, contrast, and dominance. If all are properly coordinated, harmony will be achieved in the display.

Balance

Asymmetrical Balance Grouping of items with no apparent plan; the opposite of formal balance, in which each half of a composition is identical with the other.

The display artist has a choice of either symmetrical or asymmetrical balance. Symmetrical, or formal, balance is more precise than **asymmetrical balance.** In either case, the display is divided in half by an imaginary line that serves as a central axis. For formal balance, every object on the left-hand side of the line must be repeated on the right-hand side. In informal balance, the shapes and spaces on either side of the line do not repeat each other.

Repetition

Repetition is the regular occurrence of an object or element throughout a display. Repetition may be accomplished through the use of color, such as variations of blue; the appearance of a design element, such as a seashell; the use of similar shapes, such as coral and sea horses; the use of one texture, such as glass; or anything else that is repeated. Using the same background in a series of windows can also create repetition. Because the customer registers the merchandise or the theme through visual impact, repetition is important to continuity.

Proportion

Proportion is a proper relationship between objects and spaces. To create a certain impact, items can be purposely out of proportion. An example is the samurai warrior in Wanamaker's court.

Contrast

Contrast may be created between the props and the merchandise or may come between any one of the elements of visual-merchandising design. It must be dealt with carefully and skillfully. Contrast should be used as an attention getter so that props attract the customer to merchandise that is specialized enough to sell itself.

Dominance

A focal point, or dominance, is necessary if a display is to be entirely successful. This is the main point to which the customer's eye is drawn.

FROM THE FIELD

Accessories Presentation at Bradlees

In an effort to move away from the concept of discounter, Bradlees now calls itself "the department store with a difference." The chain is based in Braintree, Mass.

In the remodeled Framingham store (91,000 square feet) located in suburban Boston's retail zone known as Shoppers World, two merchandise areas are new and experimental. One is the big, flashy junior sportswear department, projecting a trendy feeling akin to The Limited Express. The other is the "new focal point of the store," according to Harry Kohn, Jr., president. The women's accessories area was transformed into a 4,400-square-foot series of separate accessories shops with 50 percent more space than in the Bradlees prototype.

A wood-slat, dusty-rose dropped ceiling, with track and spotlights above the entire area, makes the accessories' presentation more distinctive. Because ac-

cessories are opposite the store entrance, the combination of lower rose-colored ceiling, lighting, and the lineup of accessories shops gives customers a new first impression. (See Figure 17.6.)

Like accessories, junior sportswear has been given a decor and presentation treatment totally different—from floors to ceiling to fixturing—from the rest of the store. Setting the area apart is a canopy of shiny aluminum slat fascias. The ceiling is also peppered with neon lighting, and background music is the expected-for-juniors rock. At the corners of the department, white mica cube platforms hold mannequins wearing the latest in trendy junior garb.

Bradlees has once again demonstrated that, regardless of its definition, it is a gutsy retailer, one that its competitors have learned bears constant watching.

Source: *Apparel Merchandising,* December 1984.

Dominance can be accomplished through unusual placement of merchandise, eye movement, use of color, or lighting.

EXTERIOR DISPLAY

A window, it is said, has only three seconds to convey a message to passersby that will cause them to stop. For the more receptive and usually slower moving shoppers who are already in the store, an interior display is calculated to have ten seconds in which to make its point and induce the shopper to stop and examine the merchandise.[4]

---

[4]Pieter Oschmann, *Visual Merchandising* (New York: National Retail Merchants Association, 1976), 93.

Figure 17.6   Accessories Shop at Bradlees

Source: Courtesy of The Stop & Shop Companies, Inc.

Windows should be warm and inviting in order to bring the customer into the store to spend money. Because the customer's first impression of the store comes from its exterior and its windows, the windows act as a bridge between the outside and the inside. They project the image of the store and indicate the character and the quality of merchandise carried.

Kinds of Windows

Open-back windows are often used by the smaller store because they create the illusion of more interior space than really exists. They combine the window and the selling floor itself into a unified display. An open-back window may be entirely open to the sales floor; it may have a clear glass panel separating it from the sales floor; or it may be lightly screened off by a transparent curtain at the back. Glass panels or transparent curtains permit the customer to see through the window, but provide some security protection for the merchandise in the window display.

Closed-back windows are the favorite of creative display people because they are like a stage on which to practice stagecraft. The most important design element is proper lighting. The visual merchandiser must work closely with the store planner so that proper space is allocated in the building design for closed-back windows. Alternatively, they can be designed as bay windows that protrude past the building line so as not to cut down the interior space. Store planning was discussed in Chapter 11.

Windows as Sales Producers

In recent years the value of store windows has been questioned by some retailers. These merchants consider modern glass fronts, through which passersby look directly into a store's interior, more valuable than street windows. In these cases, the entire store interior becomes part of the window display. The interaction of customers, merchandise, and salespeople produces a lively setting with lots of movement by day and, if properly lighted, an attention-getting scene at night.

Before blocking off windows, or bringing the sales floor up to the window line, or framing windows down to inconsequential shadowboxes, these retailers might consider the example of some of the great older stores on the great shopping streets.

INTERIOR DISPLAY

The interior display must attract the customer already in the store by registering an idea, color, or an item, and induce the purchase of the merchandise. Store layout was discussed in Chapter 11. Here the various types of display arrangements available within the layout will be considered. Display areas include cases, platforms, ledges, islands, and simulated rooms.

Display cases serve a triple purpose. First, they act to form a selling area on the floor by physically enclosing space. Second, they serve for storage of merchandise; goods can be stacked in the cases. Third, they are a display unit in themselves. Cases should be simple and uncluttered and, as in all displays, the merchandise should be dominant rather than the display props. (See Figure 17.7.)

Platforms are used to distinguish a display from the floor of a department store. Either rectangular or round in design, they are available commercially or can be constructed by the display department from

Figure   17.7   Display Case

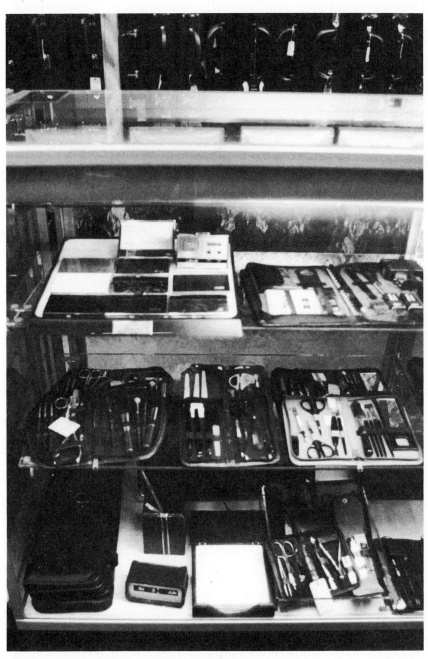

The Putumayo Environment

Dan Storper, the innovative, young president and owner of Putumayo, turned his fascination with Latin American folk art and crafts into a thriving specialty store operation in New York that features a variety of traditional cultures. They are a tantalizing mix of crafts, folk art, apparel, and accessories.

Storper cultivated his interest in folk art and crafts while majoring in Latin American studies at Washington University in St. Louis. After graduating in 1973, he set out to see South America with the idea of starting an import business.

With his $3,000 savings, Storper bought handmade jungle baskets, tapestries, and carved figures and gourds from remote tribes, and then went to New York to do a series of folk art shows in Manhattan galleries. The success of his early shows led to further South American trips and eventually to what he describes as a "fortuitous sale" to Bloomingdale's.

What does Dan Storper think about visual merchandising? "I think how you display the merchandise is almost as important as what you have to sell," says Storper. "In the third store, we tried to create an unusual environment where the clothing and accessories and folk art worked together."

The background environment in the store is based on colonial New Mexico of the 18th century. The walls are adobe and there are wood-beamed ceilings with a primitive style of slatting called latia. The floors are made of Mexican clay tiles, and structural columns in the store have been hand-stenciled in the style of the period.

There are lots of stripped trees and wood fences and lattices for displaying sashes, shawls, skirts, and accessories by simply spreading them out around the area. This effect, which Storper calls "ordered chaos," enables the customers to see the enormous variety of merchandise, while making it easy to find things.

Probably the most interesting touch is how the store's collection of folk art and craft pieces are used in the visual scheme. They literally become part of the display environment. A hand-painted Mexican chair is draped with sashes. So is an African pigskin chair. The paintings that hang innocently around the room represent a style of folk art called naive painting, are done by artists from 12 different countries, and include a well-known French artist named Dechlette. A collection of textiles also helps give the store its own look—especially several Navaho blankets.

"We have a person who is in charge of store displays," says Storper, "but we also hope the store manager and sales staff will participate in the display effort by keeping it going."

Source: "Putumayo," *Stores*, February 1984, 44. Reprinted with permission from *STORES* Magazine, © 1984 National Retail Merchants Association.

Shadowboxes
Display fixtures
usually located
behind the
counter; they are
often illuminated,
sometimes enclosed
in glass, and often
used to display
luxury items.

wood and then covered with a variety of suitable material. Platforms are particularly important in the home furnishings department, where they are used to create vignettes.

Interior **shadowboxes** are usually located behind counters, especially in the jewelry and cosmetics departments. Lighting is from concealed fluorescent tubes or spotlights in the top of the shadowbox.

Ledges are used in a different manner from other display areas. One type of ledge is recessed into the wall above a set of shelves so that it shows the merchandise stored below—or merchandise from the entire department. The space is sometimes distorted and often difficult to work with. This type of ledge arrangement is often used in the table linens department to highlight placemats. A second type of ledge, found along the main floor aisles, consists of the top of the center unit in a selling area. It is normally trimmed and decorated according to the store's main promotion or for special holidays. This type of ledge is usually visible from all four sides and must be designed accordingly.

Island areas are similar to platforms except that they are stationary and are planned in the preliminary layout of the store. They may be located in all parts of the store, but are most likely near entrances to important shops, escalators, elevators, and other high-traffic areas. Islands are finished to coordinate with the general decor of the store, and different moods are achieved through backgrounds and props. Permanent spotlights have been installed above these areas for maximum lighting effect.

**Environmental
Setting**
Simulated room
with three walls
used to display
single items of
furnishings and
accessories in a
coordinated group.

Simulated room settings are called **environmental settings.** They have furniture, carpeting, and all appropriate accessories installed in a three-walled area with appropriate wall covering. This type of display area allows the customer the opportunity of seeing exactly how a grouping of furniture will look. Usually designed by the home furnishings coordinator, environmental settings are then assembled and maintained by the display department.

The key to a successful display—whether a series of windows, cases, a room setting, or a special promotion—is coordination and a unified presentation. Continuity is necessary not only in the individual displays but also in the store as a whole.

**SELF-SERVICE
DISPLAYS**

Point-of-purchase (P.O.P.) display areas are expanding dramatically as manufacturers provide bigger, more complicated permanent displays to give them an edge on their competitors.

Recognition of the profitability of the rapidly expanding instore display field, along with market forces, is threatening to change the face of retailing. Too, designers are increasingly required to serve two masters—the store clerk or store manager who must assemble the displays and the manufacturers who initiate them. The displays must be attractive enough to gain retail acceptance but must not be an intellectual challenge to use.

The tobacco industry has been a mainstay user of permanent displays for many years, but several other industries are emerging as heavy users. These include computer firms, telephone manufacturers, the automotive aftermarket, hosiery, cosmetics and skin care, and the do-it-yourself field. (See Figure 17.8.)

Figure   17.8   Self-Service Display: Shower Mates

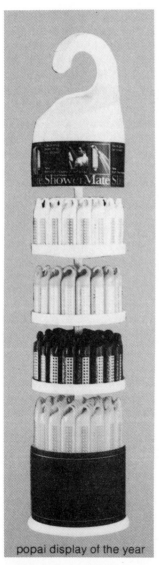

popai display of the year

Source: Courtesy of R.T.C. Industries Inc., Chicago, Illinois 60623.

Talking displays are becoming more interesting, although they are not popular with retailers because extended exposure to a sales message that repeats itself tends to unnerve salesclerks. The use of interactive displays is growing among large retailers and shopping mall operators. Another exciting development is a revolving unit powered by solar cells that capture light energy from a store's fluorescent bulbs. Budweiser has placed 30,000 revolving units in liquor departments throughout the country.[5]

For certain products cardboard is still the preferred material to use in making displays because the merchandise changes so fast. On the whole, the trend is toward permanent displays that are as flashy as possible within a limited budget. Cosmetics displays will use gingerbread such as lights, computers, mirrors, and other elements. The basic rule in display design, however, is to put as much merchandise as possible in as attractive a package as possible using as little space as possible.

Summary

The store as theater has emerged as one of the dominant themes in retailing today. The visual merchandiser has become the last link between the product and the customer. Not only must the display be artistic, but it must generate sales, especially when it occupies valuable retail space.

Three common display formats are being used: the step, the pyramid, and the zigzag. Within these formats, certain elements of visual merchandising must be considered if the display is to work. These are line, texture, weight, lighting, and color.

Merchandise must be worked into the display according to the principles of visual merchandising—balance, repetition, proportion, contrast, and dominance. Color and lighting are keys to the successful play of the elements.

The two major types of display are exterior and interior. Exterior focuses primarily on windows, which are generally of two kinds: open-back and closed-back. Window displays bring customers into the store, where the interior display must attract them to buy. Interior display areas may be display cases, platforms, shadowboxes, ledges, islands, or environmental settings.

In addition to interior and exterior display areas, self-service displays are growing in importance as a way of communicating excitement and selling messages to customers.

---

[5] "Display Makers Serve Two Masters," *Marketing News*, December 7, 1984, 15.

Questions
for Review

1. Differentiate between *window trimmer/display person* and *visual merchandiser*.
2. Explain the phrase "the store as theater" in terms of visual merchandising.
3. List the three display formats and give a short description of each.
4. List the five principles of visual merchandising design.
5. Discuss the psychological overtones and associations of color.
6. Exterior display is usually concerned with store windows. Differentiate between open-back and closed-back windows.
7. List the various types of interior displays and give a short description of each.

CASE STUDY | **Schofield's Department Store** |

Appraising the Boutique Concept

If Betty Taylor's recent experience at Schofield's Department Store was typical, the boutique concept had almost certainly outlived its purpose. Instead of making shopping easier for the consumer, the overabundance of shops or boutiques scattered throughout most department stores was causing confusion, frustration, and loss of sales.

At 11 a.m., Betty had entered Schofield's downtown store to purchase a ski sweater she had seen advertised in *Vogue*. The ad had indicated that the sweater could be found, in her area, at Schofield's.

Betty logically assumed when she entered the store that the sweater would be in the Better Sweater Boutique on the second floor, because it was priced at $60; however, the salesperson there suggested she try the new Ski Chalet adjacent to the sporting goods department on the seventh floor. There she learned that a few of the sweaters had been in stock but were sold out. Next she tried the Vacation Corner on the fifth floor, which also carried ski sweaters, because many people bought them for their winter vacation wardrobes. She had no luck there. Up and down the escalators she went until nearly 1 p.m., when she found herself in the Skirt and Sweater Shop on the third floor.

Betty sat down on the nearest chair to collect herself. This was not the Schofield's that she knew—a store in which she had thoroughly enjoyed shopping since she was a child, the store where most of her friends had purchased gifts for her engagement and wedding, and the store where she had previously been able to expend a minimum of effort to fill her needs.

Betty had not been in Schofield's downtown store for a few years because of the greater convenience of shopping at a branch store in a suburban mall near her home. In the central city on other business, however, she had decided to try the main store. After two tiring hours, she decided not to do it again. In the two-floor branch unit where she was accustomed to shopping, similar merchandise was located in one section, and the frustration level was a lot lower.

A few years earlier, Schofield's had completely revamped the interior of the main store, while keeping most of the departments in the same locations. Then, when boutiques became popular, Schofield's and other downtown department stores adopted the new "shop concept." From that point on, many customers began to feel like strangers in a foreign land.

At the same time, the idea of finding one's total needs in one area was appealing. When buying summer vacation clothes for the men in the family, it was no longer necessary to go to the boy's department on the third floor, the men's department on the fifth floor, the notions counter on the street floor, and the sporting goods section on the eighth floor. The Swim and Surf Shop had everything from bathing suits to sunglasses. For a customer looking for a wedding gift, The Bridal Bridge overlooking the main floor carried a variety of gift items ranging from silver, crystal, and china to small appliances. The boutique idea, which brought together a variety of items from different departments within the store and placed them in one shop for the convenience of the customer, was a boon to one-stop shopping.

Eventually, however, boutiques had proliferated to the point where the customer was afraid to shop in only one. Similar merchandise was being placed in a number of boutiques, and the shopper was never sure that a better selection was not available elsewhere in the store. Moreover, with more locations in which to place the same total number of items, merchandise was spread thin and there was little depth in any one area.

Schofield's customers could no longer be sure of finding the style, color, and size of sweater they were looking for in one place. There were ladies' sweaters in the sportswear department, the Sweater Bar, the Ski Shop, the Vacation Corner, the Better Sweater Boutique, and the Skirt and Sweater Shop. It was becoming more and more difficult to think of Schofield's as a department store when sometimes—increasingly so it seemed—merchandise could not be found in the department where it had been traditionally stocked.

Betty Taylor approached a young woman who was arranging a display under the Skirt and Sweater Shop sign and asked if she had the new Gem ski sweater in a size 38 in blue and white. The answer was yes. Betty was ecstatic; her search was over.

As the salesgirl wrapped her purchase, Betty described the difficulty she had encountered that day. The salesgirl asked Harriet Bogart, the ladies sportswear buyer, to join them. Ms. Bogart listened to Betty, nodding her head with every sentence. She had heard this story before and each time she wondered if the boutique concept was not being overdone.

When the idea for one-stop shopping areas within the store had first been presented in the late 1960s, and later executed, there was no doubt that it was a clever idea in store layout. The store had become impersonal following World War II. A return to small selling sections with related goods was one way to combat impersonal discount stores, which were cutting into Schofield's market. Also, customers had less and less time to shop, and they resented going from department to department to satisfy their needs for one activity. The boutique, which carried related merchandise from the various departments, was the perfect solution. The customer was happy, and management was happy because each sale in a boutique was usually a multiple sale.

Each year more boutiques appeared, stealing space from the home departments that were feeding them. With less space in each department, merchandise could not be stocked in depth. Rather, it was scattered throughout the store, often resulting in problems like those encountered by Betty Taylor.

A great innovation in store layout, the boutique could be a detriment to merchandising if not handled intelligently. Harriet Bogart did not believe that boutiques should disappear. She herself had experienced increased sales every year since her merchandise began to receive the extensive exposure that boutiques offered. The store was more attractive with interesting shops nestled in unexpected corners but, as with any good technique, it could be overdone.

When customers became frustrated instead of pleased, it was time to review the benefits of boutiques. It was time to halt the growth of these shops that seemed to be taking over each floor like an invading army. Was balance the answer to the use of boutiques within the department store?

Questions

1. Is the boutique concept detrimental to good merchandising? Defend your answer.
2. Do you agree with Harriet Bogart about the future of boutiques in department stores? Why or why not?
3. Design a layout for a full-line department store using boutiques to enhance the appearance and increase sales.
4. Explain the benefits of your layout in terms of increased sales, flow of traffic within the store, effective use of available space, and store appearance.

Chapter 18

Promotional, Sales, and Service Strategies

Source: Courtesy of Great State Beverages.

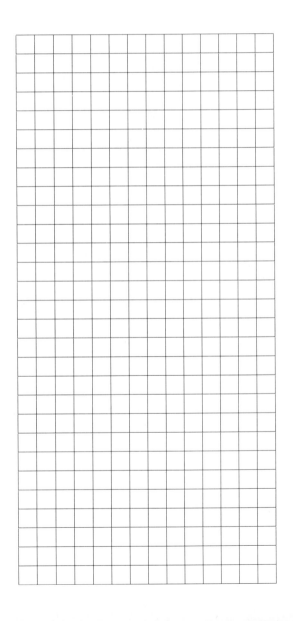

Industry Statement

Arleen F. Weiner
Divisional Director of Expense Control
Filene's, Boston

In today's business environment, fierce rivalry exists between the traditional department store and its competition. The department store finds itself vying for market share with off-price retailers, factory-owned outlets, and discount department stores as well as specialty shops. The department store must distinguish itself from its competition in order to attract and retain its customers.

The most important elements in attracting business are offering fine quality merchandise, competitive pricing, and a pleasant shopping environment. The department store must be aware of the latest fashion trends and offer a fair cross section of fashion forward as well as traditional merchandise. Timing is important. The store must carry appropriate merchandise during the right season. Merchandise presentation and effective signing are also essential. A customer must be able to find what she or he is looking for with ease.

However, merchandise cannot be the only element in attracting customers to a store. Most major competitors carry the same in-season stock at the same prices. The department store of today looks for other means of establishing itself in the community and differentiating itself from the competition.

In the past five years, customer service has emerged as the major priority for most retailers. Many have developed formal programs to provide and measure customer service in their stores. These programs include formalized training for the sales associates, customer comment cards, professional shopping groups, and customer service survey weeks during which the store invites customers to evaluate customer service. Through these programs, stores recognize sales associates who provide outstanding service and reward them for their performance. Today's consumers are well educated and respond positively to stores' efforts.

A fair, liberal return policy is essential in today's competitive market. The store must stand behind its merchandise and be willing to satisfy its customers.

467

For those customers with little time to shop, retailers are providing personal shopping service. Alterations, gift wrapping, package delivery, and shopping by mail or phone are other functions designed to facilitate the shopping experience. Stores may also offer a travel bureau, repair center, shoe shine, or food service.

Groceries are the most recent commodity to associate with the department store. Some retailers are teaming up with prominent supermarkets to offer the finest in gourmet foods for the young, upwardly mobile consumer. With the addition of groceries, the department store can truly become a one-stop shopping experience.

Credit promotion is another method department stores utilize to enhance their own selling environment. Besides the obvious benefits to the store in offering its own credit, the store makes the customer feel special because of owning a personal credit card. Some stores offer two levels of credit—a regular charge and a preferred charge for those customers meeting higher criteria.

The department store employs many credit promotion strategies to promote store credit. Services range from instant credit, which allows a customer to open an account within a matter of minutes, to pre-approved credit. When credit is pre-approved, a customer is sent an invitation to open a charge account by simply signing her or his name.

Department stores may also distinguish themselves by their involvement in community affairs. The corporation generally supports a major charity. The branch stores honor local charities, arts, or civic organizations through special events hosted by each location.

The retailer of today understands the importance of positioning within the marketplace. By providing high levels of customer service and other selling enhancements, the department store can distinguish itself from its rivals and maintain its competitive edge.

Learning Objectives

Upon completing this chapter you should be able to:

1. List the four major determinants of a retailer's promotional activities mix.
2. Discuss the three major types of retail promotional activities.
3. Name at least ten nonpersonal sales promotion activities.
4. State why personal selling is a key promotional device in all service-oriented retail stores.
5. Explain sales personnel budgeting.
6. Differentiate between image-enhancing and primary-income retail services.
7. Name six image-enhancing services.
8. Name six primary-income services.

Like advertising and visual merchandising, promotional, sales, and service strategies are vitally important to profit because they help retailers to attract and retain customers. Retailers who successfully employ these strategies often outperform both direct and indirect competition. This is especially important at a time when there is little product differentiation and the buying public is very price conscious.

Although attracted by the various forms of advertising and visual presentation discussed in Chapters 16 and 17, customers may not move from square one unless the interest that has been aroused at the time of attraction is turned into desire and action. This can be accomplished by careful selection and use of promotional activities and services. They must suit the particular target market and must be cost effective for the times and the particular type of retail operation.

Today, little difference exists between sales promotion activities and services in department stores (except perhaps for salespeople) and sales promotion and services at the mass merchants. Discounting in its infancy offered hardly any services beyond checkout personnel and in-store signs. Promotional activities were confined to newspaper advertising. As the years passed and price competition from department, specialty, and the national chain stores diluted the market, discount retailers began to take notice of all of the elements in the retail promotion mix—sales promotion activities, personal selling, and the service mix.

SALES PROMOTION ACTIVITIES

The list of sales promotion activities can be as long as the imagination of the most creative retailer. It may even include publicity and point-of-purchase displays, which are usually discussed along with advertising and visual merchandising. Both will be included here, however, because, as with most promotional activities, they are designed to stimulate consumer purchasing. A few retailers offer gifts, prizes, or even print messages in the sky to get attention. Most, however, count on the ten major types of retail sales promotion activities to attract and keep their customers.

Promotion changes with the market, the competition, and the stage of the retailer's life cycle. Very few supermarkets give away trading stamps, but in the 1950s Green, Gold Bond, Plaid, and other stamps were a successful promotional device that often drew customers into a particular store. Saving stamp books was the only way some people could acquire luxuries they could not afford after paying for their homes and cars and buying food and clothing for the family.

Publicity. Publicity is any form of nonpaid, commercially significant news or editorial comment about ideas, products, or institutions.[1] Some retailers hire public relations specialists or staff publicists in order to get as much publicity as possible. Typical coverage can be found in *Women's Wear Daily,* whose reporters appear at events such as store openings or fashion shows. To enhance a store's image, publicity must be current, credible, and newsworthy. It also helps if the story is dramatic and has human interest.

Point-of-purchase promotions. In-store displays are designed to increase sales. They remind customers about shelf items, stimulate impulse buying, encourage self-service, and best of all, reduce retailers' promotion costs because they are furnished by the supplier of the product being promoted. (See Figure 18.1 on page 472.)

Coupons. Consumers clip coupons from magazines and newspapers, receive them in the mail, or find them on product packages. They use them to get a price reduction on specific items. Couponing is big business, and many supermarkets have bins for coupon exchange between customers. The bins encourage customers to visit the store in search of coupons they can use. Some supermarkets even have on-site computers that dispense coupons. Consumers saved $1.7 billion through coupons in 1983, while retailers received $390 million for handling redeemed

---

[1] James F. Engel, Hugh G. Wales, and Martin R. Warshaw, *Promotional Strategy* (Homewood, Ill.: Irwin, 1971), 3.

FROM THE FIELD

Public Relations at Gimbels

Media coverage of a planned store event can mean the difference between a so-so and an outstanding result. Just how should you use PR as a marketing tool to support major promotional efforts? Some illustrations were presented by Roy Boutillier, senior vice president of marketing for Gimbels Midwest, at the 63rd Annual Sales Promotion/Marketing Conference and Business Equipment Exposition of the National Retail Merchants Association.

"Getting the press involved is a good marketing tool that isn't being used quite the way it could be in a lot of stores. Without spending a great deal of money, if PR is used correctly you can have an edge over your competition," Boutillier said.

One example of a success that the marketing man scored for Gimbels was having Daniel J. Travanti, star of television's "Hill Street Blues," appear at an Opera Guild benefit party, sponsored by the store concurrently with a total renovation of its Hilldale branch in Madison. Travanti was to be in the state capital visiting his alma mater, the University of Wisconsin. The store offered scholarships in his name, and the appearance deal was struck. Boutillier exclaims, "The press out of that was incredible!"

In another instance, Boutillier participated in the production of a show for Liberace that seated 16,000 to tie in with a four-city-block mall.

When the store decided to give away its entire inventory of Cabbage Patch dolls (60) rather than sell them, it was included in a cover story by *Newsweek.* Boutillier said, "We're still getting letters from all over the country on that. The press is there as a consumer if you have interesting, exciting ideas for it."

Source: "Using PR As a Marketing Tool," *Stores,* May 1984, 19. Reprinted with permission from *STORES* Magazine, © 1984 National Retail Merchants Association.

coupons. The total value of coupons distributed that year was $143 billion.[2]

Sampling. Sampling places the product in the customer's hands. This is effective because the customer whose senses are aroused—for example, the sense of smell by perfume, taste by chicken, or touch by facial tissue—often purchases the item on impulse.

[2] Lisa Belkin, "Hunting Buyers with Coupon Promotions," *The New York Times,* January 26, 1985, 44; and "Coupons," *Progressive Grocer,* September 1984, 186, 188.

Figure 18.1   Point-of-Purchase Display

Source: Courtesy of Great State Beverages.

Contest/sweepstakes. Contests and sweepstakes are similar yet different. In a contest the customer must demonstrate some skill in order to win, while participation is all that is required to win a sweepstakes. Both are used to attract and keep customers through participation in events that could lead to large rewards.

Giveaways. Pens, calendars, shopping bags, or matchbooks imprinted with the retailer's name are given away to shoppers, who carry them to their homes or businesses. They become visible reminders of the store to all who see them.

Demonstrations. Demonstrations of products or services in retail stores attract potential purchasers from among customers in the store. Cosmeticians representing a cosmetic manufacturer draw large crowds when demonstrating how to apply new makeup. The smell of frying sausage and the taste of a sample cause many nonusers to buy a package when it is being cooked in front of them.

Shelfvision

Shelfvision is a permanent shelf-talker system developed by Marketplace Communications Corporation, Portland, Ore. The system delivers the added sales associated with point-of-purchase advertising while overcoming the problems of traditional shelf talkers, which are viewed as "a legendary pain in the neck," according to the company.

"While traditional shelf talkers are recognized as a very effective advertising tool, they have always been a problem for both the store manager and the manufacturer," noted Charles H. Boggess, president of Marketplace Communications. "They generally don't stay up. Most get knocked off by inside store stockers, customers, or competitors."

Shelfvision debuted in the 2,000-store Safeway chain in August 1985. Advertisers and retailers really began to take notice after a three-month test of the system's effectiveness. The test in Denver and Seattle, involving 25 stores with Shelfvision and 25 control stores without any shelf talkers, showed an incremental sales gain of 1.5 to 24 percent with Shelfvision. The average gain was 8.6 percent.

Retailers and manufacturers alike find those figures appealing, but an added benefit for the stores is a share of ad revenues from Shelfvision, Boggess said. Up to 60 product categories can be accommodated. Advertisers receive category exclusivity. Coca-Cola already is aboard, so Pepsi, Seven-Up, Hires, and other soft drinks are frozen out.

Signs are placed directly below the products they advertise (signs for products stocked on the bottom shelf go above), and the swivel-hinged frame that holds the ad extends into the aisle and is almost impossible to remove. Field representatives of RGIS/Marketing Force, Rochester, Minn., maintain the units, visiting stores once each four weeks.

Advertisers are required to provide new copy every four weeks so ads remain clean and fresh. The 4½-inch by 7-inch ads are visible from about 5 feet. "They're not so obtrusive that they clutter up a retailer's store," Boggess said.

Based on the number of shoppers who see the ads, Shelfvision provides a very competitive cost per million (CPM) of 18 cents. Boggess compared that to Actmedia's 85 cents to $1.05 CPM for shopping card ads or a typical $5 CPM cost for a daytime television spot ad.

A&P demonstrated the value of shelf talkers in a late 1960s study that showed product movement increases of up to 244 percent, Boggess said, and the more than 1,000 A&P stores became part of the Shelfvision network in February 1986. Other participating chains include Waldbaum's, Cristedes, Big V stores, and Grand Central stores in the New York area.

National advertisers in the program include Campbell Soup, Chesebrough Ponds, Lever Brothers, and Allen Products, maker of Alpo dog food. (See Figure 18.2.)

Source: Excerpted from "Permanent Shelf-Talker System Eliminates 'Hassle' of Displays," *Marketing News*, April 1986, 14. Reprinted with permission from *Marketing News*, published by the American Marketing Association.

Figure   18.2   Shelfvision in a Supermarket

Shelfvision is a permanent shelf-talker system in supermarkets, drugstores, and mass merchandising outlets.

Source: "Permanent Shelf-Talker System Eliminates 'Hassle' of Displays," *Marketing News*, April 11, 1986, 14. Reprinted with permission from *Marketing News*, published by the American Marketing Association.

Trading stamps. Popular in the 1950s and early 1960s, trading stamps have actually been around since 1896, when Sperry & Hutchinson (S&H) founded the industry. Highly cyclical, trading stamps have moved from one of the prime sales promotion tools of the 1950s and 1960s to near oblivion today. At the peak of trading stamp popularity, supermarkets were the biggest retail users, and they still are.

Premiums. Desirable items are offered to customers at substantially reduced prices or, in some instances, for free. The idea behind giving premiums is to generate immediate sales. A special 29-cent coloring book that a four-year-old can take home after lunch is often the deciding factor in selecting one fast-food retailer over another. When both mother and child are happy, repeat business is the result.

Special events. Fashion shows, art exhibits, holiday tie-ins, and celebrity appearances generate great consumer enthusiasm. The events promote the store as an institution whether they are held on site or off. Probably the best known example of a retailer-sponsored special event is the annual Macy's Thanksgiving Day Parade, viewed on television by people from coast to coast. Most of them have never visited Macy's Herald Square store. This parade has helped make Macy's name synonymous with the best in retailing. Special events draw crowds and are considered worthwhile by most retailers even though it is almost impossible to measure direct return on investment.

PERSONAL SELLING—A COMBINATION OF PROMOTION AND SERVICE

The most important element in a store's image may be its personnel, particularly those in a service capacity. From credit office clerks to alteration people, all employees who interact with customers face to face or on the phone have a tremendous influence on how customers perceive the store. No group has a greater impact than the sales force.

Personal selling can be viewed as both a form of sales promotion and as a service. Good salespeople move customers to the cash register and also give the kind of attention to potential purchasers that turns them into long-term loyal customers. To exert a positive influence on the behavior of customers, salespeople must of course be sales–service oriented.

At Miss Jackson's, a high-fashion specialty store in Tulsa, Oklahoma, 70 percent of the volume is believed to be generated in the fitting rooms, which the store calls presentation rooms. Miss Jackson's has 20 such rooms, none smaller than 9 feet by 11 feet, to accommodate and, most important, to pamper coveted patrons. The store's C.E.O. has explained, "A clerk does not sell $17,000 in an afternoon in a fitting room. In a presentation room, you sell. In a fitting room, you fit."[3]

Miss Jackson's C.E.O. believes that the key to selling in any fine specialty store is personalized service: "That's the difference between clerking and serving. Clerks are baggers and sackers. Servers keep black books that have the name, address, daughter's name, son's name, husband's name, husband's secretary's name, husband's private telephone line; a history. The shrewder the sales associate, the better history built, succinctly, quietly, secretly. The better history, the better business."[4]

The selling floor can be the key to productivity and profit for retailers who offer personal selling as part of their promotion mix. Retailers must plan for, recruit, train, and compensate salespeople with the same care they take in managing the other retail functions. Is productivity low because the help is insufficient for handling the traffic, because no one cares whether customers buy or not, or because salespeople simply do not know how to sell?

Planning the Sales Force

Walkout Statistics Numbers of store visitors who leave without making a purchase.

Planning human resources is not revolutionary; it is not even new. Covering the floor with enough salespeople during the hours of greatest demand is a concept as old as retailing itself. What is new is the idea of an actual budget, a scientific plan or blueprint for doing this. With high wage–cost ratios and high **walkout statistics** something is needed, and

---

[3] "Miss Jackson's' Building on Tradition," *Women's Wear Daily*, June 7, 1984, 19.
[4] Ibid.

Salesperson Scheduling at Adam, Meldrum & Anderson

Salespeople in three of Adam, Meldrum & Anderson's ten stores in and around Buffalo are, on average, ringing up $10.40 more per hour than they did two years ago. This has come about by their being scheduled, more closely than before, into the right places at the right times. There is, in other words, a more perfect matching of salesperson count to customer count in every sales floor location, every moment the stores are open. Salespeople relish this, with a "we come to play ball" spirit. Customers relish it, and tell management with purchases and letters. Management relishes it, for results show up both in tangible figures and in expressions of good will for the 120-year-old company.

A selling floor coverage program was installed in the downtown headquarters store and two branches by the Garr Corporation, Marietta, Ga. The first step in the Garr procedure is to count traffic passing through its density square—recording the count by half-hour segments each full day for a two-week period. Density square at the downtown store was a rectangle of the street floor encompassing its escalator terminals. In a branch store, the square might encompass the main floor's prin-

ciple aisle intersection. At each day's end, the count for each half-hour segment is percentaged against that day's total count, and a graph line is drawn. This graph line curve or profile for any given day, obtained from the density square, will be the same as would be obtained from any other area of that store. It will also be the same for any other same day (say, Thursday) of the year, except in weeks involving a holiday. On each day's graph sheet for each store is also plotted the number of salespeople actually on floor in each half-hour segment. Thus are given first hints as to actual correlation between customers' presence with salespersons' presence. The disparities revealed are almost invariably of an extent that amazes store management, as was the case at Adam, Meldrum & Anderson. (See Figure 18.3 on page 478.)

The next step in the program's preparation is dividing each store's total sales floor area into selling centers, adhering closely to departmental boundaries while also considering at-glance visibility. With data in hand from the half-hour segmented customer and salesperson counts, past and projected departmental sales figures, and trained observations, computer-aided experts in Garr's home office focus on each selling center in each store. They make preliminary note of what shiftings of salespeople, reassignments of lunch and break periods, and resettings of part-timers' arrivals and departures might result in better matching customers' presence (work load) with salespersons' presence (work force).

Of great importance before any changes are actually made, the idea and aims of the whole program are explained to the store's salespeople in a body. Each of them is given an individual lifestyle interview to make sure any reassignment does not adversely affect his or her established personal habits or family routine. These are then all painstakingly given consideration in a draft of a best-now-possible schedule for each selling center in each store.

While the best-now-possible schedule is being prepared, Garr's headquarters experts also start drafting an ideal schedule for each selling center of each store—a schedule to be implemented gradually through attrition.

Ideal scheduling calls for a basic staff force consisting of full-time regulars and part-time regulars given specific selling center assignments, and for an army of on-call contingents trained for cross-sell floating. A Garr-supplied hiring guide reveals special techniques for attracting both regular and short-hour people, and for holding their loyalty to the store.

Also woven into the ideal schedulings are these considerations:

- Required travel time from racks to fitting rooms, and from sales floors to stockrooms
- Hand motions required on registers

and for making out stock transfers
- The complexity/simplicity of such forms
- Varying work burdens in the selling of various items
- Nonselling responsibilities of salespeople

Starting with best-now-possible but ever heading into ideal, Garr's sales floor coverage schedules continually give management selling-cost and productivity standards for achieving profitable operation while assuring high standards of customer service.

Responsibility for meeting the standards that bring about benefits is assigned to a staff of selling service supervisors in each store. Each supervisor is assigned certain specific selling centers for direct coverage and, in a buddy system, each coordinates with others in the store as necessary for coverage through meals, breaks, unexpected customer surges, security episodes, and so on.

If a major imbalance of customers to salespeople is found in any selling center—say, more than three to one—the surveying supervisor investigates and takes action on the spot, while giving assurances to the unattended. Otherwise correctional questionings and helpful recommendations are held for a come-back visit or phone call.

Source: Extracted from Lewis A. Spalding, "Better Service," *Stores*, January 1984, 72–75. Reprinted with permission from *STORES* Magazine, © 1984 National Retail Merchants Association.

Figure   18.3

Example of Salespeople/Customer Matchups before and after Initiation of a Scheduling Program: Adam, Meldrum & Anderson Downtown Store

A—Customer count Mondays, Tuesdays, Wednesdays, Fridays.
B—Salespeople available for customer service before installation of the Garr program. Too many from store opening until 11:00 or 11:30. Too few from then until 2:00 or 2:30, with peak disparity at 12:30 or 1:00. Too many again from 1:00 until closing.
C—Salespeople available for customer service after installation of Garr program, under best-now-possible scheduling. The early-morning disparity has been almost perfectly corrected by rescheduling of start times and coffee breaks. Fairly good adjustment has been made for much of the midday period and for the afternoon hours.
D—Ideal (or goal) matching of salespeople available for customer service with customer count. This is to be realized as inevitable attrition permits new sales staff hirings on terms favorable to most effective scheduling, under the Garr program.

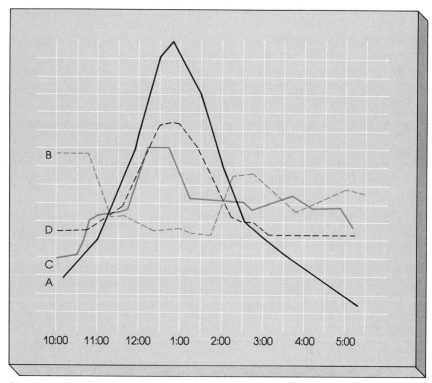

Source: Lewis A. Spalding, "Better Service," *Stores*, January 1984, 72–75. Reprinted with permission from *STORES* Magazine, © 1984 National Retail Merchants Association.

human resource budgeting could be the answer to low people productivity. The key to high people productivity for merchants is having the right people in the right place at the right time—right not only in terms of personality, aptitude, and interest, but right in terms of numbers—not too many on a slow Monday morning or too few on a busy Saturday afternoon. A properly planned sales force can be a retailer's greatest secret weapon.

Needs Analysis
A study to determine how much of a specific resource is required for a given purpose.

The first step in human resource budgeting is **needs analysis.** Statistics are gathered from previous years on the number and type of salespeople used in each selling area during each week of every season. These figures might even be broken down on a daily and hourly basis. The data is then compared to sales peaks and valleys in each of the same selling areas for the same time periods. From this a picture emerges that shows the existing relationship (if any) between sales volume and sales help.

Information about which areas are overstaffed, which are understaffed, and at which times becomes the basis for the human resource budget. The result of such a budget is the optimum use of salespeople, who can be peaked along with anticipated sales both in terms of numbers and qualifications. (See "From the Field: Salesperson Scheduling.")

The Selection Process

After planning, the next major task is to select salespeople, making sure that the right number and type are chosen and matched to the needs indicated in the human resource budget. Salespeople are selected by application, interview, and possibly personality and aptitude tests. Many retailers hire people with good selling skills, but the wrong personality. This almost guarantees failure. If tests are not used, an astute interviewer with an idea of what is needed to be a successful salesperson should be able to pick applicants with potential.

Training

In many retail establishments, titles such as sales associate or sales consultant are given to salespeople. These may help with orientation to the job, but title alone does not make an expert salesperson. The key is good training, as discussed in Chapter 5.

The corporate personnel manager for Mothercare U.S.A. has developed a unique training program for store employees that not only helps store managers train employees in the individual stores, but allows both employees and managers to enjoy the learning process. The program is illustrated in the Mothercare memorandum (Figure 18.4) and sales training cards (Figure 18.5).

Whether simple or sophisticated, training must go beyond the basic system because, to the customer, salespeople *are* the store. Part-time salespeople in branch and specialty stores have to have the same knowledge as full-time staff people, and their training, often neglected by management, is as important as training for full-timers. When customers are

Figure   18.4

Memorandum Introducing Sales Training Cards (Figure 18.5) to
Mothercare Managers

To: All Store Managers
      District Managers
      Regional Vice Presidents

Re: Sales Training Cards

Learning how to sell can really be a lot of fun! To prove it, we've developed Sales Training
Cards, which cover all the basic selling skills as well as the more difficult situations. Each
store will receive one package containing 36 training cards. Put these cards to use and see
just how much fun learning can be. Here's how they work:

PURPOSE

These cards are an excellent way to train new employees as well as reinforce the selling
skills of more experienced ones. Each card covers a different selling situation.

On the front of the card is a question regarding a specific selling situation. The back of
the card gives a preferred answer. However, you can use other approaches that have been
successful for you!

A "Remember" point is also included on the back of the card explaining Mothercare's
philosophy of customer service.

GENERAL RULES

Our selling situations are numbered by level of difficulty and frequency of occurrence.
Start with card No. 1 and work your way up to No. 36. Answer only a few at a time to retain
what you've learned. Put what you've learned into practice.

Each week review the cards you know, and add a few new ones. Progress at your own
pace. Have fun by using these cards as a tool to assist you in achieving greater sales.

Of course, customers always come first, so learn and review these cards only during slow
traffic times.

Managers can get a good "feel" of how well a candidate will be able to sell by using some
of these questions during their interviews.

So have fun while you learn. Here's just one game you can play, called sales pursuit. Or
be creative and create your own games.

SALES PURSUIT

Number of Players: One or More

Objective: To score the highest number of points by answering a selling situation correctly,
knowing the "Remember" point, and putting into practice what you have learned.

Gives correct answer	= Point value on front of card
Knows "remember" point	= Add 10 points
Uses selling approach on customer	= Add 25 points
Makes the sale	= Add 50 points

Penalty Points: To be subtracted from the score.

Salesperson waits longer than two minutes to acknowledge customer	= Lose 25 points
Salesperson uses "Can I help you?" as her opening approach	= Lose 10 points

Directions: Keep a separate score card on each employee. The daily, weekly, or monthly
winner would be the employee with the most points. Have fun while learning.

Source: Mothercare Stores Inc., 529 Fifth Avenue, New York, New York 10017.
Reprinted with permission.

Figure 18.5   Sales Training Cards Used at Mothercare

How do you approach a customer?

Greet her in a friendly manner: Say "Hi", "Hello" or "How are you". If she's **obviously** pregnant, ask her when her baby is due. When a child is present, greet him or her also and ask his or her name and age.

REMEMBER Treat every customer as an individual, and make her feel welcome in your store. Your customer should always come before **anything** you're doing.

mothercare.

A customer is returning an outfit and definitely wants her money back. What do you do?

"We will be glad to refund your money....I will call our manager. while you're waiting you might want to look at our new merchandise" (Ask her why she is returning the merchandise so you can help her make a better selection).

REMEMBER The suggestion of merchandise might interest the customer and turn the refund into a sale.

mothercare.

Source: Mothercare Stores Inc., 529 Fifth Avenue, New York, New York 10017. Reprinted with permission.

seeking help, they aren't interested in a person's work schedule, but they are interested in that person's knowledge of both the state-of-the-art and specific items. The same in-depth training has to be given to all salespeople if sales goals are to be realized. Proper training can lead to profit. A confident employee can sell, but confidence only comes with knowledge.

Brooks Fashions, the specialty apparel store chain, teaches salespeople two types of selling techniques: GET SALES and HUG. These are acronyms for:

G   Greet the customer
E   Engage in conversation
T   Tag-line promotion

S   Select items to try on
A   Accompany to fitting room
L   Leave customer in fitting room while you select other items to try on
E   End sale with a coat try-on
S   "So long and thanks for shopping Brooks!"

H   Highlights
U   Usage
G   Gratification

GET SALES is the basic routine for handling customers, and HUG is used when trying to sell a specific item.[5] Training techniques such as these give all retail salespeople (full- or part-time) the kind of confidence needed to make sales.

Profile of a Retail Salesperson

Salespeople are almost like counselors to their customers. That is the reason their appearance, product knowledge, and method of presentation of goods must match customers' expectations and taste level. One trait common to all successful salespeople is a superabundance of confidence in their own ability to sell. The following is a list of personal qualities of the ideal retail salesperson:

1. Attractive appearance; careful grooming aimed at the target market(s)
2. Enthusiasm for the selling process and the products/services to be sold
3. Product/service expertise
4. Good business etiquette that includes prompt, friendly attention to customers

[5] Theresa Caron, Internship Report, New Hampshire College, 1984.

5. A positive attitude and the ability to handle rejection
6. Expert oral communication skills including the knowledge of when to talk and when to listen
7. Adaptability to different customer types
8. Credible, sincere attitude

A successful salesperson can earn an excellent living. Salesmen in the men's suit departments of stores like Jordan Marsh, Woodward & Lothrop, Dayton Hudson, or Rich's often earn $500 a week. These salesmen have regular clients and, like other professionals, take care of their clients' needs on a continuing basis—calling them when new merchandise that seems to fit their image arrives in the store; ordering items not in stock; supervising fittings; and helping wives, family, or friends select gifts.

Because selling can be a very satisfying and financially rewarding job, some men and women elect to make sales their life's career. Others, willing to start at this level, see it as the first step along the road to becoming a buyer or merchandise manager. Another attainable goal for the salesperson is **entrepreneurship.** What better way is there to learn about the desires of a particular market than to sell to it? After a stint as a salesperson, the individual with management, financial, and merchandising skills is sure to be an excellent shopkeeper.

Entrepreneurship
Capacity to organize, own, manage, promote, and assume the risks of an organization, usually a small business enterprise.

Some people move from retail sales to selling in the channel, representing the producers whose merchandise they had formerly sold to the consumer. Having seen firsthand the customer's acceptance or rejection of particular items, these salespeople are of great value to vendors. When such representatives speak to retail buyers, they speak with authority.

The Selling Process

The seven steps in the retail selling process are (1) customer approach, (2) need determination, (3) presentation of merchandise, (4) overcoming objections, (5) closing the sale, (6) suggestion selling, and (7) postsale public relations.

Customer Approach

The salesperson asks, "May I help you?" The customer replies, "No, thank you, I'm just looking." If the salesperson continues to pursue the question, he or she will be considered pushy, and no one wants to buy from a pushy salesperson. As bad as this approach is, some retailers still tell salespeople to use it, probably because it requires little training.

The best approach is a greeting: "Hello, how are you today?" or "Good morning, please look around. I'm here to help you if you have any questions." A customer who appears confused by an array of stereo equipment might like to hear, "Please let me explain the difference between Brand A and Brand B, and then you will have a better understanding of each system." Regardless of the exact words, the greeting approach should make the customer feel welcome and should show a friendly interest in being of service.

A salesperson should be prompt in approaching each customer, even if only to indicate awareness of his or her presence. Nothing is as discouraging as waiting and waiting and waiting, finally giving up in vain and ending up as a walkout statistic. Proper training ensures a proper approach.

Need Determination

To determine a customer's needs, the salesperson must have a good understanding of consumer motivation. Many underlying, not necessarily obvious, reasons exist for the purchase of a sailboat or a pair of designer jeans. Even direct questions may not bring out the real reason, the one the salesperson must isolate. A combination of observation and questions, plus the ability to look beneath the outward image, will help a salesperson to determine his or her customer's needs.

Signature
Special rendering of a designer's name that provides quick recognition.

A middle-aged woman wearing a number of **signatures** is relatively easy for a salesperson to fathom, but what about the young career woman with more taste than money whose appearance belies her self-image? This is the challenge in determining needs. It requires patience, probing, and perseverance.

Merchandise Presentation

The salesperson must not confuse the customer. A famous cartoon shows a customer in a shoe department, surrounded by piles of shoes, pointing to one from pile A and one from pile B, and saying to the obviously frustrated and harried salesman, "I'll take those." Exaggerated perhaps, but such a situation could result from being faced with too many items to choose from at one time. The general rule is never to present more than three items at the same time. If a decision is not made from the three, remove the one that seems least desirable to the customer. (A need for good judgment and understanding of the customer's motivations is apparent here.) Bring the total back to three by adding an item. Continue to take away and add until it is obvious that one item is of more interest than the rest. The better the sales techniques, the quicker this will happen unless, of course, all of the merchandise is undesirable and poorly selected for the market.

Other rules for effective presentation are these:

- Know the location of the stock.
- Know the selling points of merchandise.

- Show, demonstrate, or describe how to use the merchandise.
- When it is feasible, place merchandise in a customer's hands or on his or her person.

Overcoming Objections

Objections
Reasons given by a customer for not purchasing an item presented by the salesperson.

An expert salesperson can often omit this step by presenting the merchandise effectively and stressing the selling points. If **objections** are overcome before they are even raised, the sale can be closed after Step 3. However, most customers have some sales resistance and ask questions that demand answers before they will agree to purchase.

Some customers have genuine objections; for example, the price of a refrigerator is too high or the shoulders of a suit are too padded. The salesperson with in-depth product knowledge can deal with these more easily than with objections such as, "I'm not sure my husband will like it" or "I really would buy it if it were available in another color." These are only excuses.

Objections can be met head-on and cast aside if the salesperson (1) does not argue with the customer, (2) anticipates the objections when presenting the merchandise and answers them before they can be raised, (3) shows respect for customers' opinions even while disagreeing with them, (4) offers tactful answers, and (5) does not belittle the competition.

Closing the Sale

Some salespeople seem to know instinctively when the time is right to conclude a transaction. For example, they realize that when a customer's interest keeps coming back to the same item, it is time to ask the questions that will lead to the close: "Will you charge this, or would you prefer to pay cash?" or "Will you take this with you now, or would you prefer to pick it up later?"

Salespeople also know that once all objections have been overcome, it is time to close. They can direct customers to this conclusion by physical maneuvers such as moving toward the register or even starting to wrap the merchandise.

Some salespeople are guilty of overkill. They keep on talking after they have said it all. This can raise new questions in the customer's mind and open up a closed issue, thus delaying or losing the sale. If the steps in selling are followed, the closing will come naturally. The more a person sells, the easier this becomes.

Suggestion Selling

A sale does not always end with the purchase of the one item the customer has originally requested. Customers can be led into multiple purchases by creative selling. For instance, before completing the transaction, the creative salesperson might suggest shoes and a handbag to go with a dress—or a shirt and a sweater with a skirt.

All retailers are interested in increasing sales volume in all classifications, yet many create barriers to multiple sales through their organizational structure and store layout. When a salesperson is not allowed to cross department lines, adding shoes, handbag, or jewelry to a dress sale is very difficult. Even if the suggestion is made to the customer that these items would enhance the dress and should be purchased, momentum is lost when the major purchase has been completed. Under these conditions, many customers leave the store without making a second or a third stop. The advantage of a specialty shop or department store boutique is that there are no lines to cross, and the salesperson in these situations has the freedom to help with the selection of additional items.

An obvious way of practicing suggestion selling in ready-to-wear is to bring additional merchandise into the fitting room. Salesmen in men's clothing stores have been employing this technique for years. The man who wanted only a sport coat when he entered the store often ends up with a sport coat, two pairs of slacks, a few shirts, and two or three ties. Busy executives appreciate this type of service because it saves time. Today many shoppers who have limited time not only appreciate suggestion selling; they expect it.

Postsale Goodwill

Every potential customer does not make a purchase even though the salesperson has devoted a great deal of time and expended a great deal of energy in the selling process. Regardless of the outcome, once the sale (or nonsale) is over, the customer should be left with a feeling of goodwill and a desire to return to the store.

Sincerity and a pleasant, friendly manner are prerequisites for success in selling. This is especially true at the conclusion of a sale. The last impression is the one that customers take with them. The memory of a smile and a friendly good-bye will often be the reason customers elect to return to one store instead of another.

There is no substitute for goodwill. When salespeople offer information about a store's return policy, gift wrapping, delivery, and other services at the conclusion of a sale, they are saying, "We care." Couple this with a genuine smile, and the result is sure to be postsale goodwill. (See Figure 18.6.)

Compensation

A paycheck is one of the most valuable forms of recognition a salesperson can receive. If salespeople are not satisfied with their earnings or potential earnings, they will not be productive. Without a productive

Figure   18.6   Thank-You Letter

Neiman-Marcus

Mrs. Howard Nelson
3365 W. Spring Dr.
Northbrook, Ill.
60062

Dear Mrs. Nelson,

It was a pleasure to be able to assist you with your
holiday shopping. I hope that your selections will
bring your family and friends pleasure.

Please accept my best wishes for a happy holiday season.
I look forward to seeing you again in the very near
future.

Sincerely,

Beth Anders
Accessories Department

5000 Northbrook Court
Northbrook, Illinois 60062
312 564 0300

Source: Courtesy of Neiman-Marcus.

staff, both sales and profit will fall and, even at minimum wage, an un-balanced wage–cost ratio is possible. Any compensation plan must consider both the employee and the employer, keeping both happy by allowing for satisfaction, productivity, and incentive. These five traditional plans for compensating salespeople were described in Chapter 5.

Straight salary. Straight salary is the most common method for compensating retail salespeople. An advantage is that it does not encourage overly aggressive sales tactics, because pay is based on service to the customer more than on sales volume. The disadvantage is the lack of incentive to do more than the minimum amount of work. Salespeople on straight salary may neglect customers.

FROM THE FIELD

New Interest in Commission Programs

Beth Davis, a tall, vivacious college graduate, speaks frankly in her Alabama lilt. "I've worked in stores with commission and without, and there's no question the customer gets better service with it. You help her and she helps you."

Davis is not alone in her attitude about commission selling in retailing. Her colleagues on the floor of a Parisian store in a Birmingham mall seem to come straight from the set of a chain store "Happy Days." The figures are astounding. "I did $225,000," says a salesman in men's wear. "I did $180,000," says a newcomer. A department manager says, "$320,000." In the 71,000 gross square feet of that store, these figures add up to $25 million in sales, or $352 per square foot, near the Parisian average. Three Parisian stores are "well over $400 a square foot and none less than $250," boasts Tom Amerman, Parisian's vice president of personnel. A few are reaching for the $500 mark. Parisian is five years into a commission program.

On a quest for higher productivity, many retailers are looking at results like these with great interest. "The industry is definitely moving toward incentives and rewards," says Tom Harms, director of human resources at J. L. Hudson. "It's absolutely necessary to improve productivity." The better department stores, in particular, are facing slower expansion just as the off-pricers are cutting into their flanks. Commissions may be one way to boost sales and solve the serious "clerk-versus-the enemy" customer service problem.

While commission selling lost popularity during the 1960s as stores turned to self-merchandising and slashed labor costs, several department and specialty stores have stuck with incentive systems with great success. Nordstrom uses commissions. So does Neiman-Marcus, one of the nation's premier department stores.

Not all commission systems are the same. They run from straight incentives to the team approach. But their evolution has piqued the industry.

Source: Excerpted from "With Commission Programs, Selling Is Its Own Reward," *Chain Store Age Executive*, March 1984, 29, 30. Reprinted by permission from *Chain Store Age Executive*. Copyright 1984 Lebhar-Friedman, 425 Park Avenue, New York, NY 10022.

Salary plus commission. Because the commission added to the straight salary is comparatively low (1 to 3 percent), the incentive does not cause intense rivalry. It is just enough to encourage more productivity on the part of the sales staff.

Straight commission. Straight commission is often paid to top salespeople if they sell high-ticket merchandise or have a following of loyal customers. Of all the compensation plans for salespeople, it offers the greatest incentive: the more merchandise sold, the greater the income. Straight commission also offers the most flexibility to both employer and employee because wages and costs are directly tied to productivity. One possible disadvantage is a highly competitive sales staff that pushes customers into buying merchandise, which will result in a high rate of returns and a negative feeling toward the company.

Quota bonus. A quota bonus compensation plan provides the stability of straight salary and the incentive of commission on a long- rather than short-term basis.

Sales supplements. To make room for new merchandise, management may pay push money (P.M.) to each person who sells an item from the old group. Retailers may hold contests in which customers select the most courteous or helpful salesperson on the staff. Votes are cast, and the winning salesperson receives cash, merchandise, or even a week at a resort. A specialty chain may hold a contest to stimulate sales in a particular classification in each of its stores and award a prize to the salesperson in each store who sells the greatest number of units.

THE SERVICE MIX

Service Mix
All services offered by a particular merchant.

Retailers offer two major types of services to their customers: (1) services that enhance either their merchandise or their image and (2) services that are sold. The goal of both elements of the **service mix** is the same—to increase customer satisfaction, sales, and profit.

Customers become more demanding as they achieve a higher standard of living and aspire to a better lifestyle. In order to meet their constantly increasing demands, competing retailers must offer a wide variety of services. The exclusive dress shop that advertises free alterations may have an advantage over the dress department of a competing specialty store where there is a charge for alterations. The retailer with an appliance service department will stay in business despite the somewhat lower prices at the discount house three blocks away. Customers flock to the general merchandise chain for help with tax returns or for stock market advice. While one retailer engages in conglomerate merchandising, another offers free delivery. Both realize the necessity of including service as a promotional strategy.

**Horizontal
Competition**
Competition
among firms at the
same level in the
distribution
channel.

**Vertical
Competition**
Competition
among firms at
different levels in
the distribution
channel, as when
suppliers compete
with the retailers
they supply.

Image-Enhancing Services

Today's retailer has to contend with both **horizontal competition** and
vertical competition. It comes from many sources—those who have an
identical mix, those whose mix of merchandise and/or services is totally
different, wholesalers selling at retail, and manufacturers' outlets stocked
with everything from fashion to furniture. Image-enhancing services can
make a difference.

The retailer must decide which of the many image-enhancing services
will help in reaching his or her specific goals. The first step, of course, is
to establish the goals. They may include:

1. Increasing utility. Examples are form utility (altering clothes to fit
   individual customers), time utility (offering credit to the customer
   who will not put off until tomorrow what he or she wants today),
   place utility (delivery of kitchen appliances at the customer's
   convenience), and possession utility (personal shoppers for busy
   professionals).
2. Increasing convenience. Examples might be in-store restaurants
   and restrooms.
3. Creating a desired image. This might mean few services, if the
   desired image is one of self-service and lower prices.

With goals in mind, the retailer must consider other determinants: type
and size of store, location, type of goods and services sold, service levels
of all competitors and, finally, both company financial and human resources.

Even after goals have been set and then looked at in relation to other
determinants, the selection of services is not an easy task. In general, the
six most important image-enhancing services are store hours, credit, delivery, alterations, repairs, and returns. Also, services that are essential
for one type of retailer may be nonessential for another.

Store Hours

Store hours are determined by the market. Many grocery stores are now
open 24 hours a day. Stores in suburban malls usually open at 9:30 or
10:00 a.m. and close at 9:30 or 10:00 p.m., Monday through Friday.
Saturday closings are usually 6:00 p.m. Sunday hours vary, depending
on community lifestyles and/or legal constraints.[6]

---

[6]"Blue laws" that exist in some states determine (1) whether Sunday openings are allowed,
(2) what types of products can be sold on Sunday (necessities versus nonnecessities), and
(3) when and how many hours stores can be open (for example, Sundays 1:00 to 6:00 p.m.).

Credit

Credit is a way of life for such a large majority of American consumers that, for most retailers, the only question concerns what types of credit to offer.[7] The four following types of basic credit plans are available.

1. *Open account.* This allows customers who hold a particular retailer's charge card to buy merchandise and/or services from that retailer and to pay for them within a specific time period without charges or interest. Usually this is within 30 days of the billing date; however, some retailers extend the due date to either 60 or 90 days, to promote special occasions or to distinguish their credit services from their competitors'. Beyond the due date, if full payment is not received, a finance charge can be assessed. Given the free nature of the service, retailers generally reduce both credit costs and risks by limiting open account credit to customers who have established records of good credit.

2. *Installment credit.* Installment credit is used by most customers buying large-ticket items such as automobiles, furniture, and appliances. The installment credit plan allows consumers to pay their total purchase price (less down payment plus interest charges) in equal installment payments over a specified time period. Usually, equal installment payments are due monthly, although weekly and quarterly payments are optional. Retailers prefer to receive a down payment on installment purchases that equals or exceeds the initial depreciation of the product. Some retailers require only a minimal down payment or no down payment at all in order to make the sale.

   Installment credit agreements are legal contracts between retailers and consumers. The terms and conditions of the contract include the total amount of each payment, the number of payments, and the dates the payments are due. In addition, the contract specifies what financial charges are being assessed (interest, service, insurance) and the penalties for late payment or nonpayment.

3. *Revolving credit.* This system incorporates some of the features of the open account and the installment plan. Several variations of revolving credit plans are used but two of the most common ones are the fixed-term and the option-term plans.

   The *fixed-term* revolving credit plan requires the customer to pay a fixed amount on any unpaid balance at regular scheduled intervals (usually monthly) until the amount is paid in full. Under

---

[7]The changes in federal tax legislation starting in 1987 will result in future changes in retail credit offerings.

this plan, customers have a credit limit, for example $500, and may make credit purchases up to this limit as long as they continue to pay the agreed-upon fixed payment (for example, $50) each month. (See Figure 18.7.)

The *option-term* revolving credit plan provides customers with basically two payment options. Customers can either pay the full amount of the bill within a specified number of days (typically 30 days) and avoid any finance charges or they can make at least a minimum payment and be assessed finance charges on the unpaid balance. Like the fixed-term account, a credit limit is established and customers are free to make purchases up to the established limits. (See Figure 18.7.)

4. *Universal credit cards.* As an alternative to offering in-store credit, many retailers accept one or more of the universal credit cards issued by outside institutions. (See Table 18.1.) The most common

Figure 18.7   Application for Revolving Credit: Fixed-Term and Option-Term

The Forecast Account is expressly designed to give you this choice: you may pay the full amount of your bill each month without incurring a finance charge; or, if you prefer, you may elect to pay 1/2, 1/3 or as little as 1/5 of your total balance each month. A small finance charge is added only in those months where you choose not to pay the balance in full. This is a marvelous opportunity to buy as much as you need during peak periods, such as back-to-school, Christmas, storewide sales — and have the convenience of gradual payment.

The Forecast Account is your easiest way to shop at Lord & Taylor by mail, phone or in person. There's no need to carry extra cash, never any waiting for change. Your monthly statement serves as an important, permanent record for all purchases.

Lord & Taylor cordially invites you

to open a Charge Account

Source: Courtesy of Lord & Taylor.

▆ ▁▁

Table 18.1   Universal Credit Cards

Advantages for Retailers	Disadvantages for Retailers
1. No need to establish and maintain a credit department.	1. Costs of the service can be prohibitive.
2. No need to become involved in investigating credit applications, billing customers, and pursuing collections.	2. Depersonalization of the relationship between retailer and customers.
3. Broader customer base. Credit can be offered to consumers who otherwise would not qualify, such as out-of-towners.	3. Reduced store loyalty. Customers can shop anywhere the card is accepted.
4. Steady cash flow. Financial institutions convert credit card sales quickly and regularly into cash minus agreed-upon service charges.	4. Reduced sense of belonging. Consumers no longer have a personal account with the store.

types of credit cards are those issued by banks (MasterCard and VISA) and credit card companies (American Express, Diner's Club, and Carte Blanche). Gasoline companies also issue credit cards that consumers can use at stations carrying their brands or brands of other companies with whom they have an agreement. (See Figure 18.8.)

Delivery

Delivery must be geared to the market, the merchandise mix, and the method of distribution the retailer employs. Customers who shop in an urban flagship store and use public transportation cannot possibly take a new VCR or microwave oven with them. Those who drive to a nearby regional mall and buy the same VCR or microwave oven in one of the company's branch stores can easily place the items in their cars. The fact that not all customers require delivery becomes a major determinant when retailers make a decision concerning the extent of their delivery services. Stores that sell major appliances and furniture must offer delivery, as must catalog/mail/telephone order merchants.

The two basic types of delivery systems a retailer may elect to use are in-store and independent.

Cooperative Delivery System
A delivery system owned and used jointly by several retailers.

An in-store (wholly owned) system has the advantages of control, flexibility in adjusting to customer's needs, vehicle personalization (advertising value), and store-trained personnel. It also has one major disadvantage—expense. Some retailers, because they prefer a private system but cannot handle the expense, form a **cooperative delivery system** in which each member–retailer shares the total services and costs.

Figure   18.8   Application for a Universal Credit Card

Source: Courtesy of American Express Travel Related Services Company, Inc.

Independent systems are owned and operated independently from any one retailer (or any one group of retailers). They either offer their services on a contractual basis (consolidated systems) or are open to the general public (parcel post and express services). Consolidated delivery systems deliver a store's packages for a fee based on the number, size, weight, and handling characteristics of the packages. A consolidated operator picks up the store's packages on a regular schedule, takes the

Consolidated Delivery System
Independent delivery system that works for a number of retailers on a regular schedule set by contract.

packages to a central facility where they are sorted to facilitate efficient routing, and delivers the packages to customers on a specific time schedule. Most **consolidated delivery systems** perform C.O.D. functions, make callbacks, and assume full liability for packages that are damaged or lost.

Express and parcel post delivery systems such as United Parcel Service (UPS) serve the needs of the general public. As an alternative, retailers resort to these systems when the delivery destination lies outside of their delivery service area. Retailers often use express and parcel post to deliver goods ordered by mail and telephone.

Alterations

Alterations are offered by many retailers, in some cases as a supplement to the sale of certain products (men's suits) and in others as a revenue service (alteration fee for women's apparel).

Repairs

Retailers usually charge for repairs of durable merchandise they have sold unless the product is under warranty by the manufacturer. As with a delivery system, repair service can be in-store or independent, and the same advantages and disadvantages exist.

Returns/Complaints

All retailers—whether they offer minimum service or full service—must have a system for handling customer complaints and returned merchandise. Not to have one is almost like proclaiming, "We are a perfect store, with perfect buyers, perfect goods, and perfect service," which could not be lived up to and would certainly present a negative image. A return/complaint service is therefore essential even if the Consumer Rights Act of 1962 had not identified four basic consumer rights—the right to safety, the right to be informed, the right to choose, and the right to be heard.

How a retailer handles a customer's complaint or return can often be more important to the customer than the solution. A sincere willingness to listen and help goes a long way in retaining the goodwill and future business of someone who has come to the store for a negative purpose.

Other Image-Enhancing Services

In addition to the six image-enhancing services described, others may include gift wrapping (free or for a fee), parking (free or for a fee), valet parking, restrooms, child-care facilities, pay telephones, layaway plans, a bridal registry, fur storage, and personal shopping.

FROM THE FIELD

Appointment Shopping at Kabachnick

Terri Kabachnick, president and part owner of a specialty store in Middletown, Conn., is doing so well with appointment shopping that she expects 80 percent of her business will be geared to this Executive Express Service in three years.

She started the service three years ago in Kabachnick, a store founded in 1961 by her husband, Phil, and Harold Reibman, because many customers were confused about styles, colors, and other details, or had limited shopping time. Many of these women were secretaries, bank tellers, or junior executives. Ten percent were senior executives. Others were housewives.

An initial interview lasts about one and a half hours. Each woman fills out a questionnaire designed to elicit "lifestyle audits and fashion and physical profiles." A more lengthy second session is devoted to testing cosmetics selected by one of the three image consultants, after which the woman is escorted to one of five 9-foot by 10-foot fitting rooms. There, a suggested wardrobe is waiting for her. All the merchandise is from regular stock. Details of the transaction are computerized for future reference.

Upon request, a limousine will take a woman from her home and back. Customers are also pampered with a special lounge for lunch, drinks, and television viewing, and with a white terry-cloth robe to make them comfortable in the fitting room. Women who wish to come in before or after normal store hours or on Sunday are likewise indulged. A quarterly newsletter is published. Members pay $50 a year.

Most customers are drawn by word of mouth. The service runs two major ads a year in local newspapers and in the monthly *Connecticut* magazine. The ad budget represents from ½ to 1 percent of sales.

Terri Kabachnick reports that about 350 women spend an average of $1,500 in the fall and $800 in the spring plus an average of $200 on each of two visits in between.

The service's volume has grown in three years from zero to $500,000. Within a year, Terri Kabachnick plans to open a complete grooming salon in the store. She now has her own cosmetics and skin-care line called Terenia, her original given name. Another aim is to rent space in shopping centers or office buildings in other Connecticut cities to expedite the service. In October 1984 she began actively enrolling franchises. The first two were Sheila, of Boise, Idaho, and Green's, Middletown, N.Y.

Kabachnick has a total of 68 employees, most of them part-timers, about half in sales. Five buyers are under a general merchandise manager. Total sales have risen in the past three years from $3 million to $4 million.

Source: Excerpted from Samuel Feinberg, "From Where I Sit," *Women's Wear Daily*, May 17, 1985.

Most retailers agree that a service mix is necessary and that good management must include a customer satisfaction management system. They do not agree on details. In 1985, Gimbels Midwest redefined customer service with a CARE (customers are really everything) program. This service strategy increased sales and gave Gimbels a competitive edge in a highly competitive market. At the 1986 meeting of the National Retail Merchants Association, Walter K. Levy, president of Walter K. Levy Associates, reported on a nationwide survey of 2,045 women and major retailers. It showed that although improved service is being used by many stores as a way to build a distinct company image, the consumer is not overly concerned with improved service.

Primary-Income Services

In the retail world of today, Sears is quickly becoming an important source for financial service as well as for appliances, and many retail malls have H & R Block as a tenant. Conglomerate merchandising was defined earlier as a mix of unrelated goods and services sold under one roof. That roof might cover a Sears or J. C. Penney store or it might cover a shopping mall where one store sells men's apparel and another repairs shoes. It might cover a European hypermarket or a K mart. The setting is less important than the concept. Service stores and service departments today are producing as much income for their owners as product retailing, and the added benefit is—no inventory!

Retailing during the final decade of the 20th century will be characterized as much by the selling of services as by the sale of products. Total sales will increase. Consumers will be purchasing more and more services and will be drawn to retail centers that offer one-stop shopping for goods and all types of services, whether image enhancing or to produce direct income. Some primary income services to look for are dry cleaning, shoe/jewelry repair, financial advice, insurance, stock/bonds, tax returns, mail service, fitness centers, diet centers, electronic banking services, restaurants, and beauty salons.

Summary

Promotional activities are a necessary component of the retail marketing mix, but how many and which ones selected depends to a great extent on the stage of the particular retailer's life cycle, the market sought, the type of operation, and the competition. The retail promotion mix consists of (1) sales promotion (nonpersonal promotions), (2) personal selling, and (3) the service mix.

Nonpersonal sales promotion includes a variety of activities and events, the most common ones being publicity, point-of-purchase displays, couponing, sampling, contests, sweepstakes, giveaways, demonstrations, trading stamps, premiums, and special events such as parades, fashion shows, or arts and crafts exhibits.

The most important element in the retail image is almost universally believed to be personnel, especially sales personnel. As a result, personal selling becomes a key promotional device in all service-oriented retail stores. Salespeople must be planned for, recruited, trained, and compensated with great care whether they are full time or part time. Shoppers are not aware of, nor are they interested in, the working hours of the person helping them select merchandise. Many retailers pay too little attention to the needs of their part-timers, who in turn, pay too little attention to the needs of the customers they serve.

The service mix includes both image-enhancing and primary income services. There is only a fine line between the two. Image-enhancing services may include store hours geared to the market, a variety of credit plans, delivery, alterations and repairs, returns and complaints, gift wrapping, parking, restrooms, child-care facilities, layaway plans, pay telephones, a bridal registry, fur storage, and personal shopping. Included in the primary-income category are dry cleaning services, shoe and jewelry repair service, financial services, tax return service, insurance, stocks/bonds, maid service, on-premises restaurants and beauty salons, fitness and diet centers, and electronic banking.

As an affluent buying public becomes more demanding, retailers will probably add more services to their total mix and, at the same time, eliminate those that are no longer relevant. The many faces of retail promotion may change in the years ahead, but one thing is certain: As long as there is a retail industry, there will be a retail promotion mix.

Questions for Review

1. List the three major types of retail promotional activities.
2. Name at least ten nonpersonal sales promotion activities.
3. Why is personal selling considered a key promotional device?
4. List at least five personal qualities of the ideal retail salesperson.
5. List the seven steps in the retail selling process.
6. Name at least six image-enhancing services.
7. Name at least six primary-income services.

CASE STUDY

Chase's Furniture Store

Evaluation of Selling Personnel

Ben Chase began to look over the reports that were the basis for the yearly evaluation of his staff, a practice started by his father Ben, Sr., the first year he opened Chase's.

Ben, Sr., had known that one of the best promotional devices available to any specialty retailer is a good sales staff. Because of this he had always paid particular attention to the hiring, training, and evaluation of every employee. He knew that whether or not customers left Chase's with merchandise, they did leave with an impression of the store. This impression would come to mind when future purchases were being considered.

Comments like these were typical over the years: "Chase's is a nice place to shop because the salespeople are always so pleasant. . . . You can always count on getting advice from the sales staff. . . . The salespeople really "know their stuff" and are never pushy. . . . I was treated with great courtesy even though I did not find exactly what I was looking for. It's the first place I intend to look the next time I am in the market for furniture."

The people who worked at Chase's were loyal and happy. Their employer cared about them and treated them as individuals rather than as mindless clerks. They were given periodic salesmanship sessions, and sales techniques were constantly being updated. As a result, yearly evaluations were usually very good. This meant increased pay. In such an atmosphere there could be no doubt about salespeople earning their wages although, on occasion, a poor performer did surface. When this happened, the individual was given every chance to become a better salesperson and was terminated only when all else failed.

Ben, Sr., had always evaluated his employees by the observation method. From his balcony office he could observe without being observed. Because his criticism was always constructive, no one felt spied on. In fact, when he himself handled a transaction he always discussed the sale, at its conclusion, with the salesperson nearest to him, asking, "Was there anything I should have done to improve my salesmanship?"

Ben, Jr., had learned the value of personal selling from his father. When he took over the business, he had tried to use his father's simple method of evaluating the floor personnel. When he became too busy, he had hired an outside agency that sent "shoppers" to Chase's on a bimonthly basis. Each year every salesperson was observed once or twice. Ben, Jr., used the agency reports as the basis for his evaluations.

Ben, Jr., picked up the reports on three salespersons hired in the current year. The way new people handle themselves is of utmost concern. These reports, written by the "shopper," recreated the actual scene.

Salesperson 1, Johnathan Curtis

(Shopper, a conservatively dressed woman about 50, approached Johnathan Curtis, who was standing just to the right of the main door.)

Shopper: Could you help me please: I am in a terrible hurry.

Curtis: Certainly, madam, what can I do for you?

Shopper: Our daughter is paying us an unexpected visit and we don't own a crib.

Curtis: How old *is* your daughter?

Shopper: Oh, the crib is for our grandson, her little boy. He is three years old.

Curtis: And he *still* sleeps in a crib?

Shopper: Yes he does! However, I am not here to discuss his sleeping habits. I came to see if I could purchase an inexpensive crib so that we can have it on hand whenever they visit in the future.

Curtis: What did you do when they visited in the past?

Shopper: Well, I recently gave away an old crib that I had in the attic for years. We did use that.

Curtis: Don't you really think you'd be better off with an extra bed? After all, at three years old he should be sleeping in a bed.

Shopper: Really young man, I don't think it's any of your business where my grandson sleeps. I came here for a crib, not advice on child rearing.

Curtis: Don't get upset, I only thought that a bed might be more practical. If you want a crib, I'll show you a crib, although I think it's a waste of your money. (He starts to direct the woman toward the back of the store.)

Shopper: I told you and I'll tell you again, I want a crib, not advice!

Curtis: OK, OK, lady. I'll sell you anything you want. I make the same salary whatever I sell.

Shopper: Young man, *you* are very rude. Chase's is not the *only* furniture store in town and I don't have to stay here and be patronized.

Curtis: I'm sorry, ma'am, but how can I help you if you won't listen to me?

Shopper: *I* should listen to *you*? You are the one who is supposed to listen to *me,* and I said I wanted to look at cribs. Now are you going to show me the cribs or shall I leave?

Curtis: Right this way, madam. Far be it from me to interfere with a grandmother's desires. (He turns around just in time to see the woman hurrying toward the front door.)

Salesperson 2, Jane Murphy

(Shopper, a well-dressed woman in her late 20s, was inspecting some pillows stacked on floor-to-ceiling shelves in a corner of the first floor.)

Murphy: Aren't those lovely pillows? You know, we have the best selection in town.

Shopper: Yes, they are attractive.

Murphy: Just what kind of pillows were you looking for? We have a wonderful collection of both casual and dressy types.

Shopper: Well, I wanted something for my sofa. I have a rather modern studio apartment with a large black leather sofa that opens into a bed, and I want something colorful, practical, and not too expensive.

Murphy: Did you have any special colors in mind?

Shopper: Just something bright.

Murphy: (picking up a large emerald green corduroy pillow from the first shelf) How about something like this?

Shopper: No, I don't think so.

Murphy: Would you prefer another color or fabric?

Shopper: I really don't know just what I want.

Murphy: How about the yellow burlap up there next to the beige group?

Shopper: Could I see it please?

Murphy: Certainly. (She climbs on a stool to reach one of the upper shelves and is just about to step down with the pillow.)

Shopper: No, I don't think so. It's too *yellow*.

Murphy: (still on stool) Let me take down a few different pillows and arrange them for you so you can get an idea of how a group would look.

Shopper: All right! What about that red one on the top shelf, the blue one just below it, and the plaid one with the fringe over there, next to the wall?

Murphy: (arranging the three pillows on a black sofa nearby) That's a handsome arrangement and should look great on your sofa.

Shopper: No, I don't like it.

Murphy: Would you like to try another combination? I'll be glad to take down any others that might appeal to you.

Shopper: Oh, all right, how about those pastels way up there?

Murphy: But I thought you wanted something bright?

Shopper: I'm not sure.

Murphy: (reaching for pastel pillows) How does this look?

Shopper: No, I don't like those.

Murphy: Why don't I leave you alone for a while so that you can really study the different groups?

Shopper: Oh, never mind, I'm only looking anyway.

Murphy: (surrounded by pillows) That's what we want you to do, so please don't leave. Look around and I'll be right over here if you need me.

Shopper: Maybe I'll come back another day. (turns to leave)

Murphy: Please do, Miss, and here's my card. I'll be glad to assist you whenever you return.

Salesperson 3, Jack Mattson

(Shopper, a man in his mid-30s, dressed in work clothes, was wandering among the kitchen sets.)

Mattson:	Can I help you?
Shopper:	I'm just looking.
Mattson:	OK.
Shopper:	How much is that table and chairs over there? (pointing to a glass and chrome table with chrome and brown chairs)
Mattson:	Oh, that's a very expensive set.
Shopper:	How much?
Mattson:	Wouldn't you prefer this maple set?
Shopper:	I'm really interested in that glass and chrome set. How much?
Mattson:	As I said, it's *very* expensive. I think you'd be better off with something a little cheaper.
Shopper:	(annoyed) Why don't you let me be the judge of what's too expensive and what isn't?
Mattson:	I just thought . . .
Shopper:	That I couldn't afford the glass and chrome set?
Mattson:	No sir, not at all. It's just that—well, you looked more like the maple type.
Shopper:	The maple type, hum? Just what is the maple type?
Mattson:	Look, let's forget the whole thing. The set you like is a great buy and I know you'll enjoy it.
Shopper:	It's a good thing I really like it, because after your remarks you're lucky I'm buying anything.
Mattson:	Then you'll take it?
Shopper:	Yes.
Mattson:	Would you please step over to the office so that I can complete the sale. Will this be cash or on installment?
Shopper:	Cash.
Mattson:	Fine, sir. And, sir, I really am sorry if I offended you. I guess I just wasn't thinking.
Shopper:	OK, OK. (He takes his wallet from his pocket.)

Questions

1. Devise a rating scale that could be used as the basis for personnel evaluation.
2. Using the scale developed in Question 1, rate each of the three salespeople at Chase's.
3. Analyze each of the three sales presentations in terms of the functions of retail salesmanship.
4. What is your opinion of the method of evaluation used by Ben, Jr.? Explain.

Part VII

The Future of Retailing

Chapter 19

Managing Retail Change

Managing Retail Change

Source: Jack Gifford, Professor of Marketing, Miami University of Ohio.

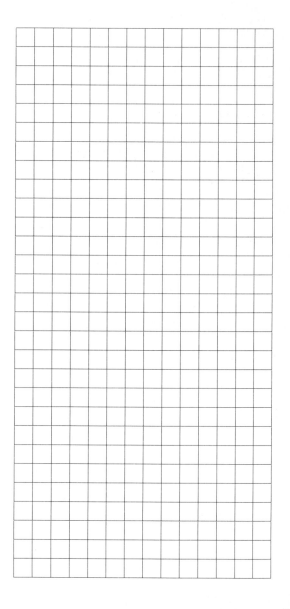

Industry Statement

Leon Gorman
President
L. L. Bean

Retailing, by its nature one of the most competitive industries in the United States, will become even more competitive in the years ahead. Rapid growth of general merchandise sales in the 1970s, exaggerated by high rates of inflation, caused an overabundance of retail square footage to be built. A study by the Marketing Science Institute of Cambridge, Mass., has concluded that "more than sufficient retail store space exists for the present and any reasonable population growth" and yet "plans for expansion continue." In contrast to this high-supply situation, M.S.I. projects a modest 2 to 3 percent real growth in retail sales through 1990.

Increased competition means more promotional pricing and reduced margins as retailers contend for the lowest price reputations. Product introductions multiply along with product obsolescence as retailers chase the ever-changing fashion trends or attempt to create demand with products of real or perceived technological improvements. Differentiation is difficult to achieve in our mass media society and competitive edges are difficult to maintain. Discount department stores are taking market share from the department store chains. Specialty stores are taking share from traditional department stores. Off-pricers and factory outlets are taking share from everyone. And always ready to take advantage of any exposed niche are the catalogers, whose own ambitious circulation plans compare with the excesses in retail square footage.

Changes in the supply side are compounded by several broad demographic trends. These include the social and economic transformation of American women, the higher education level of all consumers (the smart shopper), population shifts to the South and West and from urban to suburban, the aging of American society including the baby-boomer generation, the changing profile of families and households, the changing racial and ethnic characteristics of Americans, and the apparent disappearance of the middle class as economic groups divide into upper and lower income segments. The resulting proliferation of lifestyles and value systems is causing American consumers to significantly alter their traditional buying patterns.

Success in this changing environment requires constant innovation. Retailing is an incremental business and retail innovation means paying attention to the thousands of details and minor enhancements that add real value to product selections and customer services. There are few, if any, breakthroughs. Retailing is not a long-range process. The customers have a short-range buying horizon, and the retailer cannot get too far ahead or behind them. Being close to the customer is required, along with timely and flexible responses to their current and emerging needs.

Elements requiring continuous innovation for retail success include a product line of superior quality and functional or fashion value, one that is both differentiated and appropriate to specific customer segments; a highly efficient fulfillment system that adds value by delivering these products to customers when and where they want them at the lowest possible prices; sophisticated information systems for managing inventory and customer-oriented marketing techniques that clearly understand and communicate with the relevant market segments; highly motivated people who put the customer first and have a deep feeling for personal service; innovation and productivity that provide the ideas and profits for reinvestment in the future; and a profound sense of working for the common good, of balancing and advancing the composite interests of customers, employees, suppliers, shareholders, and community.

Learning Objectives

Upon completing this chapter you should be able to:

1. Predict two or three fundamental changes in consumer behavior.
2. List 16 technological changes possible by the year 2000.
3. Describe electronic banking, computer-based information systems, and electronic marketing.
4. Discuss some future changes in traditional retailing that will be based on future societal changes.
5. Discuss changes in the discount segment of retailing.
6. Explain the differences between supermarkets and superstores.
7. List eight trends in shopping center development.
8. Apply the basic principle of retailing to future retail strategy development.

Retail trends of the future, as in the past, will depend to a great extent on the external environment. The retail student and practitioner must adapt the fundamentals of retailing to society as it exists in every era. The basic principle of retailing does not change: Retail success requires the right merchandise or service at the right place, at the right time, at the right price, and in the right quantity. To apply the basic principle of retailing to the successful retail models of the future will be easier in some ways and more difficult in others.

Long-range planning in retailing is no different from long-range planning in any market-oriented industry. Before strategies can be developed, a thorough study of past and present facts, figures, principles, and theories must be undertaken and measured against external uncontrollable variables. Considering the dynamic nature of retailing and the changing value system in the marketplace, future projections have to be considered in the light of historical data. For that reason, the material in this final chapter is aimed at recycling old thinking and old values while pointing out new choices for the decades ahead.

PLANNING FOR THE FUTURE

A director, partner, and national service director for retailing at the accounting firm of Touche, Ross & Co. said in the mid-1980s:

In the next 30 years, many of the fundamentals of retailing will change because of changes in society, the consumer, and commerce in general.

First and foremost, the retail store will continue to be the dominant form for general merchandise distribution for at least 20 years, but the store of 2004 will be different. Retail forms will have to be structured to appeal to a highly informed, intelligent, short-of-time consumer. Customer bases will be in the home, workplace, and other public places that are not thought of as retail environments today. The consumer will be able to price-shop easily and gain the necessary product information in those classifications where marketing is done through brand identification.

The store of the future may concentrate its in-store merchandise

FROM THE FIELD

Predictions of Futurist Alvin Toffler

Civil War in Mexico, the return of a barter economy, and an era of personalized shopping were among the predictions futurist Alvin Toffler had for retailers attending a mid-1980s meeting of the National Retail Merchants Association. The author of *Future Shock* and *The Adaptive Corporation* said the telecommunications revolution has led to "the most important moment in retail history since the change of the century."

While Toffler's crystal ball did not have many specific visions of the retail future, it did contain concepts with retail implications. The era of the mass production society is ending in the demassified society, manufacturing will become much more customized, and shopping will be much more personalized.

Toffler said two retail experiments in Japan and in the United States fit into his demassified society theory. Electronic shopping services being developed allow a consumer through the telephone and television to shop for products. "By pushing the buttons, a consumer gets information and an electronic auction occurs. Eight manufacturers will bid for the business and there will be no standard pricing. It's a move that resembles the bargaining of the past."

In Japan, "fresh ladies" are saleswomen going door-to-door with consumer catalogs. The women not only dispense merchandise information but become a friend of the family and provide tips on nutrition, education, and other family needs. "It's a personalized experiment in which Japan is going back to the era of the peddler. I believe in less price-comparable inventory classifications while offering merchandise with relatively easy price comparisons through other mediums or not at all. It may also differentiate itself by services, adding some that have been dropped in the past or new services not contemplated today. These services will be matched to target customer groups, using the store's technology to direct promotional efforts.

Productivity is a second factor that will continue to be important. New methods and standards will meet the challenges of new retail forms.

As successful retailers grow across the country, today's overstored condition heightens. It is unlikely that this expansion and the resulting fierce competition it creates among already strong

---

both CompUcard and the Japanese fresh ladies are returns to the past made possible through high technology. They are dramatic expressions in demassifying distribution."

Toffler said that loneliness is the single biggest epidemic in U.S. society, and retailers that can address the problem in a store environment could enhance their business tremendously. Loneliness has become a problem because of the emphasis on individuality in America.

In trying to forecast the future, Toffler believes low probability predictions often have the greatest impact. In the mid-1970s, the Republican party was seemingly crushed by Watergate, and OPEC was wielding clout. The Bell System was intact, Latin America's economies were strong, and China was still closed to development.

Toffler's low probability predictions include a civil war in Mexico. "There has been low-grade terrorism in Mexico for some time but it has been kept under control. Could you imagine in the time of economic crisis if this ter-

rorism suddenly blossoms into a civil war? It would be like having Vietnam on our doorstep. We would have to send help before it spread over into Texas and California. The first national security priority of our government should be to make sure of the economic stability of Mexico."

Other Toffler low probability predictions include Iran obtaining nuclear weapons, the United States helping OPEC, the spread of neo-Nazism, and a Sino-Soviet rapprochement.

In the business world, Toffler foresees full-time employees becoming much less important, nepotism coming back out of the closet, whole families being hired as a work unit, and the barter economy expanding. He said there will be continued corporate upheavals, pointing to AT&T and Beatrice. "Many companies are going through radical reorganizations and it is no accident. It reflects the environment at large."

Source: Steve Ginsberg, "Alvin Toffler Warns Retailers That Huge Changes Are Coming," *Women's Wear Daily*, January 15, 1986, 16.

competitors will soon abate. The challenge will ultimately have to be the innovative and profitable redeployment of existing store space into new retail classifications or services or into other commercial uses.

The most threatening phenomenon may be the challenge to established retailers by the vertical integration of manufacturers and wholesalers as they use the easily reached customer population to expand their sales and profits.[1]

The Touche, Ross national service director for retailing also suggested the following responses:

1. Some form of joint ventureship with manufacturers or, perhaps, retailer-owned vertical integration in certain important merchandise categories.
2. Finding and hiring the best and brightest men and women and compensating them accordingly.
3. Staying current on technological advances, researching, studying, imagining, and experimenting with the changing tools, and adopting those that fit within plans for the particular company.
4. Providing training at all levels of an organization, as technology changes, to deal with the newly enlightened consumer and the changing environment.
5. Evaluating, changing, and streamlining management teams to deal with scientific management methods and plan and execute new strategies.[2]

TECHNOLOGY

In looking at the first decade of the 21st century, forecasters agree that the successful retailers will be risk takers and leaders who understand how to operate in the information age.

The points listed below describe what is possible after the year 2000:

1. At-home, listed networks will be commonplace.
2. Nonstore shopping will account for 20 to 25 percent of retail sales.
3. Buyers will have on-line, real-time information about inventories, rates of sales and lead times, and three-dimensional **holographic displays** that will enable them to select merchandise from distant points without buying trips.
4. The computer will prepare the merchandise mathematics and present suggestions based on manufacturers' databases. These will include visual images of available merchandise.

Holographic Displays
Three-dimensional pictures made without the use of a camera.

---

[1]Samuel Feinberg, "From Where I Sit," *Women's Wear Daily*, September 26, 1984, 15.
[2]Ibid.

5. The computer will access a public database with the latest economic projections for the particular goods, combine the data with visual information on manufacturers' offerings, suggest dollar and unit purchases, and highlight the previous year's winners and losers.

6. Merchandise managers will review each buyer's plans to determine not only the financial impact but also the influence on the store's image.

7. The computer will communicate information on the retailer's final plans to the manufacturing network, thereby shortening need and distribution lines and increasing inventory turns.

8. Basic and commodity buying decisions, such as on jeans and towels, will be made centrally, as will some selections of national brand and private label merchandise.

9. When a buyer wants to review open-to-buy status, he or she will talk to a computer that will recognize the voice, call up the merchandise plan and latest open-to-buy figures, and display three dimensionally the styles that have been moving. The buyer then will ask the computer to go into the purchasing process.

10. Advertising and promotion programs will be directed at specific consumer groups, sometimes at individual consumers through at-home or public access networks.

11. Ad and promotion staffs will sit at a telemarketing terminal with voice and photographic capabilities and describe to the computer the ad or promotion they want to run.

12. The retail inventory method will have given way to the unit cost method of calculating gross profit. The computer will be relied on to calculate or project results of store receipts, price changes, interstore transfers, and sales.

13. A customer will approach an apparel shopping service terminal and identify himself or herself by voice. The terminal will ask what assistance is required. Given a response, the computer will display several outfits three dimensionally on a mannequin. The customer will make a selection and the computer will tell where to find the items and suggest matching items. In a high-service store, the customer will be met by a salesperson with the merchandise.

14. The customer will have a wide choice of payment options, including old-fashioned cash. Financial institutions and retailers will have moved into each other's domains. New payment services will be available—payroll deductions, savings plans, and debits to stocks, bonds, and liquid assets.

15. Computers will also help improve the patterns, staffing and personnel functions, and the running of the physical plant.[3]

---

[3] Samuel Feinberg, "From Where I Sit," *Women's Wear Daily*, August 21, 1984, 10.

Electronic Banking

Automatic Teller Machine
A terminal located on or off bank premises that allows customers access to their accounts up to 24 hours a day.

Electronic banking, which involves the use of **automatic teller machines (ATMs)** and the instant processing of retail purchases, will increasingly be used in retailing. More customers than ever imagined during the 1980s will have the purchase price of an item automatically deducted from their bank accounts and entered into the retailer's account without cash changing hands. This will be accomplished as computer terminals are located not only in banks and shopping malls but in stores, airports, gas stations, and restaurants.

In spite of the great increase in electronic banking, individual store credit cards will still exist. Many people have the need to identify with their stores. Others feel secure only if they can control payment (review cancelled checks). These are the same type of consumers who need to squeeze the tomatoes when buying produce.

Cash Dispenser
A terminal located on or off bank premises that dispenses cash to customers and debits their accounts.

By the year 2000, electronic banking will increase cashless retailing but it will not do away with credit options in either the United States or in Europe. Automated teller machines, quick **cash dispensers (CDs), electronic fund transfers** at point of sale (EFT/POS), and terminals for teleshopping and telebanking are being promoted more by the banking industry than by retailing. Even so, paperless transactions will increase in importance when the technology is adequately developed.

Computer-Based Information Systems

Electronic Fund Transfers
Computerized systems that process financial transactions, exchanges, or information.

Executive decision making in the future will be supported by personal computers, large databases, computer networks, color graphics, and computer-based modeling, all of which should improve the quality of the process and the resulting decisions. Computer-based decision support systems (DSS) are already allowing retailers to review past performance, analyze alternatives, and project results if certain decisions are made. They are a combination of the evolutionary process in retail information systems and allow interaction between decision makers and the system.

Decision Support Systems
Evolutionary computer-based information systems that allow interaction between decision makers and the system.

The retail information system began with the accumulating cash register, moved on to electronic data processing (EDP), and then to management information systems (MIS). **Decision support systems** will become the next standard decision aids. They will be just as much a part of the retail management system as today's computerized checkouts, which instantly record and display sales, give customers detailed receipts, and store inventory information in the computer's memory bank.

Every January at the annual meeting of the National Retail Merchants Association, both large and small computer companies display new electronic point-of-sale systems that do everything from verify charge transactions to give instant sales figures. These systems become more sophisti-

Management Information Systems
Data processing systems designed to furnish current information to several levels of management for operational, decision-making, or objective-evaluation purposes.

cated each year and will eventually be an integral part of every retailer's computer-based **management information system.**

Electronic Marketing

Is a society where most homes have a terminal for buying merchandise or transferring money a futuristic dream or reality? Electronic shopping is already beginning to offer the retailer incremental sales, improved productivity, and higher net profit. In October 1983, the first commercial interactive videotex operation was launched in the greater Miami area as an at-home shopping service by Knight-Ridder Newspapers. At the same time two Melvin Simon centers in San Antonio, Texas, installed computerized mall directories, offering merchandise, weather, sports, and other information. Electronic marketing systems that will be an integral part of the future in retailing are videotex, teletext, and videodisc.

Videotex. A bundle of information available to subscribers through existing telephone or two-way cable television hookups, videotex is the dominant technology in the at-home market. It has a number of advantages over mail order procedures, one being that it can be updated quickly. Videotex includes text and graphic information, such as news, weather, sports, and airline flight times, as well as interactive shopping and banking. When the consumer selects shopping, a menu lists different types of shopping, brands, models, prices, and stores. If the viewer decides to buy, a charge card number is entered and the item is ordered. Videotex may be used for comparative shopping. Consumers using it to cross-reference brands, models, and prices can also compare ratings before making a decision.

Teletext. This system beams information similar to videotex over regular television airways or through special cable television networks. Teletext customers cannot reply directly to the service but can place orders over the phone.

Videodisc. This means of storing digital information on a disc looks much like a phonograph record. Up to 30 minutes of text-type information, photographs, and videotapes (including sound) can be stored on the same disc. Videodiscs are being used successfully to inform consumers about microcomputer hardware and software for high-tech products.

Merchandise types of particular interest to consumers in electronic selling are appliances, home furnishings, toys, sporting goods, electronic and photographic equipment, and luggage. A retailer with in-store terminals can offer 15,000 types of towels and sheets while having only

FROM THE FIELD

Electronic Marketing

Videotex has been called the marketer's dream come true. In concept it's efficient, it's fast, and it's the future. However, it has also been called a medium without a market, or worse, a failed experiment.

True, videotex has failed to deliver many of its early promises. On the other hand, a number of major companies see sufficient promise in videotex to invest what is estimated to be upward of $500 million in this emerging technology. They include IBM, CBS, and Sears through a company called Trinitex; Bank of America, AT&T, Chemical Bank, and Time Inc. through a company named Covidea.

Like other communications media, videotex can be used to inform, educate, entertain, and sell. Unlike many others, it can aggressively promote direct transactions and highly targeted, personalized communications. Because the computer can track what people are browsing, as well as what they are buying, extremely powerful marketing information can be gathered.

Here are some of the more important tools available today:

Electronic brochures and catalogs. Available from the services that provide color graphics and animation, electronic brochures and catalogs can be used in much the same way paper literature is used—with color illustrations of products or services, copy describing features and benefits, information about the company, and order forms.

With videotex, color and motion can be combined to create what is, in effect, a living brochure or catalog. In one example, the marketer illustrated a briefcase as it opened up. Prospects can see products built before their eyes or moved through space—the keyboard of a typewriter appears . . . then the body of the unit . . . then the operator who is using it. Water pulsates, lights blink. These capabilities engage and involve the user by giving life and vitality that only graphic electronic communication can give.

Product advertising. Some services allow you to create ads, complete with color graphics, 800-numbers, instructions, and information, to lead customers to select your electronic brochure or catalog to take action directly on the service. Ads can be run during different weeks of the year or tested head-to-head in different sections of the service during the same week.

Image building. Through what is called *sponsorship advertising,* or through quizzes and contests, advertisers can communicate image-related messages to a specific market. For example, by sponsoring a financial section on a service, every service subscriber who chooses to look at that section, 365 days a year, will receive a message or will see a logo. This subtle but powerful tool is available on most services.

Direct electronic mail. On many services, the marketer and the prospect can exchange messages. The marketer can send messages to classes of prospects or blanket all or part of the subscriber base with outbound electronic direct mail. Previous purchasers can be singled out for follow-up with what amounts to an electronic "bounce-back." Customers can also send a message: "If you are out of blue, send red" or "If I can't get my order by October 15, please cancel."

Calculators, interactive quizzes, and surveys. These are probably the most powerful, but least understood, capabilities of videotex. With so-called calculators, you can create an interactive quiz or questionnaire that allows the consumer to share personal information that is calculated by the sending computer. A computer program matches the answer to a preselected offer—depending on how the quiz turned out. You know what the individual prospect wants, needs, and feels because, through the calculator, the prospect has told you.

Research. Many services offer the marketer detailed research options. For example, response and nonresponse analyses can be made down to the individual family member level. Consumer attitudes toward your products and services, as well as toward electronic shopping, are monitored through telephone research and some focus groups.

Coupons, electronic surveys, direct ordering. Many new capabilities are in the planning stage. For example, with the increased capability of home computers to communicate and to print paper coupons, redeemable coupons can be transmitted over the phone lines into a subscriber's printer.

Consider the evolving role of the computer in direct marketing. Marketing intelligence is being gathered at a startling rate as a result of the continued lower cost of computer processing time. Direct marketers have been using computers for years, first for label production and list management, and later for computerized letters and tracking analysis.

Now, through videotex, the computer is becoming a new medium in its own right. Videotex is a way to examine what the future holds for all of us—computerized home, voice-activated command points, and electronic "life schedules" will be part of the electronic marketing revolution.

The innovators and those who adopt videotex may be the marketing giants of the 1990s and beyond. The cost is relatively low today, and the potential is truly enormous.

Source: Excerpted from Kathryn Moeller, "Electronic Marketing Is Here to Stay—and to Grow," *Marketing News,* March 14, 1986, 42–43. Reprinted by permission from *Marketing News,* published by the American Marketing Association.

1,000 styles and colors in the store itself. Retailers consider in-store terminals to be of value in high-service departments to support sales personnel who are inexperienced or decreased in number.[4]

Electronic marketing will become a more important means of selling goods and services to more and more customers. In the future, Sears, J. C. Penney, or Spiegel will very likely have a central database with a potential reach of millions of people. Teleshopping in the late 1980s was only one more alternative to in-store retailing. After the year 2000 it will have a much more profound effect on the industry.

INSTITUTIONAL CHANGES

Emerging Countries
Countries moving out of Third World status.

Many changes in both the type and nature of existing retail institutions will take place in the next few decades. Some may disappear through mergers, acquisitions, or bankruptcy, while others emerge and thrive. **Emerging countries** will need more retail institutions as they move into the economic mainstream. This will mean worldwide expansion opportunities for many established Western retail companies.

As in the past, the changing lifestyles of consumers and the influence of the external environment will have an impact on all institutions through which goods and services are sold. Nontraditional retailing should continue to grow as mail and telephone ordering through classic catalog operations keep pace with electronic retailing. (See Figure 19.1.)

Retailers must pare down their stores for profitability and sharpen up their marketing in order to survive the challenges of the coming years.

---

[4]Samuel Feinberg, "From Where I Sit," *Women's Wear Daily*, August 22, 1984.

Figure   19.1   Response to Catalog Customers

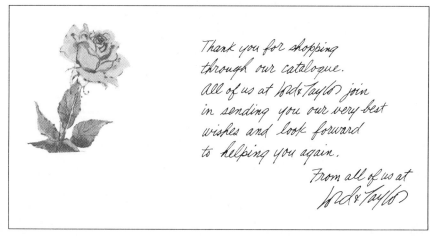

Source: Courtesy of Lord & Taylor.

They must think more in terms of profit than of volume, be more specific in targeting businesses, improve service, become bolder, and take more risks, while adopting a more enlightened attitude toward developing management talent.

Changes in Traditional Stores

On the traditional retail scene, high-tech tools will never completely replace the human element, although most stores of the future will use high technology to its full capacity. Computers may take over inventory control, sales tabulation, customer complaints, and regulation of lighting, heating, and telecommunication services. They may even be used for some advertising—videocassettes of designer shows, visual screens of projected photographs, and videotaped interviews with prominent designers or demonstrations of how to wear apparel. Yet high tech cannot possibly replace the joy of shopping, of finding surprises, of seeing what is new and exciting.

The biggest problems facing traditional department and specialty stores toward the end of the 20th century are overbuilding and underpricing. Profit margins will continue to be squeezed. The response from some stores may be a cutback in service and ambience and merchandise assortments that suffer from the sameness syndrome because buyers fear that straying too far from center will be too risky. If this continues, perhaps the broadly based department store carrying everything for everybody will be a thing of the past.

Price cutting, the number-one problem facing retailers during the 1980s, gets customers into the habit of expecting sales and thus waiting to buy goods at sale prices. If this continues, traditional stores could lose their image to discount merchants. This could mean the end of traditional stores because a fuzzy image will hurt market share.

Walter K. Levy, the retail consultant, has said of traditional retailers: "A willingness to break away from what they have always been doing will be critical. Department stores should enter a marketing phase [in which] they will introduce new private-label products and market them as national brands just like a Sears Diehard battery."[5]

The future will belong to department and specialty stores that offer service and are able to differentiate themselves from their competitors, present a strong identity, and concentrate either on a geographic market or a specialty.

Customer Segmentation

Customer segmentation will be one of the most important strategies of the 1990s and beyond. Consumers will be divided into categories by age,

---

[5]"Experts Say Stores Can't Rest on Laurels," *Women's Wear Daily,* January 13, 1986, 7.

income, sex, lifestyle, taste, and preferences. Products will be targeted at each group with great precision. Retailers of the future will target products much more narrowly—for example, to the female teenaged audiophile or the paperback book–oriented young male.

The big stores will rearrange their major departments and their goods. Some will have departments that cater to teenagers, young marrieds, working men and working women, successful career executives, and senior citizens. Within those groups, the products offered for sale will be targeted to different income levels and tastes.

Customer segmentation will go beyond focusing on maternity clothes, for example, which is fairly common today. The pregnant working woman might be the target of a separate shop in a department store. Segmentation will apply in all classifications. In a home electronics department, products may be broken down into subcategories distinctly aimed at three different groups: young people, men, and women. Within those categories, the intended uses of the products will be further broken down very specifically—for example, audio equipment bought exclusively for listening, equipment purchased as part of a general home decorating plan, or equipment for the professional who works from his home and uses it for business.

All retailers will not open up scores of distinct departments or even small separate shops, but most are expected to do so. The strategy for retail companies could very well be to divide and conquer and then subdivide their buying and even operations according to specific consumer groups.[6]

Entrepreneurship

There will be a resurgence of the entrepreneurial spirit and a movement away from the kind of large corporate management that is often completely unfamiliar with daily operations. A perfect example took place in 1986 with the leveraged buyout of R. H. Macy's by 300 members of its management group. They bought 20 percent of the company and, at this same time, sold its Midwest store division. By becoming owners, top managers have a real stake in Macy's success.

Changes in the Discount Segment

Discount retailers should continue to flourish, although those who try too hard to imitate department stores may lose out to those that stay with their low-price image. In addition to the old mass merchants such as Zayre, Caldor, and K mart, major department store groups are making a commitment to discounting. They believe that new discount divisions will provide them with a future in a large market segment. Penetration of

---

[6] Isadore Barmash, "What's New in Retailing," *The New York Times*, September 19, 1982, 23.

the department store into the mass merchant's market is growing in all merchandise categories and should be an important trend in the 1990s.

Some experts believe that warehouse-type operations have a great future. Home Depot, Price Club, Cub, and other food outlets all fall into this category. To open a warehouse-type operation in a former discount store, the drop ceiling is taken out, the vinyl tile is scraped off the floors, and a moderately nice store box is converted into a building that a shopper will believe is truly a warehouse. A warehouse conveys an impression of savings. Customers must go through some physical abuse in purchasing, for this is the way they believe that they are saving money. The question is, will warehouses stay warehouses?

To see the Price Clubs, the Home Depots, and Cubs of the 1990s, visit an upgraded local Levitz store. This company now offers decorator service. Delivery is commonplace; trailers and hitches are no longer available at the stores. Store hours are shorter. Satellite stores are operated without warehouses. Competition forced this change. Tomorrow it may well do the same thing to today's warehouse operations.[7]

Discount stores may have robots and computers to handle merchandise, and manufacturers may deal directly with computers that will actually buy goods. Computer terminals will distribute merchandise by special robot-driven carts or dollies. In the next century, high-tech will help the growing middle class to use its money more effectively.[8]

Packaged Goods Firms in Retailing

Smart packaged goods firms like General Mills and Pillsbury are using marketing research techniques to choose the right retail opportunities. During the mid-1980s, General Mills acquired Eddie Bauer and The Talbots as well as the LeeWards crafts-supply chain and Wallpapers To Go.

Packaged goods companies can bring to retailing the same marketing techniques used in selling cereal and flour. Planners and human resources people at these companies therefore view retailing as the direction of the future, one of the few growth areas still open to them, and perhaps a means of dealing with the consumer directly and efficiently. This has appeal to marketing-oriented companies capable of building a strong image among consumers.

From Supermarket to Superstore

In every city, food chains are gambling on huge emporiums to restore profits. From small local chains like Alexander's Supermarkets in Man-

[7] Robert Kahn, *Retailing Today* (Lafayette, Calif.: Robert Kahn & Associates, 1984), 2.
[8] Samuel Feinberg, "From Where I Sit," *Women's Wear Daily,* January 13, 1986, 7.

Figure 19.2   Supermarket Shopping Guide

Source: Courtesy of Alexanders Supermarkets.

chester, New Hampshire, to the nationwide Grand Union chain, the emphasis is on service and one-stop shopping. (See Figure 19.2.) Stores are striving to create an air of festivity. Employees wear color-coordinated jackets or smocks. Balloons sway above cash registers, and in almost every aisle a producer's representative is cooking or serving everything from sausage to ice cream. These stores have on-premises bakeries, delis, fish markets, liquor stores, flower shops, custom butchers, and lunch counters (for those who are not satisfied with the free samples). In some of them as much as half of the inventory is nonfood items, including clothing and appliances. At some stores the doors never close; the hours are 24 a day, 7 days a week. (See Figure 19.3.)

Figure   19.3   Profiles of America's Supermarkets

Warehouse store: Essentially low-price and no-frills, stocking mostly food. Superstore: More nonfood items and more specialty services, such as cheese and delicatessen counters. Combination store: Superstore with nearly half the space devoted to nonfood items. Conventional supermarket: Self-service grocery with at least $2 million in annual sales.

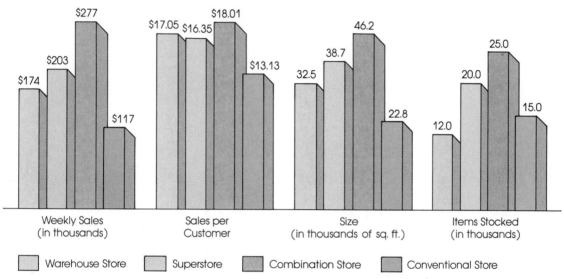

Source: Food Marketing Institute, "Food Marketing Industry Speaks," 1987. Data is for 1986. Reprinted with permission.

A complete and unusual view of this retail segment was offered by the *Today Show* in a series on the "Supermarket of the Future," which aired in 1984.

U.S. and Japanese Supermarkets

Supermarkets in Yokahama, Japan, and Rochester, New York, were featured in one program. The Japanese supermarket was shown as having daily specials moving through the store on a track and impulse items coming to the customer. Meat products were sliced by computers. By pushing a button, the shopper could make a selection. On each shopping cart, a calculator enabled the shopper to keep a total of the cost of items put in the cart. Even the stockboys were computerized robots.

The Rochester, New York, store could be the market of the future. Although it looked like any other supermarket at first glance, it had over 85,000 square feet of shopping space. What made it special was the convenience extras. In a computerized pharmacy prescriptions were analyzed for customers for possible dangerous interaction with other drugs they might be using. To help lower prices, the store provided the largest bulk-food selection ever seen, with barrel after barrel and container after container of everything from baking mixtures to soft drinks to potato chips. Even plastic forks could be purchased by the pound. Each item was bagged and marked with the **universal product code** (for faster computerized checkout) by a clerk right on the spot.

Universal Product Code
Product identification consisting of a series of bars and a 10-digit number, used with an optical scanner for computer checkout.

A game room kept shoppers' children busy. A customer could do all of his or her banking on an automatic teller machine without leaving the store. This was also the first food market in the country to computerize the counting of cents-off coupons. The checker no longer counted out each coupon. It was done as fast as they could be passed over the scanner. To find what he or she wanted, the customer simply touched the screen of one of the computerized store directories, and an alphabetical listing was provided. Touch again, and the computer indicated where it was.

Debit Cards

Another program focused on debit cards, then in very limited use in the states of California, Florida, and Maryland. The Hy-Vee Food Store in Des Moines, Iowa, was one of the first to try them. The customer bought her groceries as she normally would, and the cashier rang them up as normal. The customer then simply put her card with the magnetic strip on it through the reader, punched in the four-digit security number, and hit the enter button that sent the transaction on through the banking channels. It took five or six seconds at most.

As more people use the debit card and see its advantages, the volume will increase at a rapid rate. Nevertheless, the day of the checkless or even cashless society is still a long way off.

Supermarket Theft

The program devoted to supermarket theft indicated that California grocery and liquor stores were being stuck with more than $400 million worth of bad checks every year. As a result, a California law passed in the middle 1980s allowed merchants to collect triple the value of a bad check plus court costs. That threat alone was often enough to force the person who wrote the check to make it good. Steve Koff, of the Southern California Grocers Association, was quoted as saying:

> Most of the stores do try contacting the individual on several occasions, be it either phone, letter, or turning it over in some cases to a collection agency. This new bad check law has been a vast improvement for us. Raising the risk of writing a bad check now is recognized by customers and, in most cases, they are thinking twice before writing that bad check.

Technology is also being used in the fight against bad checks. Stores in the East, Midwest, and in California are experimenting with debit bank cards. If the money is not in the account, the machine will say so.

The typical shoplifter usually takes no more than three or four items at a time. The total value averages just over $10. Multiply that by eight thefts a day, 365 days a year, at more than 37,000 supermarkets nationwide, and the losses add up to more than a billion dollars a year.

Technology is also being used in this fight. **Checkstand detectors** are similar to those used at airports. A hidden sensing device on the merchandise triggers the detector if a shopper tries to carry it out past the checkstand without paying for it. When the merchandise is paid for, the salesperson removes the sensor. Jan Charles Gray, of Ralph's, said: "There have been hundreds of stops, and thousands of dollars in merchandise have been recovered. But more important than that, professional shoplifters, and even the amateurs, do not want to shoplift in this environment."

Shoppers' Attitudes

A program was devoted to the results of a market survey that indicated shoppers' attitudes, which are important to supermarket merchants planning for the future. The survey showed that 54 percent of shoppers expected food prices to increase, but only moderately. Those asked said they thought food prices would go up more than clothing or gasoline prices, but less than utility or housing costs in 1984.

Surprisingly, low prices were not what most shoppers looked for first in a supermarket. A third of those surveyed said fast checkout was the most important service a store could offer. Many said they go where the lines are usually shortest or shop during the hours when their favorite market is least crowded. Twenty-seven percent of shoppers said they shop where they can get the widest variety and best selection of merchandise. Only 25 percent gave low food prices as their priority.

Nevertheless, nearly half checked the newspaper ads for weekly specials. Thirty percent used manufacturers' and store coupons regularly. Twenty-nine percent compared prices from market to market. Only 12 percent, however, would actually shop somewhere other than their regular market to take advantage of a particular advertised special. Nearly everyone seemed to care about the nutritional value of what they ate. The survey showed that 95 percent of shoppers are at least somewhat concerned about the nutritional value of the foods they buy. Specifically, 25 percent said they worry about chemical additives and artificial coloring and flavoring in their food. The next highest concern was sugar content, followed by the vitamin and mineral content of packaged foods. Way down the list in ninth place was calories. Only 9 percent of shoppers put calories at the top of their list of nutritional concerns.

Many people were also concerned about food safety. Eighty-seven per-

Checkstand Detectors
Detection devices, usually located near store exits, designed to sound an alarm if sensing devices attached to merchandise have not been removed by a salesperson.

FROM THE FIELD

Videotex Advertising at Winn-Dixie

When shoppers enter any of 90 Winn-Dixie supermarkets in the Dallas–Fort Worth area, they do not have to stroll down the aisles to discover what is new in the cereal section or is marked down in the meat department. Two small video screens do the walking for them. The Winn-Dixie chain has added videotex advertising systems to boost sales and profits.

The chain's video system runs short, animated advertisements to alert shoppers to special buys. Two screens are suspended from the ceiling, one typically in the produce section, the other at the checkout counter. On them, customers can view weekly specials, new products, and special promotions.

The system was developed to increase sales and attain a higher market share by using advertising and sales promotions in a multimedia program. Results of a seven-week pilot program involving 20 Winn-Dixie stores—10 with the system, 10 without—showed that the new advertising medium increased sales 32 percent for six major products. In addition, customer counts increased in the stores with the system.

The videotex system is the heart of a four-part advertising program developed by Stan Rubinson, president of Marketing Technologies, Inc., Long Island; his brother, Dr. Kalmark Rubinson; and Stanley Roban, a veteran of mass merchandising promotions.

The program includes some of the more traditional supermarket advertising and promotion, including shelf talkers, special circulars, and newspaper ads, in addition to the 15-second ads on the video screens. Winn Dixie, pleased with the program, asked for monitors to be installed permanently in its two newest stores, in Bryon and College Station, Texas.

Source: Excerpted from "Texas Supermarket Chain Installs Videotex Screens," *Marketing News,* March 14, 1986, 37. Reprinted by permission from *Marketing News,* published by the American Marketing Association.

cent checked the packaging closely to make sure it was in good condition. Seventy-nine percent also checked the expiration date on perishables. Only 40 percent really read the ingredients on food labels.[9] Obviously, the food industry has learned what customers want. The future will test their response.

THE NEW SHOPPING CENTERS

A virtual revolution is taking place in the development, operation, retailing, and financing of U.S. and Canadian shopping centers. In 1986, a shoppers' paradise opened in Edmonton, Alberta, on the northern

[9]David Horowitz, "Close-up Reports," *Today Show* (NBC), New York, July–August 1984.

fringe of Canada's flat, frozen prairie. West Edmonton Mall, the largest shopping center in the world, was built as a way for 817 stores to sell everything from blouses to automobiles. Officials said that early sales averaged $360 [Canadian] for each of the mall's 3.8 million leasable square feet, compared with a Canadian industry average of $240. Along with Fantasyland, it represents a sort of Canadian fulfillment of the postwar dream—a dream of cars, consumerism, and convenience.[10] Shopping centers of the future will build on the same type of excitement and changes seen in the West Edmonton Mall.

Before World War II, there were only about 10 shopping centers in the United States. By 1980, there were more than 19,000, handling some 40 percent of the nation's retail trade. In 1986, there were more than 26,000 in the United States and 2,000 in Canada. These were places where new generations learned to eat, drink, and socialize. The shopping center will continue to be a social gathering point for generations to come.

Trends in shopping center development that retailers can look forward to were described by Eric Peterson in *Stores* magazine.[11]

Mixed Uses

More developers are deciding that retail complexes alone will not pay the freight. They are adding buildings, recreational and entertainment facilities, residential units, and hotels to make their projects more cost effective. Shopping center developers are crossing over into the commercial markets, and office project developers, in turn, are crossing into the retail market.

Mixed-use complexes once only associated with urban settings are going suburban as well and becoming a staple in planned communities, providing everything from the basic retail needs to typical suburban mall shopping. Some are on a grand scale, like the $165-million Trillium at Warner Center in Woodland Hills, California, a project its developers are calling a total environment, with a pair of office towers joined by a retail promenade. (See Figure 19.4.) Trillium even has a tennis stadium, and plans include a full-health spa, 12 tennis courts, and a hotel. Some centers will combine retailing with office buildings, apartments, medical facilities, restaurants, and health club facilities.

Urban Projects

The mixed-use trend in city centers is typified by Metro Center in Stamford, Conn., a $50 million office–retail complex. Its location adjacent to

---

[10] Douglas Martin, "A Shoppers' Paradise on the Prairie," *The New York Times*, February 23, 1986, business sec., 27, 28.
[11] Eric Peterson, "Shopping Center Futures," *Stores*, January 1986, 147–157.

Figure   19.4   A Retail Promenade Linking Two Office Towers: Trillium Shopping Center

Source: Courtesy of Trillium.

the city's transportation center makes commuting by office workers and shoppers seem like little more than a subway ride.

Access to transportation is a key factor at urban mixed-use developments. The $120-million, 728,000-square foot Concord Cal Center retail–office complex is right across the street from the Concord BART station (Bay Area Rapid Transit). Its two office towers have a retail complex as the link.

In Tampa, public transportation plays a key role in the success of Harbour Island, but the massive project was not simply plopped down in the middle of downtown. Development has been in phases, at a total cost of $1 billion, on a previously undeveloped 177-acre island south of downtown Tampa. The transportation link consists of two vehicular–pedestrian bridges. Harbour Island's retail portion embodies another subtrend, the festival marketplace. Created in the spirit of Boston's Faneuil Hall Marketplace and Baltimore's Harborplace, its retailing elements are linked by an expansive brick piazza and a 730-foot waterwalk featuring a waterfront amphitheater.

Festival shopping is also a buzzword in Richmond, Virginia, where a variety of urban retail projects are changing the city's shopping habits. The $25-million 6th Street Marketplace is transforming a three-block area into a glass-enclosed promenade of shops, kiosks, and restaurants, as well as galleries and landscaped plazas. Not far away and much bigger is the $450-million James Center, a retail, office, and residential complex that also includes a $33-million hotel. James Center was designed by the same architects who created New York's World Trade Center. Finally, Shockoe Slip is a cobblestone riverfront area that many years ago was a cotton and tobacco trading area.

On the more upscale side of urban mixed-use development is Fort Lauderdale's Broward Financial Center, a $40-million office tower attached to a retail complex where quality is represented by the tenants and the decor.

Suburban Niches

The big suburban mall is not dead yet. At Riverchase in Birmingham, Alabama, for example, retailing does not share the spotlight with other uses. Although they are there, the mall part of the project is definitely the star, all 1.5 million square feet of it. The anchor lineup at Riverchase is impressive: Macy's (300,000 square feet), Rich's (245,000) Pizitz (135,000), J. C. Penney (165,000), and Parisian (145,000). It covers the price spectrum, and the overall layout leaves room for two more department stores.

New Communities

Many new communities are springing up, especially in the high-growth parts of the country. No better way exists to handle a major influx of people than to master plan a community for them.

Retailers as Developers

A variety of anchor-type department store, drug, and supermarket chains have always forged their own shopping center opportunities to a certain extent by simply developing their own projects. Homart, part of Sears, is one of the leaders.

Developer Diversification

In order to maximize the opportunities and find the niches, the country's biggest developers are doing different things at the same time. The Rouse Company perhaps led the way, spinning off into urban specialty centers—festival marketplaces—at the same time it was developing suburban and urban regional malls.

Redevelopment

In the late 1980s, many or most of the record number of shopping centers built during the 1960s are coming to the end of their useful lives. That means redevelopment, and lots of it. It also means a whole slew of retail expansion opportunities. As malls outlive their usefulness, it is time for change. Thus, redevelopment will create retail opportunities in many settings nationwide. New types of tenants will contribute to the growth of existing and planned shopping centers.

Summary

Advanced technology will aid retailers in presenting the right merchandise and services to tomorrow's consumers. Each retailer will be better able to analyze consumer behavior, needs, and ability to pay than ever before. This analysis will result in better assortment planning and more business. On the negative side, with technology available to more retailers, competition will be greater.

With the use of advanced technological tools, market analysis and site selection will be more accurate. As the computer zeros in on special market segments, retailers will be able to make better decisions about in-store or nontraditional means of reaching their markets. On the other hand, all retailers will have these tools, and competition will be greater.

One of the biggest retail problems of the future will probably be time and timing. With electronic marketing, 24-hour business hours, and competition coming from every segment in the marketing channel, it will be more difficult than ever before to make time decisions. Traditional store hours will no longer be the criteria for success. The malls of the future will reflect these changes.

Price will be influenced by inflation, recession, export–import regulations, labor relations, and other variables that will probably be as difficult to measure in 2001 as they were in 1981. Retailers of the future must continue to be aware of world political and economic events that affect both wholesale and retail prices.

Quantity decisions will also result from a study of future societies. Developing countries will need more retail institutions along with more goods and services as they move into the economic mainstream. This opportunity for international expansion by many established retail companies may offset diminishing demand here for certain categories.

The retailer of the future will have to pay attention not only to new shopping centers in the United States and Canada but, when purchasing goods and services for resale at these centers and elsewhere, he or she must be aware of the shopping habits and needs of customers everywhere. Superstores, mixed-use complexes, electronic funds transfer, and in-home shopping are all major trends that will characterize world retailing as we enter the next century.

Questions for Review

1. List at least ten technological changes in retailing that are possible by the year 2000.
2. Describe electronic banking, computer-based information systems, and electronic marketing, and their implications for retailing in the near future.
3. Discuss some future changes in traditional retail stores as we approach the year 2000.
4. Discuss some future changes in the discount segment of retailing.
5. Differentiate between supermarkets and superstores.
6. List seven trends in shopping center development predicted by *Stores* magazine.
7. How do you see the field of retailing in the year 2000?

CASE STUDY   R. R. Richards

The Feasibility of Day-Care Service in a Furniture Store

R. R. Richards, a household furnishings chain offering a complete assortment of both hard and soft goods for the home, was one of the region's leading chain stores and had been competing successfully with large national general merchandise chains that had had outlets in the area for more than 40 years.

Roy R. Richards, founder and current chairman of the board, had opened the first store when he returned from duty in the navy at the end of World War II. His idea was to serve the complete household needs of the many families like his own who were buying their first homes and having children.

Many young couples had saved money during the war years, planning for the day when the war would be over and they could begin to lead normal lives together. When the day arrived, they were an entirely new customer group with more money to spend than any previous generation. Couples who had delayed careers, children, and the lifestyle they wanted were finally ready to buy the possessions they had been denied for so long. Roy Richards meant to supply these needs.

Because his father had opened a small furniture store in the city where Roy grew up, he was familiar with retailing. With his father's help and the backing of a local bank that had the foresight to recognize, as Roy did, the tremendous potential market that existed for household goods of all types, R. R. Richards became a reality.

The first store was opened on the east side of the city, where new housing was being constructed at a fast pace, with homes ranging from $15,000 to $22,000. Richards soon achieved a fine reputation and a very satisfactory level of profit as Roy provided in-depth assortments of moderate-priced merchandise for the home—furniture and appliances, bedding, draperies, and kitchen utensils of all types. Richards offered credit, delivery, and appliance service. This was a major factor contributing to success.

Mrs. Jones might find a refrigerator for less money at a discount store, but no service was offered. Mrs. Green might find draperies that were comparable elsewhere, but a drapery purchase at R. R. Richards included the service of an expert decorator, who hung the drapes in her living room. Mrs. Mason enjoyed the ability to charge her furniture purchase at Richards, and Mrs. Denton did not have to worry about carrying home two dozen sets of bed linen. From the outset, Richards was a full-service retailer, using service as a sure way of combating the discounters who were proliferating almost faster than new homes needing furnishing.

Success led to more success as Roy carried his formula to other cities and suburbs that were experiencing a postwar boom in both housing and population. The R. R. Richards store became a well-known landmark all over the region, bringing quality goods at a fair price to the average household.

Customers who, right after the war, had been willing to settle for almost anything as long as it was new, became more sophisticated. They too began to patronize Richards, realizing the value of the peripheral services that accompanied their purchases. Sales increased each year, and charge accounts became so numerous and credit so important a part of the operation that a separate credit department was established in 1960 with a director of credit services. By 1975, the entire system was computerized; with 22 stores in the chain, running a manual system was becoming impossible.

Much of R. R. Richards' success was obviously due to its unwavering service policy. At more meetings over the years than Roy cared to remember, discussions centered on Richards' services. Should they be cut down, expanded, or eliminated? Even when he began to share the decision making with a large staff of executives who made up a management team, the service policy did not change. Richards was a service chain, and a service chain it would remain as long as the year-end figures verified the wisdom of this decision.

Competition was tougher each year, but so were the customers, who were educated, smarter shoppers and more knowledgeable about what they wanted. They were also much more discerning about what they liked and did not like.

As more women entered the work force and leisure time became more precious, the demand for different kinds of services increased. Richards, the service store, thus began to sell a wide range of services in addition to offering the traditional product-oriented ones such as repair, delivery, credit, and decorating. If Sears could sell a tax-return service, theater tickets, and even funeral arrangements, then why not Richards? Their customers expected Richards to keep up with demands and this meant flexibility and expansion to suit changing needs.

Some needs had changed considerably over the years; for example, young mothers-to-be not only planned the nursery but often thought ahead to child care. Career mothers were increasing in number. Retailers everywhere were providing all types of appliances and services to make the working mother's life easier, but what about actual quality care for the baby when mother went back to her job? Could a retailer provide day-care centers in the store? Could a mother leave her baby at Richards in the morning to be picked up at the end of the workday? What were the ramifications for retailing in general and more specifically for R. R. Richards if such a service were to be established?

This was a new service problem born of a new need in a new age. Should the chain that had done such a good job of filling its customers' needs from the postwar days through the cold war, the youth rebellion, and women's liberation take this revolutionary step? What would the benefits be to Richards and to its customers? Was it time for Richards to open a day-care center?

Everyone agreed that the growth in sales would continue in the service sector of the economy and that a store that sold many services as well as products could continue to meet the competition and draw customers in large numbers. The question was, exactly where did the retailer stop? Did day-care centers belong in a retail store?

Richards executives had to weigh both sides of the question. On one side of the ledger were two positive factors.

1. Customers who bought the service would be in a Richards store twice a day at least five days a week. If they had to purchase any home furnishings, most likely they would make the purchase in the store that had become part of their daily lives. All sales would increase.
2. With the day-care centers Richards would become more than an impersonal retail institution. A family attachment would develop and this attitude would also contribute to increased sales.

On the other hand there were some obvious potential problems:

1. Would the cost per square foot outweigh the increased income if valuable selling space in each store were allocated to a day-care center?
2. If no space were available, what would be the cost of building the necessary addition to a store?
3. Day-care centers could not be run by part-time minimum wage employees. What would a qualified staff cost? Again, would the costs outweigh the benefits?
4. Government inspection and regulations would bring more red tape into the life of the retailer, already overwhelmed in this respect.

These were only a few of the factors that would have to be given consideration. Management was sure that a much more intensive study would be needed before a decision could be reached. As one executive mentioned, the foremost thought in everyone's mind should perhaps be ethics and responsibility. Would Richards truly be making a contribution to society by filling this growing need or should day-care centers be left to agencies that best understood child care? What did the store owe society? Could a profit-oriented industry do a better job than nonprofit agencies or would the profit motive get in the way of the human side of this service? How far should the service orientation be carried in the future?

Questions

1. In your opinion, can a service-oriented retailer continue to compete successfully with a cut-price retailer in the same field? Explain your answer.
2. Make as extensive a list as possible of the kinds of services a retail store might successfully sell to working mothers.
3. Do you think that a profit-oriented industry (such as retailing) can do a better job of providing quality day-care then the nonprofit sector of society? Why?
4. Address Question 3 from an ethical point of view: do day-care centers belong in retail stores? Why?
5. Discuss the regulatory problems Richards might face in opening day-care centers.
6. Should Richards open day-care centers in all its stores or only in those that will be built in mixed-use development centers? Why?

Appendix

Starting a Retail Business*

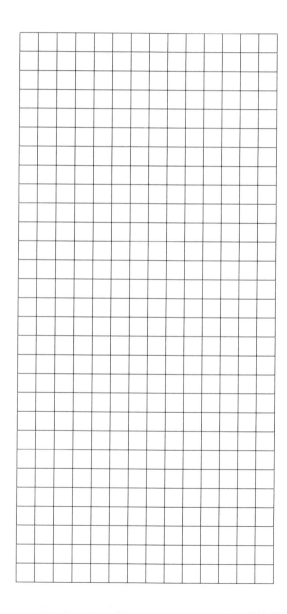

*This appendix was written by James F. Wolter, Ph.D., Associate Professor of Marketing at Grand Valley State College, Allandale, Michigan.

Learning Objectives

Upon completing this appendix you should be able to:

1. Understand the role of small business in a retail economy dominated by large firms.
2. Assess your personal readiness to act as an entrepreneur and innovator.
3. Develop a retail business plan—a pro forma store on paper—that includes analyses of target market needs and competitor's offerings, and formulation of plans for the structure, location, financing, merchandising, and operating policies of your store.
4. Know when you need help and where to find the help you can trust and afford.
5. Evaluate opportunities for buying a franchise or an existing business.
6. Compare your hopes and plans to the success stories of some retail entrepreneurs, both large and small.

THE SMALL BUSINESS CONNECTION

This appendix is intended to start you thinking systematically about opening your own retail business. The major focus of this book has been to guide your career choices and give you professional training for employment in an established retail business. For a majority of retail students, entering an ongoing business is a good place to start, because the existing organization and job structure are a good match with college training in business. People with greater entrepreneurial interests, however, are willing to accept the unique challenges of starting their own businesses. This appendix asks personal questions about your readiness to start a business and gives a comprehensive outline of the planning necessary before any money is spent on business assets.

Small in Dollars, Large in Numbers

Although the retail industry is dominated financially by large firms, small businesses outnumber large ones by far, both in numbers of store

Figure   A.1   Distribution of U.S. Stores by Size and Share of Total Retail Sales, 1982

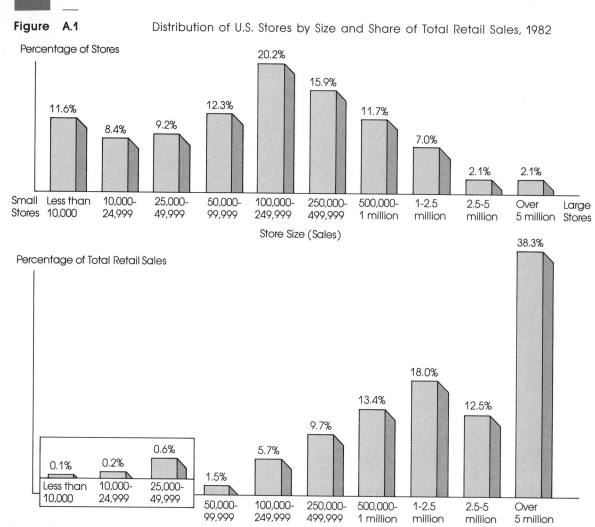

Source: E. Jerome McCarthy and William D. Perreault, Jr., *Basic Marketing: A Managerial Approach* (Homewood, Ill.: Irwin, 1987), 316.

locations and in employees. Firms with sales in excess of $500,000 are responsible for 74.4 percent of all retail sales but only occupy 15.4 percent of the retail stores by number. Therefore, 85 percent of retail stores are small businesses with annual sales of less than $500,000.

A small store revival was described in Chapter 10. Smaller private retailers dominate certain specialty markets, such as sporting goods, hardware, and eating and drinking establishments. (A majority of restaurants, including nationally recognized fast food chains, are privately owned or franchised businesses.) Most new and used automobile, boat, and appliance dealerships are private businesses. Others that are usually private are service and repair businesses, numerous specialty apparel and gift stores, greenhouse and flower shops, and on and on.

Clearly, no shortage exists of opportunity or of chances to match hobbies, interests, or specialized training to retail opportunity. What *is* typically missing for first-time would-be retail entrepreneurs is an objective assessment of the challenges and dangers of ventures in new businesses. Seasoned retailers often say, "I wouldn't have done it had I really known beforehand what I was getting into!" Although there is some risk that hearing about the pitfalls may be discouraging, serious marketing students should consider the differences between large and small businesses and serious entrepreneurs need to be forewarned. Probably the best test of "entrepreneurial quotient" is indicated by willingness to proceed while knowing that it is a difficult path.

The Advantages of Size and Large-Scale Operation

In many ways, if you are a small retailer, the deck is stacked against you, especially if you are competing against larger firms with a similar retail mix. A lot of power comes with size, including the power to recruit and adequately pay staff, either experienced help or the best of the bright, newly graduating retail merchandising or marketing majors. Large firms also have leverage in buying inventory, leasing top mall space, and sharing system-wide costs for administrative services, market research, and promotional programs. Large firms can create national images and induce top vendors to create special privately branded products. One of the most serious challenges in starting your own business, that of obtaining money, is not a serious problem for healthy firms with established credit and ratings in equity markets.

The Disadvantages of Size

Before losing heart, realize that there are weaknesses in the structure of large firms that open the door for small business opportunity. First, large firms are neither entrepreneurial nor typically innovative. Over the years large firms have watched the wheel of retailing (Chapter 1) roll over them, too caught up in internal affairs to respond to changing market needs. The very nature of bigness requires large firms to select product markets that are large enough to support the scale of their operations. These policies leave countless specialized market niches unsatisfied. Then too, the trend toward centralized merchandise planning predominates in large firms and ignores specialized local market needs. The responsive, smaller retailer can move quickly to close this gap, offering the highly differentiated products and services ignored by larger chain stores.

The following is not meant as a criticism of large store employees as much as a warning to you, the potential entrepreneur. Large firms typically do not ask employees to work the long hours for low pay that you will demand of yourself. Your advantage is, of course, that unlike your counterparts in large firms, you are a stakeholder in your business and accept full responsibility for its success or failure. Frequently, management trainees in large establishments are young, mobile professionals who are as interested in their next job assignment as they are in their present one. This sometimes leads to trade-offs that produce short-term results, perhaps at the cost of sacrificing long-term growth. You will not be tempted with such choices because the future belongs to you.

ASSESSING YOUR PERSONAL READINESS

The inventory that follows is a self-assessment questionnaire. With it you can make an honest appraisal of your strengths and weaknesses compared to generally accepted criteria for success in private business. For simplicity's sake, a simple three-point scale is used (-1, 0, $+1$) to help you add up your entrepreneurial quotient. Comments on summary scores follow the questionnaire.

1. Are you a self-starter?

    $\frac{\quad\quad}{+1}$ I start on my own, no prodding needed.

    $\frac{\quad\quad}{0}$ If someone starts me, I can carry through.

    $\frac{\quad\quad}{-1}$ Someone has to tell me to move.

2. How do you get along with other people?

    $\frac{\quad\quad}{+1}$ I get along with everyone; I like people and don't make enemies.

    $\frac{\quad\quad}{0}$ I have a few friends I get along with.

    $\frac{\quad\quad}{-1}$ Most people are boring or irritating.

3. How well developed are your leadership skills?

    $\frac{\quad\quad}{+1}$ I have been a natural leader and have exploited it.

    $\frac{\quad\quad}{0}$ If I'm given the authority, I can direct others.

———— I let others get the ball rolling.
  −1

4. How well do you accept responsibility?

   ———— I make the outcome of things my personal responsibility.
     +1

       ———— I try hard but blame others when things go wrong.
         0

         ———— Other people are always fouling up.
           −1

5. How good are your organizing skills?

   ———— I can see what needs to be done, plan ahead, and follow
     +1
   the plan.

       ———— I get things done but there is never enough time.
         0

         ———— The best-laid plans often go astray, so I just
           −1
         do my best.

6. Describe your work habits.

   ———— I enjoy my work and do whatever is necessary to finish
     +1
   the job.

       ———— I work hard but I know when to quit.
         0

         ———— I'm careful not to burn out at too young an
           −1
         age.

7. Rate your decision-making ability.

   ———— I make decisions and live with the results.
     +1

       ———— I take a long time to make decisions and then
         0
       worry over whether I was right.

         ———— Most problems will go away if ignored.
           −1

8. Do you have tenacity?

————— I'm like a postage stamp; I stick to a job until it's done.
+1

————— I hang in there as long as things are going well.
0

————— If I run into a brick wall, I won't beat my
−1
brains out.

9. Describe your personal integrity.

————— My word is my bond; I don't say things I don't mean.
+1

————— Trust is a mutual thing; I give it if I get it.
0

————— I like to keep them guessing.
−1

10. How is your personal health and energy level?

————— I'm never sick, and I get more energy by spending what
+1
I've got.

————— I take pretty good care of myself.
0

————— You've got to be on your guard against
−1
people who will use you until you're sick
and tired.

Now count your responses.

————— How many plus-ones?
+1

————— How many zeros?
0

————— How many minus-ones?
−1

Subtract minus-ones from plus-ones to arrive at your *net score.*

If you were honest, the questionnaire gives you some idea of how strongly you feel about qualities that are found in successful retail entrepreneurs. The more ones and the fewer zeros, the better your chances are. If you had a number of minuses, you need to seriously consider either changing your attitudes or modifying your career choices. At the very least, find partners or employees whose strengths complement your weaknesses.

THE REWARDS AND PITFALLS OF MANAGING A SMALL BUSINESS

The leading causes of failure in small businesses are (1) poor marketing and (2) poor business management. The *marketing concept* is a sound philosophical approach to retail business. No amount of luck can replace careful market research, customer segmentation, and preparation of a differentiated marketing mix for your retail business, large or small. The second problem, that of poor execution, encompasses many pitfalls. The following list is adapted from a Dun and Bradstreet report on nine roadblocks to success in business.[1]

1. Lack of experience and an unwillingness to seek help.
2. Running out of money or becoming overextended.
3. The wrong location. An inexpensive lease is no bargain if the location is not suitable.
4. Poor inventory management—having too much of the wrong merchandise or too much or too little inventory.
5. Overspending on capital assets—buildings and equipment. These commitments limit working capital.
6. Granting uncontrolled credit to customers or getting caught short on cash to pay suppliers.
7. Taking too much, too soon out of the business. Many small businesses do not break even in the first or second years. Raiding the cash drawer or the inventory is very tempting.
8. Uncontrolled growth or contraction in business activities. Getting big too fast and falling short of cash budgets both spell trouble.
9. Poor attitudes. In general, the small business owner must be willing to work long hours, curtail outside activities when they interfere, and be honest and ethical in business dealings.

Assuming that your personal assessment went well and that you can avoid the pitfalls leading to failure, you pass the screening process to this point. Remember that, for the entrepreneurially inclined, there is no higher calling than being independently successful.

CREATING YOUR BUSINESS ON PAPER—THE RETAIL BUSINESS PLAN

The need for up-front planning cannot be overemphasized. Putting a business plan on paper is a demanding yet low-risk process that will lead to much higher chances for success. Because every business opportunity is unique, the plan elements are generic. Some will be more important to special situations than others. In general, the more detailed and objective

---

[1]"Business Failure Record," Dun and Bradstreet Corporation, New York, N.Y., 1987.

the plan is (and quantitative where applicable), the more useful it becomes as a blueprint for success.

Good planning requires both doing the right things and doing things right. This means that having the most eloquent plan (doing the right things) is of little use unless you have also thought through the tactics used to implement the plan (doing things right). Your chances of getting support from bankers or venture capitalists and help from small business consultants, lessors, or prospective vendors are also enhanced with a good plan.

The five elements of the business plan are (1) a description of the business, (2) the marketing plan, (3) the location of the business, (4) the merchandising plan, and (5) the financial plan.

Business Description

Choice of the Legal Form of the Business

Changing tax laws, fluctuating availability of capital, and methods of distributing risk must be evaluated before selecting a proprietorship, partnership, or corporate structure. U.S. Government Small Business Administration publication MA 6.004 asks the questions that must be answered to plan business structure.

Store Type and Location

Will your business be in-store or nonstore? Changing lifestyles suggest looking at ways to innovate in nonstore retail systems, which take products and services to customers instead of the other way around. SBA business development pamphlet MA 2.002 discusses location questions.

Product and Service Mix

Be creative by defining your product in terms of all of the needs it satisfies. Most retail business offers a product that is a mixture of tangible (physical product) and intangible (service product) elements.

Competitors

Competitors are direct and indirect. As an example, direct competition might be among furniture stores competing for a family's living room furniture replacement. This competition occurs within the furniture product market. On a broader scale, a family might choose, as a status investment, a new automobile instead of new furniture. This competition occurs within the generic market for status. In this part of your plan, identify all direct competitors and carefully analyze their retail mixes.

Marketing Plan

Market Description

Markets are people with common needs, who live in a defined geographical locale, and whose travel and shopping habits favor your business offering. Retail businesses have a characteristic range (drawing power in terms of how far people are willing to travel to shop for the merchandise in question) and threshold (how many total customers are needed to be successful).

Target Market—Understanding Segmentation

Naming market segments requires careful research of relevant markets to determine the reasons behind buying. If you name product markets too narrowly, you are inclined to systematically omit potential customers. Conversely, naming segments too broadly may lead you to leave special-needs segments unsatisfied.

The Retail Strategy—Target Market plus Retail Mix

Now match your target market to a carefully designed retail mix. It is critical that you consider all of the marketing mix elements (4 Ps). Retailers commonly ignore the place variable, for example, because they assume that place decisions are complete when location is decided. Actually, place decisions extend up the marketing channels to vendors as well as down to customers. Unique opportunities in on-line computer ordering, or new drive-through convenience stores, or home delivery systems are place decisions. Having an active channel—for instance, a pizza delivery van that cooked pizza in transit, giving faster and fresher service—would be a place decision. Match your creativity with comprehensive planning when designing your retail mix and your business will be perceived as being unique.

Business Location

The Importance of Location

Chapter 10 is devoted to location. Small, start-up businesses will not usually be able to afford helicopter rooftop analyses or many other primary data-based locational analyses. This means that careful use of less expensive secondary data and some limited personal inquiries are about all that prospective entrepreneurs use. Be wary of gross traffic counts; many small businesses have failed because they located where it was either inconvenient or unlikely for passersby to stop and shop. Neighborhoods, like shopping centers, have a characteristic of attracting a certain clientele. Spend time walking through proposed sites on different days and hours. Ask local merchants about different seasons of the year.

Customer Counting and Projections

Many of the issues are discussed in U.S. Government publications SBA MA 2.021, *Using a Traffic Study to Select a Retail Site,* and MA 2.024, *Store Location: Little Things Mean a Lot,* which discusses landlords, leases, merchant associations, and zoning and planning.

Merchandising Plan

Store Image—Layout, Design, and Fixturing

Chapter 11 discusses store image issues for existing businesses. The atmosphere of the store creates a lasting first impression on shoppers. "Getting it right" before grand opening avoids confusion for first-time shoppers.

Finding and Keeping Good Vendors

The best vendors offer merchandising help, along with product. Chapter 12 discusses how vendors should be thought of as partners in your business. Direct contact with manufacturers or importers of goods will result in their introducing you to their distributors and wholesalers. Chapter 13 offers suggestions on negotiating with suppliers. Usually small businesses must make prompt payment to assure supply.

Stockkeeping and Inventory Policy

Inventory budgeting is discussed in Chapter 12. Because of the importance of having the correct inventory mix, you should stress this part of your plan. Get the best information possible from the market and from your suppliers.

Financial Plan

Start-up Capital Needs (multiply by 2)

Two kinds of capital demands occur in a new business. First, one-time start-up investments must be made. Second, ongoing expenses are incurred in running the business. Probably the most useful tool for determining financial needs for ongoing cash flow is a three-year financial plan (below). Experienced operators warn that first-timers chronically underforecast their start-up cash needs and overforecast their sales revenues. Unplanned and underbudgeted expenses cause the former and overoptimism causes the latter. Either or both would leave you short on cash.

Sources of Capital

Only two sources of money exist—yours and other people's money (OPM). Before spending either, you should document your personal and business financed position. This requires four financial documents. First you need a personal net worth statement that includes liquid assets and borrowing power. Next, your business plan must include (1) the income statement, (2) cash flow statement, and (3) balance sheet. These documents are needed for planning both the equity (your money) and debt (OPM) sources of capital.

In addition to the four statements, you should prepare a capital equipment list to help maintain control over assets and to assist in the creation of a cost budget. Capital equipment includes furniture, machines (both office machines and equipment used in creating your product or performing your service), store fixtures, and delivery vehicles.

The primary sources of financing are:

- Banks (Banks almost always require secured loans for start-up businesses.)
- U.S. Small Business Association (Almost 95 percent of SBA loans are placed through private banks in the 7A program. Unless you are woman- or minority-owned, these programs are as restrictive as direct bank loans.)
- State Chartered Small Business Investment Companies (SBICs) are licensed and regulated through the SBA but use state sources of capital. For availability in your state, check with the SBIC Central Office: U.S. Small Business Administration, 1441 L Street N.W., Washington, D.C. 20416.

Other sources of financing are:

- Consumer finance companies
- Leasing companies
- Commercial loan companies
- Savings and loans
- Life insurance companies
- Credit unions
- Individual investors (Check law and tax firms who "look for opportunities" for their clients.)
- Suppliers and franchisers (Especially look for qualified minorities.)
- Venture capital funds (Most large cities have venture clubs meeting monthly; see your local chamber of commerce.)

Remember that borrowing creates a special responsibility on your part to manage the risk your business presents and to provide a fair return to investors. Carefully prepare yourself to answer investors' questions regarding the six Cs of credit:

- Character: your integrity, honesty, reputation
- Capacity: the power of your business to pay back
- Collateral: surety—assets used to guarantee loans
- Capital: your personal investment in the business
- Conditions: business and economic signs of the times
- Communication: how well you present yourself and your plan.

Financial Documentation

Four areas need to be documented: (1) personal net worth, (2) income projections, (3) cash flow projections, and (4) balance sheet. Space does not permit developing detailed instructions for these documents in this appendix.

For personal net worth (item 1), availability of capital, and borrowing power, your banker or accountant should be consulted.

For the other three items, see Chapter 14 and Appendix 14A. In addition, order SBA publications:

- *Keep Pointed toward Profit*   MA 1.003
- *Basic Budgets for Profit Planning*   MA 1.004
- *Cash Flow for a Small Business*   MA 1.006
- *Business Plan for Retailers*   MA 2.020

Other published resources that are helpful include "Steps to Starting a Business," Bank of America, *Small Business Reporter* 14: 7, 1980; "Financing Small Business," Bank of America, *Small Business Reporter* 14: 10, 1980; and "Understanding Financial Statements," Bank of America, *Small Business Reporter* SBR 109.

Breakeven Analysis

The ideas behind breakeven analyses are simple. Your business sales should provide enough profit margins (flowing in) to offset the money costs of being in business (flowing out). In practice, breakeven analyses are complicated by definition of fixed versus variable costs, long- versus short-term debt service, and time phasing of financial flows. These analyses are further complicated by whether the business provides financial support to you, the owner, and by the possibility that it may take more than a year (or two) of operations to actually break even on an accumulated basis. The following calculation gives a simplified example.

First, separate costs into fixed and variable components:

$$\text{Breakeven Point (in sales dollars)} = \frac{\text{Total Fixed Costs}}{1 - \dfrac{\text{Total Variable Cost}}{\text{Corresponding Sales Volume}}}$$

Every cost element must be stated in terms of the same period (day, week, month, or year).

Suppose that Jill Smith is opening a small specialty athletic and dance shoe store in Los Angeles. She estimates her fixed expenses at $12,000 for the first year. She estimates that variable expenses will be about $600 for every $1,000 of sales (40 percent contribution margin). How much sales must her store gross for her to break even?

$$\text{Breakeven Point (in sales dollars)} = \frac{\$12,000}{1 - \left(\dfrac{600}{1000}\right)} = \frac{\$12,000}{.40} = \$30,000 \text{ (per year)}$$

Figure A.2 gives the same example as a graph.

Two cautions: First, as you can see from Jill's example, profits (or losses) for the retailer are very sensitive to sales volume. Second, just breaking even does not provide profits. In Jill's case, every $1,000 sales

Figure   A.2   Breakeven Point

Jill Smith's shoe store must have sales of $30,000 per year to break even.

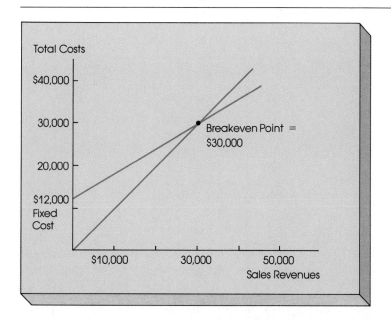

over $30,000 contributes $400 to profit. If she could, for example, have sales of $50,000 the first year, she would have gross profits of $8,000 (.4 C.M. × $20,000 excess over breakeven).

GETTING AFFORDABLE YET EFFECTIVE HELP

Fortunately, there are numerous sources of help for the new business entrepreneur. The costs of this help vary from the hourly or contract rates of professional attorneys, accountants, and consultants to the free assistance of volunteer and agency help.

Accountant and Attorney

Take your time selecting an attorney whose client base includes small business people. Ask for references and don't be afraid to check them out. Select an accountant who will provide (1) competent tax planning, (2) direction for cost control, (3) credibility in your reporting, and (4) compliance with the law. Shop for accounting firms whose reputation confirms that they will become committed to and involved in your business.

Other Service Providers

1. *Your insurance agent:* You will need proper liability coverage and contingency planning.
2. *Your board of directors,* if you are incorporated: Pick advisors who can and will help.
3. *Financially involved people and institutions:* After all, it is their money.
4. *Government publications and assistance networks (SBA).*
5. *Trade associations:* These range from the National Retail Merchants Association to more specialized offerings, such as *Nation's Restaurant News* or *Women's Wear Daily.*
6. *State and local chambers of commerce:* Especially well suited to help in specific planning. Most local chambers have a small business development specialist offering essentially free help.
7. *Community and regional colleges:* Look for ones with small business assistance offices.
8. *Turnkey vendors and franchisors.*

FRANCHISING VERSUS BUILDING OR BUYING A BUSINESS

Franchising has been called the wave of the 1980s, and new franchise systems are indeed popping up like mushrooms. In examining franchise opportunities, several issues should be considered.

Advantages of Franchising

Franchising offers easy entry into established markets as well as proven production and marketing techniques. Properly administrated franchises give help in starting and managing businesses and have been proven to reduce the risk of failure. To a greater or lesser extent, franchises *can* offer national brand images, synergistic promotion, and systematic sharing of the secrets of success across the system.

In franchising, shortcomings match the advantages. Many a naive investor has lost money because of dishonest or incompetent operators peddling dreams on paper. Some investors have found that the up-front fees and royalties are so high that making a profit is difficult at best. Even for successful and legitimate systems, a franchise is not a shortcut to success. The same personal commitment and hard work are required to learn and operate franchises as any other business.

Sources of Franchise Information

You will need information from the following sources as well as experienced professional advice to choose from among competing franchise opportunities.

Directories of Franchisors

- *Franchise Opportunities Handbook,* U.S. Department of Commerce, The Superintendent of Documents, U.S. Government Printing Office, Washington, D.C. 20402.
- *Entrepreneur* magazine's annual "500 Franchise" directory, usually the January issue. This shows categories, size, costs, expected performance, and year-to-year growth of the top 500 franchisors. A unique rating system has been developed by the editors. (Note: It is not clear that the published information has been uniformly audited.)
- *Venture Magazine,* February 1987. This contains a report of the 50 fastest growing new franchises.
- Business reference services in local libraries.

Disclosure Documentation

The Federal Trade Commission requires a franchisor to give you a detailed disclosure document at least ten days before you pay any money or legally commit yourself to a purchase. This document gives information on at least 20 items, including:

- Names, addresses, and telephone numbers of other purchasers
- A fully audited financial statement of the seller

- The background and experience of key executives
- The costs required to start and maintain the business
- The responsibilities you and the franchisor share once you buy.

Other Relevant Sources

Call and visit existing franchisees. Check all references, including better business bureaus, chambers of commerce, and the *International Franchise Association,* 1025 Connecticut Avenue N.W., Washington, D.C. 20036.

Analyses of Franchises

Pay careful attention to the cost-for-value ratio. What are you really getting for your money? Be very wary of newly founded franchises that demand large investments but have no history of successful operators. Be wary of franchisors who will arrange for your financing, especially for very low down payments. They may end up owning your house and car and some future wages. The best guideline is to deal with proven success—companies with a solid reputation in the market and among their franchisees.

The acid test is always performance in the market. Look for profits and long-term growth. Faddish foods or entertainment can be here today, gone tomorrow. Be sure to try the product yourself and try the business. McDonald's franchisees spend a minimum of two weeks at Hamburger University and 500 *volunteer* hours behind the counter of a store before they own a franchise. By that time, they know what they are getting into.

Check into the products offered by the franchisor beyond the trademark and name. Look carefully at the operations manuals, real estate and construction services, equipment packages, inventory control, and field consulting services. Make sure that your fees earn benefits for both you and the franchisor.

Success Stories from the Field

Stories abound of how large successful retail dynasties started from small beginnings. In recent history, Les Wexner's family apparel store has grown into The Limited Stores, Inc. R. David Thomas opened the first Wendy's hamburger store in the late 1960s. Their successes are chronicled in business school case studies and the popular press. Also interesting, but less often told, are stories of retail entrepreneurs who have contained their growth and are running a much more personalized business. Two such stories are told below.

Moser's Dried Flower Barn

Reini Moser, born and educated as a horticulturist in the Netherlands, came to the United States as a young adult. In the mid-1970s, when her three daughters were becoming more independent, she turned to an earlier love, dried flower arranging. At first it was a hobby. As friends encouraged her and her reputation spread, she began commercial contract work. Her business reputation and the demand for her work spread almost too fast, requiring long days of tedious production. Part of their home, located on a state highway just out of town, was converted to a retail shop and soon became a regular stopping point on the tour bus circuit. By the 1980s, several people had been trained to produce Reini's designs, although she refuses to give up production work herself. She says, "You have to love this work to get others in your shop interested in maintaining quality and production."

By the mid-1980s, the Mosers were crowded out of their family home by the business. Reini has a successful nationwide business promoted by an annual catalog and monthly newsletter. Soon, a married daughter opened a satellite store in a nearby community. Employing several people and having two stores open and growing catalog sales seem like a reasonable plateau to Reini. She has both financial success and an excellent reputation. Becoming larger poses special problems because her product requires custom and artistic work. Any cookie-cutter attempt at increasing production would threaten what she considers the integrity of her unique product.

Wise's Patio Shop

Al Wise is an engineer who wanted more contact with people and greater autonomy in his life. After searching for attractive opportunities, he decided that a small retail business specializing in outdoor furnishings was needed in his Midwestern city of about half a million residents. Because he was an engineer, Al carefully and systematically planned his business on paper before he started. Using most of the techniques suggested in this appendix, he created the plan that he took to lenders, suppliers, and builders. He is careful to point out that one must enter a new business with both head and heart. In other words, even after months of planning, the time came for him and his wife to say, "OK, that's it! Quit the secure job and put the plan into action." That was 11 years ago.

Al says that at first he was too scared of failing to notice how demanding his new business was. He had to get used to wearing the many hats of buyer, seller, stockkeeper, delivery man, and repairman. Mrs. Wise soon became a full partner and admits that being together 24 hours a day requires some personal adjustments. The last of the Wises' three children has graduated from the state university, and there are now three patio shops open in a triangle about 55 miles on a side. The Wises still manage the original store themselves but have trained managers for the other two stores. Al often visits the local college and talks to retailing students about his experience. His message is punctuated with reflections of the several stages of growth their business has passed through.

Perhaps because of his early engineering experience, Al leaves nothing to chance. He still budgets his store's cash and inventory position carefully. He constantly monitors competitors' advertisements and shops their stores. He pays himself and Mrs. Wise a salary and never helps himself to something extra out of the cash drawer. "This is a job like any other," says Al. "As soon as you get sloppy, you get fired."

Glossary

Access Road Approach road to a store or shopping center from a highway.

Advance Dating Added time allowed to pay for goods, following the invoice date when the ordinary dating period begins, that results in a discount for the purchaser.

Analog Method Method for obtaining a sales forecast by comparing potential new sites with existing sites.

Anchor Tenant Major mall tenant occupying a large, usually corner, store.

Anticipation Payment of an account before the due date; also, the resulting discount.

Art Deco Style from the 1920s and 1930s that combines exotic (1920s) or sleek (1930s) design with new materials.

Artificial Texture An illusion of surface feel created by the design artist to enhance a display.

Asymmetrical Balance Grouping of items with no apparent plan; the opposite of formal balance, in which each half of a composition is identical with the other.

At-Home Electronic Market Potential customers reached at home through personal computers or videotex terminals linked by the telephone system to a computer center.

Atmospherics Interior design intended to create or suggest a particular mood.

Attrition Shrinking of employee roles through resignation, retirement, or death.

Automated Storage and Retrieval Warehousing system that combines the use of computer control of stock records with mechanical handling.

Automatic Teller Machine A terminal located on or off bank premises that allows customers access to their accounts up to 24 hours a day.

Baby Boom The record 76 million Americans born between 1946 and 1964.

Basic Stock Method Inventory method in which estimated sales for the month are added to a basic minimum stock to determine the beginning-of-month stock.

Branch Store An outlet owned and operated by the flagship store, often carrying a modified line of merchandise.

Bridge Line A line of apparel by a name designer that is priced considerably lower than usual designer fashions.

Brood-Hen-and-Chick Plan Management plan under which the parent store organization operates the branches.

Bytehead Computer industry buzzword for those who create computer systems.

Career Path The planned sequence of jobs that leads to a career objective.

Case Allowance Rebate offered by a manufacturer or wholesaler to retailers who advertise and sell a specific product at a reduced price.

Cash Dispenser A terminal located on or off bank premises that dispenses cash to customers and debits their accounts.

Catalog/Warehouse/Showroom Merchant Discounter who sells through catalogs mailed to customers' homes or displayed in a showroom adjoining the warehouse.

Caveat Emptor "Let the buyer beware." This is applied to merchandise sold without a warranty.

Central Business District Usually downtown; a grouping of stores that offers a broad range of products/services and prices.

Chain Decentralization Transferring of certain functions from central headquarters to regional offices or individual stores.

Checkstand Detectors Detection devices, usually located near store exists, designed to sound an alarm if sensing devices attached to merchandise have not been removed by a salesperson.

Classification Planning A system that breaks major categories of merchandise into smaller, manageable classifications for the purpose of inventory control.

Cluster Analysis Technique for analyzing markets that uses a computer to search among data for patterns and to group consumers according to attributes and behaviors.

Combination Store Supermarket plus discount store or supermarket plus drugstore.

Commissionaire A purchasing agent in a foreign market acting on commission for retailers or others importing from that country or area.

Commission Buying Office A resident buying office that is paid by manufacturers for placing orders with them.

Community Shopping Center Strip center expanded to serve a trading area of 40,000 to 150,000 people.

Comparison Shopper A store employee sent to competitors' stores to determine goods carried and relative prices charged.

Conglomerate Merchandising Carrying unrelated goods and offering unrelated services that can be sold profitably in the same store.

Consolidated Delivery System Independent delivery system that works for a number of retailers on a regular schedule set by contract.

Construction Documents Working drawings and specifications prepared by the store designer for use by contractors.

Consultive Selling In-home selling by specialists whose expertise is valued by the customer.

Convenience Goods Products purchased with a minimum of effort or time.

Converting Business Turning imported raw materials into finished goods before resale, instead of simply selling the raw materials, to increase the importer's profit margin.

Cooperative Delivery System A delivery system owned and used jointly by several retailers.

Cooperative Education An educational methodology that employs alternate periods of formal study and successful work experience as a prerequisite for graduation.

Customer Segmentation Dividing customers into segments by social, psychological, demographic, economic, geographic and lifestyle characteristics.

Decision Support Systems Evolutionary computer-based information systems that allow interaction between decision makers and the system.

Demographics Statistics on human populations: size, distribution, age mix, ethnic mix, education, income.

Department Stores Retail outlets organized into separate departments for purposes of promoting and controlling a wide variety of goods, such as apparel for men, women, and children; home furnishings; linens; and dry goods.

Depātos Japanese department stores, which offer a mind-boggling array of goods and services.

Designer Licensing Designer contracts a manufacturer to produce specific items for distribution to selected retail stores.

Direct Marketing Nonstore retailing, including vending machines, door-to-door, and catalog sales.

Discount Stores Stores that buy and sell "low" and depend on fast turnover to make a profit.

Discretionary Income Money available after necessities are paid for; money available for optional spending.

Display Element Component with some functions of a fixture but more dramatic, less well constructed, and with about a five-year life.

Disposable Income Personal income after taxes are paid; income available for consumption or savings.

Drawing Account A regular allowance, available to salespeople working on straight commission, to be balanced at intervals against commissions earned.

Easement Agreement Agreement that allows limited use of land owned by someone else.

Economic Utility The power to satisfy consumers' needs and wants. Utility created by the movement of goods results in employment within an economy.

800-Number Retailing Telemarketing that allows the potential customer to telephone the retailer toll free.

Electronic Fund Transfers Computerized systems that process financial transactions, exchanges, or information.

Electronic Retailing Space-age retailing that combines television for presentations with computers for order taking.

Embargo Government order prohibiting the handling of certain goods.

Emerging Countries Countries moving out of Third World status.

Engel's Laws Theory of 19th-century German statistician offering basic view of how consumers spend their income on goods and services.

Entrepreneurship Capacity to organize, own, manage, promote, and assume the risks of an organization, usually a small business enterprise.

Entry-Level Position A job that requires little or no related work experience.

Environmental Setting Simulated room with three walls used to display single items of furnishings and accessories in a coordinated group.

Equal Store Plan Plan for managing branch stores that separates the buying and selling functions, with buying done centrally and sales planning done by branch managers.

External Media Various means of communicating ideas to potential customers not in the store.

Factory Outlets Stores that sell manufacturers' seconds, irregulars, overruns, and samples.

Festival Marketplace Specialty marketplace in a dramatic setting, characterized by excitement and activity; also called marketplace center.

Fixture Showcase, table, gondola, or rack used to house and display merchandise, usually with a useful life of about 20 years.

Flexible Pricing The setting of prices that are open to bargaining.

Focus Group Panel of a dozen or fewer people, typical of a target market, invited to discuss a product, service, or market situation.

Follow-Up Interview In-depth interview of a job applicant who is being seriously considered for a position.

Franchise Retailer An independent store owner who sells branded items or service under licensed agreement with the franchise holder (franchisor).

Free on Board (FOB) Term identifying the point from which the retailer is to pay transportation charges for merchandise purchased; also called freight on board.

Freestanding Store Store located away from any traditional commercial area.

Freight Forwarder A firm that groups small shipments of several manufacturers into truckload or carload shipments.

Fringe Trading Area Wide area located outside the primary and secondary trading areas, containing 5 to 30 percent of the store's potential customers.

Generic Goods Plain-label goods, often priced much lower than advertised brands.

Gondola Hutch-type display cabinet designed to be placed against a wall.

Grievance A complaint that is handled formally through fixed procedures.

Gross National Product (GNP) Total retail value of all goods and services produced by a country during a specific time period.

Headhunters Individuals or agencies who are paid to find managers or executives for a client company.

Hierarchy of Needs Maslow's theory that people seek to satisfy needs in this order: biological, social, psychological.

Holographic Displays Three-dimensional pictures made without the use of a camera.

Homogeneous Merchandising Merchandising philosophy that limits goods presented to items similar in nature.

Horizontal Competition Competition among firms at the same level in the distribution channel.

Horizontal Cooperative Advertising Joint advertising by a group of retailers for their mutual benefit, usually to increase store traffic or interest in a product.

Image Advertising Advertising intended to convey positive mental pictures of the advertiser; institutional advertising.

Impulse Goods Items that are likely to be purchased on the spur of the moment.

Initial Interview Preliminary or screening interview of a job applicant.

Initial Mark-on The first markup on a single purchase or a single article among the purchases.

In-Store Retailing All types of retailing except direct marketing.

Internal Media Various means of communicating ideas to customers inside the store.

Interns Students in a formal training program that allows them to learn on the job by working closely with professionals.

Items Hot items; any goods that exhibit quick salability.

Job Bank Computer listing of job openings in private companies, developed by the U.S. Employment Service and updated daily.

Job Enrichment A way to improve an employee's efficiency and satisfaction by increasing the challenges, opportunities, and rewards (non-monetary) provided by the job.

Lifestyle Network of possessions, affiliations, behavior, opinions, and attitudes: virtually everything a person owns or does.

Lifestyle Segmentation Dividing of trading areas into segments on the basis of the way people live and how they spend their money.

Line Haul Movement of goods between cities and towns, as opposed to local delivery.

Loss Leaders Items sold below cost to pull customers into the store. This practice is forbidden in some states.

Maintained Markup Gross margin.

Management by Objectives A process in which a superior and a subordinate jointly set job objectives for the subordinate and then meet periodically to evaluate progress.

Management Information Systems Data processing systems designed to furnish current information to several levels of management for operational, decision-making, or objective-evaluation purposes.

Marketplace Center Center oriented toward entertainment as well as goods; also called festival marketplace.

Market Representative The person in a resident buying office who concentrates on a particular grouping of goods.

Market Week Scheduled showing of merchandise by manufacturers in one area; unlike trade shows, for which merchandise is brought together from many areas.

Mark-on The difference between the gross delivered price of merchandise and the original retail price.

Mass Merchants Group of retailers engaged in discount merchandising.

Mazur Plan A plan for department store organization based on only four functions: finance, merchandising, promotions, and operations.

Media Buying Service Organization of media specialists that buys blocks of advertising time and space on behalf of a group of retailers.

Media Mix All of the media chosen by an advertiser for a particular message or campaign.

Membership Retailing Discounting operations that require payment of a membership fee in order to shop in a warehouse.

Merchandise/Service Mix Merchandise or service assortment.

Minimum Wage Smallest hourly rate that may be paid to an employee, sometimes established by a union or others, but usually the federal minimum wage law.

Ministry of Trade Foreign government office able to assist local businesses in their importing and exporting activities.

Mixed-Use Center Downtown center with two or more uses, such as an office building with retail promenade.

Model Stock Plan Inventory method based on model stock lists that show different assortments needed at specific dates during a budget period.

Multiple Pricing The offering of a discount for buying in a preset quantity, such as 12 for $1.

Multiunit Department Store Department store organization consisting of a flagship store and two or more branch stores.

Needs Analysis A study to determine how much of a specific resource is required for a given purpose.

Neilsen Reports Reports to manufacturers on products sold through food stores, drugstores, and mass merchandisers, giving such information as brand shares, sales, and trends.

Networking Creating an effective and organized system that helps in establishing support for job search activities.

Nonstore Retail Mail order houses, vending machine operators, and other forms of direct selling.

Objections Reasons given by a customer for not purchasing an item presented by the salesperson.

Odd Pricing The setting of prices that end in an odd number, often a 9, as in $1.99.

Off-Price Retailers Stores with turnover double that of traditional apparel shops, with prices as much as 60 percent lower on brand merchandise.

Ombudsperson A person outside the normal chain of command who handles complaints and grievances.

On Consignment Turned over by an owner to a retailer. The retailer pays only when and if the goods are sold.

One-Stop Shopping Concept of convenience promoted by shopping centers and malls.

On Line Under the control of the central processing unit of a computer.

On-the-Job Training (OJT) Instructing employees during regular working hours while they are also doing productive work and are being paid normal wages.

Open-to-Buy Position Amount a buyer is in a position to spend on merchandise to replenish supplies for a period.

Opinion Leaders Trendsetters within a group.

Optical Scanner An electronic wand that picks up information from a product and enters it into a computer.

Optical Weight The amount an object appears to weigh rather than what it actually weighs.

Orientation Program Program that familiarizes new workers with their roles, the company, its policies, and other employees.

Original Retail Price The first retail price placed on merchandise; must be distinguished from prices that are reduced by taking markdowns.

Party Plan In-home selling to groups invited by the consumer/hostess.

Peripheral Land Land on the fringes of a shopping center, owned by the owner of the center.

Peter Principle Principle that people in an organization tend to rise to their highest level of incompetence.

Pirating Luring personnel from other firms.

Point-of-Purchase (P.O.P.) Displays In-store displays such as special racks and printed materials, usually furnished by manufacturers.

Point-of-Sale (P.O.S.) Terminals Terminals that supply information on sales, inventory, and commission earnings.

Preferred Nation Status Situation of developing countries that are granted special trade privileges by the United States, including lower tariffs on their goods.

Price Lines Distinguishable price levels, set by store policy, that must be applied to all merchandise.

Primary Trading Area Area located closest to the store, containing 55 to 70 percent of the store's potential customers.

Private Labeling A way of differentiating and enhancing a store's image by offering exclusive items bearing the store's name.

Product Developers Buyers with expanded duties that involve generating ideas and specifications for new or replacement products and arranging for their manufacture.

Promotional Markup (PMU) A higher price used during a short, initial sell-off period and then later in comparative advertising.

Protectionism Government policy of using high tariffs or other import restrictions to enable domestic products to compete with imported ones.

Psychographics The study of combined demographic and psychological factors.

Public-Access Electronic Market Potential customers reached through computer terminals in shopping malls, hotels, offices, and other public places.

Push Money (P.M.) A special bonus paid to a salesperson who is successful in selling a specified item.

Pyramid Format Display that is geometric and often follows the lines of a perfect triangle, beginning at a broad base and progressing to an apex.

Random Storage Computer model for optimal use of stock storage space.

Reference Group Group such as family, social, or professional, which a person identifies with and looks to when forming opinions.

Referrals The names of an informed person's acquaintances who might be potential employees.

Regional Shopping Center Center consisting of at least two department stores and 50 to 60 smaller stores, serving a minimum of 150,000 people.

Remerchandising Altering the tenant mix of a refurbished shopping center.

Resale Price Maintenance Supplier's control over selling price at various stages of distribution.

Resident Buyers Individuals or members of a service firm employed by a group of noncompeting retailers to provide market coverage of the world's major markets.

Resident Buying Office Link between a buyer and distant manufacturers, paid by the retailer to provide market coverage.

Résumé A brief history of education and experience that job applicants prepare for prospective employers to review.

Return on Investment (ROI) Net profit in relation to total costs, given as a percentage.

Role Playing Exercise in which individuals experience a situation through a trainer's dramatization, often by participating as actors.

Scrambled Merchandising Carrying unrelated types of goods in the same store, where they can be sold profitably.

Secondary Trading Area Area located just outside the primary trading area, containing 15 to 25 percent of the store's potential customers.

Self-Actualization The desired result when a person sets out to become all that he or she is capable of becoming.

Service Mix All services offered by a particular merchant.

Shadowboxes Display fixtures usually located behind the counter; they are often illuminated, sometimes enclosed in glass, and often used to display luxury items.

Shopping Goods Consumer goods purchased only after the buyer compares the offerings of more than one retailer.

Sight Line Line of vision at eye level.

Signature Special rendering of a designer's name that provides quick recognition.

Single-Country Promotions International merchandise promotions (in-store or catalog) featuring a single country's products and culture.

Socioeconomic Class Social situation of a person or group, indicated by a combination of social and economic factors.

Specialty Goods Consumer goods with special features for which buyers are willing to make a major purchasing effort.

Specialty Store Chains Chains that concentrate on a limited line of merchandise, such as groceries, automotive parts, hardware, or fashion apparel.

Specialty Stores Retail outlets that maintain a large selection of a limited line of merchandise.

Split Run Practice of national magazines selling advertising space at reduced prices to regional retailers; the ads appear only in magazines sold in their region.

Staple Goods Goods bought because of an actual need.

Step Format Display that begins at a low point on one side and climbs smoothly to a higher point; sometimes called diagonal arrangement.

Stockkeeping Unit (SKU) A unit controlled by the inventory control system; generally an item with a specific description, such as No. 327 shoe, black, size 7½D.

Store Design Design of exterior features; interior configuration; and decoration, fixtures, and display elements.

Strategic Career Search Systematic job hunt matched to one's career plan.

Strip Center Relatively small group of stores in a trading area that serves 7,000 to 40,000 people; also called a neighborhood shopping center.

Subliminal Cues Messages below receivers' awareness level intended by the sender to register subconsciously.

Superclass Households earning more than $50,000 annually.

Superette Self-service food store with annual sales of less than $2 million.

Supergraphics Billboard-sized graphic shapes, usually brightly colored and of simple design.

Supermarket Self-service food store with minimum annual sales of $2 million.

Super Regional Mall Shopping mall consisting of three to six department stores, hotels, office buildings, and recreation centers.

Superstore Giant supermarket that carries a full line of food items plus hard and soft goods.

Supplier-Controlled Cooperative Advertising Advertising initiated and controlled by a supplier or manufacturer, often for a type of product or service not sold by major retailers.

Tearsheet Page torn from a publication and sent to an advertiser or agency to prove that an ad is in the publication.

Teleshopping An electronic system for buying merchandise at home.

Track Lighting Display lighting that consists of movable units mounted on vertical or horizontal tracks.

Trade Discount A deduction from the agreed price, normally granted by manufacturers to wholesalers but sometimes also to large retailers.

Trade-Off Analysis A study of the gains and losses when one option is exchanged for another.

Trading Area Area from which a location attracts its customers, usually determined by asking the owner, checking license plates, or checking competing locations.

Traditional Shopping Center Downtown grouping of stores.

Trickle-Down Process Theory that economic changes eventually work their way through the system.

Turnaround Time Response time; the time that passes between an action and the response to it.

Typographical Display Type used to make a design statement.

Underwriters Laboratories Large, independent, not-for-profit testing group whose UL mark means the product has been safety tested against nationally recognized standards.

Unit Pricing The quotation of prices in terms of a standard measure such as ounces, feet, or dozens.

Universal Product Code Product identification consisting of a series of bars and a 10-digit number, used with an optical scanner for computer checkout.

Vending Machines Automatic retailing via coin-operated machines that satisfies customers' need for convenience even at higher prices.

Vertical Competition Competition among firms at different levels in the distribution channel, as when suppliers compete with the retailers they supply.

Vertical Cooperative Advertising Retailer advertising of a specific product for which wholesaler or manufacturer agrees to share costs; also, ready-made advertising furnished to retailers.

Videodisc Sales tool designed for in-store and public-access terminals that conveys product information via text, photographs, and videotapes with sound.

Videotex Subscription service that provides information and services (such as shopping and banking) via telephone or cable television hookups.

Walkout Statistics Number of store visitors who leave without making a purchase.

Wall Systems Wall selling fixtures that include full-height perimeter partitions and high partitions between departments or zones.

Want-Driven Society Society in which consumers purchase goods/services because they satisfy the 3rd, 4th, and 5th levels of Maslow's hierarchy of needs, rather than levels 1 and 2.

Weeks-of-Supply Method Inventory method in which stocks on hand are kept at a level representing projected sales for a predetermined number of weeks.

Wheel of Retailing Theory that retail businesses evolve through three stages: entry, trading up, and vulnerability.

Zero Population Growth (ZPG) The goal of bringing to a halt the growth of world population.

Zigzag Format Display resembling a modified pyramid that begins at a broad base and zigzags to the top, with no two heights the same.

ZIP Codes Codes assigned by the postal service (to speed mail sorting) that enable marketers to reach specific market segments.

ZIP-Market Clusters Segments (40) of the U.S. population determined by applying geodemographics to ZIP code neighborhoods.

Name Index

Subject Index